THINGS INDIAN

THINGS INDIAN

Being Discursive Notes on Various Subjects Connected with India

by

WILLIAM CROOKE

GYAN

Published by

GYAN

Gyan Publishing House
5, Ansari Road
Daryaganj, New Delhi-110002
Phone: 011-47034999, 9811692060
E-mail: books@gyanbooks.com

Distribution Network
gyanbooks.com
India, USA, Canada, UK, Australia, France

ISBN : 978-81-212-2653-0 (PB)
First Published, 1906

2nd Impression 2021

Printed at: Gyan Press, Delhi.

Things Indian
Author: William Crooke

THINGS INDIAN

BEING DISCURSIVE NOTES ON VARIOUS SUBJECTS CONNECTED WITH INDIA

BY WILLIAM CROOKE
OF THE BENGAL CIVIL SERVICE (RETIRED)

NEW YORK
CHARLES SCRIBNER'S SONS
153-157 FIFTH AVENUE
1906

PREFACE

THIS book is intended to form one of the series which already includes "Things Chinese," by Dr J. D. Ball, and "Things Japanese," by Professor B. H. Chamberlain. The selection of subjects for treatment and the form of the present book naturally differ from those of its predecessors. India is much better known to the English reader than either China or Japan, and there is a large library of works on special questions connected with the country and people, not to speak of encyclopædias like the "Imperial Gazetteer." Hence it has not been considered advisable to discuss at length the history, religion, literature, geography, geology, or natural history of the Empire, subjects which cannot be dealt with in a satisfactory way within the limits of short articles. It has been my object to search in the by-ways of Anglo-Indian literature, and discuss some of the quaint and curious matters connected with the country which are not specially considered in the ordinary books of reference.

This method of treating "Things Indian" was suggested to me in the course of reading which I was obliged to undertake in the preparation of a new edition of the "Anglo-Indian Glossary" of Sir H. Yule and Mr Burnell. It seemed to me that it would be interesting to deal in a similarly discursive way, but with more detail, with some of the subjects already included in the Glossary, to which the present work may be regarded as in some degree a supplement. These articles have in this book been marked with an asterisk, and the same course has been followed in the case of native words which have passed into Anglo-Indian speech, and are to be found fully explained in the pages of "Hobson-Jobson."

India forms a continent rather than a country. The Panjábi, for instance, differs as much in physique, character, language, and traditions from the Madrási, as the Scotchman from the Neapolitan. Hence, when a writer attempts to deal with subjects which concern the Empire as a whole, the difficulty of the task becomes apparent. A statement which may be true as regards Northern India may in no sense apply to the land or races of the South. For matters, therefore, which lie beyond my own experience, confined as it was to the United Provinces of Agra and Oudh, I have been obliged to rely on the best available authorities. A bibliography of this literature will be found prefixed to the new edtion of "Hobson-Jobson."

I have to acknowledge much assistance from many friends, and particularly from Colonel D. D. Cunningham and Mr Vincent A. Smith, who have kindly read the first rough draft of the book, and have favoured me with numerous valuable suggestions, while saving me from committing many errors.

TABLE OF CONTENTS

THINGS INDIAN

AGRICULTURE.—Immediately on the arrival of the Aryans in India the agricultural seems to have replaced the pastoral type of culture, and since then farming has been by far the most important of Indian industries, directly supporting at the present time no less than 65 per cent. of the total population. Its importance to the community from the earliest times ensured the protection of the farmer. Megasthenes, writing about 300 B.C., tells us that "an enemy coming on a husbandman at work on his land would do him no harm, for men of this class, being regarded as public benefactors, are protected from all injury." In later days historians of our Indian wars have described with wonder how the peasant continues to plough, sow, and reap amidst the clash of battle. But Bráhmanical legislation, as we find it in Manu, whose work in its present state dates five centuries after the time of Megasthenes, looked on farming with some measure of contempt, and confined it to one special class, that of the Vaisya. The Buddhist theory of the sanctity of life is thus reproduced in the maxim of the sage: "It is a mode of existence which the benevolent greatly blame; for the iron share not only wounds the earth but the creatures therein." The Indo-Chinese races, on the other hand, regarded the king as the patron of agriculture, and, like the Emperor of China, the Burmese King solemnly began the year by ploughing a field with his own hands, while his Bráhman astrologers repeated prayers for a successful crop. It was left to the wisdom of Akbar to ordain that the collector of revenue should be "a friend of the farmer," and should assist him in every way—a rule which our Government has steadily enforced, even though some of its efforts may have failed to attain success.

We find at the present day, side by side with modern scientific methods, such as those of the tea or indigo planter, some of the most primitive forms of agriculture. The earliest of all is probably that popularly known as *jhoom.** In this form of shifting cultivation the farmer begins by ringing the trees along the hillside. These soon die, the leaves drop off, and the effects of dry-rot and white-ants soon become apparent. In the first season the branches and brushwood are collected and burnt, and, as a beginning, a crop of pulse or millet is sown, the seed being scattered on the highest point of the slope so that the first heavy fall of rain may wash it down and cover it with the ashes. Next year the dry, bare trunks are set on fire at the roots, and as they gradually smoulder away the ashes improve the soil. A rude fence of matted branches is raised round the plot to keep off deer and wild pigs, or, as in parts of the Central Provinces, the farmer prepares craftily designed pitfalls, or he fixes lines of broad-bladed spears in the ground, and drives the bison or wild buffalo upon them. Before long the fertility of the plot becomes exhausted, or weeds grow so vigorously as to choke the seedlings. The owner then abandons his clearing, and selects another patch of hillside, where he repeats the process. Besides the destruction of valuable timber, which is the result of this method of farming, the system enforces a nomadic habit of life, and prevents the growth of permanent villages. The crop, being dependent upon a timely rainfall, is most precarious, and is much injured by wild animals.

The next stage is the system of terracing the hillside, which is a decided advance on the jhoom. It comes into operation when irrigation is found necessary. In many such holdings along the lower Himálaya, the central hills, and the eastern frontier of Bengal, the water supply is arranged with remarkable ingenuity.

It will be noticed that, as in many other countries,

agriculture starts on the hillsides, not in the richer valleys where the density of the forest defies the efforts of the pioneer, and the danger of malaria and wild beasts checks cultivation. Gradually the richer valley lands are cleared and come under the plough, and here cultivation is permanent, while the poorer upland slopes continue to be worked by rotation.

In the rule which prevails in all primitive village communities of periodically redistributing the land we see a survival of this shifting method of farming. With settled government, and the growth of the desire for individual property, this has now practically disappeared. It survives in some parts of the Panjáb, as in Gurgáon, and in what is known as the *vesh* system of the frontier Patháns. The Marris of Balúchistan redistribute their holdings every ten years, and allot the shares by drawing marked pellets of goat's dung from a bag. In parts of the Central Provinces the practice is so well established, and the style of farming so lax, that if redivision be refused, the tenants will abandon the village.

Much ill-informed criticism has been directed against the methods of the Indian farmer. When he is charged with merely scratching the surface of the soil, he replies that deeper cultivation is impossible with his present type of plough, half-starved oxen, and insufficient manure supply. If his ploughing is shallow, he makes up for it by the number of times he ploughs each field. His plough is merely an improved form of the mattock with which the hill-man tills his jungle clearing. One fork of a branch makes the share, and the straight part the handle, the hand-plough used by some tribes in the Central Provinces forming the link between the ox-plough and the mattock. The Aryan plough was dragged by men and women, and a relic of this custom survives to this day among the Káfirs of the Hindu-kush, where the woman directs the ox by means of a long pole attached to the yoke. For raising water from the well he has never adopted any kind of pump, and relies upon the Persian wheel, the leather bag raised by oxen hauling a rope over a pulley, or the weighted lever worked by manual labour. His harrow, in its rudest form, is a bunch of thorns tied to the tail of his bullock; in its highest, a plank on which he stands while it is being dragged over the fields.

This condition of things is largely due to the innate conservatism of the farmer. He suffers always from lack of capital, and more particularly in the congested districts, like the Gangetic valley, his want of progress depends on causes which are beyond his control. Lack of grazing land and dearth of fodder weaken his plough cattle; lack of fuel compels him to burn their manure, which thus loses much of its valuable elements; the rude village craftsman is unable to supply him with better implements than those which he uses at present; he cannot select his seed grain when he is obliged to borrow it for each sowing. At the same time, the possibility of reform does not lie in the introduction of English or American implements. In the first place, labour-saving appliances are useless where labour is cheap, and, secondly, most competent authorities believe that the adoption of the English plough would be a mistake, because the wet soil, when deeply stirred by such an implement, soon hardens like a sun-dried brick.

But with all these drawbacks, nothing in its way is finer than the *petite culture* in places like Gujarát and the Gangetic valley. The farmer, it is true, works under the rule of custom; but custom with him is the accumulated experience of countless generations. He wins success by his own unremitting industry, and by the devotion of the labour of his whole family to the soil. It is only the higher ranks of the rural population who relieve their women from the burden of field work. The woman in the Plains does not plough, nor, except occasionally, does she drive the oxen at the well; but she distributes water in the fields, reaps and gleans, winnows the grain, tends the cattle. Among the semi-aborigines of Bengal the distribution of work between the sexes is different. Ploughing and sowing the rice are the task of the men; transplanting and weeding that of the women. Once the land is ploughed, and the seed-beds planted, the men rest till harvest time, leaving the women to do the rest, while the children scare bird and beast from the crop. This must have been the rule in Aryan times, because the fact of the woman sharing in the harvest festivals and offerings proves that in early ages the duties of farming lay, for the most part, in her hands.

The hope of improvement in agriculture depends on such a rise in the condition of the farmer that he can buy and keep better cattle; that he can select his own seed grain, instead of taking any rubbish the money-lender chooses to give him; that he can afford to purchase fuel and save manure for his fields. But this is an ideal, the attainment of which it is useless to expect under existing conditions.

Meanwhile the State has not been backward in considering measures for the improvement of agriculture, and investigations have been made by many experts, like Sir James Caird, Professor Wallace, and Dr Voelcker. All these observers have been struck by the many good qualities of the Indian farmer—his care in keeping his land clear from weeds; the skill with which he raises water from his well, and suitably distributes it over the various crops; his knowledge of soils and their capacities, of the times for sowing, watering, and reaping; his mastery of the system of rotation, of growing mixed crops, where one supplies the chemical constituents which another demands from the soil, and where in a season of drought, if one crop fail, another succeeds.

"Certain it is," writes Dr Voelcker, "that I, at least, have never seen a more perfect picture of careful cultivation, combined with hard labour, perseverance, and fertility of resource, than I have seen at many of the halting-places of my tour. Such are the gardens of Mahim, the fields of Nadiad (the centre of the 'garden' of Gujarát, in Bombay), and many others."

Nor is the farmer, though he may be slow in taking up an improvement, indisposed to adopt it if he becomes convinced that it will be to his advantage. Five-and-twenty years ago the sugar industry in the Gangetic valley was conducted in the rudest way—the cane imperfectly crushed with stone or wooden rollers, the juice boiled with so little care that the product was most inferior. But on the introduction of a cheap and efficient steel-roller mill and the vacuum boiling-pan, the ancient rude appliances soon fell into disuse.

The climates of India are so diverse (no less than five have been distinguished in the Madras Presidency alone), the soil of such varying qualities, the agricultural population displaying such differences of skill and industry, that it is impossible to suggest any general programme of reform which will suit all the provinces and peoples of the Empire. Though it is probable that the nitrogenous elements of the soil are reconstituted to a large extent during the periodical rains, the standing difficulty of the peasant is the scarcity of manure. His caste prejudices prevent him from utilising, as the Chinese do, bones and night-soil. When he does collect manure it is often stored and distributed in a wasteful manner; and when, as is generally the case, it is used for fuel it loses a large part of its valuable constituents. This difficulty cannot be removed except by the establishment of fuel and fodder reserves, an enterprise which the State is not in a position to undertake at present. Much, no doubt, can be done to improve the existing stocks of cattle, not so much by importation from abroad, as by selection and crossing of the best native breeds; and a similar improvement may be effected in the chief crops by selection of seed and transmission of the best varieties from one part of the country to another. Model farms, unless worked on purely business principles, can be of little use to the farmer. Finally, the lack of education and intelligence among the rural classes is likely for many a long year to debar them from sharing in the general industrial development of the country.

The prospects of a general and decided improvement in agricultural methods are thus not promising at the present time. India moves slowly, but it does move; and if by an extension of the irrigation systems the risk of periodical famine could be abated or entirely removed, there is no reason to fear that, with the immense reserves of waste land which still remain unoccupied, the danger of the population outrunning its means of support will become urgent. To quote the latest official annalist, Mr Risley:

"With canals to enable crops to grow and ripen when the rainfall is insufficient either in quantity or distribution, and with wells for high cultivation on a small scale, with the double-cropping that these appliances tend to foster, and with the economy of animal and vegetable manure that characterises the farming of the best agriculturists in India, and is spreading from them downwards, the ability of the soil under the plough to support on the whole a very much larger population than that which now depends upon it can be confidently assured."

[Sir J. Caird, "India: the Land and the People"; Wallace, "India in 1887"; Voelcker, "Report on the Improvement of Indian Agriculture"; "Census Reports for India and the Provinces," 1901.]

AMULET.—An amulet is primarily a relic of some sacred personage, powerful animal, or the like, worn with the object of coercing hostile spirits, or securing the good offices of those that are benignant. Thus, Sir J. Hooker describes the Tibetans as wearing "square amulets on their necks and arms, which are boxes of gold and silver, containing small idols, or the nail-parings, teeth, or other reliques of some sainted Lama, accompanied with musk, written prayers, and other charms." The rule of Sir J. Malcolm is commemorated to this day in Central India by women, who tie a string round a child's arm to ward off evil spirits, and call it "the Malcolm string." The same result is secured by Musalmáns, who wear a passage from the Korán tied round their necks. When General Nicholson was once attacked by a Gházi fanatic, he was obliged to shoot his assailant, and the ball passed through a religious book which the man had tied on his breast, apparently as a charm. Hindus bring themselves under the protection of the divine powers by wearing a medallion with an image of a god or goddess. A figure of Sítala, the small-pox goddess, or of the malignant Devi, is often worn in this way as a protection against disease. When a widower marries again, his second wife wears an amulet, which she calls the "crown of the co-wife," and to this she makes gifts to avert the hostility of the ghost of her predecessor.

Animal substances are constantly used in this way, the object being to invest the wearer with some of the qualities of the beast whose relics he carries with him. The fangs, claws, whiskers, or fat of a dead tiger form valuable protectives, and the hill-man wears a necklace of wild boar tusks. Wool, possibly with some totemistic idea, is constantly used as an amulet, hung to doors, or on the legs and necks of horses. To this is often added a *cowry* *-shell, which is supposed to crack when the Evil Eye falls upon it.

The use of the amulet largely depends on what is called sympathetic or symbolic magic. Thus, the hill-man of Central India, to cure colic, ties round the waist of the patient a vermiform root. Chin women in Burma wear fowls' merry-thoughts round the throat to guard against a class of disease which, it is believed, can be cured only by the sacrifice of a fowl.

The Burmese are specially addicted to wearing amulets, the virtue of which depends on the sympathetic principle. Balls of mercury, gold, iron, orpiment, and various other substances are embedded in the flesh, which is allowed to heal over them. Careful jailors sometimes operate on refractory convicts, and extract amulets of this kind. The removal of the magical substance is found to make them much more amenable to discipline. In the Burmese war of 1845 some of their generals rushed on our troops holding quicksilver in their mouths. Charms embedded in the flesh seem almost peculiar to the Indo-Chinese races, and the practice is of ancient date, as Marco Polo describes the Japanese protecting themselves in this way against the forces of the Great Kaan. But it occasionally occurs in

India, as in the case of Muhammad Yúsuf Khán, the famous Madras mutineer, who was said to have a magic ball in his thigh which made him invulnerable. Natives still declare that he did not die until it was extracted.

In Rájputána the Rákhi, or wrist-string, of which Colonel Tod tells romantic tales, is a well-known amulet, and it was regularly worn by the Emperor Akbar, doubtless under the influence of the Hindu ladies of his harem. The Hindus of North India have a regular festival in the rainy season, at which a thread amulet is tied on the right wrist. The wristlet is first consecrated by an offering, and the gods who rule the four quarters of the heaven are invoked with appropriate texts.

Throughout the country the use of amulets of one kind or another is universal, and the rules for preparing and wearing them form a sort of science, the details of which it is difficult to discover, because natives are not communicative about them. Like charms all the world over, half their virtue lies in the observance of secrecy. Protection is generally provided for those parts of the body which are specially exposed to the attacks of spirits—the head, particularly the forehead, nose, ears, and neck; the chest and waist, as containing the chief organs of the body; the wrist, the seat of the pulse; the fingers and toes, because they are liable to danger from touching and grasping. The ear is a most vulnerable point, and when the Hindu ascetic abandons all other kinds of ornament, he is careful to retain his ear-rings. In fact, the line separating the amulet from the jewel is only vaguely defined, and in our time both are so closely associated that it is difficult to distinguish one from the other.

AMUSEMENTS.—Though the native of India takes his pleasures sadly, there are many forms of amusement in which the people freely indulge.

The Aryans were a pleasure-loving race, and in the Vedas we find constant references to amusements—gymnastics, cock and ram fighting, shooting with arrows, theatrical performances, and picnics, in which ladies joined their husbands. Among these early Kshatriyas gambling was much in vogue, and a true warrior could not refuse a challenge to the dice. In later times, under the code of Manu, dicing and gambling were denounced. But even now, at the Diwáli, or feast of lamps, it ranks as something like a religious observance, and in many of the Native States, and even in some of our larger towns, it is on this occasion tolerated. In Nepál on this night gambling is universal, and the mania extends to all classes of the city population. In former days endless quarrels arose from the system of credit gambling, and finally Jang Bahádur was obliged to issue an order that all bets were to be staked in cash. In our cities, gambling with dice, cards or cowry-shells is common, and has been controlled by special legislation. A curious form is that of rain gambling, against which recently in Bombay special regulations were enforced. The players during the monsoon sat round a vessel placed under a spout connected with the house roofs, and bets were made on the event of rain falling in sufficient quantities within a given time to fill the tub. In Burma the game of the thirty-six animals is popular. The banker selects a certain animal, and writes its name on a slip of paper, which he places in a box or bamboo tube. Punters go round asking the players to back their fancy, and whoever selects the right name wins thirty times his stake.

The wilder jungle tribes have many games of their own. The Meos of Rájputána amuse themselves with dancing and rude singing, throw javelins, or play with clubs, while fencing and the use of dumb-bells are common. The eastern frontier tribes play what is called the *konyon*, the Oriental equivalent of one of our boys' games of "marbles." It takes its name from the seed of a creeper about the size of a horse-chestnut. Several of these are set up on end, and the players, propelling their nuts with the middle finger of the right hand, endeavour to knock down as many of their adversaries' nuts as possible. In the same region the Lepchas play at quoits and games like the Highland "putting," or "drawing the stone." "Chess, dice, draughts, punch, hockey, and battledore and shuttlecock are all Chinese, Indo-Chinese, or Tartarian," writes Sir J. Hooker. In the Hindu-kush Káfir girls play at ball, knuckle-bones, or swinging, while boys prefer rougher games, such as dashing at a companion and knocking him down. They mimic the national dance, throw walnuts into a hole, and play a kind of "prisoner's base," quoits, run and jump. Even such a degraded race as the Andamanese have a sort of "blind man's buff," which Sir R. Temple believes to be indigenous. With them leap-frog, hide-and-seek, mock pig and turtle hunts, with mimic burials and ghost-finding, are favourite sports.

Animal fights go back to the time of the Mauryas, who ruled Northern India after the campaign of Alexander, and they were a favourite amusement of the Moghul Court. Tavernier tells us of the elephant fights in the sandy bed of the Jumna beneath the Agra Fort. Of these, Tom Coryatt says:

"Twice every week elephants fight before the prince, the bravest spectacle in the world; many of them are thirteene foot and a halfe high, and they seem to jumble together like two mountains; and were they not parted in the midst of their fighting by certaine fireworks, they would exceedingly gore and cruentate one another by their murdering teeth."

In our own times such exhibitions were common at Native Courts, like Baroda and Lucknow. Lady Dufferin, at Udaypur, saw elephants, quails, partridges, rams, pigs, deer, buffaloes, and cocks fight before the Viceroy.

"Though there was a total absence of cruelty in the performance," she writes, "and though it was worth seeing as a peep into a bygone world, I feel almost sorry I had been present, for it does seem rather barbarous."

Cock-fighting was an amusement in South India, in the days of Fryer, at the close of the seventeenth century.

"They have," he says, "a Breed of Cocks as big as

Turkies, which they Arm with Razors, tied flat under their Claws, and faulched Two Inches instead of Gavelocks, with which they slash one another Mortally; so that the Dispute endures not long, for most an end the first or second Blow decides it."

The famous cock-fight between birds owned by Asaf-ud-daula, Nawáb of Oudh (1775-97), and the Resident, Colonel Mordaunt, formed the subject of the well-known picture by Zoffany, which was destroyed in the Mutiny. Mrs Fanny Parkes quotes a native proverb which says that "Cocks fight for fighting's sake, quails for food, and láls, or amadavats, for love." Even now, when they can evade the eye of the policeman, bazaar ne'er-do-wells match quails, láls, and partridges.

Another city sport which has no element of cruelty is that of pigeon-flying. It is a pretty sight at a place like Lucknow to look down from a minaret and watch the flocks of birds circling in the sunshine, while the owners frantically wave flags from the house-tops to attract them. If they can entice a rival's bird they hold it to ransom.

Another popular spring game is kite-flying, which seems to have come to India from China through the Malays. Matches are often made for considerable stakes. The strings are coated with crushed glass smeared on with glue, and each player seeks to manœuvre his kite so as cut his rival's string. It is curious to watch the interest which respectable, elderly gentlemen take in the amusement. Like most games it has its special season, and when the spring is over the kite-makers turn their attention to toys.

Children's games are innumerable. One of the most popular is a sort of "prisoner's base," of which a variant in the Panjáb is called "Kabadhi," or "touch"; and "fox and geese," which is called "tiger and goat." Little girls with their strong dramatic sense delight in dolls, and Miss Billington gives a pleasant account of a kind of Maypole dance at Madras, in which strings of flowers replace ribbons, and the girls, crossing hands, swing round in "a giddy crescendo of speed," while one girl sings and the others circle round her. Little village children make mud pies, or cluster in amazement behind their elders when a party of gipsy rope-dancers visits the village, or watch the Kathputli *Nautch*,* a sort of marionette show, in which all the well-known members of native society and, in particular, the Sahib and the English lady are freely satirised. All these performers, even the monkey-man with a skull into which he pretends to whisper charms, strive to import a suggestion of magic into their performances. Dr Buchanan-Hamilton was gravely told that in order to do the common Mango trick, it was necessary to take the kernels of a certain shrub, "grind them between two stones for seven days and nights, without ceasing. Then place a sword upright, with its point in a cup. Rub the pulp of the kernel, expose it to the sun, and an oil will run down into the cup. Put the oil into a bottle to be preserved for use. In order to perform the experiment, take a ripe Mango stone, rub it over with the oil, and place it in a pot of earth properly watered. The young shoot will be immediately formed." Later he learnt that he had been deceived.

In Coorg the people, perhaps the most manly race in Southern India, have all kinds of village athletics, wrestling, and quarter-staff, played with a shield and bludgeon, in which the players often get so excited that the bystanders are obliged to interfere. One of their games seems never to have reached the north. A peg is driven into the ground in the centre of the arena. To this a rope is fastened with a loose knot, and one of the players holds it by the other end. A set of wooden balls is placed along the circle marked by the outer end of the rope, and one ball is laid close to the peg. The object of the game is to recover the balls without being touched by the rope-man. The winner is the man who seizes the ball near the peg, and escapes without being touched. If he is caught, the penalty is a scourging with nettles.

Football seems to have come from the Malays to the Burmese. Here the ball is made of wicker-work, and must not be touched with arm or hand during the game.

One man begins by knocking it into the air with knee, foot, or shoulder, and then passes it on to another, who keeps it up as long as he can, or until it pleases him to pass it on to some one else. The indigenous cricket or hockey of Bengal, called *danda-guli*, is played with a thick acacia stick two feet long, and a ball of the same wood, five inches in diameter. It is almost needless to say that both these games, in their European form, have become widely popular among natives.

Juggling and performances such as rope-dancing, sword-play, and the like, are almost confined to the gipsy races, like the Nats of Upper India and the Kolhátis of the Deccan. The performers are often little girls, who roll themselves into balls, tie themselves into knots, and go through a bewildering amount of dislocation. They will pick up with their eyelids two straws stuck in the ground, and while their eyes are bandaged, thread a needle with their toes. More unpleasant to watch is the trick of raising a weight with strings attached to buttons placed under the eyelids, fire-eating, and sword-swallowing, done in a peculiarly realistic style. In the sword game a girl balances herself on the back of her head and her heels. Two swords, with blades pointed inwards, are crossed on her chin, and two under her neck. She then revolves rapidly, and twists her body over the swords with admirable deftness.

The Indian juggler in his way is an excellent performer. All his feats are done in the open and without the use of elaborate appliances. He has an admirable stock of "patter," and he is skilled in the art of distracting the attention of observers at the critical moment. His most familiar tricks are those of the Basket and the Mango. In the former a child is enclosed in a basket, a sword is thrust through it, piteous yells are heard, and blood, or what looks like blood, drips through the bottom. Presently the child appears safe and sound amidst the crowd. The Mango trick is seldom well done, and the process of making the seed throw out roots, then branches, then flowers, and finally a ripe fruit, is sufficiently obvious.

It is perhaps too much to say that all games have a basis of magic, but some performances are certainly done with this object. Thus the Khásis of Assam have the annual game of "Tug-of-War," in which one side representing the village and the other a gang of demons tug at the ends of a rope passed across a stream, the intention being that the evil spirits may lose and quit the neighbourhood. In Burma a similar game is intended as a rain charm. The Gonds and Bhíls of the central hill-ranges have their harvest games, without which they think that the crops will not ripen. The men have to climb a pole, on the top of which a piece of coarse sugar is fixed. Each player is armed with a sort of shield, by means of which he tries to protect himself from the women who thrash him with light tamarind rods. It is not child's play, as the backs of the men attest next morning, but all is done with perfect good-humour.

For Pachísi, and similar games played on a board, see under CHESS.

ARMENIANS.—The last census records only 1,053 of this once important people now resident in the country. There is no means of determining the date of their first arrival, but at an early time they seem to have established themselves in some of the marts of the West Coast. An Armenian traveller, Nikitin, has left an account of his visit to India in 1470 A.D. Terry (1615) speaks of Armenians as the chief wine-merchants, and Tavernier (1665) writes: "Whenever the Armenians see that money is to be made, they have no scruples about supplying materials for the purposes of idolatry." They established close relations with the Moghul Court. European and Armenian merchants used to bring China silks and other foreign goods for the inspection of Akbar, and Bernier tells of an Armenian envoy sent by the King of Abyssinia to Aurangzeb.

One of their chief settlements on the West Coast was Súrat, where they seem to have acquired considerable influence about the end of the seventeenth century. They are mentioned as residing in Bombay in 1676, but Pársi competition resulted in their almost complete disappearance from Western India, and passing eastward, we find them established at Sútanati, in Bengal, at least sixty years before Job Charnock raised our flag on the Húgli. Their influence with the native powers was largely utilised by the early English officials. Captain Hawkins, on his mission to the Emperor Jahángír, was much aided by his wife, an Armenian lady, who subsequently accompanied him to England. The success of the famous embassy to the Court of Farrukhsiyar in 1715, as a result of which, through the loyalty of Dr Hamilton, the grant of the right of free trade was conferred upon the Company, was largely due to the influence of Khwája Israel Sarhad, the Armenian who was attached to it. In Madras, too, the Armenians became an important community, and in 1724 we find them engaged in a serious quarrel with the officers of the Company, who charged them with "interloping," in other words, with interfering with their trade monopoly. At a later period Armenians had some share in military operations. Mír Kásim, about the time of the Patna Massacre of 1763, had at least two Armenian generals in his pay, Marcar and Gurjin Khán or Gregory.

During the early years of the Company's rule in Bengal the Armenians formed an influential trading community, and the first Christian church built in Bengal was that of the Armenians at Chinsura. They have always shown their readiness to adopt the manners of the land of their adoption. Burnes, who found them at Cábul, describes how they used to take off their shoes and turbans when they entered their church. In Calcutta, about 1830, they used to wear at home the loose, Oriental robe, but out of doors they copied European fashions. They were wealthy, and they had no poor among them. Their ladies are described by a writer of the time as "the fairest of the daughters of Eve." They then followed the occupations of hawking goods, selling precious stones, and money-lending. In more recent times they have adopted English habits and speech; wear English clothes at home and abroad; and their names have become Anglicised. In former days many an Englishman married an Armenian wife, but improved facilities for visiting home have made such marriages much less numerous. The last Census returns show only a couple of hundred speakers of Armenian, who are scattered all over the country. The majority use English as their vernacular tongue.

The Armenian Church, which claims as its founder the Apostle Thaddeus (A.D. 34), now holds doctrines closely resembling those of the Orthodox Greek Church. Of its four patriarchs, who have their seats at Constantinople, Sis, Jerusalem, and Etchmiadzin, near Erivan, the last controls the congregations in India. The kindly Bishop Heber in 1824 records his meeting their Archbishop, who used to visit India once in four or five years. Later on he met the Episcopal Commissary from Shiráz, and entered into correspondence with the authorities, his constant aim being to encourage friendly intercourse between the Churches of England and the East.

["Calcutta Review," xxx. 305; lxxiii. 382; xciii. 1; xcviii. 132.]

ARMS, ARMOUR.—India supplies a series of arms of offence and defence, ranging from the most primitive to the most highly developed types.

Some of the jungle tribes, like the Keriyas of Central India, are in, or have only quite recently emerged from, the Age of Stone. As in other parts of the world, these weapons are either palæolithic or neolithic, the former having so far been discovered only in the South. Stone weapons are found more or less extensively over the whole Peninsula, from the south districts of Madras, along the Western Coast to the Indus valley: all through the central plateau of the Deccan with its flanking ranges of hills. They have been discovered isolated at considerable depths in the alluvium, and beneath the sites of the oldest human settlements in the country. In some places, as at Mirzapur, what seem to have been factories of these implements have been observed. True flints are rare, their place being taken by the allied horn-stones and agates. These implements were used for various purposes—for scooping out boats and other hollow vessels after the wood had been previously charred; up to quite recent times, until they were replaced by iron, they were used as plough-shares; the jungle tribes made of them the blade of the spud for digging roots, or fixed them in cleft sticks as battle-axes; others were employed as skin-scrapers, and the ring-stones as spindles, net-sinkers, or, when of larger size, as parts of querns; some formed a sort of knuckle-duster. The smaller flakes supplied the place of lancets, knives, or arrow-heads. Even at the present day the Andamanese use splinters of glass for the same purposes. Nowadays the use of stone is confined to a few tribes on the very confines of the Empire, those bordering Assam and Burma on the north-east. The geological evidence in South India discloses a wide gap in time between the palæolithic and neolithic periods. On the other hand, the neolithic people and their successors, who gradually acquired a knowledge of the use of the metals, seem to have been identical. In modern popular belief the stone axe is regarded as a "thunder-stone," or an uncanny object, in other words, the abode of a spirit, and it is therefore found on the rude pile of stones which form the village shrine.

The existence of a well-defined Bronze Age has not been established in India. On the other hand, that of copper is well marked in the Central Provinces and the Gangetic valley. In the former region more than four hundred pure copper implements were found at a village named Gungeria, in 1870, specimens of which are in the British Museum and other collections. In this find two forms are peculiar to India, heavy celts with recurved points, and the long crowbar-like implements, to which the name of "bar-celt" has been given. According to some authorities these implements date back to a period perhaps as early as 2,000 B.C.; others, on the evidence of silver ornaments found with them, assign them to a much later age. The bronze articles found in graves in South India seem to be mostly articles of luxury, and may have been imported from the West in the early centuries of the Christian era.

Gradually the Copper Age was replaced by the Age of Iron, the ore being found in great quantities in the central and southern districts, where it is still worked in a crude way by the Agariyas and other forest tribes, their present methods probably reproducing those of the period when the metal first came into use. The manufacture of the celebrated Indian steel was developed at a very early period, and was brought to great perfection. It formed the material of the splendid swords of Persia, such as those which Ctesias claims to have received from the King of that country and his mother. This steel was extensively exported from India in Greek and Roman times. The well-known *Wootz* * of Madras is probably identical with it.

When we come to the Vedic period the bow, made of bamboo or horn, was the chief weapon, and with it arrows tipped either with deer-horn or iron were used. The Buddhist sculptures supply numerous representations of early Hindu weapons—javelins, spears, lances, battle-axes, swords and daggers of many shapes, and coats of mail. This people seem also to have possessed some mechanical means of flinging boiling oil and fire-tipped darts at the enemy, such as were employed by the Oxydracae in the campaign of Alexander. Iron weapons of offence and defence were the sole equipment of the Indian soldier up to the time of the introduction of gunpowder. Barbosa (1514) describes the equipment of the Bijapur army in his day as consisting of long light lances, quilted cotton tunics, coats of mail and iron caparisons for the cavalry; for the infantry, iron maces, battle-axes, swords and bucklers, and Turkish bows, with a large supply of arrows. This combination of weapons lasted until quite modern times in the armies of the native princes. Thus, Wilks, describing the horse of Nizám Ali in the campaign against Tippoo in 1790-92, writes:

> "It is probable that no national or private collection of ancient armour in Europe contains any weapon or article of equipment which might not be traced in this motley crowd; the Parthian bow and arrow, the iron club of Scythia, sabres of every age and nation, lances of every length and description, and match-locks of every form; metallic helmets of every pattern; simple defences of the head, a steel bar descending diagonally as a protection to the face; defences of bars, scales, or chain-work descending behind or on the shoulders, cuirasses, suits of armour, or detached pieces for the arm, complete coats of mail in chain-work, shields, bucklers, and quilted jackets, sabre-proof."

Such strange weapons are occasionally worn in our days by troops of the Native States at ceremonials like an Imperial Durbar at Delhi.

There is no satisfactory evidence that Asia anticipated Europe in the knowledge of fire-arms or of gunpowder. Fire-arms were probably introduced into India through Egypt from Venice in the end of the fourteenth or beginning of the fifteenth centuries, and the influence of Venice appears in the name *Bundook* * applied to the Indian matchlock, which is derived from the name of that city. An attempt has been made to push back the date of the introduction of gunpowder into India on the ground that the destruction of the Kashmír temples at the close of the fourteenth century was affected by its means. But it is now generally admitted that their ruin was the result of earthquakes and the imperfect bonding of the masonry.

The first distinct evidence of the use of artillery is by Bábar at the battle of Pánipat in 1526. His infantry was armed with the sword and bow, six-bladed maces, javelins, and axes. The matchlock was being then gradually introduced, but he tells us in his "Memoirs" that the people of Bajaur on the Indo-Afghán frontier had, in

1519, never seen such a weapon. His son, Humáyun, had swivel guns carrying a heavy ball, "which would strike anything that was visible at the distance of a parasang." Still larger were Akbar's guns, each dragged by several elephants and a thousand oxen.

Later on the size of artillery largely increased, and it is to the period of decadence of the Moghul Empire that we owe the enormous pieces still to be seen in many parts of the country, which were constructed of iron bars welded and banded together, like Mons Meg of Edinburgh. The Moghuls followed the example of the Portuguese in giving special names to each piece. Such are the Malik-i-Maidán, or "Lord of the Plain," and the Lamchhari, or "Long Tom," of Bijapur, the former weighing 42, the latter 22 tons. The Lílam Top left by the Turks at the siege of Diu, and now at Junagarh, is 17 feet long and 9½ inches in calibre; that at Asírgarh, made in 1663, and called "Terror of the Land," is somewhat larger. At Visapur, near Poona, is a large gun, apparently of the time of Queen Elizabeth, with the letters E. R. and the Tudor rose, which was probably captured by West Coast pirates from an English ship, and presented by them to the Mahrattas. In Upper India there was the great gun of Dacca, weighing 27 tons, which has now disappeared; the sister gun at Murshídábád, dated 1637, weighs nearly 8 tons. The great gun of Agra, 43 tons, sank in the Jumna in the course of an attempt to remove it to England, and in a spirit of pure Vandalism was blown to pieces in 1833. The Bhangiyán-wála Top of Lahore, familiar to readers of Kipling's "Kim," was used by Ahmad Sháh at the battle of Pánipat in 1761, and thence passed into the hands of the Sikhs. Burma has the great gun of Amarapura, about 29 feet long; the piece of Ghazni, which carried a 64-lb. ball, received from the British soldier the title of "Long Tom," a name revived in the South African War.

Guns like these have always been regarded with veneration. At Udaypur in Tippera is an old cannon, 8 feet long, before which every native bows, and places on the top a leaf or branch, believing that if his offering is accepted it will be miraculously removed from the position in which he placed it, and be covered by the gun. That of Lahore is worshipped as a representation of Siva; that of Banáwar in Mysore, if duly worshipped, cures the stomach-ache. The most curious modern artillery is that of the *Guicowár* * of Baroda, who made a battery of gold guns, manned by gunners with pink fleshings.

The bow was long the distinctive Indian weapon, and is still largely used by the forest tribes. Herodotus tells us that his Indian contingent with the army of Xerxes (480 B.C.) were armed with cane bows and cane arrows tipped with iron, an interesting proof of the early use of this metal. It assumes many forms, the most primitive that of the jungle folk, who make it of bamboo, with a string of the same material. They have various kinds of arrows, some with iron heads ingeniously barbed, others with a blunt point for shooting little birds. The Indian archer raises his hand over his head when drawing the bow, but in the Buddhist sculptures of Orissa the prince draws it in the perpendicular fashion of the European archer. The Kol of the central hills places one end of the bow on the ground, kneels on his right knee, and, pressing his left foot against the bow, discharges the arrow. The Greek writers attest the skill of the archer; "nothing can resist an Indian arrow," says one of them. If the tale told of Sháh Sikandar at the siege of Delhi in 1452 be true, that he sent an arrow right through the body of an ox at 800 paces, the archers of that day must have greatly surpassed their successors. The Assam frontier tribes are said to shoot at 30 yards; when they get to 50 their practice is indifferent. The same may be said of the forest tribes of Central India. The Káfirs of the Hindu-kush, who pride themselves on their prowess, shoot, according to Sir G. Robertson, with accuracy up to 80 yards.

Even in quite modern times the bow has been used with some success against our riflemen. Forbes Mitchell describes a body of archers, who formed part of the garrison of the Sháh Najaf at Lucknow during Sir Colin Campbell's attack in 1858, and shot arrows with great force and precision. The Syntengs of the Assam border in 1862 opposed our troops in the same way, and on the same frontier in 1883-84 the only weapons of the Akhas were bows and arrows. Of the Bhotan campaign of 1865 Sir C. Macgregor wrote:

"It has been the fashion to laugh at such weapons as bows and arrows and stones; and yet I doubt . . . if we would have lost more men if the enemy had been armed with muskets. The arrows are all sharp-pointed, and fly with great precision, having penetration enough to go through a man's body; while on this occasion a man was killed, and several received very nasty gashes from stones."

Some Tibetans, who resisted our Mission in 1903-4, were armed with bows and arrows.

The practice of applying poison to arrows dates from very early times. The Rigveda speaks of two kinds of arrows, one of copper, and the other of stag-horn, the latter being poisoned. The historians of the campaign of Alexander, as in the case of Ptolemy, refer to this custom, and we also read of the poisoning of weapons by the liquid distilled from the carcasses of snakes. At the present day Gonds in the Central Provinces, Jaintiyas on the eastern frontier, Kachins in Burma, and many other jungle tribes poison their arrows by fixing a little cotton soaked in aconite near the barb. The Lepchas freely eat the cooked flesh of game killed in this way. It may go to the credit of the Andamanese, or be regarded as a proof of their low standard of culture, that they never use poison for their arrows.

But it is on the sword that the Indian soldier has always placed his chief reliance. The histories abound in tales of great swordsmen. Bakhtiyár Khilji fought a savage elephant with his sword, and routed it by a blow on its trunk; Sher Khán killed an enormous tiger with a blow of his sabre; Sher Afkan, who was slain, like

Uriah the Hittite, that Jahángír might possess his wife, the fair Núr Jahán, cut off the trunk of a State elephant, and clave the Súbadár of Bengal in two by a single stroke.

The forms of the sword are infinitely varied. The Rájputs preferred the Sirohi, a slightly curved blade, formed like those of Damascus; but they also used the long cut-and-thrust, like the Andrea Ferrara, and the double-edged sword. Some of those in the Alwar armoury have pearls enclosed within the breadth of the blade, so that they run down to give weight to the stroke, a device which was also adopted in Europe. Wilks describes the sword used by the Nairs, noted in Southern India for their skill with the weapon, as "a thin, but very broad blade, hooked towards the edge like a bill-hook or gardener's knife, and about the length of a Roman sword." In this they followed ancient precedent. The coins of the Indo-Scythian kings show them armed with a sword, short, and sometimes straight, sometimes curved. Megasthenes says: "All wear swords of a vast breadth, though not exceeding three cubits in length; when they engage in close fight they grasp with both hands to fetch down a lustier blow." A figure in the Buddhist Stúpa at Bharhut shows a soldier armed with a long, straight sword, at least 2½ feet in length, which is suspended from the left shoulder by a long belt. The weapon of the Kandhs is a battle-axe, but they use a curiously curved sword with singular force and dexterity.

Naturally the sword has been valued and respected. Each of Akbar's weapons had its own name. He had thirty swords, one of which was sent in rotation every night to his bedchamber. At Mewár there is an annual worship of the sword. The double-edged sword of State is carried in procession, made over to the leader of the warrior ascetics, and the Rána does sacrifice and bows before it. Hence special veneration is paid to swords once wielded by national heroes. It was considered a marked instance of loyalty when the Rája of Kolhapur, in 1875, presented the sword of Sivaji to His Majesty the

King. But Grant Duff tells us that the Bráhmans in charge of Sivaji's cenotaph at Málván claim to have his real sword in their possession. Possibly the warrior had more than one special sword. The Zamorin of Calicut possesses the sword of the Malabar hero, Cherumán Perumál, the blade of which is now rusted to the scabbard; it is protected by a covering of copper, and is daily decorated with garlands. In Mewár they still treasure the sword of the hero Bappa, which is said to have been presented to him by the Saint Gorakhnáth, who pronounced over it the incantation that it should sever rocks. The Mahrattas claim to have the sword of Afzul Khán, whom Sivaji treacherously assassinated, and at Amritsar are preserved and worshipped the mace of the Guru Har Govind, and the swords of two other Sikh heroes.

Akin to the sword are the Dáo [*Dow* *] of Assam and Burma, which, according to Sir H. Yule, "serves every purpose, from making a tooth-pick to felling a tree, or killing a pig, or an enemy," and the Kúkri [*Kookry* *] of the Gurkha, which is used for equally varied purposes.

A word may be said about three remarkable weapons — the Vághnakh, the Chakra, the Boomerang. The Vághnakh, or "tiger-claw," consists of three or four sharp steel claws, with side rings attaching them to the fingers and wrist. The classical instance of its use is in the assassination of Afzul Khán by Sivaji, familiar to English readers in Meadows Taylor's story of "Tara." This weapon is said to have been presented in 1826 by Rája Pratáp Singh of Satára to Mountstuart Elphinstone; but such relics have a curious way of multiplying themselves in India, and some thirty years after it was again shown at Satára to Lady Falkland. Four examples of the weapon are found in the India Office, and one in the Meyrick collection, all received from one or other of the Mahratta States.

The chakra or steel quoit is an old Hindu weapon. In mythology it is assigned to Vishnu, and is said to have given a title to the Chakravarti, or world-wide

Emperor of old Hindu times, though this title perhaps more properly means "Ruler of a Chakra, or tract of country." Later on it became the special weapon and symbol of the fanatical Sikh Akális. The Sikh twirls it swiftly round the forefinger, and, raising the hand, launches it with deadly aim, so as to kill an enemy at a range, they say, of 80 paces. General Mundy, who witnessed a display by an expert, says that the quoit flew at half a man's height from the ground, with great force, for about 60 yards; but the wielder did not seem to have a very accurate control over its direction. It is curious that the Bhuiyas, a forest tribe of Orissa, use a similar weapon. It is a ring of iron, 6 to 8 inches round, with the outer edge sharpened. Swinging it round the index finger and then releasing it, the Bhuiya will, it is said, sever a 2-inch sapling at 40 yards.

More remarkable is the case of the boomerang, generally supposed to be confined to the Blacks of Australia. The early Hindus had a weapon called Bráhmastra — "Bráhma's missile," of which little is known, save the tradition that it possessed the power of rebounding in the direction from which it was discharged. A weapon of this kind is used to this day by the Tamil tribes, the Maravar and Kallar.

"The Australian boomerang," writes Professor Tylor, "has been claimed as derived from some hypothetical high culture, whereas the transition stages through which it is connected with the club are to be observed in our own country, while no civilised race possesses the weapon."

Bishop Caldwell has argued that its presence in South India is evidence of some connection between the people of that region and Australia, but it seems quite possible that it may have been independently invented in both countries.

[Hon. Wilbraham Egerton, "An Illustrated Handbook of Indian Arms."]

ARMY.—The growth of the Indian Native Army may be summed up in this way. We started our conquest of the country by overthrowing the weakest Native Governments and races, and we gradually proceeded to utilise for military purposes the more vigorous and manly elements of the people. We began with the effeminate population of Southern India, where we first raised a native, mercenary army. By its aid we effected the conquest of the Bengal Delta. We were thus brought into contact with the more martial races of Oudh and the Ganges-Jumna Duáb, and by the help of the Bráhmans and Rájputs from that region, we overthrew the Mahratta and Sikh Governments, and checked the expansion of the Gurkhas of Nepál. Our wise and sympathetic management of the Panjáb brought the Sikhs, the most formidable native troops we had hitherto encountered, on our side; and it was largely by their aid that we overcame our own mutinous regiments. After the mutiny the Bengal army was reorganised, and for its most efficient regiments we now depend on Sikhs and Panjábi Musalmáns, Gurkhas, and the stubborn Afrídi, and other Pathán tribes on or beyond our north-western frontier.

Alexander first proved that a small disciplined force could beat enormous native levies, and Bernier predicted that a small European brigade would overthrow the unwieldy masses of the Moghul armies. The French put the idea into practice, and it was they who first, at Pondicherry, began to drill sepoys, and afterwards to organise the forces of the Native States on their borders. Following their example, we enrolled sepoys during the siege of Madras in 1746. These were at the outset levies raised by native soldiers of fortune, ill-armed, ill-paid, and ill-disciplined. Our earliest native cavalry consisted of regiments borrowed from the Nawáb of the Carnatic, who believed this to be the only army in which a gentleman could serve. It was not till 1759 that the Madras army was formed into battalions; the first chaplain, it is interesting to note, was the devoted missionary, Schwartz. It was not till 1767 that an attempt was made to care for the wounded by establishing a corps of *Dooly* * bearers, and providing native doctors.

It was in 1681 that Mr Hedges, Governor of Bengal, brought from Madras a small force of semi-disciplined factory guards, and in 1695 a similar force was locally enlisted. Thus the Bengal army started; but it was left to Clive, in 1757, the year of Plassey, to form the Bengal force into battalions, to supply them with European accoutrements, and to subject them to regular drill and discipline.

The Bengal Cavalry began with the irregular horse, known as the Moghul Horse, which were raised in 1762. The present Body Guard of the Viceroy are the representatives of a troop of "Moghuls," raised in 1773. The first really disciplined native cavalry was that known as Bruce's Hindustani Horse, which was raised by, and attached to the person of, the French adventurer, De Boigne. When he left the service of Scindia he brought them over with him, and they were in 1769 received into our army.

In the early days of our rule the authorities depended for the defence of their factories on their own clerks and other servants. It was just at the close of the seventeenth century when the historian, Kháfi Khán, visited Bombay, and gives a remarkable account of the English forces.

"When I entered the fortress," he writes, "I observed that from the gate there was on each side of the road a line of youths, of twelve or fourteen years of age, well-dressed, and having excellent muskets on their shoulders. Every step I advanced, young men with sprouting beards, handsome and well-clothed, with fine muskets in their hands, were visible on every side. As I went onwards, I found Englishmen standing, with long beards, of similar age, and with the same acoutrements and dress. After that I saw musketeers, young men, well-dressed and arranged, drawn up in ranks. Further on I saw Englishmen with white beards, with muskets on their shoulders, drawn up in two ranks, and in perfect array. Next I saw some English children, handsome, and wearing pearls on the borders of their hats. In the same way, as far as the door of the house where the Governor abode, I found, drawn up in ranks on both sides, nearly 7,000 musketeers dressed and accoutred as for a review."

There were, then, three periods in the history of the native army of India: first, from the raising of sepoys to fight the French in the Carnatic up to the battle of Plassey, when the army was only in its early stage, and no effective organisation was possible. The second stage occupied one hundred years, and closed with the Mutiny. During this time the Madras army attained a high degree of efficiency, due to the constant war service in which it was engaged. When the South Indian campaigns ceased it naturally deteriorated. Meanwhile the northern army, under the leadership of Sir A. Wellesley, became a most formidable force, and it was at the close of the Mahratta war that it attained its greatest strength and probably its highest point of efficiency. From this period the signs of that demoralisation which culminated in the Mutiny of 1857 were perceived by many careful observers. It emerged from the Panjáb campaigns with no increase of reputation, and it was only the incorporation of the valuable Gurkha element which began after the Nepál war of 1814-15, and that of the Sikhs which followed the annexation of the Panjáb in 1849, which stiffened its ranks, and provided the force which was destined to reduce its mutinous regiments.

Since the reorganisation which followed the Mutiny the progress towards efficiency has been continuous. South India and the Deccan, as the result of a long period of peace, now fail to supply the class of men we require. The Rájputs and Bráhmans of the Ganges valley, who filled the pre-Mutiny army, have also to a great extent lost their martial renown. The flower of the modern army consists of Gurkhas, Sikhs, and the hardy frontier races. For hill fighting the best troops are the Gurkha and Pathán regiments; in steadiness and devotion none surpass the Sikh. The danger from regiments drawn from the frontier tribes is their liability to sudden outbreaks of fanaticism, which leads them to attack their own English officers; and though they are as a rule to be depended on even when fighting people of their own race, instances of treachery, as at the night attack of Roberts on the Peiwar Kotal, have occurred. In its Bengal cavalry regiments the army possesses perhaps the finest light horsemen in the world, and a fresh source of strength shows itself in the trained contingents of the Native States. Its weakness lies in its officers. The number of Europeans attached to the regiments is much too small, and we have hardly yet reached the highest type of native officer. This difficulty will be removed as we gradually open the commissioned ranks of the army to the cadets of the Indian nobility.

[Wilson, "History of the Madras Army"; Cardew, "Sketch of the Services of the Bengal Native Army"; "Calcutta Review," lxxxix, 225; Lord Roberts, "Forty-one Years in India."]

ART.—The influences which have contributed to the development of Indian art are as various as the races out of which the present population has been composed. As Aryan and Dravidian, Turk and Iranian, Scyth and Mongol are represented in the Indian people of to-day, so each of these races has had its share in the art and architecture of India. The pre-historic intercourse between Babylonia and the West Coast was afterwards resumed by the Arabs, and in medieval times China was closely connected by trade with the South. The savage arts of the pre-Aryan races are now found only in the hills, or among the rural population of the plains, but survivals of them may be found in the rough gold and silver work of Madras and in the jewellery of the peasant woman. Much of the modern jewellery worn by town-folk is merely the translation into metal of the ornaments of grass or straw worn by the jungle tribes. Aryan art, modified by its Dravidian environment, has resulted in the modern Hindu style. This in its turn has been influenced by later emigrants, who have brought with them the artistic feeling of the older civilisations in the valleys of the Tigris and Euphrates, Central Asia, and China.

Indian art, like Indian religion, is essentially catholic and receptive. The craftsman, as was remarked by the Greek historians of Alexander's campaign, is particularly skilful in imitation. Terry, writing in 1665, says:

"The truth is, that the natives of that monarchy are the best apes for imitation in the world, so full of ingenuity that they will make any new thing by pattern, how hard soever it seem to be done, and therefore it is no marvel if the natives there make boots, cloaths, linen, bands, cuffs of our English fashion and habits, and yet make them all exceeding neat."

The result of modern British influence has been disastrous. It shows itself in the Berlin-work taught in Mission schools, the adoption of European patterns in plate and jewellery, the use of crude aniline colours in place of the delicate vegetable dyes. A good authority, Mr Val. Prinsep, writes:

"These people, directly they touch European tastes, seem to lose their inherent feeling for the right thing. The worst shoddy is not so bad as the mass of objects heaped together in their palaces; yet they have beautiful things, and dress themselves with some feeling for colour, barring a taste for aniline dyes, which I see growing all over the country. Is it, perchance, that they see so little good taste among Europeans out here, whom, of course, they copy? If so, Europeans have much to answer for."

The Ajanta frescoes, probably of Persian origin, show that in the early centuries of the Christian era painting was appreciated. But in our days many natives are incapable of understanding our prints, drawings, or photographs.

"Landscapes," says Sir H. Yule, "are absolutely unintelligible. If portraits, they may know them to represent humanity, but the most striking likeness they scarcely ever recognise. Maps rarely can be made intelligible to them. As to rough pencil sketches, they convey to the natives of India as little intelligible meaning s the graven edicts of Asoka did to the world before James Prinsep."

So, writing of the Hindu-kush Káfirs, Sir G. Robertson says:

"No Káfir ever recognised pictures of buildings and landscapes. Boys and girls recognised the originals of the photographs at once, and shouted out their names; men between twenty and forty took time to consider, frequently held the pictures upside down, and required to have them readjusted before they discerned their meaning, and recognised the features portrayed; while those a few years older could never make anything out of them at all."

At the same time, Sir H. Yule's statement is perhaps put too strongly in reference to the ordinary native of our day. Colonel Cunningham remarks that the assertion could never have been correct in the case of hill people, like Lepchas or Bhotiyas. Even thirty years ago a map was comprehensible and interesting to the cooly of Sikhim.

Here it is possible only to consider some of what Sir G. Birdwood calls the Master Handicrafts of India.

To begin with gold and silver plate—we meet with beautiful work from Mysore, Lucknow, and Kashmír, the last introducing the shawl pattern into the chasing. Here and in Burmese work we see the only Indian use of ruddy gold. Next comes the Swámi [*Swamy* *] work of Madras, with its Dravidian tone, representations of Hindu gods in high relief, either *repoussé* or screwed and welded on the surface. The hammered *repoussé* work of Cutch, Lucknow, and Dacca is all of foreign origin, that of Cutch from Holland, the other Saracenic or Italian. The cased parcel-gilt work of Kashmír is a Moghul art, but has been developed by the artistic taste of local craftsmen.

Of work in brass, copper, and tin there are several well-known varieties, from Ahmadábád and Ahmadnagar in Bombay, Benares, Madura, and Tanjore. The last is by far the finest style, recalling, says Sir G. Birdwood,

"the description Homer gives of the work of Sidon in bowls of antique frame. Some are simply etched, and others deeply cut in mythological designs, and others are diapered all over with crystæ of the leaf pattern, seen in Assyrian sculptures, copper on brass, or silver on copper, producing an effect often of quite regal grandeur."

The older Benares work, with its deep, boldly-cut designs, is in its way excellent. But competition and the craze for cheapness have robbed the industry of nearly all the value it once possessed. The same may be said of the Moradábád work, tin soldered on brass, or designs etched on the metal, and filled in with lac, like Niello work.

Damascened work is almost peculiar to the Panjáb, where it is known as Koft, and to the Nizám's Dominions, where it is called Bidri [*Bidree* *]. This art is peculiarly Oriental, and originated in Damascus. It was brought to India from Persia, where it is still practised with success, by the Muhammadans.

In the art of enamelling Jaypur is supreme. According to Sir G. Birdwood, it is probably in origin Turanian.

"It was introduced into China, according to the Chinese, by the Yuechi, and was carried as early, if not earlier, into India. From Assyria it probably passed into Egypt, and through the Phœnicians into Europe."

Arms, trappings, and caparisons have been from the earliest times one of the leading art industries. Sir G. Birdwood recognises a strong resemblance between the forms of Persian and Arabic ornamentation and those of India, the former closely allied to the sculptural representations of Assyria, and Babylonia, and the hieroglyphic paintings of Egypt.

The well-known *Blackwood* * furniture of Bombay owes its inspiration to the Dutch, while the Bombay inlaid work came through Sind from Shiráz, whence it was introduced rather more than a century ago. Similarly, the inlaid marble work of Agra originated in the exquisite decorations of the Táj Mahal, attributed by some to the Frenchman Austin de Bourdeaux, but which are almost certainly of the Persian school.

Among minor arts may be mentioned the ivory carvings of Amritsar, Benares, and Travancore; the marble work of Agra and Jaypur; the clay figurines of Krishnagarh and Lucknow; the *papier maché* of Kashmír; the Delhi paintings on ivory—all the details of which may be found in Sir G. Birdwood's admirable monograph.

The future of Indian art can only be a matter of speculation. It is doubtful if the leading art industries will long survive their exploitation by ill-instructed collectors of curios. If they are to progress they must be supported, not by large miscellaneous orders from European tradesmen, but by the encouragement of the individual craftsman, who is allowed to treat each subject in his own fashion, and is warned to resist the influence of all foreign models and ideas. He must be allowed leisure and liberty to turn from one piece of work to another as the spirit moves him. At present the necessity of working under pressure to execute large orders tends to destroy the individuality of his work. Also see CARPETS, EMBROIDERY, JEWELLERY, POTTERY, WEAVING, WOOD-CARVING.

[Sir G. Birdwood, "Industrial Arts of India"; Mukharji, "Art Manufactures of India"; Articles by Lockwood Kipling in "Panjáb Gazetteer"; "Art Monographs," issued by the Governments of the Panjáb and United Provinces; Hendley, "Art Industries of Jaypur"; "Journal of Indian Art."]

ARYA SAMÁJ.—The tendency of modern Hinduism, with all its electicism and elasticity, to develop more on indigenous lines than in response to any foreign teaching, is shown in the quasi-religious organisation known as the Arya Samáj. This includes at present about 92,000 members, of whom three-fourths come from the Panjáb and the remainder from the United Provinces. It is rapidly increasing its numbers, the total membership in

1891 having been only about 40,000. Its teaching has some analogy to that of Nának, the Sikh Guru, inasmuch as both profess a purely theistic creed in place of the polytheism of the later Hinduism. It encourages the observance of caste rules in regard to persons who are not Hindus, while intermarriage and commensality with all Hindus are recognised.

The sect was founded by Dyanand Sáraswati, a Gujaráti Bráhman, born in 1827, who died, some say of poison administered by a rival sectarian, in 1883. The peculiarity of his teaching was the assertion that the four collections of Vedic Hymns, as distinct from the later Bráhmanas and Upanishads, are the only true revelation, and that hymns addressed to Agni, the fire god, Súrya, the sun god, and Indra, the god of the firmament, are really addressed to one god under various names. While he wished to lead his followers back to the Vedas, as the only true revelation, he adopted other doctrines, such as metempsychosis, which have no Vedic authority. He also advocated social reform, and preached against child marriage. In its spirit his teaching was strongly opposed to Western thought and science.

Since the death of its founder the sect has suffered from internal dissension, the question on which its members are at present divided being that of the lawfulness of the use of animal food, the vegetarians representing the conservative element, while the "cultured" party advocates the use of meat. According to Mr Burn, who has given a full account of the sect, while it is possible that Christian teaching has given the impulse to this form of enquiry into Hinduism, there is little reason to believe that the Samáj has been directly influenced by mission work.

"Almost all the distinctive features of its creed, such as monotheism and the vanity of idol-worship, and its social reforms in connection with child and infant marriage and caste restrictions, have been anticipated in the tenets of the Vaishnava reformers. Where it differs completely from these is in its having a more intellectual foundation, and while many of them have ended in the deification of their founder, the members of the Arya Samáj regard Dayanand Sáraswati as a great teacher, but merely human, and subject to rebirth."

In strange contrast to this advanced theistic teaching is the exaggerated belief in the sanctity of the cow, and the preaching of some members of the sect is believed to have encouraged the fanatical movement against cow-killing, which led, a few years ago, to serious disturbances in parts of Northern India.

["Census Reports," Rájputána, 1901, i. 53ff.; United Provinces, 1901, i. 82ff.; Rev. F. Lillingston, "The Bráhmo Samáj and Arya Samáj in their bearing upon Christianity"; Pramátha Náth Bose, "Hindu Civilisation during British Rule," i. 96ff.]

ASTROLOGY.—This, one of the most ancient of the world's superstitions, is based on the belief that the changes and chances of a man's life depend on the motions of the heavenly bodies. Chaldæa seems to have been the scene of its origin, and thence it spread to the East as well as to the West. As early as 50 A.D. the Indian astrologers practising at Rome were expelled by Nero. One of these is said to have been Apollonius of Tyana, who travelled in India to learn the science of the Bráhmans, and returned to Rome with seven magical rings, each made under the influence of one of the planets, and prescribed that they were to be worn on the corresponding days of the week. Albirúni (c. 1030) speaks rather contemptuously of Hindu astrologers, and charges them with relying for their prognostications more on augury and physiognomy, and neglecting to draw conclusions, as they ought to do, from the stars.

The Moghul Emperors paid great attention to astrology. Terry, writing of Jahángír, says:

"The great Mogul puts so much confidence in his Astrologers, that he will not undertake a journey, nor yet resolve to do anything besides of the least consequence, unless his wizards tell him it is a good and prosperous hour to begin and set upon such an undertaking; and at the very instant he hath his directions from them, he sets upon the thing he undertakes, and not before."

In this he followed the example of his grandfather, Humáyun, who was noted for his skill in the art. Later on, in the time of Aurangzeb, Bernier speaks of Delhi as swarming with Hindu and Musalmán astrologers, whose methods he describes.

"The most ridiculous of these pretenders to divination was a half-caste Portuguese, a fugitive from Goa. This fellow sat on his carpet as gravely as the rest, and had many customers notwithstanding he could neither read nor write. His only instrument was an old mariner's compass, and his books of astrology a couple of old Romish prayer-books in the Portuguese language, the pictures of which he pointed out as the signs of the European Zodiac. '*A tal Bestias, tal Astrologuo*'—'For such brutes, such an astrologer,'—he unblushingly observed to the Jesuit, the Rev. Father Buze, who saw him at his work."

Even Europeans in India have depended upon the predictions of Bráhman astrologers. James Forbes describes how an astrologer predicted that Mr Hodges would be Governor of Bombay, and he, when the prediction was fulfilled, consulted him about all he did. Finally the Governor died on a night which the Hindu Calendar recorded as unlucky. In later times Meadows Taylor tells how an astrologer gave a remarkable forecast of his life, and predicted with wonderful accuracy the fate of the young Rája of Satára.

Nowadays the astrologer flourishes in India. He is consulted on all the affairs of life—whether a marriage will be prosperous, what will be the sex of an expected child, whether a favourable verdict will be given in a law-suit, whether a speculation will prosper, how long the enquirer will live, and so on. In some cases he decides the favourable time for such a modern operation as vaccination. For these purposes the astrologer uses an almanac, various editions of which are issued at the great seats of Hindu learning, like Benares or Násik, containing a record of lucky and unlucky days, directions of journeys and the like, predictions of the prospects of the season, and the stars dominant on each day of the year. The lunar mansions are carefully defined, for on them depends in a great measure the fate of a child. If it be born in one of them, Múl, the fact is most inauspicious, and the father dares not look on the baby until a rite of expiation is performed. In former times such children were exposed or made over to one of the wandering ascetics.

In Upper India there are two branches of the profession, that of the Jyotishi, who prepares horoscopes, and that of the Joshi, a much lower practitioner, who never casts nativities, but is employed to dispel the evil influence which attaches to Saturn and the demons which rule eclipses. He practises the ancient art of palmistry, but has, of course, no connection with the gipsy palmist.

In South India he is known as a Panchángi, who is a well-recognised village official, and consulted on every matter affecting the welfare of the community. Mr Logan, writing of Malabar, says that there are two things he must have, a bag of cowries and an almanac.

"When any one comes to consult him he quietly sits down, facing the Sun, on a plank-seat or mat, murmuring some sacred verses, opens the bag of cowries, and pours them on the floor. With his right hand he slowly moves them round and round, solemnly reciting meanwhile a stanza or two in praise of his teacher and of his deity, invoking their help. He then stops and explains what he has been doing, at the same time taking a handful of cowries from the heap and placing them on one side. In front is a diagram drawn with chalk on the floor, and consisting of twelve compartments. Before commencing operations with the diagram, he selects three or five of the cowries highest up in the heap, and places them in a line on his right-hand side. These represent Ganapati, remover of obstacles; the Sun; Jupiter; Sáraswati, goddess of speech; and his own preceptor. To all of these the astrologer gives due obeisance, touching his ears and the ground three times with both hands. The cowries are next arranged in the compartments of the diagram, and are moved about from compartment to compartment by the astrologer, who meanwhile quotes the authority on which he makes such moves. Finally, he explains the result, and ends with again worshipping the deified cowries, who were witnessing the operation as spectators."

But the chief business of the astrologer is the preparation of horoscopes. In order to prepare this the exact time of birth must be ascertained, and the astrologer then works out from his almanac the asterism and planet dominant at the moment. When the asterism is ascertained the horoscope name is fixed, having as its first letter the initial of the asterism of birth. If the astrologer be afterwards accused of making a wrong prediction, all he has to say is that the parent has failed to give the exact moment of birth. From time to time he is called in to advise in the event of illness, or at any crisis in the life of the child. When illness occurs he generally advises an offering to appease the wrath of the angry star, and to avoid any mistake he appropriates this for himself. At marriage he has to compare the horoscopes of bride and bridegroom, and decide whether or not in one of their former lives they may perchance have been members of different castes, a fact which would be fatal to the engagement. In ordinary marriages this is a necessary condition; but in the case of a Bráhman, he may marry a girl who was once of lower caste than himself; but if the horoscope show a condition the reverse of this, no alliance can take place. When the match is finally arranged, it is his business to fix an auspicious hour for the ceremony.

The Bráhman astrologer can also act for the lower castes, and this is one of the means by which the forest tribes are brought within the fold of the Church. Musalmáns have a method of their own for drawing a horoscope and fixing a lucky birth-name; but, as a matter of fact, it is to the Hindu astrologer that all the lower class Musalmáns resort. In the same way the court of Burma, like that of Siam, kept up a staff of

Bráhman astrologers, who were regularly domesticated in the country. There the rural astrologer decides the proper time for ploughing and sowing, by ascertaining the position in which the Nága, or great serpent, is lying beneath the earth. In Tibet the Lamas encourage astrology as the chief means of gaining a livelihood at the expense of the laity.

"The astrologers," writes Colonel Waddell, "have always a constant stream of persons coming to them for prescriptions as to what deities and demons require appeasing, and the remedies necessary to remedy these portending evils."

Many are the ways in which evil predictions may be counteracted. Thus, we read of Rája Dáhir of Sind:

"Dáhir then said to the astrologer, 'I must fight to-day; tell me in what part of the heavens the planet Venus is, and calculate which of the two armies will be successful, and what will be the result.' After the computation, the astrologer replied, 'According to the calculation, the victory shall be to the Arab army, because Venus is behind him and in front of you.' Rái Dáhir was angry on hearing this. The astrologer then said 'Be not angered, but order an image of Venus to be prepared of gold.' It was made and fastened to his saddle-straps, in order that Venus might be behind him, and he be victorious."

Unfortunately, the device failed and Dáhir was slain. Another instance of an astrologer causing the ruin of his master is that of the Rája of Nadiya. When Bakhtiyár Khilji, in 1202, marched on the city, the Hindu Rája was advised to wait nine hours before attacking. Meanwhile the Musalmáns entered the city, and the Rája had to fly for his life.

[Shway Yoe, "The Burman," i. 9, ii. 95; Waddell, "Buddhism of Tibet," 450ff.; "Bulletin of Madras Museum," iii. 305ff.; Logan, "Manual of Malabar," i. 141; Dosabhai Framji Karaka, "History of the Pársis," i. 161; "Calcutta Review," lxxxiv. 273ff.]

BABOO.*—The term Baboo, really a respectful form of address, used in North-east India, has come to be appropriated by Europeans to the Bengal clerk, who, excellent though he be as an office hand, has many eccentricities, and in particular uses English in a most amusing way. No one has yet dared to make a collection of the solecisms which the majority of Englishmen commit when they endeavour to express themselves in the native tongue, and many natives speak and write English with remarkable ease and correctness. But to the jaded English official the curiosities of the so-called "Baboo English" are a perennial source of amusement.

It is not difficult to discover the origin of this curious "Pidgin" dialect. It is the result of the system of education in the Indian Universities, which busy themselves about the superstructure when they ought to be digging the foundations of learning. In most of the schools which prepare students for the University examinations the teaching of English has been inferior. Too little regard has been paid to elementary instruction in grammar and idiom; up to recent times the reading books consisted of selections drawn far too largely from the Johnsonian school of eighteenth-century literature, and later writers, who cultivated a crisper and less cumbrous style, were neglected. A large part of the instruction used to consist of the so-called paraphrasing of poetry. Thus, Sir G. Trevelyan describes a visit to a school in which

"the class was engaged on the 'Deserted Village.' Each scholar read a few lines, and then gave a paraphrase of them in the most grandiloquent and classical English. I sat aghast at the flowery combination of epithets which came so glibly and naturally to their lips, not knowing at the time that the natives who have been brought up at the Government schools, having learnt our language from Addison and Goldsmith, use, on all occasions, the literary English of the eighteenth century."

One youth, on being asked to define Goldsmith's phrase "unwieldy wealth," replied: "Dazzling gauds and plenty too much elephants."

The possibilities of Baboo English first became known to the West in the delightful "Memoir of Justice

Onoocool Chunder Mookerjee," published in 1873. An English humorist has adopted the dialect in "Mr Jabberjee" of *Punch*, but he has hardly caught the true Oriental flavour of his original.

A few instances of the style in later days may be given. A school-boy writes:

"The headmaster is a man of great anger, the boys suffer so much from corporal punishment that no man can return from school without shedding his tears. Under him the school is changed to butcher's shop."

A gentleman writes to his physician:

"While walking last evening, by riding on the road, I tumbled my steed, and have broken my arm, and waist. Therefore be pleased to send me some oil, pill, or a leach (*sic*) for remedy."

The following are two letters from the husband of a patient, addressed to the Matron of a Female Hospital:

"Dear She. My wife has returned from your hospital cured. Provided males are allowed at your bungalow, I would like to do you the honour of presenting myself there this afternoon. But I will not try to repay you. Vengeance belongeth unto God. Your's noticeably.——"

"Dear and Fair Madam. I have much pleasure to inform you that my dearly unfortunate wife will be no longer under your kind treatment, she having left this world for the other on the night of 27th ult. For your help in the matter I shall ever remain grateful. Your's reverently.——"

The following gives a lively picture of an outbreak of plague:

"The Sub-Postmaster report that last evening a mice come out from behind office door and after walking a little stammered and breathed its last in the presence of Sub-Postmaster. As this is prognostic of plague, please arrange."

The following announced cholera:

"All Railway Babus assembled. To stay here is instantaneous death. What can Babu give in exchange for his soul? In anticipation of sanction, will leave to-night."

The following is from a servant to his master:

"Honourable Sir. Yesterday vesper arrive great hurricane. Valve of little aperture not fasten; first make great trepidation and palpitation, then precipitate into precinct. No tranquility in house since valve adjourn. I send for carpenter to make re-unite. God grant master more long life and more great post."

From an essay on Cardinal Wolsey:

"Cardinal Wolsy was an eminent man and also a minister of Henry the V. Monmouth, he was a rude gray headed man and a strict English and his death was a remarkable one. As Bishop of Yourk but died in disentry in a church on his way to be block-headed."

An English gentleman was startled to find himself addressed as "Honoured Enormity." A youth writes an essay on the horse: "The horse is a very noble animal, but when irritated he ceases to do so." Another thus sums up human life: "In short, the rich man welters on crimson velvet, while the poor man snorts on flint." Another defines a bat as "a featherless bird given to grazing at night"; while another describes the distance between two places as "Thirty miles as the cock crows." Another, acknowledging a favour, writes: "You have been very good to me, and may God Almighty give you tit for tat." Mrs Fanny Parkes, when her head servant died, promised to pay his funeral expenses, and was amazed to receive a bill: "For roasting Sirdar Bearer, five rupees." At a recent examination in Bombay a candidate, in an essay on Matrimony, remarks: "I do not believe in polygamy, but am one."

["Indo-Anglian Literature," Calcutta, 1887; "Life of Onoocool Mookerjee."]

BAMBOO.—"Among the Indo-Chinese nations the staff of life is the Bamboo," writes Sir H. Yule; and it is hard to say how the native of India could do without it. But though he values it for its practical uses, he seems never to realise, as the Japanese do, its artistic grace and beauty. It is the hill-man who best appreciates its manifold utilities. Thus, Captain Lewin writes of the Eastern frontier tribes

"He builds his house of the bamboo; he fertilises his fields with its ashes; of its stem he makes vessels in which to carry water; with two bits of bamboo he can produce fire; its young and succulent shoots provide a dainty dinner dish; and he weaves his sleeping-mat of fine slips thereof; the instruments with which his women weave their cotton are of bamboo. He makes drinking cups of it, and his head at night rests upon a bamboo pillow; his forts are built of it; he catches fish, makes baskets and stools, and thatches his house with the help of the bamboo. He smokes from a pipe of bamboo; and from bamboo ashes he obtains potash. Finally, his funeral pile is lighted with bamboo. The hill-man would die without the bamboo, and the thing he finds hardest of credence is that in other countries the bamboo does not grow, and that men live in ignorance of it. Throughout the whole of India, indeed, the bamboo occupies the foremost place in the domestic economy of the inhabitants."

A curious use of the bamboo is seen among the vagrant hunting tribes and the bird-catchers, who supply birds in the larger cities. They arrange a set of bamboo slips somewhat like the joints of a fishing-rod. The thinnest piece is smeared with bird-lime. This is passed up through the branches of a tree; joint after joint is added, till the first piece approaches the top, when it is deftly pressed against the feathers of the unhappy bird. The skill of the sportsman is shown in the care with which he avoids making any rustling of leaf or branch.

It is among the forest tribes that we find the bamboo worshipped. Some hill tribes of Assam and Chota Nágpur worship it as their tribal god; with others it is a sacred tree, round which the bride and bridegroom revolve at marriage. The athletes of Central India, who perform most of their feats by its aid, make an offering to it before they begin their exhibition. Some worship a single bamboo fixed in the ground; others a collection of three; others a split bamboo. At most of the village shrines in Northern India a bamboo may be seen fixed in the ground as a convenient perch for the god when he feels disposed to visit the place.

Many are the varieties of the bamboo, but the economic values and peculiarities of these have not been as yet fully investigated. The popular classification is into "male" and "female," the former term being applied to any solid bamboo used for spear- or lance-staves, walking-sticks, and the formidable *lathee*,* or quarter-staff, which every rustic carries. More particularly the name defines the variety known to botanists as *Dendrocalamus strictus*. "Female" is the name applied to the hollow and weaker varieties, and is sometimes restricted to *Bambusa balcooa*.

One peculiarity of the bamboo which has attracted considerable attention is its habit of flowering.

"All the species," writes Sir G. Watt, "commence to flower when in full leaf, but as the inflorescence expands, the leaves as a rule fall off, until when in complete flower the clump, or certain portions of it, are leafless. In some cases special flowering culms are produced; at other times every culm flowers, the flowering portion or the entire clump dying off after the seeds are mature. In a few instances the plant continues to flower as a perennial, while some bamboos are entirely annual, flowering and dying down to the ground every year. With all the larger species the flowering stage is reached after a prolonged period of vegetation, variously stated at from twenty-five to thirty years, and is almost regularly followed by the death of the whole stock."

This flowering seems to be decidedly influenced by some of the causes which produce famine. At any rate, the providential supply of its wheat-like grain has saved the lives of thousands during the great famines. The question remains whether the bamboo flowers when it reaches a definite age, or only at any period when mature, provided the circumstances of the season are favourable. On the one side is the great authority of Sir J. D. Hooker, who holds that the flowering is not due, as some suppose, to the life of the species being of a certain duration—for the bamboo flowers only to die down to the ground—but to favourable seasons. Others adopt the view that the flowering occurs at a definite stage in the life of the plant. Sir G. Watt thinks that both theories may be true:

"And this is probably the wiser solution of the difficulty

—that is to say, a bamboo may not flower before it has attained a certain age, but its flowering is not fixed so arbitrarily that it cannot be retarded or accelerated by climatic influences."

A curious product of the bamboo is the Bamboo Manna, or *Tabasheer*,* which possesses an interest for the antiquary, as it has been supposed to be the substance referred to by authors like Dioscorides and Pliny, when they speak of sugar. The view of Sir H. Yule, that the hydrate of silica found in the bamboo cannot be the Saccharum of the ancients, seems now to be generally accepted.

No bamboo in India seems to equal in size the giant plants in the Botanic Gardens of Peradeniya, Ceylon, which are 2 feet in diameter. The Bengal varieties, according to Linschoten, "are so thicke, that a man can hardly gripe them with both his hands"; and Pyrard de Laval speaks of those in the same region "as big as a man's thigh," which is the size of the great Lepcha bamboo which was described by Sir J. D. Hooker. The rate of growth is remarkable, the more important varieties seeming to grow chiefly at night, on an average 3 inches a day, and horrible tales are told of torture by fixing a criminal on one of the shoots and allowing it to penetrate his body gradually. All natives believe that the bamboo does not shoot until thunder comes, an idea possibly based on the fact of the greater amount of nitrogen compounds in the air during electrical discharges. The belief that jungle fires are caused by the friction of one dry bamboo upon another is rejected by Dr Ball, who prefers to attribute them to human agency, accidental or wilful.

[J. S. Gamble, "Bambusiae of British India"; A. B. Freeman-Mitford, "The Bamboo Garden"; Watt, "Economic Dictionary," i. 370ff.]

BANYAN TREE.—Two species of the genus *ficus*, or the fig—the banyan (*ficus bengalensis*) and the Pipal [*Peepul**] (*ficus religiosa*)—have for many ages received homage from Hindus. The banyan with its numerous stems was fitly regarded as the home of gods and spirits.

Even Bishop Heber, when he saw a great banyan tree in Central India, could exclaim, "What a noble place of worship."

"There is," says Terry, "one very great and fair tree growing on that soil, of special observation, out of whose branches or great arms grow little sprigs downwards, till they take root (as they will certainly do if they be let alone), and taking root, at length prove strong supporters unto those large branches that yield them. Whence it comes to pass, that those trees in time (their strong and far-extended arms being in many places thus supported) grow to a very great height and extend themselves to such an incredible breadth, they growing round every way, as that hundreds of men may shade themselves under one of them at any time; the rather, because these, as all other trees in those Southern parts of East India, still keep on their green coats."

The anthropomorphic worship of the banyan appears in its representation on a Buddhist sculpture from Malwa, as the Kalpa-druma, or "wishing tree," with long pendent roots, from which untold wealth is dropping in the form of square pieces of gold, in such quantities that all the vessels placed below are overflowing; while in the sculpture at Mahábodhi, near Gaya in Bengal, two human arms are extended from the tree, one holding a plate with food, the other wine or water, towards a man, who is stretching out his right hand to receive them.

The famous Akshaya Vata, or "undying banyan," at Alláhábád, is mentioned in Hindu legend as the place where Ráma, his wife Síta, and his faithful brother Lakshmana, took refuge. The Chinese pilgrim, Hiuen Tsiang, in the seventh century A.D., describes it as a tree with wide-spreading branches, which was said to be the dwelling-place of the man-eating demon; it was surrounded with human bones, the remains of pilgrims who used to fling themselves into the water at the sacred river-junction, a custom which, he says, had been observed from time immemorial. The successor of this sacred tree is still worshipped in an underground temple near the fort of Alláhábád. One small sect in Baroda, the Lálvadias, take their name from the banyan tree, which is their sole object of worship.

Of the sacred pípal trees the most famous is that at the Mahábodhi temple near Gaya. It was here that the Buddha sat when he gained perfect wisdom, and hence it got the name of Bodhi-druma, "the tree of knowledge." It, or one of its successors, seems to have survived the downfall of Buddhism, although, according to tradition, cut down more than once by enemies of the Buddhist faith; but it was, according to General Cunningham, probably destroyed by the western king, Haimanta, in the first century of our era. Even the fanatical Bakhtiyár Khilji, in his invasion of Bengal, seems to have spared it, or one of its successors, as the Muhammadans spared the famous tree at Pesháwar. The pípal is a quick-growing tree, and perhaps as many as twenty successors of it have sprung from seed from the time of Asoka to the present day.

When Buddhism was established in Ceylon, the King Tissa begged for a branch of the holy tree under which Buddha had received enlightenment.

"The difficulty," writes Sir Emerson Tennent, "of severing a portion without the sacrilegious offence of 'lopping it with any weapon,' was overcome by the miracle of the branch detaching itself spontaneously, and descending with its roots into the fragrant earth prepared for it in a golden vase, in which it was transported by sea to Ceylon, and planted by King Tissa in the spot at Anarajapoora, where, after the lapse of more than two thousand years, it still continues to flourish, and to receive the veneration of all Buddhist nations."

"This," says Mr Fergusson, "if not the oldest, is certainly among the most ancient of the idols that still command the adoration of mankind." The cult is closely connected with the Indo-European cosmic tree, which produces ambrosia and dispenses salvation.

Another famous banyan tree is the Kabír Wad [*Cubeer Burr* *], of which the scanty remains still survive on an island in the Narbada in the Broach district. That observant traveller, P. della Valle, saw "this great and fair tree" in 1623. When James Forbes visited the place (1776-83) it had already suffered much from floods, but even then enclosed a space 2,000 feet in circumference. Nearly fifty years later Bishop Heber writes that "enough remains to make it one of the noblest groves in the world." Since that time, floods, storms, and old age have almost completed its ruin. The place where the central stem stood is marked by a shrine sacred to the Saint Kabír, though it is practically certain that it is only by a later legend that it is connected with this holy man, who died early in the fifteenth century, and that its sanctity dates from the time when Buddhism was a power in the land. In many places we find legends of such trees springing from the tooth-twig of Buddha. The story has passed on to the saints who succeeded him, but all such places were originally seats of the older worship. It was this, or a similar tree under which Arrian says that the Indian sages used to sit in a state of nudity, "the shadow whereof Nearchus says extends to five plethra," adding that even ten thousand men could be covered by the shadow of a single tree. Thence the story passed down to the days of Milton, who took from Gerard's "Herbal" his account of the fig tree:

> "Such as at this day to Indians known,
> In Malabar or Decan spreads her arms."

Some of the existing banyan trees are of remarkable size. One at Wái, in the Satára district of Bombay, is described by Lady Falkland as covering an area of $3\frac{3}{4}$ acres; in 1882 its circumference was 1,587 feet. When Sir J. D. Hooker, in 1850, saw the tree in the Botanical Gardens at Calcutta it was sixty-eight years old, 80 feet high, and threw its cool; dark shade over an area of 300 feet in diameter. Quite recently it was found to have 232 aerial roots, the main trunk had a girth of 42 feet, and the circumference of its leafy crown was 857 feet. It still grows vigorously, and there seems no reason why it should not increase in size for many a long year to come. A tree which grew near Hardoi, in Oudh, now destroyed, is said to have sheltered two regiments in the Mutiny.

[On the Bodhi Tree, see Cunningham, "Mahàbodhi," 13, 30; Tennent, "Ceylon," ii. 611ff.]

BARASAUL GUNS.—This is a name given to mysterious sounds heard occasionally in the neighbourhood of Bárásál, in the Bakarganj district of Bengal. They are described as resembling the dull, muffled boom of distant cannon. Sometimes they sound like a cannonade between two widely separated opposing forces; at other times seeming to come from different directions, but always from the southward, or seaward.

Many explanations of this phenomenon have been suggested, and it can hardly be said that the question has as yet been definitely decided. Natives, in their usual way, attribute them to the supernatural commemoration of the marriage between Ganga, the goddess of the Ganges, and the Bráhmaputra, or "son of Bráhma." Some modern enquirers have suggested that they are merely the sound of fireworks at native weddings; others that they are due to the falling in of river banks, landslips, thunder-claps, or seismic disturbances. The theory that they are caused by the crackling of bamboos during forest fires is confuted by the fact that there are no jungles in the direction from which the sounds arise.

Two theories possess a higher degree of probability—that of Professor Tomlinson, that they are due to the discharge of ball-lightning; or that of Mr Pellew that they proceed from the noise of waves beating on the shore of the Bay of Bengal.

In the discussion which took place at a meeting of the Asiatic Society of Bengal in 1870 it was urged by Mr Pellew that

"the waves of the length of a mile or so, advancing

obliquely from the S.S.W., would break successively on the coast from W. to E. To a person close by the sound of each wave would be somewhat continuous: but to a person forty or fifty miles off, if the waves broke simultaneously, the sound would be a boom like that of a gun, because both extremities of the wave would be at the same distance from the hearer at the centre."

On the whole, the wave theory seems best to account for the facts.

Other mysterious sounds have been heard in the neighbourhood of Purniya in Bengal, which have been attributed to landslips in the hills or to seismic disturbances. Others heard in the deserts of the South Panjáb and Rájputána are almost certainly due to movements in the sand-hills under the influence of wind. Here the lonely herdsman hears voices at night calling out, "Strike! Strike!" the cries, as he believes, of men slain in ancient frontier raids. Dean Stanley records similar sounds at the mountain of Jebel Musa, in the Sinai Peninsula, where the hill of Nakús, or "the Bell," takes its name from the idea that the sounds are those of a convent enclosed within the mountain.

["Journal Asiatic Society of Bengal," 1870; "Nature," January-May, 1896; Yule, "Marco Polo," ch. xxxix; "Cathay and the Way Thither," 156-8, 398; "Calcutta Review," ciii. 332ff.]

BATHING.—Bathing in India is enforced by reasons based on ceremonial rather than on sanitation. The average Hindu, in spite of his frequent dabbling in water, is not in other ways a cleanly person. In the disposal of sewage, for instance, he defies all the laws of health. He is, however, much cleaner than the low-class Musalmán. The dress of the cooly woman obviously shows her disregard of personal cleanliness. Still more is this the case with visitors from beyond the northern frontier. The Kábuli horse-dealer seldom washes or changes his clothes. As winter comes he piles one garment over another, and reverses the process with the advance of summer.

The Tibetan, who comes down to the Plains with borax, equally dislikes a bath. Colonel Dalton writes that when a party of Bhotiyas from the hills came to obtain a certificate of naturalisation as British subjects, he refused it till they had washed themselves, probably for the first time in their lives. The Káfirs, Sir G. Robertson tells us, have their faces always sooty from smoke, and are most reluctant to wash. At the same time these people on the north frontier are not influenced by a constitutional distaste for cleanliness; the rigour of the climate prevents the use of the bath. The Wás, a forest tribe in Burma, have not this excuse. Sir J. G. Scott writes: "The state of dirt of both men and women is absolutely beyond belief, and is limited by the point beyond which extraneous matter refuses to adhere to human flesh."

When the Hindu, then, takes his morning bath, he does so in order to remove the pollution which would prevent the due performance of his daily worship. In this respect the man of high caste in Northern India is usually much less sensitive than those of Madras. But this is not always so. A well-known Rája in the United Provinces always bathed after an interview with a European. For a Nayar of Malabar the mere approach of a low caste person anywhere in his vicinity involves pollution which can be removed only by bathing. The Nambútiri Bráhman men bathe three times a day; women and children only once. The men may be recognised by the thick, indurated skin between the first finger and thumb of the right hand, where the loin-cloth is held while being wringed dry. The bath to avoid ceremonial pollution must in Malabar extend to complete immersion. Even to use hot water seems to be against the canon, and many are the devices by which they endeavour to turn the flank of the law. The water must be in a natural tank or stream; even Ganges water, if confined in a tub, would fail to secure the object. Hence some of the strictly orthodox are driven to emptying big kettles of boiling water into the stream above the bathing place, in order that the health of the bather may not suffer.

"The orthodox fashion," writes Mr Logan, "is to hold the nose with finger and thumb and dip completely under the surface, when nothing more loathsome than the polluting touch of a European's friendly hand has to be washed off. This bath is necessary before food can be partaken, or a sacred place entered, or several other acts performed."

People who dip into the Ganges or some other holy river realise to some extent that to be pure in body renders them more susceptible to the health-giving influences which pervade the sacred place; but the pilgrim's bathing is generally intended to bring himself into communion with the spirit which animates the water into which he plunges.

The Buddhist of the Himálaya also recognises that purity of body is emblematic of purity of mind, and that ablution is a sacerdotal act preliminary to worship. But he seldom does more than dip the tips of his fingers in water, and often not so much as that.

With the Musalmán, too, the bath is a ceremony; but in some of the larger cities they have adopted the ancient Roman bath, which was used to secure personal cleanliness. They are careful to divide pollution into two classes, the greater and the less; and prescribe total immersion as a remedy only for the former and less common variety. Where water is not readily procurable, according to the original Arab rule, a handful of sand or earth will answer the purpose. In a similar way the Dárds of Kashmír effect the same result by fumigating themselves with the smoke of cedar twigs.

[Logan, "Manual of Malabar," i. 118; Fawcett, "Bulletin of Madras Museum," iii. Pt. I. p. 53; Waddell, "Buddhism of Tibet," 423; Dalton, "Ethnology of Bengal," 97; Robertson, "Káfirs of the Hindu-kush," 169; "Upper Burma Gazetteer," Pt. I. i. 510; Drew, "Jummoo and Kashmír," 431.]

BAZAAR.*—The great markets of the Indian cities, each with its quarter allotted to a special trade, its lines of small shops open to the roadway, displaying piles of cloth of many colours or masses of brazen vessels, the heaps of grain in the open air, the thronging crowds, the din and dust, all under a glaring tropical sun, have always interested the traveller; but in modern times the chief bazaars at the capital cities, Delhi, Agra, Lahore, Lucknow, have lost much of their splendour during our rule, since the hordes of courtiers, troops, and hangers-on which followed the sovereign have been dispersed. New bazaars, like those of Calcutta and Bombay, have arisen to meet the increasing home and foreign trade, but they have little of the picturesqueness of the older bazaars.

Of the four great bazaars of Southern India of which accounts survive—Goa and Calicut, Bijapur and Vijayanagar—the two last are in ruins, and the two former have little left of their original magnificence.

The Goa bazaar has been described by Linschoten (1583) and Pyrard de Laval (1605). The former tells us of the Leylon or auction-mart, the "outroop," as he calls it.

"There are certain Cryers appointed by the Citie for ye purpose, which have of all things to be cryed and sold; these goe all the time of the Leylon or outroop, all behanged about with all sorts of gold chaines, all kindes of costly Iewels, pearles, rings, and precious stones; likewise they have running about them, many sorts of slaves, both men and women, young and old, which are daylie sould there, as beasts are sold with us, where everie one may chuse which liketh him best, everie one at a certaine price. There are also Arabian horses, all kinde of spices and dryed drugges, sweet gummes, and such like things, out of Cambaia, Sinde, Bengala, China, etc., and it is wonderfull to see in what sort many of them get their livinges, which every day come thether to buy and at another time sel them again."

Pyrard describes the long street—

"Very handsome and broad, full of shops of jewellers, goldsmiths, lapidaries, carpet weavers, silk mercers, and other artisans. While this market is afoot, there is so great a crowd in the street that one can hardly pass. They fear neither rain in winter nor heat in summer, by reason of the large *sombreros* or parasols, which every one carries; these are 6 or 7 feet in diameter at the least, in such wise that when the crowd is assembled they all touch one another, and the whole seems but one covering."

After speaking of the trade in slaves, he adds:

"In this market are also to be seen a great number of other slaves that are not for sale, but themselves bring the work they have done, such as tapestry, embroideries, and needle-work; as also preserves, fruits, and other things. Others earn money by fetching and carrying anything required. The girls deck themselves out in fine style, so as to be more attractive, and to sell their goods the better. In short," he continues, "one sees there the wealth of the Indies in all kinds, and jewels the finest that can be seen. There are also the money changers, of whom there are several at other points. Their shops are at the ends of the streets and at the cross-roads, all covered with money, whereof they pay a tribute to the king. Their gains are very great, for it is necessary at Goa to have money to go to the market, where everything is of the very cheapest, and one only buys what is required for the hour, and not even for the whole day. So that one is half-burdened with this money, which is bulky and heavy, and of small value withal."

In Calicut, according to Pyrard, the arrangements were more elaborate. The market

"is opened at seven o'clock, and one of the king's officers has the duty of sounding a bell to warn the king's servants and purveyors to go buy what is necessary for his house, for none would dare to buy anything ere the king's household was supplied. This done, the bell is sounded a second time to call the merchants; but before the merchants enter, the tax-farmers take their dues off even the smallest of the goods. Before the king's officers have taken what is due to them, no one would dare to go near or touch any goods, least of all anything eatable. Even after that, unless they be Bramenis or Nairs, they would not dare so much as touch any goods that are for sale ere a price has been made, and then they are obliged to take them. Care has to be taken also in going through the market, where all those that sell are seated, not to touch either their persons or their goods, unless they be of the same caste and religion."

The third great bazaar of the South, Vijayanagar, the splendid Hindu city which lasted only a couple of centuries, and was overthrown by the Musulmán kings of the Deccan in 1565, is described by Abd-er-razzák, who visited it in the middle of the fifteenth century. There were four bazaars near the king's palace, and at the head of each a lofty arcade and magnificent gallery.

"The bazaars are extremely long and broad. The rose merchants place before their shops high *estrades*, on each side of which they expose their flowers for sale. In this place one sees a constant succession of sweet-smelling and fresh-looking roses. . . . Each class of men belonging to each profession has shops contiguous the one to the other; the jewellers sell publicly in the bazaar, pearls, rubies, emeralds, and diamonds. In this agreeable locality one sees numerous running streams and canals formed of chiselled stone, polished and smooth."

Bijapur was another of these short-lived capitals. Founded early in the fifteenth century, it was destroyed by Aurangzeb in 1686, and is now little more than a ruin. Asad Beg, who was there in 1604, has left an enthusiastic account of its bazaar:

"Before each shop was a beautiful green tree, and the whole bazar was extremely clean and pure. It was filled with rare goods, such as are not to be seen or heard of in any other town. There were shops of cloth-sellers, jewellers, armourers, vintners, bakers, fishmongers, and cooks. . . . In short the whole bazar was filled with wine and beauty, dancers, perfumers, jewels of all sorts, palaces and viands. In one street were a thousand bands of people drinking, and dancers, lovers, and pleasure-seekers assembled; none quarrelled or disputed with another, and this state of things was perpetual. Perhaps no place in the wide world could present a more wonderful spectacle to the eye of the traveller."

Another type of bazaar is that of the great camp of

Aurangzeb, which, Bernier tells us, was laid out daily by the Grand Quarter-master.

"All of them are distinguished by extremely long poles stuck in the ground at the distance of 300 paces from each other, bearing red standards, and surmounted by the tails of the Great Tibet cow, which have the appearance of so many periwigs."

Similar to these were the bazaars of the Mahratta Camp, which Wilks tells us

"to their famished visitors exhibited a picture of the spoils of the East, and the industry of the West. From a web of English broadcloth to a Birmingham pen-knife; from the shawls of Cashmere to the second-hand garment of a Hindoo; from diamonds of the first water to the silver ear-ring of a poor plundered village maiden; from oxen, sheep, and poultry, to the dried salt fish of Concan; almost everything was seen that could be presented by the best bazaars of the richest town, but above all, the 'tables of the money-changers,' overspread with the coins of every country of the East, in the open air, and public street of the camp, give evidence of an extent of mercantile activity, utterly inconceivable in any camp except that of systematic plunder, by wholesale and retail."

To pass on to North India, the traveller, Fra Sebastian Manrique, thus describes the Lahore bazaar in 1641:

"But what I most admired was the moderate price at which these things might be had. A man might eat abundantly and royally for two silver reals (five pence) per day. The abundance of the provisions and the cleanliness of the streets surprised me much; also the peace and quietness with which everything was conducted, as well as the justice and rectitude of the people towards each other; so that merchant and merchandise remain perfectly secure from thieves."

Of the modern Indian bazaars perhaps the most remarkable are those of Bombay, Calcutta, and Benares. In the Bhendi [*Bendy* *] bazaar of Bombay the ethnologist will observe specimens of many races—Arabs, Somális,

Zanzabaris, all the races of Continental India, traders from Persia and Central Asia, Jews, and every nation of Europe. The wealth of colour in dress and merchandise, silks of China and Japan, piece goods from Manchester, piles of brass-ware, and every kind of food, cooked and uncooked, is amazing. The smells, of which those of ghee, assafœtida, and cow-dung smoke are perhaps most obvious, vie with those of Cologne. The China bazaar of Calcutta is famous for the pushing Baboo, Jew, and Pársi merchants, who shout and squabble and tempt the visitor to purchase ullaged stores and cheap trumpery of every kind.

Benares or Mathura are types of the pilgrim bazaar, full of brass idols and all sorts of cheap souvenirs which the pilgrim carries home as mementoes of his visit. Crowds of worshippers throng the shrines, and bow before the idols which line the roads; great white Bráhminy bulls stalk solemnly along, and levy toll from every corn-chandler's grain pile, while the owner looks askance at the sacred beasts which he dare not molest.

He that desires to traffic in the wealth and curios of the East will seek the Chándni Chauk [*Chowk* *] of Delhi, the marble-workers' quarter in Agra, or the Rúmi Darwáza of Lucknow. Here, though the shopkeepers are mostly Hindu, the predominant tone is Muhammadan. This is the favourite haunt of the young Musalmán who pretends to be a man of fashion, where he lounges along in his white pyjámas, gaudy velvet cap, short embroidered waist-coat, his lovelocks plastered down with ill-smelling oil, and leers at the dancing-girls on the balconies. Nothing in these modern bazaars strikes one more than the combination of wealth and squalor. The trading classes are only just getting rid of the belief, which dates from the times of anarchy, that a rich man is wise not to make his wealth too conspicuous; so a really great merchant squats in a mean verandah, and stores his goods in a tiny closet behind. Sordid huts and rubbish heaps surround respectable buildings. The air is full of dust, and the whole place resounds with the gossip and chaffering of the seething crowd. But for those with a taste for curious things the bazaar has infinite possibilities—an old coin from the board of a money-changer, a piece of ancient brass, quaint pottery or embroidery will often reward the visitor who understands the language, and knows enough of the manners and customs of the people to overcome that reticence and shyness which they always show in the presence of a stranger, whose race and religion are different from theirs.

[Linschoten, i. 185; Pyrard de Laval, i. 411, ii. Pt. I. 64; Abd-er-razzák, in "India in the XVth Century," 24; Elliot, "History of India," vi. 163f.; Bernier, ed. Constable, 365; Wilks, "Historical Sketches," ii. 208; "Lahore Gazetteer," 160.]

BIRTH-RITES.—Birth ceremonies are partly a form of initiation, marking the formal introduction of the child into the sept of its parents; partly, as in the use of lustration or baptism, they are a method of repelling the evil spirits which are most dangerous at the main crisis of human life. For the Indian baby the sixth day after birth is the most dangerous. Hence Shashti, the "Goddess of the Sixth," is specially worshipped. Surgeons tell us that this is just the period when infantile lockjaw, caused by want of care and cleanliness, is likely to attack the child. On this night a fire is kept lighting in the room, and the bed is surrounded with iron and other things which scare evil spirits.

In India we find many instances of the curious institution of the Couvade, the father, at the birth of a child, being treated as an invalid, instead of, or in addition to, the mother. The ruling idea on which this practice is based seems to be that there is an invisible connection between the father and child, so much so that the spirit of his child is likely to accompany him in his wanderings, and might unwittingly be injured by him in the course of his daily work. So he lies up for a while, does not work in his field or hunt, and does not go far from home lest the tiny spirit of the baby might be tired.

Albirúni (c. 1030) thus writes of the Hindus: "When a child is born people show particular attention to the man, not to the woman." Ethnologists have collected numerous instances of the custom in modern India. Thus, among the basket-makers of Gujarát, the wife goes to work immediately after her child is born; but

> "the presiding Mother (Máta) of the tribe is supposed to transfer her weakness to her husband, who takes to his bed, and has to be supported for several days with good, nourishing food."

Among the Erekulas of Madras, when the mother is taken ill,

> "she informs her husband, who immediately takes some of her clothes, puts them on, places on his forehead the mark which the women usually place on theirs, retires into a dark room where there is only a very dim lamp, and lies down on the bed, covering himself with a long cloth. When the child is born, it is washed, and placed on the cot beside the father. Assafœtida, *jaggery** (molasses), and other articles are then given, not to the mother, but to the father. During the days of ceremonial uncleanness, the man is treated as the other Hindus treat their women on such occasions. He is not allowed to leave his bed, and has everything needful brought to him."

This habit of the husband taking a purifying dose after his wife has borne a child is very common among many of the forest tribes of Central India. The father is purified in a different way by the Deshasht Bráhmans of Bombay, who insist, when a birth occurs in his family, on the father jumping into a well with all his clothes on; after which he is allowed to pour a couple of drops of honey and butter into the child's mouth, as a sign that it is admitted into the caste.

The first feeding of the child on grain is the occasion for a most elaborate rite. The Madras Nairs, who are specially careful in observing domestic ceremonies, insist that the first meal of rice given to a child should be taken from the temple offerings to the family god. The ceremonial feeding of the child is carried out in the presence of the relations and friends, by the tribal priest, or by the father, when, with the recital of appropriate sacred texts, a morsel of various kinds of food is placed between the baby's lips with a consecrated spoon.

There is a widespread prejudice against the birth of twins or triplets, which is supposed to be natural among animals, not human beings. In former days in Burma and elsewhere such children were killed; in other places it was the habit to make them over as disciples to some wandering Fakír.

It is the universal rule among Hindus to bury, not to cremate, young children. On the one hand, a child until initiated is not supposed to be a member of the tribe, and not entitled to the privileges which its seniors enjoy. In the Panjáb, again, the dead child is buried under the threshold in the hope that it may be reborn in the family.

[Alberuni, "India," i. 181; Monier-Williams, "Bráhmanism and Hindúism," 229; Oppert, "Original Inhabitants," 206; Fawcett, in "Bulletin of Madras Museum," iii. 242ff.]

BORE; MACAREO.—These are names given to the unusally high tides which occasionally rush up the estuaries of the Indian rivers, as they do in that of the Severn. The phenomenon was first noticed in India on the West Coast in the Bay of Cambay, and is thus recorded, evidently from personal experience, by the author of the Periplus, who probably wrote in 80-89 A.D.

"India," he says, "has everywhere a great abundance of rivers, and her seas ebb and flow with tides of extraordinary strength, which increase with the moon, both when new and when full, and for three days after each, but fall off in the intermediate space. About Barugaza [*Broach* *] they are more violent than elsewhere; so that all of a sudden you see the depths laid bare, and portions of the land turned into sea, and the sea, where ships were sailing but just before, turned without warning into dry land. The rivers, again, on the access of flood tide rushing into their channels with the whole body of the sea, are driven upwards against their natural course for a great number of miles with a force that is irresistible."

Linschoten (1584) describes the phenomenon, and adds:

"The Indians say that Alexander the Great came into this place, and perceiving the speedie ebbe that ranne there; he returned back againe, thinking it to be a miracle and worke of the gods, or else a foreshewing of some evill fortune."

The same phenomenon has been constantly noticed in the Húgli, Meghna, and other rivers of the Bengal Delta, and in some of the rivers of Lower Burma, as described by Cæsar Frederick, who was in Pegu in 1569. The historian, Kháfi Khán, speaks of a disastrous tide of the same kind in the Húgli soon after Job Charnock founded Calcutta.

In later times it suggested a fine simile to Captain Grant Duff, writing of the battle of Kirkee in his "History of the Mahrattas":

"Those who have witnessed the Bore in the Gulf of Cambay, and have seen in perfection the approach of that roaring tide, can form the exact idea presented to the author at the sight of the Peshwa's army."

In all these cases the origin is the same. The great tidal wave, originating in the Indian Ocean, or Bay of Bengal, breaks in an angry surf on the Eastern or Western Coasts, and, when aided by the Monsoon, rushes up the rivers of the Deltas, where it meets the flushes that descend from the upper country during the rainy season. In the Húgli its height has varied from 5 to 12 feet. On its approach the cries of *Bán! Bán!* ("The Bore! the Bore!") are the signal for all the smaller craft to move into mid-stream to avoid being dashed against the bank, or stranded on the retreat of the tide. In some cases it has caused widespread destruction. In 1876 heavy floods in the Meghna, combined with a strong south-west gale, caused an inundation of the Delta in Lower Bengal, resulting in the death of 74,000 people in Bakarganj, and 12,000 in Chittagong. A cyclone-wave like this twice devastated the settlement of Masulipatam in Madras in 1679 and 1864.

BRÁHMAN.—This is the general term applied to the functional group or caste which holds the highest rank in the Hindu system. Generally speaking, they may be regarded in relation to the Hindus as equivalent to the Levites among the Jews. It is true that they have secured the monopoly of performing priestly duties to all Hindus except some of the lowest rank, who employ officiants drawn from their own or some other group of the same standing. But it would be a complete mistake to class all Bráhmans as priests: on the contrary, only a small proportion of Bráhmans practises any religious function. In Bengal Proper, for instance, only one Bráhman in six is a priest; in Behár one in thirteen; in Orissa one in thirty-four. Bráhmans, in fact, freely engage in all occupations which do not involve personal pollution, and are found in large numbers among agriculturists, soldiers, and policemen, clerks, and other more respectable callings. It would, again, be an error to suppose that all Bráhmans form one homogeneous caste, that is to say, a group the members of which freely intermarry and dine together. On the contrary, the subordinate groups classed under the general name of Bráhman are practically independent of each other, and occupy very different positions in the social scale.

By the usual division there are ten great Bráhmanical sections, divided according to the regions which they occupy, of which five are supposed to include the Bráhmans of North India and five those of the South. But the severance between the various classes of Bráhmans goes much further than this nominal division into ten local bodies. In Bombay, for instance, the Bráhmans number slightly over a million, and have more than two hundred groups, none of which intermarries with another. In Madras the Bráhmans fall into six linguistic groups, each speaking a different tongue, and no member of any one group will marry or eat with a member of another. Further, each of the six groups has rules within rules regarding the persons within its own circle with whom its members may marry or eat cooked food.

The social position of Bráhmans is, then, infinitely varied, and it is extremely difficult to arrange in order of respectability people who practise such diversity of function. The highest in the list of those devoted to religious functions are those priests who profess to celebrate the purest Vedic ritual; next come those who pretend to perform any priestly function of the higher class. In the third grade come astrologers, family priests, and the lower class of instructors in the mysteries of Hinduism. The fourth group includes the sorcerer, the fortune-teller, the river-priest, who frequents places of pilgrimage, and the temple-priest. In the lowest rank of all, comes the funeral-priest, who is an object of abhorrence to all respectable Hindus.

This rough classification at once suggests that the so-called Bráhman caste is made up of very diverse elements; and this is certainly the case. The physical appearance alone of the Benares Pandit as contrasted with the lower village Bráhmans, shows that these two classes have nothing in common. Some of the higher grades of priests may be the descendants of the ancient priests of Vedic times. But the lower classes, the sorcerer and the fortune-teller, for instance, are probably, in origin, "medicine-men" of the non-Aryan tribes, who, when Bráhmanism absorbed and sheltered much of the beliefs of the Dravidian races, were admitted as priests of the new creed, but confined to the lower grades of the hierarchy. In Bengal, and possibly in other parts of North India, some of the Buddhist priests or monks, when their religion was swept away, may also have been included.

In the early Aryan times the house-master was the priest. By degrees families of priestly singers appear to have grown up in the royal courts, and gradually monopolised the duty of performing sacrifice and reciting hymns of praise and prayer. This naturally led to the elaboration of ritual, which finally came to be the business of a close guild of priests, who, to secure their own position, prohibited marriage beyond their own circle. The priest, in short, who was selected in early times on his merits, gradually acquired the right to pass on the office to his sons, and the priesthood came to be based on descent, ra*her than on personal qualities or aptitude. This account of the position of early Bráhmans depends on the evidence of a literature composed by Bráhmans, and, as was recently proved by Professor Rhys Davids, its statements must be received with caution.

The inferior position assigned to the temple priest is noteworthy, as marking the comparatively late introduction of image worship, and its adoption by the lower grade of officiants. It may also be remarked that the Southern Bráhman claims to enjoy a higher rank of purity than his brethren of Northern India. Unlike the Bráhman of the north, there is no lower caste from whose hands he will take water. The reason which he would assign for this is that Hinduism in the north has been defiled by one conqueror after another, while, isolated in the south, it has remained untouched by foreign influence. But his title in the south of Ayyár, or "father," indicates his position as a missionary and founder of a new order among a non-Aryan population. He is thus obviously a newcomer, an upstart, and hence no Bráhman in India is more bigoted and exclusive, less willing to permit the inferior castes to rise in the social scale. On the other hand, in spite of the fact that Bráhmans acted as Mayors of the Palace to the Mahratta rulers, there is no part of India in which they are held in less estimation.

A Hindu of North India should properly have three priests: first, his Purohit, or family priest, who attends domestic ceremonies and receives fees. He need not necessarily understand the ritual, and is chiefly employed at marriages, and to act as an intermediary between the families of husband and wife, because the former by social etiquette cannot visit his wife's relations. Next comes the Panda or Pádha, who must be learned in ceremonial ritual; and lastly, the Acháraj, whose business is the due performance of obsequies. But it is important to note that none of these priests has any necessary connection with moral teaching. This is the business of the Guru, who need not necessarily be a Bráhman, and is more often a member of one of the ascetic orders.

The Gurus, then, represent the working clergy of Hinduism, and Mr Nelson, writing of Madura in Southern India, remarks that they stand in much the same relation to the lay population as the parish clergy of the present day in Italy and Spain, with this difference that they belong to various sects, and do not look up to one common superior. It is in this part of the country that they are most influential. They are the guardians of morality, punish offenders against the laws of caste, restore penitents to caste communion, and give instruction in religious duties. Some are attached to different sects; others have territorial jurisdiction, and make progresses and visitations, which, in the case of the chief pontiffs, are accompanied by gorgeous ceremonial. Fees are levied from their constituents, and religious and social pressure is enforced against those who fail to discharge this obligation. In Northern India their organisation is less powerful. Here a pious Hindu usually has a Guru, who acts the part of a father-confessor, advises him on sacred matters, and is consulted on all business of importance. The institution of the Guru, though sometimes open to serious objection, is the one force in modern Hinduism which serves to promote that ideal of morality which the faith seeks to attain.

It has often been asked whether in the present day the Bráhman is increasing or losing his influence over the people. On the one hand, the rise of the modern theistic sects, like the Bráhmo and Arya Samáj, undoubtedly marks a reaction among the more enlightened portion of the community against the pretensions of the Bráhman and his ritual. But this movement is of limited extent, and although among many classes there is a growing tendency to sneer at the claims of the Bráhman to possess a special sanctity, still the mass of the people shows no tendency to revolt. Hinduism, as has been often observed, is more a social than a religious system, and the offices of the Bráhman include all that part of his religion which the Hindu values most highly—the initiation rites after birth, the ceremonies attending marriage, and the obsequies which assure him a seat in Heaven. Even among the more intelligent classes the influence of women is strongly in favour of maintaining these traditional observances. Sects like that of the Jains, for instance, who have severed themselves in a large degree from official Hinduism, still employ the services of a Bráhman for family rites. The vast majority of the people is so wedded to custom and so unintelligent that they show no disposition to escape from the Bráhman's yoke. And this yoke is easy to bear, because it involves no inconvenient moral restrictions, and merely requires the payment of dues, which is regarded as a respectable incident in rites such as those of marriage and death. Railways now offer increased facilities for visits to holy places, and it might be expected that they would increase the revenues of the local priests; but the Bráhman loudly complains that this is an Iron Age, and that he has not on the whole benefited. The fact seems to be that the pilgrim of our days distributes in alms at half a dozen shrines what he used in former times to spend at one. So long as Bráhmanism continues to lay no heavier burden upon the people than it does at present there seems no immediate prospect that its influence will rapidly decline.

[For the Northern Bráhmans, Nesfield, "Calcutta Review," lxxxiv, 257ff. ; Risley, "Tribes and Castes of Bengal"; Crooke, ditto "North-Western Provinces and Oudh"; Ibbetson, "Panjáb Ethnography"; Hunter, "Orissa," i. 238ff. ; Monier-Williams, "Bráhmanism and Hindúism." For South India, Nelson, "Madura," Pt. III. 160ff.: Fawcett, "Bulletin of Madras Museum," iii. 33ff. : Abbé Dubois, "Description of the People of India."]

BRÁHMO SAMÁJ.—This, like the Arya Samáj (q.v.) is one of the modern theistic sects, established with the object of reforming Hinduism, and, in particular, of abolishing image worship. Founded by the celebrated teacher, Rám Mohun Roy (1774-1833), it has been carried on by his successors, of whom the best known is the late Keshub Chunder Sen.

Its chief principles are a belief in the unity of the Godhead, the brotherhood of man, and direct communion with God in spirit without the intervention of any intercessor. Like all sects of the kind it has shown a tendency to fission, and now consists of three groups, the differences between them being ritualistic or social, rather than religious. The Ádi Samáj, the oldest and most Conservative section, clings more closely to Hindu beliefs and to the system of caste; the Nabidhan Samáj, or "New Dispensation," is more advanced, and seeks to assimilate what it finds best, not only in the sacred books of Hinduism, but in those of Islám and Christianity. The third section, the Sadháran Bráhmo Samáj, is the most Liberal in its views, as shown in the rejection of caste and of all that is ordinarily regarded as essential to Hinduism.

Bráhmos, according to the last census returns, number only 4,000, of whom three-quarters come from Bengal. Doubtless a much larger number is in sympathy with their views, but is naturally reluctant to break away definitely from Hinduism. In any case the progress of the sect has not been rapid and Mr Gait, writing of Bengal, remarks:

> "The general opinion is that although a large section of educated Hindu society is becoming distinctly monotheistic in its tenets, it is not attaching itself to the Bráhmo sect, but finds room within the limits of orthodoxy for its interpretation of Hindu theogony."

The advanced Hindu has thus little temptation to become a nonconformist, and sever himself from the family life which is the ideal of his social system.

[Lillingston, "The Bráhmo Samáj and Arya Samáj in their Bearing upon Christianity"; "Census Report," Bengal, 1901, i. 159f.; Pramátha Náth Bose, "Hindu Civilisation during British Rule," i. 132ff.]

BUDDHISM.—Originally founded in Northern India during the sixth century B.C. by the great teacher Gautama, the Buddha, or the "Enlightened One," the faith has now practically disappeared from the Peninsula, and possesses its only adherents within the Empire in Burma and along the mountain frontier to the north. In the third century B.C., under the great king Asoka, it became the State religion. As time advanced it was debased by contact with the idolatry and foul Tantric beliefs which it had never succeeded in extirpating, and Bráhmanism reconstituted on a more popular basis, and giving shelter to the Animism of the lower races and village gods, gradually reasserted its superiority. Buddhism survived in an attenuated form up to the end of the twelfth century of our era, when the Muhammadan invasions upset the Hindu dynasties of North India. Finally, it disappeared, not so much as the result of direct persecution, but rather from internal decay, the main cause of which is that it was, and is, in a great measure a religion for monks, with which the laity had little concern.

The study of Indian Buddhism has greatly advanced in recent years. The chief Scriptures of the faith are being gradually collected and translated; increased knowledge of Tibet and Upper Burma has thrown much light upon its later developments; and the chief sites connected with the life of Buddha have been more carefully explored. Recent archæological enquiries prove that the identifications by General Cunningham of Kusanagara, the site of the death of the Master, with Kasia, in the district of Gorakhpur, must be abandoned. It is now established that the monuments commemorating his birth and decease are to be found within the limits of Nepál, in the Himálayan Tarái, the region of fen and forest lying beneath the lower range of hills. The jealously suspicious rulers of Nepál are only now making up their minds to afford facilities for research in a region which certainly contains the more important monuments and inscriptions connected with the creed in its earlier stage.

Buddhists at present number in the Indian Empire 9,500,000, of whom the vast majority are found in Burma; a small body of 300,000 is scattered along the lower Himalayan range, from the Panjáb on the west to Nepál on the east. Sir J. G. Scott is of opinion that Buddhism, as it appears in Burma, is much nearer the original creed of Gautama than anywhere else, having been derived from Ceylon, where the faith is equally pure. But, to quote Mr Lowis:

"At no period of history has a nominal profession of faiths less exacting than the Buddhist been found incompatible with a genuine, if surreptitious, allegiance to the gods of an earlier age."

In illustration of this he refers to the late survival of old-time idolatrous rites centuries after the introduction of Christianity into Europe, and to the persistence of similar beliefs in parts of India, where Islám has long been the nominal faith of the people. So in Burma,

"as elsewhere, the existence of spirits, kindly or malevolent, as the case may be, is the fact that from time immemorial has been laid hold of and assimilated by the religious instinct of the native, and this ingrained conception the Burman has refused to cast off, with his acceptance of the loftier truths of Buddhism. He has disguised it, that is all; if, in truth, it can be called a disguise, which is so unblushingly apparent." Hence Burman Buddhism, "is a thin veneer of philosophy laid over the main structure of Shamanistic belief."

In the Himálayan border-land the case is even worse; for here, as has been already said, Buddhism has absorbed not only Shamanism and idolatry, but has added to these the impure mysteries of the Indian Sákta and Tantric schools.

[For early Buddhism, Kern, "Handbook of Indian Buddhism"; Rhys Davids, "Manual of Buddhism," "Buddhist India"; Smith, "Asoka"; "Early History of India"; For modern Buddhism, Waddell, "Buddhism of Tibet"; Sir J. G. Scott, "Upper Burma Gazetteer," Pt. II. i. 1ff.; Shway Yoe, "The Burman"; Fielding, "The Soul of a People"; "Census Reports," 1901, Burma, i. 31ff.; Bengal, i. 157, 201, 427; Panjáb, i. 141.]

BUNJÁRA.—This is the general name for a number of tribes, of gipsy appearance and habits, who are found throughout North and Central India, as far south as the Nizám's dominions, being most numerous there and in the Bombay Presidency. They now number about three-quarters of a million, and the great majority of them are Hindu by religion. Some vague references to them have been quoted from Arrian and the medieval Hindu dramatists; but the first literary account of them appears in the description of Sikandar Lodi's attack on Dholpur, in 1504 A.D. From that time they appear prominently in the records of the Muhammadan campaigns in the Deccan; and about 1630 two of their noted leaders had, one 180,000, and the other 52,000 pack oxen attending the Moghul army. Sir A. Wellesley, in his "Dispatches," constantly refers to the services rendered by them in his Mahratta campaigns. Good soldier as he was, he spared no pains to provide supplies for troops, and it was on the Bunjáras that he mainly depended.

Since the introduction of roads adapted to wheel traffic, and of railways, the great Bunjára caravans have nearly disappeared, and it is only occasionally that a band of these picturesque wanderers is seen in our time. They still observe the methods adopted after long experience of a nomad life. They carry their grain in W-shaped bags, adapted to balance on the ox-pad, which are never tied with girths or cords, and each contains rather less than 2 cwt. of grain. At night they pile their sacks in L-shaped walls, 3 or 4 feet high and 6 or 8 paces long, each family having a block to itself. When rain falls they spread a canvass to protect the grain and its carriers. They never load up before daybreak, and in these days of peace they allow the cattle to straggle and graze along the road. After a stage of about 10 miles they halt in the early afternoon, graze their beasts, and then make a short march to the camp, where they tether their oxen to a long rope for the night. In most cases women and children accompany the caravan, and when it halts the women start at once to prepare the food.

They are terribly vexed with witchcraft, to which they

attribute diseases like fever and rheumatism, the natural result of exposure.

> "Solemn enquiries," writes Sir A. Lyall, "are still held in the wild jungles, where these people camp out like gipsies, and many an unlucky hag has been strangled by the sentence of their secret tribunals."

Their own tribal council of elders decides the cases which arise in the course of their journeys, and they seldom trouble British courts. This is perhaps partly due to the fact that they are themselves, on occasion, addicted to serious crime, such as dacoity, and some of the gangs are notorious for cattle-lifting; others kidnap children, coin false money, and they were in the old times closely associated with the Thugs, using, as General Hervey tells us, the noose which they now employ dexterously for lassooing cattle to strangle their victims. When asked by General Wilks from what country they claimed their origin, one of them, pointing to the tent which covered their grain-bags said: "This is our country, and wherever it is pitched is our home; my ancestors never told me of any other."

With the partial disappearance of the Bunjára from Indian roads and camping-grounds a picturesque element amidst the general squalor of rural life is lost.

> "The women," writes Mr Mullaly, referring to the Deccan, "are comely and above the average height of the women of this country. They are easily distinguished by their dress and profusion of jewellery they wear. Their costume is the gown of brownish-red cloth, red or green, with a quantity of embroidery. The bodice, with embroidery on the front and on the shoulders, covers the bosom, and is tied by variegated cords at the back, the ends of the cords being ornamented with cowries and beads; a covering cloth of the same reddish colour with embroidery is fastened in at the waist, and hangs at the side with a quantity of tassels and strings of cowries. Their jewels are very numerous, and include strings of beads of ten or twenty rows with a cowry as a pendant, threaded on horse-hair, a silver necklace, a sign of

marriage. They wear brass or horn bracelets, ten or twelve in number, extending to the elbow on either arm with a piece of embroidered silk, one inch wide, tied to the right wrist. Anklets of ivory or bone are worn only by the married women; they are removed at the death of the husband. Silk embroidery adorned with tassels and cowries is also worn as an anklet by all women. Their other jewels are a nose ornament, a silver pendant from the upper part of the right ear, attached to a silver chain. which hangs to the shoulder, and a profusion of silver, brass, and lead rings. Their hair is, in the case of unmarried women, unadorned, brought up and tied in a knot at the top of the head; with married women it is fastened in like manner with a cowry or brass button, and heavy pendants are fastened to the temple. The latter is an essential sign of marriage, and its absence is a mark of widowhood."

In Upper India the women braid their hair on a sort of horn, which adds greatly to their height.

The race is probably largely mixed, some in appearance and stature resembling the finer races of the north, others squat in figure and dark in complexion approximating to the Dravidians, by whom they are surrounded. And this is admitted in their legends, which describe one body of them as originally men of high caste who, through neglect of the ministration of Bráhmans and the duties of pious Hindus, fell from their high estate and took to a nomad life.

[Gunthorpe, "Notes on Criminal Tribes," 29ff.; "Census Report," Mysore, 1901, i. 554f.; "Berar Gazetteer," 195ff.; Crooke, "Tribes and Castes," s.v.]

CAMBAY STONES.—This is a term applied to two classes of gems—agates found in Gujarát, and other foreign stones brought to Cambay to be worked by its lapidaries. The trade is a very ancient one, as it is described by the author of the Periplus (c. A.D. 80); but the stones to which he refers seem to have come from a place further inland than Gujarát — Palithána, perhaps represented by the modern Paithan on the Godávari, and from Ujjain in Málwa.

"A few cos from the City of Broach," writes Pietro della Valle, "is a mine of Calcidonies and Agates, white and green; but these stones are carried less into Barocci than to Cambaia, although it be further from the Mine, because there is a Sea-port, and a greater concourse of Foreign Merchants; and in Cambaia they are wrought into little Globes either round or oval, to make Coronets or Necklaces, and also little Cups, and divers other curious vessels for ornament."

Much discussion has arisen on the question whether the Murrhine cups, so highly prized by the Romans, were the moss-agate cups of Cambay, or some kind of Oriental pottery. Pliny mentions the fragments of such a cup being exhibited in the theatre of Nero, "as if they had been made of the ashes of no less than Alexander himself." On the whole, we may accept the opinion of Dr Ball that these Roman cups were probably of agate; the custom of roasting the agates (which must be done with no other fuel than dry sheeps' dung) having perhaps given rise to the idea that they were some kind of porcelain. He adds that the suggestion that they were made of fluor-spar may be rejected on the grounds that this mineral has never been found in India, and that there is no trace of its having been imported or worked by the West Coast lapidaries.

Three varieties of the Cambay stones are left unbaked —two kinds of onyx and the cat's-eye. The agate, known as carnelian from its fleshy colour, is baked in earthen pots placed in a trench and surrounded with fuel, to bring out the colour. The beads called Sulaimáni, or "those of Solomon," are made of onyx brought from the Narbada valley. Of the agates, four kinds, the common, moss, Kapadvaj, and veined, rank next to the Rájpipla carnelians. Besides these the Cambay lapidaries use jasper and chocolate stone from Morvi in Gujarát, lapis lazuli from Persia, jet from Bassora and Aden, and blue stone, not a turquoise, but a composition, from China. Crystal comes from a mine in Morvi, and was much valued in the Moghul Court. Tavernier tells us that

Aurangzeb, when seated on his throne, "had brought to him upon a golden saucer, enriched with diamonds, rubies, and emeralds, a large cup of rock crystal, all round and smooth, with the same decoration as the saucer." Dr Ball notes that some very fine crystal cups were found in the Delhi Palace during the Mutiny, some of which are probably included in the collection now in the Green Vaults at Dresden.

The trade of Cambay stones is divided between China, Arabia, and Europe. The Chinese prefer flat carnelians to wear as armlets or dress ornaments, and necklaces of plain round beads. The Arabs use agates, carnelians, cat's-eyes, and bloodstone; while to Europe all sorts of fancy articles are exported—watch-stands, knife-handles, paper-cutters, studs, and the like. It is probably from the same source that many Musalmán Fakírs obtain the rudely cut necklaces which they wear; some probably come from Tibet or Central Asia. Some of the rivers of Upper India, like the Son and those of Bundelkhand, produce a coarse agate, which is largely worked up into knife-handles and other ornaments. Some time ago a leading craftsman excused himself for delay in completing an order on the plea that he was busy making prehistoric stone implements for a well-known collector.

[P. della Valle, i. 61; Tavernier, i. 389, ii. 205; Watt, "Economic Dictionary," ii. 168ff.; "Bombay Gazetteer," vi. 198ff.; xviii. Pt. III. 267.]

CAMEL.—Of the two varieties of camel, the Bactrian, or two-humped variety, is found tame in Central Asia; the dromedary, or single-humped species, is that so largely bred and used in North-western India. These are so nearly allied that the hybrid between them is fertile. The Bactrian camel, which requires a colder climate than the dromedary, is found in a wild state, or as the result of escape from domestication, in the neighbourhood of Lob-nor. But it is remarkable that the dromedary has never been found wild, unless, as Sir G. Watt says, we accept the extreme view of its identity with the Bactrian. A recent authority, Professor W. Leeke, states that the wild Bactrian camel differs from the domesticated breed of Central Asia in having a smaller hump, not so much long hair; the colour is more rufous, and the ears and muzzle shorter. The wild variety he regards as much nearer to the fossil type than the domesticated, and hence he believes that it cannot be derived from the domesticated breed.

Some writers have regarded the camel as one of the oldest existing mammals, fossil remains of two extinct species having been found in the Pliocene deposits of the Indian Siwálik hills. One of these belonged to a species, which, though larger than the single-humped variety, is hardly distinguishable from it, and the animal, at least in Pliocene times, was probably wild in Northern India.

By breeding and selection, two varieties of the Indian camel have been developed: the Sowári, or riding-camel, and the baggage-camel. The best specimens of the former come from Bikanír and Jaysalmír in Rájputána, where, as Mr L. Kipling observes, the dry desert air "suits the austere Arab constitution of the beast." It differs from the baggage-camel much as a thorough-bred differs from a cart horse. In this region experts distinguish various breeds—that from Narwár being more enduring than that from Bikanír, but not its equal in seed; that of Jaysalmír, a dark, small, ugly animal, but very docile and the laziest of all in its paces. In the time of Akbar, according to Abul Fazl, the best varieties of the Indian camel used to come from Cutch, the swiftest from Ajmír, the best for burden from Sind. Jang, in the Panjáb, is the main breeding-ground of the baggage animal. Experience in the Afghán war graded the Indian breeds as first Bikanír, second the Panjábi, especially those from Ráwal-pindi, both of which surpassed those from Sind. In Bombay they are bred in Káthiáwár, where, curiously enough, they seem to have overcome their aversion to water and live in swamps. The dromedary accompanied the Muhammadan in his wanderings as far as Spain, and has recently been introduced to Nevada and Australia.

Opinions differ with regard to the time camels can endure want of water. Skinner says that his camels once went nineteen days without drinking, but in this he was probably mistaken. The general belief in India is that the beast will die if kept without water for three or at most five days, unless the fodder supplied be green and moist.

The Indian camel is an excellent beast of burden. It has been estimated that seven camels will carry a ton 20 miles a day in marches of eight or ten hours. Burnes, after careful experiments, fixed the pace of loaded camels at 2 miles 300 yards per hour. The great fault of the camel is that he is practically useless in muddy ground and that his temper is abominable. This last is certainly in a large degree due to the way in which he is treated by his Kábuli, or frontier-dwelling master. For his ailments the cautery is the standing remedy, and the scarred hide of the elderly baggage-camel shows permanent marks of the popularity of this treatment. He is one of the cheapest of baggage animals, as he practically finds himself on the camel-thorn and other rough herbage on the roadside.

All along the western frontier the Musalmán tribes freely eat camel's flesh, and among Indian Muhammadans the old Arab practice survives in the annual camel sacrifice at the Id [*Eed**] festival. But one Baloch tribe rigidly avoids the use of the meat, and in making a solemn engagement, says: "If I fail in this, may I be made to eat camel's flesh."

[See the excellent monograph in Watt, "Economic Dictionary," ii. 50ff.; Blochmann, "Ain-i-Akbari," i. 143.]

CARPETS.—"It would appear," writes Sir G. Birdwood, "that carpets originated in embroidery, and that carpets were first used, like embroideries, for hangings and palls." Such was, perhaps, the origin of the carpets of silk, gold, and silver, which Tavernier describes as made at Súrat and Ahmadábád.

Various materials go to the making of Indian carpets—

wool, cotton, silk, the hair of the yak, and that of the goat, specially in the form of *pashm*, the undergrowth of hair in various species of that animal, or mixtures of those materials. They differ, again, according to the mode of manufacture, the cotton carpet being generally made with a horizontal, and the woollen with a vertical warp. In both cases this consists of cotton.

Cotton carpets are known as Daris or Durries, "door-mats," or Shatranji [*Sitteringy* *], the latter generally larger than the former, and, as the name implies, of a chequered pattern. They are made of thick, strong cotton thread in a loom such as that used for weaving the ordinary cotton cloth. Bands of blue in alteration with white, produced by using different coloured threads, form the usual pattern. Special care is devoted to weaving the small cotton prayer carpets used by Musalmáns, which often have the figure of a mosque as part of the design. The best cotton carpets come from Agra and the neighbouring districts.

Far more important is the woollen pile carpet, known as Kálín or Kálícha. It is probably of Saracen origin, and is hence known as "Persian." Here the foundation of the carpet is a warp of strong hemp or cotton thread. Into each of these threads short hanks of coloured wool are twisted so that the ends stick out in front. As each line is completed the ends of these hanks are shorn down to a uniform length; a single woollen thread is passed across the breadth of the carpet so as to keep the tags of wool upright, and the whole is compacted by beating with a fork-like instrument. Finally, the whole surface is shorn smooth. The design consists of a series of hieroglyphics, intelligible only to a master of the craft. A boy sits with the pattern before him, and drawls out the number of loops to be made and the colours to be used. "Lift five and use red," he says, or "Lift one and use green," and this is repeated by the workman.

Mr L. Kipling thus points out the superiority of the Indian pile carpet over those of English make:

"The warp is of strong, elastic cotton threads, which are

soft in texture, and not made over-hard and tight by over twisting and sizing. On these wool thread is tied, and the allowance of wool is very liberal. The looms are large enough to make any size of carpet, and there are therefore no seams. For ordinary English carpets the warp is of hard, fine cords, and there is very frequently an underlay of jute, which does not appear either on the back or front of the carpet, and which gives substance and firmness to the fabric. . . . The jute is exceedingly hard and sharp, and as the wool is pressed against it by use, the softer material wears and cuts away. In an Indian carpet, the whole fabric sinks together under the foot. Moreover, very few of the English Jacquard looms are more than three-quarters of a yard wide. Hence the necessity for seams, which are the first places to wear thread-bare. So it may be said that it is more economical, when buying a carpet, to give three or four times the English price for an Indian hand-woven fabric. Multán," he goes on to say, "is probably the only town in the Panjáb which can claim woollen carpet-weaving as an independent, if not absolutely indigenous manufacture."

He thinks that the original inspiration came through carpets imported from Turkistán by the caravans from Central Asia. These carpets are in the Tartar style, and are woven in pieces, which to English eyes are disproportionally long for their width, "a peculiarity noticeable in all carpets that come from countries like Persia and Turkistán, where wood for roofing timber is small, and apartments in consequence are long and narrow." An old Persian test for a good carpet is to drop a piece of red-hot charcoal upon it. This leaves a singed brown spot. If the carpet be a good one, you can brush off the singed wool with the hand, without leaving any discernible trace.

One of the most famous Persian carpets now in existence is that presented to the Girdlers' Company by their master, Robert Bell. It bears the arms of Mr Bell and those of the Company, with the motto, "Give thanks to God." It was woven in the Royal Carpet Factory, established by Akbar at Lahore. The traditions of this school of craftsmen is still maintained by the Kashmíri carpet weavers at Srinagar and Amritsar, who founded the manufacture on the ruin of the shawl industry.

With foreign demand for cheap work and gaudy colouring the carpet industry has deteriorated. The wool has been adulterated, the quantity used skimped, and worst of all aniline compounds have taken the place of the native vegetable dyes. This deterioration is obvious in many of the carpets of Sind, Jabalpur, and Mirzapur, where, under a better system, admirable specimens were produced. Those of Malabar, according to Sir G. Birdwood, are

> "the only pile carpets made in India, of pure Hindu design, and free at present from European as from Saracenic influence. . . . No other manufacture of carpets known could hold a pattern together with such a scheme of colouring and scale of design. The simplicity and felicity shown in putting the right amount of colour, and exact force of pattern, suited to the position given them, are wonderful, and quite unapproachable in any European carpets of any time or country. They satisfy the feeling for breadth and space in furnishing, as if made for the palaces of kings."

[Birdwood, "Industrial Arts of India," 283ff.; Mukharji, "Art Manufactures of India," 392; Coxon, "Oriental Carpets"; L. Kipling, in "Gazetteers of Hoshiárpur and Mooltan"; Watt, "Economic Dictionary," ii. 176ff.; Lawrence, "Valley of Kashmír," 377.]

CARRIAGES, CARTS.—It is not till the era of the monuments that we can form any distinct idea of the early Hindu carriage. The Vedas, it is true, speak of tricolumnar, triangled, three-wheeled cars, of one-wheeled chariots, and of litters drawn by horses, asses, and deer. But the accounts give no real picture of these conveyances. The Greeks probably derived their war chariots from Egypt, or Semitic Asia Minor, and Dr Schrader believes that the Indo-Iranian use of the chariot may belong to the same cycle of culture. The Aryans probably brought the use of the chariot with them from Central Asia. The Hindu war-chariot held two fighting men besides the driver; it was carried along the road by oxen to spare the horses, as Strabo tells us, and, according to his account, the Hindus were skilful in driving a team of four high-mettled steeds when whirling round a circle. Arrian, writing in the time of Alexander the Great, remarks that

> "it is the elephant which carries royalty. The conveyance which ranks next in honour is the chariot and four; the camel ranks third; while to be drawn by a single horse (as in the modern *Ekka* *) is considered no distinction at all."

In the Sánchi sculptures the chariot has one long pole in the middle, curving upwards to the horses' necks, with two short shafts at the sides reaching as far as the flanks, but it had no yoke. That of Rája Prasenajit, depicted on the Bharhut Stúpa, is a two-wheeled vehicle with a high ornamental front and lower sides. It is large enough to hold four men, the Rája himself standing in the mid-front with the driver on his left, a man with a fly-flap on his right, and an umbrella-bearer behind him. The vehicle is drawn by four horses, with plumes on their heads, long-plaited manes, and tails tied up on one side to prevent the animals whisking them in the face of the charioteer. Like the chariots depicted on the Egyptian monuments it must have been a very light vehicle, capable of moving over rough country at a rapid pace. After this, apparently in the reign of Harsha in the seventh century A.D., the horse chariot disappeared from India, never to be revived; but the type persists in the many references in Buddhist writings to the small two-wheeled cart, dragged by a pair of oxen, like those of the present day.

India still, however, possesses vehicles of a very primitive type. Dr Ball describes at Chattísgarh in the Central Provinces a conveyance consisting simply

> "of a stout pole, which connects the axle tree with the bullocks' yoke; on this the driver and one or more passengers sit straddle-wise, with their legs hanging down. A more rudimentary wheeled equipage it is difficult to conceive of; yet some of them are made of choice wood, are highly ornamented, and are drawn by sleek and well-fed cattle."

In the early Aryan car, again, the wheel had no spokes, the wheel and axle tree being hewn out of the same tree-trunk. This exact style does not seem to have survived. But in the wilder parts of Basim in Berar stone wheels are, or were till quite recently, in use, and among the forest tribes, like the Kols of the Vindhya range and in parts of Berar, solid-wheeled carts are still in vogue. Bishop Heber describes a solid-wheeled cart used at Banswára in Central India, which had "no axle trees of the kind used in Europe, but the wheels are placed below the carriage, and seemed like those of wheel-barrows." The primitive solid, wooden, or stone wheel persists in the great idol cars of some of the southern temples. As late as 1895, according to Sir W. Lawrence, the only wheeled carriages in the Kashmír valley were low trollies, resting on wheels rudely fashioned from tree-trunks, which were used for hauling the crops. The Santál cart shows an utter contempt for all rules of mechanics. The wheels are solid, and placed parallel to each other at one end of a couple of bamboo poles, which are pegged to the axle, and meeting at a point at their other extremity, rest upon the yoke which crosses the necks of the buffaloes. This long, narrow cart was adopted because it could easily be steered through the devious jungle paths. The same type survives in places like Baroda, where the roads are mere water-courses, below the level of the country, and closely confined by hedges. Here the cart is a long, cumbrous, wattle-sided vehicle, tilted high in front above the heads of the majestic cattle, depressed behind so that when loaded it sweeps and drags along the road.

This principle of high yoking is seen best in the common *Ekka*,* or pony-carriage, which is so hung that little or no weight falls upon the pony's shoulders. One of these little carts easily accomplishes 30 or 40 miles a day, the pony being kept up to the mark by stimulants, of which hemp and treacle are the chief constituents.

The coach which travellers in Moghul times speak of must, if four-wheeled, have been much the same as the Rath [*Rut* *] of our day in which women and portly merchants travel, or, if two-wheeled, was identical with our *Bylee*,* a lighter and less pretentious vehicle. Pietro della Valle compares these coaches with the chariots described by Strabo.

"They are generally," he says, "covered with crimson silk, fring'd with yellow round about the roof, and the curtains; and the oxen . . . are fair, large, white, with two bunches like those of some Camells, and run, and gallop like Horses; they are like wise cover'd with the same stuff, but beset with many tufts or tassels, and abundance of bells at their necks; so that, when they run, or gallop, through the streets, they are heard at a sufficient distance, and make a very brave show. With these kind of Coaches in India, they not onely go in Cities, but also for the most part travel in the Country."

In Vedic times the ladies drove in cars; but when we come to the era of the Purános we hear of them travelling in litters. These were probably of the very primitive type in which we nowadays see the bride starting to begin her married life — a pole, to which is hung a sort of framework, surrounded by a dirty curtain, beneath which the lady squats. This was gradually developed into the *Palankeen*,* of which Tavernier gives us an elaborate account, and which Grose, the first literary Indian Civilian, speaks of as "the utmost stretch of invention for humouring the constitutional indolence of those people, as surely a more lazy conveyance could not well be imagined." Among the Portuguese and our early officials this was a vehicle reserved for persons of rank, and rigid sumptuary laws prohibited underlings from using it. In Grose's time, that of the battle of Plassey, only the Governor and Second of Council were allowed to have a gold or silver "tyger's head" on the end of the poles of their vehicles. Up to about sixty years ago most officers used the palankeen to reach up-country stations. Then an inventive genius laid it on a wheeled platform, and had it dragged by coolies, which later on were replaced by ponies. Thus was evolved the *Dawk Garry** of our times, which in its turn is being rapidly ousted by the railway and motor.

One mode of conveyance which Tavernier describes has quite disappeared—ox-riding. It seems to have obvious disadvantages, because he warns the traveller—

> "You should take care when you buy or hire an ox for riding that he has not horns longer than a foot, because, if they are longer, when the flies sting him he chafes and tosses back the head, and may plant a horn in your stomach, as has happened several times."

Possibly one of the first European carriages which reached India was the "gallant Caroch of 150 pounds price," which Sir Thomas Roe brought as a present to the Emperor Jahángír. Quite a rage spread among the nobility to have similar vehicles, and it speaks highly for the artisans of the time that several like it were made in a few weeks. Sometimes, as at the Court of the late King of Burma, difficulties arose about the position of the box. When it was found that His Majesty had to sit inside, below the level of the driver, he boiled with indignation, and suspected a plot against his dignity. So the carriages which had been presented to him were laid aside as lumber, until an ingenious craftsman crowned one with a Buddhist spire. The King could now use them without loss of honour, when dragged by men. But the spires were so heavy and unwieldy that the improved carriage could not be used on the rough roads of Mandalay, and they were finally brought out only as a show on feast-days.

Native fancy has often exercised itself in devising eccentric vehicles. Abul Fazl tells us that Akbar invented "an extraordinary carriage. When the carriage is used for travelling, or for carrying loads, it may be employed for grinding grain." The courtly historiographer adds that "it has proved a source of much comfort for various people. His Majesty also invented a large cart, which is drawn by one elephant. It is made sufficiently large so as to hold several bath-rooms, and thus serves as a travelling bath. It is also easily drawn by cattle." Of the same type is the extraordinary carriage of the Nawáb of Rámpur in the United Provinces. It has two stories, the lower big enough to allow of a nautch being performed inside, while the upper chamber, to which you mount by a flight of stairs, is for the accommodation of servants.

CASTE.—This is a word introduced from the Portuguese to express what the old Hindus called Varna, or "colour," or Jati, "birth." What is now implied in the term is thus defined by Mr Risley:

"A caste may be defined as a collection of families or groups of families, bearing a common name which usually denotes, or is associated with a specific occupation; claiming common descent from a mythical ancestor, human or divine; professing to follow the same professional calling, and regarded by those who are competent to give an opinion as forming a single homogeneous community. A caste is almost always endogamous in the sense that a member of the large circle denoted by the common name may not marry outside that circle, but within the circle there are usually a number of smaller circles, each of which is also endogamous. Thus, it is not enough to say that a Bráhman at the present day cannot marry any woman who is not a Bráhman, she must also belong to the same endogamous division of the Bráhman caste."

Side by side with castes of this kind we find what may be called the tribe, such as that of the Santáls or Nágas. It differs from the caste inasmuch as the common name does not usually imply occupation; its members generally occupy, or profess to occupy, a definite tract, but they do not necessarily marry only among themselves. The modern tendency is for such tribes to be transformed into castes. Thus, among the hill tribes of Central India the leading men often profess to be Rájputs, in the sense that they call themselves "sons of kings," and gradually become promoted to membership in the Rájput caste or tribe. A good illustration of this is found among the Gonds of the Central Provinces, who pretend, or at least the higher grades among them pretend, to the rank of Rájputs. Or again, tribesmen join some Hindu sect and take its name. More frequently still they keep their old name, but begin to employ Bráhmans and practise the outward usages of the Hindu rule, and end by becoming a caste like those of the Hindus in the Plains.

Thus there are many varieties of castes; some tribal, which have become modified in the manner already described; some occupational, where the members are linked together by a common occupation, from whence they often take their name, and which they follow, or pretend to follow; some are sectarian, where the bond of union is a common faith; some are mongrel castes, formed by crossing with members of other groups. There are, again, national castes, like that of the Mahrattas, based on actual or traditional sovereignty; castes which have become separate unities because their forefathers migrated from their birth-place, and made a fresh start in a new land; other castes, again, have arisen by fission owing to a change of custom, one part of a caste, for instance, breaking off because a section of its members refused to permit the marriage of widows, or because they quarrelled with their brethren over some question connected with food, or some social etiquette.

When caste thus presents itself in so many varied forms it is plainly impossible to frame any single theory which will account for its origin. The modern Hindu, when he speculates at all about the basis of an institution which he takes for granted, tells us that it has existed from all eternity, since the time when the World-Soul created the Bráhman from his mouth, the Kshatriya or warrior from his arms, the Vaisya or trader from his thighs, the Sudra, lowest of all, from his feet. Mr Risley plausibly suggests that we have in this legend the Indian version of the Iranian fourfold division of the people. At any rate, we now understand that caste was not a social institution of the early Aryans, that in Buddhist times it was only in the making, and that the first literary evidence of its existence in a definite form is to be found in the earlier law treatises like the Institutes of Manu.

The Hindu, again, regards caste as immutable. But even now we can see with our own eyes new castes coming to birth, and old castes in constant process of modification.

At present we are unable to give more than plausible suggestions regarding the origin of such a complex institution. To some it has appeared probable that a common occupation was the original basis of caste, and that the impulse towards its formation was given by the Bráhmans, who, as ritual became more and more complicated, formed themselves into a Levite guild, an example which other groups of workers followed. This theory, though clearly applicable to a large number of existing castes, does not cover the whole ground.

M. Senart, again, seeks to show that caste is a normal development of Aryan institutions in an Indian environment, and that its analogue is to be found in the Gens of Rome or the Greek Phratria.

Mr Risley, on the other hand, is disposed to lay stress on the difference of colour between the dark Dravidian or pre-Aryan races and their conquerors, the fair Aryans. The conquerors take the daughters of the land as concubines or wives, but give their own daughters in marriage only among themselves.

"The principle," he writes, "upon which the system rests is the sense of distinctions of race indicated by differences of colour, a sense which, while too weak to preclude the men of the dominant race from intercourse with the women whom they have captured, is still strong enough to make it out of the question that they should admit the men whom they have conquered to equal rights in the matter of marriage.

"Once started in India, the principle was strengthened, perpetuated, and extended to all ranks of society by the fiction that all people who speak a different language, dwell in a different district, worship different gods, eat different food, observe different social customs, follow a different profession, or practise the same profession in a slightly different way, must be so unmistakably aliens by blood that intermarriage with them is a thing not to be thought of."

An interesting development of caste is that of the so-called Left and Right Hand castes of Southern Madras. The latter include all the more respectable castes, with the pariahs or menials; the former the five varieties of smiths, leather-workers, and certain other of the lower castes, while Bráhmans, Muhammadans, and certain others are neutral. The result of this division has been considerable friction between the two groups. Mr Nelson is inclined to believe the cause of this division, which is quite modern, to lie in the opposition of the Panchálas, or five classes of artisans, to Bráhman supremacy.

"Perhaps, too, the immigration of the Vellálans, an agricultural caste, into the country, and the assumption by that caste of superiority over others added strength and vitality to the contest."

Dr Burnell prefers to attribute the movement to the time when Jainism gave way to Bráhmanism, and the adherents of the latter beliefs asserted their rights against their opponents, who represented the national party. It is a remarkable feature of this division that in the Shakilli [*Chuckler* *] caste, who are cobblers, the women belong to the Right and their husbands to the Left Hand division.

The question of the social and economical effects of the caste system is one of considerable complexity. On the one hand, the hereditary transmission of occupations obviously tends to restrict progress, in so far as it confines special trades and handicrafts within a closely limited circle; on the other hand, in the case of the master handicrafts of India, such as weaving and embroidery, woodcarving and work in metal, there can be little doubt that this specialisation of function has led to the transmission of special aptitudes from one generation to another, a result which appears in some of our more important English industries, such as that of Lancashire weavers and Sheffield cutlers.

From the social point of view the system presents some obvious advantages. It takes the place of our European Trades Unions and Provident Societies, in so far as it secures a member the sympathy and support of his fellows. In troublous times, like the period which immediately preceded the establishment of our rule, it supplied the only influence in opposition to the prevailing anarchy, and in a great measure prevented the complete disorganisation of society.

Hinduism, again, practically disclaims the desire to exercise any moral restraint over its adherents, and the only effective check on licence is that of the caste council, which by sentences of excommunication reproves the grosser kinds of social offences. Its methods of conducting investigations may not always conform to our ideas of justice; but they are based on rules familiar to the people, and are gladly accepted by them.

The main result of the caste system is to stereotype existing conditions, to repress the desire of the individual to advance his own interests at the expense of, or in opposition to, those of the community in which he is included. It thus conforms to that respect for ancestral custom which is one of the main principles of Hindu life.

It may be asked if there are any indications that the people are gradually becoming released from the bondage of caste. The construction of railways and the increased desire for travel have certainly tended towards the relaxation of some of the most vexatious restrictions in the matter of food. The preaching of Christianity and the rise of the modern theistic sects have an influence in the same direction. But among those classes of society who possess a caste which they value there seems no desire to escape from its restrictions. Were they to lose their caste they would identify themselves with the menials whom they despise, and at present the influence of such people is too weak to render any agitation on their part in this direction likely to have any tangible result.

[On the general subject see Risley's review of the subject in chap. xi. vol. i. "Census of India Report" of 1901, with the remarks in the Provincial Reports of the same Census. On caste in Buddhist times, Rhys Davids, "Dialogues of the Buddha," 97ff.; For Left and Right Hand castes, Nelson, "Manual of Madura," Pt. II. 7ff.; Buchanan, "Mysore," i. 77; Oppert, "Original Inhabitants," 57ff.]

CATTLE.—In India where cattle are used not only to provide milk and the *Ghee*,* or clarified butter, which is so largely used in native cookery, but to drag the plough and cart and serve as beasts of burden for nomad tribes like the Bunjáras, their importance in the rural economy cannot be overrated. Pliny, indeed, speaks of the elephant as the working animal of India; but here he must have been misinformed. Tillage by means of cattle was much later than hoe husbandry. Dr Buchanan-Hamilton came to the conclusion that cattle were little used in agriculture in Bengal until after the Muhammadan invasion.

It was no doubt on account of this economic value of the animal that it was protected by a religious sanction. But the belief in the sanctity of the cow did not arise till the value of the ox in ploughing was well recognised. It did not prevail in early Aryan times, when there was no restriction of the use of beef, and it seems to have been prescribed under Bráhman influence. It may possibly mark the transition from the pastoral to the agricultural stage. In later times various attempts have been made to secure the protection of the animal by special legislation. Akbar, probably under the pressure of his Hindu wives, prohibited the slaughter of kine during the autumnal Jain festival; in 1802 Daulat Ráo Scindia offered an additional cession of territory on condition that the British Government prohibited cattle-slaughter in the territories which he had been compelled to surrender; in the following year Lord Lake prohibited slaughter in the neighbourhood of the holy land of Mathura. In States under a purely Hindu government, like that of Nepál, cow-killing is strictly prohibited. Some years ago the Mahárája of Bharatpur, a State to the west of Agra, commenced buying up worn-out cattle and releasing them in a jungle close to our frontier, where they inflicted so much damage on our villages that it became necessary to erect an enormous wire-fence to prevent their ravages. In some jungles the common cattle become feral. But it must have been one of the greater bovines that Nicolo Conti in the fifteenth century makes the subject of a remarkable story. In the neighbourhood of Calicut, he writes:

"Wild cattle are found in great abundance with manes like those of horses, but with longer hair, and with horns so long that when the head is turned back they touch the tail. These horns being extremely large, are used like barrels for carrying water on journeys."

In recent years the Hindu revival has led to a serious agitation in favour of prohibition of cattle-slaughter. To this appeal the answer of the Indian Government has always been that while not only the British troops and residents, but also a large Muhammadan and menial population consume beef, prohibition of slaughter is out of the question. At the same time, arrangements were made for the erection of slaughter-houses at a distance from Hindu quarters, and for the regulation of the exposure of beef in public market. In spite of these measures serious *émeutes* occurred which caused much embarrassment to the Government. Where the people can act themselves, as in their caste tribunals, the penalties for killing a cow even by accident are very severe. Fra Paolino, writing at the close of the eighteenth century of South India, says that if a Bráhman killed a man or a cow, all his caste-fellows unite against him: cut off his scalp-lock, deprive him of his sacred thread, and expel him from their caste. "He is then put upon an ass with his face towards the tail, and in that manner conveyed beyond the boundaries of the place." In Upper India many a poor creature convicted of cow-slaughter has been forced to march up one bank of the Ganges from the sea to its source, and back again by the opposite bank.

But while the Hindu professedly venerates the cow, he will shamefully ill-treat the animal, and will leave it to die in a ditch in preference to ending its life mercifully. To quote Mr L. Kipling: "The same code which exalts the Bráhman and the cow, thrusts the dog, the ass, and the low-caste man beyond the pale of merciful regard." In contrast to the Hindu's respect for the cow, the feeling of the hill and border races is very different. Thus, on the northern frontier the Dárd looks on the cow as the Musalmán looks on the pig; will not drink cow's milk, nor make nor eat butter; nor will he burn the dung as fuel. He keeps cattle for ploughing, but has as little as possible to do with them. When his cow calves he pushes the calf to its mother's udder with a forked stick, and will not touch it with his hands. It is, of course, possible that this taboo may be the survival of a belief in the sanctity of the animal, as was the case with the pig among the Semites, once sacred, now an object of abhorrence. So among the Gonds part of the worship of the dead was the sacrifice of a cow. This was doubtless a rite shared with the early Hindus, from which the Hindu of our day escapes by dedicating a bull-calf to Siva, branding it, and letting it loose. The Gonds, though they have now given up the rite of cow sacrifice, condone their neglect of the ancient custom by holding a secret service every four or five years, in which they place to their lips beef covered with a piece of cloth.

The objection to the use of milk, which they regard as an excrement, appears among the Dravidian tribes of the Central hills, like the Mundas, and is widespread among the Indo-Chinese and Malay races, including the Khásis of the eastern frontier, Gáros, Nágas, Burmese, and Nicobarese, while it was adopted by the stricter Buddhist sects. The late kings of Burma used to receive milk by purchase from Bráhmans, but it was a foreign usage. Further east the same feeling extends to the Sumatran and Javanese tribes, and widely prevails in China.

The main type of Indian cattle, for which zoologists have adopted the curious name of *Zebu*,* includes the domestic breeds, and some which have lapsed into feral habits. It differs from the domestic cattle of Europe not only in possessing a hump, but in the number of the sacral vertebræ. Their voice, says Professor Wallace, "is a hoarse, guttural grunt or half cough, instead of the ringing bellow of the European species, in which both lungs and throat play an important part." The same writer is of opinion that the fact that all Indian cattle, irrespective of the colour of their hair, have black skins, has much to do with their ability to withstand heat; and for this and other reasons he maintains that experiments for improving the native varieties by the introduction of European blood are not likely to succeed.

The native breeds may be divided into the southern and the northern. The main distinction in outward appearance is that in the cattle of Bengal the horns project forward and form a considerable angle with the forehead; while in the south they are nearly on the same line with the *os frontis.* The Mysore breeds, writes Professor Wallace,

> "occupy among cattle a position for form, temper, and endurance, strongly analogous to the thoroughbred horse among horses. The animals representing it are light in build, and their greatest defect for army purposes is their moderate size."

They appear best in the Amrit Mahal, or State breed, which was produced by crossing the best Mysore varieties, and enabled Hyder Ali and Tippoo to make such wonderful marches in their campaigns against the British. Further north, the Kistna breed, for size, massiveness, and general symmetry of parts, are in the first rank of the larger Indian cattle.

Passing further north, the finest large cattle are those of Gujarát, unequalled except by those of the Kistna. Much resembling the Amrit Mahal strain are the Khilári cattle, called after the breeders of that name in Khandesh, the most valuable draught cattle in Central India. Next come those of Málwa, great favourites of the Bunjáras, by whom they are brought south, being adapted for steady work rather than speed. From Káthiáwár come heavy, loosely-made beasts, better suited for pack transport and well work, but with hoofs too soft to stand the rough Deccan roads. Hariána in the south-west Panjáb supplies a short-legged, compact animal, excellent for plough and well, while the cows are famous milkers. The English lady in the Gangetic valley looks to Mathura, the land of Krishna and his milkmaids, for her milch cows. The little red ox from the banks of the Ken in Bundelkhand is an excellent farm worker.

But it is to the unwieldy, ugly buffalo that the peasant looks for his supplies of milk and ghee.* She can be grazed in the rough marshes of the plain country, needs much less care than a cow, and gives more milk. Its natural fancy for water adapts the animal to regions where the rainfall is heavy, and in the rice districts, where much of the ploughing must be done under water, they are largely used. The worst point about the buffalo is the delicacy of its constitution, and it succumbs to heat much sooner than the ox. It is undistinguishable from the feral variety, with which it interbreeds. It still shows its wild nature in its detestation of Europeans, and it is a nasty customer to meet in a narrow lane. There are many varieties, of which that of Bombay is most highly prized.

The Gayál [*Gyaul* *], *Bos frontalis*, an animal closely allied to the Gaur [*Gour* *], *Bos gaurus*, has been domesticated; but all attempts to tame the Gaur, the finest bovine in India, have failed. As Captain Forsyth remarks, the most difficult of all animals to reclaim from a wild state are those whose congeners have been already domesticated—the wild horse and ass, the wild sheep, goat, and dog, the jungle-fowl. The Gayál is the milch animal of Assam, Chittagong, and the Mishmi Hills, and is a most valuable source of meat and milk. In the Himálaya we have, again, the Yak, whose scientific name, *Bos grunniens*, "the grunting ox," is derived from its peculiar call, undoubtedly one of the Bovidae; but during the Tibet war of 1854-55, when the Nepalese troops suffered from want of food, Jang Bahádur induced a complacent high priest to declare that they were deer, not oxen, and that the meat might be lawfully eaten by Hindus. It is amongst all quadrupeds the one found at the highest elevations, as high as 20,000 feet. The cross-breeds of the Yak and Indian cattle are also used; that between the male Yak and the Indian cow, called Jubu or Zobo, is superior to the Garju, of which the sire is a Yak, and the mother a hill cow.

[Wallace, "India in 1887"; Watt, "Economic Dictionary," v. 659ff.; Blanford, "Mammalia," 483ff.]

CHESS.—To India mankind is indebted for the invention of chess.

"A collection of fables and fairy-tales on the one hand," to quote Professor Macdonell, "and the most intellectual game the world has known on the other, start on their wanderings from India, in all probability at the same time, and after a lapse of centuries are again found side by side in Europe, whiling away the tedium of myriads during the monotonous life of the Middle Ages."

In its origin chess was the oldest form of Kriegspiel known to history. Its original Indian name was Chaturanga, which means "four-membered," and may be regarded as the technical name for "army" in the Epics, the four members representing elephants, chariots, horses, and infantry. The original board was called Ashtapada, "eight-square," which apparently meant that it had sixty-four spaces. Dice date from the very earliest period in India, and Professor Macdonell thinks that backgammon, the rules of which were practically the same as at present, was played on such a board. The earliest chess seems to have been a game played with dice.

Literary evidence now proves that chess certainly existed in India by the middle of the sixth century A.D. Soon after this time it spread to Persia and Arabia on the west, and to China on the east. The very name Chaturanga was adopted in Persia as Chatrang, and by the Arabs as Shatranj, which proves clearly that the route of the game to the Arabs was *viâ* Persia. The Arabs brought it to Spain probably at the end of the tenth century, and by the end of the eleventh it became a familiar game in Europe.

"The order," says Professor Macdonell, "in which the sixteen pieces were arranged on each side of the board in the Indian game, when it first became historically known, appears to have been practically the same as in the chess of the present day. The king, accompanied by his councillor, occupies the middle of the first line; while on each side of them were placed an elephant, a horse, and a chariot, the latter occupying the corner. Eight foot-soldiers were drawn up in the second line."

As for the moves, those of the knight, the king, and the pawn, have never changed since anything has been known about them.

When Alberúni describes the Indian chess of the eleventh century, his account implies that it was played in two forms, one much the same as the Arabic game, the other a four-handed game, in which dice were used, each piece moving according to the number of the throw. The second form has been shown to be a later invention than the two-handed game. Professor Macdonell thus sums up the matter:

"It is quite possible that dice were combined with the primitive form of chess; but they could very well have been used by two players, as in backgammon. The ordinary game, with figures moving independently, might have been a development of a more mechanical game, in which the moves depended on the throw of dice. The latter might have survived beside its more intellectual successor by becoming modified as quadruple chess, just as backgammon in the form of the Indian Pachísi can be played by four players. Chess would thus in its primitive state have been an applied form (like backgammon) of the far more ancient game of dice. This development seems more probable than that the highly intellectual game of double chess, which it is natural to suppose was the result of a prolonged evolution, should, after being independent of dice from the beginning, have, when fully developed, relapsed to a primitive stage in the form of quadruple chess."

In India at the present day the game of Shatranj is very popular. In general, it seems to differ from our chess in the prohibition against the pawns moving two squares at first; and the king of one party is placed opposite the queen or Wazír of the other, instead of the queen being always on her own colour. Colonel Welsh describes a game played in "the true native style," in South India:

"The ground being smoothed and checkered with *Chunam*,* and the queen cut out of the stalk of a plantain leaf; the queen and bishop alone differing in their moves and value from ours. The Queen, or Wazeer, moving diagonally, backwards and forwards, one square, and taking like a Pawn; and the Bishop clearing over everything, within its range, but taking or checking only on the second square diagonally; so that the Castle is the only piece which can move and take, from one end of the board to the other."

Another kind of game played on a board is Pásha, or Pachísi. Here the board is arranged in the form of two long rectangles intersecting at right angles in the middle. There are thus ninety-six squares, excluding the large square or space in the centre. Sixteen pieces are arranged on each side of the board, and the moves are regulated by throwing dice. Pásha is played by two or four players, and in contrast to the decorum of Shatranj, the Pásha board is the scene of noisy vociferation.

[Macdonell, "Origin and Early History of Chess," "Journ. Roy. As. Soc." 1898; Forbes, "History of Chess."]

CHILDREN. — What strikes the observer first in regard to native children is their extreme precocity. The parent makes no attempt to shield his child from knowledge which may pollute its early innocence, and from the time it is able to comprehend anything no mystery of life is kept secret from it. Tavernier, writing of the diamond mines of Golconda, expresses astonishment at the cleverness of quite little boys, who knew every trick of the trade, and used to barter and sell stones amongst themselves. Grose, writing in 1757, speaks of Musalmán boys in Western India having their education supplemented by their introduction into all companies, and scenes of public business in their tenderest youth:

"Where their fathers carry them, not without due preparation and instruction how they are to deport themselves, and by this means, under their watchful eye and control, enter them early into that great University, the world."

Of the Hindu boys he writes that the merchants initiate them into all the mysteries of trade,

"insomuch that it is not uncommon to see boys of ten or twelve years of age, so acute and expert, that it would not be easy to over-reach them in a bargain."

He had a very high opinion of the boys, and speaks of them in a tone which seems to us exaggerated.

"And, in truth, their docility, sedateness, and awful regard for their parents are surprising, considering the extreme fondness of these for their children, which, however, they temper so judiciously as not to spoil them; their whole study being to make them consider them as the best and tenderest friends they can have in the world, which point once carried, the rest may be imagined to follow in course."

Even among well-to-do people boys and girls disport themselves literally naked up to about the age of five. To the north, when a boy is two or three, a string is often tied round his waist, to which is sometimes attached a key or some metal charm; to the south little girls are provided with a silver or bell-metal "fig-leaf." Girls begin clothing earlier than boys; the first dress of a boy is a short shirt, or shift, with a scanty waist-cloth, and for girls a little petticoat. In 1891 the Census Commissioner attributed the high mortality among female children to the fact that they are generally unprotected above the waist, while the boy is provided with some sort of an upper garment to cover the more vital organs. When the child is dressed in a more or less imperfect way, the inference is that he or she has been initiated into caste, up to which time the Hindu thinks that children have no souls, and that it does not matter what they eat, or whether they do or do not observe the rules of ceremonial purity. The jungle tribes extend still further this period of licence, and among some of these people in Central India the girls may eat anything till they bind up their hair — that is to say, are marriageable — and boys may do the same till they marry.

The evil custom prevails widely of loading little children with jewellery, a fertile cause of the numerous murders of infants.

A common way of treating little children is to rub them all over with oil and lay them in the sun. This habit did not escape the eye of Marco Polo, who, writing of Maabar * or the Coromandel Coast, says:

"The children that are born here are black enough, but the blacker they be the more they are thought of; wherefore from the day of their birth their parents do rub them every week with oil of sesame, so that they become as black as devils."

The Bengalis believe that rubbing the child with oil and exposing it to the sun makes it able in later years to stand heat bare-headed. They do it, says Ward, to dry up the juices and harden the bones.

It is perhaps in a large degree poverty which establishes a Malthusian check by the prolonged lactation so common in India. Ward says that in his time Bengali children were kept at the breast till the age of five. Sir J. Hooker saw a boy of four being nursed by his aunt, and afterwards chewing hard dry grains of maize. Captain Lewin speaks of Chakma boys of three sharing their mother's milk with an infant, and Mr Malabari says that the Marwári boy of eight in Gujarát is nursed. The Ját woman in Rájputána, to find time to discharge her heavy household duties, drugs her baby from its infancy with opium, as the Karen mother in Burma gives it spirits from its early years; if she is unable to suckle her child immediately after its birth, she takes a mouthful of spirits and feeds it with this from her own lips.

Even more curious is the habit of putting a child to sleep by letting water drip upon its head. In the western Himálaya the child is laid on a sloping bank, and a tiny stream of water is directed on its head through a spout of bark. Lady Dufferin saw a mother lying flat alongside and nursing her baby while the douche fell upon it. One woman told her she should stay there all day; others spoke of half an hour, or an hour or so. The treatment is continued even in winter. In some cases permanent depression of the skull is the result.

Actual deformation of the heads of children is practised on the Panjáb frontier. According to Mr Thorburn, women in Bannu press the child's head daily to make the forehead broad and flat, and pinch and pull the nose to a point, and elongate it. Some even use clay moulds to shape the skull, or the child is laid with the head a little below the level of the body, so as to throw part of the weight on the skull. The practice prevails in other parts of the Panjáb, where the head is moulded in a cup. The treatment produces that bullet-shaped head which we associate with low, intellectual development, but it does not seem to impede the growth of the brain. The Nicobarese also deform the heads of infants by flattening the occiput and forehead. Around the shrine of the Saint Sháh Daula, at Gujránwála in the Panjáb, a number of children, known as "Sháh Daula's Rats," are kept and exhibited. They are probably congenital idiots, with small heads, large ears, and generally stunted growth. They take their name from the peculiarly rat-like form of the skull. A recent observer remarks that they look exactly like Aztecs.

Considerations, generally based on astrology, decide whether a child is lucky or not. Thus, in the Panjáb, births in certain months and under certain lunar asterisms are held to be lucky or unlucky. A first-born son, according to Mr Rose, is particularly uncanny, subject to magical influences, and invested with supernatural powers.

"On the one hand, his hair is useful in magic, and on the other, its possession gives a wizard power over him, so that he must not leave the house on the night of the Diwáli, or feast of lamps. He should not be married in May, nor should the mother eat first-fruits in that month."

The position of the first-born is probably due to the belief that, if a son, his father is reborn in him, and some tribes go so far as to perform the obsequies of the father on the birth of his son and heir. Mr Rose explains on this principle the curious Panjáb custom of the "Divine Nuptials," which provide for the remarriage of the parents after the birth of their first son. The wife leaves her husband, and goes, not to her parents, but to the house of a relative, whence she is brought home as a bride.

"These ideas are an almost logical outcome of the doctrine of metempsychosis; and it as inevitably results that if the first-born be a girl, she is particularly ill-omened, so that among the Khatris of Multán she used to be put to death. And so too it is said of the Peshávar district that it is considered a misfortune, almost a disgrace, for a woman to bear a daughter, especially if it is a first child."

The third and eighth son is also dangerous, and folklore traditions thus familiarise the people with the idea of infanticide.

CHINESE.—The last Census returns show that the Chinese population in British India amounts to 67,000, of whom the vast majority are Buddhist by religion and resident in Burma.

There is ample evidence of long-established intercourse between China and India. China seems to have first come in contact with the tribes bordering the northern frontier after its conquest of the Northern Turks in 630 A.D. After this its influence weakened, but was revived in the beginning and ended in the middle of the eighth century. Meanwhile the spread of Buddhism to the north of the Himálaya encouraged the visits of pilgrims to visit the sacred sites, and to procure copies of the Scriptures. Such were Fa-hien, whose travels began in 399 A.D., and Hiuen Tsiang, who followed in 629. The records of these journeys supply most valuable materials for the study of Indian Buddhism. The figures in the Ajanta Caves (200 B.C.-600 A.D.) are by some supposed to show traces of the influence of Chinese art in the suppleness of the figures, the drawing of the human eye, and other details. Marco Polo, at the end of the thirteenth century, records that there was a considerable trade between Manzi, or South China, and the Indian ports of Kaulam, Hili, and Calicut in Southern India; while Ibn Batuta, in the middle of the fourteenth century, tells us that the Chinese used to moor their ships during the winter or rainy season at Pandarani, a port of Malabar. Chinese pottery and coins have often been found in South India, and the curious building at Negapatam, known as the "Chinese Pagoda," though probably Buddhistic, shows that the tradition of Chinese influence long survived. We hear of thirteen China ships "made of double firwood, fastened with good iron nails, and daubed with lime, chopped hemp, and wood-oil," passing the stormy months of 1292 in Bombay harbour. During the first half of the fifteenth century they were acknowledged as over-lords by the kings of Ceylon. Soon after this their political influence seems to have ceased; but since that time the commercial intercourse of the two countries has been uninterrupted. John Deza, the Portuguese admiral who destroyed the fleet of the Zamorin, found it under the command of a Chinaman. Some Chinese under Portuguese rule seem to have become Christians, for Fryer (1673), on his visit to Goa, put up in "a tavern kept by a Chinese, who are White, Platter-fac'd, and Little-eyed, tolerated on account of embracing Christianity."

Again, many of the industries of India are traditionally or actually connected with the Chinese. Though the art of sugar-making seems to have come from Gangetic India to China, it is curious that white sugar in India is still called Chíni [*Cheeny* *], or Chinese. The Sind potters claim descent from a naturalised Chinaman introduced by one of the Mírs of Haidarábád. A colony of the same race brought the art of leather-making to Cawnpore. Mr Keene finds traces of Chinese carving side by side with Italian painting in Akbar's palace at Fatehpur-Sikri. It was a gang of Chinese convicts who started the thriving cultivation of potatoes and other vegetables at the hill-station of Mahabaleshwar.

The Chinese in Burma enter the country through Bhamo, the Ruby Mines, and Rangoon. They are divided into two classes: first, merchants who come round by sea from Canton, and, secondly, those from Yun-nan, who cross by land to trade in petty wares and forest produce, and whose language is different from that of the former. The Chinese in this province are gradually increasing, and it seems likely that through their aptitude for amalgamating with the Burmese, they will before long form one of the leading elements in the population. Their children by Burman mothers are a finer race than the Burmese themselves, and their daughters are reputed the handsomest women in the country. On the other hand, the natives of India, owing to caste scruples and religious differences, do not get on with the Burman so well as the Chinaman does. As merchants and traders, Chinese are firmly established in the chief commercial centres, while as petty contractors and carpenters they supply a much-felt want throughout the province. In agriculture they have as yet done little, but Mr Lowis writes:

> "If Chinese agriculturists as enterprising and law-abiding as the present generation could be introduced into the country, I have no hesitation in saying that the economic welfare of Burma would be assured, for the Chinese amalgamate with the Burmans far more readily than do the natives of India."

The important Chinese colony in Calcutta, which is

recruited from the Hakka districts in the province of Canton, has a quarter of its own, where its members work as carpenters and shoemakers, boil down pig's fat into lard, and deal in opium and hemp drugs. Formerly they used to perform the orthodox marriage rite by lifting the bride over a pan of charcoal; but at present practically no women are imported from China, and they merely take a woman, generally a Roman Catholic, into the house, to be turned out if there be any incompatibility of temper, or to be discarded when the man returns to China. The girls are married off, and sink into the class libellously called Portuguese. They bury their dead in special cemeteries, most of the tombs being of the orthodox horse-shoe form; but the young China party follows the European fashion of monument. One characteristic of them is the cool way in which they treat their customers. If they be shoemakers, it seems a matter of perfect indifference to them whether the shoes fit or not. But this is not so with the tailors. The poor Eurasian in Calcutta, when he wants a suit of clothes, stands in the middle of their bazaar, and tradesmen, putting their heads out of their shop doors, bid excitedly in a sort of Dutch auction, till the lowest price is reached. They copy a pattern only too faithfully, reproducing all its faults and imperfections with a kind of religious scrupulosity. There is no trick of the trade, such as a liberal use of shoddy in clothes and pasteboard in shoes, with which they are not acquainted.

The Chinese temple in India, which seems usually to be the seat of Buddhist, as well as Shinto worship, or a combination of the two, serves, not only as a place of worship, but as a club-house. Sir H. Yule describes one at Amarapura in Burma:

"As usual, like an old curiosity-shop rather than a place of worship; full of all sorts of quaint carved cabinets or shrines, fantastic lanterns and censers, curious bronzes, life-size grotesque figures ranged in cupboards on the wall, teapoys, altars, furniture of inconceivable purpose, stands of imitation antique weapons, such as halberts, pitch-forks and morning-stars, possibly intended for use in their plays, etc. The principal figure was of Sagyin marble. Differing from the Burmese and Indian Gautamas, it still seemed to me to resemble the prints of Fo, or the Chinese version of the Buddha. But the people evaded our question as to the person represented. A shelf of minor figures stood below, and among them was a regular Burmese Gautama in the normal attitude. The wood-carving about the pillars and brackets was thoroughly Chinese, showing much more finish and executive expertness in the *tours de force* of its fantastic under-cutting than any Burmese work, but decidedly inferior to much of the latter in real artistic design and effectiveness."

The Calcutta temple is dedicated to Kwan-te, generally called the god of war. In the courtyard is the god's horse, comfortably stabled. Climbing a flight of steps you reach the chapels, and rooms for attendants, in which you find cooks sacrificing fowls, sucking-pigs, ducks, and kids, which when stewed the worshippers eat, while the god and his attendants satisfy themselves with the savour of the offering. In a niche are the Lares and Penates of the community, and on either side of the god's altar are placed his seal and sword, a sort of scythe made of wood.

On the Burmese frontier, Sir J. G. Scott describes a Chinese shrine. It consists of a couple of long, rude sheds, with an entrance in the middle of the side.

"There is nothing within but a line of tables and altars, with erections on them like troughs reared on end and inscribed with Chinese characters. There is no suggestion of an image of any kind; the offerings of food, fruit, and flowers are placed on the tables; candles and joss-sticks burn outside the shed and at the foot of the pillars, but there is no priest or monk in charge, and there appears to be no regular service, or days of worship. The whole in its simplicity and vagueness recalls the State religion of China, the worship of the Tien or Hwang-Tien, the imperial concave expanse of Heaven, rather than a form of Buddhism."

["The Chinese Colony in Calcutta," in "Calcutta Review," xxxi. 368ff.; Yule, "Mission to Ava," 143; "Upper Burma Gazetteer," Pt. I. i. 584; "Census Report," Burma, 1901, i. 131.]

CHOLERA.—This terrible epidemic disease, long known to the Hindus before the arrival of the Portuguese under the name of Visucika was first described to Europeans by Correa and Garcia in the sixteenth century with the title of *Mordexin* * or *Mort-de-Chien.** We have an account of an epidemic in Colonel Pearce's force at Ganjam in 1781; of a severe attack in Jessore in 1817; and of its appearance in the army of the Marquis of Hastings, where the outbreak was attributed by the natives to the slaughter of cows in a grove sacred to Hardaur Lála, a deified hero of Bundelkhand.

The disease is due to a micro-organism, once called the Comma Bacillus, but now found to be a vibrio or spirillum. Few micro-organisms have been more studied, but many of the facts of its life history are still doubtful. The organism displays much variability, and hence arises the difficulty of tracing the origin of isolated epidemics. One of the centres of its diffusion is the Bengal Delta. Here it is endemic, but remains quiescent for a time; it becomes periodically diffused, but the causes of its occasional activity and diffusion are still not satisfactorily determined. It is distributed by human agency, and even by soiled clothing, rags, or other articles which have become infected.

"There is no reason to suppose," writes Dr Shadwell, "that it is air-borne, or that atmospheric influences have anything to do with its spread, except so far as meteorological conditions may be favourable to the growth and activity of the micro-organisms. Beyond all doubt the great manufactory of the poison in the human body, and the discharges from it are the great source of contagion."

It may be communicated by food and drink, or by the agency of flies; but the most important source is water, because it affects the greatest number of people. But it is not altogether a water-borne disease, because it may infect the soil of localities which have a pure water supply, but have none or ineffective drainage. And here it is more difficult to get rid of than in cases where water is at the root of the mischief.

There can be little doubt that one of the main sources of the diffusion of the disease, which has periodically spread along the sea routes to Europe and through Central Asia, is the large concourse of pilgrims at places like Hardwár and Alláhábád in Upper India and Násik in Bombay, or along the pilgrim route to Juggurnaut. The source of more than one of the epidemics in Central Asia and Europe has been traced to Hardwár. It has also appeared among the crowds of half-starved labourers on famine relief works. Much has been done in recent times by improved sanitation and the provision of a pure water supply at the sacred places of the Hindus to repress the outbreaks, and we now seldom hear of the visitations of the disease at the cantonments of European troops, which were so frequent and destructive in pre-Mutiny days.

The terror which natives feel on an outbreak is shown by their deification of a special cholera goddess, Mari Bhaváni, to whose wrath the plague is universally attributed. On such occasions an image of the goddess is solemnly paraded and led in procession beyond the infected area, and the disease is supposed to depart in her train. The ruder hill-man employs his priest to parade the village streets and take a straw from every thatch. These are burnt with an offering of rice, butter, and turmeric at a shrine to the east of the village site. Chickens, smeared with vermilion, are then driven in the direction of the smoke, and carry off the disease. If these methods fail, goats, and finally pigs, are used as scape-animals. These never disappoint expectation, the explanation being that the proceedings of the priest are so leisurely, and so much time is spent in collecting subscriptions to provide the victims, that in the interval the disease has usually worked itself out. More sensible people demolish their flimsy huts and fly into the depths of the jungle, where they usually free themselves from the infection. The Burmese Buddhists have adopted a similar form of worship, derived from the primitive animistic beliefs of the race. In Nepál any year in which the figure 8 appears is said to be surely visited by an epidemic. The favourite remedy among the early Europeans in India, as described by Dellon and Thevenot, was to apply a heated sickle to the soles of the feet.

[Dr Shadwell's article in "Encyclopædia Britannica," 10th ed. xxvii; "Central Provinces Gazetteer," Intro. cxvii; Crooke, "Popular Religion and Folk-lore of North India," i. 140ff.; Shway Yoe, "The Burman," chap. xii.]

COFFEE.—Coffee was probably introduced into India by the Arabs trading with the Malabar Coast. It is said to have been brought to Mysore by a Musalmán pilgrim, Bába Búdan, who returned from Mecca some two centuries ago with seven seeds of the plant, probably originally introduced into Arabia from Abyssinia. This legend is to some extent corroborated by the fact that the observant traveller, Linschoten (1576-90), does not mention having seen it, though it is alluded to by his editor, Paludanus.

Attempts were made, it is said with some success, to grow it in the Botanical Gardens at Calcutta. But it has been ascertained that it is impossible to grow it with success in the Plains, and plantations are now found only in the Nilgiri hills, the Wynaad, Salem, and Coorg in South India. There are also some few plantations in the Malabar States of Cochin and Travancore, and in the western part of Mysore. The total value of coffee exported from India in 1903-4 was £912,000.

It can hardly be said that the industry is in a satisfactory state. It commends itself even less than tea to the native public, and the total value of the imports from India, including Ceylon, to the United Kingdom have fallen within twenty years from five and a quarter to two and a half millions. It is also exposed to a host of enemies—fungoid disease, such as leaf-blight and leaf-rot; and to many insect plagues, such as the dreaded Borer, a species of beetle; various bugs, distinguished as brown, black, and white; black grub, the larva of a moth; locusts and weevils, rats, squirrels, monkeys, and jackals. Many devices have been suggested to overcome these pests, but only indifferent success has been achieved. One plan tried was to introduce the red ant to attack the bug ; but the remedy was worse than the disease, their bites being so painful that the coolies refused to enter a plantation infested by them.

[Watt, "Economic Dictionary," ii. 460ff.]

COOLY.*—This is a term applied to the common unskilled native labourer, and especially to the emigrant workmen enlisted for service in the tea-gardens of Assam or Ceylon, and the plantations of Mauritius or the West India Islands.

There is a curious difference in the manner in which the coolies of various parts of India carry their loads. Thus, writing of Kashmír, Mr Drew tells us that in the outer hills they carry the load on their heads, first making a soft pad with their turbans, a method ineffective over difficult ground. Further up, in the middle mountains, they bend the head forward and fix the load on the shoulder and back of the neck. The most business-like method is that of the Kashmíris, Ladakhis, and Baltis, who load the back by means of a light framework of sticks and rope suspended from the shoulders. Further east, in Nepál, the Bhotiyas always carry the load on the back, supported by a strap across the forehead, while the Newárs use a pair of baskets suspended from a pole balanced across the shoulder, which is the method employed by the *Banghy-burdár** of the Plains. The cooly in Sikhim has a wooden frame strapped over his shoulder like a knapsack, and supported by a broad band of plaited cane passed across his temples. Further east, again, the Jaintiyas use the wide, plaited band across the forehead.

In the Plains the ordinary cooly carries his load on his head, unless he uses the *Banghy*,* which is on the plan of the London milk-woman's yoke. Some years ago, it is said, a railway contractor imported wheel-barrows, but after a while he found, to his amazement, that the coolies were carrying them filled with earth on their heads. There is even a caste etiquette in such matters. The Beldár of Bengal carries earth only on his head, while the Koras, a somewhat similar caste, use a pair of baskets and a shoulder-yoke. Any violation of these rules involves expulsion from the caste. Among the Nicobarese the distinction is one of sex, men using the yoke, women resting the load on their heads.

A camel load in Turkey is said to be 300 lbs., but, according to Curzon, an Armenian porter at Constantinople will carry 600 lbs. a short distance. A cooly woman is said to have carried a piano up the hill to Naini Tál, but probably no Indian cooly can vie with the brawny Armenian. Hodgson, when Resident at Nepál, investigated the question of cooly carriage very carefully, and advised the Indian Government that goods for Nepál should be packed in loads of 160 lbs., adding that "a single mountaineer will carry that surprising weight over the huge mountains of Nepál." Mr Drew tells of one man who carried four dozen large bottles of beer in a case; another 192 lbs.; and one well authenticated case of a load of 240 lbs. This was over a hundred miles of uneven Kashmíri roads, with many long rises and several passes, one of 9,000 feet elevation. On such a journey coolies take their own time, doing a ten days' march in eighteen or nineteen days, and all this work is done on a diet of unleavened bread and rice. Further east, in the Sikhim hills, Colonel Waddell fixes the standard load of a cooly travelling at a decent pace, about 14 miles a day, to be 60 lbs., and this inclusive of his wraps and bedding.

CROCODILE.—The great Saurians, which the Anglo-Indian persists in calling *alligators*,* consist of two species belonging to one genus, and a third quite distinct from these. First comes *Crocodilus palustris*, which has the shortest snout, inhabits fresh water, and is the true and dreaded Magar [*Mugger**] of our Indian rivers. Secondly, *Crocodilus porosus* has a much longer head, inhabits tidal creeks and estuaries, and is the only Indian crocodile ever to be found in salt water. Quite distinct from these two species is the Ghariyál, a name which has been corrupted into the *Gavial* of zoologists, the long-nosed reptile which never frequents swamps or stagnant water like *C. palustris*, and never enters salt or brackish water, like *C. porosus*.

The true Magar lives partly on fish, partly on bodies of men or animals floating down the stream. He is often a man-eater, lying in wait near fords and bathing-places, where he seizes his prey. Hence such spots are often protected by lines of stakes; but these, he, being amphibious, is often able to turn. Mr Baker tells of one shot by Mr Chapman in one of the Bengal rivers, from the stomach of which were taken about 30 lbs. weight of gold, silver, copper, brass, and zinc, all women's ornaments. From a Ghariyál shot by Mr Carlleyle near Delhi were taken the following:

> "About a dozen large bunches or pellets of hair, probably human; sixty-eight rounded pebbles; one large ankle-ring; twenty-four fragments of Chúris or glass bangles; five bronze finger-rings; a silver neck-charm; a gold bead; thirty small red coral beads."

This disposes of the assertion, sometimes made, that the Ghariyál never preys on human beings.

The Magar is thus described by Linschoten:

> "In the River of Bengala, called Ganges, and by Malacca there are Crocodiles, and other sea Serpents of an unspeakable greatness, which oftentimes doe overturne smal fisher boates and other scutes, and devoure the men that are therein; and some of them creeping out of the water unto the lande do snatch up divers men, which they hale after them, and then kill them and eate them, as it dayly happeneth in those Countries."

As to their size, the largest Mr Baker ever saw in the Sunderbunds was 24 feet long. From the fact that there is a special provision of nature for replenishing their teeth, Sir S. Baker infers that the crocodile is a creature which surpasses all others in duration of life.

Crocodiles have been utilised in India to prevent the escape of prisoners from forts, in the moats of which they used to be preserved. Captain Hervey describes the fort of Vellore as guarded in this way by Hyder Ali. Tavernier, writing of Bijapur, says of the king's palace:

> "What causes the approach to it to be difficult is, that in the moat which surrounds it, and which is full of water, there are many crocodiles."

General Mundy gives a similar account of the fort of Barabati, near Cuttack; and the old traveller, Cæsar Frederick, describing Pegu in Burma, says:

> "It is a great citie, very plaine and flat, and four-square, walled round about, and with ditches that compass the wals round about with water, in which ditches are many crocodiles."

These creatures, according to Sir H. Yule, were there as late as 1830.

The dangerous nature of the reptile has invested him, like the tiger, with sanctity. Tame crocodiles are protected and fed in many places, as in the famous Magar Taláo, or "Crocodile Tank," near Karáchi. The Rája of Jaypur protects them in the lake at Amber, and will not allow a shot to be fired in their neighbourhood. At the tank at Khán-Jahán Ali in Jessore young married women feed the monsters in the hope of being blessed with off-spring; and at the tank at Pír Pokhar, near Pandua in Bengal, one of them, called by the name of Fateh Khán, "Lord of Victory," when called, comes to the surface and is fed. Buchanan-Hamilton describes a tank at Purneah in Bengal dedicated to a saint, and inhabited by a pair of crocodiles which are identified with the saint and his wife. When deprived of the usual victims supplied by pilgrims they became exceedingly voracious, and just before the traveller's visit carried off a young man who was watering a buffalo.

> "The natives, far from being irritated at this, believed that the unfortunate man had been a dreadful sinner, and that his death was performed (sic) by the Saint merely as a punishment."

This veneration for the crocodile may be a survival of

the old worship of the Nága, or dragon; or, when the worship is performed to promote fecundity, may be connected with similar powers ascribed to fish all over the world.

Though some Hindus worship them, the fishing tribes have no scruples about eating them, in spite of the unsavoury taste of their flesh. Sir S. Baker says:

"I have eaten almost everything, but although I have tasted crocodile I could never succeed in swallowing it. The combined flavour of bad fish, rotten flesh, and musk is the *carte de diner* offered to the epicure."

The Kanjar gipsy of Behar rejects beef, but loves crocodile flesh; and so do the Irulas of Madras, the jungle tribes of the Central Provinces, the Mor fishermen of the Indus, and the Malláhs and Koch fishermen of Bengal.

In spite of the savagery of the brute many Englishmen have risked their lives in bravado by going within his reach. Lord Valentia mentions a sergeant of the Scotch Brigade at Vellore, who for a small wager entered the moat, which was infested by them. He was several times dragged under water, but eventually escaped with many severe wounds. Outram, while looking at the crocodiles in the Udaypur lake, was asked by the Maharána if any man living would dare jump in. He sprang at once into the water and escaped safe to land. Rice, the renowned tiger-killer, once ran over the backs of the crocodiles in the Magar Taláo. The Maharája of Jodhpur told Colonel Tod that he had ridden alligators in the lake near his palace. But Tod did not believe him, and explains that he acquired his "talents for amplification" by residing at the Jaypur Court.

[Baker, "Sport in Bengal"; Sir S. Baker, "Wild Beasts and their Ways," chap. xiii; Chevers, "Indian Medical Jurisprudence," 367; Buchanan-Hamilton, "Eastern India," iii. 59; Eastwick, "Dry Leaves from Young Egypt," 218.]

CURRY.—In discussing this well-known article of native diet we must distinguish between the original Indian variety and that introduced at a later date, which was derived, as Sir H. Yule suggests, from the spiced cookery of medieval Europe and Western Asia.

As an example of the first kind of curry we may take that used by the Nambútiri Bráhmans of Malabar, perhaps the most Conservative people in India. It consists of two varieties, one made of chopped vegetables fried in *ghee*,* cocoa-nut, or *gingelly* * oil, and seasoned with sesamum, salt, and *jaggery*,* or coarse sugar; the other of *jack-fruit* * mixed with sundry vegetables.

This, it will be noticed, omits capsicum or red pepper, the most common ingredient of the curry of our times, a condiment which was introduced by the Portuguese. That careful observer, P. della Valle, writing in 1623, describes the curry of his day:

"Caril is a name which in India they give to certain Broths made with Butter, the Pulp of Indian Nuts (instead of which in our Countries Almond Milk may be us'd, being equally good and of the same virtue), and all sorts of Spices, particularly Cardamoms and Ginger (which we use little) besides herbs, fruits, and a thousand other condiments. The Christians, who eat everything, add Flesh, or Fish of all sorts, especially Hens or Chickens, cut in small pieces, sometimes Eggs, which, without doubt, make it more savoury; with all which things is made a kind of Broth, like our Guazetti, or Pottages, and it may be made in many several ways; this Broth, with all the aforesaid ingredients, is afterwards poured in good quantity upon the boyled Rice, whereby is made a well-tasted mixture of much substance and light digestion, as also with very little pains; for it is quickly boyled, and serves both for meat and bread together. I found it very good for me, and used it often."

When we come to the recipes used in Akbar's kitchen, as described by Abul Fazl, we find an increased use of ghee and of spices, like cardamoms, cummin, pepper, coriander, and assafœtida, all of which are ingredients of the modern Musalmán curry, and some of its European imitations. To this day the Hindu of North India uses as a condiment, eaten with his rice or cakes, pulse, cooked with turmeric, capsicum, and salt.. The high-caste man rejects both unions and garlic as impure; both these are used by the Muhammadan and low-caste Hindu.

As for European curry, none is superior to that of Madras, where cocoa-nut milk is a leading ingredient. This is not procurable except in the neighbourhood of the sea-coast, and hence the so-called Bengal or North Indian curry is an inferior article. What makes the curry of India superior to imitations provided by English cooks is, that to make a good curry the turmeric and other spices must be quite fresh, and ground for each dish; while the English cook depends on curry powder and pastes, which soon lose their delicacy of savour. She also notably fails in producing the floury rice which every native can prepare.

The Chatni [*Chutny* *], or relish, which accompanies the curry is a very important part of the dish, and here, too, the English cook is handicapped by the inferiority of that procurable in England. The basis of the best chatni is mango,

> "gathered," as Linschoten says, "when they are green and conserved, and for the most part salted in pots, and commonlie used to be eaten with rice, sodden in pure water, and so eaten with salt mangas. . . . These salted mangas are in cutting like the white Spanish olives, and almost of the same taste, but somewhat savorie, and not so bitter, yet a little sowre, and are in so great abundance, that it is wonderful."

The European occasionally adds the dry fish known as the *Bummelo* * or *Bombay Duck*,* for which the Burman substitutes the *Ngapee*,* or *Balachong* * of the Malay races, which consists of various kinds of fish, in an advanced state of putrefaction, pressed into a mass with salt. To give increased pungency to the relish he sometimes adds to this the big stinging red ant. The Burman, too, uses for his curry a variety of vegetables, such as wild asparagus, the succulent stems of acquatic plants, the leaves of the mango, which are somewhat acrid, and those of the tamarind curiously aromatic. The Hindu of Upper India substitutes for these, under the general name of Ság, various herbs which the women pick in the fields.

If the English working classes could only be taught the virtues of the moist curries above described, and of the dry curry, consisting of cold meat cut into pieces like dice and fried in spice, a condiment known in India as Jhál fraisseé, their food would be infinitely more wholesome and savoury.

[P. della Valle, "Travels," ii. 328; Linschoten, ii. 26; Blochmann, "Ain-i-Akbari," i. 59; Shway Yoe, "The Burman," i. 84; Riddell, "Indian Domestic Economy," 383ff.]

DACOITY.*—This is the term applied to gang-robbery, and under the present law the gang must consist of at least five persons associated for a common purpose. The organisation of these gangs in modern times has been compared to that of the Thugs (q. v.), but among dacoits an actual or assumed religious motive is absent.

Dacoity, however, is a very wide term, and includes several varieties of crime. Thus, we have gangs raised and led by some famous leader, who claims to be influenced by political motives, like Tantia Bhíl of the Central Provinces, captured in 1889, about whom tales are current like those of Robin Hood, and some of the Bohs who fiercely resisted the annexation of Upper Burma. Such gangs are easily organised in half-settled tracts like Káthiáwár, where outlawry has always been the last refuge of the aggrieved, and in more troubled times used to grow into a regular profession. In a sort of Alsatia, like that on the Rájputána frontier, where the four native states of Dholpur, Bharatpur, Karauli, and Gwalior meet, an active leader has always been able to raise a gang of desperadoes and raid the British villages in the Ganges-Jumna valley.

Of quite another type are the gangs which have from time to time been formed within our own territories. These consist either of local criminals, or are often drawn from the gipsy-like wandering tribes. Such in Upper

India are the Sánsiya or Habúra. A similar tribe in South India, the Maravans of Tinnevelli, though only one-tenth of the population of the district, committed in recent years seventy per cent. of the dacoities. General Hervey describes the rude comfort of the Mínas of the Rájputána-Panjáb frontier, who habitually raid the neighbouring districts and bring home valuable plunder. They live in excellent masonry houses, with underground passages, arranged to facilitate escape and for the storage of loot. They have fine camels for use in these raids, are well supplied with the best food and spirits, load themselves and their women with jewellery, and are noted for their charity and hospitality.

"But a curious observer might detect that a close intelligence was withal a part of them all; that the eye is restless and watchful, the child is signalling something, the woman's song is the voice of warning, whether by word or intonation; and that the man's hang-dog look cloaks furtive glances which connect him with persons who are peering through the high thorn fences of the cattle yards which project from each dwelling, or with others who flit from window to window or terrace of their labyrinthine and subterraneous abodes."

The same is the case with the Gújars of North India, who, as in the times of the Mutiny, take advantage of any relaxation of authority to pursue their trade of rapine. Not long since it was fairly well established that outrages of this kind were committed in Bombay by jungle tribes, with the support of the factious, high-class Mahratta Bráhmans.

It is from Bengal, in the early days of our rule, that we have the fullest accounts of the ruin to which dacoity can reduce a province. It began long before our Government was established, during the anarchy attending the decay of the Moghul Empire. It gained strength in the transition period before our power was consolidated, and the great famine of 1770 greatly extended it.

"The Dacoits of Bengal," says a State paper of 1772,

"are not, like the robbers of England, individuals driven to such desperate courses by sudden want. They are formed into regular communities, and their families subsist by the spoils which they bring home to them."

Warren Hastings reported that the whole province up to the boundary of Calcutta was a prey to dacoits. In 1780 they burned 15,000 houses and 200 people in the capital itself. In the country districts many avoided arrest by the use of stilts, which enabled them to escape in the marshes. Active measures were, of course, taken, but it was more than three-quarters of a century before this crime was really put down.

River dacoity is another variety; and nothing surprises the modern Anglo-Indian more than accounts written in the early years of the last century, and even later, of the insecurity of the Ganges, then the great highway to Upper India. The Sunderbunds, a labyrinth of swamp and forest in the Gangetic Delta, were a safe refuge for such ruffians, who went so far as to plunder and murder Europeans. This also used to occur up country. General Sleeman tells the strange story of Ravenscroft, a Bengal Civilian, who embezzled the Company's funds, retired into Oudh where no writ ran, and was finally murdered by dacoits in 1823. In the next year the good Bishop Heber bewails the cruelties committed by the Bengal dacoits on any one suspected of concealing treasure. Even quite in our own times the Law Reports show cases in which the dacoits, like the robbers of the treasury of King Rhampsinitus, cut off the heads of their wounded comrades to avoid detection. On the Ganges river dacoity still survives. Quite recently a party of boatmen from Benares organised a raid on the dacoit boats in the lower reaches of the river, and returned after a successful expedition with a number of pirates' flags, which they solemnly presented to the Lieutenant-Governor.

In Lower Bengal a new source of danger has recently come to light in the outrages by bands of Kábuli ruffians, who are permitted to enter India on pretence of trade, and have committed many serious gang robberies.

It is only within the last few years that the gangs which have always flourished in Burma have been broken up. Dacoity there assumed the character of a manly sport, in which every young man of spirit should at one time or another have engaged. The object was often not plunder, but to carry off a girl who resisted the advances of a suitor. It was members of these gangs who organised themselves at the annexation of the Upper province, and kept the country in a state of turmoil for several years.

Dacoity is the one branch of his business in which the native policeman is least successful. His impulse is always to harry the local ex-convict and ne'er-do-well, while the professional robber is safe miles away with his booty. But happily for the interests of justice the robber gang has generally an informer in its midst; and though it may for a time flourish by the aid of the jewellers and traders who act as receivers, the end comes sooner or later. Dacoity, in short, is one of the last survivals of an age of anarchy, and it still offers a career to the wilder and more enterprising elements in the population, whose hopes of distinction through a life of adventure have been checked by the pressure of British law. If that control were once removed, the men are ready to raid and murder as they did in the good old days.

[Arthur (A. T. Crawford), "Reminiscences of an Indian Police Official"; Hervey, "Some Records of Crime"; Kitts, "Serious Crime in an Indian Province."]

DANCING.—Dancing appears in the oldest Indian literature. In the Veda, Ushas, the Dawn, robes herself in the attire of a dancing-girl, and in the Mahábhárata we have a curious account of the Rájput lords and ladies going on a picnic, where they are entertained with dancing. Dancing is frequently represented on the Buddhist monuments; but on the revival of Bráhmanism we find Manu prescribing that the dancer is impure, and the twice-born are directed to abstain from the amusement.

"There can be no doubt," writes Sir M. Monier-Williams, "that dancing in the East was once exclusively connected with religious devotion, especially with homage paid to Siva in his character as Lord of dancing."

On this was possibly based the Greek belief, as reported by Arrian on the authority of Megasthenes, that it was Dionysus who taught the Indians the Satyric dance, "or, as the Greeks call it, the Kordax." But at the present day it is only in South India, where troops of Dási<s [*Deva-dasi* *] are attached to the greater temples, and among the jungle tribes that this connection of dancing with religion is recognised. These Dásis consist partly of superfluous girls who are presented by their parents to the Pagodas, and, partly, of those devoted to a temple in fulfilment of a vow. They are married to the god at an early age, but seldom continue to live the life of vestal virgins. Their female children are brought up to the same degrading profession; some by connection with men of low caste lead a better life. Mr Nelson describes the Dásis of Madura as "very deficient in good looks, and very bad dancers." The rise of the caste and its euphemistic name, according to Mr Francis, seem to date from the ninth and tenth centuries of our era, during which time in South India much activity was shown in temple-building and elaboration of ritual. Their duties then, as now, were to fan the idol with ox-tail flappers, to bear the sacred lights, and to sing and dance when the idol was carried in procession. With their own laws of inheritance, their special customs, and rules of etiquette, enforced by a caste council, they hold a position which is, perhaps, without parallel in any other country.

The better-class Hindu of our day never dreams of dancing himself or permitting the women of his family to practise what he holds to be a degrading art. If he wishes to be entertained with dancing he hires a troop of professional *nautch-girls*.* Hence one of the many things in our Western customs which he cannot understand is a ball, in which ladies and gentlemen dance together. Mrs Parkes tells us that the ladies at Lucknow were not allowed to dance in the presence of the Nawáb, since the occasion when, supposing that a quadrille was being danced in his honour, he called out, "That will do; let them leave off!" It is, in fact, only under the influence of strong religious excitement that the men of North India break out into dancing. Broughton, in his account of the Mahratta camps, describes the young sepoys imitating nautch-girls on Krishna's birthday, "though to dance in public, upon any other occasion, would be reckoned a disgrace to which no decent man could possibly submit."

The really interesting Indian dances are those of the jungle tribes. Here they still retain their religious character, being performed at the chief agricultural seasons, seed-time and harvest, in the belief that the beating of the dancers' feet on the ground will arouse and please Mother Earth, and cause the crops to prosper. It is particularly at harvest-time that the wild tribes inhabiting the central hills break out into unrestrained merry-making and license.

We may distinguish two main varieties of the aboriginal dance. In one, that of the Kols of Chota Nágpur, which is called the Karama, because it is danced at the cutting of a branch of this sacred tree, the women stand in line, each with her arms round her neighbour's shoulder, bend their heads modestly, and advance and retreat slowly opposite a band of men, who beat their drums violently and encourage the women to greater exertions. Occasionally the latter bend down and pat the ground with their hands, invoking Mother Earth. The observance is now rapidly passing away as the tribes become Hinduised, and many of the songs are merely invocations of the Hindu gods. When danced before Europeans it is rather a monotonous, spiritless performance, but at the regular feasts under the influence of copious draughts of native spirits the performance rapidly becomes an orgy. When they perform in an officer's camp the ladies of the ballet are permitted to refresh themselves only with a little coarse brown sugar.

In the Santál dance, as described by Captain Sherwill, the figure is very different. A lofty stage is erected in a plain, on which a few men seat themselves and seem to act as masters of the ceremonies.

"Radiating from this stage, which forms the centre of the dance, are numerous strings composed of from twenty to thirty women, who, holding each other by the waist-band, right shoulder, arm, and breast bare, hair decked with flowers or bunches of *Tusser** silk, dance to the wildest and maddest of music, drawn from monkey-skin covered drums, pipes, and flutes; and, as they dance, their positions and postures, which are most absurd, are guided and prompted by the male musicians, who dance in front of, and facing the women; the musicians throw themselves into the most ludicrous positions, shouting and capering, and screaming like madmen; and as they have tall peacocks' feathers tied round their heads, and are very drunk, the scene is a most extraordinary one."

The Bhíl dance is even wilder. Men and women, keeping time to the music in a double shuffle, wheel round the musicians in an irregular circle. Men at these dances often dress up as women, impersonate Hindu Fakírs, or animals. Sometimes they roll along the ground, rise, and joining hands, bound backwards and forwards with a double shuffle of the feet, or a step like that of the Irish Jig. But this is surpassed by the dance of the Kurumbas of South India, who perform before their chief at their great festival. Their heads are covered with long, flowing plumes, and at the end a member of the ballet sits down quietly, while cocoa-nuts are broken on his bare skull to the music of a drum.

Another form of the circular dance is that round a fire, as among the Khattaks of the Panjáb and some of the Burmese tribes. The Khattaks, a Pathán tribe of the frontier, with swords drawn revolve to the music of pipe and drum. At first the movement is slow, but it soon quickens, and the dancers slash with their swords at imaginary enemies. Quicker and quicker goes the music; the swords flash through the dust and smoke, till the performers are quite exhausted. The audience enters into the spirit of the performance as ardently as the dancers do, and nothing much wilder or more passionate than a Khattak dance can be witnessed in India. The Khásis of the Assam frontier and the Wás of Burma have a similar dance. The Wá dance begins with a dignified walk to the sound of a rhythmic chant, broken at intervals by a choric shout, when all leap with both feet off the ground. Another dance of the Káws, an allied tribe, has been compared to "a Highland Fling, performed by a man in the last stage of physical exhaustion."

An interesting point about this circular aboriginal dance is that it has probably been adopted into Hinduism in the form of the Rás Mandala, the dance traditionally performed by the Gopis, or milkmaids, round their lord, Krishna, which has in later days become an important part of his worship, and is performed in Rájputána and other places which are the chief centres of his cultus. The more prominent figure in the centre, around whom the dancers revolve, impersonates the deity. In the pictorial representations the number of figures of the god equals that of the dancers, a crude materialising of the poetry of the old sacred song, in which each girl, as she dances, dreams that she, and she alone, has a divine partner.

To return to the aborigines—no tribe has developed dancing so elaborately as the Oraons of Chota Nágpur. They possess an unusually fine musical taste, are good tonists, and can sing in unison. Their children, says General Dalton, dance as soon as they can walk, and sing as soon as they can talk. Each of their villages has a dancing circus, with stone seats for the spectators in true Homeric fashion. At festive seasons the dance begins at sunset and lasts till sunrise, if the supply of home-brewed beer holds out. The dust raised by the feet of the dancers spreads a brick-dust hue over the ballet. But after a night's dancing they start off cheerfully to their day's work.

The Khási dance of Assam is remarkable for the dress of the dancers.

"The men, decked out in jackets of satin or velvet, or broad-cloth of the brightest hue, red, green, purple or yellow, with silken turbans, plumed with peacock or other feathers, with gold and silver ear-rings, bangles and charms, with silken dhooties, and often with a bright *chudder** of silk or broad-cloth, a gaily decorated quiver with arrows hanging at their back, and armed with the two-handed sword and shield which they continually clash together, dance in a circle a wild but monotonous measure, accompanied with discordant music, firing of musketry, and long-continued howling."

The Káfirs of the Hindu-kush, again, are dancers in a different way. Sometimes they dance for mere amusement; but more generally for a solemn purpose. The war dance, performed by the women while their men are absent on a raid, is intended to give the warriors strength and courage, and to keep them wakeful lest they should be surprised by the wily foe. It is thus one of the forms of mimetic magic which is such an important element in their religion. They dance, again, to propitiate the gods, to celebrate the death of a clansman, or at the solemn erection of an effigy in his honour.

To an Englishman the modern *nautch** is destitute of interest or excitement, but the native never tires of this, his chief amusement. In Western India the performance is sometimes enlivened by the egg-dance, in which a number of eggs are attached to a wicker wheel on the dancer's head, in slip knots kept open by a glass bead. The girl whirls round, and at each turn places an egg in a loop, and without breaking them withdraws them one by one as the dance goes on. The nautch-girls are chiefly drawn from the professional dancing castes, but they are quite ready to welcome outsiders who voluntarily enter their community, or to kidnap little girls who are trained in the art. In former days, Seroda, near Goa, was one of their main centres, and romantic tales are told by travellers early in the last century of the beauty and accomplishments of the residents of this charming village. But now its palmy days are over, never to return.

It is nowadays only in the courts of Rájputána that the nautch-girl holds a recognised place. "They are," writes Mr Val. Prinsep, "a kind of privileged people, and wander through the palaces unveiled and unmolested." They do all the shopping and commissions for the veiled ladies of the Prince, and their dancing is more interesting than the ordinary nautch. Mr Prinsep describes with admiration the dance at Jodhpur in honour of the hero Rájas of olden time, when

"one hundred women dance round in a kind of stately measure, with 'woven paces and with waving hands.' They keep beautiful time, and in the strong light and shade of torch-light, with the glitter of many a bangle, armlet, and anklet, the effect is most striking. Ever and anon the great drum in the centre gives a boom, when the women all throw up their arms together, and behind all the great moon rises over the dark trees. I never was more 'fetched.'"

In South India these dancers in old times used to accompany armies in the field. In Malabar, Barbosa says:

"Whenever there is war, according to the number of men-at-arms whom the king sends there, he likewise sends with them a quantity of women; because they say that it is not possible to bring together an army, nor carry on war well, without women. These women are like enchantresses, and are great dancers; they play and sing, and pirouette."

P. della Valle describes one of these South Indian dances performed by the temple ballet at Ikkeri:

"Hither almost the whole City flock'd, Men and women and all the companies of the flower'd Virgins, who, putting themselves into circles, here and there danc'd and sung; yet their dancing was nothing but an easie walking round, their sticks alwayes sounding; onely sometimes they would stretch forth their legs, and now and then cowre down as if they were going to sit, one constantly singing, and the rest repeating the word Cole, Cole [Káli]."

The dress of the nautch-girl is highly decorous, but arranged with little elegance or grace. It often consists of skirts of scarlet and gold, spangled sáris [*Saree* *], trousers of silk brocade, and they wear masses of jewellery, the anklets of silver or gold with little bells making a soft tinkling as their brown feet move. The grave Bishop Heber describes a ballet at Delhi:

> "Their dresses were rich, but there was such a quantity of scarlet cloth petticoats and trousers, so many shawls wrapped round their waists, and such multifarious skirts peeping out below each other, that their figures were quite hidden, and the whole effect was that of a number of Dutch dolls, though the faces of two or three out of the number were pretty."

The costume of the Madura dancers baffled the comprehension of Lord Dufferin: "the front part hangs in petticoats, but the back is only trousers," in fact, a sort of divided skirt in a new and striking style.

The dance itself is a series of slow posturings, with graceful movements of hand and arm representing in dumb show a love scene, the wiles of a serpent charmer, the motions of a lutist.

> "Nothing," writes Lady Dufferin, "could be more strictly proper, and nothing could possibly be more languid and gentle than the dancing, if dancing it can be called." The Burmese dancing she thinks more interesting than the Indian. "Still it consists almost entirely of bending about the body into extraordinary positions, many of them suggestive of a bad pain somewhere. The movement which is most admired is made with the arm, and consists in bending the elbow the wrong way; it looks as if it had a double joint."

What is most remarkable is the wonderful sensitiveness to time, and the extreme tension in which every muscle is constantly kept, with the power of moving local muscles, while the rest of the body is motionless.

[For the organisation of the South Indian Dasis, see C. Ramachendrier, "Decisions on the Law relating to Dancing Girls."]

DEAD, DISPOSAL OF.—India is simply a museum containing examples of the varied methods of disposing of the dead. These may be roughly classified into those which have as their object the preservation of the corpse or of some relics of it ; secondly, those in which the ruling intention is to put the dead out of sight.

Of the first class the most familiar example is the Egyptian custom of mummification, where the intention was to provide a refuge for the Ka, or separable soul. Beyond some isolated examples and folk-lore traditions we have no distinct evidence that the custom of embalming extended to India. But even at the present time the Khásis of the Himálaya preserve in honey those who die in the rainy season, and cremate them when the weather clears. The Maghs of Bengal and the Kúkis of Assam smoke the bodies of their priests and chiefs, and keep them in the house for a time, finally disposing of them in the usual way. A survival of the same custom may perhaps be found in the rule of some of the ascetic bodies, who bury their dead in salt.

Next comes platform burial, of which many suggestions have been made to explain the origin. It may have been intended to protect the body from profanation, or, the dead being taboo, to prevent the corpse touching the ground until the perishable part has disappeared, lest the productive powers of the soil may be affected ; or the idea may have been to keep a refuge for the ghost until it passes into another state of being ; or a desire to keep the bones as relics. Platform burial is practically now confined to the Nágas of the Assam frontier.

The habit of exposing the dead to birds and beasts of prey was imported from Central Asia, and now prevails only among the Pársis. Colonel Waddell has recently shown that this method is inevitable in Tibet, owing to the severity of the winter, which prevents the digging of graves, and the absence of fuel for cremation.

Excavation shows that in South India at least inhumation was the practice of the earliest races found in that region. In early Aryan times both inhumation and cremation prevailed. Before the separation it seems probable that the Aryans exposed their dead. Later on, under Bráhman influence, it became the rule to cremate the corpse and bury the ashes in or near the spot occupied by the pyre. This, again, was modified into the present custom of cremating the corpse and consigning the ashes to a sacred stream. This may have been also the Dravidian rule, unless it may be due among them to Hindu influence. The Santáls of our day bring the ashes of their dead long distances to their sacred river, the Damúda. It is a curious instance of the effect of modern ideas on Hinduism that not long ago a pious Bráhman suggested to the Indian Government that the State should co-operate in disposing of the ashes of the dead. His plan was that at all the well-known places where the ashes are committed to a holy river, Hardwár, Benares, Násik, a trustworthy funeral priest should be appointed to perform the rites, the ashes being consigned to him by parcel post.

When the Hindus abandoned the custom of earth burial they still retained traces of the more primitive method. They prescribed burial for the bodies of persons dying in a state of taboo, like ascetics, lepers, women dying in child-birth, and young children. These last are in North India very generally buried under the threshold, possibly with the hope that they may be re-incarnated in the family. So the primitive rite of providing a funeral feast, at which in its earliest form the corpse was consumed by the survivors by way of a sacrament, was modified into the modern Sráddha, at which food is presented to the dead and the sainted ancestors of the family.

Among the existing jungle tribes the primitive practice still prevails. The Berads of Poona simply leave their dead in the forest, "to become spirits." Others bury the corpse in a rude way in the jungle, and pile a few stones to mark the grave; others perform a farce of cremation, merely singeing the face and feet of the corpse and exposing it in the forest. But the rule is subject to constant modification. Thus, among the tribes of the Hindu-kush cremation used to be the common form, the ashes being collected in rude wooden boxes or in earthen jars and buried. Now Muhammadan influence has taught them to bury the corpse, and the same change of practice has, of course, occurred among the lower Hindu tribes who have in recent times adopted Islám or Christianity.

The rule against cremation of the unmarried dead can be removed by a sort of post-mortem marriage. The natives of South Malabar marry a dead girl to a cocoa-palm or to a young Bráhman, and when this is done the death rites are performed in the normal way.

One of the leading motives of the death rite is to propitiate the ghost, which becomes offended at any ill-treatment of the corpse. Hence probably arose the custom of shelf or niche burial, in which, after the grave is dug, a chamber is excavated on one side, into which the corpse is placed so that it may not be crushed by the overlying soil. This is the rule among some of the ascetic classes and certain vagrant races of the Deccan. It has also been adopted by the Musalmáns. The transition from this to dome or vault burial can be easily traced.

Of another form of burial, that in a crouched or sitting position, India supplies many examples. It has been supposed to symbolise the pre-natal position in the womb, or more probably it is a survival of the binding of the corpse to prevent the ghost from "walking." In later times it seems to have been regarded as honorific, the chief being buried in the posture he occupies at the tribal fire, or the ascetic teacher as he addresses his pupils.

We find also various devices to prevent the ghost from "walking" after death. Such are the plan of binding the corpse on its way to the pyre; or removing it by a special door so that it may not be able to find its way home; or burying the dead face downwards, or filling the grave with thorns, all based upon the same idea. Others, again, bury the dead for a time, and when corruption has done its work, remove the bones to a tribal ossuary. Here the theory may be that the bones must be purified to form a home for the ghost. The Todas of the Nilgiri hills have a "green" and a "dry" funeral, the first carried out immediately after death; the latter in about a year. It may be suspected that the Todas, who now cremate the dead, formerly practised the custom of inhumation, and that the "dry" funeral marks the time for the removal of the bones to an ossuary. For the same reason it seems likely that the Hindu death rites, performed on the anniversary of the death, also mark this period.

Mourning under Bráhman guidance has been elaborated into a system. The mourners, after contact with the dead, undergo a special ablution to remove the death pollution, and to prevent the danger of the ghost clinging to their clothing when they leave the cremation ground. Another set of observances is intended to baffle the ghost. When more advanced races assume mourning garb few suspect that the idea underlying the practice is that the ghost may not recognise them, and so be prevented from plaguing them. In the same belief the Hindu shaves and carries about with him a piece of iron, which protects him from the ghost.

The Hindu passion for symbolism appears in the custom of funeral rites done in effigy. In Bombay the Prabhu clerks have a mock funeral when a relation dies in a distant land or at sea, and there is no corpse to cremate; the same rite done when a person is alive signifies that he is dead to his family and caste. Thus, a husband will have a funeral in effigy for a wife who has deserted him, or parents for a son who has left his father's religion and becomes a Christian or a Musalmán. An image is made of three hundred and sixty leaves of the holy Palása tree, with a cocoa-nut representing the head, a plantain leaf for the brow, thirty-two pomegranate seeds for the teeth, two cowry-shells marked with red lead for the eyes, and so on. The effigy is laid upon the skin of a black antelope, and on it is placed a lighted lamp. The soul of the dead man is then charmed into the image, and as the lamp flickers and dies the mourner performs the rites for the departing soul, raises a pyre, cremates the image, and carries out the usual death ceremonies.

[W. Crooke, "Primitive Rites of Disposal of the Dead, with special reference to India," "Journal Anthropological Institute," xxix. (1899), 271ff.]

DEMONOLOGY.—From the cradle to the grave the Indian rustic, whether he be by religion Hindu or Musalmán, is oppressed by dread of the demons who surround him. Spirits of all kinds, some malignant fiends, some merely mischievous sprites, ever dog his earthly path; to their working he attributes all the evils of his existence, plague or other disease, loss of crops or famine; it is they who impede every work of piety which he undertakes. Hence the main object of his religious life is to identify the particular demon which for the time besets him, and to devise appropriate means by which he can be scared away or propitiated.

Many of these malignant spirits are the ghosts of those who have died an untimely death, the young man snatched away by sudden disease, the hunter slain by the tiger; in short, the ghost of any one who has died in an unusual or tragical way, and is hence likely to resent being so unceremoniously hustled from this life. As an instance of the really dangerous fiend we may take the Rákshasa, who is of the ogre-vampire type, disturbs sacrifices, animates corpses, and is generally the foe of the human race. In many of his characteristics he is the impersonation of the savage aboriginal tribes who resisted the Aryans. Of another type is the Churel, the ghost of a woman who has died in child-birth, who goes about with her feet turned backwards and abducts comely young men. Of the merely malicious sprite we have an example in the "Boy Satan" of Travancore, an imp about the size of a twelve-year-old boy, who showers stones at night on those who offend him and makes their couches regular beds of thorns. But he may be propitiated by offerings of food, and then acts as a guard over the goods of his protector.

Superstitions of this kind prevail most generally among the jungle tribes, who are exposed to sudden and unexpected death by malaria or the attacks of wild beasts. Among the peasantry of the Plains it is those who are most secluded and ignorant, and especially the degraded outcast tribes, who are influenced by such beliefs.

The business of identifying and propitiating the spirits of evil is not entrusted to the Bráhman priest, who is mainly concerned with the worship of the higher gods. The exorciser is generally drawn from the lower castes. The cases which he is usually called to treat are what a physician would diagnose as hysteria in some of its myriad forms, or the sudden and often unaccountable maladies of infant life. His procedure may be illustrated by Captain Macpherson's account of the Kandhs of Bengal:

"Seating himself by the afflicted person, the priest, taking some rice, divides it into small heaps, each dedicated to a god whom he names. He then balances a sickle with a thread, places a few grains on each end, and calls all the gods by name. The sickle is slightly agitated. A god has come perching by the offering. The priest declares his name and lays down the sickle. He then counts the heaps of rice dedicated to that god; if odd in number, the deity is offended; if even, he is pleased. In the former case, the priest becomes full of the god, shakes his head frantically with dishevelled hair, and utters wild, incoherent sentences. The patient addresses the god in his minister, enquiring humbly the cause of his displeasure. He refers to his neglected worship, sorrow is professed and forgiveness prayed for, and the sacrifices prescribed by the priest are instantly performed. Deceased ancestors are invoked in the same way as the gods, and appeased by offerings of fowls, rice, and liquor. The consecrated rice and the brass vessels are the perquisite of the priest."

If the evil be averted, well and good; but if the treatment fail, all the exorciser has to say is that some more formidable spirit has taken the field and brought his work to naught.

In Southern India as well as among the Lamas on the Tibetan frontier the rite of so-called "devil-dancing," a form of the Shamanism prevalent among the lower races all over the world, is commonly performed. Thus, Mr Logan, writing of Malabar, describes the Tiyars, who are much given to "devil-charming," or "devil-driving," as it is called. Their priests are of the washerman caste, who with chants, clashing of cymbals, magic figures, and waving lights expel the evil spirits from their votaries at certain epochs of their lives. Before child-birth a leafy arbour is made, and in front of it is placed an image of the terrible Chámunda, queen of the demons, made of rice-flour, turmeric powder, and charcoal. A gang of washermen represents the demons. On being invoked they bound on to the stage in pairs, dance, caper, roar, fight, and drench each other with saffron-powder water. Soon they seem to become verily possessed of the devil. Fowls and other animals are thrown to them to appease their fury. These they tear with their teeth, as the tiger rends his prey. By-and-by the convulsions cease, the devils depart, and the cure is supposed to be complete.

A similar account is given by Pyrard de Laval of what he saw at Malabar.

"As for their sicknesses, they have no medicines or cures but sorcerers, which are equipped like very devils, and come only by night to see the sick, with fire in their mouths, at the ears, feet, and hands, and are all covered with a false skin, and having upon them an endless number of bells that make a strange and horrible din. They also perform divers gestures, grimaces, and superstitious tricks, and make offers and promises to the devil, and all this in the presence of the sick person, who deems himself much relieved thereby." While he was there the king sent for a diviner to predict the result of a dispute with the King of Cochin. "I saw a most hideous man appear, all covered with a false skin, the hair of his head so long as to touch the ground, tall man as he was; he had also bells at his neck, on his arms and legs, and round his waist, which do make a wondrous jingling din. He ran five or six paces forward, then as many back, and kept roaring unceasingly all the time he was before the King . . . I believed that he was a sorcerer, but every one told me he was a devil."

By Hindus no ghost is more dreaded than the Mamduh, the spirit of a Musalmán of evil life. Muhammadans have much the same theory of evil spirits. The ghost of Muhammad bin Tughlak, the ruthless Emperor of Delhi, who lived in the middle of the fourteenth century, would have walked the earth to this day had not his pious successor, Fíroz Sháh, sought out all who had been wronged, paid them compensation, and received their acquittances, which he placed in a box beside the coffin of the sinner, that he might have them ready to present before the Judge at the Last Day.

When a Musalmán woman in Upper India is attacked with hysteria, she is supposed to be possessed by one of the Jinn. She is taken to the shrine of some noted Saint, like that of Sakhi Sarwar in Dehra Gházi Khán district. The sacred drum is beaten, and the woman begins to sway her head and body in time to the music. The keeper of the shrine appears, and subjects her to a lawyer-like examination to find out the tribe and name of the Jinn. The demon answers through the woman in various ways. He saw her and fell in love with her; or he admits that he is tormenting her because she will not return his love. This is usually the answer of a woman who wishes to leave her husband, or fears that he will beat her. The priest then requires the Jinn to leave the woman. He promises to go, but for a consideration, a calf or a goat, money or clothes, all of which are the perquisite of the guardian of the shrine. If the Jinn gives no satisfactory assurances more drastic measures are employed. The woman's hands are bound, and wedges of wood are forced between her fingers until the spirit becomes more compliant. At other shrines the woman is beaten with a sacred whip or chain, and thus the devil is driven out of her.

From this last account it would appear that fraud, or at least collusion, between priest and patient is not uncommon. But in some cases there is undoubtedly a form of genuine hysteria, and Captain Sherwill, who frequently witnessed such scenes among the Kandhs, was satisfied that there was no deception. When, however, as in the Panjáb instances, the devil-priest has a direct interest in the offerings, it is not difficult to believe that he adapts his treatment to the circumstances of his patient.

DIAMOND.—Diamonds were from very early times valued in India. The Puránas speak of them as divided into castes, and Marco Polo describes them as found in the kingdom of Mutfili, the modern Motupalli in the Gantúr district of Madras, where they were found in the beds of mountain streams after floods.

> "Moreover," he adds, "in these mountains great serpents are rife to a marvellous degree, besides other vermin, and this owing to the great heat. The serpents are also the most venomous in existence, insomuch that any one going into that region runs fearful peril; for many have been destroyed by those evil reptiles."

And he goes on to tell the famous story immortalised in the "Voyage of Sindibad," how the diamond-seekers throw into the valleys pieces of meat to which the diamonds adhere; when the eagles bring the meat to the summit of the cliffs, the watchers shout and frighten them away, or search the nests and find diamonds in the droppings of the birds, or sometimes when the eagles are taken diamonds are discovered in their stomachs. This tale, as Sir H. Yule shows, is as old as the time of Epiphanius in the fourth century, and was reproduced by later Arab travellers; it was told by Nicolo Conti in the fifteenth century. Dr Ball thinks that the mines of Albenigaras, mentioned by the last authority, were those of Wairagarh in the Central Provinces, and that the story arose from the custom of sacrificing cattle when a mine was opened to propitiate the evil spirits who guard treasure. An echo of the same tradition has been traced in the story told by Pliny and other early writers that the diamond was softened by the blood of a he-goat. If this explanation of the myth be correct, the early diamond-diggers must have been non-Aryans, who did not regard the cow as sacred.

Later on the trade in Indian diamonds is mentioned by Linschoten, who says that it was carried on by the Christians of Goa. It was left to Tavernier in his second journey (1638-43) to give the first complete account of the Indian diamond mines. But even this observant traveller was not aware of their extent.

The area in which diamonds were, or are, found consists of three distinct regions. First, the eastern side of the Deccan, from the river Pennár to the Son, the country of the Golconda diamonds, most of which seem to have come from Partiál, on the south-east frontier of the Nizám's dominions; secondly, the Madras Presidency, especially the deltas of the Kistna and Godávari; thirdly, Chota Nágpur and the Central Provinces as far as Bundelkhand. Here are the mines of Panna, about which a curious legend is told. Once upon a time a holy man came there with a diamond as large as a cart-wheel. The Rája tried to seize the treasure, but it burst into fragments, and all the diamonds now found are only fragments of it. None of the great historical diamonds are traceable to Panna. Those now found are of inferior size, but of excellent water, varying in colour from the purest white to black, and passing through all the intermediate shades of milky, roseate, yellow, green, and brown. Sir M. Gerard states that most of the stones now sold there come from South Africa.

Diamonds of considerable value have undoubtedly been found in Chota Nágpur and Sambalpur, but the history of the mines, which has been investigated by Dr Ball, is still obscure. General Dalton tells a story of one of these diamonds which illustrates the old method of "shaking the pagoda tree." The Rája of Chota Nágpur had a diamond valued at Rs.40,000. Captain Camac with a force visited his country in 1772, and proposed to the Rája to exchange his hat for the Rája's turban, which was adorned with the diamond, as a mode of swearing eternal friendship. The Rája was afraid to refuse, and could never be brought to see that he had got the best of the bargain. A Portuguese, it is said, went to dig at Karur in the Bellary district. He spent all his money to no purpose, and in despair was just about to take poison when his men found a stone weighing 434 carats, by which his fortune was assured.

Tavernier says that in his time the largest cut stones in the world were one belonging to the Grand Duke of Tuscany, which he valued at £200,000, and that of the Great Moghul, worth £900,000. The history of the latter stone is still obscure, but from the investigations of Dr Ball and Mr Beveridge we may identify it with the Kohinúr. It has also been suggested that in conformity with the Eastern practice of changing meaningless names into something more intelligible, the fact that the diamond was found at Kollúr on the Kistna suggested the name Koh-i-núr, or "Mountain of Light." Legend tells that the stone was worn by one of the heroes of the Mahábhárata; but the first historical notice of it is that the Emperor Bábar states that his son Humáyun acquired it at Agra in 1526 from the family of Rája Bikramajít. Previous to this it appears to have been in the hands of Sultán Ala-ud-dín, who acquired it from the Rája of Málwa in 1304. In the revolution which led to the flight of Humáyun from India he presented it to Sháh Tahmasp of Persia, and as Abul Fazl does not mention it among the valuables of Akbar, it apparently found its way into the Deccan, whence it came into the treasury of Aurangzeb, as a present from Mír Jumla. Mr Beveridge suggests as a reason for the gift that it was given to Aurangzeb because it had originally belonged to his ancestors. Some have supposed that while the gem was in Persia it was cut or broken by cleavage, and that one fragment is the Orloff diamond, now in the sceptre of the Emperor of Russia, and that another portion is a gem at present in Persia. At any rate the Kohinúr was taken from the Moghul treasury in 1738 by Nádir Sháh of Persia, from whom it passed in succession to Ahmad Sháh, and thence to Sháh Zamán and Sháh Shuja, from whom it was taken by force by Ranjít Singh in 1839. He bequeathed it to the temple of Juggurnaut, but ten years later, on the downfall of the Sikh power, it came into the hands of the British, and in the Life of Lord Lawrence may be read the curious story how he put it in his waistcoat pocket, and forgot all about it, until some days after, when his bearer brought him what he thought was a piece of worthless glass.

The history of another famous Indian gem, the Pitt Diamond, has been fully investigated by Sir H. Yule.

Thomas Pitt, who began as an interloper or unlicensed trader, and ended his Indian career as Governor of Madras, bought it there in 1701 for 48,000 pagodas, or rather more than £10,000. Pope unfairly described what was quite an honest transaction:

> "Asleep and naked as an Indian lay,
> An honest factor stole a Gem away."

It was finally sold to the Duke of Orleans in 1717 for 2,000,000 livres, or about £133,000.

In the beginning of 1905, at Messrs Streeter's sale, the Agra Diamond came for sale. It had been taken as loot from the King after the capture of Delhi in 1857. It was resolved to smuggle it to England, but how to get it safe out of the country was a matter of difficulty. Finally it was administered to a horse in a ball. The horse was taken to Bombay, fell ill, and was shot. The diamond was brought to England and sold to the Duke of Brunswick, by whom it was recut. It is now a perfect stone of a lovely rose-pink colour.

Perhaps the finest stone now in India is the "Star of the South," which was found in Brazil in 1853. It was purchased by Khanderáo, Gaikwár of Baroda, for, it is said, £90,000, and before he would wear it he dedicated it to the temple of Ganpati. Below it in the Gaikwár's necklace is a flat, heart-shaped diamond, the "Star of Dresden," which is said to have cost £45,000.

[Ball, "Tavernier," ii. App. I., II., III.; H. Beveridge, "Calcutta Review," cvi. 188ff.; Sir H. Yule, "Hedges' Diary," III. cxxxii.; "Times," 6th February 1905.]

DIVINATION.—The art of obtaining knowledge of secret things, or of the future, has been practised in India from the earliest times, and still exercises a powerful influence over the people. Arrian describes how the sages used to predict the character of the seasons and any calamities which might befall the State:

"The private fortunes of individuals they do not care to predict, either because divination does not concern itself with trifling matters, or because to take any trouble about such is deemed unbecoming. But if any one fails to predict truly, he incurs, it is said, no further penalty than being obliged to be silent for the future."

Most varieties of divination found in other parts of the world occur also in India; artificial divination, by haruspication, prodigies, lightning, augury, astrology, and lots; and natural divination, by dreams and prophetic oracles. All the artificial methods rest ultimately upon some form of sympathetic or mimetic magic. Haruspication, or examination of entrails, a primitive Roman practice, has been traced by R. von Ihering to nomadic Aryan times, when it was adopted as a means of ascertaining whether a new country was a healthy place of abode or not. It appears now to be confined to people like the Abors of the Assam frontier, and the Kachins and Karens of Burma; some divining by examination of the entrails of pigs and cattle, the brains and sinews of fowls; others using only the liver of a pig, which, if dark or malformed, indicates an unlucky marriage engagement; if smooth, straight, pale-coloured, the reverse.

Osteomancy, or the inspection of the marks on a fresh shoulder-blade of a sheep, was, according to the Arab historian, Ali Sher Káni, practised in Sind. It is now employed by the Tibetan Lamas, and we meet with a modification of rhabdomancy and osteomancy among the Karens of Burma, who divine by chicken-bones. The thigh or wing-bones of a fowl are scraped till holes appear in the bone. When the number of holes is even on one side of the bone, this is used. Pieces of the bamboo are placed in the holes. If these slant inwards the omen is unlucky; if outwards, favourable.

Augury, too, traced by Ihering to the wandering Aryans before the dispersion as a means of finding their way over the mountain passes, has left its mark on the beliefs of the modern Hindu, who looks on the flight or croaking of the owl as an evil omen, and prognosticates good or evil from the call of the partridge and other birds.

Rhabdomancy, the taking of omens from wands or arrows, appears all through Indian literature. Marco

Polo describes how Chingiz Khán, when he was at war with Prester John, tested in this way the skill of the pagan and Christian diviners, the latter gaining the victory. Of the modern Káfirs of the Hindu-kush Sir G. Robertson says:

> "The wise women stand opposite to one another, each balancing two arrows in the palms of her hands. They then approach one another, and allow the free ends of the arrows to touch, whereupon, in a supernatural way, all the arrows shuffle together, and it is by noticing which arrows emain on the top that they know whether the raiding party will be successful or the reverse."

Many forms of divination are practised at the present day. It is often used to ascertain the result of a marriage engagement. In Gujarát, for instance, the bride and bridegroom play a game of chance, with betel-nuts, dried dates and coins, seven of each being placed in a cup. The result is decided by the way in which these fall, and the victor is supposed to have the mastery in married life. The Koch of Bengal make the pair exchange a handful of cowries, which are then laid on the ground. A woman counts them, and if the greater number are found lying with the hollow side upwards, the girl will triumph in matrimonial disputes. The Kachins of Burma give the diviner a piece of the clothing of the intended bride. He thus gets *en rapport* with the lady, and is able to predict her destiny.

Naturally things which are sacred, or mysterious, and hence holy, are employed for this purpose. The egg, the seat of life, is often used in this way. Among the Khásis of Assam, the seer places an egg on a few grains of rice spread on a board. After calling on the egg to speak the truth, he sweeps the rice off the board, except one grain, which he leaves on any spot that his fancy dictates. Then naming a particular spirit, he asks that if he be the cause of the evil, a part of the shell of the egg may be deposited near the rice grain. He then strikes the egg sharply on the board, and repeats the process until the desired result is secured. The mystic cocoa-nut is used at the far western shrine of Hingláj. One is flung into the water, and according as the bubbles rise in large or small numbers, the person consulting the oracle will be happy or miserable.

Sacred plants and grain are used in the same way. The Kuravas of Madras tell fortunes by shaking rice in a winnowing fan, an instrument which itself has mystic power, and prophesy good or evil by counting the grains left behind. The Mundas of Chota Nágpur, when selecting a site for a house, lay a little rice at each corner of the site, and if it be found undisturbed in the morning, building may commence. In sickness the same people drop oil into water, and name a god with each drop. When the oil forms a single globule on the surface, that god is the one to whom sacrifice should be offered. The Kachins of Burma use the bamboo, which is their sacred tree. A piece is laid on the fire, and as it splits and crackles omens are taken. Or they sever the membranes of a leaf, knot the fibres together, and from the number and position of the knots foretell the future.

A favourite method of the Sikhs is by the Dhal, a little wooden hexagon, on each face of which are engraved certain letters of the Gurmukhi alphabet. This is thrown twice, and the letters which come uppermost are compared with a little book, called the Paintís Akhari, containing a series of lines each beginning with one of the thirty-five letters of the same alphabet. This is done before undertaking a journey or enterprise, and the verses thus selected give an omen which foretells whether the result will be lucky or unlucky.

When Musalmáns and those Hindus who follow their guidance in such matters divine, they take a copy of the poems of Háfiz, and select at random a verse which is supposed to solve the difficulty. Or they apply lamp-black to a child's eyes and make him stare until he sees, as in a vision, where stolen goods or treasure are concealed. Or they light a charm-wick, and the boy describes the scenes which he beholds in the glare.

Lastly, the interpretation of dreams is a science in itself, and possesses a literature of its own. Every chapman's stall contains a manual in which the method is described, with an almanac defining the lucky or unlucky days, or the points of the compass towards which a journey is likely to be fateful or prosperous. No wise man, in native belief, rejects the warnings which are given in this and many other ways.

DOG.—In India, as elsewhere, the domestic dog is "the descendant of several different wild forms, amongst which the common wolf and the common jackal are two of the principal." The *Dhol*, or Indian wild dog, is in general form more like the jackal than the wolf. It is found in packs of as many as twelve, from Gilgit and Ladakh in the north, to the forests of the south, living on wild sheep and antelopes in Tibet, and on deer and wild pig in the Indian jungles. In size it is about as large as a small setter, in colour like the old "mustard" breed of terrier, and in shape more vulpine than any European breed. It is said to attack and kill the tiger, and tigers will certainly not remain in forests frequented by a pack of these animals. Mr Sanderson thinks that they may kill tigers; but Mr Blanford believes that the disappearance of the tiger from their haunts is more usually the result of their dispersal of the game on which the tiger lives. It is more nearly allied to the wolf and jackal than the domesticated dog, and is more difficult to tame than either of its wild kinsfolk. It does not bark, but howls and yelps more like a jackal. At the same time all observers note how readily the tame dog reverts to the howl of the jungle animal. Hence it is as inaccurate to say that the pariah is the wild dog domesticated, as it is to suppose that the jungle dog is the pariah gone wild.

In ancient times the Indian hound was held in high repute. Strabo describes them as

"animals of great strength and courage, which will not let go their hold till water is poured into their nostrils; they bite so eagerly that the eyes of some become distorted, and the eyes of others fall out. Both a lion and a bull were held fast by a dog. The bull was seized by the muzzle, and died before the dog could be taken off."

Herodotus tells of Tritantæchmes of Babylon, who kept such a great pack of these dogs, that four large villages were assigned for their support; and a bas-relief of one of these dogs found at Babylon can be easily identified with the great Tibet mastiff of our days. In fact, Dr Kræmar has recently shown reason to suppose that the St Bernard dog is a branch of the same breed. Marco Polo describes them as being as large as donkeys, and says that the Great Kaan had so large a pack of them that he kept two thousand keepers in charge of them. They are mentioned in Chinese literature as early as the twelth century B.C., and are said to have come from the West. They spread from Tibet to India, China, and Europe through Babylon and Assyria, and thus became known to the cultured races of the Mediterranean. We find them represented on Buddhist monuments in India of the third century B.C. Nowadays in Tibet they are employed as beasts of burden. Sir J. Hooker describes a train of them laden with salt:

"A huge, grave, bull-headed mastiff, his glorious, bushy tail thrown over his back in a majestic sweep, and a thick collar of scarlet wool round his neck and shoulders, setting off his long, silky coat to the best advantage."

In the early days of European influence, the West began to send its breeds of dogs to India. Terry gives an amusing account of two mastiffs brought by Sir T. Roe to the Emperor Jahángír. Each was carried in a little coach, and one of them showed his pluck by attacking an elephant. The Moghul was so pleased that he allowed four attendants to each dog to fan the flies from them, and had them carried about in palanquins. He had a pair of silver tongs made so that he might feed them with his own hand. He commissioned Roe to procure him another pair of mastiffs, and some Irish deer-hounds. Blood-hounds were imported at an early date by the Portuguese. Under the liberal ideas of Akbar the Musalmán prejudice against the dog began to pass away. He used to import dogs from Kábul and the Hazára country, and Abul Fazl records with some wonder that people in his day began "to ornament dogs, and give them names." Bernier tells us that Aurangzeb used to keep Uzbeg or Central Asian dogs, and had a little red coat made for each of them. The bull-dog caused a tragedy in the early days of our rule. Captain Hamilton describes how, in 1670, the Chief of the Honore Factory on the west coast procured a bull-dog from a ship's captain. The dog killed a sacred cow, and the Bráhman mob murdered every European in the place. The monument to John Best and seventeen Englishmen thus slain records that "they were sacrificed to the fury of a mad priesthood, and an infuriated mob."

The best known Indian dog is the Pariah or Pye, "whose home is Asia, and whose food is rubbish,"—"the victim," as Mr L. Kipling says, "of an implacable socialism, the slave of a sharp-toothed Trade Union." He is best seen in the Ganges Plain, where there are more dogs, and fewer stones to throw at them, than in any other part of the world. The breeds vary greatly. In the Central Provinces the Gonds have a red-coloured breed, quite distinct from the pariah of the Plains imported by the Hindus. Captain Forsyth is probably mistaken in supposing that it is descended from the wild jungle dog. The dog of the Burmese Wás, again, is supposed by Sir J. G. Scott to be a dwarf Indian pariah; he is quite unlike the Chow dog of China and the black variety of Tongking. A finer variety is the Bunjára dog, bred to guard the camps of these nomads. Captain Forsyth describes the true Bunjára dog as

"a fine, upstanding hound, of about 28 inches high, generally black, mottled with grey or blue, with a rough but silky coat, a high-bred, hound-like head, and well-feathered on ears, legs, and tail. He shows a good deal of resemblance to the Persian grey-hound, but is stouter built, and with a squarer muzzle. Probably this wandering race of gipsies may have brought the originals with them from Western Asia, the subsequent modification being due to a cross with some of the indigenous breeds."

He has a deep bay, quite unlike the currish bark of the pariah. Mr Webber found a pair of them invaluable for cutting off a wounded buck, as they hunted by sight as well as by scent. They were quite as fast as his Scotch deer-hound, but very different in disposition, being sulky and treacherous with strangers and other dogs, though faithful to their master. They always went for the hind-quarters of a deer, while the deer-hound seized by the throat. The Bunjára dog has admirable pluck; he can go as fast as a greyhound, and will run all day. His nose is superior to that of any domesticated breed in a hot climate; with a little better speed he would be excellent for coursing deer.

A similar valuable breed is the large, hairless, Poligar dog of Madras. The Musalmáns brought the greyhound from Persia, and the breed is now best represented by the Northern Rámpur breed. There is a peculiar breed of lap-dog in the Nepál valley which is a special favourite with the nautch girls of Khatmándu and Pátan.

Writing of Assam, Tavernier says:

"Although the country abounds with all things necessary to life, among all articles of food the flesh of the dog is specially esteemed; it is the favourite dish at feasts, and every month, in each town of the kingdom, people hold markets where they only sell dogs, which are brought thither from every direction."

Though the gipsy tribes, like the Sánsiya, will on occasion eat dogs, the Eastern Frontier is still the chief home of the practice. The Kúmi tribe of Arakan, whose name Captain Lewin interprets as "dog-men,"

"because they wear a very scanty breech-cloth, which is so adjusted, that a long end hangs behind in the manner of a tail," are also very fond of dog-meat. "A favourite festival dish among them is a dog stuffed with rice. The young cur is plentifully fed with cooked rice about an hour before cooking time, and when stuffed to repletion is knocked on the head, skinned and roasted. The rice is left in the stomach and eaten with the dog's flesh as a concomitant relish."

Before our time the Garos of Assam used to sacrifice slaves when their chiefs died; now they kill a dog to guide the dead man's spirit to Chikmang, the tribal Paradise.

But there is a standard of taste even in dog-eating. The Annamese will eat only black dogs that have a black palate; the Chinaman will eat only the Chow dog, which also has a black palate, but he does not mind what the colour of his coat may be; the Wá of Burma fattens his dwarf pariah for the table; the Akha will eat any dog he can lay his hands on.

The feeling towards dogs varies with the variety of the Indian races. The ancient Aryan seems to have respected the animal. In the Mahábhárata Yudhishthira reaches the gate of heaven with his dog; Indra expostulates with him, but in vain. He replies: "Never, come weal or come woe, will I abandon yon faithful dog"; and he has his way. Later on, when ritualistic feeling became intensified, the dog's habit of foul and indiscriminate feeding offended the Bráhman, and Manu's rule that the out-caste tribes should keep no other animal but dogs and asses has produced a feeling of aversion which has clung to both these beasts ever since.

But the Hindu tenderness for animal life, largely due to Buddhist teaching, has in some cases overcome this prejudice, and we meet instances of dog-worship, as in the Khichi Púja of Nepál, at which annually dogs are worshipped, and every cur in the country has a garland of flowers hung round his neck. At Loháru in the Panjáb a brave dog that saved his master in battle is worshipped; the Mahratta Sáhu Rája, when his dog saved him from a tiger, gave him an estate, allowed him the use of a palanquin, dressed him in rich robes and jewels at his Durbar, and put his own turban on the head of his favourite. A tomb in the Satára district still bears an image of the animal. In folk-lore the famous tale of Bethgelert, in which the faithful hound saves his master's child from the wolf, and is killed by mistake, appears in various forms. In the common version the dog belongs to a Bunjára, who in his need mortgages him to a banker. The banker is robbed, and the dog detects the thief. In his gratitude the banker sends the dog home with an acquittance for the debt tied round his neck. His old master upbraids the dog for deserting his post, and slays him without looking at the paper. When the tale fell into the hands of the Bráhman reciter the hatred for the dog caused him to be replaced, in the popular version of the story, by a mungoose, which kills the cobra in the baby's cradle.

In concession to Bráhman prejudice, when the modern Hindu worships the dog he does so in connection with low-grade gods like Khandoba or Bhairon. He is still invested with some mystic power. As the people of Northern India sent round cakes as a signal for the Mutiny, so in Gujarát they passed on a pariah dog with a packet of food tied round its neck.

The Pársis have the curious custom of exposing the dying man to the glance of a dog. They seem now to be half-ashamed of the rite, as is shown by the elaborate method by which they endeavour to explain it away. Mr Dosabhai Framji writes:

"The face of the deceased Zoroastrian is exposed to the gaze of a dog three or four times during the recitation of the funeral sermon or oration. This seems to have led to the erroneous supposition, caused doubtless through ignorance, that before the dead body is removed from the house, a dog is made to lick it, or to eat some portion of its flesh. It is scarcely necessary to say that this belief has no foundation whatever. The exact object and meaning of the ceremony has not been properly ascertained; but, according to popular belief, dogs are considered sacred animals. They are supposed to guide the souls of the dead towards heaven, and to ward off on their way the influence of evil spirits to which they may be exposed. This belief, however, is not generally shared in by the educated Pársis of the present day."

By many it has been connected with the custom of exposing the dead to wild beasts. A dog that has a yellow spot on each side of the eyelids is called the "four-eyed" dog, because he is believed to have two additional eyes, a peculiarity which gives him a special power of seeing evil spirits.

From the time of the Prophet the dog has been unclean to the Musalmán. Pyrard de Laval tells us that when he came to the Maldives the Portuguese sent the king a dog as a curiosity, "which he incontinently drowned. If a native had been touched by one of them, he would go at once to bathe and purify himself." The Hindu-kush Káfirs under Musalmán influence have the same feeling. Sir G. Robertson had to tie up his dogs when people in a state of ceremonial purity approached him.

But there is a change going on in native feeling, and many people now imitate Europeans in loving and valuing their dogs. The Mahrattas in particular have always loved the dog, and early in the last century Broughton describes the ladies in their camp petting little lap-dogs which they obtained from the French officers. The love of dogs extends to Burma, and not long ago a Shan prince, who was the lucky possessor of a dog with nine tails, was greatly respected. In fact, it is only the Musalmán of the old school who maintains his detestation of the dog, and year by year the habit of keeping them as pets is growing.

DOLMEN.—The special interest of the Indian megalithic monuments lies in the fact that they form a continuous series from prehistoric times down to the present day. But as the building of these structures has continued to modern times the difficulty of fixing the probable dates of their erection is greatly increased.

Those of the early age are found in the largest numbers in the south of the Peninsula. In Malabar Mr Logan divides the monuments into five classes: first, megalithic remains; secondly, excavated caves, which are probably synchronous with the first class; thirdly, caves with massive urns, and massive sepulchral urns not found in caves; fourth, modern sepulchral urns of small size; fifthly, the Topikallu, or "hat-stone" monuments, which have not as yet been proved to be sepulchral, but evidently belong to the first class. In these constructions nothing has hitherto been found in the hollow space between the stones which support the flat covering slab, and which themselves were placed on the solid rock. It has been suggested that they may have been tribal ossuaries.

Megalithic remains of the cromlech type are common, and invariably contain remains of iron implements and weapons, all covered with fine sifted earth. The stones composing the ends of these places of sepulture are sometimes fully exposed, sometimes half buried, and sometimes only just showing themselves above the surface. Occasionally the cromlech has a stone circle round it. The caves cut in the soft rock are probably of the same age ; but those containing a large sepulchral urn inside an excavated chamber, in addition to the usual earthernware pots and iron implements characteristic of the earlier interments, are apparently later in date. The pottery is of a more advanced type, and ornamented ; beads are found, and iron implements of a more varied form. Even now, following the old habit, the Malayális use earthen pots to hold the cremated remains of relations until an opportunity occurs for their removal to a holy river.

These Malabar monuments are attributed by the people to the mythical age, and are called Pandu-kuri, or house of the Pándava heroes of the Mahábhárata. Their age is very uncertain, and in some cases secondary interments may have occurred on the same site. Bishop Caldwell records the finding at the excavation of one of the Coimbatore monuments of a coin hoard, including a silver denarius of Augustus.

The Nilgiri Hills are studded with cairns, barrows, kistvaens, and dolmens, many of which were excavated by Mr Breeks. The age of these monuments is very uncertain. The Todas even to the present day make stone circles for their funeral rites. The builders of what appear to be the more ancient monuments were skilled in the making of pottery, used weapons of iron, and wore ornaments of silver and copper. The few articles of bronze may have been imports from Babylonia. What relation these people bore to the earlier palæolithic or neolithic people there is at present no evidence to determine.

The monuments of the Deccan, investigated by Colonel Meadows Taylor, are often found in considerable groups, accompanied by cairns and barrows. When excavated they were found to contain human remains, portions of bone and charcoal, broken pottery, red and black. As usual, they fall into two groups, dolmens and kistvaens, the latter small and closed, the former large, three-sided, and open at one end. The stone forming the door is often pierced with a hole. Much speculation has been devoted to explain this. Some have believed that the intention of the opening was to allow offerings of food and other things to be passed in for the use of the ghost. Others think that the intention was to allow a sick child or an ailing limb to be thrust into the sacred place as a mode of cure. Many of the three-sided, open dolmens may have been used as ossuaries, such as are now constructed by the Nágas of Assam.

The Coorg monuments have recently been investigated by Mr Rea, but the megalithic monuments of India still await thorough investigation. The literature of the subject is scattered through a number of articles in scientific periodicals and journals of learned societies, and little has as yet been done to collate and co-ordinate the available information.

Of the modern stone monuments the most remarkable are those of the Khásis of Assam, first described by Sir H. Yule, Sir J. Hooker, Major Godwin-Austen, and other writers. In their most common form they appear as erect, oblong pillars, intended as monuments of, and refuges for, the ghosts of the honoured dead. Some are unhewn, the work of the chisel being supposed to scare the indwelling ghost; sometimes the more modern pillars are carefully squared. They usually appear as trilithons, but as many as thirteen have been found in a single group. The highest pillar is often in the centre, covered by a circular disc, and to right and left they gradually diminish in height. The scale on which the monument is constructed depends on the amount of rice-beer which the relatives are able to provide for the men engaged on the work of hauling and erecting the pillars. Some of the pillars are of considerable size. They are dragged to the spot on a rough sledge, and raised to their position by gangs of men, who haul cables made of bamboo. In some cases the monument consists of a square sarcophagus of slabs, through the chinks of which may be seen earthen pots containing the ashes of the honoured dead. These appear to have been tribal or family ossuaries. The method in which they are raised throws useful light on the construction of monuments such as Stonehenge.

Another group of such monuments is found among the Kols of Chota Nágpur. Dr Ball describes their gravestones as of a truncate, pyramidal shape, marked superficially with groovings which may have some significance. He gives an interesting account of the mode of construction.

> "Partly according to the estimation in which the deceased was held, partly according to the amount of refreshments, chiefly rice-beer, which the surviving members of the deceased's family are prepared to stand, a greater or less number of men assemble, and proceed to the spot where the stone is to be raised. If the flag selected be not very heavy, it is placed on a wooden framework, and so carried on men's shoulders to its destination. When, however, the stone is of large size, it is placed on a kind of truck with enormously massive wheels, which is specially constructed for the purpose. Sometimes it is necessary to make a road for the passage of such a truck; at others, the pushing and pulling with ropes is sufficient to carry it over the obstacles which are encountered in the way."

In the Deccan we find numerous stone circles erected in honour of Vetála, the Ghost King, or Demon Lord. They are in form analogous to the European monuments of this class. The centre is occupied by a large stone in which the demon lives, and the surrounding ring represents his followers. The circle was probably intended as a "ghost-hedge," to restrain the spirit within these assigned limits, or a sign that the site was taboo. Mr Fergusson's view that structures like these were built on the model of the rail which is found to surround the Stúpas or relic mounds of the Buddhists is not now generally accepted. The order of development seems rather to have been, first, the ring of stones surrounding the earthen tumulus; next, the stone circle from which the tumulus has usually disappeared; lastly, the elaborate rail of the Buddhists.

The hill tribes in the centre of the Peninsula raise rude stone cairns in memory of their dead. Further west the Bhíls erect stone tablets to record the death of their chiefs, never in honour of women. As a rule, the dead man is represented on horseback, armed with sword, lance, and shield, and dressed in flowing robes, a mode of attire to which he was quite unaccustomed in life. Similar to these are the Páliya, or guardian stones of Cutch and Gujarát, which are generally erected in memory of Chárans, or bards and their women, who were either slain in some raid, or immolated themselves in pursuance of a vow, or in defence of property committed to their charge, a mode of death known as *Trága.** The deceased is usually represented in the act of death, killing himself on horseback with sword or spear; the woman committing suicide by thrusting a dagger into her throat. In Cutch, when the Muhammadans came, they destroyed the images on these stones, particularly those which represent the deceased as received into the heaven of the gods. Hence in more modern times the Hindus carved only a tree, possibly the tree of life, on their monuments.

Further north, the Káfirs of the Hindu-kush erect a menhir in honour of the dead, sacrifice a goat and pour its blood upon the stone, which is regarded as the resting place of the ghost. In like manner the Wás of Burma erect a sort of cromlech, which may have been originally a place of sepulture, but is now said to be the abode of the house spirits. One theory does not necessarily exclude the other; in fact, the development is just what might have been expected in the evolution of savage religion.

[Borlase, "Dolmens of Ireland," iii. 750ff.; Fergusson, "Rude Stone Monuments," chap. xiii; Meadows Taylor, "Trans. Royal Irish Academy," xxiv. 329ff.; Logan, "Manual of Malabar," i. 179ff.; Sir H. Yule, "Journal Asiatic Society of Bengal," xiii. Pt. II. 618, xvii. 494; Ball, "Jungle Life," 64, 164; Rea, "List of Architectural and Archæological Remains in Coorg"; Godwin-Austen, in "Journal Anthropological Institute," vols. i. iv. v.; M. J. Walhouse, *ibid.* v.]

DRAMA.—The origin of the acted drama in India is very obscure. We have, it is true, in the Vedas a series of rhymed dialogues; but the real drama first appears as a sort of mystery-play in connection with the cult of Krishna, and it seems to have consisted of scenes from the legendary history of the god, carried out with song and dance, and with patches of prose dialogue improvised by the actors.

At the same time we find among the wilder tribes a regular form of folk-drama, not intended to teach the spectators the mysteries of their religion, but a sort of magic, operating through mimicry and sympathy. It is in these rude village dances, intended to promote the growth of the crops, the cessation of plagues, success in sport or war, that the beginnings of the Indian drama may be recognised.

Attempts have been made to trace in the later Sanskrit drama the influence of the Western world. The running-slave, the parasite, the Indian name for the curtain, the prologue, the acts, incidents like the ring of recognition, have been cited in support of this theory. But the evidence is far from complete, and though the Sanskrit drama may have been to some extent affected by the neighbouring Græco-Bactrian kingdom, it seems, in a large degree, to be of indigenous growth. It has peculiarities of its own. It has a jester who plays a leading part, and a hero and heroine who are often plunged in the depths of despair; but the plot usually ends happily, and nothing sensational or affecting occurs within the view of the audience. The characters, again, speak in different dialects; the leading personages use Sanskrit; women and men of the lower orders *Prákrit*,* or the older vernacular derived from or akin to Sanskrit. A sign of the age of the appearance of this form of drama is that the buffoon is always a Bráhman. Each play has a prologue, in which there were never more than two actors, and it was not, as ours is, detached, but led immediately to the business of the play. The first act furnishes the clue to the story, and closes, as it begins, with a prayer. These plays were performed on lunar holidays, at a coronation, at fairs and festivals, marriages, and other special occasions. The courtyard of a palace, or house, of a man of rank was the theatre, and, like our Shakespearian drama, there was little scenery and few stage properties. Each play was generally three times as long as an ordinary European piece.

The modern drama follows much the same lines. Sir E. Arnold describes a piece which he witnessed at Bombay, advertised in the bills as a "Sataric Drama," in twenty-six acts, with countless scenes. The female parts were sustained by Hindu girls—a vast innovation, as women never appeared on the earlier stage. These were nautch-girls trained to mingle dancing and singing with acting. The subject was the loves of Krishna, and one of the characters was a Rámúsi, one of the criminal tribes of the Deccan, who coolly proposes to set fire to the house containing the god and his ladies for a small bribe.

Somewhat similar is the Rámlíla of Northern India, which is based on the Rámáyana epic. Here we see represented the story of the banishment of Ráma, the abduction of his faithful wife, Síta, by the monster Rávana; the monkey army led by Hanumán, which effects her release; and the drama ends with the blowing-up of the gigantic wicker-work and paper figure of the monster, amidst the acclamations of the delighted crowd. The god and his spouse are always represented by Bráhman boys. Bishop Heber was told the almost incredible story that the boy and girl, as he describes them, were in former times always poisoned with sweetmeats given to them on the last day of the show, so that it might be said that their spirits were absorbed into the deities whom they had represented.

Similar to this is the Kathakali, or national drama of Malabar, based originally, like the Rámlíla, on the Rámáyana. A single play lasts through a whole night, and a multitude of Bráhman performers take the parts of warriors, demons, monkeys, birds, women and men of the woods, each defined by special dresses and properties. But all is in dumb show, and no performer speaks his part on the stage. The only vocal accompaniment is that of a bard, who recites or chants ballads at intervals in the performance.

Another development is the Burmese Pwé, well described by Sir J. G. Scott:

"There is no nation on the face of the earth so fond of theatrical representations as the Burmese. Probably there is not a man, otherwise than a cripple, in the country who has not at some period of his life been himself an actor, either in the drama, or in a marionette show; if not in either of these, certainly in a chorus dance. It would be wrong to say that there is no other amusement in the country, but it is indisputable that every other amusement ends up with a dramatic performance."

He goes on to show that every act of the Burman's life, from the cradle to the grave, is celebrated by a Pwé, held in the open air. The subjects are taken from the Játaka, or legends which the Buddha told of his former existences, or from events in the lives of Indian kings and heroes. The Burmese drama is thus a direct off-shoot from the early Sanskrit drama.

Much more solemn and impressive is the sacred mystery-play which the Shiah sect of Musalmáns performs at the feast of the Mohurrum. The subject is the martyrdom of Hasan and Husain. Excited crowds, lamenting and beating their breasts, follow the Táziyas or cenotaphs of the martyrs, and during ten days of the feast singers chant the tale. It ends with the death scene, a story which Gibbon says, "in a distant age and climate will awaken the sympathy of the coldest reader."

[Sylvain Lévi, "Le Théâtre Indien"; Wilson, "Theatre of the Hindoos"; Mantzius, "History of Theatrical Art in Ancient and Modern Times"; "Calcutta Review," xv. 97ff.; Arnold, "India Revisited," 89; Yule, "Mission to Ava," 368ff.; Shway Yoe, "The Burman," i. 342ff. For the Mohurrum, Pelly, "Miracle Play of Hasan and Husain."

DRESS.—Absolute nudity is a condition now prevailing only amongst the most secluded and backward races. In early days in South India, to judge from Marco Polo's account, dress was limited.

"You must know that in this Province of Maabar *

[the Coromandel Coast] there is never a tailor to cut a coat or stitch it, seeing that every one goes naked. For decency only they do wear a scrap of cloth; and so 'tis with men and women, with rich and poor, aye, and with the King himself."

Even at the present day all over India young children go about nude, and the custom has come down to our times among the most conservative class of the community, the ascetic bodies, some of whom up to quite recent times wore no clothing of any kind. Nowadays in several of the Nága tribes of Assam the women are perfectly naked; in others the men. When left to themselves, the Andamanese men go stark naked, the women wearing only a tassel of leaves before and behind. Among the most savage tribe of these people, the Jarawas, both sexes have been seen naked. The Nicobarese are recorded as naked by a traveller of the seventh century, and even now the men wear only a scanty loin-clout fastened behind with a waggling tag, which gave rise to the fable of a race with tails. The Wá women of Burma wear only their jewellery in their villages, and have no hesitation in appearing thus before strangers.

The next upward stage is the wearing of grass, leaves, or bark. In South India the Paliyan women sometimes go about clad only in leaves, which are generally those of a water plant, cut into lengths about a foot long, and tied round the waist so as to provide a bushy tail behind and an apron in front, reaching nearly to the knees. Buchanan-Hamilton, in the beginning of last century, found the Korars of Mysore wearing little more than a bunch of grass. The Kadavas of Coorg dress in leaves, which they change four times a day. Going further north, Mr Hislop found the Mariya Gond women wearing nothing but bunches of twigs fastened to a string round their waists; when Captain Glasfurd met them they wore a scrap of cloth suspended in the same way.

The leaf-wearing tribe to whom most attention has been attracted is that of the Juángs of Chota Nágpur. General Dalton describes the sufferings of some girls in his camp, whose covering of leaves became dry and crackling, and who were too shy to ask leave to go to the jungle and procure a fresh suit. The same people a little further south support the leaves with a girdle of bark or a chain of earthenware beads. In 1871 an English officer supplied them with clothes; the foreheads of the women were marked with vermilion as a sign that they had entered civilised society; their leaf bunches were solemnly burnt, and the men promised not to allow their women to resume their primitive dress. But, to quote a recent report, "the innovation of waist-cloths issued to the Juángs did not outlast the material." This is, in fact, an instance of the reaction which has recently set in among these tribes against Hinduism. Not long ago the Santál women broke their lac bangles, abandoned the use of foreign cloth, and went back to their home-made calico.

The use of these leaf garments is still traditionally connected with the worship of the aboriginal gods. In South India at the worship of the Mother-goddess, Mariyamma, the lower castes, when visiting her temple, substitute garments made of leaves of the Margosa tree for their ordinary dress.

Bark formed the dress of the ancient Hindu ascetics, and in the Mahábhárata when the Pándavas retired to the Himálaya they wore garments of this kind. Even now the bark of what is called the "Sacking tree" is used for clothing in West India, and the male dress of the Abors of Assam consists chiefly of a loin-cloth made of bark.

The use of clothing of this kind survives in the girdle, which is so prominent an article of dress in the early sculptures. Even now the men of the Oraons of Chota Nágpur wear always round the waist a girdle made of cane or *tusser* * silk. Since they have taken to a more decent dress this has become superfluous, but it is retained as a survival of the band which supported the primitive fig-leaves. We see this in the case of the Abors, among whom the women wear suspended from a string a row of shell-shaped, embossed pieces of bell-metal, and the Kachins of Burma hang from their belts a double row of cowry-shells.

Of early Hindu dress we have numerous representations

on the monuments. Both at Sánchi and Amaravati the women are laden with jewellery, but their dress is only remarkable for its scantiness. They generally have a broad waist-belt, from which strips of cloth are sometimes suspended, and sometimes also a waist-cloth is added, but this is usually represented as transparent. This may have been the Court dress of the time, or a conventional mode of representing the female form, because Rajendralála Mitra points to passages in early authors insisting on modesty of dress. General Massey writes:

"It is quite a mistake to suppose that nudity is the rule among the female figures at Sánchi. Some who appear at a cursory glance to be totally nude only appear so because the sculptor, like the early Greek artists, represented their drapery over the lower limbs by simple lines. A woman in the sculptures at Mahábodhi wears a long loin-cloth reaching to her ankles, with an embroidered or jewelled belt in three rows. Her breast is covered with a large bead necklace, and on her head is a high worked cap, beneath which the hair is arranged in rolls stretching over her ears and forehead."

The women on the Buddhist rail from Mathura appear to be naked, wearing only jewellery and the bead belt round the waist. On the Bharhut rail, on the contrary, no woman is entirely nude.

When we come to early travellers, like Nicolo Conti and Barbosa, the modern style of dress is well established. All over India the basis of men's dress is the Dhoti [*Dhoty**], or waist-cloth, wrapped round the loins and passed between the legs. This among women is represented by the Sári [*Saree**]. The drawers, or *Pyjammas*,* came in with the Musalmáns. Miss Billington thus describes the mysteries of the sári:

"A full sized sári should be about 5½ yards long, and from 36 to 40 inches wide. To put it on, a woman makes a few pleats at one end in her hand, which she draws through in front of a band or string already round her waist. The length of the material is then carried round her figure towards the left, and when it has been brought completely round, the end is taken over the shoulder and draped over the head. It is only, of course, from long practice that the perfect art of disposing of it is reached, but one sees tiny girls of three or four emulating the example of their mothers with pieces of calico about as large as a pocket-handkerchief; for the Indian girl longs as keenly to leave the shapeless sacque, which is the first garment of her baby years, and attain to the dignity of a sári as her sister of the West desires a long skirt and its attendant privileges."

In South India the cloth is wound several times round the body from waist to knee, and at last brought over the right shoulder and down to the left side, so as to fall in front in ample folds. This is the general arrangement, but each caste may be distinguished by special modes of tying the cloth.

The low-caste women in Upper India make the sári serve for upper clothing as well as to drape the waist, and its filthiness is remarkable even in India, the land of dirt. Those of higher rank supplement the sári by the Chádar [*Chudder**], or the Angiya, or bodice. But in South India it has long been the habit among some castes to wear nothing above the waist; and this is regarded so clearly as a mark of social status that in 1858 a riot occurred in Travancore because Christian convert women gave up the practice of going about without an upper cloth. In contrast to her working sister of the North, the Nair woman, one of the most beautiful in India, dresses in the cleanest clothes.

The sári, again, among some of the Northern races has developed into the petticoat. While the Mahratta women of the Deccan pass the sári through their legs like a man's Dhoti, Bráhman women in Khandesh wear it in petticoat form; and further north Musalmán women wear it over the unsightly drawers, certainly the most unbecoming fashion of Indian female dress. The petticoat sometimes assumes enormous proportions. The Cutch lady has about 75 feet long of Turkey-red cloth sewn into a number of folds. It reaches the acme in the costume of a Nepál princess described by Lady Dufferin:

"The first view of her was that of a mass of light

gauze above, and a pair of legs clothed in white trousers below. . . . The thin pink and yellow striped material was not a petticoat, and I am quite at a loss to imagine how it was put on, or how many hundred yards were in it. It looked just as if a great piece had been unrolled, and unrolled, and then picked up and half wound round and half carried by the wearer. When she sat down it was in a great fluff, and when she got up she took it in her arms, and it overflowed everything except the trousers."

So far for the dress of the married woman. When she loses her husband all is changed. The Bráhman girl-widow in Western India when she comes of age has her head shaved, her glass bangles broken, her bodice taken off, and she is allowed to wear no robes except white and red, and no ornaments except gold finger rings. Generally in Upper India her dress consists of a single dirty white sheet.

In the representations of the Hindu ladies in the early sculptures nothing is more remarkable than their coiffure. Some of the Orissa dames have a great chignon piled at the back or on the top of the head, or projecting on both sides, or only on the left, or arranged in fantastic braids and folds which are sometimes fixed upright on sticks or wires. In the Saiva shrines of the same province Sir W. Hunter writes:

"Both sexes have their hair done in a sort of tower over their heads, but some of the ladies have also a braid falling over the bosom to the waist. In the more modern sculptures the hair is brushed back, and either falls in a braid as above, or is arranged in a fillet behind. The horizontal chignon projecting from the back of the head does not come into fashion until the twelfth century." In the sculptures of Kanárak of the early thirteenth century the women have "enormous chignons, projecting horizontally from behind. A head-dress falls in graceful festoons across both temples, ending in a golden boss at either ear, from which hang elaborate earrings."

Modern custom does not prescribe such an elaborate

arrangement as this. Everywhere the binding up of the hair marks that the girl has come of age. In the Central Panjáb there are four styles prescribed in accordance with the time of life. With little girls the front hair is cut straight across the forehead, and the back hair hangs loose. As they grow up, the hair is plaited on each side of the forehead, and the unplaiting of these plaits is a solemn rite which takes place at marriage. After marriage the front hair hangs loose, and the back hair is plaited in a tail. No high-caste woman uses bone combs; they must be of wood or ivory. Generally the Northern woman wears her hair in a knot on the top of the head, while her Musalmán sister prefers plaits hanging down. She does not, of course, wear false hair. This is a privilege reserved to women outside the pale of Hinduism, like the Gonds or Oraons, or the Burmese, who collect the hair of their male relations when they shave the head on entering a monastic life, to add it to their own. The Panditáni or Bráhman woman of Kashmír wears her hair in a peculiar arrangement of many plaits, in which black wool or silk is interwoven. Up to marriage the plaits are separate, but after marriage they are gathered together and fastened with a heavy tassel.

The graceful use of flowers to decorate the hair is also barred to the respectable Hindu woman as savouring of the licence of the nautch-girl. Some of the Christian women of West India wear flowers, a practice supposed to be borrowed from the Portuguese of Goa; but we find the habit well established at Kunáwar and in the Turi country of the Western Himálaya, where the lads wear the little red and yellow tulip in their turbans to fascinate their lady-loves. Central hill tribes, like Santáls, Oraons, and Mundas, also wear flowers in the hair.

Men wear the hair in various ways. The custom of shaving the head, wholly or in part, is a modern innovation. Curtius, writing of the time of Alexander, states that the hair of the head was seldom cut, but that the face was shaved, except the beard. The wilder tribes leave it uncut and hanging behind in rough masses, or in ringlets, like the Balúchis. Many wear the moustache, which the Musalmán cuts short over the upper lip. The beard is everywhere a sign of manly dignity. Writing of the Maldives, Pyrard de Laval says that with precise Muhammadans the rule is

> "to wear the beard as long as possible, and only to shave it under the throat, and above and below the lips; for they would not for the world have anything they eat or drink touch their hair, that being one of the most disgusting pollutions; therefore they have no hair round the mouth."

The Musalmán dyes his beard with various preparations. Chalk and soap are rubbed on it, followed by a fermented paste of wheat-flour, pulverised iron filings, and yeast. Finally it is washed in a strong infusion of galls, or *Phyllanthus emblica*. Another method is to rub henna leaves on the hair, followed by a paste of indigo or indigo leaves, which produces a bluish black. The variety of shades produced by these processes is remarkable, and was noticed by Megasthenes, who says:

> "Their beards, Nearchus tells us, they dye of one hue and another, according to taste. Some dye their white beards to make them look as white as possible, but others dye them blue; while some again prefer a red tint, some a purple, and others a rank green."

The Sikh or Rájput ties a scarf round neck and head, which curls out the ends of his whiskers in a style which he thinks becoming to a fighting race. In the figures at the Caves of Elephanta many of the women and boys wear wigs, and Garuda, the bird-god, has one shaped exactly like that of Dr Johnson in his portrait by Sir Joshua Reynolds.

The costume of the Pársi lady, perhaps the best dressed woman in India, is a combination of the Hindu and Musalmán styles, with hints derived from old Persian models. She has the short body and sári of the Hindu, with the full trousers of the Musalmáni.

She covers her head with a white kerchief, worn in the style of the European nun, and in her robe of China or Japan silk she revels in a luxuriance of colour, shell-pink, straw-peach, mauve of the tint of the palest Parma violets, pale sky and twig-green being the most favourite tints.

In quite another style the Banjára woman stalks along, dressed in a long boddice and strong dark blue kilted petticoat, decked with fine embroidery, with her hair arranged in a horn-like peak, which, curiously enough, is also the fashion of the Káfirs of the Hindu-kush.

Men's dress is much less varied and interesting. As we see it at present it is a combination of the Hindu and Musalmán styles, the latter owing to long-established Court usage having displaced the former for all occasions of dignity. Thus with the Hindu the loin-cloth gives way to the tight drawers, and a man of taste wraps himself in a Kashmír shawl, while the cooly wears in cold weather a narrow loin-cloth and a blanket with which he ingeniously drapes himself so as to keep out rain and cold. In the Plains you may know a Hindu by his jacket being fastened on the right, while that of the Musalmán is buttoned to the left. In Kashmír the rule is exactly the reverse, and here the Hindu Pandit mounts his pony on the near, the Musalmán on the off side; the Pandit begins his ablutions from the left leg, the Musalmán from the right. All this seems to have been the result of definite rules intended to distinguish the rival faiths.

Nothing can be more graceful than the simple white flowing robes of the old-fashioned Musalmán gentleman, which the "advanced" youth of our day replaces by a caricature of an Englishman's frock-coat, and wears the Egyptian fez in place of the healthier and more dignified turban. The Musalmán of the Panjáb has a fashion of his own in the matter of pyjammas. Mr Val Prinsep got the Nawáb of Baháwalpur to show him a pair of his inexpressibles, which were about six yards across, and gathered up with a string round the waist. As the foot and ankle pass through a hole in the extreme corner of this bag, the drapery between the legs is very voluminous, and getting twisted round the ankle, gives the impression that the wearer is bandy-legged.

No costume, effective though it may be, is less becoming than that of the respectable yeoman of the North, who wears a jacket and trousers of rich-coloured chintz stuffed with cotton, a fashion as old as the eleventh century when Albirúni mentions it, and a cap of the same material with great flaps to cover his ears. Cold, he thinks, chiefly attacks him through the ears and mouth; so he keeps these carefully wrapped up.

It is in his head-dress that the native gentleman strives to display his taste and originality; and the monuments show the same diversity of fashion in early times. The importance of the turban is shown by the custom of exchanging it as a pledge of brotherhood. Sir H. Edwardes states that in the old times no Hindu in the frontier district of Bannu was allowed to wear a turban, "that being too sacred a symbol of Muhammadanism, and a small cotton skull-cap was all they had to protect their brains from the keen Bannu sun." In West India the best people wear the small, flat, white Moghul turban; the Bráhman of the Konkan a disc of artfully-folded red calico, 3 or 4 feet in diameter; the Bhatiya curves the tip above his forehead like a rhinoceros horn; the Mahratta winds round his head a bundle of tightly-twisted ropes of cloth; the Baniya merchant's turban is round and elevated, like a shako, or rolled in conch-shell shape. The Rájput prides himself on a variety of the most delicate tints, and he adopts various styles, from the heavy cone worn by the Háras to the graceful, jewel-besprinkled turban of the nobleman at Court. Their greatest chief, the Mahárána of Mewár, wears a low, round turban with two rows of jewels in front, stretching from ear to ear. The turban has even affected Anglo-Indian politics. The Madras sepoy used to wear a hat, and the ill-advised attempt to replace it by a turban was the main cause of the Vellore Mutiny in 1806.

All these forms of head-dress are in picturesque

contrast to the Bengali hat or cap, or the muslin cap with gold embroidery in which the Musalmán young man of fashion swaggers down the bazaars of Delhi or Lucknow. Most eccentric of all is the hat of Sind or Balúchistán, which looks like a gold brocade chimney-pot worn the wrong way up. Quaint in appearance, but much more practical, is the umbrella-like hat of straw or bamboo worn by peasants or fishermen in Western India or Bengal, or the cane war helmet of the Nágas. Least useful of all is the Pársi hat of black oil-cloth, which is not only ugly, but useless as a protection against sun and rain. For really savage dress we must go to people like the Nága, with his dark blue or black kilt decorated with cowry-shells, his feather plumes and boar-tusk ornaments, his leggings of cane dyed in curious colours. The Lepchas, again, wear an ample robe of flossy silk, and over it a small, sleeveless cloak, covered with crosses and fastened with a girdle of silver chains. Others wear a blue and white striped cotton rug, caught up on the shoulders and fastened round the waist by a belt, so as to form a loose and graceful tunic ending at the knees. Their head-dress is a sort of wicker flower-pot of a reddish colour, with a peacock feather stuck at the top.

The observer of a crowd at a fair or place of pilgrimage notices at once the varied colours of the women's dress. Colours, which under a grey western sky would look gaudy and bizarre, seem to match the bright sunshine and cloudless blue of the Indian summer. The choice of colours is regulated by certain well-defined rules. According to the Atharva Veda, the old Hindus believed that a combination of blue and red savoured of witchcraft; but there seems to be no prejudice against them now. In North India the special colours of the Hindu and Buddhist are red and saffron, and the former detests indigo blue; the Sikh wears blue or white, and dislikes saffron; the Musalmán colour is indigo blue or green, which last is specially worn by those who claim direct descent from the Prophet, and they will not wear red. To take a few instances from other parts of the country—in Baroda the turban is usually red, a white or green head-dress denoting that the wearer is in mourning, though most elderly Bráhmans reject the showy colour. The favourite colours of the Cutch lady are blue, red, and green; yellow and purple are seldom worn; iron-grey on a red ground, the colour of old age and mourning, is sometimes worn by young women whose friends have been widowed. In the Deccan widows can wear any colour except red, white, and black. In Kashmír the Hindu lady often wears a deep, rich red, and the men turbans of red or blue.

"And in every turban," writes Mr Prinsep, "red, blue or white, these people stick great clusters of yellow flowers, or crimson poppies, which shine like jewels against turban and skin."

"Certain districts," says Miss Billington, "have favourite colours, and throughout Gujarát this is a very warm, deep crimson, enriched with beautiful embroidery. On the West Coast the women of caste usually wear white; while those of the lowest order have small checks or stripes in various mixtures, a dull yellow and red being much affected. In Calcutta scarlet divides favour with lilac and white—but white is generally preferred—while indigo-dyed blue is more or less common everywhere. Bandhna, or 'tie and dye' cloth, in cotton as well as silk, is much used in the Central Provinces and Native States."

Shoes, too, have their fashions. The Hindu lady usually goes barefoot, slippers marking the Musalmáni or dancing-girl. Usually the man's shoe is a heelless slipper, with turned-up toes, and is embroidered with coloured strips of leather or decoration in silk or gold. The chief fault of the native slipper is that it imposes a shuffling gait on the wearer. But fashions are here rapidly changing, and the use of European boots and shoes, which began with the hangers-on of our cantonments, is rapidly spreading all over the country. It has raised the "shoe question" to the dignity of a matter of internal politics. [*See* ETIQUETTE.] But Mr Bose tells us that the "Europe" shoe so loved by the Baboo is not admitted at the Hindu marriage rite. The importance of the etiquette of wearing shoes is shown by the fact that before our rule no one in Assam was allowed to use them without a special licence from the king, an indulgence very seldom granted. His long white stockings mark the Baboo as clearly as short deer-skin socks distinguish the Afghán. The hill-men of Chamba wear the Chapli, a soft leather shoe excellent for mountain climbing, which in the neighbouring hills of Kashmír is replaced by the grass sandal. The Chapli, however, is of little use in wet, as the foot slides too much, and on gravel, because small stones penetrate between the foot and sole.

[J. F. Watson, "Textile Manufactures and Costumes of India"; Miss M. F. Billington, "Woman in India."]

EDUCATION.—The causes which have opposed the progress of education in India are sufficiently obvious—in the first place, the want of intelligence among the people in general, and the rural classes in particular; secondly, the necessity of using child-labour in agricultural, pastoral, and many industrial occupations. Under native rule only the specially literate classes were educated to any extent, and this tradition has lasted to the present day. The priestly classes, again, are opposed to general education on modern lines. To these influences may be added the prejudice felt by those of high caste against sitting side by side with low-caste students, a feeling specially noticeable in Southern India; and early marriage and the seclusion of women, which check female education. The result is that at the last Census only fifty-three persons per mille were literate in the limited sense in which this term was employed.

Of all the provinces, Burma, with its Buddhistic system of teaching, stands easily first, while at the bottom is Kashmír, and only a little higher Chota Nágpur, with its large forest population. Travancore shows best in female education. In order of religions Pársis come first, and are followed by Jains, Buddhists, Christians, Sikhs, Hindus, and Muhammadans, while last of all are the Animistic tribes.

The question of education under our rule is too wide for treatment here; but something may be said about the native system of teaching. The purely native school is now exactly the same as it was when P. della Valle described it in the Deccan in 1623. Then, as now, the scholars repeated their lessons

> "with a certain continu'd tone (which hath the force of making deep impression on the memory)." In arithmetic they "writ down the same number not with any kind of Pen, nor on Paper, but (not to spend Paper in vain) with their fingers on the ground, the pavement being for that purpose strew'd all over with very fine sand." "I ask'd them, if they happen'd to forget, or be mistaken in any part of the lesson, who corrected and taught them? they being all Scholars without the assistance of any Master; they answer'd me and said true, that it was not possible for all four of them to forget, or mistake in the same part, and that thus they exercis'd together, to the end that if one happen'd to be out, the others might correct him. Indeed a prety, easie, and secure way of learning."

About two centuries later Buchanan-Hamilton found the same system of education in the Patshálas or indigenous schools of Bengal. Boys used to start at the age of six by drawing on the floor with a steatite pencil, commencing with the consonants, and afterwards joining the letters so as to form syllables. When they learned in this way to read and write a little they were promoted to arithmetic, the figures being drawn on palmyra or plantain leaves with a reed dipped in a white liquid prepared by dissolving clay in water. In the second year they began to do accounts on paper.

In Muhammadan schools the chief exercise is the recitation of the Korán, which a pious follower of the Prophet should know by heart. The boy sits with the book before him, of which he often cannot read a single line. But such is the force of habit on the native mind, that if the book be closed while the boy is reciting, he will be unable to continue his task.

The mild nature of the Hindu did not prevent the infliction of severe discipline. The Bengal dominie was most ingenious in the invention of punishments. A boy was made to stand with back bent and a brick on his neck, which, if he dropped, he was caned; refractory scholars were put in a bag with nettles or a cat, and rolled about; another was forced to mark out so many yards on the ground with the tip of his nose, or two boys were compelled to pull each other's ears. Punctual attendance was ensured by the last comer receiving as many stripes as the number of boys who came in before him. It was a common sight to observe the master sally forth, cane in hand, to hunt up truants.

Most of these native schools have now been absorbed in the State system of primary education. But here and there a native merchant or landowner, who is too proud to send his son to the village school, keeps an ill-paid Pandit or Maulavi to carry on private teaching, of which the chief part is the droning out of passages from religious books in Sanskrit or Arabic, which no pupil understands.

["Calcutta Review," ii. 334ff., lxxv. 293ff.; Chevers, "Indian Medical Jurisprudence," 529; "Census Report," India, 1901, i. 158ff.]

ELEPHANT.—The Indian elephant, differing from the only other existing species, the African, in many points, such as shape of head, smaller size of ears, and fewer and differently shaped molar tooth ridges, is found in a single variety from the base of the Himálaya to Ceylon. The remains of fossil elephants found in the Siwálik hills form a link between the modern variety and the mastodon. It has hence been asserted that the evolution of the modern animal took place in Eastern Asia.

The male does not usually exceed 9 feet in height, which is twice the circumference of the fore-foot. The largest known tusk, that of an animal shot by Sir Victor Brooke, was 8 feet in length, and weighed 90 lbs. According to Megasthenes, most elephants live to the age of an extremely old man, and the most aged reach two hundred years. Mr Sanderson, one of the best authorities, fixes the age from one hundred and fifty to two hundred years. Many fables about the animal have passed into current belief, such as that it has no joints, "an old and grey-headed errour, even in the days of Aristotle," says Sir Thomas Browne, based on the account of Ctesias. Pliny knew enough to discredit the tale that when it lies on the ground it cannot get up by itself. Tavernier seems to imply that elephants were in his time imported from Melinda in East Africa to India, a story hardly credible in the light of our present knowledge. An occasional specimen even now crosses the sea. One was kept and ridden a few years ago by a Rája in the United Provinces. This variety is more powerful and less amenable to discipline than the Asiatic beast. The real difficulty in using them for the service of man is the impossibility of obtaining them in considerable numbers. The African native, with his instincts for the destruction of animal life, seldom captures or tames wild creatures.

The points of a good Indian elephant are thus summed up by Sir S. Baker:

"An Indian elephant to be perfect should be 9 feet 6 inches in perpendicular height at the shoulder. The head should be majestic in general character, as large as possible, especially broad across the forehead, and well rounded. The boss or prominence above the trunk should be solid and decided, mottled with flesh-coloured spots; these ought to continue upon the cheeks, and for about 3 feet down the trunk. This should be immensely massive; and when the elephant stands at ease, the trunk ought to touch the ground, when the tip is slightly curled. The skin of the face should be soft to the touch, and there must be no indentations or bony hollows, which are generally the sign of age. The ears should be large, the edges free from inequalities or rents, and above all they ought to be smooth, as though they had been carefully ironed. When an elephant is old, the top of the ear curls, and this symptom increases with advancing years. The eyes should be large and clear, the favourite colour a bright hazel. The tusks ought to be as thick as possible, free from cracks, gracefully curved, very slightly to the right or left, and projecting not less than 3 feet from the lips. The body should be well rounded, without a sign of any rib. The shoulders must be massive, with projecting muscular development; the back very slightly arched, and not sloping too suddenly towards the tail, which should be set up tolerably high. This ought to be thick and long, the end well furnished with a double fringe of very long thick hair or whalebone-looking bristles. The legs should be short in proportion to the height of the animal, but immensely thick, and the upper portions above the knee ought to exhibit enormous muscle. The knees should be well rounded, and the feet be exactly equal to half the perpendicular height of the animal when measured in their circumference, the weight pressing upon them when standing. The skin generally ought to be soft and pliable, by no means tight or strained, but lying easily upon the limbs and body."

The cult of the white elephant, practised by the kings of Siam and by the late dynasty of Upper Burma, probably had its origin in India, and was based on the Hindu worship of Airavat, the sacred elephant of Indra. It was a Buddhist idea that the Máha-Chakravartti Rája, "the great wheel-turning king," or universal sovereign, should be endowed with seven precious things, one of which was a white elephant. Aelian, quoting the account of Megasthenes (306-298 B.C.), describes the fidelity to its master shown by a white elephant; and Horace refers to it—"*Sive elephas albus volgi converterit ora.*" From the Ceylon Chronicle, the Mahavanso, we learn that the King of Anuradhapura had one in the fifth century. We next hear of the Muhammadans seizing a white elephant from Rája Dáhir of Sind in the eighth century, and at the end of the twelfth they captured one which Rája Jay Chand of Kanauj used to keep at Benares. In Moghul times we have accounts of at least two, one captured from the Chief of Mulher in the Násik district, and of another which had the peculiarity of never throwing dust upon his head, and called by the curiously inappropriate name of Syáma Chandra, "Dark Moon." To obtain this animal Sher Sháh warred with the King of Jhárkhand, or the central Indian hills, believing that its possession would ensure him the throne of Delhi. So late as 1813 a white elephant caught in Travancore was believed to indicate a prosperous reign for the young Mahárája.

The elephant plays an important part in early Indian history. Seleucus failed to overcome Chandragupta, but his object was gained by his exchange of a large part of Afghanistan for the elephants which won the victory for him at Ipsus. This, as Mr L. Kipling observes, is the only animal on the Buddhist sculptures carved "with true knowledge and unvarying truth of action."

The Moghuls dealt largely in elephants. Akbar used to hunt them in parts of Upper India, like Agra, Málwa, Narwár, and Behár, from which in a wild state they have long since disappeared. Tom Coryatt tells us that the Moghul kept 30,000 elephants; "In feeding of whom, and his lyons, and other beastes, he spendeth an incredible masse of money, at the least tenne thousand pounds sterling a day." Tavernier says that Aurangzeb used to allow Rs.500 a month for the support of one of his favourite elephants. "It is fed on the best food and quantities of sugar, and is given spirits to drink." Our less liberal Government allows only Rs.24 a month for the keep of its Bengal elephants. Every Hindu Rája should have a stable of elephants, and it is very lucky to have at the gateway an animal that has the habit of swaying its body to and fro. The Maháraja of Alwar drives an elephant team, a four-in-hand with a carriage gondola-shaped, two stories high.

The use of elephants in war dates from very early times. Strabo speaks of three men carried in the "tower," or on his bare back, of whom two shoot from the side and one from behind, while the driver urges on the beast with his goad. In the Mahábhárata we have a trained elephant corps, an example followed by the Sassanians of Persia, who recruited them from India. Sir H. Yule remarks on the difficulty in understanding the accounts of the number of men carried on a war elephant. The writer of the Book III. Maccabees tells us of thirty-two, besides the Mahout, while Ibn Batuta describes twenty or thirty on its back, which was the number borne by the great elephant sent by Timúr to the Sultan of Egypt. Livy says that there were four men on each elephant at the battle of Magnesia, which is probably true, the other writers obviously speaking without knowledge of the facts.

The Moghuls, and in imitation of them the Nawábs of Oudh, delighted in elephant fights. The Moghuls also used the animal for the execution of criminals, as is attested by Terry and Badauni. As late as 1801 the Peshwa caused Wittuji Holkar to be executed in this way, and the custom prevailed till quite recent times in some of the Himálayan States.

Elephant shooting, says Sir S. Baker, is, when fairly followed for a length of time, the most dangerous of all sports. Many elephants may be killed without the sportsman being in peril, but once a wounded elephant does attack his charge is most dangerous.

"A tiger's charge," says Sanderson, "is an undignified display of arms, legs, and spluttering; the bison rushes blunderingly upon his foe; the bear's attack is despicable; but the wild elephant's onslaught is as dignified as it seems overwhelming; and a large tusker's charge, when he has had sufficient distance to get into full swing, can only be compared to the steady and rapid advance of an engine on a line of rail."

The animal is one of the worst enemies of the cultivator. It is difficult to imagine the ravages committed by them in Bengal at the close of the eighteenth century. Hon. R. Lindsay writes:

"Most fortunately for the population of the country, they delight in the sequestered range of the mountains; did they prefer the plain, whole kingdoms would be laid waste."

We now know, from Mr Sanderson's observations, the character of the *Rogue** elephant. He is not, as a rule, a male driven from the herd by rivals; more usually he is the lord of some herd in the neighbourhood, and visits fields where less bold animals and females with calves fear to venture. He keeps more or less to the jungle occupied by his herd, and follows its movements. Sometimes he is a young male as yet unable to assert a position in the herd, or one who from choice separates himself for a time, if not completely. But Mr Sanderson believes that a really solitary elephant is uncommon, and that an elephant cannot actually be driven from the herd. Such an animal remains in the neighbourhood, but avoids molestation.

Opinions differ as to the degree of intelligence possessed by elephants. Hindus represent Ganesa, god of wisdom and remover of obstacles, with an elephant's head; but popular belief does not regard the animal as the impersonation of wisdom. He can be educated to perform certain acts, but he has little or no power of initiative, and has not even sufficient intelligence to save his master from drowning or attack. In tasks where he seems to show most cleverness, as in shifting logs, he acts almost entirely under the influence of quite imperceptible hints from his driver. Some have doubted his power of remembering wrongs, and Mr Sanderson laughs at the tale of the elephant that soused the tailor who pricked him with his needle, on the ground that being himself fond of water he cannot infer that man dislikes it. But Linschoten was probably nearer the truth: "But he that hurteth them, he must take heed, for they never forget when any man doth them injuries until they be avenged." Darwin, it may be noted, accepts the evidence of similar intelligence in many animals, and Sir S. Baker notices particularly the elephant's power of remembering localities. A good *howdah* * elephant shows splendid courage before a tiger, but such animals are rare, and the ordinary beast is subject to fits of senseless panic which often endanger the life of the rider.

Ivory carving is an industry carried on all over the country, animal and other figures, hunting, feasting, and mythological scenes being the most common subjects. The art is of great antiquity, as, according to Mr Stubbs, the oldest set of chessmen in the South Kensington Museum was discovered about fifty years ago in the ruins of the city of Bahmanábád in Sind, which was destroyed by an earthquake in the eighth century. An important branch of the industry is the making of ivory combs and bangles, the latter largely worn in the Panjáb and in some other parts of the country. It is a curious instance of the localisation of trades that ivory turnery still clings to the old town of Páli in Rájputána, where it has been a specialty for centuries. The ivory used in North India comes from Africa, Burma, and from local sources. African is the favourite, as when cut it is of a warm, transparent tint, with little grain, and as it dries from exposure, it lightens in colour. Indian ivory, on the other hand, when cut, acquires by degrees a pale yellowish tint. The African variety is harder, closer in texture, and takes a finer polish, the lack of polish being the best proof that the material is Indian. A good deal of ivory is used at Delhi in the production of the pretty little miniatures which are the work of sharp-sighted boys. The use of ivory bangles is so well established in the marriage ceremonial that it will be interesting to watch what material, as ivory grows scarcer, will be substituted for it.

[Sir S. Baker, "Wild Beasts and their Ways," chaps. ii., iii., iv.; Sanderson, "Thirteen Years," 48ff.; Stubbs, "Monograph on Ivory Carving for the N.W.P. and Oudh"; Ellis, Ditto for the Panjáb.]

EMBROIDERY.—Embroidery is one of the old handicrafts, and has been brought to great perfection in India. Marco Polo thus writes of the Gujarát leather embroidery:

"They also work here beautiful mats in red and blue leather, exquisitely inlaid with figures of birds and beasts, and skilfully embroidered with gold and silver wire. They are marvellously beautiful things; they are used by the Saracens to sleep upon, and capital they are for that purpose. They also work cushions embroidered with gold."

This work still survives in the form of leather mats embroidered in silk, or painted.

The fabrics ornamented with this work are of various kinds. Thus, from Dacca we have the famous embroidered muslins, the pattern being either worked by hand in the loom or done by the needle. Another variety is the Chikan [*Chicken* *] work, or hand-worked flowered muslin. It is done in Lucknow by Musalmán men, but sometimes little girls may be seen at work, and some very fine pieces are made by the secluded women of the banker class. From Murshídábád and Patna comes the Kárchob or gold and silver embroidery applied to horse-trappings, jackets, money-bags, belts, and the like. Agra, Benares, and Lucknow do a large trade in embroidered caps, while the floss silk-work of Delhi on table-covers, cushions, and the like is largely bought by Europeans. At Amritsar and Ludhiána embroidered shawls and dressing-gowns are made. In fact, there is hardly a city throughout the whole Peninsula which does not make a specialty of some kind of embroidery, most of which is done by men and boys.

It is only embroidery for family use which is the work of women. A good example of this is the Phúlkári [*Phoolkaree* *] of Northern India, which has in recent years become fashionable among Europeans for curtains and other forms of decoration. A Ját girl of the Eastern Panjáb is expected to embroider at least one of these sheets for use at her marriage. The beauty of such a garment depends greatly on the material. Originally the embroidery was done on a coarse cotton stuff, dyed in rich deep tints of blue or chocolate, all produced by vegetable dyes. The coarseness of the material permitted the counting of the threads, and threw out the rich hues of the silk-work. When, however, a demand arose for these fabrics the old domestic industry was unable to supply the market, and the business passed into the hands of the professional embroiderers, who used finer materials and silk dyed with aniline colours, a result disastrous from the artistic point of view. In the real phúlkári used for personal dress, wilful defects in the design or colouring, as protection against the Evil Eye, are noticeable.

Perhaps the most important branch of the embroidery art is that applied to what are known as Cashmere shawls, though the manufacture is not now confined to that province. Delhi does a large business in a long, loose stitch in white filoselle applied to European fabrics; but the demand for such work in articles like ladies' opera-cloaks has now almost quite ceased. Much of the work is now applied to the satin of Europe.

"Some of the recent patterns," writes Mr L. Kipling, "notably one counterfeiting the markings on peacocks' feathers, are brilliant and effective." But he adds, "There seems to be a touch of flimsiness in most Delhi work, and this characteristic is not likely to be cured by the determination of the public on the one hand to pay cheap prices, and of the dealer on the other to secure large profits."

[H. C. Cookson, "Monograph on Silk in the Panjáb," with note on Phúlkáris by Mrs F. A. Steel; L. Kipling, "Delhi Gazetteer," 136; Birdwood, "Industrial Arts of India," 278ff.; Mukharji, "Art Manufactures of India," 368ff.; Miss Billington, "Woman in India," 194.]

EMIGRATION. — The causes which dissuade the Indian peasant from leaving his native land have struck their roots deep in the social needs, religion, and superstition of the people. The Hindu, with his intense reverence for family life and membership of his tribe or caste, depends probably more than any other peasant in the world on the sympathy and co-operation of his brethren. All the affairs of life are regulated by the opinion of the group in which he is born, and severed from that group he finds himself a hopeless outcast, the last penalty for any grievous breach of social law being ostracism. The European of our day finds it difficult to understand fully such a feeling as this, but memories of it live in George Eliot's pictures of rural life in England at the beginning of last century.

Secondly, being a member of an endogamous group, and the marriage of his children being one of his clearest duties, he knows that if he removes to a distance the ever-present difficulty of negotiating suitable marriages will be indefinitely increased. He may even be forced to incur the disgrace of seeing his daughter grow up an old maid, or he may imperil the happiness of his ancestors and of himself by failing to provide a line of male descendants competent to perform the obsequies.

Thirdly, the gods in whom the rustic really believes are not the great world gods, but the minor gods of his hamlet, whose shrine is under the village tree. The jurisdiction of these gods is purely local, and when he once leaves his village he finds himself in the land of new gods, whose hostility he knows not how to appease.

Hence the Hindu, and the Musalmán in imitation of him, prefers to stay at home, and the bribe of higher wages abroad does not appeal to him as it does to the man of the West. If he does emigrate, he always tries to return to the village of his birth and end his days among his own people.

Of emigration to foreign lands there is little in India. Before the Hindu lies the Kála Páni [*Kalla Pawnee* *], the "Black Water," with all its danger and mystery. Madras coolies go to Ceylon, if this be reckoned a foreign country, and both Madrasis and Bengalis cross the sea to Burma. The man who wanders most is the Sikh and Panjábi Musalmán, whom the prospect of good pay and a pension attracts to service in China, the Malay States, or Uganda. A small stream of emigrants passes to the plantations in Mauritius and Réunion; some go as hawkers to Natal; a few Afghâns find service as camel-drivers in Australia. But this movement of Indian emigrants abroad is not largely encouraged by the Government, owing to the difficulty of securing fair treatment to the coolies.

Internal migration is more important. This assumes various forms: first, temporary, such as that in times of famine from want of food or fodder, and the movements of gangs of labourers to large public works; secondly, periodic, when the changing seasons drive men, their families and cattle, to and fro from cool mountains to warm plains, for caravan transport, trade, and so forth; thirdly, permanent, caused by overcrowding and distress on the one hand, or by political advantages on the other; lastly, reciprocal, where persons passing in one direction are replaced by others moving in the opposite direction.

The first variety of internal migration has been unhappily considerable in recent years. To the peasant of Upper India Málwa is pictured as an El Dorado, the land of prosperity, where the rain never fails. So when famine appears in the Ganges valley, streams of miserable people press south with their families and cattle to the land of promise, distress and disease levying a heavy toll on them in the march. When they reach their destination they find the land already overcrowded, and conditions little more hopeful than at home. It lies, in fact, distinctly in the danger zone, and has suffered severely in recent famines. Similar movements of labour are seen in the direction of our great railway and canal works. The professional digger caste, the Waddars or Ods, move about as freely as the English navvy. It was mainly migration of this kind which remedied the distressing social difficulties of the Santáls, and the Kashmíris were driven by distress and misgovernment into the Panjáb.

Instances of the second type, or periodic migration, are found in the movement to and fro of the tribes on the Panjáb frontier, or of the herdsmen of the Ganges valley, who drive their cattle in summer to the hills of Central India. There is an annual vernal and autumnal movement of great flocks of goats and sheep up and down the upper valley of the Sutlej, and of herds of yaks in search of pasture from one part of the snowy range of the Himálaya to another. In Balúchistán the people migrate annually to India for commerce, the carrying trade, and in search of work as labourers, while the Brahuis come down for the sake of the cheaper living and grazing facilities which the lowlands offer. The extent of this movement may be measured by the fact that as many as 15,000 of their camels have traversed the Bolán Pass in a single month. They come with their families, cattle, cocks and hens; set up a goat-hair rug on poles to serve as a tent, and stay on grazing their flocks till the increasing heat of April drives them back again to their highland home.

The third, the permanent or quasi-permanent type, is found in the movements of the Panjáb farmers to the new irrigation colonies, or the sturdy peasant of Behár to Calcutta, where he finds service as an orderly or door-keeper. When the artisan moves to seats of industry like Bombay or Cawnpore, he often leaves his women folk behind, and if he does not start a new household in the land of his adoption, returns home when he has the means to do so.

The fourth, or reciprocal form is mainly the exchange of brides. The Hindu dislikes marrying in his own village, and prefers to seek a wife at a distance. The usual reason he assigns for this habit is that when his wife's parents' home is near, she is apt to run away if any petty family quarrel occurs, and so he can keep her in better order if her home be distant. But the custom is really based on a law of exogamy, which regards the residents of a village as united by some vague tie of blood. There is thus a constant movement of young women backwards and forwards between the home of their parents and their husbands. This reciprocity is seen most clearly among the Rájputs of North India, who seek a husband for a daughter among the prouder western septs, and these give in turn brides to those of the east whose blood is not so blue. In Rájputána itself the movement is not confined to women. An heiress is accompanied to her new home by a staff of servants, or a bridegroom marrying into a rich family comes to the house of his father-in-law attended by a body of retainers, and often lives there for long periods.

At present a constant stream of emigrants sets in from the hill tribes of Central India towards the tea-gardens of Assam. The Government has endeavoured to enforce rules for the protection of these labourers; but the result has often proved unsatisfactory, and great difficulty has been experienced in the attempt to reconcile the claims to protection of an ignorant class with the legitimate demands of an important industry.

In some districts, like parts of the Gangetic valley and Behár, the Census figures show extreme congestion; in others the requirements of advancing industries are in excess of the supply of available labour. In many cases the systems of labour enlistment are inadequate, and outbreaks of plague in industrial centres like Bombay have obstructed the supply of labour. Even with its enormous population it does not seem likely that in the immediate future India will be in a position to supply its own industrial needs, and at the same time furnish bodies of colonists for places like our new dominions in Eastern Africa.

["Census Report," India, 1891, i. 66; 1901, i. 88ff.; Bengal, 1901, i. 127; Panjáb, 1891, i. 273; 1901, i. 273.]

ETIQUETTE.—More than two hundred years ago when Mr Hedges, agent in Bengal, wrote: "A gaudy shew and great noise adds much to a Public Person's Credit in the Country," he only expressed one of the leading principles which influence the life of the East, and which is nowhere more effective than in India itself. India is the land of custom, and in religious thought and social life its people have from the earliest times laid special stress upon ritual and formalism. The Hindu conception of sacrifice and the worship of the gods is founded on an elaborate symbolism and ceremonial which dates from remote ages. The due recitation of spells and sacred texts, the intonation of the voice in prayer, the acts of the worshipper, the symbolical nature of the offerings, are not a modern accretion, but depend on the very nature of their religious system. To use the words of Mr Herbert Spencer: "What we think the essential parts of sacred and secular regulations were originally subordinate parts, and the essential parts consisted of ceremonial observances."

This belief in the efficacy of ritual in matters of religion has been extended to the domain of social life, and has gained force through the distinctions of rank and the division of the people which are the result of the caste system. Hence the social intercourse at tribal gatherings, marriage, and other ordinances of social life, and attendance at the Royal Courts, have all come to be regulated by intricate rules of etiquette and class precedence. No people in the world enjoy a show as they do, and no people are more desirous that functions of this kind should be done "decently and in order."

In process of time, of course, old ceremonial observances tend to decay, or rather to assume other forms; so that we now see in many of these customs only obscure survivals of the original rite. Thus the tribute-present, without which no Oriental presents himself before his lord, has become the *Dolly** of fruit and vegetables which the native gentleman presents to his European superior, or the gold coin wrapped up in a handkerchief, which he knows will be merely touched and returned. The Tibetan, when he wishes to be polite, puts out his tongue and presses forward his left ear, because the ancient Chinese rule was to cut off the left ear of captives for presentation to the chief. In the usual Eastern fashion the host assures his guest that his house and all it holds are at his disposal.

But familiarity with the European and the pseudo-independence resulting from popular education naturally tend to check the innate courtesy of the people. The town-dweller now often passes the magistrate in the bazaar without a salute; it is only in remote villages that the rustic stands on one leg, takes off his turban, or dismounts from his pony when the Englishman rides by. But even in these later days there is nothing finer than the tactful courtesy of the native gentleman of the old school. He does not like the brusqueness of manner which the European too often displays, he particularly objects to "chaff," and dislikes familiarity of any kind. The result is that he becomes watchful and on his guard. He is so anxious to please that he is afraid to speak freely, or give an opinion which may be quoted against him and bring him into conflict with a neighbour or fellow-casteman. Hence the duty of interviewing a succession of native magnates becomes a tedious labour to the busy official. The conversation tends to become limited to an exchange of compliments, which the Englishman thinks forced and unmeaning, and he soon finds that at interviews of this kind he cannot gain from his visitors the clear information which will aid him in the business of administration. It is in his winter marches and camp life, when he meets the rustic alone in his field, or chats with the beaters when in search of game, that he sometimes penetrates a little behind the screen which perpetually veils the real life of the people from the foreign observer.

Salutation is regulated by elaborate rules. The Hindu has at least five forms of obeisance; the most servile when he touches the ground with eight, and the less abject with five members of his body. Next in order come a prostration, the forehead touching the ground; bringing the hands to the forehead and touching it with the thumbs; raising the right hand (never the left) to the forehead and bowing, which last is the usual respectful form. These are carefully appropriated to special occasions and persons, and the degrees of reverence when the persons meeting are of unequal rank are carefully defined. Women, again, have their special rules. A Rájput lady in Cutch begins the day by making three bows to her mother-in-law and to all women in the house, even servants, who are older than herself. Covering her right hand with the end of the head-cloth, she stretches it to the ground, and then twice raises it to her head. Weeping is the sign of both joy and sorrow, and women when they meet a relative or friend after a long absence think it necessary to fall into her arms and weep. Kissing is naturally restricted by rules of caste. We see it in its original form among the Kyoungtha of the Assam frontier, who apply mouth and nose to the cheek and give a strong inhalation. They do not say in their tongue "Give me a kiss," but "Smell me!"

The Moghuls prescribed an elaborate style of Court etiquette, and much of the current practice is a survival from their time. They used only their Central Asian speech in Durbars, and in imitation of them the late Burmese kings had not only a special Court language, but appointed a language for courtiers when speaking to each other about Royalty. To quote Sir J. G. Scott:

> "An ordinary man 'walks,' a mendicant 'stalks,' or 'strides,' or 'passes with dignified gait' . . . while a King 'makes a royal progress.' The latter expression is emphatically correct as far as personages of the Burmese royal blood are concerned, who never go on their own legs in the open air. If they do not mount an elephant, some official is honoured with the weight of Majesty on his back."

The Moghuls did not observe the modern rule that punctuality is the virtue of princes. To keep a stranger waiting was a way of asserting the great man's dignity. But it may also be said that failure to keep an appointment is in the East often not intentional. When people are bound by the law of omens, lucky or unlucky times and seasons, the fault more often lies at the door of the astrologer rather than at that of Royalty.

Another habit of the Moghuls, which even petty Rájas of our time imitate, was to pretend not to converse directly with a visitor, his requests being communicated to the Emperor through an attendant, and the reply given in the same way. Tavernier describes how a stranger had to stand beyond a small marble channel outside the hall of audience. His arrival was announced by two officers to His Majesty, "who very often does not appear to hear, but some time after he lifts his eyes, and throwing them upon the ambassador, makes through the Secretary a sign that he may approach."

They were also careful in their rules of salutation. Abul Fazl defines the Taslím as consisting

> "in placing the back of the right hand upon the ground, and then raising it gently till the person stands erect, when he puts the palm of his hand upon the crown of his head, which pleasing manner of saluting signifies that he is ready to give himself as an offering."

In another form of salutation, the Kornish, which in some ways resembled the Chinese *Kowtow*,* the palm of the right hand was placed on the forehead and the head bent downwards. It was also prescribed that when anything was said, it was in a low whisper, a rule which Lord Valentia found to prevail in the Court of the Peshwa at Poona.

The persons attending the Durbar were seated in order of rank, a rule which is observed in our days. This has given rise to a regular scale of precedence, which often leads to disputes and intrigues. A nobleman of our time will do almost anything to secure a place higher than that of a rival, and nothing causes more excitement than any alteration in the number of guns which natives are entitled to receive as a salute. The Indian nobles within our territory are careful to claim this honour when they visit one of our cantonments. But our thrifty Government always sends them a bill for the gunpowder expended in their honour.

Much of this etiquette is maintained in native Courts. In Rájputána the Mahárája of Jodhpur leads the fashion. The highest honour he bestows upon a visitor is to receive and dismiss him standing, and to raise his right hand on the arrival and departure of his guest. To men of the second rank he merely rises when they come and go; to the third grade he rises only on arrival. His great drum is beaten in the palace four times every night, and it is held the highest compliment on the death of one of his nobles that one beat is omitted.

The etiquette of sitting is also carefully prescribed. Pyrard de Laval writes of the Maldive Court:

> "When they are seated in any place, others must take care to pass behind them, for to do otherwise would be held a great indignity, and would bring about some untoward result; but if it be necessary to go in front of another, the one who does so crouches full low and holds his hands close to the ground, saying *Assa*, as who should say 'Be not displeased.' It is a grave indiscretion for one seated in the presence of others to swing the legs; they are much offended at it, and hold it to be a sign of bad luck and a piece of bad manners."

Youths of respectable rank are still carefully taught the mode of sitting with the legs crouched under the body. When a well-bred native gentleman is given a chair he is careful to arrange his robes decorously over his knees.

Whether the visitor is or is not to receive the dignity of a chair is a question of no little difficulty, and the young Englishman soon learns that in the days of his griffinhood he was grossly deceived in granting this honour to unworthy persons, at the suggestion of his orderly, for a consideration. But it is the great Shoe Question which has led to really acute controversy. The native rule is that a visitor on entering a house does not uncover his head, but removes his slippers so as not to defile the clean white cloth with which the floor of a gentleman's sitting-room is covered. The European in return claims that he does all that civility requires by removing his hat, and in the old days he never dreamed of permitting a native gentleman to enter his private room without removing his slippers. Nothing was more characteristic of General Nicholson than when, in the crisis of the Mutiny, he insisted on a Patiála officer removing his shoes before entering his tent. The present position of the question is not satisfactory. Those who wear the native slippers remove them, those who wear boots or shoes of European fashion retain them.

The question was a burning one even in the days of Tavernier:

> "In the islands of Manilla or Philippines there are blacks so rich that some of them have offered the Viceroy up to 20,000 croisats (£6,500) for permission to wear hose and shoes; this was not allowed them. You see certain of these blacks with bare feet, though followed by thirty slaves and superbly clad."

The Court of Burma was naturally precise in such matters, and Sir H. Yule describes the wearisome negotiations to decide the exact point at which the members of the embassy were to remove their shoes when entering the palace. In former days, even outside the palace, no European wore shoes in the king's presence. The shoe, in fact, in native belief, represents the wearer. The Moghul emperors went so far as to send their slippers under escort to represent them at the Courts of tributary princes. All South India rang with surprise when a Rája of Madura ordered the envoy to place the Royal slipper on the floor, pushed his own foot into it, and asked where was its fellow. What did they mean by bringing him an old shoe as a present? Then he had the embassy beaten with canes and turned out of his fort. Well it was for the Rája that it is a long cry from Madura to Delhi, otherwise he would have found cause to repent his assertion of independence.

The permission to retire must, of course, be given by the host, and inexperienced English officers have often been embarrassed by a visit prolonged until at last the signal was given. At a ceremonious visit the host presents betel and rosewater as a sign that the interview is closed. In his "Travels," Lord Valentia, a great stickler for etiquette, tells how he refused to receive the otto of roses from the Nawáb of Murshídábád, "a mark of inferiority I could not allow." Finally he insisted on helping himself. "According to strict etiquette it ought to have been given me at the door, and standing, for the further the advance before giving it, the higher the compliment." When he visited the Peshwa, the Minister for British Affairs gave rosewater, *pawn*,* and attar to all the party except to the Resident and Lord Valentia.

"He began at the lowest, contrary to the etiquette of other Asiatic Courts that I have visited. The Dewán gave pawn, rosewater, attar, and spices to the Colonel [Barry Close]; to me he gave attar and rosewater. We then arose, and His Highness presented me with the gold box filled with pawn, from his own hands."

The Portuguese, great sticklers for etiquette, brought their own code with them to the East, and carefully observed its regulations. Linschoten describes how the host

"commeth unto the doore of his house, with his hatte in his hand, and with great curtesie to receyve him that commeth to visite him, and so leadeth him up into his hall or chamber, where hee offereth him a chaire to sitte down, and then he himselfe sitteth, then he asketh him what hee woulde have, which having understoode hee bringeth him downe againe to the doore in the like sort, and so with *Besolas manos* biddeth him farewel, and if he should not doe so, or when hee giveth him a stool, shold give him one unlined or one yt is lesse or lower than that he taketh for himselfe, he that visiteth him woulde take it in evil parte, esteeming it a great scorne, and seeke to be revenged on him for the same."

Stavorinus gives much the same account of the Dutch:

"Above all things the master of the house must attend to the seating of every guest, and drinking their healths in the exact order of precedence," especially with ladies, who "are particularly prone to insist upon every prerogative attached to the station of their husbands. Some of them, if they conceive themselves placed a jot lower than they are entitled to, will sit in sulk and proud silence for the whole time the entertainment lasts."

Such occurrences are not unknown in our days, but Anglo-Indian society has succeeded in freeing itself from much of the etiquette which was so burdensome to an earlier generation.

EURASIAN.—This is the modern term for persons of mixed European and Indian blood, more euphemistic than "Half-caste," and more precise than "East Indian" or "Anglo-Indian," which last is the title adopted by members of this community.

The Eurasian problem has engaged the attention of sociologists from the earliest period of European intercourse with India. It first arose in the Portuguese settlements on the West Coast, and it is easy to account for the degeneration of this mixed breed from the description given by travellers, like Pyrard de Laval, of the lazy and dissolute habits of the settlers at Goa—the men attended always by male and female slaves, the women spending their whole time gazing from their latticed windows, and living most dissolute lives. Linschoten writes:

"The children of the Portingales, both boyes and gyrls, which are borne in India, are called Castisos, and are in all things like unto the Portingales, only somewhat differing in colour, for they draw towards a yealow colour; the children of these Castisos are yealow, and altogether like the Mesticos [*Mustees* *], and the children of Mesticos are of colour and fashion like the naturall borne Countrimen or Decaniins of the countree, so that the posteritie of the Portingales, both men and women being in the third degree, doe seeme to be naturall Indians, both in colour and fashion."

In the Portuguese settlements this amalgamation of the races was more rapid than elsewhere, owing to the existence of a large Christian native population.

The evil results of this state of things soon attracted the attention of the English rulers. About 1670 Gerald Aungier, Governor of Bombay, sent home for English wives for the factors and other European residents. In 1700 the Council of Hugli reported:

"It is alsoe of very ill consequence that your Covenant Servants should intermarry with any of the people of the country or those of mixed race or Musteechees, therefore we desire your Honour would continue it as a Standing Rule that none Doe Rise in your Service, or rather be not Retained in your service a Covenant Servant, as Factore or Merchant, that shall marry with any of the Country not of Europe parents."

Grand Pré describes another class of Eurasians at Chinsura, the old Dutch settlement near Calcutta:

"Here, as in all the Dutch establishments, some Malay families have settled, and given birth to a description of women called Mosses, who are in high estimation for their beauty and talents. The race is now almost extinct, or is scattered through different parts of the country."

Early in the last century Captain Williamson, fearing that the Eurasians of Bengal would mutiny and join the natives, opposed giving them any public employment. Lord Valentia was also very nervous, and proposed that every father of a half-caste should be required to send them to Europe, and that their return to India should be prohibited. The wise and kindly H. T. Colebrooke discussed the matter in a much more sensible way about the same time.

"A gradual increase of the bastard race from continual accessions to it, joined with the augmentation of numbers in its posterity, may be expected to take place, and to constitute a progressive colonisation in fact, notwithstanding the opposition ineffectually given to it. This doubtless is in some degree actually in progress; but it proceeds less actively than might have been anticipated. The mixed race melts quickly on either side; into the white Creole, on the one part, by the intermarriages of the women with the European sojourners (for settlers they are not permitted to be); and into the dark native Christian, on the other, by the mixture of the men with native women more swarthy than themselves."

On the whole, he welcomed the increasing colonisation of India by such people:

"In a political view a Christian population, holding a decent rank in the motley throng of tribes and castes, would add to the strength of the State and probable duration of the Empire."

These hopes, it is needless to say, have not been realised, mainly because the problem of the education and settlement of the Eurasian community has never been seriously undertaken. The first attempt to improve them was the opening of a school at Calcutta by Mrs Hodges about 1760, in which she taught French and dancing. The girls married off quickly, but their character was described as "childish, vain, imperious, crafty, vulgar, and wanton."

Easier communication with the home country has checked the growth of this class. It is very difficult to estimate their exact numbers. According to the last returns, they number, including the Firingis, or half-caste Portuguese of Bengal, about 90,000, of whom rather more than half are in Bombay and Madras. They are exceedingly fertile and are probably increasing; but their numbers in the Census returns are kept down by their habit of recording themselves as Europeans—Scotch or Irish by preference. In Madras it appears that many native Christians, who have taken to European ways and dress, have, with a view to enhance their social position, returned themselves as Eurasians.

An important Eurasian centre in South India is Vepery, a suburb of Madras, of which Captain Hervey, in the early part of last century, gives a lively account. He describes some of them as

"rolling in wealth, and aping all the airs and following all the customs of consequential importance which that wealth can command. They live in excellent houses, furnished in first-rate style, keep up splendid establishments, and do all they possibly can to vie with the European residents in the elegance of their abodes or the brilliancy of their equipages. . . . They try, however, all they can to induce European gentlefolks to enter within the precincts of their houses, by holding out to them all manner of allurements to join their company. . . . Those, however, who are known to associate with these sable-browed individuals are kept at arm's length by respectable people, and never allowed to enter the circles of the select community of the place. Time was when officers of the Madras army used to mix promiscuously with them, but such things never occur nowadays." He says that they were called "Vepery Brahmins," and he speaks of the danger to officers who "are frequently among these dark-eyed, bewitching syrens, and are very liable to become smitten with their charms."

The best class of Eurasians are probably those of French descent at Pondicherry. As for the Portuguese East Indian of Malabar, the only links which connect him with Portugal are his religion, his language, and his name. But the tongue which he speaks is as much Dravidian as Portuguese, and his religion is much debased by the animistic atmosphere in which he lives. The most degraded of all are the Firingis [*Firinghee* *] of Eastern Bengal, who were originally of Portuguese descent; but it is now impossible to say how much foreign blood flows in their veins. They are darker than the natives among whom they live. They are intensely ignorant, too proud to do any manual labour, and their condition is steadily deteriorating. Midway stand the Goanese of Western India, who are largely employed as domestic servants, and as stewards on the English steamer lines.

Among Eurasians, as a whole, there is no uniform standard of character or ability. Some of them are very respectable and intelligent, and have reached a high position in Government service, the learned professions, and commerce; others, again, are mere helots in the slums of native bazaars, for whom there is no present and no future. Their worst faults are instability of character, extravagance, and a contempt for the native races, which the latter return with interest. To quote the Bengal Census Report of 1881:

> "The stigma which in all countries attaches to the half-breed is perhaps nowhere felt more keenly than in India, where the Eurasian is rejected both by the pure European whom he imitates, and by the natives of the country whom he affects to despise."

It is encouraging that their progress in education has been noteworthy. In Madras, 70 per cent. of them are literate in English, and here they are not merely clerks or machinists, but practise a greater variety of occupations than the members of any other community.

It is difficult to forecast the future of the race. They are generally admitted to be unsuited for the Army. An Eurasian regiment would cost nearly as much as one formed of Europeans, and though some of them fought gallantly in the Mutiny, they are generally considered less trustworthy than soldiers of pure European descent, and they are less amenable to discipline. The idea of planting them out as colonists in the hills seems to be impracticable, as agriculture, stock-raising, and market-gardening have little attractions for them, and these occupations are already well filled by natives. Now that special measures have been taken to educate the poorer class, it may be that a future lies before them as overseers of native labour in the rapidly developing industries of the country, or by emigration to Australia or New Zealand. But until the race developes more self-reliance, and ceases to depend on official patronage, its prospects of rising in the social scale are far from promising.

["Calcutta Review," cvii. 79ff.; "Life of Colebrooke," 317ff.; For Bengal Firingis, "Census Report," Bengal, 1901, i. 409; "Calcutta Review," liii. 57ff.; lxx. ii., lxxii. 177; "Bulletin of Madras Museum," ii. 70ff.]

EVIL EYE.—"There be none of the affections," says Bacon, "which have been noted to fascinate or bewitch, but love and envy; they both have vehement wishes, they form themselves readily into imaginations and suggestions, and they come easily into the eye, especially upon the presence of the objects which are the points which conduce to fascination, if any such there be."

Thus envy is at the root of the Evil Eye superstition. Hence, the man blind of an eye, or afflicted by any other infirmity, is certain to envy those who are in good health, and blessed with strength and beauty. It is, therefore, the old hag, the cripple, the hunchback, who are naturally prone to cast their malicious glances on the young and beautiful. Again, it is at one of the crises of human life—child-birth, the coming of age, marriage—that the subject is most exposed to this dangerous influence, and most of the rites performed on such occasions are intended to avert "over-seeing."

The belief in the Evil Eye is a widespread superstition accepted by the Fathers of the Church, by medieval authorities, and it flourishes among ignorant and superstitious races, even among the English peasantry of our day. But nowhere does it thrive more vigorously than in India. Here the belief slides easily into those connected with witchcraft and demoniacal influence, which are all so closely linked that it is difficult to disentangle them.

When we realise that the Evil Eye superstition is largely based upon the feeling of envy, it is easy to understand some of the popular remedies which are adopted to neutralise or repel it. Hence we can explain the idea that if you make an intentional blot of imperfection on anything you value, it will cause in the mind of one able to "overlook" you a feeling of dissatisfaction, which is fatal to the complete effect of the evil glance. Accordingly, in the case of a child who is specially liable to fascination, the Indian mother smears its face with lampblack, or dresses it in dirty clothes, or calls it some opprobrious name, such as "Beggar," "Grasshopper," or "Three-farthings." In the last resort, if the child be a boy, it is dressed in girl's clothes, a pathetic proof of the low estimation in which the mother holds her baby girls. They are so worthless that no one thinks it worth their while to fascinate them. For the same reason a native gentleman thinks it no compliment for his child to be praised by a European. He dreads what a Scotchman calls "fore-speaking," when praise beyond measure—praise accompanied by a sort of amazement or envy—is believed to forebode disease or accident. Such praise is most dreaded from the lips of a foreigner, who is naturally an eccentric, uncanny person.

The dread of the Evil Eye is responsible for some of the squalor of a native bazaar. When you build a house it is unwise to finish it; it is safer to leave a beam projecting from a wall, or part of the front unplastered, that the malignant passer-by may find occasion for amused contempt, rather than for unstinted praise of the owner. Again, building is an act of virtue, and the heir can win no merit by completing his father's design; he prefers to leave the old dwelling incomplete and build a new one elsewhere. The superstition in the same way affects native art by insisting on irregularity of pattern and an occasional error in the outlines. Dr Westermarck has recently shown that many or most Eastern art patterns represent devices to repel the Evil Eye.

When we come to actual protectives their number is legion. A frightful figure of a demon or of an European soldier painted near the door is thought most effective. For the same reason a milkman puts charcoal in his pail to prevent the contents being soured by fascination, or because it represents a blot of imperfection. Hence, too, when one of the Karens of Burma falls ill, the first stage of the cure is to powder him all over with charcoal.

All metals, and especially iron, a late discovery which must have been looked on with wonder and dread by early man, are useful in this way. This explains the religious taboo of iron, the vessels and other things used in worship being of copper or brass. For the same reason the Doms of Behár, one of the most expert criminal castes in India, excommunicate any member of the tribe who uses an iron "jemmy" in committing a burglary. Equally valuable are things which come from the great, mysterious sea, like coral and shells. The cowry-shell is particularly valued because the evil glance is supposed to be so concentrated upon it that it finally cracks from the amount of venom it has absorbed. Hence we reach the explanation of the rude ornaments worn by the most primitive tribes, and we finally come to the jewellery, which in its primary conception is an amulet or talisman. Many pets are kept by natives with a view to absorb the evil influence of the malignant glance. Grooms keep a monkey in the stable to shield the horses, and a wise merchant hangs a parrot in an iron cage at the door of his shop, and is thus doubly guarded.

As we have seen, it is hard to draw the line between fascination and witchcraft. Both these superstitions lead to the practice of "devil-murder," which perplexes officials in the Andaman Islands. If any unaccountable sickness or death occur, it goes hard with any morose or unpopular person who may be really suspected of casting the Evil Eye. Even his wife and children are hunted down as his accomplices.

[Elworthy, "The Evil Eye"; Crooke, "Popular Religion and Folk-lore of North India," ii. 1ff.; Westermarck, "The Magic Origin of Moorish Designs," "Journal Anthropological Institute," N.S. xxxiv. 211ff.]

FAIR.—There are two classes of Indian fairs: the village fair, where petty articles of food and products of the local handicrafts are sold, generally by barter; and secondly, the religious fair, in which a visit to a place of pilgrimage is combined with a considerable trade in all kinds of merchandise, cattle, etc.

The most primitive form of Indian trade is that which has been called Dumb Barter. It consists in the seller laying down his goods in a fixed place and then hiding in the vicinity. The purchaser appears, places what he considers an equivalent beside the wares exposed, and then in turn disappears. If the offer be accepted the bargain is made; if not, one party adds to his pile of goods until an agreement is reached. According to Albirúni this was one of the ways in which the early trade in cloves was conducted in South India; and we have accounts in the old travellers of the same custom among the Veddahs of Ceylon and the Poliyas of Malabar. Quite recently the

Rája of Bastar, in the Central Provinces, used to collect his tribute from the Gonds. An officer on his behalf visited their domain yearly, beat a drum and hid himself in the neighbourhood, whereupon the Gonds used to bring out what they had to give and deposit it at an appointed spot.

It is easy to understand how this mode of trade developed into the village or tribal fair, which was held on the boundary of two tribal areas, and this spot, as Sir H. Maine shows, became a neutral meeting-ground of the people of both regions. A place like this, where the people were safe from the danger of sudden attack, would come to be regarded as specially under the protection of the local deity. A shrine would be erected to him, and the beginnings of a common worship created. The village fair would thus be the first attempt to encourage the union of hostile tribes, and would pave the way towards the establishment of a place of national worship. As social life progressed a special mercantile class came into existence, the Vaisyas of the caste system. But in the early stages of the growth of the Indian village they were not admitted to membership of the community. They did not live within the village site, but on its outskirts, and beyond them rose the flimsy huts which sheltered the outcast serfs who ministered to the wants of the land-owners.

The village mart still shows a close affinity to this, the oldest form of fair. It is held outside the village site, generally at the boundary of two or more villages; there is no market-house, all the business being done in the open air. Very little money passes, pots and pans, country-made cloth, glass bangles, and other trumpery being exchanged for grain and vegetables. The Garos of Assam, a very primitive tribe, use no coin at their fairs, the small change consisting of little bundles of cotton. As in all such modes of traffic, "every bargain is a battle," and the din and confusion are so great that it is impossible to watch any single transaction. It is in the frontier fairs that the difference between the Hindu merchant and his jungle customer appears most clearly. The latter quivers with excitement at the strange goods exposed for sale, and is all eager to negotiate. The tradesman knows the ways of his constituents. To their eagerness he opposes a chilly indifference, pushes aside the forest man's gum or dyes or simples with contempt, and it is only at the close of the fair that he gracefully exchanges his trumpery wares at four times the proper price.

In the great medieval fairs of Europe it has been supposed that trade was an offshoot or development of the cult of the local Saint. But sometimes the Church utilised to its advantage already existing assemblages for trade. In India, as we have seen, trade often opened the way to worship; but in some cases the process was reversed, religion first occupying a site marked out by some natural feature which suggested sanctity, and trade following in its wake. At any rate the fair at present equally serves both purposes. It is hardly an exaggeration when General Sleeman states that during the bathing season at the opening of the cold weather the greater part of the Hindu population, from the Himálayan slopes to Cape Comorin will be found assembled at these fairs. Every twelfth year the planet Jupiter is in the sign of Aquarius, and then enormous gatherings of pilgrims collect to bathe at the more sacred sites along the banks of the holy rivers, such as Hardwár, Alláhábád, and Sonpur on the Ganges, and Mathura and Batesar on the Jumna. The great rivers being unsectarian, these fairs are attended by all classes of Hindus. It is the one holiday for the women-folk, and it is a pleasant sight to watch whole families jolted along in clumsy bullock-carts, or trudging through the dust, all animated with the hope of washing away their sins in the holy water; or when the bathing is over, to observe the happy girls haggling for cheap trinkets or picnicking by the river-side. A more serious side of such gatherings is the epidemic disease which originates from them, and it needs all the energy of the authorities to guard against the dangers which arise from these enormous crowds. Crime at such places is quite trivial, while the patience of the people in the face of much toil and discomfort, and their orderly conduct, are admirable.

Each religion has its own fair. While the Hindu resorts to places like Hardwár, Benares, or Ságar Island, the Sikh visits the holy places of his faith, Amritsar, Siálkot, Anandpur; the Musalmán visits the shrines of Saints, like that of Pákpattan in the Panjáb, where, if he can crush through a narrow door at the holy time, he believes that his salvation is assured. Of a grosser type are the fairs in honour of Káli Devi, the grim goddess of destruction, at whose shrines, like those of Devi Pátan and Bindháchal in North India, her altar reeks with the blood of countless victims.

In most of these fairs trade is a very important element. Batesar on the Jumna is one of the great horse fairs, as Sonpur in Behár is renowned for elephants and cattle. Here dealers and remount agents attend from all parts of the country, and haggle and bargain with farmers, or gangs of Kábuli or Central Asian merchants. Equally important are fairs, like Bagesar and Pálampur to the west, and Sadiya to the east, which have been started to attract the shy mountaineers of the Himálaya or Tibet, and to bring them into communication with the merchants of the Plains. On the other hand, to the rude hillman the fair has dangers of its own. Captain Harcourt states that in Kulu, one of the Panjáb hill districts, the fairs are much too frequent and most hurtful to the well-being and moral tone of the people, leading to drunkenness and debauchery.

More romantic than these were the fairs in the Moghul Seraglio, the favourite amusement of Akbar and Sháh Jahán, the account of which supplies Bernier for the materials of one of his most effective pictures. It must have been a pretty sight to see the fairest ladies of the Court selling

"beautiful brocades, rich embroideries of the newest fashion, turbans elegantly worked on cloth of gold, fine muslins worn by women of quality, and other articles of high price." "If any Omrah's wife," he slyly tells us, "happen to have a handsome daughter, she never fails to accompany her mother, that she may be seen by the King and become known to the Begums." The stall-holder, if the King offers too low a price for her wares, "fearlessly tells him he is a worthless trader, a person ignorant of the value of merchandise; that her articles are too good for him, and that he had better go where he can suit himself better."

Needless to say sports like these offended the sour-faced Puritans of the Court, like Budáoni, who described them as "another blow at the honour of our religion."

FAKÍR.—This is a term very loosely and inaccurately used by Europeans to describe various classes of mendicants and ascetics, who have no connection with one another. They may be divided into two great classes: the religious Orders, and a miscellaneous group containing some respectable people, but most of them little short of impostors and sturdy rogues.

The ascetic Orders may be compared to the Franciscans of the Christian Church. Many of these are excellent men, some of whom live peaceful lives in monasteries and shrines, entertaining travellers, educating neophytes, and exercising a wholesome influence upon the people around them. Some adopt a wandering life, make periodical visits to their disciples in the capacity of Gurus, and, as has been explained in connection with Bráhmans, exercising the only influence in support of morality which Hinduism provides. Some are celibates, and some family men. The institution is a very ancient one, the early Hindu rule, which was followed by the Buddhists, providing that each "twice-born" man should, as a recognised part of his career in this world, retire to the woods and adopt the life of an ascetic. Buddhism, with its Church largely under the influence of monks of the Order, gave a decided impulse to the growth of monasticism, and there seems little doubt that on its downfall many of its monks became absorbed in some of the numerous Orders which then took their rise, while much of their subsequent development proceeded on Buddhist lines.

Besides this respectable body of ascetics there are hosts of wandering rogues who infest the country. These make no real pretence to leading a religious life, and practise all sorts of trickery upon the simple-minded rustics with whom they come in contact. It is practically impossible to discover from the Census returns the numbers of these two classes, or indeed of the persons classed under the general head of Fakír. Out of the 5,000,000 beggars in India 700,000 are religious mendicants or inmates of monasteries, but the wandering Friars, if they may be so designated, must be far more numerous.

A large body of these disreputable Friars is known by the name of Jogi, and forms a very miscellaneous class. Some practise extreme austerities; others lay claim to miraculous powers, asserting that by abstinence and abstract devotion they acquire Yoga, or union with the Divinity. An old Arabic story describes how they used to prolong life by means of the elixir of immortality, a mixture of sulphur and mercury, and Marco Polo asserts that they lived as long as two hundred years. Fortunately the prescription by which they attained this longevity has been lost. In Bengal they claim Bráhmanical origin, but opposed to this is the fact that they and other religious sects in Northern India freely admit outsiders to their brotherhood. Mr Gait suggests that they may have been originally Buddhists, and that their present degraded condition is due to their having retained that faith after the mass of the people had reverted to Hinduism. They still call their priests by names which were used by Buddhists; and bury their dead with the legs crossed in the conventional attitude of Buddha, and with the face turned to the north-west. Many of them have now adopted the trade of weaving, which was often resorted to by decayed religious communities. Even in the Panjáb at the present day, the connection between weaving and religion is shown in the fact that in some Musalmán tribes the same persons perform indifferently the function of the weaver and of the Mullah or priest, and the leaders of some of the modern reforming sects in Northern India followed the same trade.

Among those Fakírs, who, as studies of the combination of dirt with sanctity, are well worth the attention of the artist, the most remarkable are the loathsome Aghoris, who are happily extinct in the more frequented parts, and now appear only in the darker corners of the land. They preserve the ancient cannibal ritual of the followers of Siva or of the Mother-goddess, eat all kinds of filth, and carry about a human skull as a drinking-cup. These abominable habits they represent to be merely the practical expression of the Saiva belief that the whole universe is co-extensive with Bráhma, and consequently that one thing is as pure as another.

As has already been suggested in connection with dress, the nudity of the ascetic orders is a survival of primitive belief. Under our rule the habit has ceased, and all Fakírs wear, or are supposed to wear, some pretence to clothing. Another of their habits is smearing themselves with ashes, which they themselves believe to be connected with fire-worship. Dr Frazer has suggested that the smearing with clay or ashes may indicate that by a new birth they have changed colour.

Another fact in the development of the monastic Orders is the readiness with which they form new sections based on some trifling modification in current belief or custom, or a new body is recruited under the leadership of some one eminent for piety, or believed to possess miraculous powers. The most curious development of this idea is seen in the so-called Nikalseni Order, who professed to have as their Guru the famous General Nicholson. They have now disappeared from the Census returns, and Nicholson, so far from encouraging them, is said to have flogged any he could arrest. The fact seems to be that their veneration for him was really a pretence. Our Government, after the fall of the Sikh power, continued the practice of the former rulers, and conferred small grants of land on the religious Orders. The Nikalsenis seem to have thought that by adopting as their Guru a powerful official like Nicholson they would have a better chance of receiving a share of the bounty.

Many Fakírs have pretended to possess the power

of remaining completely buried underground for a considerable time without detriment. Cases of this kind have been reported from the Panjáb by travellers like Dr Honigberger, Lieutenant Boileau, and Captain Osborne. Some of these are obviously impostures, some, as in a case reported from Bengal in 1868, the acts of ignorant fanatics. Others, again, like that of a Guru at Dehra Dún, are possibly cases of hypnotic trance. This man is said to have possessed the power of dying at will, and returning to life after a concerted interval. In the end he mistook his reckoning, was not awaked at the proper time, and never revived.

Never has the influence of the so-called Musalmán Saints over an ignorant people been better described than by Sir H. Edwardes at Bannu on the North-west Frontier. To the people of that district

"blood was simply a red fluid; and to remove a neighbour's head at the shoulders, as easy as cutting cucumbers. But to be cursed in Arabic, or anything that sounded like it; to be told that the blessed Prophet had a black mark against his soul, for not giving his best field to one of the Prophet's own posterity; to have the saliva of a disappointed Saint left in anger at his door-post; or to behold a Hájee, who had gone three times to Mecca, deliberately sit down and enchant his camels with the itch and his sheep with the rot; these were things which made the dagger drop out of the hand of the awe-stricken savage, his liver to turn to water, and his parched tongue to be scarcely able to articulate a full and complete concession of the blasphemous demand."

The wandering friar extorts alms in many ways by practising on the superstitious beliefs of the villager. His methods now are much the same as those described in Gujarát by Barbosa:

"The Moors who beg for alms . . . take great stones and strike themselves with them on the shoulders, and the breast, and on their stomachs, as if they were going to kill themselves with them, and they receive alms not to do it, and go away in peace. And others bring knives and stab themselves in the arms and legs before them, in order to extort alms; and others come to the door to decapitate rats and snakes and other reptiles, and they give them money not to do it."

The Fakírs of whom he speaks were Musalmáns, and though the Prophet said, "Let there be no monkery in Islám," they have established numerous fraternities and Orders of Dervishes, partly formed under Turanian influence, partly in imitation of the Hindu and Buddhist Orders.

The tortures inflicted on themselves by Fakírs have been described by many observers. Bernier writes:

"I have seen several who hold one, and some who hold both arms, perpetually lifted above the head; the nails of their hands being twisted, and longer than half my little finger, with which I measured them. Their arms are as small and thin as the arms of persons who die in a decline, because in so forced and unnatural a position they receive not sufficient nourishment; nor can they be lowered so as to supply the mouth with food, the muscles having become contracted, and the articulations dry and stiff."

Fryer gives a similar account, and speaks of a Hindu Fakír "enjoined for Forty days to endure the Purgatory of five Fires." Colebrooke tells of a Musalmán Fakír who demanded a horse and a thousand rupees from a merchant, and stood for a fortnight before the man's door, on one leg, and resting his arms on a crossed bamboo. "Finding no prospect of succeeding, he departed when tired of his posture." This is a form of the coercion known as "Sitting *Dhurna*,"* which has always been common in India. Tavernier tells of a Fakír who dragged an iron chain, 2 cubits long and thick in proportion, and pretended to be able to cure barrenness. A man dragging an enormous chain loaded with masses of iron recently travelled all over Northern India by rail.

Many rogues of this kind still infest the rural districts, and we sometimes see at places of pilgrimage men with distorted limbs, or one lying on the "arrowy bed," a couch covered with nails, in imitation of Bhíshma, one of the heroes of the Mahábhárata. Asceticism will ever be the refuge of the weaker minds impressed by the earnestness which such tortures and macerations are believed to inspire. But increasing good sense and the influence of British law are gradually tending to the discontinuance of austerities such as these. They are practised by only a small minority of the begging fraternity, and the comfortable sleekness of the majority shows that they are not common in our time.

[Oman, "The Mystics, Ascetics, and Saints of India"; "Census Report," India, 1891, i. 206; Bengal, 1901, i. 381; Panjáb, 1891, i. chap. iv.]

FALCONRY.—The royal sport of India dates from a remote antiquity. Representations of it are found on the sculptures of Khorsabad, near Nineveh, and Ctesias speaks of it in India. Central Asia was perhaps the scene of its origin, but it is remarkable that Indian forest tribes, like the Bedars of Sholapur, the Hos and Mundas of Chota Nágpur practise the sport, and it may have arisen independently among them. As for Central Asia, Marco Polo tells of the Great Kaan going out with ten thousand falconers, "and some five hundred gerfalcons, besides peregrines, sakers, and other hawks in great numbers; and goshawks also to fly at the water-fowl." Thence perhaps the taste spread to the Indian Musalmáns. The Emperor Tughlak Sháh had ten thousand falconers, and three thousand men to beat up the game. When Humáyun retreated to Persia, the Sháh ordered that he was to be provided with gerfalcons, sakers, sparrow-hawks, royal falcons, and peregrines. Akbar was a great lover of the sport. Abul Fazl, in his usual style, writes:

> "His Majesty, from motives of generosity and from a wish to add splendour to his Court, is fond of hunting with falcons, though superficial observers think that merely hunting is his object,"

and he gives full details of his staff of falconers and of the varieties of his birds. It is still a favourite sport in the Panjáb and Sind, where Sir R. Burton has well described it.

The birds used fall into two great classes: long-winged

falcons, like the peregrine, and short-winged hawks, the former preferred in Europe, the latter in India, where the principal varieties are the Jarra or Sháhbáz, "Hawk-king," or goshawk; the Bahri and Shahín, or peregrine falcon; the Lagar and Jagar, the hobby; the Básha and Báshin, a sparrow-hawk; the Shikra of the goshawk genus; and the Besra, a true sparrow-hawk. Where a double term is used it marks the sexes.

General Mundy, who loved the sport, gives a good account of it:

"With the long-winged, soaring bheiree [*bahri*] we had a best-speed gallop of five miles after a black curlew, a bird giving flights almost equal to the heron, and the bhauses [*báz*] or short-winged, killed for us a couple of wild geese, some teal, and several partridges. This latter species of hawk does not soar, but darts from the wrist with the speed of lightning, and seldom fails to strike its quarry within two hundred yards, generally in a much smaller distance. Another kind of falcon is a small bird, perhaps barely so large as a thrush, and its prey is proportioned to its strength. It is flown at quails, sparrows, and others of the feathered tribe of the same calibre. The mode of starting it is different from that of any other hawk. The falconer holds the little well-drilled savage within the grasp of his hand, the head and tail protruding at either opening, and the plumage carefully smoothed down. When he arrives within twenty or thirty yards of the quarry, the sportsman throws his hawk much as he would do a cricket ball in the direction of it. The little creature gains his wings in an instant, and strikes the game after the manner of the bhause [*báz*]."

The Lugger [*Lagar*], he goes on to say, when flown at a hare, has not strength to stop it by one swoop, but he and his confederate alternately swoop and strike her, and she soon becomes exhausted. The blow inflicted by the heel talon is very severe, scoring the flesh, and stripping off the fur.

Indian hawks are obtained either young from the aery, or captured in a snare composed of running loops of strong gut, fastened to bamboo pins firmly planted in the ground. In the centre, as live bait, a pigeon is secured with a string round its leg, which the falconer concealed close by pulls occasionally to make her rise and attract the hawk. When captured the hawk is "seeled": that is to say her eyelids are sewn together with fine silk in order to tame her, and she is thus gradually broken to the hood, the hole in which is every day enlarged, and her food increased, until she finally becomes docile. Her chief enemy is the vulture, which often swoops down upon her from a higher altitude as she seizes her prey. A well-trained falcon will not strike a bird when flying over water, as she understands the danger of being drowned with her victim. Many will agree with General Sleeman: "Hawking is a very dull and very cruel sport. A person must be insensible to the sufferings of the most beautiful and most inoffensive of the brute creation before he can feel any enjoyment in it. The cruelty lies chiefly in the mode of feeding the hawks," on living animals or birds.

In the few places where it is still pursued in Northern India it is the sport of Musalmáns. Hindus very properly dislike it for humanitarian reasons, and the more extended use of better guns and rifles will probably tend to make it less popular.

"I strongly suspect," says Mr L. Kipling, "the best of the business is the riding and the company. Any one in the habit of looking at birds in India may see free hawking enough: the shrike, which in a town garden brings down a sparrow nearly as large as himself, the gallant and tigerish sparrow-hawk, and on far hill-sides falcons of two or three kinds."

A meaner creature is the common kite, who harries the cook's fowls, and swoops down on a dish of mutton chops on its way to the table.

[Burton, "Falconry in the Valley of the Indus"; "Calcutta Review," xxviii. 151; cvi. 184.]

FAMINE.—Famine in India is the result of the meteorological conditions which prevail in the Peninsula, and there seems no reason to believe that these conditions have in the modern period undergone such a radical change as to increase the risk of this terrible visitation. The records which we possess of the famines which occurred before our time are not precise enough to afford a satisfactory basis for investigation. Megasthenes, it is true, says that in Magadha, or modern Behár, famine was unknown owing to the successful use of irrigation; but the Buddhist books contain numerous references to famines in that part of the country. In Káthiáwár, a region specially liable to failure of the monsoon, we have before the British occupation about 1820 records, dating from the middle of the sixteenth century, of no less than twenty-three years of drought or famine. On one occasion (1631-32) we read harrowing accounts of dog's flesh sold as mutton, bones ground for flour, and of cannibalism. This is generally supposed to have been the worst famine that ever visited India. Again, in 1747 the people were reduced to eating wild plants and cattle. In the Deccan also we have records of about twenty-five famines in five hundred years, beginning with the terrible Durga-devi of 1397-1408, which devastated Southern India. The early years of our rule in Bengal were marked by the awful famine of 1769-70, in which the province lost one-third of its people, and one-third of its area became waste. In 1778 Burma, a region generally immune from disasters of this kind, was the scene of a terrible scarcity, in which the people kept themselves alive only by eating their half-starved cattle, and it is said that even human flesh was consumed. Between 1780 and 1783 the Carnatic was devastated by a terrible famine, largely due to the ravages of Hyder Ali's army, a disaster which was immortalised by Burke. Similarly in the Upper Provinces terrible suffering was the result of the famine of 1838. In more recent times Orissa in 1866, Madras in 1876-78, and finally Western India during the 1891-99 period, have suffered severely. Mr Risley estimates the total loss of life from famine and plague during this last visitation as not less than 5,000,000, and this is probably a moderate calculation, because, between 1892 and 1901 in British territory in Western India, official reports state that 2,500,000 perished, while 2,000,000 died in the Native States under the Bombay Government.

It must be remembered that in Indian famines the most severe mortality is due not to actual starvation, but to diseases such as dysentery produced by unsuitable diet, and to epidemics like cholera breaking out among the crowds of debilitated labourers collected on relief works, who are too ignorant to submit to sanitary regulations. Besides these there are numbers of people of a better class who will starve rather than degrade themselves by appearing on public relief works, just as persons of the same class in England refuse the hospitality of the workhouse. The problem of providing for people of this kind, and in particular for women accustomed to a life of seclusion, is one of the most serious with which an Indian famine official is required to deal.

Sir John Elliot has recently given a full account of the meteorological conditions which produce these calamities. Severe droughts and famines occur at irregular intervals, and a noteworthy feature is that they frequently follow in pairs, separated by intervals of from two to four years. They result either from a general weakness of the south-east trade winds, diversion of an unusually large proportion of this current to South-east or East Africa, a larger diversion than usual of the monsoon to Burma or Abyssinia, or, lastly, to very unequal local distribution in India itself, due to local causes established during the antecedent hot weather. The meteorology of the period 1892-1902, corresponding as it did in length to a sun-spot period, is of especial interest as confirming these inferences. The influence extended beyond India, as is shown by the droughts which prevailed in Australia from 1896 to 1902, in the Karoo region of South Africa, and in the Nile valley. "The examination of the whole of the facts emphasised the necessity for the co-ordination and systematisation of the work of observation in the Indo-Oceanic meteorological province."

Beside the Carnatic famine already mentioned only one great scarcity has been attributed to any cause but drought. This occurred about 1345, when that madman, Muhammad Tughlak, by cruelty and misgovernment, and his wild schemes for the conquest of China, reduced the land to a state of desolation. But even in this case the ruin was aggravated by seasons of insufficient rainfall.

A curious point illustrated by recent famines is that women suffer less than men in these calamities. Some have suspected that this is due to the facility with which women cooks can pilfer food. But this does not seem to account for all the facts. Experience appears to show that, for reasons as yet imperfectly understood, women in India are constitutionally stronger than men, and are less liable to succumb to the effects of insufficient or unsuitable food, and the diseases which accompany such a condition of life.

A remarkable accompaniment ot Indian famines, particularly in Western India, is the Rat Plague. Various species of Muridæ have from time to time caused enormous damage to crops during seasons of drought. The same result has followed the incursions of the field-vole in Europe. In some cases in India the common house rat, deprived of its ordinary sustenance, has migrated to the fields and attacked the standing crops. But the chief damage is done by the Indian Jerboa (*Gerbillus indicus*), the Metad (*Mus mettda*), and the Kok (*Nesocia bengalensis*). In 1814-15 in Káthiáwár Captain Le Grand Jacob thus describes the plague:

> "They appear in dense masses past all counting, as if springing from the earth, about the harvest season. Nothing can stop them—fire, ditches, and water have been tried in vain; they move along, a mighty host, eating up all that comes in the way. All at once they vanish, as if by magic, and for years not one is to be seen. They are about double the size of the common rat, and are of a reddish sandy colour."

When they appeared at Ahmadnagar in 1879, the natives believed them to be the spirits of those who died in the recent famine. Sacrifices were made to the village gods, and Bráhmans were fed. The efforts to destroy them were hardly more successful than the incantations of the priests. Finally, a heavy fall of rain, followed by frost, ended the plague. A similar phenomenon has been noticed on the eastern frontier. Swarms of rats appear from time to time, coming, as the people suppose, from the south, and destroy everything, attacking the house granaries as well as the standing crops. In 1864 an extraordinary belief spread among these jungle tribes that the rats disappeared because they were transformed into jungle-fowl. In proof of this they still point out a peculiar draggled feather in the plumage of the bird, which they say is the tail of a rat.

As causes contributing to famine or scarcity may be mentioned the numerous fungoid pests which produce the diseased conditions known as mildew, mould, rust, or smut. Some of these have been satisfactorily identified; of others, owing to the difficulty of determining their life history, little is known. Of insect pests the name is legion. First come locusts, a term loosely applied to various species of Acrididæ, which occasionally invade India. Many of them lay their eggs in the sandhills of Sind or Rájputána, and the progeny appears in Bengal and the lower Himálaya 1,000 miles to the east. Then come the granary weevil, and various insects, each of which has a special taste for particular crops, fruit, and forest trees, such as the Rice Sapper, the Sorghum Borer, the Red Spider of the tea plant, the Opium Cut-worm, the Cotton Boll-worm, and a myriad others.

["Census Reports," India, Bombay, and the Central Provinces, 1901. For Fungoid and Insect Pests, Watt, "Economic Dictionary," iii. 455; vi. Pt. I. 142.]

FESTIVALS; FASTS.—The most primitive Indian festivals are those based on the idea of sympathetic or mimetic magic. These fall into two main groups: first, those intended by the use of magical rites to promote the fertility of the soil, the fall of rain, the intensity of sunshine, the growth and due harvesting of the crops; secondly, those performed with a view to expel evil and the influence of demons.

We have good examples of the first class in the festivals of the Hos and Santáls. The Hos have seven annual feasts; the first represents the symbolic marriage of the earth, and takes place when the Sál, their sacred tree, is in flower; the second, at the sowing of the rice; the third, when the seed is sprouting; the fourth, when it is being transplanted; the fifth, an offering of first-fruits; the sixth, the clearing of the threshing-floor; the seventh and last, when the granaries are full of grain, and the people give themselves up to riot and debauchery.

Many of the early Hindu festivals probably in the same way were connected with the seasons of agriculture. But the dates of their celebration have been modified under the changing conditions of the lunar calendar; they were appropriated to the service of special gods, and provided with new forms of ritual. But the connection with the primitive ideas on which festivals were established can in some instances still be traced. Thus the opening of the agricultural year is marked by the Uttaráyana or Makara Sankránti, which occurs at the winter solstice, and is now devoted to the worship of the sainted dead, the Lares of the household, and by a further extension to that of the Visva Devas, or universal gods. This is represented by the *Pongol** of South India, when offerings of new rice are made, and, as in the Holi of North India, fires are lit as a magical way of making sunshine. The Nairs of Malabar seem to observe the same feast under the name of Onam, when there is a mock fight of boys armed with toy bows and arrows, the object being to scare the powers of evil.

This is followed by the Vasanta Panchami, or spring feast, and for the next forty days the Rájputs give themselves up to licence, both in word and action, drink intoxicating liquors, and eat stimulating food. Even respectable people roam about the streets like Bacchanals, vociferating songs in praise of the powers of nature. In Kashmír on this occasion every one appears in a costume of yellow, the colour appropriate to the season. This spring feast is specially celebrated by the forest tribes of Assam.

"It is as gay as a carnival," says Colonel Dalton, "and while it lasts, the women, especially the maidens, enjoy unusual liberty. For many days before the actual festival, the young people in the villages may be seen moving about in groups, gaily dressed, or forming circles, in the midst of which the prettiest girls dance with their long hair loose on their shoulders. The first day of the festival is devoted to interchanges of visits, the next to the bathing and worshipping of all the cattle, and on the third day the inhabitants of several groups of villages, old and young, meet at some appointed place, and give themselves up to thorough enjoyment. The girls on these occasions do not like to dance before the men of their own village."

The climax of this feast in North India is the Holi, when bonfires are lit, and the people abandon themselves to rude debauchery. Next comes the Nág-panchami, or "Dragon's Fifth," at which veneration is paid to the great serpent on which the world rests, and which is regarded as influencing the work of ploughing and sowing of the autumn rice harvest then beginning. The autumn harvest rites are similarly represented by the Durga-púja, "the worship of Durga," and the Rám-líla, or "play of Ráma," at the end of the season. The miracle plays then performed are probably survivals of the original mimetic magical ceremonies, which are still carried out at this time by the forest tribes.

The second group of festivals contains those which are intended to symbolise the expulsion of evil influences. This also is in part the motive underlying the agricultural feasts, but we find it to this day undisguised in the village and domestic rites. Thus, at the harvest-home of the Hos Colonel Dalton describes how

"at the time an evil spirit is supposed to infest the place, and to get rid of it men, women, and children go in procession round and through every part of the village with sticks in their hands, as if beating for game, singing a wild chant, and shouting vociferously, till they feel assured that the evil spirit must have fled."

In the Himálaya the rite is performed much in the same way, and is known as "Devil-driving." The well-known Diwáli, or "Feast of Lights," is another form of the same rite. The lights are supposed to scare the evil spirit from the household, and the oldest woman of the family goes outside and beats a winnowing basket or corn-sieve, shouting "God abide! Poverty depart!"

Much a later stage in the development of festal rites is reached when usages such as these are specialised in the service of different gods. Hence arises the bewildering variety of Hindu festivals, each sacred place being the favourite home of one of the deities, Benares of Siva, Mathura of Ḳrishna, and so on, each of which has its own festal calendar in which the varied incidents of the life, or one or other of the powers or attributes of the divinity, are celebrated at a special feast. Thus, the calendar of Brindaban, the birth-place of Krishna, contains forty-six festal days, in some of which the incidents of the life of the god are commemorated, side by side with devotion to other gods and the primitive sun-making magic, the sleeping and awaking of the deities, who are supposed to rest in the period between the summer harvest and the first ploughing after the start of the autumnal rains.

Hence, too, these feasts come by degrees to be appropriated to special classes of the people. Thus, in August is the great Bráhman feast, when the Bráhmans provide magical string amulets, which they tie round the wrists of their constituents in return for gifts, the old magic of cords and knots found all over the world. The Rájputs have appropriated to themselves the Dasahra in October, which partakes of the nature of the Saturnalia, a period of licence, when, as at Satára, the king himself used to parade a buffalo round the town, and slay it at the temple of the guardian goddess, as a scape animal to carry with it the sins of the people. The Feast of Lamps is similarly specialised by the merchant class, who light lamps to scare away ill-luck. But in its more primitive form it is celebrated by the cow-men of Behár, who drive their cattle over a pig, and when the wretched animal is dead, cook and eat it in the fields. Hence, too, it is associated with the cult of the dread goddess Káli, at whose shrine myriads of animals are sacrificed. Lastly, the lowest classes use the Holi bonfire with the same object.

A study of Hindu festivals thus illustrates in an interesting way the process by which the village and domestic rites of mimetic magic have been introduced into Bráhmanism, and under new titles and amidst new surroundings adopted in the service of the newer gods.

It would not be difficult to show that some of the Musalmán feasts, though the original meaning is now disguised by special observances and the dates obscured by the variability of the calendar, are based on the same principle. Thus, Muhammadans have in their feast of Ramazán the exact equivalent of the Christian and Buddhist Lent, followed by an outburst of rejoicing at the Id with which it concludes, the practice of abstinence being, as Mr Frazer has shown, a sympathetic charm to foster the growth of the seed, which is forced into vitality by the mimetic observance of the Saturnalia, which brings the festival to a close. Finally, in the animistic environment of India they have adopted at the shrines of their Saints many of the magical usages which the Hindus prescribe in the service of their village gods.

Fasting is not so prominent a feature of Eastern as of some other faiths. A fortnightly fast is part of the worship of Siva and Vishnu. Many Hindus who revere the sun fast on Sunday, and do not eat at all on cloudy days, when the sun is obscured by clouds. With the Indian Musalmáns, too, the older rule has gradually fallen into disuse, and of the many fasts ordained by the prophet few observe more than the Ramazán [*Ramdam*].* Owing to the fact that their calendar is lunar, this fast gradually moves round the whole circuit of the year. While it occurs in the cold season fasting is not a severe ordeal, but in the hot weather the prohibition against eating, drinking, and smoking from sunrise to sunset is a serious tax on the strength of even robust people.

[For South India, "Census Report," Travancore, 1901, 304, 327; ditto Cochin, 1901, 164; for Kashmír, Lawrence, "Valley of Kashmír," 264; for the Deccan, "Calcutta Review," cxiii. 264; for North India, Growse, "Mathura," 267.]

FEVER.—Of all the diseases which menace the health of Europeans in India, fever, either in the typhoid or malarial form, is far the most deadly. Typhoid produced by the special *Bacillus typhosis* is primarily disseminated by polluted soil, the contagion being communicated through dust and flies, infected food and drink, especially milk and water. It seems not to be directly infectious, but secondary infection, either direct or indirect, appears to occur in some epidemics. It is particularly a disease of early life, and though in some cases protective inoculation seems to have been successful, the evidence that it is a real prophylactic is at present insufficient. Under the influence of this disease some of the finest Indian cantonments have become veritable death-traps to the young European soldier.

Malarial fever, due to the attacks of the *Anopheles* genus of mosquito, appears in many forms. The ordinary symptoms have been well described by Sir R. Burton:

> "Fevers, I may inform you, in this part of Asia are of two kinds. One is a brisk, bold fellow, who does his work within the day, permitting you to breakfast, but placing his veto upon your dining; the other is a slow, sneaking wretch, who bungles over you for a week or a fortnight. The former appears as a kind of small shivering first; then as a sick headache, which, after a few minutes, feels as if a cord were being tightened round your pericranium; your brain burns as if it were on fire; your head throbs as though it would burst; your skin is hot, and hard as a driving glove. Presently your senses leave you; to delirium succeeds congestion; you pant and puff, all your energies being applied to keeping the breath in your body. You fail therein, and are buried that evening. The slow form attacks you much in the same way; only it imprudently allows you leisure to send for a doctor, who pours cold water from an altitude on your shaven poll, administers mercury sufficient to stock an average-sized thermometer, blisters you, generally with mustard and other plasters, from the nape of your neck down to the soles of your feet."

This was in the prehistoric ages of pathology. Now the doctor prescribes quinine, and directs that the stagnant pools near the house be dosed with kerosine oil to destroy the *Anopheles*.

A peculiarly dangerous form of this disease is the Kála Azar, or "Black Sickness," which was first recognised among the Garos of the Assam frontier in 1869, and gradually spread into the lowlands, where, as Mr Risley writes:

> "Its track is marked by deserted villages, untilled fields, a land revenue reduced by 23 per cent., and a disheartened population which, after nineteen years of steady increase, has now receded to the figure at which it stood nearly thirty years ago."

The origin of this disease has recently been traced to a parasite called the *Trypanosome*, which in Central Africa causes the "Sleeping Sickness." It was found in numbers in mud fish taken from ponds in the neighbourhood of infected villages.

Another form of the disease, known as Dumdum or Bardwán fever, seems to have a like origin. It was first noticed in Jessore about 1837, where it continued till 1843, and then seemed to disappear. But it came again in 1863, and lasted twelve years. It gradually worked its way from east to west, reaching the United Provinces in 1887, and the Panjáb in 1891-92. In the twelve years' epidemic in Bengal and the Ganges valley it killed more than 2,000,000 people. Accurate diagnosis of disease is, of course, not to be expected from the village watchman who furnishes the statistics, and is prone to class all diseases of the inflammatory kind as "fever." Even allowing for these, fever is by far the most dangerous ailment of the peasant. In the period 1891-1901 nearly 12,000,000 deaths were attributed to fever in the United Provinces; in the same period two-thirds of the total mortality in the Panjáb were assigned to this cause.

Compared with this terrible fever mortality the death-roll from cholera or plague sinks into insignificance. The Indian village, utterly destitute of drainage, inhabited by a people ignorant of the most elementary principles of sanitation, deriving its water supply from shallow, unprotected wells and foul tanks used indiscriminately for drinking and ablution, is a hot-bed for the germs of zymotic disease. And when, in addition, we have a race many of whom are habitually under-fed and exposed to periodical drought and famine, the terrible mortality disclosed by the official statistics is easily accounted for.

In India, as elsewhere, nature vigorously resents any interference with her operations. The crying need of the country is irrigation, but in parts of Northern India this boon has been obtained only at the expense of an increase of malaria. Unless side by side with canals an extensive drainage system be provided, the remedy is often worse than the disease. No sight in rural life is more touching than to visit malaria-stricken villages at the close of the annual rains, to find the fields unploughed and unsown, because practically the whole adult population has been incapacitated by fever. As the day goes on, lines of sickly wretches, insufficiently fed and clad, sit shivering in the sunniest spot they can find.

The problem of alleviating these evils is almost beyond the power of the State to solve. Some little relief it can and does supply by rural dispensaries, the free distribution of quinine, and its sale in penny packets at every post-office. In an epidemic the native is apathetic; he regards illness as an inevitable evil to be alleviated only by prayer, charms, and sacrifices. He is quite insensible to the lessons of sanitary science, and resents any effort to enforce rules of health and cleanliness. The population is so immense that village sanitation can be carried out only by the agency of venal native subordinates who are beyond the control of the small, overworked staff of Europeans. While these conditions last the prospects of checking this terrible mortality are not hopeful.

[For the Bengal Fever, "Census Report," Bengal, 1881, i. 57ff.; 1891, i. 112ff.; for Kála Azar, ditto Assam, 1901, i. 19; India, 1901, i. 47.]

FIRE-WORSHIP.—Fire-worship among the early Aryans included not only that of actual fire on earth, but of its manifestations in heaven, the lightning and the sun. It is more than probable that the same respect for fire, produced in a mystic way either by friction or from the rays of the sun, was shared by the races whom they found in occupation of the land. But these people seem never to have advanced to the higher generalisation that fire was the manifestation of a fire-god, as the Hindus did in the case of Agni. It was worshipped, on the one hand, because it was a powerful means of purification, especially for the expulsion of demons; and, secondly, most of the fire festivals were probably mimetic charms to secure a due supply of sunshine for the crops.

But while the Aryan occupation was one chief factor in the growth of this cult, it seems to have reached India by other sources direct from Irán. On the Indo-Scythian coins we find the king represented as worshipping at a fire-altar, and in the works of the early Muhammadan historians there is evidence of the existence of fire-worshipping tribes in the Panjáb as late as Timúr's invasion at the end of the fourteenth century. Meanwhile, with the arrival of the Pársis on the West Coast the cult was again established. It was probably from them that it was adopted by Akbar, who employed a Pársi priest and had a fire-temple in his palace. A curious print in the *Aín-i-Akbari* represents him worshipping fire with twelve candles before him, while a singer chants the ritual. He especially worshipped the sun on New Year's Day, and ordered his courtiers to rise when the palace lamps were lighted.

Probably the oldest sacred fires in the world are those of the Pársis at Yezd and Kirmán. From thence, they say, the seed of it was brought to India, not, as they strongly assert, being an object of worship, but as a symbol of divinity, and nothing more. In establishing a fire-temple great efforts are made to obtain fire produced by lightning. A tree fired in this way was found by a Pársi near Calcutta some years ago; and from it fire was carefully conveyed to Bombay. Over the fire thus obtained is held a perforated metal tray in which are chips and dust of sandalwood. Thus a new fire is created, and this process is repeated nine times, when the fire is finally pronounced to be pure. Akbar used to make his sacred fire by exposing a piece of cotton to the sun's rays passing through a crystal lens. It was thus made annually, and all the fires of the household were lighted from it.

Among the Hindus the cult of the sacred fire is specialised by a class of Bráhmans known as Agnihotri. The fire for special sacrifices must be made with the Arani, or fire-drill, constructed from the wood of sacred trees. The sparks fall into a pit in which the fire is received on the dust of holy wood. The Rájput legend asserts that the tribes had their origin from a fire-pit of this kind.

In many places in India the sacred fire is carefully preserved. Hindu pilgrims with infinite difficulty find their way to Baku, near the Caspian, where fire issues from the petroleum beds. Juálamukhi [*Jowaulla Mookhee* *] on the lower slope of the Himálaya, where jets of combustible gas issue from the earth, is one of the very oldest sacred places. At two of the great Nepál temples the fire is guarded by special priests. Even the Musalmáns, apparently in imitation of the Hindus, have adopted the cult, and maintain their own sacred fire. It is found even among the indigenous races. At the devil dances of the Mishmis of Assam the lights are all extinguished, and then relighted by a spark from a flint, which is struck by a man suspended from the roof of the house. He must not touch the ground, as the light thus obtained is supposed to come direct from heaven. In the same way among the Nágas when they remove from a village under tabu, all fires are put out, and new fire is obtained by friction, from which the torches are lit to fire the jungle for their rude mode of farming. On the Sabbath of the Káfirs of the Hindu-kush the headman lights a sacred fire in honour of the god Imra.

All the forest tribes understand the art of making fire by friction. This is done either by revolving a pointed stick in a hollow cut in a flat piece of wood, or by rubbing one stick against another in a saw-like motion. It is very remarkable that the Andamanese have never acquired the art; the Nicobarese, on the other hand, have learned to make fire, and insist that the fire intended for ceremonial purposes must be made in this way. It is only among the Indo-Chinese races of Burma, like the Kakyens, that the piston and cylinder is employed.

The custom known as fire-walking has attracted much

attention from anthropologists; but though it has been witnessed by many observers, it is still difficult to account for the facts. Buchanan-Hamilton thus describes the rite at Mangalore:

"Women who suppose that the goddess has inflicted on them barrenness or other great infirmity, vow to walk barefooted on red-hot coals before the temple. If the goddess hears their prayers, she prevents the coals from burning their feet. My informants impudently assert that the ceremony is frequently performed. A quantity of red-hot coals are spread before the temple, and the woman, after having fasted a whole day, walks three times slowly with bare feet over the coals."

There are numerous accounts of devotees walking barefoot along a pit filled with hot charcoal in pursuance of vows made to the village goddesses of South India. In some cases the priest is said to pour red-hot embers on the hair of women who escape unhurt. In Gujarát the rite is performed by the village sweeper and headman at a famous Bhíl temple, and by the Dosádhs, a menial tribe of Bengal and the United Provinces, at the annual worship of their god Ráhu, who is supposed to cause eclipses. A somewhat similar custom prevails in North India, of Hindus walking through the Holi fire, and Musalmáns over that burnt in honour of their Saint Madár. Some have supposed that the performance is a mere trick, the pit being so narrow that the fire-walker treads on the sides of it, not on the burning coals; others, that the ashes formed over the burning charcoal saves his feet from injury; others, that some protective is applied to the feet; others, again, that hypnotic phenomena are at the root of the matter. The accounts of the custom collected from various parts of the world do not help us much to ascertain the meaning of the custom.

Among modern Hindus the chief fire rite is the Homa, or fire-sacrifice. The fuel must consist of wood from holy trees, and the pieces must not be crooked, broken, or decayed. In the more important rites the fire is obtained fresh by friction, and the offerings of each god are thrown into the fire, while the priest recites the appropriate formula. At meals the rite may be done in a less formal way by throwing a portion of rice and butter into a little copper or earthen vessel, the officiant all the time repeating the names of the gods. In Nepál, under the influence of the foul Tantrik cult, in one form of the Homa the offering is not rice, flowers, and butter, but flesh, which apparently was once that of a human being. Sometimes the rite is indefinitely prolonged. At the inauguration of a temple by Jang Bahádur it is said to have been done a million times.

The sacred fire enters also into domestic rites of the Hindus. At marriage the fire is solemnly lighted by a priest, and the bride and bridegroom are made to step seven times round it. This is the binding part of the rite.

[For the Sacred Fire, see J. C. Nesfield, "Calcutta Review," lxviii. i.ff.; 360ff.; for Fire-Walking, A. Lang, "Modern Mythology," 148ff.; Crooke, "Popular Religion and Folk-lore of North India," ii. 317; Oppert, "Original Inhabitants," 98ff. 480; for the Pársi Fire, "Bombay Gazetteer," ix. Pt. II. 213ff.]

FISH, SACRED.—Though fish are freely caught and eaten by many castes in India, there is still a good deal of sanctity attached to them. First, they are regarded as one of the creatures into which the soul of the dead migrates after death; secondly, they are considered to be an emblem of fertility and good luck.

The traveller Fra Paolino describes how in 1780 the Rája of Travancore, after the death of his mother, implored the English commander at Anjengo to issue an order that no one was to fish in the sea for three days, lest the fish that had received his mother's soul might be caught. For many years a great carp in the Jhílam at Srinagar was well known to be the late Mahárája of Kashmír, and at Mandi in the Himálaya, according to Mr Gore,

> "standing on the iron Victoria Jubilee Bridge, you can gaze into the deep green pool below and see the great Máhasír swimming lazily along which bears the soul of the Rája's late lamented grandfather in his capacious bosom."

A week after a death the Gonds perform the rite of

bringing back the soul of the deceased. They go to the riverside, call out the name of the dead man, catch a fish, and bring it home. In some cases they eat it in the belief that by so doing the deceased will be born again as a child in the family.

The fish as a symbol of fertility has an important part in the marriage rites. The Bráhmans of Kanara take the married pair to a pond and make them throw rice into the water and catch a few minnows. They let all go, save one, with whose scales they mark their brows. If there be no pond near, the rite is done by making a fish of wheat flour, dropping it into a vessel of water, taking it out and marking their foreheads with the paste. The Emperor Jahángír, before undertaking a journey, used to have a huge carp brought into his presence, followed by a dish of starch, into which he plunged his fingers and rubbed them between the eyes of the fish and then on his own forehead. He probably got the idea from the Kashmíri ladies of his harem; at any rate, Mr Val Prinsep describes the Mahárája of Kashmír doing exactly the same rite a few years ago.

The reverence for fish naturally grew under Buddhist teaching, and has passed with its principles into the rules of the modern Vaishnava sects. Krishna, for instance, has his sacred fish at Kotah; Zálim Singh, when Colonel Tod wished to fish there, wrote to him: "Kotah and all around are at his disposal; but these fish belong to Krishna." Along the banks of the Ganges and Jumna fish are carefully preserved at places like Hardwár, Mathura, and Benares, and attempts made by Europeans to catch them have sometimes led to frantic excitement among the Bráhmans. In some places, as at a pool in Kanara, the fish have gold rings fixed in their fins, and are specially sacred. The fish in a tank at Kolába, the people say, can never be destroyed; an Englishman once tried to catch them, but he failed, got sick, and died. One of the most remarkable exhibitions of sacred fish is in a pond at a shrine near Khatmandu, in Nepál, where the ever marvellous transparency of the water allows an exceptionally clear view of its revered inhabitants. The Buddhists on the Irawadi honour their sacred fish in a curious way The creatures are so tame that they allow themselves to be caught, and pilgrims stick gold-leaf on their heads as they do on the images in their pagodas. But the famous fish at the Thikadaw Pagoda are now neglected, and have grown wild and timid.

FOLK-TALES.—Much energy has been displayed in recent years in collecting Indian folk-tales. Story-telling flourishes among the Hindus, as it does among all the unlettered people of the East, who have nothing in the way of popular literature. Muhammadans who have any literary taste enjoy the "Arabian Nights" in the original, or more usually in Persian translations, and town book-stalls are full of chap-books containing folk-tales and love stories. You do not hear story-telling going on in an Indian bazaar as you do in Egypt; but in most of the larger towns there is usually some person skilled in the art, who attends evening parties to amuse the guests. In the villages it is often a blind man, whose memory has been improved by his infirmity, who recites tales to the peasants as they rest and smoke after the labour of the day. Old ayahs tell stories to little European children. In short, any one interested in folk-lore can have no difficulty in finding an almost inexhaustible stock of tales.

The materials are at present insufficient to attempt a classification of the various streams of influence which have contributed to the present stock. If we accept the most plausible theory, that the folk-tale is in the main based on the customs and ritual of the people among whom it originates, we should be able to bring under some system of classification the tribal elements which go to make up the current tales. It is possible, nay, probable that when the Aryans entered the country they brought with them a store of legend different from that of the Dravidian races whom they found in occupation, and the same may be the case with the Scythic, Turanian, Turk, or other races which have at one time or another entered India. But as is the case with the existing population, the elements of the current tradition have been so thoroughly mixed and combined that it is all but impossible to disentangle them. Language, it may be said, ought to help us, and we should be able to distinguish, at least, the foreign tales from those of indigenous origin. But here, too, we find that the titles of the actors have been intermixed. The same tale told by a Musalmán will speak of Jinns and Paris, while the Hindu narrator will introduce the Rákshasa or the Deo. The best chance of finding the purely Indian tale, unaffected by foreign influence, is among the forest tribes, and some of those collected from people like Santáls and Kols do, in their incidents and the custom and ritual which they depict, seem to mark a more archaic stage of tradition than those which come to us from other and more accessible sources. This is about all that we can safely say at present. We must remember, too, that there has been a constant interchange of tales between India and other countries within historical times.

Some authorities have suggested that a large number of the current European folk-tales have been derived from India. It has been argued that these tales found their way to Europe in various ways—by the ancient trade routes along the coasts of the Indian Ocean and Red Sea, or by caravan tracks though Central Asia; by Buddhist missionaries to the west; by crusaders and gipsies. One famous medieval romance, that of Barlaam and Josaphat, for instance, is merely a Christianised version of the life of Buddha. It is quite possible that folk-tales, the small change of literature, may have been carried about in this way. But another view is gradually gaining ground, that many of these tales, based on analogous custom and similar phases of social life, may have been independently invented.

Whatever view may be taken of such coincidences of tradition, the resemblances between some Indian folk-tales and those of Europe are startling. "Cinderella," and "Bethgelert," "Moorachug and Meenachug," "The Giant who had no Heart in his Body," are all well represented in Indian versions. But here caution is required, for such tales once told in India by a European rapidly pass into

Oriental tradition, and, equipped with fresh characters and new incidents, may soon become naturalised, and may be supposed to be of indigenous origin. Thus, Sir R. Temple has recently shown how the tale of Shoan, who married a sea-maiden, told to the Nicobarese by a European, has been adopted by them, and now forms part of the island folk-lore.

The literary collections of tales are very numerous. The Epics, the Mahábhárata and Rámáyana, like the Odyssey, are based on folk-tales. Of the standard collections, the Panchatantra, which is perhaps as old as the beginning of our era, was the model of tales like those of the "Arabian Nights," where one story is dovetailed into another, and the whole work is like a set of Chinese boxes. These tales largely owe their inspiration to Buddhism, and this is more particularly the case with the Játaka, which gives a series of stories showing the lives of the Buddha in a succession of previous births. These passed largely into the collections made to illustrate the sermons of the Middle Ages. The Hitopadesa is more a collection of moral epilogues. The most voluminous of all is the Katha Sarit Ságara, which may go back to the beginning of our era.

One great cycle of tales, that of the Panjáb hero, Rája Rasálu, based either on the adventures of a real personage or on a confused recollection of gallant struggles by the Hindu Rájas against the Musalmán invaders of the seventh or eighth century of our era, has been thoroughly explored by Sir R. Temple and Mr Swynnerton.

[See the "Katha Sarit Ságara," translated by Mr Tawney, and the "Játaka," edited by the late Professor Cowell; of modern collections may be mentioned Miss Frere's "Old Deccan Days," Mrs Steel and Sir R. Temple, "Wide-awake Stories," Miss Stokes' "Indian Fairy Tales," Mr Knowles, "Folk-tales of Kashmír," Sir R. Temple's "Legends of the Panjáb," Mr Campbell's "Santál Folk-tales," and large collections in the "Indian Antiquary" and "North Indian Notes and Queries."]

FOOD.—The idea, commonly accepted even by well-informed writers like Buckle, that the Hindu usually eats rice, results from the fact that up to comparatively recent times most authorities derived their impressions either from Madras or Bengal. As a matter of fact, throughout

Northern India the main food of the poorer classes is, according to the season, millet, barley, or gram; while the richer chiefly eat wheat, and sometimes rice. In Bengal Proper and Orissa, and in the eastern part of Central India, rice is the chief food, the distinction being that the poor eat the coarse, early rice, the rich that which is later and finer. In the Mahratta country, the Deccan, and North Madras, the two great millets are mainly used; in Mysore, Raggy, or the small millet. Rice and millets are the staples of South Madras and the West Coast. Everywhere pulse is largely used, supplying the nitrogenous matter wanting in cereal grains, and essential to those who rarely use meat.

The jungle tribes naturally use the food provided by the forests in which they live. When the scanty supplies of grain fall low they supplement them with various fruits, berries, and bulbs, generally most unappetising and indigestible, perhaps the best being the succulent corolla of the *Mohwa*,* to which they add any animal food which they can shoot or snare. Their tastes in food are very catholic. When an Oraon lover presents a maiden with a dish of grilled mice it shows that he entertains a really serious affection for her. The Black Shans of Burma prefer snakes to any other food, and all the tribes of that region eat lizards. The Lepcha of Sikhim dines off the dragon-like lizard generally called the *Biscobra*. The Bágdis of Bengal eat tortoises, many of the fishing tribes crocodiles, and boiled frogs are exposed for sale in Burmese bazaars. Perhaps the foulest eaters in India are the vagrant Doms, who will eat any kind of meat, even carrion, and the leavings of any other caste.

Cookery in its most elementary form is seen among the Irulas, a jungle tribe of Madras, of which an account is given by Captain Harkness. They grow a little grain near their huts, and when it is ripe pluck as much as they may require for the day's consumption. A fire is kindled on the nearest rock, and when it is well heated the embers are brushed away and the ears laid out to parch. The grain is then rudely crushed between two stones and made into cakes with water; the rock is again heated, and the bread toasted upon it. They never dream of storing their grain, and when it is consumed, fall back upon the roots and berries of the jungle.

The well-known principle that witchcraft may work through scraps of food accounts for many customs of eating. In the first place, *confarreatio*, the rule of eating together, is based on the suggestion that when all members of a group eat together no one will devise mischief, which would be as dangerous to the plotter as to his victim. Hence, when a bride from another group joins the tribe she eats ceremoniously with her new relations, and thus obtains franchise in the household of her adoption. Hence, too, all natives strongly object to any one, Europeans in particular, watching them while they eat. As the early traveller, Nicolo Conti, says: "On this account many eat in secret, fearing lest they should be fascinated by the eye of lookers-on." Barbosa describes in detail the extreme care with which the King of Malabar used to eat so that no one saw him, and his meal was preceded by the most elaborate ablutions.

In fact, by the high-caste Hindu eating is regarded as a sacrament, and can be done only under the most rigid rules. A Bráhman dinner in the Deccan has been thus described:

"The head of the house, his sons, and guests of superior rank sit on low, wooden stools in a row, and in the second row facing them are guests or male relations of inferior rank. Metal or leaf plates are laid in front of each stool; to the right-hand side is a water pot, and to the left a cup with a ladle in it. On the top to the right are cups for curries and relishes. The pulse and grain are served by a Bráhman cook, and the vegetables and butter by one of the women of the family, generally the host's wife or his daughter-in-law. The dinner is served in three courses: the first of boiled rice and pulse and a spoonful or two of butter, the second of wheat-bread and sugar with salads and curries, the third of boiled rice with curds and salads. With each course two or three vegetables are served. The plate is not changed during dinner. In each course the chief dish is heaped in the centre of the plate; on the right the vegetables are arranged, and on the left the salads, with a piece of lemon and some salt."

It was a primitive Aryan practice that the sexes ate apart. Like the women of Homer, who usually ate in their own room, the Hindu woman eats by herself when her husband has finished his meal.

To secure purity the pious Hindu usually cooks for himself, first plastering a sacred circle, within which he can conduct the operation without danger of interference from men or demons. But the peasant who is engaged in work in the fields eats food cooked by his wife. When a low caste is on the way to promotion to a higher rank they usually mark the fact by refusing to eat food not cooked by a Bráhman. The Musalmán of rank usually eats food cooked in the ladies' apartments, whence it is sent out to the guests. One of the many trials of the official Englishman is the necessity of at least pretending to eat a banquet sent to his tents by a local magnate. The food is generally much richer and more highly spiced than that which he is accustomed to eat, and in its journey from his host's kitchen it arrives stone cold.

The foods prohibited to the twice-born are defined by Manu as mushrooms, salted pork, barn-door fowls, garlic, onions, turnips, and carrots; the eating of all these involves degradation. The rules, however, vary throughout the country. In the Central Provinces, where customs are comparatively lax, most Bráhmans eat goat's flesh, venison, some birds such as the green-pigeon, and fish. Rájputs eat meat and game, and the lowest septs of them even eat fowls. The mercantile classes are the most particular of all. The sect of the Satnámis do not eat chillies, tomatoes, or other red vegetables, because their colour is supposed to resemble blood. A clear distinction is drawn between the wild and the domestic pig. Rájputs will eat the former; none but the lowest menial castes, the latter.

These rules involve curious inconsistencies. While a high-caste man is very careful about the cooking of his flour, he never troubles to enquire through whose hands it may have passed in the course of manufacture. The Baiti, a caste in Bengal who make the shell-lime used with betel, are so impure that no good Hindu will touch their water-vessels; but no one dreams of refusing to chew lime moistened with water from these very vessels. There is, again, a clear distinction drawn between food such as boiled rice and bannocks prepared with water and food cooked with *ghee*,* such as sweetmeats and confectionery. Food of the first variety can be prepared only at home, under the careful rules which regulate the family kitchen. With regard to the second the theory is that the product of the sacred cow which enters into their composition ensures their purity. In other words, Hinduism is elastic enough to ignore its own rules when they are practically unworkable, and provides one class of food for the traveller and another for the man living at home. Hence, no one will hesitate to eat sweets in the bazaar, or parched grain, which is purified by passing through the fire, and he never thinks of the caste of the shopkeeper. But he salves his conscience by not eating such things out of a regular dinner plate, but from a leaf platter or his hand.

Musalmán Fakírs, again, have their special rules of food, many of which they have borrowed from the Hindus. The well-known fanatic priest on the Afghán frontier, the Akhúnd of Swát, has the seed of a kind of grass grown for him and eats nothing else. A noted Hindu ascetic in Berár eats and drinks only once a day. At this meal he stoops down, and, dispensing with the use of his hands, takes from the floor, freshly plastered with cow-dung, a ball of meal and water prepared by a Bráhman.

The Musalmán's dietary is much more liberal than that of the Hindu, and this is one of the main reasons for the spread of Islám in Eastern Bengal. He eats mutton, fowls, eggs, and fish, with wheat cakes and rice in the form of Puláo [*Pilau**], and curry.

"Whoever," says Buchanan-Hamilton, "has travelled much with natives, and been witness to the weakness of their constitution in resisting changes of air and water, will agree with me in saying that those who enjoy a diet of animal food and strong liquors in moderate quantities, are best able to resist the influence of unhealthy climates, and the sudden changes of air."

Natives are, as a rule, moderate eaters, but some of the

stories of the amount of food eaten by them almost pass belief. It used to be said of the old Bengal sepoy that he would fix his ramrod in the ground and string on it his bannocks as fast as they were made. When the pile reached the top his ration was complete. More extraordinary are the tales of Abul Fazl, the historiographer of Akbar, who used to eat 20 lbs. of food per diem. Afzul Khán, treacherously slain by Sivaji, used to eat a large goat daily. Most remarkable of all was Mahmúd Begada, King of Ahmadábád, who ate 20 lbs. of cooked food daily and had 3 lbs. parched grain for desert. His breakfast was a cup of honey, a cup of *ghee*,* and fifty plantains. Every night he had placed by his bedside two dishes of mutton sausages.

It can hardly be said that the Anglo-Indian has been successful in adapting his food to the climate. Things have certainly improved in modern times; but the stock dinner of earlier days, of which a saddle of mutton and a turkey were the chief dishes, is sometimes to be met with still. Few Indian cooks are skilled in the delicate, appetising dishes of France which admirably suit the climate. The fact is that cookery for Europeans is thought degrading, and the profession is occupied either by low-class Musalmáns, half-caste so-called Portuguese, or outcast tribes like the *Mughs** of Bengal. The cook begins as a scullion in some rich man's house, and gradually picks up a little knowledge in the kitchen. Such a thing as a school of cookery is unknown. A Frenchman like Tavernier saw the deficiencies of the *cuisine* of his day.

"I have been very careful," he writes, "in all the places where the Dutch have settlements, to contribute as far as possible to the amusement of their ladies. As I never came from Persia to India without bringing good wine and fine fruits, and always had some one with me who understood cooking better than the Dutch in India, and knew how to make good soup and bake, I entertained them often with collations, where pigeons in pyramids, flavoured with pistachios, were not lacking."

Teaching of this kind is badly wanted even at the

present day, and in particular in British army barracks, where badly cooked food, prepared by dirty cooks, is one of the main causes of the prevalence of ill-health.

FOOTPRINTS, SACRED.—The myth of footprints stamped on the rock by gods and mighty men is found in all parts of the world. Its analogue, as Professor Tylor points out, is to be found in the fossil footprints of birds and beasts which are often imitated by savages in their rude carvings. We find also in India the respect paid to the feet, as shown in the customs of kissing or touching the feet of a superior; the drinking of the water in which the feet of priests or holy men have been washed; the widespread folk-lore idea that the feet of eminent men are distinguished by special mystic marks. The footmark, then, in a sacred place is the appropriate symbol of the presence or visit of a sacred personage. It has been supposed by General Cunningham that the Buddhist reverence for these supposed relics of the Master began with the prostration of his disciples after his death. But more probably it is one of the early animistic ideas imported into Buddhism.

The most celebrated of these marks is that at the summit of Adam's Peak in Ceylon, a hollow 5 feet long and 2½ wide, which Buddhists venerate as the mark of the Master; Saivites as that of Siva; Musalmáns as that of Father Adam. One of the most sacred Hindu marks of this kind is the Vishnupada, or footmark of Vishnu, at Gaya in Bengal, which is preserved in a silver basin under a canopy and within a shrine. But all sorts of deities, saints, holy animals like the cow, heroes like the Mahratta Sivaji, are commemorated in this way all over India.

The Muhammadans have appropriated the idea, and reverence in many places the Qadam-i-Rasúl, or footprint of the Prophet. One of these was brought from Mecca by a pilgrim in the days of Akbar, who ordered the grandees of the Court to meet it and carry it themselves by turns. But he paid no particular respect to the relic, and allowed the discoverers to keep it in their own house.

The Indian fancy for exalting their deities by portraying

them of monstrous size is shown in the dimensions of some of these relics. The Chinese pilgrim, Hiuen Tsiang, saw a footprint of the Buddha in the Deer-park at Benares which was 500 feet long. Their love of symbolism is shown in the emblems which they carve upon it—in Tibet, the Eight Glorious Marks—the golden fish, umbrella, conch-shell, victory trumpet, lucky diagram, victorious banner, vase, lotus, and wheel. The Burmese make it nearly square, with the toes all of the same length, and divide the sole into 108 squares, in which they represent all sorts of things—monasteries, tigers, fish, priests, and the like—signifying that all these things are under the feet of the Master.

[Yule, "Marco Polo," 3rd ed. ii. 321f. ; Kern, "Manual of Buddhism," 97 ; Waddell, "Buddhism of Tibet," 293 ; Shway Yoe, "The Burman," i. 201 ; 9th Series, "Notes and Queries," iv. 463.]

FOREST or JUNGLE TRIBES.—This is a conventional term for a mass of tribes of different origin, who, under varying conditions of livelihood and culture, occupy the more hilly and inaccessible parts of the country. In speaking of forests of the central part of the Peninsula, we must carefully distinguish them from those of other tropical countries, like, for instance, the Amazon Valley or Ceylon. Here we have none of the masses of giant trunks, the dense foliage which often excludes the sunlight, the great tangled creepers and impenetrable underwood. Here there is no gloom or silence ; the trees, as a result of improvident forestry, are generally low and stunted ; from the scantiness of water, animal and bird life is not abundant. With its occasional patches of brushwood or coarse grass the Central Indian jungle is more a copse than a primeval forest. The truly tropical forest is found only in the Eastern Himálaya where close heat and abundant rainfall encourage a wild luxuriance of vegetation like that of Brazil.

Ethnologically speaking, these people may be roughly divided into three groups. To the north of the Peninsula, starting from the west, along the lower slopes of the Himálaya they have been classed as Mongoloid, with a considerable Indo-Aryan admixture, the advancing Aryan having here penetrated and annexed the more fertile valleys. Further east, as we reach Nepál and Assam, the Indian influence is much less apparent, the people of the Plains being too unwarlike to enter the hill tract, where the tribes have remained almost purely Mongoloid. Passing south, we find a body of tribes like Bhíls, Gonds, Santáls, who are primarily of Dravidian origin, but have been largely influenced by the Indo-Aryans or Aryo-Dravidians who occupy the Plain country of North India. Further south, again, we have tribes of a still lower type—Dravidians less exposed to outer influence—who inhabit the forests of the Eastern and Western Ghâts, the hills which flank the south of the Peninsula.

It is impossible to fix with precision the numbers of these forest tribes. In the course of the last Census those people who professed to worship a tribal deity, not any of the Hindu gods, were classed as Animists, and amounted to 8,500,000. But everywhere tribes of this class are largely influenced by Hindu religious beliefs, and by the customs and mode of life of the Hindus on their borders; and it is as difficult to draw the line between Animism and Hinduism as it is to define the point where the simple forest life of the more isolated hill tribes merges into the ordinary type of Indian culture.

A few typical instances will best describe the present condition of these tribes.

The Rájis of Kumaun and the neighbouring hills of the West Himálaya live in the forest, make wooden bowls for sale, and live in temporary huts, supporting themselves on wild herbs and fruits and occasional supplies of cooked food, which they receive in exchange for their wares from villagers of the settled tract. When they acquire any grain by barter or by the rudest form of farming they hide it away in caves, or hang it, bound up in leaves, from the branches of trees.

Further east, the Thárus live in the Tarái, or marshy tract below the lower range of the Himálaya, clear the forest, cultivate for a time, and then retreat before the people of the Plains who occupy the land. They are thus the real pioneers of agriculture. They are not, as some have supposed, immune to malaria. But they suffer less than the men of the Plains, chiefly because they raise their huts on high platforms and clear the jungle round their villages. It was a tribe like this which was the first to tame animals useful to man—the hog, the wild cow, the jungle-fowl, the buffalo, the elephant; and Manu, in his spirit of Bráhman exclusiveness, directs that such people should be carefully avoided by the twice-born. The Thárus are admirable hunters, and to this day furnish the best elephant-drivers in Northern India. In rather a lower social stage are the Korwas of the Central Hill tract, who do little farming, but support themselves on the roots and berries of the jungle, so much so that when a girl is married, a well-defined tract of jungle is allotted to her as her dower, and no one ventures to intrude on her domain.

As types of the more eastern Himálayan tribes we may take the Nágas and Lusháis. They are much more warlike than any of those already described, and their propensity for raids, with the object of procuring slaves and heads of their enemies, has repeatedly brought them into conflict with the British Government. In spite of their savage mode of life, they are skilled in various industries—weaving cotton cloth, the material of which they grow and spin themselves, and making baskets. The Lusháis are able to mould brass, and some of their blacksmiths can make a gun-lock.

Perhaps the most degraded of these tribes are those of South India—the Yanadis of Nellore—living in rude, conical huts of brushwood, and supporting themselves on jungle fruits and wild honey; the Malayális of Salem, and the Kádirs of the Anamalai range—all jungle-folk, the latter in particular being so shy that little is as yet known of them by British officers.

It is difficult to realise the feeling of fear and contempt with which from the earliest times these tribes were regarded by the Aryans. The Vedic singers satirised their flat noses, and spoke of them as "eaters of raw flesh," "lawless," "disturbers of sacrifices." Their habit of distending the lobe of the ear with heavy rings led to the fable told by Strabo, of men "who had ears reaching down to the feet, so that they could sleep in them." The broad nose of the Dravidian originated another fable of men "who dwell near the sources of the Ganges, and subsist on the savour of roasted flesh and the perfumes of fruits and flowers, having instead of mouths orifices through which they breathe." Like demons all over the world, "their heels are in front, and the instep and toes are turned backwards."

All these tribes are being gradually drawn, in social custom and religious belief, within the Hindu fold. The stages of this transformation are usually as follows: first, they abandon forest life and migratory modes of farming, and settle down in villages; next, they begin to learn the names of Hindu gods, and by the cajolery of missionaries drawn from the ascetic Orders insensibly adopt the external observances of Hinduism; then Bráhmans are established among them, who depose the tribal gods. These henceforth are worshipped only in a clandestine way, or by women, and are finally included in the Hindu pantheon as local manifestations of this or that principle, or are relegated to the class of household or village deities. At the same time they abandon or modify the tribal vernacular, and adopt the Aryan tongue of the locality. Socially, they enter the Hindu system and adopt Hindu rules of marriage. Finally, they come under the bondage of Hindu money-lenders, who, trading on the ignorance of the tribes, and availing themselves of unfamiliar codes of law, gradually acquire possession of their land and other property.

Such a reversal of the original tribal and religious life has from time to time led to unfortunate disturbances, as among Santáls, Mundas, and Bhíls. Much has been done to avert the economic ruin of these tribes by the introduction of codes of law more suitable to them, and by putting them under the more immediate supervision of British officers. But it is obvious that the process of Hinduising will gradually extend, and that, except in the case of the more isolated and warlike tribes, within a generation or two most of them will lose their distinctive beliefs and customs. Even now among tribes included within the Hindu fold some curious survivals mark their once dominant position, such as the rights of investiture claimed by tribes like the Bhíls and Mínas at the election of their Hindu rulers.

An interesting chapter in the relations between our Government and these tribes tells of the ascendancy and civilising influence acquired by some British officers over these people. Cleveland in the Bhágalpur district worked for the regeneration of the Santáls; Outram raised the Bhíl Battalion; Hall and Dixon civilised the Mhairs. In the Mutiny troubles it was the Mhairwára Battalion and the Mewár Bhíl Corps who alone in Rájputána remained true to their colours, and many officers in our day have done similar services to the wilder races on our frontiers.

[For the Rájis, Crooke, "Tribes and Castes," s. v.; Thárus, ibid., and Risley. "Tribes and Castes," s. v.; For the Assam and Chota Nágpur tribes, Dalton, "Descriptive Ethnology"; for the Central Indian tribes, Hislop, "Papers regarding the Aboriginal Tribes," "Gazetteers Central Provinces," and "Berar" and "Bombay"; for those of South India, Breeks, "Primitive Tribes of the Nilagiris"; various papers in "Bulletin of Madras Museum"; "Census Report," India, 1901, Ethnological Appendices.]

FRUITS. — "Goa," writes Tavernier, "produces numerous fruits as Mangues, ananas [pine-apples], figues d' Adam [plantains], and cocos [cocoanuts]: but certainly a good pippin is worth more than all these fruits."

Bernier, also, decides that the fruits of India are inferior to, and not so varied as, those of Europe. This he attributes to the ignorance of the gardeners, who do not attend to the planting of fruit trees, the selection of suitable soil, and the introduction of grafts from foreign countries. In spite of the improvement in fruit culture which dates from Muhammadan times, most observers will accept his opinion that the fruits of India are distinctly inferior to those of Europe.

The list of the fruits of India shows that the best varieties have been introduced from abroad, and that it is only in recent times that the native varieties have been really improved.

To begin with the indigenous fruits—we have, first, the mango. The multitude of the varieties and the number of ancient common names show that its original home was in the South of Asia or the Malay Peninsula. This is admitted in the Hindu legend which tells that the monkey god, Hanumán, first brought the kernels from the garden of the demon Rávana in the south. The indigenous variety is abominable, leaving on the teeth masses of fibre, and its taste has been described as a combination of the essences of carrot, geranium, and turpentine. Its improvement seems to have been largely the work of the Portuguese, as is shown by the names of the best strains. Popularly speaking, the best mangoes are supposed to fall into three classes, Bombay, Langra, Malda; but the native grower divides them into innumerable varieties, which have been gradually improved by selection, those of Mazagaon in Bombay, and Multán being recognised as the best varieties. The original Mazagaon mango tree was in existence in 1838, and was considered so valuable that a guard of sepoys was posted round it to protect the fruit. From here, in the times of Sháh Jahán, couriers conveyed the fruit to Delhi. Moore in "Lalla Rookh" ascribed the crusty temper of Fadladeen to an unexpected failure in the supply of his favourite fruit.

The other Indian fruits which are probably indigenous, but now much improved by culture, are the *jack*,* the citron and lemon, the mulberry, *banana*,* pear, apple and tamarind, plum, walnut, bitter cherry, pomegranate, and grape. All these fruits are, as a rule, disappointing to the European palate. For most people the odour of the jack is a sufficient deterrent. Mulberries are inferior to those of Europe; the pomegranate contains mostly seeds with a modicum of pulp. The little lady-finger plantain and the variety with a red rind are the best, and grow only within reach of the sea-breeze.

With these indigenous fruits we may compare those of foreign origin—the pine-apple, custard-apple, tomato, cape-gooseberry, and guava from America; the papaw from the West Indies; the *orange*,* *leechee*,* and peach from China; the *pummelo** from Java; the *loquat** from Japan; the *mangosteen** from the Malay Archipelago; the date-palm from Arabia; the almond from Persia; the apricot either from China or Armenia or Caucasia. Many of these are excellent. Pine-apples from Burma, where an ingenious gentleman proposes to manufacture champagne from them; oranges from Sylhet, perhaps the original home of the tree, Sikhim, Gujarát, and Nágpur; leechees from Bengal, Lucknow, or Sahâranpur; peaches from various places in North and South India are all excellent.

To quote Sir G. Watt:

"It is remarkable that while the wild forms of many of the fruits of Europe are abundant, as indigenous plants in the Himálaya, a very few only were cultivated before the arrival of Europeans; and the gooseberry, the currant, and the bramble, which have been carried to such perfection in Europe, are still uncultivated in India. The peach succeeds in the plains of India, but the effect of climate upon it is marked. In Bengal excellent peaches are to be had attaining much of their European flavour and ripening into a soft, pinkish separable pulp. . . . . The apricot shows a somewhat similar behaviour. In Afghánistán, Kashmír, and Chamba excellent apricots are obtained, and indeed the tree, if not indigenous to Afghánistán, is quite naturalised. . . . The grapes of Kashmír and Afghánistán are famous, but owing to the period of plucking and the method of packing, they have lost their natural flavour before they reach the plains of India. A very considerable trade, however, is done by the Kábuli merchants in small circular boxes of grapes. H.H. the Maháràja of Kashmír, has successfully introduced the wine grape into Kashmír, from which wine and brandy of good quality are obtained."

Next to the Portuguese, India owes the naturalisation of its best fruits to the Moghuls. A tray of musk-melons drew tears from Bábar when he remembered his native land of Ferghána, and it was he who seems to have brought the better kinds of grapes, pine-apples, and musk-melons to Agra. Bernier tells us that the Moghuls used to import immense quantities of fresh fruits, melons, apples, pears, and grapes, from Kábul, Bokhara, and Persia, and also dried fruits of all kinds. The Ágha, or gentleman, in whose suite he travelled, used frequently to spend twenty crowns a day on fruit for breakfast. As we have seen elsewhere it was the Musalmáns who brought the taste for fine gardens to India, and to ornament them they imported all kinds of fruit trees from Persia and Central Asia.

[P. Robinson, "My Indian Garden," 49f.; Lawrence, "Valley of Kashmír." 348ff.; and excellent articles on the chief varieties in Watt, "Economic Dictionary."]

FURNITURE.—The needs of a people low in the scale of culture are few, and the furniture of the peasant consists exclusively of necessaries—granaries of clay, from the size of a small room to that of a beer barrel, which are now disappearing in the Panjáb as grain is sold on the spot and not stored; spinning-wheels, of which there should be one to each woman in the family, but which have now much decreased owing to the use of foreign cloth; churns; cotton hand-gins; baskets and winnowing-fans for cleaning grain; earthen pots and pans; others of wood for mixing dough; an iron sieve; a pestle and mortar; a griddle; a few stools and cots—these make up the furniture of the peasant's hut in the rural parts of India. In Burma the house furniture is equally simple. A chair is of no use to the Burman, and without chairs tables are equally useless. A few mats and hard bamboo pillows are laid on the ground, for the law of Buddha forbids the use of cots. A box, a few simple cooking utensils, two or three earthen pots with lids, and a wooden stirrer; a water jar, a ladle made of cocoanut shell, a large lacquered dish, out of which the family eat, complete the outfit.

The monuments and early literature represent the furniture of palaces as characterised by much beauty and grace. We have elaborate bedsteads and thrones, seats of cane and of wood finely carved, long benches, chairs of a form curiously like those of our day, footstools and little tables, or *teapoys*,* depicted in great abundance. The designs of some of these show a remarkable similarity to the art of Egypt, Nineveh, and Babylon, and were possibly obtained by early trade intercourse between India and the Euphrates-Tigris valley. Megasthenes says that in his time the people ate from tripods or teapoys; perhaps he specially refers to Court custom; if he be right, the fashion now in vogue of sitting cross-legged and eating from plates or leaf platters would be a later habit, which is hardly probable.

It is on her metal vessels, however, that the Indian housewife of to-day specially prides herself. Though none but gold cups are mentioned in the Rig-veda, it is certain that copper and silver were used from early times. Bronze came probably in the form of vessels from abroad, such as those found in the prehistoric interments of South India. The earliest vessels were gourds and leaf platters, which are still used by Fakírs, and it was from the gourd that the forms of the modern drinking-vessels were evolved. Copper, an indigenous metal, was regarded as the purest of all, and until recently all sacrificial vessels were made of it. Even now little copper saucers and spoons are used by careful Hindus for making oblations. For most purposes brass has now superseded copper, and a sensible rule, framed in the interest of the traveller, has made it safe from pollution by the touch of a low-caste person. The difficulty of cleaning it led to the use of bell-metal, but this, a newer and less holy compound, does not enjoy the privilege possessed by brass. Hence in North India a bell-metal tray is polluted if a man of a different religion or of lower caste than the owner touches it. Each member of the family, therefore, has, or should have, a set of such vessels. If it becomes impure it cannot be cleaned in the ordinary way like brass, but must be melted down and remoulded. Yet it is, except earthen pots, the only sanitary vessel which the Hindu owns, because milk sours in brass pots, and bell-metal is alone safe for cooking. While the Hindu uses vessels of brass or alloy, the Musalmán prefers copper, usually tinned. But there are exceptions—Gujarátis using all copper, except a brass *Lotah** for ablution; and Musalmán villagers have vessels like their Hindu neighbours.

The number and value of the vessels in a house are considerable in comparison to income. This is one of the ways in which the peasant invests his savings, because they are easily pawned or sold in times of distress. A small peasant family in North India will have pots and pans worth five or ten shillings; when we come to the family of a rich merchant, the number is enormous. Besides vessels in which food is cooked for guests and at feasts, he must have betel-boxes, lamp-stands, perfume-sprinklers, pipe-stands, many of which are fine specimens of artistic work in metal.

The earthenware vessels so largely used are supplied by the village potter, who is one of the servants on the village establishment, and is remunerated for his work by a dole of grain from each farm at harvest time. The number of such vessels used is enormous, because the traveller flings away or breaks them at each halting-place, and it is only in very economical families that they last for any time. The mounds on which the oldest villages stand consist largely of masses of potsherds. The type is very constant, and many of the existing shapes closely resemble those found in neolithic interments.

A remarkable form of vessel is the Kangar or Kangri, the portable brazier of earthenware or metal which every Kashmíri, asleep or awake, in winter, carries under his long loose garment. It is usually protected by a wicker-work covering, and held over the stomach and loins. The practice is very dangerous, and there is hardly a Kashmíri who has escaped burning from using it. In spite of its general adoption in Kashmír, it does not seem to have been introduced till Moghul times.

[For ancient furniture and vessels, Rajendralála Mitra, "Indo-Aryans," i. 243ff.; for modern furniture and vessels, Birdwood, "Industrial Arts of India," 199ff.; Mukharji, "Art Manufactures of India," 196f.; Dampier, Monograph on Brass Manufactures in the N.W.P. and Oudh"; Shway Yoe, "The Burman," i. 94f.; Drew, "Jummoo and Kashmír," 177.]

GARDENS.—Of the ancient Hindu garden we know little. Babylon, with its hanging gardens, has been supposed to be the centre from which the taste spread, and its influence probably extended to India in very early times. At the same time it reached the Central Asian tribes by way of Persia, and when they occupied India they brought the love of gardening with them. The Buddhist cave-dwellers planted gardens for the culture of vegetables, flowers, and fruit, and some of the plants which these old monks grew exist in the neighbourhood of their hermitages to the present day—for instance, in the garden at Lonála near the Kárli Caves. When we come to the dramatic literature we have many references to gardens. In the "Necklace" one is thus described in the true Oriental style:

> "The garden is now most lovely. The trees partake of the rapturous season, their new leaves glow like coral, their branches wave with animation in the wind, and their foliage resounds with the blythe murmurs of the bee. The Bakula [*Mimusops*] blossoms lie round its root like ruby wine; the Champaka [*Michelia champaka*] flowers blush with the ruddiness of youthful beauty; the bees give back in harmony the music of the anklets, ringing melodiously as the delicate feet are raised against the stem of the Asoka tree."

But here we have no flower culture or landscape gardening; the scene is rather that of a Hindu garden of our day, where the owner sits under the cool shade of the trees. When we come to Musalmán times we learn that Fíroz Sháh, at the end of the fourteenth century, planted twelve hundred gardens near Delhi; but these were probably in the Hindu style. For the higher type of Indian garden India is indebted to Bábar. In a well-known passage in his "Memoirs" he laments among other deficiencies of Hindustán its lack of beautiful gardens.

> "Formerly," writes Abul Fazl in the time of Akbar, "people used to plant their gardens without any order, but since the time of the arrival in India of the Emperor Bábar, a more methodical arrangement of the gardens has been obtained, and travellers now-a-days admire the beauty of the palaces and their murmuring fountains."

The art of making fountains and artificial waterfalls was introduced in Moghul times by a Persian of Khurasán, who built the first in Gujarát early in the sixteenth century.

After Bábar, Jahángír was a great gardener. It was the mother of his empress, Núr Jahán, who invented otto of roses. Jahángír, in his "Memoirs," describes the gardens and fountains which he made in Kashmír. Bernier, when he visited the Shálamár gardens in 1665, writes:

"The entrance from the lake is through a spacious canal, bordered with green turf, and running between two rows of poplars. Its length is about five hundred paces, and it leads to a large summer-house placed in the middle of the garden. A second canal, still finer than the first, then conducts you to another summer-house at the end of the garden. This canal is paved with large blocks of freestone, and its sloping sides are covered with the same. In the middle is a long row of fountains, fifteen paces asunder; besides which there are large circular basins, or reservoirs, out of which arise other fountains, formed into a variety of shapes and figures."

He describes with admiration the summer-houses, but says nothing of the flowers. It is still one of the show-places of Kashmír, but its glories have departed; the plane-trees have lost much of their beauty, and of the summer-houses only the black marble pillars remain. Still, with its masses of purple rock seamed with snow, the light green foliage of the plane-trees, the shrubs and lilac blossoms, it is a pleasant place in which to dream of the glory of its founder. In Jahángír's other Kashmír garden, the Nishát Bágh, "Garden of Pleasaunce," the trees are perhaps finer, and the view of the lake, with the high cliff beyond, is entrancing.

"Magnificent Chenár trees," writes Sir W. Lawrence, "planted throughout the valley, with the ruins of cascades and summer-houses, all owe their origin to the Moghul vogue, and though it has been said of the Emperors that they were stage kings, so far as Kashmír is concerned, they would be entitled to the gratitude of posterity if only for the sake of the beautiful and shady plane-tree."

From these Moghul gardens the taste spread through the country, and no palace was complete without its garden. In South India even the ruthless Hyder and

Tippoo made gardens, the former approving of the English style then coming into fashion. The Lál Bágh, says Mr Browing,

> "looks like a purely European pleasure-ground, till the visitor advancing sees the gorgeous creepers, the wide-spreading mangoes, and the graceful betel-nut trees which characterise the East."

The formality of these Muhammadan gardens, which reflects the taste of Egypt or Babylon in the symmetry of their arrangement—trees planted according to their species in rows, one the "answer" of the other—commends itself little to our taste. Whatever beauty such gardens possess is due to the play of light and shade, as the sunlight forces its way through the dense foliage of the trees, the rich greenery nursed by constant irrigation, and the murmur of the water as it passes through the channels. Such a place is a paradise to birds which are never disturbed.

While the present type of native garden is due to the Muhammadans, scientific vegetable gardening was started by the Dutch. Tavernier in 1666 found that the Dutch at Hugli grew

> "all the delicacies that are found in the European gardens: salads of different kinds, cabbages, asparagus, peas, and principally beans, of which the seed comes from Japan, the Dutch desiring to have all kinds of herbs and pulses in their gardens, which they are most careful to cultivate, without, however, having been able to get artichokes to grow."

Just a hundred years after, Stavorinus tells us that peas, beans, and cabbages were to be had in Calcutta only during the cold season; in the hot season nothing was to be bought but some spinach and cucumbers. About 1780 potatoes, which the Dutch are said to have been the first to introduce from the Cape, peas, and French beans were in high repute.

"From them the British received annually the seeds of every vegetable useful at the table, as well as several plants, of which there appeared much need, especially various kinds of pot-herbs. They likewise supplied us with vines, from which innumerable cuttings have been dispensed to every part of Bengal and its upper dependencies."

Their garden at Chinsura, with three stone terraces flanked with groves of trees, was a model to the English settlers. The French, too, had a splendid garden at Gyretti, a place which has disappeared from modern maps, but was the site of the country-house of the Governor of Chandernagore. About this time we find newspaper advertisements of "Garden Houses" near Calcutta. But in 1674, more than a hundred years before this time, Fryer described the English garden at Bombay: "Voiced to be the pleasantest in India, intended rather for wanton Dalliance, Love's Artillery, than to make resistance against an invading Foe"; for it then became the site of a battery.

The splendid modern gardens of the native princes represent the Moghul type, improved by modern English taste. In the island of Jagnavás, at Udaypur, writes M. Rousselet:

"Each mass of buildings has a garden attached to it, surrounded by galleries, where flowers and orange and lemon trees grow near a stream, the different channels of which form a curious pattern. Immense mango trees and tamarinds shade these beautiful places, while the cocoanut and the date-palm raise above the very domes their feathery heads, which are gently swayed to and fro by the breeze from the lake." Of the hanging gardens the same traveller writes: "One of the most curious features of the palace of Udaypur is its extensive hanging gardens. It seems astounding to find trees of a hundred years' growth and lovely flower-beds situated at so great a height, and covering so many roofs of different elevations. In the centre of the garden is a fountain, from which avenues paved with white marble diverge in all directions; the water being carried off in narrow channels and lost to sight amidst groves of pomegranate and orange trees. A marble gallery encircles this entrancing spot, where the grandees of the Court, reclining on velvet sofas, indulge in pleasant day-dreams while taking their siesta."

One of the finest gardens of India is the Bani Bilás at Alwar, which covers 150 acres, remarkable for its fine drives, ornamental trees, and a profusion of fruits, flowers, and vegetables. The peaches are excellent, and the Bombay and Malda mangoes very fine. All the ordinary fruits are grown, and sometimes strawberries in great profusion.

Where Islám is the State religion, the garden is the site of the tombs of the prince and his nobles. Such are the grove gardens of Baroda, which were on the same plan as those which surround the Táj Mahal at Agra, or the tomb of Akbar at Sikandra.

Writing of Vijayanagar in the fifteenth century, the traveller Abd-er-razzák says: "These people could not live without roses, and they look on them as quite as necessary as food." The indigenous rose seems to have been much improved by the Musalmáns, and the culture spread on the discovery of otto of roses early in the seventeenth century. Nothing can well surpass the Indian rose. Lady Dufferin writes:

"The roses at Lahore are things to rave about. I never saw such a profusion; one drives through hedges of them, and there are great bushes, and arches and trees covered with them; it seems to me to be a real city of gardens."

Equally beautiful are the great rose gardens, like those of Gházipur, where the sound of the opening of the countless buds is distinctly heard in the stillness of the evening.

We have seen that many of the best Indian fruits were imported from abroad. The same is the case with many other plants. The Portuguese brought the best products of America—maize, capsicum, the agave or American aloe, which last has now become so common a plant that it is difficult to believe that its introduction was so recent. The ground-nut now largely cultivated in South India came from America either through China or Africa. Europe has given the cabbage, celery, leek, artichoke, and lettuce; the Canaries, beet; Cochin China, the *soy* * bean; Persia, the spinach. The cultivation of these vegetables, which thrive in Upper India, has done much to improve the health of European residents, and the taste for them is rapidly spreading among the better classes of the people. But among the rural classes religious prejudice still checks the introduction of valuable articles of food. The mangold wurzel, for instance, and the tomato flourish; but when cut they are supposed to resemble meat, and are consequently taboo.

It is the Himálaya, perhaps, that has given most in exchange to European gardens—the *deodar*,* rhododendron, and many splendid orchids. Few of the Indian garden flowers, save the rose, the tuberose, and jessamine, have much perfume. To Mr Massey, once Financial Member of Council, Sir M. Grant-Duff assigns the familiar epigram: "At least, Mr Massey, you will admit that the flowers here are charming." "No," he replied, "they are the only things in the country which do not smell." On the other hand, although few Indian gardens contain many herbaceous plants yielding much odour, there are so many trees and shrubs which emit powerful scents, some of the most delightful fragrance, others almost intolerably offensive, that it must be a very exacting olfactory sense which cannot meet with sufficient exercise in them.

GIPSIES.—The connection between the European gipsies and the East is obvious from philological considerations alone. But the circumstances of their westward migration have long been disputed. On one theory their arrival in Europe, which is recorded for the first time in 1417, was due to the escape of fugitives before the armies of Timúr, who reached India in 1398. Another suggestion connects them with a body of Jat minstrels imported from India to Persia by Bahrám Gúr about 420 A.D., whence they gradually worked their way into Europe. A third theory identifies them with various Indian vagrants of the present day, such as Doms, Bediyas, or Nats. Lastly, Mr F. H. Groome identifies them with a prehistoric body of wanderers from the East, who brought with them the art of working in bronze. On this view of the case, the modern Gipsies may be akin to some of the present vagrant tribes, but the separation occurred at a very early period.

Attempts have been made to identify the Gipsies in a special way with two of these wandering tribes, the Chángars and the Doms, the former name being supposed by some to be the origin of the title "Zingari," the latter of "Romani." The Chángars, whose name is supposed by Leitner to mean "grain-sifters," are a vagrant tribe of the Panjáb—the men employed in agriculture, and particularly in reaping, and the women in sifting and cleaning grain. The Doms or Dúms are a widespread race, found all through North India. The best group of them is found in the lower Himálaya, where they are mostly respectable artisans. The Dúm-Mirási, if he be really identical with these people, is a wandering minstrel. The Dom of Behár is a foul outcast, a scavenger, and eater of carrion, and is employed on the duty, odious to the Hindu, of providing the fire for cremation.

Akin to these people, in function at least, are the numerous wandering tribes found all over India, like the Bediyas of Bengal; the Nats, Sánsiyas, and Kanjars of the United Provinces; the Máng, Mahár, or Dhed of the Deccan. These tribes practise the usual Gipsy industries—mat and basket-making, knife-grinding, and the like. The facility of their occupation makes it an easy cloak for more nefarious practices, as is the case with the European Gipsy. Some, like the Gulgulias of Bengal, live by begging and pilfering, and exhibiting trained goats and monkeys. The women sell drugs to cure ear and toothache, and for less reputable purposes. The Panjáb, again, has a tribe of wandering blacksmiths, whose home is their cart, in which they carry about the tools and materials of their craft. There are, again, wandering bodies of tumblers, rope-dancers, acrobats, jugglers, and snake-charmers. Many of these groups are perhaps not ethnologically connected, but their way of life closely resembles that of their brethren in Europe.

These people speak a variety of thieves' slang, based on one or other of the dialects of Prákrit—a later tongue, allied to Sanskrit. Lahnda, "the west language," spoken in the Panjab along the Indus valley—roughly speaking from about the latitude of Delhi to the Kashmír border, the ancient country of Kaikeya—has been identified by Dr Grierson with the tongue of an Aryan race, the Kaikeya Pisáchas, of whom he thinks the modern Gipsies are the descendants. The so-called Gipsy dialects of India, of which no less than thirteen are spoken in the province of Berár, have not yet been thoroughly investigated by Dr Grierson in the course of the Linguistic Survey. Many of them are mere thieves' argot, as when a London thief transforms "police" into "icelop," and finally "slop," the Indian Dom calls a Jamadár, or police sergeant, Majadár, "the sweet one."

A large part of the crime of the country is due to these people. Their methods of crime vary in different provinces. In the United Provinces much of the dacoity and gang-robbery is their work. Some years ago the Coercion Act was applied to the most notorious tribe, the Sánsiyas. The worst criminals were interned in a reformatory, while the younger members were dispersed on the estates of native land-owners, and efforts were made to train them to agriculture and other industries. But the experiment failed, because they were indisposed to follow any respectable occupation, and constantly deserted their settlements. According to Mr Crawford, similar attempts at reformation were equally unsuccessful in the case of the criminal tribes of the Deccan:

"They are exceedingly intelligent and observant," he says, "very active in their habits, the lads being as carefully trained in running and athletic exercises as they are trained in the skilful use of their fingers. They are good actors, and able to assume almost any disguise; very plausible and insinuating in their address, scrupulously clean in their persons and habits, and somewhat addicted to finery withal. They rarely drink; their womenkind, all expert thieves themselves, have or had a reputation for virtue. They are very staunch to each other, and no police officer ever succeeded in getting any reliable information out of a Bámptia."

They are not unpopular with their neighbours, because their robberies are committed at a distance, at religious fairs and other assemblages. They now freely use the railway as a hunting-ground, constantly travel in trains, and mix with the people in the waiting-sheds. They watch for an opportunity to alight in the night at some small station with any goods which they can appropriate, or they fling the bundle out of the carriage window as they approach a station, and afterwards search the line till they find the spoil. European travellers are constantly robbed in the same way.

[Arthur (A. T. Crawford), "Reminiscences of an Indian Police Official," chap. xvii.; Hervey, "Some Records of Crime," *passim*; Leitner, "Sketch of the Chángars"; Gunthorpe, "Notes on the Criminal Tribes of Bombay, Berar, and Central Provinces."]

HINDU; HINDUISM.—To define the terms Hindu and Hinduism is one of the most difficult problems in the investigation of Indian religion. Some have proposed to define a Hindu as one who receives religious services at the hands of Bráhmans. But both Sikhs and Jains employ Bráhman priests, and in Northern India the more recent converts to Islám consult them at marriages and other family rites; while they are found at Buddhist Courts, like those of the late Kings of Burma and in Siam. Nor does the custom of cremating the adult dead mark the line of distinction between Hindus and non-Hindus, because certain Hindu ascetics, like the Jogis and Jangamas, are buried; some of the lower Hindu castes bury or cremate their dead almost indiscriminately; the modern Buddhists of Tibet sometimes cremate, sometimes bury, and sometimes expose the corpse to birds and beasts of prey.

Hence many authorities have endeavoured to define Hinduism by a process of exclusion, holding that a Hindu is one of the large residuum which does not profess one of the other well-known creeds; in other words, that a Hindu is one who is not a Sikh, a Jain, a Buddhist, or professedly Animistic—the last, according to the definition adopted at the recent Census, implying that he professes a tribal religion, such as that of the Santál or Kol—and that he is not a member of one of the foreign religions—Islám, Hebraism, Mazdaism, or Christianity. And it has been further urged that,

"thus limited, a more applicable term for it would be Bráhmanism, which connotes its two chief characteristics at the present day—the recognition of inherited status, and the authority of a hereditary sacerdotalism."

The objection to this is that in some accounts of the religions of India, such as that of M. Barth, Bráhmanism has acquired a technical meaning, and implies that development of Hindu belief from the original worship displayed in the Vedas to the advanced ritualism taught in the sacred books, the Bráhmanas, in which the predominance of the doctrine of sacrifice and of the Bráhman priesthood is asserted.

Hence, conscious of the extreme vagueness of the term, a recent native writer lays down, "what the Hindus, or the major portion of them, do, that is Hinduism," or, to put the question in another way, Hinduism is more a social than a religious organisation, placing the fact of belonging to a caste, and subjecting each of its members to the common opinion of the group to which he belongs, above and independent of considerations of a religious or doctrinal character. Hence the Hindu of our day may be a follower of the Vedanta, the highest development of Hindu philosophy; or he may be an Agnostic, the product of Western thought acting on his traditional beliefs; he may be a hill-man, as ignorant of theology as the stone he worships in time of trouble, and ready to eat without scruple any food he can procure, provided he belongs to a definite caste, and duly follows the laws of social life which his caste prescribes.

And this has been the case from the earliest times. It is doubtful, for instance, if Buddhism ever differed from the orthodox Hinduism of its day more than does at present the creed of the Vaishnavas of Bengal, or of the Lingáyats of Southern India. The Jains, again, though their beliefs conflict with orthodox Hinduism in the most vital points, do not discard the title of Hindu, and still employ Bráhman priests. The revolt of the Sikhs from Hinduism was the result of political and social causes rather than differences of doctrine. Sikhism and Jainism are commonly regarded as religions distinct from Hinduism, because they became the State religions of ruling princes. Others who hold equally divergent views, but have not been pushed to the front by political influence, remain members of sects still included within the Hindu fold.

Thus, to use the words of Sir A. Lyall:

> "Hinduism is a tangled jungle of disorderly superstitions, ghosts, and demons, demi-gods and deified saints, local gods, universal gods, with their countless shrines and temples, and the din of their discordant rites; deities who abhor a fly's death, those who delight in human sacrifices, and those who would not either sacrifice or make offering— a religious chaos throughout a vast region never subdued or levelled, like all Western Asia, by Mahomedan or Christian monotheism."

Lastly, all these multitudinous forms of belief are left without any official control from its leaders. Hinduism has never dreamed of a Council or Convocation, a common Prayer-book, or a set of Articles of Belief. Each sect goes its own way, preaching its peculiar tenets, converting to its own standard the Animists by whom it is surrounded, and never combining for action except under the influence of some outburst of fanaticism, when the sacred cow, or a shrine in which only a handful of worshippers make sacrifice, is believed to be in danger.

It is this catholicism and indifference to dogma which makes the conversion of the Hindu to the tenets of a historical religion, like Islám or Christianity, so difficult. The mass, as a whole, is so flabby and loosely organised, that any general reformation is impossible. The result of any attack from abroad is merely the creation of one more new sect.

[Barth, "Religious of India"; Hopkins, "Religion of India"; Sir A. Lyall, "Asiatic Studies"; Monier-Williams, "Bráhmanism and Hinduism."]

HORSE.—Among Indian horses the Káthiáwár breed, with the stripes along the back, withers, and legs, is a very primitive type. It is believed to be the result of a cross with the wild ass, and some have thought that this is the origin of the tale of Sindibad, where the grooms of King Mihráj or Mahárája tethered the mares somewhere on the coast of Cutch to await the coming of the sea-horse. The present breed is the result of crossing with the northern horse and Arabs imported on the western coast, or, as Professor Ridgeway attempts to show, by a cross of the Libyan with the indigenous breed. In the partially-haired tail, too, this Káthiáwár breed differs from all living horses, save the Mongolian pony, which has been regarded as a distinct variety. Mr Lydekker has recently discovered in the skull of the modern Indian horse a vestige of the pre-orbital depression or pit which must, as in living deer, at one time have sheltered a tear-gland. He regards the Arab and the English thoroughbred as distinct from the *Eques caballus* of Western Europe, of which the original tint seems to have been dun with black marking on the legs, and sparse development of hair on mane and tail, like the Káthiáwár breed. The Arab variety, with a bright bay colour, white star on forehead, and not infrequently a black bar round the fetlock, is quite different. It is almost certain that the Indian horse is a descendant of the fossil horse of the Siwáliks, in which the skull pit is larger. A similar pit was found in the skulls of "Eclipse," "Bend Or" and "Stockwell," and hence it has been concluded that the Arab stock from which our thoroughbreds are derived was originally imported in ancient times from India.

The horse was highly valued by the Aryans, and the Vedas mention the Bahlika or Balkh stock; while in the Mahábhárata we read of breeds from Tartary and the Kalmuc country, with local horses from Sind, Kámboja, on the north-west frontier, and Panchála in the upper Ganges valley. With the Muhammadan invasion a large importation of horses from Turkestan to India began. Marco Polo speaks of the large trade in horses from Arabia and Persia to South India, where the animals lived only a few years, because the climate did not suit them, and the people did not know how to manage them. On the rise of the Bahmani dynasty in the Deccan, and the Vijayanagar kingdom further south, great efforts were made to import foreign horses, and in the sixteenth century the Portuguese found that their influence over these inland powers lay mainly in the control of the horse-trade. When the Mahratta kingdom came into being, the trade again improved, and they also largely imported from Northern India. On the downfall of Mahrattas and Sikhs, Indian horse-breeding again suffered a check, and was extended in recent times only to meet the increasing demand for remounts in the Indian Army.

In Portuguese times the great loss of Arabs at sea made the animal very costly. Pyrard de Laval says that an Arab or Persian was worth at Goa over £100, and Linschoten raises the price to £224. Tavernier tells us that the least valuable of the Moghul's horses cost from £875 to £1125, and that the best were worth £2250.

At the present day India largely imports Gulf Arabs from the Persian Gulf, Kábulis from Afghánistán, Cape horses from South Africa, Walers from Australia, and New Zealanders. Of the indigenous breeds, we have the Stud-bred, the produce of local mares from English thoroughbreds, Norfolk trotters, or Arab stallions. Of these the best are provided by the Panjáb, United Provinces, and Rájputána. Breeding is encouraged by prizes at horse-shows, and liberal purchases at fairs by army remount agents. Next come the Káthiáwár horses already described, and those of Cutch, which Abul Fazl tells us owed their excellence to a cargo of Arabs wrecked on the coast. Finch describes them as in his time the best horses in the world, worth £1500 apiece.

The Deccan breed was at its best in Mahratta times. Broughton describes them in Sindhia's camp as

"seldom above fourteen and a half hands high, and the most valuable ones are often much less. They are short in the barrel and neck; have small, well-shaped heads, and slim, though remarkably well-formed limbs; they have generous tempers, and are full of spirit; and are said to be capable of undergoing more fatigue and hard fare than any horse in India. The sum of three and even four thousand rupees, is often paid for a Dukhunee whose pedigree is well-known; and so fond are the Mahrattas of these beautiful and valuable favourites, that, when they can afford it, they will feed them on wheaten cakes, boiled rice, sugar, butter, and other similar dainties."

A still more stimulating food was sometimes provided for Indian horses in a meal of boiled mutton or goat's flesh. Marco Polo tells us that in Malabar they fed their horses on boiled meat and rice. In Cutch, before hard work, the old outlaw custom of giving the horse such food still prevails. Sir H. Yule tells a tale of Sir John Malcolm, when, at an English table, a brother officer had ventured to speak of the sheep's head custom to an incredulous audience. He appealed to Sir John, who only shook his head deprecatingly. After dinner the unfortunate story-teller remonstrated, but Sir John's answer was only: "My dear fellow! they took you for one Munchausen; they would only have taken me for another!"

It was on ponies such as those of the Deccan that the Pindáris made their extraordinary rides. The North Indian country pony of to-day is an excellent, hardy beast; the *tattoo** under an *ekka** makes wonderful journeys when stimulated to exertion by a ball of sugar and spice.

The native, in buying a horse, depends on marks and colours, some of which are lucky and some unlucky, much more than on the well recognised points. In the Deccan three rings of hair, one above the other, or forming three angles, two rings in a line on the brow, various lines in the hair of the neck or chest, are all inauspicious.

But happily a horse may have one good mark which counterbalances those that are unlucky. Of these marks the most regarded are the feathers, one on each side of the neck, just under the mane. If there be two turning towards the ears, it is a good sign; one of this kind is tolerably good. But if the feather turn towards the rider, it is the Sampan, or mark of the snake, which is most dangerous. General Sleeman tells of the King of Oudh, becoming enamoured of a waiting-maid, but as she unfortunately had a Sampan, or figure of a coiled snake in the hair on the back of her head, the queen-mother remonstrated, and suggested that His Majesty's attacks of palpitation of the heart were caused by some of his wives being marked in this unlucky way. True enough this was found to be the case with no less than eight of the King's wives, all of whom he promptly divorced.

As regards colours, a Pachkalyán—that is, a horse possessing the five auspicious colours, four white stockings and a white blaze on the forehead—is highly prized. In the Deccan equally valued are a piebald horse marked in this way, and a wall-eyed, cream-coloured mare; while a mare of any other colour, or with one wall eye is most unlucky. The wily British subaltern studies marks like these, and often buys an inauspicious beast for a song. For the respectable native gentleman the ideal horse is a cream or piebald with a Roman nose, taught to amble and prance by judicious pressure of his cruel thorny bit. The beauty of such a beast is thought to be much improved if his mane, tail, and fetlocks are dyed a bright scarlet.

[Professor Ridgeway, "The Origin and Influence of the Thorough-bred Horse."]

HOUSE.—The oldest existing human dwelling-places in India are said to be the Khandagiri caves in Orissa, while the stone walls at Girivraja, in the Patna District, are supposed to be remains of the oldest stone buildings. But stone buildings are comparatively modern, and in ancient times caves were the abodes of the troglodyte ascetics, like those who still live in such places on the banks of the Irawadi. The habit of occupying caves, though infrequent, has not quite disappeared from the India of our day. Dr Ball found the Kamars of Raepur, in the Central Provinces, living in caves, and a colony of Kunjwas housing themselves in the same way at Solon, below Simla. He remarks that these modern cave-dwellers do little to protect themselves from the weather; their sole artificial shelter was a lean-to of loose branches to exclude the wind.

Next above the dwellings of these troglodytes comes the round house. This, the earliest form of human habitation, has survived for ritual purposes in the Temple of Vesta at Rome, and in a few British churches like that of the Temple; while it is the model of the Kibitka of the Tartar hordes and of the pastoral Baloch tribes. This form of house simply represents the result of bending down two or three branches to form a rude shelter. Houses of this kind are still found among the wilder races in various parts of the country, from some of the more secluded Rájputs of the west to the hill-men of Bombay and Madras and the Andamanese. At Masulipatam, says Fryer, the huts "are cast round as beehives, and walled with mud." The last Madras Census Report describes a Kuravan marching along with his round basket-work hut on his head when he changes his quarters.

The beginnings of the rectangular house may perhaps be traced in the rude shelters used by the Gipsy tribes. These are made of bamboo or palm-leaf matting, or of some coarse canvas or cloth. But some, like the Doms of Behár, have not even such a dwelling as this, and in rain cower under the eaves, or creep into the cattle-shed. Slightly superior to the nomad's shelter is the hut of the ruder forest tribes.

"The huts of the Juángs," writes Colonel Dalton, "are about the smallest that human beings ever deliberately constructed as dwellings. They measure about 6 feet by 8, and are very low, with doors so small as to preclude the idea of a corpulent householder. Scanty as are the above dimensions for a family dwelling, the interior is divided into two compartments, one of which is the store-room, the other used for all domestic arrangements. The paterfamilias and all his belongings of the female sex huddle together in this one stall, not much larger than a dog-kennel; for the boys there is a separate dormitory."

The narrow entrance, into which the owner is obliged to creep on all fours, is characteristic of the most primitive kind of Dravidian hut, and it has been suggested that this is a reminiscence of cave-life. It is also noteworthy that the Dravidians, practising the nomadic system of agriculture, do not in their most primitive stage build their houses in continuous rows or streets, but erect them on the hill-sides, in convenient proximity to the holding. The Andaman hut is merely a thatch, 4 feet by 3, sloping from 5 inches behind to 4½ feet in front, and supported by four uprights and some cross-pieces, without walls.

Very similar to these was the earliest Indo-Aryan house, the form of which has been handed down in the marriage shed of our days. The materials were wood, basket-work, and clay. The main feature was the corner-posts, which were fixed in the ground with rites, sometimes including human sacrifice, intended to conciliate the earth-spirits, and were always regarded as, in some sense, sacrosanct.

The modern house varies largely in construction and arrangement throughout the Peninsula. In Southern India, where the fear of ceremonial pollution is felt more keenly than in the north, the object is to secure the isolation of the family. To quote Pyrard de Laval:

"All the houses of the Malabars are of this sort. They have large porches at the entrance of their houses, as well poor as rich, within the enclosure; for all their houses are enclosed with walls, that is, those of the rich; the rest have ditches and good, strong palisades of wood, and note that these are so high, that when one wants to go from one house to another, one must ascend a ladder of five or six steps, and so descend, while on both sides are wooden barriers which close with locks. You never see there any house but has its garden and orchard, small or large. These porches or auiards in front of the house are for receiving passing strangers, both for giving them meat and drink, and also a place to rest and sleep; they take them not inside their houses."

The arrangement known as the Joint Family has left its mark in the Bengal house. Here the dwelling of a well-to-do merchant or land-owner generally consists of a series of rooms built round two courts, which lead one into the other—the outer to accommodate the male members of the family; the inner for the women. The peasant's hut is likewise enclosed in a yard, one side of which is occupied by the chief building, consisting of two rooms, one for sleeping, the other used as a store-house. On the other sides are the cattle-sheds, store-rooms, or cook-houses, and accommodation for those members of the family who have not set up house for themselves. When a son marries, he simply adds an extra shed to the original family house.

When we go further north the character of the house alters. Here the bamboo of Bengal is scarce, and timber is dear. Hence the walls of the house are built of mud, and while the meaner hut has a flimsy thatch of reed-stalks laid on light rafters, the better-class house has a flat roof made of rough beams covered with brushwood, on which a thick layer of clay is rammed. Sometimes the house has a tiled roof, but this is liable to destruction by hail-storms or by the squalls of the monsoon, and is often wrecked by the monkeys, who tear up the tiles to recover grain dropped between them.

In this part of the country the feeling of insecurity, which dates from the anarchy following the decay of the Moghul Empire, is marked in the castellated form of the better-class houses, huddled together with narrow intervening lanes designed for self-defence. The courtyard plan prevails also here, but it is entered from a sort of winding inside porch, where robbers may be resisted. This insecurity of life and property is illustrated not only in the arrangement of the older cities, where each class of merchant and craftsman used to occupy a separate quarter which could be barricaded at night, but in the plan of the palaces of the ruling chiefs. Mr Val Prinsep tells us that in the Udaypur palace there is not a single room through which a moderately-sized man could pass without stooping; and M. Rousselet describes a palace at Baroda to which he ascended by a dark staircase, nearly perpendicular, and so narrow that he could easily touch both walls with his elbows. This was closed at the top by a heavy trap-door.

In the Himálaya the severity of the climate has led to a modification of plan. The house in Kumaun is built of large stones, and roofed with heavy slates. In shape it is narrow and very long, with two stories—the lower used as a byre and store-room; the upper, with a long enclosed verandah, being the dwelling-house. When thatch is used, it is fastened with strips of split bamboo, to which heavy weights are attached. In Bhutan the form is more like a Swiss chalet, the want being a chimney, which the people are unable to construct.

We have seen that the primitive Dravidian hut resembles the Kibitka of the Central Asian nomads. The tradition of the *Shámyána*,* or great flat tent elevated on poles, survives in the pillared Moghul audience rooms, which are the glory of Delhi and Agra.

The finest form of town house is found in great trading cities, like those of Rájputána, or at places of pilgrimage such as Mathura or Násik. In Násik we find the wooden house of the best type. Mountstuart Elphinstone writes:

> "Houses are ornamented with wood-work and verandahs with pillars, some twisted and some straight, all newly ornamented with flowers and other patterns cut deeply in the wood; and balconies ornamented in the same way, projecting a little over the street, and supported by carved masses of wood jutting out from the walls. The beam over the front of the shops is always ornamented in this way."

M. Rousselet describes a similar and perhaps finer

type in the wonderful house of the Seth merchants at Ajmír, with two upper stories decorated with balconies and profuse carving. Ahmadábád, and many of the old towns in the Panjáb, supply examples of splendid wood carving applied to domestic architecture, which reaches, perhaps, its highest point in the streets of Nepál towns like Khatmandu, Pátan, and Bhátgaon. In the northern pilgrim cities, such as Mathura or Benares, this decoration is executed in stone. The delicate ornamentation and lace-like lattices, all derived from the original wooden type, are marvellously elaborate and effective. The finest example of the style is reached in Bírbal's house at Fatehpur-Sikri, which Victor Hugo calls "the tiniest of palaces, or the largest of jewel-boxes."

Finally, when we pass to the Indo-Chinese area, we notice a new form of house—the long house, such as that of the Gáros and Singhpos of the Assam frontier. Colonel Dalton describes one of these, 100 feet long by 20 broad, divided into rooms on both sides of a long passage open from end to end; and Sir J. G. Scott gives a plan of a Kachin house in Upper Burma, built in the form of an oblong, with a projecting porch at each end. Ascending a flight of steps you enter the house, in which the rooms are arranged in a double row, on one side being the general guest room, opposite to which is that occupied by the girls. Beyond this is the long room of the men, and fronting it is one for the parents of the family, and another for the eldest son. The boys occupy the so-called Bachelor's Hall which is common to all the village youths.

A second peculiarity of the Burmese house is one occasionally found in other parts of the country, as among some of the Panjáb Játs. To quote Sir H. Yule:

"An effectual barrier to the actual adoption of these many storied-buildings in Burma exists in the deeply-rooted prejudice of every man in the nation against allowing any one not of admitted superiority in rank to occupy a more elevated position than himself. That any one should occupy a floor above one's head would be felt as an intense degradation. Hence, though the inhabited floors of nearly all buildings in Burma are raised to some height above the ground, there is no such thing properly as a two-storied dwelling in the country, except some few belonging to foreigners."

The modest height of Burmese buildings is shown by Sir J. G. Scott to be due to the fact that

"in Upper Burma the shape of a man's house is fixed for him by law according to his station in life. All are one-storied, save where exceptional royal favour has granted a spire-like roof to a distinguished noble. No one would brave the denunciation of the religious by adding a spire to his house, or even adorning the gable with the carved pinnacles and flamboyant finials of the monasteries. Consequently the one regular form prevails everywhere."

[For houses generally, "Census Report," India, 1891, i. 55f.; South India, "Census," Cochin, 1901, i. 6; Fawcett, in "Bulletin of Madras Museum," iii. No. III. p. 303; "Panjáb Census," 1901, i. 26; Buddhist, Rhys Davids, "Buddhist India," 68; "Bombay Gazetteer," xviii. Pt. III. 286; Bengal, Hunter, "Orissa," ii. App. 13f.; Lal Bihari Dey, "Bengal Peasant Life," 28ff.; Himálaya, Gerard, "Koonawar," 84f.; Lewin, "Wild Races," 43.]

HUMAN SACRIFICE; CANNIBALISM.—The first literary evidence of human sacrifice is found in the Sanhita of the Rigveda, which records how a father vows to sacrifice his son to the god Varuna, and how the child is miraculously saved by the intervention of the deity. This rule of sacrifice to the water god possibly survives in the later sacrifice of children in honour of the Ganges at Ságar Island, where the river meets the ocean. Later, in the Yajurveda, we have the rite of Parusha-medha, or "man-sacrifice," and the same ceremony was an accompaniment of the celebrated Asva-medha or horse sacrifice. Thus it developed into what was called the Narabali, in honour of the blood-stained goddess Chámunda, and this was recognised in the foul Tantric worship as a ceremonial rite, where alone it survives in ritual form in dark corners of the land to the present day.

All through the later course of history we meet occasional instances of the custom. First we find the foundation sacrifice, either, as some believe, intended to appease the earth-deities of the place, or as a deliberate piece of god-making, to create a divine protector of the building. Many a fort and tank, as legend tells, were guarded in this way, and it has been in the wilder tracts one of the standing difficulties connected with the decennial Census that the enumerators are supposed to be making a roll of victims for such a rite. Whenever we build a great bridge or harbour mole, our engineers are suspected of being on the look-out for victims, and people are careful not to wander abroad at night during the time the foundation is being laid.

Of a different kind is the voluntary immolation of ascetics. One of the places where such self-sacrifice used to occur was the shrine of Omkár Mandháta in Central India, one of the aboriginal deities adopted into Hinduism. Here fanatics used to leap from a cliff in pursuance of a vow. There was a general belief that any one who escaped death in the leap would become Rája. To avoid such an unpleasant contingency, it is said that the ruling prince was careful to have poison mixed with the last food given to the victim. An English officer witnessed the death of almost the last victim in 1822, and since then the strong arm of the law prevents any sacrifice. By another method, known as the Jal Samádh, or "water sacrifice," the fanatic used to construct a wooden platform fixed on several earthen pots, the mouths of which were turned down. The whole was placed in a sacred tank or stream, and the victim gradually sank with the support on which he rested. Ward describes an implement used in Bengal in the early part of last century—a steel knife in the shape of a half-moon, by which devotees, pressing the edge of the blade against the nape of the neck, and violently dragging it forwards by chains attached to stirrups in which their feet rested, succeeded in decapitating themselves.

Another form, again, was the rite of *Traga*,* as practised by the tribe of bards in Western India. They were employed to act as treasure-escorts in troubled times, and vowed to immolate themselves if any attack were made on the property committed to their charge. The knowledge that such a security would wound, and, if necessary, kill himself or one of his family, prevented many an outrage.

The well-known Meriah sacrifice of the Kandhs was of quite another type. Here the victim was procured by the menial Pan tribe, usually by kidnapping from British villages. He was acceptable only if he had been bought with a price, or had been born a victim—that is, that he was the son of a victim-father, or had been devoted as a child by his parents. In some cases the youth was tied to the proboscis of a wooden elephant, a specimen of which is one of the curiosities of the Madras Museum. After death portions of the flesh were distributed throughout the country, and buried in the fields to ensure the fertility of the soil. Mr J. G. Frazer suggests that the victim may have originally represented the earth-deity, or perhaps a deity of vegetation, though in later times he came to be regarded more as a victim than a living god.

In this rite we meet with instances of substitution or commutation of the sacrifice, which often accompanied a gradual progress in civilisation. Sometimes the victim was replaced by a goat, or the father merely pricked the ear of one of his children, and the blood which trickled on the ground constituted the sacrifice. Among some of the tribes of Madras the mother, before the ear-piercing of her eldest daughter which is preparatory to betrothal, has to undergo amputation of the top joint of one or more fingers of her right hand. She offers part of herself to save her daughter from the Nemesis which dogs the fortunate. Dr Ball tells how a Santál propitiated the hill-god to secure good sport. He put a few grains of rice on a leaf, and then drew blood from various parts of his person, commencing by pricking his toe with a thorn and ending with his ear. Each drop was made to fall on a grain of rice, and this constituted the offering. Similarly the ascetic custom of jumping over a cliff was modified in some of the Native States of the Himálaya into the habit of the victim sliding down a rope suspended from a precipice. When the horrid rite of swinging a man in the Charakh Púja (*Churuck Pooja* *) was prohibited in British territory, some of the central tribes found that it answered the purpose quite as well to swing a pumpkin from a pole. A solemn farce is performed to mark the transition from the original blood-sacrifice at the installation of the Rája of the Bengal Bhuiyas. A man comes forward and the Rája touches his head with a sword; the "victim" disappears for three days, and then presents himself at Court as if he had been miraculously restored to life.

We meet with a similar evolution in the custom of head-hunting among the savage tribes on the eastern Bengal and Burma frontier. The primary object is not to collect trophies; this is quite a later development, as it appears among the Kachins. Still less primitive is the Chinaman's theory of cutting off the heads of his enemies, in the belief that it will be to their disadvantage to appear headless in the next world. The Wás of Burma preserve the original idea. They procure heads in the hope that the soul of the dead man will accompany his head, and that when hung up in its possessor's house it will scare the powers of evil. Hence they prefer the skull of a stranger, because the ghost does not know his way about in a new place, and is not likely to wander. But even among the Wás there are grades in head-hunting. The really wild Wá takes any heads he can come across, those of strangers and innocent people by preference; a little above him is the Wá who restricts his collection to heads taken in war, and those of thieves and dacoits. A person is considered well on the way to reclamation who only buys heads, though he be not careful to enquire how they were obtained. At the top of the scale is the Wá who has given up using human skulls, and exhibits only those of wild beasts. This is the shape into which the custom has developed among those Himálayan tribes who have been to some extent humanised by Buddhism.

The accounts we sometimes now read of human sacrifice exhibit its degraded, ritual form. Human blood is supposed to be a sovereign cure for barrenness and other evils which are attributed to the influence of demons, and we occasionally hear of children being immolated for such purposes. Mysterious cases of corpses found in sequestered shrines of the dread goddess Káli are either the result of actual sacrifice or of religious suicide.

From the time of Herodotus down to Marco Polo, there are numerous accounts of cannibalism among Asiatic races like the Padæans, who, perhaps, represent the Battas of the Malay Peninsula. Many of the stories told are certainly exaggerations, or based on sheer error, like that of Thevenot, who, in 1666, speaks of human flesh being openly sold in a market near Broach. But a careful authority, Mr Logan, thinks it not improbable that cannibalism occurred at times among the lower classes of Malabar; and Dr Burnell quotes a recent case in which some slaves killed a Nair, and, on being asked why they committed the murder, replied that if they ate his flesh their sin would be removed. There seems to be no evidence of its occurrence during the late terrible famines. Where it does very rarely occur, it seems to be in the ceremonial or sacramental form, based on the idea that by eating the flesh of any one eminent for virtue, courage, and the like, these qualities will be transferred to those who partake of the ghastly meal. When Colonel Dalton taxed the Kharrias of Chota Nágpur with the crime, they did not deny that the practice of devouring their parents once obtained among them; but he rejects as a fable a similar story told of the Birhors, an allied tribe. According to Sir J. G. Scott, the use of human flesh was always permitted to the Sháns of Burma during the operation of tattooing, and he points out that the accusation of cannibalism made against the Wás is as old as the "Lusiad" of Camoëns. They are not habitual cannibals, but possibly at their annual feasts human flesh is eaten as a religious rite. Their enemies say that they tempt old people to climb a tree, shake them down, and eat them.

[Human sacrifice generally, Chevers, "Indian Medical Jurisprudence," 396ff.; Crooke, "Popular Religion," ii. 285; Yule, "Marco Polo," 3rd ed.

ii. 349 ; Kandhs, Frazer, "Golden Bough," 2nd ed. ii. 241ff. ; South India, Logan, "Malabar Manual," i. 173ff. ; Oppert, "Original Inhabitants," 332 ; in North India, Malcolm, "Central India," ii. 210ff. ; Ball, "Jungle Life," 81 ; Forsyth, "Highlands of Central India," 181 ; in the Himálaya, Harcourt, "Kooloo," 206 ; Waddell, "Buddhism of Tibet," 518 ; in Burma, "Upper Burma Gazetteer," i. Pt. I. 327, 430, 498, 511.]

IDOLATRY.—In India, as in most countries, idolatry is a late development of fetishism. There were images in Vedic times, one of Rudra is specially mentioned; but there is no evidence of actual image-worship. Fetishism, of course—the worship of stock and stone—comes down from the most ancient days; every village sacred tree has its pile of stones which embody the local god. But some Central Indian tribes, like the Mundas, pay little regard to fetishes, and have no symbols of any kind; while others, like the Oraons, have always some visible object of worship, though it may be but a wooden post, a stone, or a lump of clay. The wild tribes of Burma have no images, not even a stock or stone.

We can see the transition from fetishism to idolatry in its lowest type among a degraded tribe like the Madras Yanadis, who worship pieces of wood, bricks, stones, pots of water in which are placed leaves of the sacred margosa tree, rude pictures on the walls of their huts, or mere handfuls of clay squeezed into some shape, and placed under a sacred tree.

According to one view the sacrificial post, carved and ornamented with a rude face or other symbol, was at an early period introduced into the temple to represent the god. According to another, the altar-stone or menhir—the haunt of a ghost to whom blood-sacrifice was offered—assumed the anthropomorphic form, and became the idol. Others suggest that actual idol-worship began when Buddhism had already become contaminated by Animism. There are no early statues of the Master, nor is he represented on the Bharhut Stúpa (150-100 B.C.), nor at Sánchi. General Cunningham believes that the oldest representation of Buddha is on the coins of the Indo-Scythian king Kanishka, about 100 A.D. Sculpture does appear on the Mahábodhi railing of the time of Asoka (272-232 B.C.);

but the earliest, finest, and most essentially classical images of Buddha are to be found in Gandhára or South Afghánistán, and were doubtless produced under Hellenistic influence. Thus the idol, in its modern form, owes its inspiration to Greece. Image-worship is referred to only twice by Manu, and his expression of contempt for the temple priest shows that it was regarded as an innovation on the pure Aryan household worship.

Idols fall into two classes—Svayambhu, "existing spontaneously," that is to say, stones which in their own nature are pervaded by the essence of deity; secondly, those that are artificial. The former are much the more sacred. They are generally rude stones, with little or no carving, which are supposed to have descended from heaven, or to have appeared miraculously on earth. They are so pure in themselves that they are not liable to pollution, and if defiled in any way do not require reconsecration. With the artificial stones, on the contrary, measures must be taken to cause the deity to abide in its representation. The ritual of consecration varies with the dignity of the image. Usually, when brought from the maker's workshop, it is purified by washing with the five products of the sacred cow. It is then placed in a copper jar full of water for twenty-four hours, when the priest touches the image in all its limbs, and finally breathes upon its lips. The sacred fire is lit, and the image and its temple, which also undergoes purification, become fit objects of worship. The Himálayan Buddhist pushes the anthropomorphic idea still further by inserting in the larger images internal organs made of dough or clay, and in the more valued ones filings of the nobler metals and holy rice. The final consecration is secured by inserting a scroll of the law and other sacred books.

The artificial idol may be made of various substances. The precious metals are held in the highest honour; then comes an alloy of eight metals which is highly esteemed. Those of the small-pox goddess, following the law of symbolism, are of silver. Some of the most ancient and reverend images are made of wood, and that of the *Neem* * tree is specially valued. Many persons make an image of clay for each act of worship, and when the service is over the image is thrown into running water, in many cases as a rain charm. Jaypur provides most of Bráhmanical India with images of marble, white, red, or black, plain, coloured, or gilt. If current rumour be not mistaken, Birmingham shares in the trade in metal images.

A broad line of distinction lies between the cult of Siva and that of Vishnu. In the former there is no idol, only the so-called phallic symbol, which was probably, in form, derived from the model of the miniature Dagoba or Buddhist relic-shrine. This is worshipped only with a water-oblation, a few flowers, and in some cases by perambulation round the symbol or the shrine, which must be done with the right shoulder towards the sacred object in the course of the Sun, or as we pass the decanters round the dinner-table. Hence the cult commends itself to the economical worshipper, while the banker prefers the elaborate worship of Vishnu. His image is finely chased and decorated, solemnly washed at daybreak, dressed, fed, put to bed for a siesta, and finally made comfortable for the night.

The Hindu gods are always represented in a standing or sitting posture. The Burmese, in their representations of Buddha, adopt three attitudes—standing, sitting, or lying; the first as a teacher, the second in meditation, the third as he died, and attained Nirvána. The Tibetan images of Buddha are made of *papier-maché*, clay, bread-dough, compressed incense, and butter of various tints, the larger being supported by an inner framework of wood. The Burmese and Tibetans differ from the Hindus in often making their images of perishable materials, being designed, as they say, only as a temporary representative, to keep alive the reverence for the Master. They also have the habit, unknown to Hindus, of fixing a film of gold-leaf on the image. One of these Sir J. G. Scott describes as covered by the piety of generations of worshippers with a layer of gold half an inch thick.

The idols of modern India present little of the artistic taste shown by the people in other ways, and which appears in the older Buddhist and Jain images and those found on the north-west frontier. The reason is perhaps in a large measure because the type soon becomes conventionalised, and never changes. To represent the dignity and attributes of the god they have recourse to the clumsy expedient of representing him of enormous size, or possessing many limbs, weapons, and symbols. We have thus the four-armed Vishnu, or eight-armed Devi. Colossal images are common both to Buddhists and Jains. Sir H. Yule suggested that the fashion of making these enormous images came from Ceylon, but the wide diffusion of the practice renders this unlikely. Tavernier speaks of one in Siam more that 60 feet high; Abul Fazl describes the statues at Bamian in Afghánistán, one of a man 80 yards high, another of a woman 50 yards, a third of a child 15. The Buddhist pilgrim, Hiuen Tsiang, says that the greater image, which was gilt, was of a height of 140 or 150 feet, and the second 100. The latter, he seems to say, was sheathed in copper. Still larger was a recumbent figure, which he says was about 1000 feet in length. The largest Jain figure at Gwalior is 57 feet high, while that at Shravan-belgola in Mysore, the colossal statue of Gomatesvara, cut out of a single rock, is 60 feet in height.

INFANTICIDE.—The practice of female infanticide is not of recent growth in India. It is condemned in the early law books, but it was an ancient Aryan rule that the father was entitled to "take up" the child, and thus decide whether it was to be reared or not.

At all times the birth of a girl has been regarded as a misfortune, not a blessing. Even a man so enlightened as Todar Mal, the revenue minister of Akbar, gave up wearing an aigrette in his turban when a girl was born to him. The real basis of this feeling is that rule of marriage which modern ethnologists term hypergamy, or the law of superior marriage. This compels a man to marry his daughter to a member of a group equal or superior in rank to his own; while he himself may take his wife, or at any rate his second wife, from a lower group. The custom seems to have originated in the rule of the early law-givers, which allowed an Aryan to marry a woman of the indigenous tribes, but forbade, under the heaviest penalty, an Aryan woman allying herself to one of the aborigines. However the custom may have arisen, the practical result is that there is a surplus of women in the higher groups. When the men are allowed to marry women of lower rank than themselves, competition for husbands to wed high-born girls inevitably arises. The old habit of buying the bride gives way to the custom of buying the bridegroom, and in extreme cases infanticide is a necessary result. Infanticide is thus a custom depending altogether on social considerations, and on the special Hindu marriage law.

Tavernier thus describes the custom as it prevailed in Bengal in his time:

"When a woman is delivered, and the infant, as often happens, is unwilling to take its mother's breast in order to suckle, it is carried outside the village and placed in a cloth, which is tied by the four corners to the branches of a tree, and is thus left from morning to evening. In this way the poor infant is exposed to the crows, which come to torment it, and some have been found whose eyes have been torn out of their heads, which is the reason why many idolaters are seen in Bengal who have but one eye, and others who have both injured or altogether gone."

Probably small-pox had more to say to the prevalence of blindness than child-exposure.

General Sleeman gives a terrible picture of female infanticide in Oudh in 1849. One of his Bráhman informants told him that not more than one in ten, or, as another said, one in twenty girls was allowed to live in some tribes. He records another curious fact, like the custom of "sin-eating," which is said to have at one time prevailed in England, that the family priest, while the household was regarded as under the curse of child-murder, was invited to eat in the house, and thus assumed responsibility for the sin.

The custom attracted the attention of British officers soon after we first came in contact with the races chiefly addicted to the crime in the upper Ganges valley, the Panjáb, and Rájputána. The efforts to repress it first took the form of conferences of the leaders of the guilty tribe, who were urged to form an organisation for the reduction of the cost of marriage and the removal of the other disabilities which led to the murder of female infants. The result of these measures was disappointing, and finally a special law was passed by which notably guilty clans were proclaimed, made liable to constant inspection of their infants and to the payment of a heavy police-tax, which continued until the tale of girls was again complete.

The result of this legislation has been so far successful that it is believed that actual murder of female children now seldom occurs; but the low figure of girl-infants, as compared to that of males, indicates that the former are neglected.

In the Panjáb the Játs are certainly addicted to it, but to quote the last report, actual infanticide occurs only when "the prospective difficulty of finding a husband is combined with a superstitious belief that the child is likely to cause misfortune." In Western India it seems to be confined to Baroda. As might have been expected, the difficulty of feeding little girls leads to their destruction among the hill-tribes. Colonel Dalton states that among the Kandhs the future of the child is decided by sticking an ivory stylus into a sacred book, and the fate of the infant depends upon the picture or sentence which is touched. If the parents are satisfied that the child is likely to bring trouble upon them, it is placed in an earthen jar, carried to that point of the compass from which the oracle declares that evil is to be anticipated, and there buried.

The question is thus summed up by Mr Risley:

"But if the practice of deliberately doing away with

female infants is now confined to a limited area, and even there is perhaps somewhat rare, there is little reason to doubt that in most parts of India female infants receive far less attention than males. It is almost universally the case that, whereas male offspring are ardently desired, the birth of a female child is unwelcome. It is especially so where the provision of a husband is a matter of difficulty and expense, and where there are already several female children in the family. Consequently, even if there is no deliberate design of hastening a girl's death, there is no doubt that, as a rule, she receives less attention than would be bestowed upon a son. She is less warmly clad, and less carefully rubbed with mustard-oil, as a prophylactic against the colds and chills to which the greater part of the mortality amongst young children in India is due; she is also probably not so well fed as a boy would be, and, when ill, her parents are not likely to make the same strenuous efforts to ensure her recovery. It seems clear, therefore, that even if they are constitutionally stronger than boys, girls in this country, especially amongst Hindus, are less likely than in Europe to reverse the birth-proportion of the sexes by a relatively low mortality during the early years of life."

Male infanticide, which is reported only from the Panjáb, depends on causes different from those which produce female infanticide. It is based on the belief in the blood-sacrifice, which is regarded as a remedy for barrenness; a woman should bathe over the child's body or in water in which it has been immersed. According to one account, life should be taken with a copper knife—a remarkable instance of religious conservatism—and with as much pain as possible.

[Chevers, "Indian Medical Jurisprudence," 750; "Calcutta Review," i. 372ff.; "Census Report," India, 1901, i. 115ff.; Panjáb, i. 203ff.]

INTOXICANTS.—The use of intoxicating liquor is recorded in the very early legend, which tells of its production from the churning of the mystic Mount Mandara, and there is ample evidence of its use in Aryan times. The earliest Indian drink was the Soma, regarding the nature and qualities of which there is much difference of opinion. In India the plants identified with the Soma are various species of *Sarcostemma*. The modern Pársis, who use it in their religious rites, import from Persia as Homa the stems of the jointed fir (*Ephedra vulgaris*), and use also the twigs of the spurge-wort (*Euphorbia vulgaris*). The extreme unpleasantness of the juice of any Asclepiad has been taken to prove the impossibility of this identification; but Sir G. Birdwood points out that near Bombay the hill-men drink a similar intoxicant from the root of the *Calotropis gigantea* or swallow-wort. It is possible that, as the best available substitute for the foreign beverage, the *Sarcostemma*, which grows in Bombay, was selected; and it seems, on the whole, most probable that the juice, from whatever plant it may have been originally derived, was used like hops, because it contained a bitter principle suitable to flavour the sacred drink, which may have been fermented from some kind of grain.

With the rise of Buddhism came a reaction against the use of drink, which is reflected in the directions of Manu that the higher classes should abstain, while the Sudras might drink what they pleased. For them, he says, there is no disgrace in drinking, but abstinence is a sign of spiritual advancement. He does not refer to the milder intoxicants, like toddy; but he went so far as to order that those of the higher classes who indulged in spirits were to commit suicide by drinking them in a boiling state. The historian, Ibn Khurdádba, tells of an equally drastic reformer, a king of Kumár or Cape Comorin, who used to brand wine-bibbers with a hot iron. With the rise of Saktism, or the impure rites of Mother-worship, the use of spirits became part of the ritual, and this has certainly been one of the main causes of the spread of drunkenness among the lower classes.

By the time they reached India, the Musalmáns had in a great measure come to disregard the rules of Muhammad prohibiting drinking. Nearly every Musalmán king, Ala-ud-dín in particular, at the instigation of the priestly body, tried to prohibit it, but without success. To use Gibbon's phrase, the wines of Shiráz have always prevailed over the law of the Prophet. Bábar writes openly about his drinking-parties. Akbar, to the horror of the religious orders, allowed the sale of wine in the bazaars. Jahángír, under priestly admonition, prohibited the use of beer and hemp, and, by some accounts, of wine. The order was as ineffective as his famous ukase against tobacco. He grossly exceeded himself, and even had a coin struck in which he is represented with a wine-cup in his hands. Many of his degenerate successors owed their deaths to excess in drinking. It was the Moghuls, too, who made the use of ice popular. It used to be brought to their palaces from the hills of Kumaun, whence it was floated on a raft down the Jumna to Delhi, which it reached in a journey of three days and nights.

The importation of wine—by preference Italian, and also that produced in Asia Minor and Persia—was carried on as early as the time of the Periplus in the first century of our era. There was also a demand for palm wine from Arabia. Linschoten speaks of pipes of wine as part of the cargo of ships in the Indian voyage, and Grose tells us that in his time (1757) Europeans depended on supplies from abroad,

> "few relishing the distillery of the country, which, however, produces various strong spirits, to which they give names that would seem odd, such as spirit of mutton, spirit of goat, but for the reason they annex to it, which is their throwing into the still according to the liquor they propose a joint of mutton, a haunch of venison, which give their names respectively to the distillation. This, they imagine—how justly I do not pretend to know—superadds to the liquor a certain mellowness and softness that corrects the fieriness of the spirit."

This method does not appear to have survived to our days.

Petro della Valle describes a favourite English drink called "Burnt Wine"—"hot wine boyled with cloves, cinnamon, and other spices." According to Ovington (1686), "Bengal is a much stronger spirit than that of Goa, though both are made use of by the Europeans in making Punch"; and Fryer (1674), discussing the unhealthiness of Bombay, describes a horrid decoction, *Fool Rack* *: "Brandy made of Blubber, or Carvil by the Portugals, because it swims always in a Blubber, as if nothing else were in it; but touch it, and it stings like nettle." In his curious way of explaining the term, he says that "it, distilled, causes those that take it to be Fools."

The hill-tribes have various intoxicants of their own. Those of the Central Hills make it chiefly of *Mohwa* * (*Bassia latifolia*), a spirit which, according to Captain Forsyth, when well mellowed, resembles in some degree Irish whisky. He must have been singularly fortunate, because when the British soldier drinks it in its cruder form he holds his nose as a child does when taking medicine. He adds that, though the Gonds drink occasionally, habitual excess has practically ceased under our rule. Many of the northern and eastern tribes make a sort of crude beer, which has been brewed by them from the earliest times. Thus, to the west, we have the Chang of Spiti and the Lugri of Kulu, both pernicious drinks made from fermented rice. Further east we have the Marwa of Sikhim and the neighbouring hills, and the Zu of the eastern Nágas. Colonel Cunningham notes the remarkable method in which this Marwa beer is made. It takes its name from a species of millet of which it should be made, but in default of this maize or rice is used. The grain, of whatever kind it may be, is first pulped by being exposed in baskets under a small waterfall. It is then mixed with fragments of fermentative cakes, which are stored for use. The basis of these is coarsely-ground corn, permeated throughout with the dried and empty mycelial filaments of a species of Mucor, bearing numerous reproductive bodies in the form of Chlamydospores. The curious point is that it also contains a certain proportion of the root-tissues of a species of *Polygala*, which secures the presence in the cake of numbers of reproductive fungal elements, capable of retaining their vitality for prolonged periods so long as they are kept dry. The proportion of

Polygala in the cakes has to be carefully regulated, because, on the one hand, any undue amount leads to suppression of growth of the fungal elements; and, on the other, any defect fails to suppress the common and useless aerial fructification of the fungus. It is difficult to imagine how such a difficult problem as the due relations of the various constituents of the cakes could have been worked out by any savage or semi-civilised people and yet it has been done by these tribes of the Eastern Himálaya. This beer is half a food and half a drink, and is sucked with a straw from a bamboo jug. It is a good rule among some of these tribes that the use of liquor is taboo to women. The Kandh women of Orissa merely touch the cup with their lips at a feast as a compliment to the guests, and while drunkenness is considered laudable among the men, in a woman it is uncommon, and would be thought disgraceful.

The use of liquor by the natives of the present day is a subject too wide for discussion here. There seems no good reason to believe that the immoderate use of spirits has increased, though probably the consumption is more general than in the early years of our rule. At any rate, when we first came in contact with the natives, there was much drinking. Streynsham Master, writing from Surat in 1672, says of the people: "None of them will eat the Flesh of Cows, and Oxen or Calves, and almost as few of them forbear Wine, for those that eat noe flesh will Gulch abundance of strong drink." Linschoten, at a rather earlier period, lamented that the Portuguese soldiers were learning from natives the taste for spirits, which took the place of the wine of their native land. Writing of Bengal early in the last century, Buchanan-Hamilton says:

"In no country have I seen so many drunken people walking abroad; and in more than one instance I saw men, who, from their dress, were far above the vulgar, lying on the road perfectly stupefied with drink, and that in the middle of the day, and in places far removed from the luxury and dissipation of towns."

It is also a fallacy to suppose that the habit did not

prevail under native rule. Colebrooke, when he visited Nágpur in 1800, writes:

"The number of distillers' shops is incredible. Mahrattas of all ranks drink immoderately, and so do the women. Even ladies of rank use spirituous liquors; but the women, who fetch wood and grass from the forests, are, most of all, addicted to intoxication. It is curious to see of an evening crowds of well-dressed women getting drunk at a distiller's door."

Such scenes are certainly very unusual at the present day. When a native drinks he does not, as a rule, tipple; but he drinks with the object of getting drunk. This is done deliberately. A servant will often ask leave of his master to get drunk, and he can generally state the precise amount which will produce the desired effect. The use of foreign spirits is certainly on the increase among the educated classes, who are specially fond of cheap and noxious liqueurs. One of the great drinkers of modern times was Ranjít Singh, whose tipple was raisin wine mixed with ground pearls, a liquor as strong as brandy. To promote thirst he used to eat, when drinking, fat quails stuffed with sage. Toddy, the produce of the palm, "an aerial cellar," as Sir J. Hooker calls it, when used fresh, is one of the least deleterious of Indian drinks. Even then, however, it is highly productive of gout, and, when fully fermented, very intoxicating.

Much more dangerous than spirits are the products of the hemp-plant, Gánja, Bhang, and Charas—the first, the female flowering tops holding a resinous exudation; the second, the mature leaves, and in some parts the fruit also, but not the twigs; the third, the resinous substance found on various parts of the plant. Its use is as old as the Atharva-veda, where it is ranked with Soma as one of the five plants which are "liberators of sin." Its early use in Scythia is attested by the evidence of Herodotus, and it gave the name of Assassins (Hashsháshín, "eaters of Hashish") to the Musalmán fanatics who attacked the Christians during the Crusades. Much discussion has taken place on the connection between the use of these drugs and insanity, and the question has not been finally set at rest by the recent Drug Commission. It reported, by a majority, that the moderate use of Gánja does no injury to the brain; but when taken in excess, which is rarely the case, it may be a cause of insanity, especially when there is any weakness or hereditary disposition. At the same time, the large amount of insanity in the Bengal hemp districts suggests an opposite conclusion, and many good authorities disagree with the conclusions of the Commission. In any case, it is not so serious a danger as alcoholic excess in Europe; and there is some reason to believe that these drugs act by retarding waste of tissue, and hence their use in moderation may be beneficial to those exposed to severe labour on insufficient diet. Gánja is commonly used in the form of *Majoon** or Majoom, which is a confection made of hemp, flowers of the thorn-apple, powder of nux vomica, *ghee*,* and sugar.

Last, among the milder intoxicants may be mentioned the *piper Betel*, the use of which is recorded by Marco Polo and Abd-er-razzák in the fifteenth century. Later travellers, like Linschoten, Pyrard de Laval, and P. della Valle, describe its virtues as drying the brain and evil humours of the body, and preserving the teeth. As evidence of its popularity in India, we have the statement, doubtless an exaggeration, that there were 30,000 shops for the sale of the drug in Kanauj. It is used with *Pawn*,* which, Fryer says, "makes a fragrant breath, and gives a rare Vermilion to the Lips." There are different varieties, which possess various degrees of narcotic qualities. It produces a moderate exhilaration, which makes it popular with Muhammadans, to whom the use of liquor is forbidden; and the Burmese monks, who cannot smoke tobacco, are most persistent chewers. Sir G. Watt remarks that its qualities have attracted little attention among our physicians in India, but the Dutch in Java regard it as valuable in the damp, miasmatic climate of that country, and serve it out to troops and convicts, among whom it has a favourable effect on catarrhal and pulmonary disease.

On the eastern frontier, pawn and betel take the place of love-letters. When a packet is sent with a flower, it means, according to Captain Lewin, "I love you." If much spice is added, and the corner is turned in a peculiar way, it means, "Come!" A small piece of charcoal placed inside the leaf says, "Go! I have done with you!" The leaf, touched with turmeric, shows that the sender cannot come.

[Various articles on intoxicants and drugs in Watt, "Economic Dictionary."]

IRRIGATION.—Irrigation, in which "the industry of man carefully supplements the gift of God," seems to have been first developed by the Babylonians, and was certainly applied to Indian agriculture in very ancient times. Something like the modern Persian wheel seems to have been known in the Vedic age, and the many fine weirs and tank-embankments date from the first period of Hindu settled rule. Manu directs that the breaker of a dam shall be punished by long immersion in water. The extension of irrigation was the special work of the Maurya dynasty, about 150 A.D. In early Muhammadan days the ruthless Tímúr allowed the builder of an embankment to hold the protected land free in the first year; in the second, he paid what he could afford; in the third, the regular revenue collections were made.

Our modern canals date from the reign of the benevolent Fíroz Tughlak, who used one of the drainage lines from the lower Himálaya to the west of the Jumna. But it was to Akbar that this tract owed a perennial supply from the great river itself. Sháh Jahán brought a canal into his new city of Sháhjahánábád—a work carried out by Mardan Ali Khán, to whom we also owe the beginnings of the Eastern Jumna Canal. These canals, owing to faulty alignment and ill construction, became practically useless about the middle of the eighteenth century, when they were taken in hand by English engineers like Colonel John Colvin, who framed the first scheme for the great Ganges Canal, afterwards developed by Sir P. Cautley. Works like the Son and Orissa Canals, and those on the Cauvery and Godávari constructed by Sir A. Cotton, followed, until in 1901 43,000 miles of water-ways were in operation—more than four times the length available ten years before, and watering about half the 30,000,000 acres which are now practically safe from danger of famine. It is these splendid canals which account for the fact that the supply of rain, which in the Deccan supports 150 persons per square mile, can feed double that number in the Plains of Hindustán and the Panjáb.

The only drawback to this beneficent system of Public Works is the danger of malaria, which has been discussed in connection with FEVER, and the damage caused by the efflorescence of noxious salts—sulphate of soda, mixed with common salt and carbonate of soda, collectively known as Reh. These evils are the result of reckless over-saturation of the soil, and waste of water from the canals themselves. In the case of Reh, the soluble salts are brought up from below by the force of capillary attraction, as the sun's rays evaporate the soil-water which holds them in solution. The obvious remedy is drainage, combined with the irrigation system.

Among the chief recent developments are the irrigation colonies of the Panjáb, watered by canals from the Jhílam and Chináb, which have fertilised large areas of barren soil, and provided a valuable outlet for the congested agricultural population of the province.

The canals largely provide water on what is called the "flush" system, where the supply is given at a level which enables the farmer to bring it directly into his fields. As in the case of well-irrigation, this has led to the formation of groups of farmers, who, aided by the organisation of the village community, arrange among themselves for the equitable distribution of the supply. But "flush"-irrigation naturally leads to waste of water and soil-saturation, and one of the problems of the future is the invention of a cheap and workable water-meter.

In Balúchistán the canal is replaced by the Karez, an underground water-way, often two or three miles long, with shafts at every hundred yards. It taps the hill streams at their source, and gradually brings the water to the fields.

In the case of canal or tank-water, when the supply has to be raised to fields on a level higher than that of the source, many rude but efficient appliances are used. The simplest is the basket or canoe-shaped wooden vessel, which is swung by cords, and, with each movement of the labourers who work it, raises some water from one reservoir to another until the required level is reached. Next comes the leather bag used with the well, and hauled to the surface by the labour of a team of oxen driven down a slope. In its best form nothing better illustrates the economy of labour. The bag has an appendage drawn into the trough at the mouth of the well by the same cattle that raise the bag, and this is released by a string running over a pulley. Thus a man and boy can manage three yokes of oxen, raising as many bags of water. Less elaborate is the contrivance known in North India as the Dhenkli, the *Picottah* * of Madras, the Shadoof of the Nile valley—a balanced lever, one end heavily weighted, the other supporting the water-vessel. Here the ordinary process is reversed, and it is in sinking the vessel in the well that the labour is employed.

Lastly comes the curious machine known as the Persian Wheel, of which the history is obscure. It does not seem to be used in Persia, but it is represented by the Egyptian Sakiyeh, and it appears in Palestine. Possibly the Indian title merely implies that the idea came from the West. In Egypt it was probably a late invention, as it has not been recognised on the tomb frescoes. The Burmese have a somewhat similar machine, the Yit, in which, as in the Persian Wheel, the water is raised by a wheel, to which bamboo baskets are attached. The Persian Wheel is known as far south as Malabar, and it is purely a matter of habit or tradition whether the farmer uses the wheel or the leather bag. The difference is, that in the wheel the labour falls upon the cattle alone, and is incessant; in the case of the bag, more work is imposed upon the men engaged, and though the periodical strain upon the oxen is greater, they have intervals of rest while they remount the slope.

The Deccan and Gujarát are behind the rest of the country in facilities for irrigation, because the rivers, not being snow-fed, fail when their supply is needed. It was in this tract and in Berár and the Central Provinces that the last famine was most severely felt. The recent Irrigation Conference proposes to remedy this by a reservoir at Rámtek near Nágpur, and by an irrigation canal from the Mahánadi river in Raipur.

It has been calculated that there are 106,000,000 acres of uncultivated land available for settlement by means of canals. It may be hoped that foreign capital will soon combine with the efforts of the State to develop this enormous area, thus relieving the pressure of population in the most congested tracts, and increasing the food supply for home-use and exportation. Of course, Northern India, with its snow-fed rivers, is the most promising field for experiments of this kind.

[For Reh, see Watt, "Economic Dictionary," vi. Pt. I. 400ff.]

JAINISM, JAINS.—Jainism is the Cinderella of Indian religions, and the origin and tenets of this sect, which now numbers 1,333,000 persons, of whom the majority are found in the west of the Peninsula, have been the subject of much controversy. By some it was supposed to be antecedent to, by others an off-shoot of Buddhism. Its literature is of great extent, and interpretation of it difficult; but sufficient investigation of its sacred books has now been made to enable definite conclusions to be drawn.

It is known to have been the result of a movement contemporaneous with and based on much the same grounds as those which gave birth to Buddhism. Neither of these beliefs was intended to lead to a reform of Hinduism as it then existed; rather they were developments within Hinduism itself, and the cause which led to them was the monopoly which the Bráhmans claimed of entrance into the Monastic Orders. The leaders in both these movements were members of the Kshatriya or warrior caste, and both sects had their origin about the same time and in the same part of the country, Magadha, the modern Behár.

The founder of Jainism was a prince named Vardhamána or Mahavíra, who was born about 599 B.C. He first entered one of the Hindu Monastic Orders, but subsequently founded an order of his own, of a more rigorous type, one of the chief rules of which was absolute nudity. He gained the title of Jina, or "spiritual conqueror," from the rigour of his austerities, and from this the name of Jaina is derived. The first material evidence of the faith is found in statues and inscriptions discovered at Mathura, which are assigned to the first or second century of our era.

The chief difference between Jainism and Buddhism is that the former rejects the doctrine of Nirvána or extinction, and believes that the soul, freed from the body, goes to an undefinable heaven of blessedness. Devotion is chiefly paid to the Saints who have attained this spiritual life. Buddhism, again, was more practical, and possessed more of the missionary spirit than Jainism, which preferred a career of seclusion, founding its shrines, like those at Mount Abu in Rájputána and Párasnáth in Bengal, far from the haunts of men, amid the most lovely forest and mountain scenery. Jainism also differed from Buddhism in the fact that it more fully admitted the right of the laity to admission into communion. This, as well as the speculative and unenterprising character of the creed, secured it against the attacks of the reformed Bráhmanism. Buddhism, having little support from the laity, fell into decay; while Jainism survives as the special religion of the rich mercantile classes of Western India, who have sent out colonies into all the great trading centres. While Buddhism became the State religion of powerful kingdoms, Jainism, except in Southern and Western India, where some of the local princes were converted to the faith, has exercised little political influence in the land.

Jainism is remarkable for the magnificence and profuse ornamentation of its shrines, erected by pious members of the powerful commercial class, which supplies the majority of its followers. As Mr Fergusson observes:

"Building a temple is with them a prayer in stone, which they conceive to be eminently acceptable to the deity, and likely to assure them benefits both here and hereafter."

Unlike ordinary Hindus and Musalmáns, they have no objection to restore an old temple if they cannot afford to build a new one. Hence their religious buildings are more permanent than those of other sects. Nothing in Indian architecture is perhaps finer than the groups of Jain temples at Pálitána, Girnár, Mount Abu, Párasnáth, and Khajuráhu, all in Northern India; and no modern Hindu temples surpass in magnificence the Jain shrines in the large trading cities, like Delhi. Some modern temples in the Baroda State are described by the writer of the last Census Report. Passing through the wide entrance gates, we come to a large quadrangle, with a corridor surrounding an inner square, open overhead, but protected by a ceiling of wire gauze to prevent insects falling into the lamps. The floor is of marble, and the walls decorated with frescoes. The inmost shrine, dedicated to the Tirthankara or Saint, has the usual white marble image, with glass or jewelled eyes. The other chapels contain similar images of smaller size, their faces moulded in a perpetual smile. The place is always crowded with worshippers, and the air is overladen with perfumes and incense. Songs are chanted in honour of the Saint, and here we have the remarkable innovation of a dance performed by half a dozen little boys to the accompaniment of drums, fiddles, and a harmonium;

as they dance, they bow to the image and chant their songs of praise. At the end of each scene in the service, a crier puts up to auction the privilege of making the offering to the highest bidder.

In Southern India the Jain temples are of two kinds, Bastis and Bettus—the former, temples in the usual sense of the word; the latter, unknown in the north, are courtyards open to the sky, and containing images. Like the Buddhists, the Jains used to construct enormous images, to which reference is made in connection with idols.

Jainism is thus not a separate religion, but rather a sect of Hinduism. Jains are even more sensitive than Hindus to the sanctity of animal life, and their Jatis, or priests, who wear a cloth over their mouths lest they might perchance swallow an insect, and who sweep the ground where they sit to avoid the possiblity of causing the death of a creature, have been often described by travellers. With the same object they are the chief supporters of the animal hospitals (see PINJRAPOLE). Like Hindus, they respect the cow; they visit Hindu places of pilgrimage; employ Bráhman priests for their family rites; and intermarry with families of their own caste who follow the strict tenets of Hinduism. When a Hindu bride is introduced into a Jain household, she continues to follow her ancestral rites without molestation. But in the more fanatical centres of Hinduism, the creed is regarded with feelings of hostility, and many serious encounters between bigots on both sides have followed processions of their "naked" gods. They have, it is true, some tenets which the rigid Hindu brands as heretical. Thus they do not accept the sanctity of the Vedas; they omit the usual Hindu funeral rites; and have special holy places, shrines, and ceremonies of their own. But there are many Hindu sects which differ as widely as this does from the orthodox faith, but which the eclectic rule of Hinduism never dreams of excluding from its communion.

[G. Bühler, "Uber d. indische Secte der Jaina," E.T. by J. Burgess; Jacobi, "Gaina Sutras," in "Sacred Books of the East"; "Calcutta Review," cviii. 338, cxi. 151, cvi. 315.]

JEWELLERY.—In the use of jewellery it is probable that the desire for protection by means of an amulet or talisman preceded that of personal adornment. The amulet took the shape of fruit or flowers, sacred grasses, animals' claws, and so on; and much of the rudest peasant jewellery is modelled in imitation of such things. The parts of the body chosen for protection were those specially exposed to demoniac influence—the head and skull sutures; the ears, nose, and mouth; the throat, where the motion of the uvula suggests the abode of a vital spirit; the wrist and ankles, where the beating of the pulse is attributed to the same origin; and the fingers and toes, which are specially exposed to defilement. Later on, the holy flower and leaf were supplemented by the representations of other powerful protectives—the sun, moon, cobra, tortoise. Each precious stone was, again, invested with special attributes. Though the form is modified with changes of fashion, the conservatism of the East has preserved many traces of the original conception.

It is in the peasant jewellery that we find the most primitive types, and, being made of base metal, it passes on from one generation to another; while that of higher value finds its way, sooner or later, into the melting-pot. The distinctly savage type appears among the Nágas of Assam, who wear earrings made of tusks of the wild boar, a neck-collar of goat's hair dyed scarlet, armlets of brass, ivory, or plaited cane, prettily worked in red and yellow. Their kinsmen, the Gáros, wear a peculiar ornament of brass plates joined by a string—a sign that the wearer has killed his man in battle. The Chins of Burma have the objectionable habit of using the telegraph wire for earrings. In the Central hill tract the woman's ornaments are usually of bell-metal, and the weight worn is remarkable. Captain Sherwell states that the ornaments of a fully-equipped Santál belle consisted of two anklets, twelve bracelets, and a necklace, weighing in all 34 lbs. A Gáro woman of Assam was found wearing earrings of 16 lbs. weight, which were supported by a string tied over the top of her head, the friction of which had quite worn away her hair. Such women think it a mark of distinction to have the lobes of the ears torn by the weight of their jewels. In the neighbourhood of Benares and Patna the weight of their bell-metal anklets gives the girls a peculiar shuffling gait.

The materials of jewellery are thus exceedingly varied. The jungle tribes of Matherán, in West India, make collars, anklets, necklaces, and girdles of grass, which are the prototype of the modern gold-wire jewellery. The bangles and bracelets of the Bhíl woman are generally of brass. She wears four rings of this metal on each arm and leg; and if she be married, a W-shaped ornament on the ankle, while unmarried girls have only necklaces of beads. The Kyoungtha woman of the East frontier has large, truncated, hollow silver cones in her ears, which are used as flower-holders. The low-caste woman of the Plains wears bangles of coarse glass or lac, which, when decorated with beads or metal foil, are pretty and artistic. She generally has a spangle on the forehead, which is not disturbed by washing until it becomes necessary to replace it. In fact, it is unseemly for a married woman to wash her forehead, as it is held to imply her desire to get rid of the paint mark, which is the symbol of the married state. Iron has now passed out of general use, but the habit of wearing it survives in the single iron bracelet worn on the left wrist by every married woman as a mark of wedlock, and as a protective against ill-luck to her husband. Richer women now encase the iron in a sheath of gold. Up to quite recent times no Hindu woman in Bengal considered herself pure unless she wore conch-shell bracelets. They were assumed after a special religious rite, the bracelet being honoured by an offering of vermilion, sacred grass, and rice. The habit of wearing these is now passing into disuse; but a pair still form a part of the bride's dowry, as ivory bangles do in the Panjáb.

As regards the precious metals, the customs vary all over the country. Rájput women in Cutch never wear silver, except as anklets. Gold should not be dishonoured by being worn on the feet, except by those of royal blood.

Thus the Mahárána of Udaypur wears thick gold bangles on his ankles, but no one outside the palace is allowed to wear such ornaments. Lady Falkland describes the Mahratta Ráni of Satára as hardly able to walk or even raise her feet, owing to the weight of her gold anklets. In the Burmese Court the use of anklets of gold was forbidden to all children save those of the royal family.

The jewellery worn by princes and noble ladies is of wonderful variety and beauty. Thus Mr Val Prinsep describes the Mahárája of Kashmír as wearing on his head

"a rich turban, with a plume of heron's feathers, not many, but long. On one side hung a ruby, unset, as big as a walnut; on the other, a diamond as large; in the middle, an emerald like a heart, much bigger. His staff was wound about with a chain of great pearls, rubies, and diamonds drilled. About his neck he wore a chain of three strings of most excellent pearl, the largest I ever saw; above his elbows, armlets set with diamonds; and on his wrist three rows of several sorts; his hands bare, but almost on every finger a ring."

Lady Dufferin thus speaks of the jewellery of a Nepálese princess:

"It consisted of a diadem worn just on the forehead, so as to frame the face. It was an arrangement of flowers and leaves in magnificent diamonds, with large bunches of grapes in emeralds, pendent just behind the ear, where the wreath ended. I never saw anything at all like it, and there were emerald flies settling on the flowers, which repeated the colour very cleverly."

On her hands she wore English dogskin riding-gloves, and over them enormous diamond rings and diamond bracelets.

Delhi, one of the chief centres of jewel-making, now produces little that is valuable. The tendency of our rule has been to repress the more markedly ostentatious and barbaric patterns. The Rája of our day thinks more of polo ponies, motor cars, English guns and rifles, than of jewellery. The prettiest Delhi jewellery is perhaps the Babúl-work, in imitation of the blossoms of the acacia. But the specialty of the Delhi jeweller is the arrangement of precious stones, sometimes valuable, sometimes inferior, so as to produce articles of richness, variety, and contrast. In one form of armlet, the Naunaga, we have the mystic number of nine precious stones, each of which has a special protective power. At Delhi European fashion has done much to degrade the art. The trade in precious stones, writes Mr L. Kipling,

> "is now, as always, a somewhat secret branch of commerce. German Jews, trained in Paris, are perhaps the most prominent and leading dealers. There is scarcely a wedding or an accession affording an opportunity for the sale of precious stones that is not telegraphed to Paris, London, St Petersburg, and Vienna. Delhi and the rest of India are now included in this secret syndicate, and are periodically visited by dealers, who come and go unnoticed, so that Tavernier was but the precursor of a succession of jewel merchants."

For pearls Bombay is an important mart, but the leading trader is a Delhi man.

Other leading varieties of jewellery are the work of chopped pieces of pure gold strung on red silk, which is the finest archaic jewellery in India, made in the highest perfection at Ahmadábád and Surat; the beaten silver of the Gonds and Himálayan tribes, which in ornamentation resembles the Celtic type; the silver filagree of Cuttack, done by boys, whose sensitive fingers and keen sight enable them to work the fine silver thread; the beaten gold Swámi work of Madras, of the purest Hindu style; the fine gold chains of Trichinopoly; the crude silver, ornamented with torquoises, from the Himálaya; and the superb *repoussé* work of the Nepál valley. Much, however, of the hill jewellery is of a ruder type. A special variety is that worn by the Bhotiya women on the Tibet frontier: earrings, usually of pewter, in size and shape like a massive door-key; strings of amber for the neck; and an arrangement, like the chatelaine of the English lady, holding knife, spoon, scissors, awl, packing-needle, tweezers, flint, and steel, and a tobacco-pouch, suspended by chains or leather thongs from the waist.

The tastes of Hindus and Musalmáns differ widely in the matter of jewellery. When a bead necklace is worn, the wearer is a Hindu, and it usually bears the image of some deity; while that of the Musalmáni has merely a conventional pattern or geometric ornamentation. The Hindu woman pierces her ears in one or two places above and in the lobe. When the openings are numerous, and are found extending in a line completely along the helix, and where the rings are of silver, the wearer is certainly a Musalmáni; and her nose-ring is much less conspicuous than that of the Hindu.

Another function which jewellery fulfils is to act as a savings bank. When famine occurs, vast quantities of ornaments are pledged or sold. Particularly since peace was assured under our rule, immense supplies of bullion have poured into the country, most of which have been converted into jewels. The existing stock must be of enormous value. Mr Maclagan states that a competent authority estimates that in the city of Amritsar alone the jewels are worth £2,000,000 sterling. The causes which restrict the use of jewellery are very gradual, as far as the mass of the people is concerned, and, for the present at least, its use is likely to continue unchecked. The obvious objections to the hoarding of wealth in this shape are that it is not available as trade capital, that it encourages burglary and dacoity, and that the habit of decking small children with jewels is responsible for many cases of murder.

[Birdwood, "Industrial Arts of India"; Mukharji, "Art Manufactures of India"; Maclagan, "Monograph on the Gold and Silver work of the Panjáb."]

JEWS.—The Indian Jews, who have increased in numbers during the last twenty years from 12,000 to 18,000, fall into two main classes. First are those who have arrived in modern times for the purpose of trade; secondly, two colonies of long standing on the West

Coast—one to the south in the State of Cochin, and the other at Kolába, in Bombay. The modern arrivals are inconsiderable. The rates of wages for artisans are too low to attract them, and on landing they meet a race of petty traders and hucksters even more astute than themselves.

The period of the arrival of the South Indian colony has been much disputed. Their local traditions carry back their landing to the time of their escape from servitude under Cyrus, in the sixth century B.C. But recent investigations make it probable that they arrived shortly before the first Christians, and that they must have settled in Malabar as early as the first century of our era. It is equally difficult to fix the time of the arrival of the Bombay branch. Dr John Wilson believed that these Jews were descendants of the Lost Tribes, because none of their names are later than the Captivity, and all their Scriptures are of an early date. It is now generally supposed that they came from Yemen in the sixth century of our era; their own traditions place their exodus in the second century, while other authorities fix it as late as the fifteenth.

The Jews of Cochin are of two classes, the Black and the White Jews. Of these the Black group claim to be the earlier settlers, and their more complete assimilation to the native races favours this supposition. It has been a matter of fierce controversy how much Jewish blood runs in their veins. At present the relations between the Black and White section, the latter refusing to intermarry with the former, have become strained. A further distinction has recently grown up among the Black Jews, some of whom now call themselves Brown Jews, and claim to be descended from the pure original stock. The White Jews are distinguished by a special dress, the men wearing a rich-coloured, long tunic, a waistcoat buttoned up to the neck, and full white trousers; they wear a skull-cap in daily life, and a turban when they go to a synagogue. The Black Jews dress more or less like the native Muhammadans around them. They are, as a rule, wanting in energy, and have taken little share in the progress of the State to which they belong.

Linschoten says:

"The Jewes have built very fair stone houses, and are rich merchants, and of the King of Cochin neerest Counsellers; there they have their Synagogue with their hebrue Bible, and Moses Lawe, which I have had in my hand; they are most white of colour, like men of Europa, and have many faire women. There are manie of them that came out of the country of Palestina and Jerusalem thether, and speake all over the Exchange good Spanish; they observe the Saboth, and other iudicall ceremonies, and hope for the Messias to come."

He was right in classing them as Sephardim, or Spanish Jews; very few of the Ashkenazim, or German Jews, being found in India.

The Kolába Jews, known as Ben-i-Isráel, "sons of Israel," are also divided into two sections, the White and the Black; the former claiming, as in Madras, a higher rank, and refusing to eat, drink, or intermarry with the other section. They are chiefly husbandmen, oil-pressers, and soldiers; while some are schoolmasters, or employed in the medical department. Their faults are intemperance and extravagance in costly feasts and ceremonies. But the majority of them are hard-working, own some land, and they have no beggars in their community.

In Bengal almost all the Jews are found in Calcutta, where, to quote Mr O'Donnell, "they form a well-defined and well-organised community, under the leadership of men who are alike remarkable for their wealth, their liberality, and their capacity for business." In the Upper Provinces a few small, scattered communities are found, many of whom keep "Europe" shops in our cantonments. The spread of these small communities is checked by the difficulty of finding a Rabbi to perform their services, and of providing a regular supply of Kosher meat. They live on good terms with members of other religions, but it is a never-failing source of amusement to their Hindu and Musulmán neighbours to watch a portly shopkeeper with his women-folk performing the Feast of Tabernacles under a rude shelter of boughs in his little garden.

Hebrew among most of the Indian Jews is a liturgical rather than a spoken language, the majority using the vernacular of the Province in which they reside. It is considered respectable at the Census to record themselves as speakers of Hebrew if the head of the household has any knowledge of that tongue.

[South Indian Jews, "Census Report," Cochin, 1901. i. 61ff. ; Bombay Jews, "Gazetteer," xi. 85, xviii. Pt. I. 506.]

JOHAR.—This is the Hindi term, meaning literally "taking one's life," for the desperate resistance offered by high-caste Hindus, principally Rájputs. When attacked, they were in the habit of slaying their wives and children, and finally committing suicide, in preference to surrender.

The finest stories of such tragedies are those told of the Rájputs by Colonel Tod. Thus, when in 1294 Jaysalmír was attacked by the Musalmáns under Ala-ud-dín, Rája Múlráj called on his women to prepare to meet him and his men in heaven by dying in defence of their honour and their faith. They assented, and the "Johar commenced, and 24,000 females, from infancy to old age, surrendered their lives." Four years before this event the same Musalmán Emperor captured and sacked Chitor, when thousands of Rájput women devoted themselves to death in an underground chamber of the palace. A similar case occurred on the capture of the same stronghold by Akbar in 1568. Nine queens, five princesses, and the families of all the chieftains within the fortress are said to have perished. The men assumed the saffron robe of death, ate *pawn** together for the last time, and perished to a man in the breach.

From Southern India, where the habit of running *Amuck** was much more common than in the North, we have many accounts of similar desperate acts. The King of Tanjore, when attacked by his rival of Madura, surrounded a room in the palace with gunpowder, collected inside his wives, concubines, children, slave-girls, and valuables, and, when defeated, gave the signal, on which they set fire to the explosives and perished. When M. Bussy stormed the fort of Bobili in 1757, the defenders put their wives and children to death, and perished without giving or receiving quarter. So late as 1809, when Ajaigarh was besieged by our troops, the father-in-law of Lakshman Dáwa, the chieftain, killed his whole family and four female attendants; and we have a similar incident recorded in the Pindári war of 1816.

It is not only Hindus who have shown a temper such as this. Near the great ruined city of Bijapur they show to this day eleven rows each of seven female tombs side by side, and all of uniform pattern. They are said to cover the remains of the seventy-seven wives of Afzul Khán, who, when about to start on his fatal mission to Sivaji, was told that he would never return. On this warning he proceeded to set his house in order by drowning all his wives in the palace pond. The story is quite inconsistent with the chivalrous character of the hero of Meadows Taylor's well-known story of "Tara"; but it is probably true. The same fanatical spirit, illustrated in these tales of Johar, is common in Oriental life. Cases of running amuck are still occasionally recorded.

The Musalmáns who in 1799 attacked Mr Cherry at Benares, carried with them on their mad adventure their winding-sheets, which had been dipped in the holy well at Mecca. Even at the present day what is known as Ghaza, or fanatical assassination, is one of the standing difficulties on our western frontier. It is not always the case that the perpetrator of such an outrage is influenced solely by religious motives, as expressed in the text of the Korán: "To kill unbelievers is less grievous than idolatry." Often he is suffering from some real or fancied wrong, has been maddened for a time by the loss of a relative, the taunts of women, or by unrequited love. Sometimes he will brood over his trouble for months, and he has the consolation that his crime will be counted unto him for righteousness.

[Tod, "Annals of Rajasthan"; "Census Report," Balúchistán, 1901, i. 42.]

JUGGURNAUT.—The famous temple of Jagannátha, "Lord of the Universe," at Puri, in Orissa, is one of the chief objects of Hindu pilgrimage. It was originally a seat of Buddhism. At Khandagiri and other sites in the neighbourhood we have a record in stone of the phases through which Buddhism passed. The earlier stages are marked by the caves of the ascetic period, followed by the ceremonial age, with the pillared hall, in which the monastic community met. Lastly, we have the fashionable age, represented in Ráninúr, or the "Queen's Palace," with a biography in sculpture of the founder. About the end of the fourteenth century A.D. the reformed Vaishnavism—a form of pietism to which caste considerations are subordinated—reached Puri, and the worship was then devoted to Krishna, as an incarnation of Vishnu. The movement culminated in the preaching of Chaitanya, the apostle of transcendental quietism, early in the sixteenth century. Puri thus became a chief centre of this type of Hinduism, and the shrine flourishes, so that it is now perhaps the wealthiest temple in India, its anuual revenue being estimated by Sir W. Hunter at £68,000.

The sanctuary of the shrine contains the threefold image of Jagannáth, with his brother Balbhadra and his sister Subhadra. It is a remarkable fact that this threefold image is really a perversion or adaptation to the needs of another faith of the Buddhist Triratna, or "Three Jewels," —the Buddha, the Dharma or "Law," the Sangha or "Congregation." Colonel Waddell, however, denies that the "Three Holy Ones" are ever concretely represented in Tibet by Buddha, Dharma, and Sangha; and though it has been alleged that it appears in Indian Buddhism, he questions the fact. At any rate, the anthropoid development of the Trisúla or Trident, a well-known

Hindu symbol, is quite sufficient to account for the modern triple image.

As usual, a marvellous legend is told of the appearance of the image, that it was washed up by the sea on the Orissa coast, found by a man of low caste, and finally removed to the present shrine. Another remarkable tale tells that every third year a new idol is made out of a *Neem* * tree sought for in the forest, on which no crow or carrion bird has ever perched. This is known to the initiated by certain marks. When the stock is shaped by a carpenter, it is made over to the priests, one of whom is selected to take out of the original image a box containing the bones of Krishna, which is then transferred to the new image. One account describes how this Bráhman veils his face lest he should be struck dead in gazing on relics of such sanctity. Once, it is said, a Rája of Bardwán paid the priests an enormous sum for permission to see the relics, and died soon after. Others say that the Bráhman who handles the relics is slain by his brother-priests lest he should divulge their character, or that he is always removed by the god from this world before the close of the year. These tales, in their present form, are obviously absurd. The rule of Vaishnavism is utterly opposed to the preservation of relics of the dead. The tale, in fact, points to a tradition from the times of Buddhism, when relics of the Master were preserved in Stúpas all over the land.

"Everything, in fact, at Puri," writes Mr Fergusson, "is redolent of Buddhism, but of Buddhism so degraded as to be hardly recognisable by those who know that faith only in its older and purer form."

Thus we have the Rath-játra, or procession of the idol in a gorgeous car, during which, according to the older authorities, numerous suicides of devotees used to occur. Accidents may and do occur in the dragging of the monstrous car by bands of excited pilgrims, or a stray devotee, drunk with fanaticism, may fling himself beneath the wheels in a transport of religious ecstasy; but here again the genius of Vaishnavism abhors anything like human sacrifice, and a death within the temple precincts would involve an elaborate rite of expiation. The procession of the image is doubtless a survival of Buddhism, or, as Sir W. Hunter suggests, both Buddhism and its modern successor derived the custom from the Animism, which was earlier than either. During the pilgrimage caste regulations are in abeyance, and the old practice, now somewhat restricted, was that when the holy rice offered at the shrine was being distributed to the pilgrims, the lowest caste might demand it from or give it to the highest. At present no Hindu caste is excluded from the temple, save those who still retain the flesh-eating and life-destroying propensities characteristic of the jungle and outcast tribes. Again, as the pilgrim leaves the shrine a sweeper strikes him with his broom—an indignity which no good Hindu can ever endure. This is said to free him from his sins, and he is forced to promise, on pain of losing the benefits of his pilgrimage, not to disclose the secrets of the shrine. All this points back to Buddhism, and its protests against the rigidity of the caste system.

When the invading Muhammadans destroyed every idol in Orissa, they spared Jagannáth, partly because of the revenue he could be made to yield, and partly because his rule differed so widely from the abominations of the coarser forms of Hinduism. In 1883 a serious attack was made upon the god by a party of dissenters from the Central Provinces, who, naked but for bark ropes worn round the waist, forced their way into the temple with the avowed object of destroying him. A serious riot, with loss of life, was the result of this outbreak of fanaticism.

Though Jagannáth is nominally a Vaishnava deity, his worship aims at a Catholicism which embraces every form of Hinduism. Nature-worship is represented by a shrine to the Sun-god; of 120 temples within the sacred enclosure 13 are dedicated to Siva, besides several to his queen, both of whom are the deities of the rival sect. Even the rite of blood-sacrifice was not purged from Jagannáth in the Vaishnava revival. Once a year, at midnight, sacrifice is offered to Bimala Devi, the cruel goddess who delights in blood, in a shrine apart from the great temple, but within the precincts.

"It is," says Sir W. Hunter, "this composite worship of deep spirituality and sanctioned self-indulgence, which for six centuries has been gathering round the temple of Jagannáth."

It thus represents the most liberal, comprehensive, unsectarian form of Hinduism, and, more than any other of the great gods, he may claim to be a national deity.

[See the elaborate account in Hunter's "Orissa," vol. i.; for the form of the idol, D'Alviella, "Migration of Symbols," 254.]

KÁFIR; CAFFER; CAFIRISTAN. — Káfir, the Muhammadan title for an unbeliever, the ungrateful man who attributes the blessings of life to the agency of false gods, is now specially applied to the remarkable pagan race occupying portions of the Hindu-kush range to the north-west of India. They inhabit a mountainous tract, wedged in between the dominions of the Mehtar of Chitrál and those of the Amír of Kábul, which, since 1895, has fallen under the control of the latter, and most of the people have been forcibly converted to Islám.

Much speculation has been devoted to ascertaining the origin and affinities of this remarkable people. The popular theory that they were descendants of the army of Alexander seems to appear first in Abul Fazl, who writes:

"It is said that this monarch left some of his treasures in those parts, with a few of his kindred; and to this day descendants of this band dwell in these mountains, and affect to show their genealogical descent from Alexander.'

Sir G. Robertson, while admitting that there may be some points of resemblance between the present Káfir and ancient Greek sacrificial observances and certain domestic utensils, such as the curious wooden Káfir dish-stand, thinks "it may be fairly conjectured that some of the Káfir tribes are still influenced, as the ancient Indian population of Eastern Afghánistán were also influenced, by the Greek colonists of Alexander, and that those Káfirs, having never been under the rule of Musalmáns, may possibly represent some of the people of Eastern Afghánistán as they were before the victorious Moslem defeated and converted them to Islám."

This early Indian race, refusing to accept the religion of their conquerers, may, in the tenth century, have taken refuge in the hilly country which they now occupy. "There they found other races whom they vanquished, drove away, or enslaved, or with whom they amalgamated." The existing Presun tribe and their slaves, known as Jazhis and Aroms, may possibly be remnants of this ancient people.

There is no such thing as a general Káfir language, but a number of tribal dialects, all of which Dr Grierson classes as non-Sanskritic Indo-Aryan tongues, on the ground that, while they are clearly Indo-Aryan, the speakers of them seem to have come from the north, and not from the south, where that form of the Indo-Aryan tongue, which we call Sanskrit, became developed.

The old division of this race was into the Siáh-posh, or "black-robed," and the Safed-posh, or "white-robed," a distinction based on the colours of their clothing. There is this much truth in this division, that the "dark-robed" people all understand each other's language; while the three tribes of the "white-robed" section, the Wái, Presun, and Ashkund, seem to use distinct tongues. But the "white-robed" branch are not more different from the "black-robed" than they are from one another; and the division now generally accepted is into Siáh-posh, Wáiguli, and Presungali.

"If it were not," writes Sir G. Robertson, "for their splendid courage, their domestic affections, and their overpowering love of freedom, Káfirs would be hateful people. In other respects they are what they have been made by uncontrollable circumstances. For them the world has not grown softer as it grows older. Its youth could not be crueller than its present maturity; but if they had been different, they would have been enslaved centuries ago. Their present ideas, and all the associations of their history and their religion, are simply bloodshed, assassination, and blackmailing. Yet they are not savages. Some of them have the heads of philosophers and statesmen. Their features are Aryan, and their mental capacities are considerable. Their love of decoration, their carving, their architecture, all point to a time when they were higher in the social scale than they are at present. They never could be brutal savages like some of the African tribes, for example, because they are of a different type; but they are as degraded in many respects as it is possible for this type ever to become."

And he sums up the qualities of a "good" Káfir to be a successful homicide, a good hill-man, ever ready to quarrel, and of an amorous disposition. If he be also a good dancer, a good shot with bow and arrow or matchlock, a good quoit-player, so much the better; but, to be really influential, he must be rich. It is as natural for a Káfir to steal as it is to eat, and even children are encouraged to pilfer.

Their religion was a curious mixture of low idolatry and ancestor-worship, with some traces of fire-worship. Of their gods, Imra, the Creator, identified with the Indra of India, was chief of a host of tribal, family, and household gods, with goblins, fairies, who haunted river, rock, valley, and forest. Then comes Moni, the Prophet—perhaps the Muni or deified sage of the Hindus. Gish, the god of war, seems to have some vague connection with Islám, as his name is supposed to be derived from that of the Khalífa Yazíd, who opposed the Saint Husain. But, granting that this may be the origin of the name, he symbolised hatred to the Prophet, and his worship was the chief bond which united the tribes, and for so long maintained their independence. These gods were worshipped through images of wood conventionally carved, or a fragment of stone, round white stones representing the eyes of the idol. The religious duties were performed by a hereditary priest, a well-born chanter of hymns, and a buffoon Shaman occasionally possessed by the god, who was propitiated by blood-sacrifices and offerings of flour, wine, and butter, accompanied by the thick incense-smoke of burning juniper.

Physically, the Káfirs are a splendid race, almost always in hard training, and fat men are unknown.

"Admirers of form," says Sir G. Robertson, "would delight in Káfirs in their own country. They give such an impression of gracefulness and strength, when once the eye has become accustomed to the vile robes they wear."

These are, for men, a goatskin, and, for women, a long, woollen tunic and long boots. The men never lay down their arms, which consist of matchlock, bow and arrows, spear, and dagger. Swords and shields are rarely used. They have a primitive music of their own. The dead are deposited in huge coffins, within a recognised receptacle, not buried; and effigies of them are constructed, to which sacrifice is made in time of sickness, and food is offered at the periodical feasts.

On the whole, they are about the wildest and most savage race on our north-western frontier.

[Sir G. Robertson, "Káfirs of the Hindu-kush," and article in "Encyclopædia Britannica," 10th edition, vol. xxx.; Major Raverty in "Calcutta Review," ciii. 65ff.]

LÁT *.—This, or Stambha, is a general term for the pillars common to all the styles of Indian architecture.

"With the Buddhists," says Mr Fergusson, "they were employed to bear inscriptions on their shafts, with emblems or animals on their capitals. With the Jains they were generally Díp-dáns, or lamp-bearing pillars; with the Vaishnavas they as generally bore statues of Garuda or Hanumán; with the Saivas they were flag-staffs; but, whatever their destination, they were always among the most original, and frequently the most elegant, productions of Indian art."

As for their ultimate origin, they are probably successors

of the Menhirs, or standing stones, which appear in many parts of India as the work of prehistoric peoples, and are still erected by the Khásis of Assam to form a refuge for the spirits of the sainted dead, or to serve as a memorial of them, before which their successors may offer due worship and service.

Of the inscribed pillars erected by the Emperor Asoka, about 250 B.C., we have nine examples, of which the best known are those on the Ridge and at Firozábád, near the modern Delhi, and that which stands at the Fort of Alláhábád. Of the remainder, three are in the Champáran District of Behár, two in the Nepálese Tarái, and one at the entrance of the great Stúpa of Sánchi, in the State of Bhopál. They all bear copies of the well-known edicts of Asoka; the material is a fine-grained sandstone, and they are placed often hundreds of miles from the quarries which supplied them. The abacus sometimes represents a row of geese picking their food, or "a graceful scroll of alternate lotus and honey-suckle, resting on a beaded astragalus moulding, perhaps of Greek origin."

The two pillars now at Delhi were removed in 1356 A.D. by Fíroz Sháh Tughlak—one from Ambála in the Panjáb, the other from Meerut in the United Provinces. The historian of the time gives a full account of the means by which the former monument was removed. It was packed in cotton, cased in reeds and raw hides, raised on a great wain specially made for the purpose, and dragged by an army of men to the river-bank, where it was finally placed on a boat and conveyed along the Jumna to Delhi. Most of these pillars were probably erected in front of temples or Stúpas, of which no remains survive. Later on the Gupta monarchs of the fifth century A.D. erected similar pillars, either to commemorate victories or as religious monuments.

More remarkable still, as a triumph of early metallurgy, is the Iron Pillar near the Kutab Minár, in the outskirts of Delhi. It seems to date from the period of Chandragupta II. about 400 A.D. It is over 23 feet in height, and weighs some 6 tons. How this mass of pure malleable iron, with its capital and inscription as clear as when the monument was erected, could have been forged it is difficult even to conjecture.

> "It is not many years," writes Dr Ball, "since the production of such a pillar would have been an impossibility in the largest foundries of the world, and even now there are comparatively few where a similar mass of metal could be turned out."

The Jain lamp-bearing pillars, found in their best form in the Kanara District of South India, are the lineal descendants of these Buddhist pillars. Of the pillars connected with the temples of Siva we have representations in the great copper Trisúlas which stand in front of the Himálayan shrines, and a splendid modern example at Khatmándu, in Nepál.

Of another class are the Pillars of Victory, or Jayastambhas, of which we have a grand specimen in Rána Kambha's pillar at Chitor, built in the middle of the fifteenth century, and another erected soon after at Mathura to record the self-sacrifice of a faithful wife. But the masterwork of the pillar-builder is the famous Kutab Minár of Delhi, which Mr Fergusson compares with the Campanile at Florence:

> "The only Mahomedan building known to be taller than this is the minaret of the mosque of Hassan, at Cairo; but, as the pillar at Old Delhi is a wholly independent building, it has a far nobler appearance, and both in design and finish far superior, not only to its Egyptian rival, but any building of its class known to me in the whole world."

Mr Fergusson believed that the Kutab was really a Pillar of Victory, "an emblem of conquest, which the Hindus could only too easily understand and appreciate." But in this view he was probably mistaken. It was distinctly called a Muezzin's tower, whence the Musalmán call for prayer is made, by the Syrian geographer, Abulfida. Several examples of early mosques with a single tower are known. As a prayer-tower, rising high over the fort and palaces of Old Delhi it would be hardly less effective as a symbol of victory than as a Jayasthambha, or Pillar of Conquest.

[For Láts generally, see Fergusson, "History of Indian and Eastern Architecture," chap. ii. For the Kutab Minár, V. A. Smith's Notes on Sleeman, "Rambles," ii. 146, and illustrations in Fanshawe, "Delhi, Past and Present"; for Asoka's Pillars, V. A. Smith, "Asoka," in "Rulers of India."]

LEPROSY.—The death of the heroic Father Damien, who devoted his life to the lepers of Hawaii, led to special enquiries in India regarding the incidence and pathology of this terrible disease. All misfortune, bereavement, disease appear to the fatalistic Hindu to be the result of sins committed in some previous existence. In the case of leprosy, the horror which attaches to it, the impurity which debars the sufferer from the blessings of home-life and the communion of his brethren, the mystery which attends its attacks, have served to intensify this belief. It has been regarded as a punishment for treacherous assassination, as in the case of Salím who struck the first blow at the excellent Emperor, Fíroz Sháh, and within a year or two was eaten up with leprosy; the Portuguese, Fryer tells us, ascribed elephantiasis—a disease with some superficial resemblance, but really quite distinct—to a visitation of Providence on people whose ancestors murdered the blessed Apostle St Thomas; the Thugs supposed that leprosy attacked those who betrayed or slew a member of the brotherhood; others ascribed it to the curse of a dying Suttee; others to an offence against the Sun, which, as Herodotus tells us, was the Persian belief; others, again, to the crime of killing a snake.

Hence all sorts of magical cures were, and are, prescribed for this disease. Many stories about ancient tanks and wells tell how a leper Rája, generally by the advice of his faithful wife, bathed in the water, and was made whole, like Naaman the Syrian. Many shrines make it their chief business to cure leprosy. Thus the tomb of the Saint Dáúd Jahániya at Muzaffargarh, in the Panjáb, is visited by lepers from all parts of the country, who submit to a treatment of hot and cold sand-baths, and, when relieved, deposit models of the diseased limb in silver and gold, which are exposed at the shrine. It is generally believed that if any one can swim across the tank at Tarn Táran, near Amritsar, he will be cured. As for other remedies, Fra Paolino prescribes a spoonful of the fat of the mountain-snake, followed by a drink of warm water, as an assured remedy. Others say that the flesh of the Adjutant crane, chewed daily with *pawn*,* cures the disease in its incipient stage; while others lay down that a leper will be cured if he can live exposed under a *Neem* * tree for twelve years.

The recent Leprosy Commision in India, while it left much doubtful in the pathology of the disease, cleared up some popular misconceptions. In the first place, it was proved that one-tenth of the so-called lepers produced for examination by the police were not really lepers, but were suffering from leucoderma, the white variety of the disease, which causes mere discoloration of the skin, and not from the more serious black or tubercular form. The error must be still more serious in the case of so-called lepers in secluded villages, who never come under scientific observation. Secondly, it was shown that the disease is not an imperial danger—the number of recorded lepers having fallen from 131,000 in 1881 to 97,000 in 1901. This decrease may be due, in part, to more careful discrimination at the last Census, and it must be remembered that in years of famine and epidemic disease none are so liable to death as these debilitated, homeless, repulsive wanderers. In fact, statistics of the disease supplied by natives themselves are obviously untrustworthy. Few natives are able to distinguish the milder from the more serious type; the higher castes naturally conceal a malady which is regarded as a judgment sent by an offended deity; women are more prone to disguise it than men, because it is for them a bar to marriage, and, being more fully clothed than men, they are less likely to be detected.

The Commission further held that the disease has no tendency to spread, either by hereditary transmission or by contagion, but that in most cases it originates *de novo.* No race is exempt from its attacks, even Europeans being liable to it, and the rate among the Christians and Eurasians of Madras is very high; the poor and destitute are more likely to contract it than the rich and prosperous; no article of food, such as fish, originates the plague, but some kinds of diet may predispose the system to infection. The same conclusion applies to insanitary conditions, and certain chronic, infectious diseases. No geological formation and no locality are exempt, while variations of temperature do not appear to exercise any influence. But its diffusion seems to vary inversely with the dryness of the climate, and the tracts which suffer most are generally those where epidemic cholera is prevalent.

Most of these conclusions have been disputed. The Berlin International Congress of 1897 held that it was caused by the *Bacillus lepræ*, whose life-history is at present unknown, but that it probably enters the system through the nose and mucous membrane. If this be correct, the whole question of its prevalence in India must be reconsidered. As to the theory advocated by Mr Jonathan Hutchinson, that it is due to the eating of badly-cured fish, the evidence is not conclusive. It would seem that the worst leprosy districts in Bengal are those where little or no fish is eaten, and his suggestion fails to account for the high incidence among the Christians or Eurasians of Madras. But, like most questions connected with the disease, this theory has neither been proved nor disproved.

Under stricter police regulations, the habit of leper-suicide has much decreased, though occasional instances still occur. Writing in 1800, Colebrooke tells of a Fakír who caused himself to be buried alive:

"The man had grown desperate by being separated from his family, on account of leprosy he is afflicted with. It is, besides, a notion, that when one of a family dies of a leprosy, his disease seizes one of his surviving relations; but this is obviated if he causes himself to be buried alive. Another motive for this voluntary death is to obtain obsequies, which are not legal for one who dies a leper—not, at least, without ceremonies to remove the spiritual taint, and which ceremonies do not seem to be practised on such occasions."

Buchanan-Hamilton, writing a few years later, speaks of lepers

"being placed in a boat, and, a pot of sand being tied to them, they are carried into the middle of the Ganges, and then thrown overboard. They think the sin to which the disease is attributed will be removed by their dying in the sacred stream, and they cannot afford the Prayaschitta, or expiation, which Bráhmans and wealthy people afflicted by the disease undergo."

General Sleeman tells how Raghunáth Ráo, Rája of Jhánsi, killed himself in this way in 1838.

["Report, Indian Leprosy Commission," 1893; "Census Report," India, i. 143ff.; Macalister, in Hastings, "Dictionary of the Bible," iii. 95ff.]

LION.—The Indo-Aryans, according to Professor Schrader, must have encountered the lion when they entered the Panjáb, because there is no common Aryan name for the animal, and it is not mentioned in the Avesta. The Rigveda hymns speak of it as the most dreaded foe of men and cattle. At present it is found in small numbers only in the Gir forest of Káthiáwár and in the wildest tracts of Rájputána. It is now verging on extinction, and, unless protected, will speedily disappear. But the animal is most prolific, and careful preservation would ensure the existence of the breed. In older times its range was far more extensive. The Emperor Jahángír and his visitor Terry write of it as numerous in Málwa; and Bishop Heber says that in 1824 it was found in Saháranpur, Ludhiána, and the north part of Rohilkhand, near Morádábad and Rámpur. The zoological characters of the animal have not been fully investigated, and the specimens in our Natural History Museum are unsatisfactory. It would seem that the "Maneless Lion of Guzerat" is a fiction; the specimen on which the description was founded is immature, and the adult animal is said to have a well-developed mane. Some of the African lions have manes of varying size in different parts of the country, and it has been suggested that in thorny tracts, like the Gir, the hair of the mane is liable to be destroyed. A lion shot near Ahmadábád was short-maned, like those of Persia and Abyssinia. Sir S. Baker believes that the Indian species is much smaller than that of Africa, and that the mane is seldom so dark in colour or so shaggy.

In Moghul times it is said the beast was tamed. Jahángír, Terry informs us, had a great lion which went about the Court like a dog, "and never did hurt, only he had some keepers that did constantly wait upon him." Tavernier has a curious account of the method of taming, which is still employed in the case of hunting leopards in Rájputána:

"They tie the lions, at twelve paces distant from each other, by their hind feet to a cord attached to a large wooden post firmly planted in the ground, and they have another round the neck, which the lion-master holds in his hand. These posts are planted in a straight line, and upon another parallel one, from fifteen to twenty paces distant, they stretch another cord of the length of the space which the lions occupy when arranged as above. These two cords, which hold the lion fastened by the hind feet, permit him to rush up to this long cord, which seems as a limit to those outside it, beyond which they ought not to venture to pass when harassing and irritating the lions by throwing small stones or little bits of wood at them. A number of people come to this spectacle, and when the provoked lion jumps towards the cord, he has another round his neck which the master holds in his hand, and with that he pulls him back. It is by this means that they accustom the lion by degrees to become tame with people."

Bernier, describing Aurangzeb's lion-hunts, says that, "as it is considered a favourable omen when the king kills a lion, so is the escape of that animal portentous of infinite evil to the State." Aurangzeb used to camp for three and four days in the desert, and when he killed one, had him carefully measured, and details of his teeth and claws were recorded. There was a story current, which Bernier, on the authority of the chief huntsman denies, that when an ass was tied up as a bait for the beast, a quantity of opium was poured down its throat as a dose to stupefy the lion. Bernier does not speak of such a device as unsportsmanlike; all he says is that it is unnecessary, because the gorged lion is sufficiently disposed to sleep.

Lion-hunting, as a sport, is decidedly less dangerous than tiger-shooting. When, as in a case recently reported from the Gir forest, an accident occurs, it is almost invariably in the foolish attempt to follow up a wounded animal on foot. He is hit easier than a tiger, because though fond of dense jungle, he exposes himself in a way no tiger, unless driven, ever does. Sir S. Baker says that the tiger, when springing, does not strike a crushing blow, but merely seizes with his claws. But a lion shakes his prey with terrific strength, at the same time fixing his claws upon his victim.

[Blanford, "Mammalia," 56ff.: Baker, "Wild Beasts and their Ways," chap. ix.]

MAGIC.—This is a general term, including many forms of the art of working wonders by mysterious, supernatural means. Thus augury and divination, the science of interpreting omens and dreams, chiromancy, astrology, are all forms of the craft. It is fostered by the juxtaposition of two races, one more civilised than the other—the former recognising that certain phenomena are beyond its control, and due to divine agency; the other claiming the power to produce these effects by the agency of the witch or magician. Hence, while in the primitive age the functions of the priest and the witch are united in a single person, as time goes on a sharp line marks off their operations, the priest working by the aid of his gods, the witch ignoring divine agency. Hence, too, magic is probably older than religion in the history of humanity, and it turns into religion as soon as man becomes conscious of his failure to control the gods whom he had hitherto regarded as his equals. Sacrifice and prayer then become the resort of the more pious and enlightened members of the community, while the more superstitious and ignorant cling to the old magical methods. By-and-by magic dwindles into divination, and the operations, performed to exercise a fertilising effect on men and animals, become degraded into omens.

We may recognise in India the two great kinds of Magic, the White and the Black—the former harmless devices to control weather, the growth of crops, and so on; the latter the monstrous devices to obtain by unlawful means mastery over others by spells, love-potions, and the like. In the first class we find the operations classed under the head of "sympathetic" magic, or that branch of it known as "mimetic," "homeopathic," or "imitative" magic. Its leading principle, as Mr Frazer points out, is that like produces like, that an effect resembles its cause. A mistaken association of similar ideas produces "imitative" or "mimetic" magic; a mistaken association of contiguous ideas produces "sympathetic" magic, in the narrower sense of the word.

Thus we find in the Panjáb magical remedies for barrenness by bathing over a dead body, and thus catching the soul of the dead; or by eating bread cooked on the still burning pyre of a youth who was never married, and so never had transmitted the life that was in him, or was the only or eldest son in his family, and had so received the fullest measure of vitality. Or we have the mosque in Gujarát, where in the wall is imbedded a stone of a kind of conglomerate, with flinty nodules. The softer cement which binds these together, having become worn away by weather, the nodules protrude from the surface of the stone. They thus present the appearance of boils, and, in the true spirit of "mimetic" magic, persons afflicted by this disease rub the nodules with molasses to procure relief.

We have, again, rain-charms, when water is flung on girls going in procession, and the fall of the drops on the ground is supposed to encourage the clouds to drop their fatness. If a man wants to ensure a good crop of cotton, he pulls out the fibre from some of the finest bolls in his field, making the thread as long as possible without breaking it. Then he and his family fill their mouths with rice, and blow it as far as possible in every direction, the obvious intention being that the white cotton may grow as high and as widely as the scattered grains.

Of the second stage, that of Black Magic, a good illustration is found in the use of images. The wizards of the Lusháis of Assam make clay images of those whom they wish to injure, and thrust spikes into them in order to cause sickness. Or they take a mould of a person's footsteps in mud, and put it to dry before a fire, which causes fever in the victim. If a Burman is jilted by a girl, he gets a magician to make an image of his beloved, containing a piece of something which she was in the habit of wearing or using; medicines and charms are introduced into the image, and the girl becomes mad. The Bengal wizard makes a bow out of a piece of the bamboo used as a lever to press down the corpse on the pyre, and with this uncanny weapon shoots an arrow at the image of an enemy which he has fabricated with incantations. This causes pain in whatever organ the arrow strikes. All these are methods familiar to students of European folk-lore, and they have been specialised with a regular literature of spells and incantations by the Indian Musalmáns.

The compounding of love-charms is a standing source of profit to a practitioner of this class. One of the most approved prescriptions in Bengal directs that a portion of the frontal bone of a dead man, the fruit of the narcotic Dhatúra, or thorn-apple, be mixed together in their proper proportions. If a man's forehead be rubbed with this preparation, he can bring under his control any one whom he fears or loves.

This form of magic was taken up and organised into a pseudo-science in that development of Hinduism known as the Tantrik, which is devoted to the worship of the Sakti, or female element, the most degraded form of the popular faith. Here the priest-magician is armed with a multitude of spells, incantations, magical figures, and the like. He claims, to use the words of Sir M. Monier-Williams,

to prognosticate futurity, work the most startling prodigies, infuse breath into dead bodies, kill or humiliate enemies, afflict any one anywhere with disease or madness, inspire any one with love, charm weapons and give them unerring efficacy, enchant armour and make it impenetrable, turn milk into wine, plants into meat, or invert all such processes at will. He is even superior to the gods, and can make gods, goddesses, imps and demons, carry out his most trifling behests."

It is this Tantrik element which, combined with the tenets of the northern school of Buddhism, has produced the degraded cult now prevalent in Tibet.

It is naturally the more ignorant and isolated races which are chiefly under the bondage of magic. Both in the earlier days of Buddhism, and under the rule of the later Bráhmanism, the territory on the north-west frontier was the headquarters of magic. The Chinese pilgrim, Hiuen Tsiang, describes the magical powers of the people of that region, and Marco Polo tells us that they were adepts in sorcery and diabolic arts. A writer of the time of Aurangzeb states that in Assam

"the beauty of the women is very great; their magic, enchantments, and use of spells and jugglery are greater than one can imagine. By the force of magic they build houses, of which the pillars and ceiling are made of men. These men remain alive, but have not the power of breathing and moving. By the power of magic they also turn men into quadrupeds and birds, so that these men get tails and ears like those of beasts. They conquer the heart of whomsoever they like, and bring them under their command. They can foretell the movement and repose of the planets, the dearth and cheapness of grain, the length and shortness of the life of any one."

We have thus Circe transported to Indian soil.

So with Malabar, which Mr Logan calls "the land

par excellence of sorcery and magic." He describes various magical arts still in operation. They make a wax image of an enemy, and burn it with magical rites ; take a human bone from a burial-ground, recite a spell over it, and fling it into a neighbour's house. If you procure a girl's corpse, place it on a Sunday night under a demon-haunted tree, and repeat the appropriate spell a hundred times, it will be re-animated by a demon, who, if appeased with flesh and spirits, will answer questions and foretell the future. A wise man who masters a demon in this way can carry him about, and even transfer him for a consideration to another sorcerer.

Among the lower tribes of the northern Plains the magician is known as the Ojha. His chief business is the exorcism of disease. He burns strong-smelling drugs before the patient to scare the evil spirit, or he tortures the witch vicariously by squeezing an acrid juice into the sick man's eyes, or sprinkles hot oil over him with the intent that he may name the witch who has brought the illness upon him. To the east the exorcisor strips himself naked, makes a buzzing noise as if counting how many evil spirits have a hand in the case, shakes a bundle of reeds over the afflicted part to scare them, and finally prescribes that he be provided with a couple of fowls, which he eats himself, that he may sacrifice to them, and induce them to depart in peace.

A great man who succeeds in enterprises by the sheer force of genius is naturally regarded as a magician. Akbar was supposed to possess the magical power of reducing forts, and a native historian of the time gravely records that, when the Company sent out a successor to Warren Hastings, he promptly killed him by the power of his sorceries.

[On magic generally see Frazer, "Golden Bough"; in India, Lyall, "Asiatic Studies," 1st ser., chap. iv.; Fawcett, "Bulletin of Madras Museum," ii. 50ff.]

MARRIAGE.—Marriage with the Hindu is a sacrament, and the most important occurrence in life.

"Marriage," writes General Sleeman, "with its ceremonies, its rights, and its duties, fills their imaginations from infancy to age; and I do not believe there is a country on earth in which a larger proportion of the wealth of the community is spent in the ceremonies, or where the rights are better secured, or the duties better enforced, notwithstanding all the disadvantages of the law of polygamy."

Almost every variety of marriage can be illustrated from the customs of one or other of the Indian tribes.

In the first place, we have marriage by capture—the rudest form of union. In perhaps its simplest form it appears among the Birhors of Chota Nágpur. When the marriage is arranged, the father tells his daughter to show her lover how fleet she is. She runs off to the jungle, and after a short interval he starts in pursuit. The ceremony is over when the youth's shout, announcing that he has succeeded in catching the girl, is heard. Among the Andamanese, on the contrary, it is the man who runs away, and has to be captured by force, and seated on the bride's lap. The Mutuvan bridegroom of Travancore, after the marriage is settled, lurks near the house of the bride, and carries her off when she ventures out to bring water or firewood. The pair enjoy the honeymoon in the jungle, and return quietly in a few days, when the union is sanctioned by the tribal elders. Though some of the rites of the modern Hindu marriage may perhaps be interpreted in another way, they present some interesting survivals of this primitive custom—the armed procession of the bridegroom to fetch the bride, the mock resistance of her people, the objection of the husband to visit his wife's village in after life, and so on.

Another rude form of marriage-union is that found among some of the forest tribes, where the youths and girls of the village are kept in special halls, free communication between the sexes being tolerated, and permanent cohabitation ranking as marriage. Among tribes of this class there is no infant-marriage, and the bride has the right of choosing her mate. Among the

Ullatans of Travancore, when the girl is fit for wedlock, the eligible youths of the tribe assemble and dance round the grass hut in which she is concealed. Each in turn thrusts his bludgeon through the walls of the hut, and the owner of the stick she seizes claims her as his bride.

We have again the form of marriage which ethnologists call Beena, where the bridegroom serves his future father-in-law for a time, and when he marries lives with the family of his wife. Such an arrangement is common in South India, where the wife usually lives in her own house, and is visited there by her husband. It is very popular in Kashmír, because the father of the bride thus gets a drudge who works seven years without reward. Some men are so unscrupulous as to turn out the working candidate for their daughter's hand, and give her to a stranger.

The chief form of marriage, however, is that by purchase. The purchase of the bride is the more usual form, but in those tribes which practise what is called hypergamy—that is to say, where girls must marry in a group equal or superior to their own—it is the bridegroom who must be bought with a price. It is a curious instance of the effect of civilisation on primitive practice that the marriage-value of a Bengal youth is much enhanced if he have gained a university degree.

Hypergamy, again, is mainly responsible for the odious custom of infant-marriage, which, in spite of the protests of the conservative classes, it has been necessary to control by a law raising the age of consent. Other causes, however, have contributed to the spread of the custom, such as the desire to provide for a girl before she has the chance of indulging in fancies of her own. In those castes where widow-marriage is prohibited, the bride-price is naturally high, and a man has often to wait until he can save sufficient to purchase a bride. In this case he does not, as a rule, marry a very young girl, because her relations fear that she may be left a widow. On the other hand, where bridegrooms are scarce, the girl's father is not able to provide a husband for his daughter until she is well grown up. Such castes, therefore, have little infant-marriage. Education sometimes affects the matter. Some parents think it well that a boy should not be burdened with a wife until he is able to earn his own living. But others, who are not well off, endeavour to marry the boy at an early age, so that his wife's family may share the cost of his education; and a stupid boy is often married early, before he reaches the age at which his want of intelligence may be noticed by others. In Upper India, at least, there is no evidence that the lower classes have borrowed the idea of infant-marriage from the higher; on the contrary, it is more common among the poor than among the rich.

Widow-marriage is forbidden among the higher Hindu castes, because marriage is regarded as a sacrament which a woman can perform only once in her life, and the marriage of a widow is thus regarded as a form of concubinage. The same feeling prevails among the higher Musalmáns, but not to the same extent as among Hindus, and the former probably did not borrow it from the latter, as the same prejudice exists in Arabia. The main cause of the prohibition was probably the revolt against polyandry. But the levirate in India is not based on the Jewish idea of raising up seed to the dead brother; rather the woman is regarded as a chattel who passes with the estate; or it may be a survival of the fraternal form of polyandry. In any case, no brother older than the deceased husband can claim the right to his sister-in-law.

Group-marriage has by some authorities been recognised among the Nairs of Malabar; but recent native writers strenuously deny that the present ceremony can bear any such interpretation.

Among many of the lower castes tree-marriage is a recognised form. Thus, among the Kunbis of Gujarát, if a man cannot provide a husband for his daughter, she is married to a bunch of flowers, which is then thrown into a well. The girl can afterwards marry in the less regular form. In some cases, with the same object, she is married to a man who will grant her immediate divorce. The origin of tree-marriage is obscure. In some cases the idea seems to be that the dangers attending a second marriage are passed on to the tree. The ghost of the first wife is supposed to resent the happiness of her successor. In Upper India, to avoid her wrath, a man who marries a second time wears round his neck an image of his first wife, and every present he makes his new wife he offers first to the image. In other cases the girl seems to be married to the tree with the idea that she will absorb some of its fertility. In its crudest form tree-marriage appears among the Gauras of Orissa, when the girl is taken to the forest and left tied to a tree, if not to the mercy of wild beasts, at least as a prize to the first-comer. But usually it is arranged that some youth of an inferior branch of the tribe, to whom ordinarily she would not be married, carries her away as soon as her people have left her.

Proxy-marriage takes various forms. When one of the Mahratta family of Holkar succeeded in marrying a high caste Rájput girl,

"the sword of the Mahratta ruler," writes Sir J. Malcolm, "with his handkerchief bound round it, represented the prince, and to that the female was united; she married the wearer of the sword, not the shepherd."

When a South Indian dancing-girl accepts the degrading service of the temple, she is married to a dagger. In the land of Orissa, a man who cannot find a husband for his daughter before she comes of age, marries her to an arrow.

The most curious development of this is the marriage of the dead. Marco Polo describes it as a Tartar custom, and it still prevails in China. Among the Maravas of Madura, if the betrothed husband dies before marriage, the ceremony is completed in the presence and on behalf of the corpse, which must be placed on the seat beside the bride, and represents the bridegroom. When the rite is over, the *Talee*,* or marriage-string, is taken off the bride, and she is free to marry again as soon as she pleases. Among some Bráhmans of the west coast it is not considered seemly that an adult woman who dies unmarried should be sent to the next world in that state. Under these circumstances a handsome sum is paid to secure a bridegroom for the dead, and a form of marriage is gone through between them.

The details of the marriage-rite vary throughout the country, but it always presents features intended to secure two special results—first, a kind of magical rite to protect the pair from evil, and, in particular, to annul the influences which would prevent the fertility of the union. It is with this object that rice or wheat is poured over the heads of the pair, a custom which has passed from India to Europe. The second class of rites provides for the due admission of the bride, who under the rules of prohibited degrees is a stranger, into her new family. Hence we have the solemn eating of food by the pair from the same dish, like the Roman *Confarreatio.* Next the bride's forehead is marked with vermilion, the symbol of married life. This is a survival of the original blood-covenant entered into by the pair. Thus the Háris of Bengal draw a little blood with a thorn from the fingers of bride and bridegroom, and each is smeared with the other's blood. Lastly, they march round the sacred fire, which consecrates the union.

If marriage is a simple rite, divorce is even simpler; but it is not recognised in orthodox Hinduism. Among many low castes failure of the wife to provide a son is considered just ground for divorce. All such cases are settled by the tribal council. Some formality is often used, as among the Banwárs of the Santál country, who tear a leaf of the sacred *Saul** tree in the presence of the relatives on both sides in token that the marriage bond is broken.

The Musalmán marriage ceremony provides for the formal assent of the parties before the officiant, the bride being represented by a *Vakeel,** or attorney. Among the Baloch, as reported by Mr Hughes-Buller, it assumes a remarkable form. As a rule the marriage service is performed by the Mulla [*Moolah* *]; but if one does not happen to be easily available, it is customary for the bridegroom, or one of his relations, to proceed to the Mulla's residence with an empty water-skin. The Mulla fills this water-skin with his breath, the mouth of the skin is carefully closed, and the skin brought back to the bride. The Mulla's breath is then emitted in the bride's face, and as soon as it touches her the marriage ceremony is considered to be sufficient and complete.

[Numerous accounts of marriage rites will be found in Risley, "Tribes and Castes of Bengal"; Crooke, Ditto for the "North-West Provinces and Oudh"; Thurston, "Bulletin of Madras Museum"; "Census Report," India, 1901, i. 421ff.; Bengal, i. 249ff.; Pánjab, i. 217ff.]

MEDICINE.—Medicine to the Hindu is a divine revelation, and its principles are embodied in the Ayurveda, the oldest authority on the subject. The earlier books show that their authors had attained a considerable knowledge of physiology, hygiene, materia medica, and some skill in surgery. Even in the Rig-veda we find physicians who collect healing herbs and recite magic spells, as they did in Homer's time when they applied remedies to the patient. The science reached its highest development in the Buddhist period, when Asoka established hospitals. Megasthenes, writing of this time, describes physicians as next in honour to ascetics:

"They are simple in their habits, but do not live in the fields. Their food consists of rice and barley-meal, which they can always get for the mere asking, or receive from those who entertain them as guests in their houses. By their knowledge of pharmacy they can make marriages fruitful, and determine the sex of the offspring. They effect cures rather by regulating the diet than by the use of medicines. The remedies most esteemed are ointments and plasters. All others they consider to be in a great measure pernicious in their nature."

The first great authority, Charaka, dates from the first, and Susrata from the fourth century of our era. There is little doubt that these writers borrowed from the Greeks; but, on the other hand, Hindu medical science penetrated to the Court of the Khalífa Hárún-al-Rashíd in the eighth century.

The early Muhammadans gave some patronage to medicine. Timúr claims to have established hospitals in every town and city; Fíroz certainly organised one at Delhi, and Sikandar Lodi had a Hindu text-book translated. Jahángír, too, started hospitals, and appointed doctors to attend the sick. He had a French physician, Bernard, on his staff. One day Bernard, finding the Emperor in a good humour, asked him to give him a beautiful dancing-girl as his fee. So Jahángír had her lifted on the doctor's back, and he bore her away in triumph. Akbar used to employ physicians from Goa, where Linschoten, writing at the end of the sixteenth century, says the doctors were native Christians, who gave themselves airs, and had umbrellas held over them, and were more trusted by the Portuguese, from the Viceroy downwards, than their own doctors.

From this time dates the extension of European medicine and surgery in India. Tavernier visited a young Dutch chirurgeon, whom the Envoy from Batavia, at the King's special request, left at Golconda. Bernier, the famous traveller, took service as physician with Aurangzeb, and followed his camp in the train of his patron, one of his nobles, Danishmand Khán. Fryer, in 1672, speaks of the Goa physicians as great bleeders,

"hardly leaving enough to feed the Currents for Circulation; of which Cruelty some complain invidiously after recovery." He had a poor opinion of the profession at Surat: "They will submit to spells and charms, and the advice of old women. Here is a Brachmin Doctor, who has raised a good fortune; they pretend to no Fees, but make their pay in their Physick; and think it Honour enough if you favour them with a Title of your Physician. This Brachmin comes every day, and feels every Man's Pulse in the Factory, and is often made use of for a Powder for Agues, which works as infallibly as the Peruvian Bark; it is a preparation of Natural Cinnabar."

Hamilton speaks well of the Goa Hospital, and says that the Capuchins at Súrat treated the poor gratis. But he gives a very different account of the institution at

Calcutta. There is, he says, "a pretty good hospital, where many go in to undergo the penance of physic, but few come out to give an account of the operation." We may judge of the condition of Calcutta early in the eighteenth century by his statement that in one year, out of 1,200 Europeans, 460 were buried.

Two of the doctors of those days played a worthy part in the history of the Company. Gabriel Broughton (1646), as a reward for treating with success the daughter of the Emperor Sháh Jahán, who had been terribly burnt, asked for a grant of the right to trade in Bengal. William Hamilton (1715) cured the Emperor Farrukhsiyar, who was unable on account of illness to marry. In gratitude, his patient presented him with a trade Firmán, and a model in gold of his surgical instruments. At that time the Company was certainly not liberal to its doctors. Lockyer tells us that the Company's surgeon at Madras received only £36 per annum. The only medical man who suffered in the tragedy of the Black Hole was Holwell, who had been an apothecary, and wrote a good account of the occurrence.

The difficulties of these early doctors, particularly in treating native ladies, were great. They were allowed only to feel a hand thrust out through a hole in a curtain, and it was a common trick, in order to test the doctor's skill, to make a healthy slave-girl take the place of her mistress. When De Lan attended the Queen of Golconda, Tavernier says that he was first bathed by eunuchs and old women, anointed with aromatics, and dressed in native garments. Before he bled Her Majesty, his hands and arms were again washed and bathed in scented oil. "That being done, they drew a curtain, and the young Queen, putting an arm out through the hole, the surgeon bled her." The fee was usually paid, in the case of royalty, by pouring gold coins into the basin.

The early surgeons gained all the knowledge of anatomy which they possessed from the dissection of the sacrificial victims. With the rise of Bráhmanism instruction even of this kind was disapproved, and the caste objections to touching a corpse were intensified. The first real attempt to give medical teaching to natives was made by the English, and the first batch of native students was sent to England in 1845. Another obstacle to the spread of medical knowledge in the country has been the selfishness of the class of hereditary physicians, who never disclose any discoveries they may make in pathology or materia medica.

Modern native treatment is based on a theory, apparently borrowed from the Greeks, that the body is composed of five elements—earth, water, fire, air, ether; and that physical health depends on the preservation, in exact proportions, of the three general elements, rheum, bile, and phlegm; or air, fire, and water respectively. Air, or rheum, spreads below the navel; fire or bile between it and the heart; water, or phlegm, above the heart. The tastes are six—sweet, sour, saltish, bitter, pungent, astringent, each preceding taste being superior to that succeeding it. The first three, sweet, sour, saltish, appease rheum; the remaining three, bitter, pungent, astringent, relieve bile and phlegm; while bile is appeased by bitter, astringent, and sweet. Medicines, again, are twofold, clearing and subsidiary; the first purge the irritated humours, the second establish the humours which have been disturbed.

The *Huckeem*,* or physician, follows one of two schools, Hindus preferring the Misráni, or Egyptian, which never bleeds, and is partial to the use of metallic oxides; the Musalmáns favouring the Yunáni, or Greek, which follows the good old rules of Galen, Hippocrates, and Avicenna, prescribing little physic, but much fasting, approving of bleeding, and preferring vegetable drugs. The Huckeem is a mere empiric, and, being destitute of medical knowledge, relies on some old books received from a predecessor, which he can hardly read. His patients value a dose mainly for its bulk and nastiness. A quart of noisome liquid, containing various drugs, which are, or ought to be, thirty-six in number, is often prescribed. He dissuades his patient from European medicines, because these are suited to a chilly climate and a hot constitution. The drugs used are of the worst description, often carelessly marked, incapable of indentification, and stored without care. The result can easily be imagined. Broughton, in his account of the Mahrattas, tells how a man suffering from fever was shut up in a room, dosed with strong bitters, till, as he expressed it, his body was hissing hot, and he was driven almost mad. A rival doctor was then called in, who threw open all the doors, poured cold water over him, and gave him cooling drinks. In a few days the patient recovered.

The Hindu Baid is, if possible, a more incompetent practitioner. He deals largely in simples collected by the jungle men, of the use of which he is generally ignorant. To take medicine from him is a sort of sacramental act. Some orthodox Hindus, when on the point of death, call him in, believing that by swallowing the drugs he prescribes they obtain absolution of their sins. Tavernier describes men of this class who used to appear every day in the bazaar of Bijapur: "They first feel the pulse, and when giving the medicine, for which they take only two farthings, they mumble some words between their teeth." Terry, writing of North India, says that the people made little use of them: "they fearing more *Medicum quam Morbum*." The Baid, in fact, is little better than the medicine-man of jungle tribes, like the Kacháris of Assam, who places before the patient thirteen leaves representing the gods. He causes a pendulum attached to a cord to vibrate before these, and whichever leaf it approaches, this is the god who is causing the disease, and must be propitiated. This school believes that most diseases can be cured by means of a scape-animal. Maladies are of three kinds—those due to sin committed in a previous life, or in the present birth, or those merely accidental. This last can alone be remedied by a physician.

A still lower class of practitioner is a member of one of the Gipsy tribes. The Bediya of Bengal carries about grubs in a bamboo tube, which he gravely assures his patients have been removed from carious teeth. Sometimes he prescribes the scales of the pangolin, or tiger's claws, to repel the Evil Eye; or tiger's flesh, which gives courage; tiger's fat as a specific for the infirmities of age; or jackal skins, which cure rheumatism. The wise woman of the jungle villages is more competent than a person like this, because she often has an excellent traditional knowledge of simples. The hill-man, too, escapes epidemic disease, because he follows the admirable rule of deserting his meagre hut when disease appears.

For surgery the villager largely depends on the barber, who represents our old barber surgeons. In the days of constant fighting he was employed to cure wounds received in battle. Nowadays he does little more than minor operations, dealing with petty injuries. One branch of surgery he used to practice with considerable success, rhinoplasty—the treatment of restoring the noses of faithless wives or criminals who suffered this form of mutilation.

To speak of the progress of European surgery in India is beyond our present purpose. Our modern hospitals and dispensaries are gradually becoming more valued, and the skill of our surgeons, particularly in lithotomy and eye operations, is gradually displacing native methods. The Dufferin hospitals have done enormous service to women, whose health is so often wrecked by the incompetence of the native midwife.

["Calcutta Review," xxiii. 217, "Surgeons in India, Past and Present."]

MONASTERY.—The time-honoured institution of the four Ásramas, or stages of the life of a Hindu—as an unmarried religious student, a married householder, an anchorite, a religious mendicant dead to the world—contained all the germs of monasticism. The Sannyási, or man in the fourth stage, was the prototype of the great Monastic Orders of the Buddhists and Jains, founded in the sixth century B.C., the only difference being that the Sannyási Order was never such a powerful organisation as that either of Buddhists or Jains.

The Buddhist monastery, or Vihára, resembled very closely the corresponding institution of Christianity. The original plan provided simple cells, ranged round a courtyard more or less rectangular, and with little architectural style save an occasional portico or arcade with pillars and arches. This, according to Mr Fergusson, developed in later days into a more elaborate edifice with several stories, and furnished the prototype of the modern temples, buildings like the well-known Rath at Mahábalipur representing such a structure.

Most of these Viháras were probably built almost entirely of wood, and the existing remains allow us only to judge the character of the ground plan. That at Mahábodhi, in Bengal, according to General Cunningham, was laid out in a diagram of 36 squares, 6 on each side, of which the 4 corner squares are assigned to the corner towers, and the 4 middle squares formed an open pillared court, containing a well. In the centre a Stúpa, or relic-tower, was probably built. The main body of the monastery occupied the 16 interior squares, and the open courtyard was surrounded by a pillared cloister. The outer walls were enormously strong, 9 feet in thickness. The Chinese pilgrim, Hiuen Tsiang, says that this building sheltered 1,000 monks.

Monasticism reached the Himálaya and Tibet from India. Colonel Waddell, in his account of the recent Mission, has given a very interesting description of a cave-monastery near Gyantse, in which some wretched anchorites are confined in cells little larger than a rabbit-hutch, representatives of the true Indian Ascetics. The modern Tibet monasteries, as described by the same writer, are built on inaccessible sites, because begging with the bowl, even when the monastery adjoined a town or village, was never a feature of Lamaism. The style of architecture is medieval Indian. In the outer Himálaya, cells, dormitories, and other buildings cluster round the temple, and the ground floor is often used as a store-house. The upper stories are reached by a staircase or inclined beam, in which notches are cut for steps. Some of these buildings hold 2,000 or 3,000 Lamas, or, if M. Huc be believed, as many as 15,000.

Mr Drew describes the monasteries of Ladak as the most conspicuous buildings in the country, generally placed in remote situations, or in a nook sheltered by a cliff. At the entrance of the courtyard are prayer-wheels; beyond this a fine lofty chamber, the centre space of which is supported by wooden pillars, and used as an image-room. No women, not even nuns, can pass the threshold. Two Lamas rule the monastery—one responsible for religious, the other for temporal affairs. Some of these institutions are endowed, or receive help from Lhasa; others depend on alms or contributions of grain at harvest, in return for which the Lamas dispense hospitality to strangers.

The Burmese monasteries, according to Sir J. G. Scott, are usually built of teak, oblong in shape, the habited part raised above the ground on posts. There is never more than one story, as it is an indignity for a Burman to have any one over his head. The lower space is for schoolboys; the upper, with tier on tier of roof, is reached by a carved ladder. This is divided into two parts, on different levels—the lower for teaching and ordinary work; the higher, where the monks receive visitors, has at the back images of the Buddha. The monks sometimes have special dormitories, but more usually sleep in the central hall. Detached from the main building is a room for palm-leaf scribes, as well as cook-rooms and lavatories. Some have fine libraries. The monks live a life of constant self-denial, but undergo none of the absurd mortifications of the flesh endured by Bráhman ascetics. These buildings are interesting, as they probably to some extent reproduce the ancient wooden architecture of India which preceded stone constructions, and, as Sir J. G. Scott remarks, "should help us to realise the descriptions of the temple of Solomon and the ancient wooden palaces of Nineveh."

When the Siva cult replaced Buddhism in Bengal, some of the Buddhist monasteries were converted into Hindu Maths, a transfer which probably occurred in other places also. These monasteries are occupied by various branches of the Hindu Monastic Orders, such as that at Dhinodhar, in Cutch, by the Kanphata, or "slit-eared" Jogis, so called from the massive earrings worn by members of the Order; or those of the curious Lingáyat sect of Southern India, who use the monastery, as the Buddhist monks did, for a refuge during the rainy season, when their tours are discontinued. Sir J. M. Campbell describes the monasteries of the Havig Bráhmans in Kanara as built close to forest springs:

> "They are built in two blocks, an outer and an inner, separated by a courtyard. The outer block is a high, narrow verandah surrounding the inner block, with a single entrance facing the door of the shrine, and with a high windowless stone wall on the side farthest from the shrine, and with wooden pillars on the side nearest the shrine to support the roof. The inner block is divided into two parts: an outer room, where worshippers meet, and the shrine of the god."

The plan thus conforms closely to the original Buddhist model.

The northern monasteries are on a less imposing scale. At the great pilgrim-centres, like Hardwár, Mathura, or Benares, they are sometimes brick buildings, but more often a collection of huts, in which members of the Order to which the monastery is appropriated reside when attending the periodical festivals.

The continuity of monastic life is thus clearly marked for over two thousand years. But as yet its details are little known. The modern Hindu monk is usually a sullen, unsociable creature, and particularly resents the intrusion of members of another creed. Those who follow the rules of Vishnu live in much more comfort than the votaries of Siva. These last will be seen crouched round a smoky fire, their bodies smeared with ashes, their long hair roughly bound up in a roll, generally more or less under the influence of the brain-wrecking Gánja. As for the solemn services, the care of the sick and poor, the devotion to learning which characterise many of the Western monastic communities, little if anything will be found in India. The monk seems to dream his life away in the trance of semi-intoxication, and in the monotonous repetition of the titles of the deity whom he serves. Monasticism, as it appears in India, seems less animated by nobility of purpose than in any other part of the world.

[For the early monasteries, Hardy, "Eastern Monachism"; Cunningham, "Mahábodhi"; Fergusson, "History of Indian and Eastern Architecture," chap. vi. For those of modern times, Drew, "Jummoo and Kashmír," 257ff.; Yule, "Mission to Ava," 355; Oldfield, "Sketches of Nepál," ii. 277ff.; Waddell, "Buddhism of Tibet," 255ff., "Lhasa and its Mysteries," 238; Shway Yoe, "The Burman," i. 149ff.; "Bombay Gazetteer," xv. Pt. I. 121f.]

MONKEYS.—Zoologists divide the monkeys of India into two great families—first, the Simiidæ or anthropoid apes, of which the genus Hylobates is best represented by the White-browed Gibbon or *Hoolock** of Assam, which has few of the vulgar monkey vices, and in captivity is a most gentle pet; secondly, the Cercopithecidæ, with two sub-families, one represented by the *Macacus rhesus*, the Bengal monkey, a sly, destructive, quarrelsome brute, and the other by the *Lungoor** or *Hoonimaun.** This last is a dignified creature, held in high respect by Hindus. He is generally a mild, inoffensive beast, except where they abound and take to a town life, as at Ahmadábád, when they become as great a nuisance as *Macacus rhesus*. He represents Hanumán, king of the apes, who in the wars of the Rámáyana helped Ráma to recover his wife Síta from the clutches of the demon Rávana.

To say that Hindus derived their respect for monkeys from the Hanumán legend is, as Sir A. Lyall says, "putting the cart before the horse." The Hindu worships the monkey because he believes him to be a human being who has suffered degradation. Fryer, in his usual quaint way, says: "To kill one of them the natives hold Piacular, calling them half Men; once they were Men, but for their Laziness had Tails given them, and Hair to cover them." On this feeling was tacked, in later times, the Hanumán story. He possibly represents the prognathous hero of one of the forest tribes who assisted the Aryans in their movement southwards.

But the belief in the sanctity of the monkey is not confined to the Aryans. Forest tribes, like the Suiris, have adopted the animal as their tribal god, and the Bhuiyas of Orissa identify him with the Sun-god. It may have been from sources like these that the Hindus adopted him as a deity. But it is more probable that any race, on meeting the quaint animal, would worship it. Tavernier tells a curious story of a pagoda at Goa, in which they kept, in a silver tomb, the bones and nails of a great monkey, which, they said, had rendered great service to their gods. Possibly he heard of a shrine of Hanumán; but the modern Hindu keeps no such relics of his demi-gods. In North India Hanumán is the patron of every settlement, and the setting-up of his image is the outward and visible sign of the establishment of a hamlet. Naturally he is the special patron of wandering acrobats, and his shrine is often erected near a well to prevent accidents during the work of sinking. As lord of the village, his presence ensures that the water shall turn out sweet.

The offering of food to monkeys which now goes on at the chief Hindu shrines is of ancient date, as it is referred to by Ælian, who, however, mixes up the Macacus with the Lungoor. The respect paid to monkeys at such places is shown by an incident which occurred near Mathura in 1808, when two young English officers wounded one of the sacred monkeys. They were attacked by a mob of Bráhmans, who drove the elephant on which they rode into the river, and both were drowned. The natives attributed this act of revenge to the monkeys themselves, who, they said, with sticks and stones drove the elephant before them.

The Macacus, "the incarnation of unfulfilled promises," as he has been called, is a decided nuisance in bazaars, owing to his pilfering habits and the destruction he causes to tiled roofs, which are only imperfectly protected by thorns laid upon them. Many years ago it is said that a Sepoy regiment, offended at the extortion of the corn-chandlers of Mathura, as they marched through the city flung handfuls of dried peas on the roofs. These the monkeys promptly recovered from beneath the tiles, and wrecked the bazaar. In the eighteenth century they became such a pest at Benares that the Rája of Bishanpur, a pious Hindu, petitioned the Government to send a guard of Sepoys to destroy them. He stated in his petition that they used to enter his house, carry off the meat from his table, and steal whatever they could find; while they terrified his girls, assembling round them if alone, and making the most odious noises. Nowadays, when monkeys become intolerable at Benares, it is the custom to deport them to a jungle on the other side of the river. Not long ago, when being removed in crates to a jungle in the Siwálik Hills, a consignment escaped at the Sahàranpur Railway Station, which they occupied for some days, doing infinite damage in the goods sheds. At last a wily railway-man smeared some goods waggons with treacle. Most of the monkeys invaded the train, and, when they were all well aboard, the engine-driver started at full speed. The monkeys were too much alarmed to jump till the engine slacked speed in a jungle some miles down the line, when they hastily disembarked and were no more seen. Timúr, in his Memoirs, tells how his camp in the Siwálik Hills was attacked by a multitude of monkeys, who not only stole the eatables of the troops, but carried off small articles and curiosities.

They are much dreaded by native women, who say that they are liable to attack by these semi-human beasts, bears, and monkeys. Mr Cooper tells how a band of monkeys assailed a party of women in the Mishmi Hills with intent to rob them of the rice and sweetmeats which they were carrying to the workers in the fields; and Tavernier speaks of them at Ahmadábád climbing trees and throwing down the eggs of crows. Waterton denied that any animal but man had the power of throwing things. Dr Ball, however, saw a monkey, with *malice prepense*, throwing shingle down a hill-side near Naini Tál, and elephants throw sticks at passers-by. Tavernier says that at Pulicat people used to amuse themselves by laying baskets of grain on the road, and short bludgeons beside them, which the monkeys promptly applied to each others' backs.

Many are the tales told of monkeys. Fakírs often encourage them about their hermitages, and it used to be one of the sights of Simla to see the old man who took up his post on the top of Jakko Hill calling the monkeys and feeding them. Natives all agree that they have a king, and certainly at the Durga Kund, near Benares, where hosts of monkeys are daily fed, one enormous brute was recognised as their master, and when he deigned to come to eat, his subjects scuttled away with obvious signs of reverence or fear. The great mountain, called by natives Bandar-púcch, or "Monkey-tail," rises above the sources of the Jumna. The legend runs that one monkey from the Plains retires there every year in spring, and returns in the next year, reduced to a skeleton, only to give place to another. The "Man of the Woods," seen by Fryer imprisoned "in a parrit's cage, with the head of an owl and the body of a monkey, but without a tail, and the first finger of the right hand armed with a claw similar to that of a bird of prey," was perhaps some kind of monkey. At a temple at Satára 25 acres of land form the monkeys' endowment, which supplies the grain on which they feed. Madhoji Scindiah left an endowment at Brindaban to support them, and here a lame animal was treated with special attention, as his patron was wounded in the leg at the battle of Panipat. The climax of absurdity was reached when the Rája of Krishnagarh, in Bengal, spent large sums on the marriage of a pair of monkeys. Just before the Mutiny a pious Bráhman, with a view to conciliate the natives, advised that some monkeys should be fed. Sir H. Lawrence took his visitor to a gun. "See," said he, "one of my monkeys. That," indicating a pile of round shot, "is their food," and "this," pointing to a sentry, "is the man who feeds them. There! go and tell your friends of my monkeys!"

While Hindus reverence the animal, many jungle tribes use it as food. The Behars of Chota Nágpur spread nets, into which, pious Hindus say with a shudder, these unbelievers make the monkeys take headers, and promptly eat them. The Kathkari of Ratnagiri dresses himself in a woman's sheet, and thus entices monkeys which he shoots with his bow and arrows. In Coorg monkey-soup is prescribed for sick and weakly people, while one tribe in the Central Provinces take their name from this their favourite food. From Gorakhpur comes a curious account of potters, who hunt and crucify a monkey in spring to make the crops prosper. This has been supposed to be a commutation of human sacrifice. More probably it represents the annual sacrifice of the god of vegetation embodied in monkey form.

MOSQUE.—The plan of a mosque is simple. In its rudest form it consists of a mere platform bounded by a low wall on the side facing Mecca, a type which is still that of the common Imámbára [*Imaumbarra* *], the building maintained by the Shiah sect of Muhammadans for the celebrations at the *Mohurrum.** In the more elaborate design we have an enclosure of quadrangular or rectangular form. In the centre is an open courtyard, in the midst of which is a tank for ceremonial ablutions. The mosque itself is a narrow rectangular building. Midway, in the wall facing Mecca, is a niche which marks the direction of the holy Kaaba, or tomb of the Prophet, and beside it the pulpit from which the Friday sermon is delivered.

The oldest mosque in the country is that adjoining the Kutab Minár, near Delhi, which was erected just at the close of the twelfth century. This, and the mosques at Ajmír, Kanauj, Dhár, and Ahmadábád, all of the earlier period, are merely reconstructed Hindu or Jain temples. These were at the time comparatively modern, and nothing in them can be carried back much beyond 1,000 A.D. These mosques show in their structure signs of the haste with which the reconstruction was carried out. That at Ajmír is known as the Arhái Din ká Jhomprá, "the hut of two and a half days," as if to mark this fact. In the Kutab mosque at Delhi the carved pillars of the original edifice still remain. Mr Fergusson thus describes the method by which the temple was converted into the mosque:

"By removing the principal cell and its porch from the centre of the court, and building up the entrance of the cell which surrounds it, a courtyard was at once obtained, surrounded by a double colonade, which was always the typical form of the mosque. Still one essential feature was wanting—a more important side towards Mecca; this they readily obtained by removing the smaller pillars from that side, and re-erecting the larger pillars of the porch, with their dome in the centre; and if there were smaller domes, by placing one of them at each end. Thus, without a single new column or carved stone being required, they obtained a mosque, which for convenience and beauty was unsurpassed by anything they afterwards erected from their own original designs."

This form was succeeded, in the latter part of the fourteenth century, by the so-called Pathán style, which Fergusson thinks "may have been a protest of the more puritanical Moslem spirit against the Hindu exuberance which characterised both the thirteenth and fourteenth centuries." A reaction, again, against this severe simplicity resulted in the more elaborate later Pathán style. The façade, adorned with sculptured marbles, became more elaborate; little kiosks were erected at the angles of the building; but during the Pathán period minarets, which were regarded more as a symbol of victory, were not added to the building, though we have a splendid example of the detached minaret in the Kutab Minár.

Meanwhile a somewhat different style was being evolved in other capital cities of independent dynasties, like that at Jaunpur (1419-78), which presents the first example of the great propylon or gate-pyramid, and the grand mosque at Bijapur in the Deccan begun about 1557. The only instance of a mosque in which the whole area is covered appears at Kulbarga, in the Deccan.

The Moghul style is characterised by unrivalled

magnificence, as seen in Akbar's mosque at Fatehpur-Sikri, with its splendid gateway, and Sháh Jahán's mosque at Delhi—the latter, according to Mr Fergusson, one of the few mosques in India, or elsewhere, designed to produce a pleasing effect externally. Here we have, combined with dignity of style and position, the most delicious contrasts of colour, in the red stone galleries, the black and white marbles of the façade, the white domes with their golden pinnacles, the graceful minarets with rosy stripes. Here the minaret becomes an integral part of the structure—an innovation on the Indo-Saracenic style, which appears first at Ahmadábád. But in its earliest form the minaret closely follows the model of the Hindu Tower of Victory, first utilised by the Musalmáns in the Kutab Minár. [*See* LAT.] In these Moghul mosques, beautiful as they are, the decadence of the style is already obvious; the earlier grandeur is replaced by mere prettiness and felicity of decoration. In the Moti Masjid, or Pearl Mosque, the court chapel of the palace at Agra, the style reached the highest point of purity and elegance. In these, as well as in the great reception halls, like the Diwán-i-ám at Agra and Delhi, the design suggests ideas taken from the Central Asian tent, its poles and screens. The effect is produced solely by perfection of proportion, beauty of material, and harmony of constructive design. The subtle rhythm of the three domes of the Agra mosque placed over the screen arches saves the whole design, as Mr Havell remarks, from monotony, "while the marvellous grace of the contours, which is characteristic of the finest of Sháh Jahán's buildings, makes each dome grow up from the roof like a flower-bud on the point of expanding."

With the accession of Aurangzeb, the style rapidly degenerates, as may be seen by the contrast of his Moti Masjid, in the Delhi Fort, with that at Agra, till it ends in the crude buildings erected by the Kings of Oudh. In only one of the Lucknow series is there any sign of massiveness or dignity—the great *Imaumbarra*,* with its splendid concrete dome, erected for the performance of the *Mohurrum** ceremonies of the Shiah sect. As the Musalmáns converted Jain temples into mosques, so the Portuguese constructed out of a mosque the Church in the Convent of St Francis at Goa.

The common village mosque, though possessing no features of architectural interest, is more closely linked with the religious and social life than those of the great cities. The latter are generally the work of some powerful ruler, the former is painfully erected by the contributions of the very poor. It serves as a common meeting-place for Musalmáns, and a rest-house for Fakírs and travellers. Here a little school is often carried on, where a needy *Moolah** teaches little boys to repeat passages of the Korán by rote.

[Fergusson, 'H. of Architecture," 498ff.; Havell, "Handbook to Agra"; Fanshawe, "Delhi, Past and Present."]

MUHAMMADANS.—Islám, the creed which enjoins complete submission to the will of God in perfect peace, included, according to the last enumeration, 62,000,000 of people—nearly one-third of the total population of the Empire. They are rapidly increasing, partly because the tracts where they are chiefly found—North and East Bengal, the Western Panjáb and Sind, the western parts of the United Provinces—are regions which have hitherto almost completely escaped the stress of famine and plague; partly because in the districts of Eastern Bengal, where the increase of Musalmáns is most striking, social rather than religious causes have conduced to the progress of Islám. The Musalmán, who has a strain of Central Asian blood, is of more vigorous constitution than the Hindu, lives longer, and brings up a larger family. His diet, of which meat forms a considerable part, gives him more vigorous health than that of the vegetarian Hindu, and as he more freely permits widow-marriage, the proportion of women married during the child-bearing age is larger. With its democratic constitution and partial disregard of the laws of caste, Islám naturally attracts converts from the menial tribes, and though in the recent period there is no evidence of extensive proselytism, it shelters a large number of persons with whom, for various reasons, the Hindu rule is unpopular. To this must be added the fact that the Musalmán population of Bengal is most numerous in the progressive districts to the east of the Province, while Hindus are strongest in the stationary or decadent western area. The result is that within thirty years the Musalmán population of Bengal has increased from about 20,000,000 to 25,500,000.

Islám in India differs in many respects from the original faith preached in Arabia. The early Musalmán colonies were small bodies of military adventurers. They took wives from the daughters of the land, and were thus largely influenced by their Animistic environment. This process was encouraged by the Moghul Court, when the Emperors, following the example of Akbar, endeavoured to secure their power by marrying Rájput princesses. Many of these ladies continued to practise their own religion within the palaces of Delhi and Agra, and it was due to them that the old rule of persecution was replaced by a policy of toleration.

Writing of the modern Musalmáns of the Panjáb, Sir D. Ibbetson observes:

"They observe the feasts of both religions, and the fasts of neither. A brother-officer tells me that he once entered the rest-house of a Mahomedan village in Hisár, and found the headman refreshing an idol with a new coat of paint, while a Bráhman read holy texts alongside. They seemed somewhat ashamed of being caught in the act, but on being pressed explained that their Mulla had lately visited them, had been extremely angry on seeing the idol, and had made them bury it in the sand. But now that the Mulla had gone, they were afraid of the possible consequences, and were endeavouring to console the god for his rough treatment."

This fusion of Animism with Islám is shown in the special regard paid by the Indian Musalmáns to relics of the Prophet and the Saints, the pilgrimages to the tombs of the worthies of the faith, the employment by

Hindus converted to Islám of Bráhmans for their domestic rites, the partial adoption of the usages of caste regarding marriage, the worship of the village god in time of trouble. The wild tribesman of the western frontier knows that there is only one God who is worthy of worship. But he seldom prays directly to Him, and prefers the intercession of a Saint.

"It is," writes Mr Hughes Buller, "the Saint who can avert calamity, cure disease, procure children for the childless, bless the efforts of the hunter, and even improve the circumstances of the dead."

To him vows are made and marked by rags, or some petty article left at his tomb. The child born in answer to prayer is brought there and solemnly shaved, the hair and clothes being offered up to bring the baby into communion with the holy man. The hunter brings to him a deer-horn in the hope of sport, and those afflicted by disease rub the ailing limb on the tomb-stone, and hope to secure a blessing. The same is the case in Madras, where, as in North India, the Hindus join readily in the celebration of the Mohurrum, and, strangest of all, there is a Hindu temple near Srirangam which is sacred to a goddess called the "Musalmán Lady," who is said to be the wife of the local Hindu deity.

In fact, the ordinary villager is very ignorant of the principles of the faith. If he prays, it is in a form of words the meaning of which he does not understand. Musalmáns are united in detesting pork and enforcing the law of circumcision; but in other beliefs, practices, and rules of morality they differ little from their Hindu neighbours.

In recent years there has been some reaction against this condition of things. We have seen the rise of fanatic, puritanical sects, like that of the Wahábis and Ferazis of Bengal. This has been accompanied in North India by a striving after a more intense religious life, as shown in greater attention to the doctrinal teaching of the young, the dissemination of religious tracts, and the translation of sacred books into the local vernacular tongues.

On the other hand, there has been another movement, associated with the career of the late Sayyid Ahmad. He devoted his life to the foundation of a College at Aligarh, which has already attained a high rank among the Indian educational establishments. The distinctive note of its teaching is the liberalisation of Islám, and the acceptance of the results of Western science, which are abhorred by the old-fashioned orthodox Musalmán. The advanced Musulmán is now endeavouring to rival the Bengali in aptitude for State employment.

Thus there is no evidence of the decay of Islám; on the contrary, in many parts of the empire it is rapidly progressing at the expense of Hinduism. As Judaism, divorced from a country of its own and a national polity, is more than holding its own in the West, so, if the present rate of progress be maintained, Islám bids fair in the not far-distant future to gain a position higher than it now enjoys among the religions of India.

["Census Reports," Balúchistán, 1901, i. 38ff.; Madras, i. 134; Bengal, 1891, i. 147, 1901, i. 156, 165ff.; Ibbetson, "Panjáb Ethnography," p. 142.]

MUSIC.—Music is a very ancient Hindu art, cultivated by the guilds of singers who intoned the Vedic hymns. They used three kinds of instruments, classified as those of percussion, as the drum; wind, as the flute; stringed, as the lute. Later on, in a list of callings, we find players on special instruments enumerated. The Musulmáns brought their own music with them from Central Asia, and this in an early period of their history was improved and developed by the famous Amír Khusru. But with their conquest came the end of the old Hindu ballad. It no longer breathed of patriotism and independence. In its later form it differed little from the Persian Ghazal, whose themes are women and wine, the woes of separated lovers. It is only among the Rájputs and Mahrattas that the real ballad survives.

Akbar is said to have harmonised two hundred of the old Persian tunes, and he patronised the most eminent musicians of the native school. It takes away something from the repute of his musical skill to learn that he was famous as a performer on the Nakára, or big drum. Sháh Jahán was so delighted with the performance of a Maestro named Jagannáth, that he had him weighed in gold, and gave him the amount as his fee. But the puritanical Aurangzeb dismissed the royal singers, and then the minstrels of Delhi fitted up a bier, which they paraded before the palace. When the Emperor asked what this meant, they replied that Music was dead, and that they were carrying his corpse to burial. "Bury him deep," replied the Emperor, "that no sound may ever rise from him."

The chief difference between Hindu and European music is that the native ear recognises grades of sound in which we of the West take no pleasure. One authority quoted by Sir M. Grant-Duff suggested that "the dominant factor in the Hindu system is melody, and that of the European harmony"; while another laid down that Hindu music, in its present state, is just where our music was when the genius of Palestrina put in order the Gregorian moods, which are said to have come originally from the East.

"The Hindu system of music," writes Sir W. Jones, "has, I believe, been formed on truer principles than our own; and all the skill of the native composer is directed to the great object of their art, the natural expression of strong passion, to which melody indeed is often sacrificed."

The Hindu admits the superiority of the European in many branches of art, but not in music. Our music, they say, is good, but it is all written in one or two modes, and is therefore deficient in variety as compared with their music, which employs thirty-six. To quote Sir W. Hunter:

"The Hindu musician declines altogether to be judged by the few simple airs which the English ear can appreciate. It is, indeed, impossible to adequately represent the Indian system by the European notation; and the full range of its effects can only be rendered by Indian instruments—a vast collection of sound-producers, elaborated during two thousand years to suit the special requirements of Hindu music. The complicated structure of its musical modes rests upon three separate systems, one of which consists of five, another of six, and the third of seven notes. It presents in a living state some of the early forms which puzzle the student of Greek music, side by side with its most complicated developments."

Mrs Wilson dwells on the difficulty which a European finds in following the songs of the minstrel:

"Owing to the alien time of the music, and the multiplication of quarter and half tones, one finds it quite impossible to follow or grasp the composition as a whole, or attempt to reproduce it. But this does not mitigate one's appreciation of its weird character and beauty. . . . A characteristic peculiarity of the phrasing . . . is that each note is merged in the next. If there is a wide interval between one note and its successor, grace notes lead from the first to the second, and unite them. The passage generally ends with a long vibrating note . . . which introduces an element of uncertainty into one's sense of time."

All this, however, is the scientific side of Hindu music, which has been elaborately discussed by Rája Sourindro Mohun Tagore, and English students like Captain Day and others. To Europeans in India the music with which they are unhappily most familiar is that of the hideous *Tom-tom*,* beaten at marriages and feasts, and sometimes accompanied by the still more awful *Cholera horn.** Music of this kind has the character of the band of the Governor of Surat, which Fryer describes as

"a noise not unlike that our Coopers make on their Hogsheads driving home their Hoops." He adds: "I could think of nothing but the last Trump; so that I could persuade myself that there was little Musick in it; but they say that Time will bring it to be agreeable to the Ears."

There are, however, varieties even of performances on the *Tom-tom*. Dr Ball professed to be able to identify the jungle races of Chota Nágpur merely by their night performances on the drum. On the other hand, there is something strangely impressive in the weird note of the sankh, or shell-trumpet, when heard at a distance resounding from some Hindu shrine like the great temple at Tanjore, or on the hill above Pasupati in Nepál when the evening hymn swells from the many shrines which line the bank of the river below.

While the ordinary native of the plains seems to have little music in his soul, some of the forest tribes are said to be much superior. Captain Gerard describes the music in Kunáwar on the lower Himálaya as much more melodious than the Hindustáni tunes. The music of the Lamas put him in mind of Scotch airs, and though more than a hundred were singing together, they kept the time with the greatest precision. Captain Lewin says that the Shendus of the eastern frontier have a capital ear for rhythm and tune. Sir J. Hooker writes:

> "I have often listened with real pleasure to the simple music of this rude instrument, the Lepcha flute; its low and sweet tones are singularly Æolian, as are the airs usually played, which fall by octaves; it seems to harmonise with the solitude of their primæval forests, and he must have a dull ear who cannot draw from it the indication of a contented mind, whether he may relish its soft musical notes or not."

The Santáls, too, have considerable skill on the flute. While the Nicobarese are a musical people, sing clearly and well in unison, and compose songs for special occasions, their neighbours, the Andamanese, appreciate only rhythm and time, but not pitch or tune. They sing in unison, but not in parts, and can neither sing in chorus nor repeat or even catch an air. The key in which a solo or chorus is started is quite accidental.

The Parsi ladies are perhaps the most skilled performers and vocalists among the natives of India.

The modern Rája, following old-established custom, delights in the Naubat, a noisy medley of drums and trumpets, which echoes from the gateway of his palace at break of day. As Buchanan Hamilton says, "this music, in respect of quantity, is on a very thriving footing." In olden times the music of this kind must have been much better, for Tavernier describes that played at the Moghul's receptions as sweet and pleasant, making so little noise that it did not disturb the thoughts from the serious business on which the courtiers were engaged. Bernier calls the sound of the Nakára "solemn, grand, and melodious."

The variety of instruments is infinite. Besides those of a form familiar to us, we have the remarkable Nyastaranga, which sounds when pressed against the skin over the larynx, while the vocal cords within are in active vibration; and the thigh-bone trumpet of the Lamas, in the process of preparing which the maker has to eat a portion of the bone or a shred of the skin of the corpse. In Sikhim the bone of a Lama, in Tibet that of a criminal or of one who has died by violence, is preferred; the longer the bone is, the more it is valued. Sir J. Hooker mentions a rumour at Dárjíling that one of the first Europeans buried there, being of tall stature, was disinterred for the sake of his thigh-bone by the resurrectionist Bhotiyas. An indigenous bagpipe is used in many parts of the country, and natives admire no British music more than that of our Highland pipers. The Bhíls use a hollow pumpkin fixed on two hollow bamboos, with lute-like holes, three in one and five in the other. To the end of these pipes is fastened a bison or cow-horn, and a hole is made in the neck of the pumpkin, down which the performer blows. He moves his fingers over the lute-holes, and makes a sound curiously like that of the bagpipes. The Rája of Jhínd has a regular bagpipe band, and Mr Val Prinsep tells how they "gave us 'God bless the Prince of Wales,' played by pipers as black as soot, but with pink leggings on their knees to make them like their Highland originals."

The nautch-girls and some Bráhmans are said to be the only students of music in South India. They are fond of European airs, like the barbar's band in Madras, which plays the "Dead March in Saui" at Pariah weddings. Sir

M. Grant-Duff found a ballet dancing to the tune of "Malbrook se vat'en guerre," which Bussy taught to the nautch-girls at Vizianagram, and so it has come down to our times. In North India the Mirási, or wandering minstrel, has considerable musical skill; and Mrs Wilson has given a pleasing account of their performances, with specimens of some of their airs.

[Mrs A. C. Wilson, "A Short Account of the Hindu Systems of Music"; "Calcutta Review," lviii. 243, "Bengal Music"; lxix. 18, "Music of Hindustan"; lxxxiii. 277, "Is Hindu Music Scientific?"]

NAMES.—Primitive man regards his name as part of himself, and takes care of it accordingly. It is as much a portion of his personality as the clippings of his hair or nails, and these he is careful to bury or destroy, lest a witch may gain possession of them and work evil against him. This probably accounts for the refusal of the Hindu woman to mention the name of her husband, while he addresses her as "Mother of So-and-so." Hence, every high-caste Hindu has two names, one for ordinary use and the other kept secret, and usually known only to his preceptor or his family priest. The secret name is often entered in his horoscope, but sometimes in such an obscure way that it is not easily recognised. This is one of the reasons why natives dislike to produce their horoscopes, and this is never done in a law-suit if it can possibly be avoided.

The choice of names is often influenced by the theory of metempsychosis. Thus the wild tribes of Eastern India, and many others, name the child after a deceased ancestor, whose soul is supposed to be reincarnated in the baby. When a child dies, the Andamanese, on the same principle, name the next baby after it. But in other cases, immediately after conception, the mother names it, of course, without reference to sex, by one of about twenty conventional names, to which afterwards a nickname, varying occasionally as life goes on, is added from personal peculiarities, deformities, disfigurement, or eccentricities, or sometimes from flattery or reverence. They name girls after the tree which chances to be in flower when they come of age.

Names, again, are often selected by means of omens. The Central Indian Kandhs throw grains of rice into water, and if a grain floats at a particular ancestor's name, that is chosen. Among the Khásis the grandmother selects three names. The diviner spreads turmeric on a plantain leaf, on which, with a muttered incantation, he lets fall three drops of spirits, one for each of the three names. The drop which takes the longest time to fall is selected.

The forest tribes have various ways of choosing names. Those in Central India often give two names, one that of the Devi, or tribal goddess; the other that of the tree under which the child was born, or some hill near or on which the family dwell. The Santáls name a boy after his own father, a girl after the maternal grandmother. The midwife, immediately on hearing the name uttered by the father, takes rice and water, and going round the circle of relations, fillips a few drops on the breast of each visitor, calling out the name of the child. The Kols name the eldest son after his grandfather, but they first do the rice ordeal in order to make sure that the name is not unlucky. If this should happen to be the case, another is selected. Among the Nicobarese the child is named immediately after birth by the father, and an additional name is conferred as a mark of favour by a friend. A man's name is often changed in after-life, which causes great trouble in identification. The names of dead relations and friends are abandoned for at least a generation, lest their ghosts may appear when they hear their names uttered. But when a grandfather or grandmother dies, their grandson or granddaughter must assume their name.

The first name of a Pársi is selected by the astrologer soon after birth, and the second is that of the father. A third, the family name, is taken from some craft or calling, and this may be changed at the pleasure of the family. Thus, if the name selected be Ardeshir, the father's Framji, and Ghandi, or "grocer," the family name, the child is called Ardeshir Framji Ghandi. When this child has a son called Pestanji, he is known as Pestanji Ardeshir Ghandi, and so on. Like the men, Pársi ladies have three names, their personal name, father's name, and surname. When they marry, they take the husband's name and surname. Some of the occupational names are grotesque, as "Ready Money Bottlewala," or dealer in bottles.

In Burma the letters of the alphabet are assigned in groups to the days of the month, and the child must bear a name which begins with the letter connected with its birthday. There is not a person who has the same name as his father. A man's name disappears when he gets a title of rank or office. The king was the king and nothing more, or was called by some high-sounding title, like "Lord of White Elephants." When the Burman enters a religious Order he gets an honorific title, which lapses when he rejoins the world.

The question of Hindu and Musalmán names is too wide for detailed treatment here. As for Musalmáns, the enquiries of Sir R. Temple in the Panjáb show that about half the names are distinctly religious, Abdu'l-Karím, "Servant of the All-Gracious," or Háfizullah, "Protected by God"; for women the names of ladies of the Prophet's family are often selected, like Aesha, "Life," Amína, "Security"; or fancy names like Rihána, "Sweet-basil," Yasimán, "Jasmine," and so on.

Hindu names are selected on various principles. The parents desire to place the child under the protection of the deity, and call him Ráma-autár, "Incarnation of Ráma"; or if the child is supposed to have been given in response to a vow or prayer, they call him Gangadín, "Given of the Ganges." The name, again, may be dictated by affection, and the child is called Sukhdarshan, "Beautiful to see," and so on. In Kashmír the child is named by the Pír or living Saint of the family, and the name given is often that of the month of birth.

Opprobrious names are often given to a baby after its parents have lost elder children, in the belief that, when the child bears a ridiculous name, it is less liable to be attacked by the Evil Eye or other uncanny influence. Hence the child is called Tinkauri, as if "bought for three cowry-shells"; Dukhi, "the one in pain"; or its nose is pierced, and it is dressed as a girl and called Nathu, "nostril-pierced."

[Temple, "Dissertation on the Proper Names of Panjábis"; Dosabhai Framji Karaka, "History of the Pársis," i. 163; Yule, "Mission to Ava,' 194; Shway Yoe, "The Burman," i. 4; "Census Report," Andaman Islands, i. 63, 212.]

OATHS. — The Andamanese are the only Indian people who have no oaths, covenants, or ordeals. The idea of the oath is always connected with that of the ordeal, so that it is difficult to distinguish them, and this, in part, accounts for the common objection to oath-taking. Captain Sherwill, one of the earliest observers of the Santáls, says that before they came under Hindu influence they objected to swear, because they held truth sacred. On the other hand, Buchanan Hamilton states that early in the last century the people of North Bengal considered themselves degraded by taking an oath, and preferred ordeals.

The old Hindu rule, as stated by Ward, was that a Bráhman was to swear by his veracity; a Rájput by his horse, elephant, or weapon; a merchant by his cattle, grain, or gold; a mechanic by imprecating on his own head, if he speak falsely, all manner of misfortune. Albirúni, writing about the end of the ninth century A.D., says the common oath was to swear before five learned Bráhmans in the woods in the form: "If I lie, he shall have as recompense as much of my goods as is equal to eightfold his claim." The other oaths which he mentions are rather ordeals, such as drinking poison-water, that in which an idol was bathed, judgment by weighing, the water and red-hot iron ordeals.

Linschoten records a primitive combined oath and ordeal in Madras:

"When they are to take their othes to beare witnes with any man, they are set within a circle made of ashes upon the pavement where they stand, still laying a few ashes on their bare heads, holding one hand on their heads, the other on their breasts, and then in their own speech swear by their Pagode that they wil tell the truth without dissimulation whatsoever shall be asked them, for that they certainely beleeve they should be damned for ever, if as then they should not say the truth, but conceale it."

Barbosa describes how in Malabar the king used to swear to maintain the laws of his predecessor:

"Holding a drawn sword in his left hand, and his right hand placed upon a chain lit up with many oiled wicks, in the midst of which is a gold ring, which he touches with his fingers, and there he swears to maintain everything with that sword."

The use of holy water, especially that of sacred rivers like the Ganges or Narbada, is common in Hindu oaths. Tavernier tells how the King of Kashmír swore to maintain the cause of Sulaimán Shikoh by going "into the river which runs through his country to bathe his body, as testimony of the purity of his soul." But later on, the Bráhmans made him break his oath, and save his country by surrendering the rebel. Few Hindus would dare to forswear themselves after taking an oath by the Ganges or Narbada, with a garland of flowers round the neck, and some water in the palm of the right hand. In our courts, in the early days, we used to have people sworn on a pot of Ganges water; but this, like the oath by holding a cow's tail, has long been abandoned.

The common Hindu oaths in North India are taken on Ganges water, the Sálagráma or ammonite sacred to Vishnu, on cow-dung, or the dust from the feet of a cow; or, most binding of all, by laying hands on the head of an eldest son. The leaves of sacred trees are often used, such as those of the *Bael** tree which are held specially sacred by Mahrattas; but Scindiah violated even this oath when he swore fealty to Malhar Rao Holkar. A fresh-plucked leaf of a Pípal [*Peepul**], or sacred fig, or the *Toolsy*,* or Holy Basil, is often used in this way. There is a well-known story of Hindu merchants objecting to have a Pípal planted in their bazaar, because they would be forced to speak the truth. When a Bráhman is sworn, he often lays his hand on his sacred thread. Bappa, the hero of Mewár, swore his companions to secrecy by asking each of them to take a pebble and fling it into a pit, saying, "If I be false, may the good deeds of my forefathers fall into a well defiled by washing clothes!" One of the most solemn Rájput oaths is to dip the hand in salt when swearing.

The oaths of the jungle tribes are many, and are usually taken on things which they consider valuable or sacred. In Orissa the Kandhs swear by touching the *Mohwa* * tree, or they chew rice moistened with the blood of a sheep sacrificed to the Earth goddess; if the dispute be about land, the claimant puts a morsel of the soil in his mouth. A Kol swears by cooked rice; a Juáng or Bhuiya by a tiger skin, and death by that animal is invoked on the perjurer; some take the oath by a lizard skin, "If I lie, may I become scaly like this!" or by an ant-hill, "May I fall into powder like this!" The Chakmas of the east frontier swear by the things on which their very existence depends—water, cotton, rice, and the *dow*,* or hillman's knife. Among the Káfirs of the Hindu-kush the oath of peace is made by placing the feet in the blood of a cow sacrificed to the god Imra. If a man wishes to refute a charge of theft, he strips himself naked, shaves his body, goes to Imra's shrine and swears that he is innocent. He then dresses and sacrifices a goat.

In Burma the Chins still have the rite of the blood-covenant. They slay a *Gyaul*,* and smear the blood with the tail of the animal on the faces of the parties. A big stone is then set up to remind the parties of their agreement. Sir J. G. Scott cynically remarks that such stones are found near every village to record oaths which were never kept. Buddhists take the oath with much solemnity in a temple of Gautama. In the case of conspiracy it was the rule to dip in water an image of Buddha made from the sacred wood of Buddha Gaya, and each conspirator drank of it. Those of the Himálaya swear by "the Precious Lord, Sakya Muni," or the "Three Rarest Ones," the symbol of the faith.

"Men of the Book," that is to say Christians and Musalmáns, swear on their Scriptures; the Sikhs on their Granth; the Buddhists of Nepál on a copy of one of the holy books. A story is told in one of the recent reports of a Musalmán police sergeant justifying his treachery in breaking his oath to release a criminal by urging "that he swore on a pocket-book wrapped in cloth, not on the Korán." It would have been remarkable if a native had never reached this pitch of villainy until our times. In fact, Chanda Sáhib, as Colonel Wilks tells us, cheated the Ráni of Madura by swearing to her on a brick covered with the splendid brocade in which the Korán is wrapped, and Sir John Malcolm describes a similar trick practised by the nobles of Bhopál about the same time.

OMENS.—The interpretation of omens is an old branch of science, and even now has much influence over the people. The success of a journey or enterprise largely, it is believed, depends on the object which is seen first in the morning, or observed on the road at an early stage of the march. Old-fashioned natives are very careful to arrange that on waking from sleep only objects of good omen shall meet their view. Thus, when a Prabhu or Bombay clerk wakes, the first thing he looks at is a gold or diamond ring, a piece of sandalwood, a looking-glass, or a drum. Then he rubs the palms of his hands together and looks at them, for here reside the deities of luck. He then glances at the floor, setting on it first his right foot, then his left. He walks slowly out of his room with closed eyes, and opening them only before the image he worships, he bows in succession before his household gods, the Sun, the holy basil tree, the family cow, his parents, and his priest.

The most important Hindu omens are those of meeting. By the Romans the left was regarded as the lucky side, but the Indo-Europeans preferred the right. With them this feeling originally did not depend on the points of the compass, but was based on the superiority of the right hand to the left. The rule, however, was not rigidly fixed, and the value attached to the omen depended more on the fact whether the thing seen was sacred, good-looking, or the reverse. The face of an oil-man, perhaps from the dirt which accompanies his trade, is about the worst which can be seen in the early morning. But with the curious inconsistency which everywhere accompanies beliefs of this kind, that of a sweeper is lucky. His face should be always looked at first, but on meeting a Bráhman the glance should start with the feet. The names of the persons met are also lucky or unlucky. The historian of the Emperor Humáyun tells us that, doubtful of his chance of ascending the throne, he resolved to take an omen, and was reassured when he met in succession three men named Murád, "Desire"; Daulat, "Wealth"; Sa'adat, "Prosperity."

Many tales of the foundation of cities describe how the King decides to build where he saw a weak animal defeat a stronger. The town of Deola in Rájputána was built where a she-goat was seen successfully defending her kid from a wolf; the King was hunting a hare, which on being chased into a thicket became a tiger, and Almora was founded on the spot. Something in the air or water of such favoured sites was supposed to make the residents courageous.

Omens have much influence in marriage. Captain Lewin thus writes of the Chakmas of the eastern frontier:

"Both in going and coming omens are carefully observed, and many a promising match has been put a stop to by unfavourable auguries. A man or woman carrying fowls, water, fruit, or milk, if passed on the right hand, is a good omen, and pleasant to meet with; but it is unfavourable to see a kite or a vulture, or to see a crow all by himself, croaking on the left hand. If they are unfortunate to come upon the dead body of any animal on their road, they will go no further, but at once return home and stop all proceedings."

Another form of omen is used at Bastar, in the Central Provinces. Flowers are laid on an image of the goddess

Káli; as they fall to the right or left, so her response is deemed favourable or the reverse. Lady Falkland writes that the Rája of Satára, on a question of adopting a foundling, went into the family temple, and taking some grains of rice from the dish set before the idol, stuck one on each cheek of the image. If the grain adhered longer on the lucky side, he would consider the decision in favour of the adoption. Among the Parhaiyas of Chota Nágpur *ghee*, or oil, is poured upon the forehead of the bride, and allowed to run down her face; if it trickles straight down the nose the marriage will be happy; if it run down her cheeks the girl will die or prove unfaithful, and in this case the engagement is often broken off.

Much regard is paid to lucky and unlucky days—in particular, during farming work. Near Delhi, on Monday or Saturday, a prudent man will not plough with his face to the east, because on those days the "Ruler of the Four Quarters" is in that direction. He will not go northwards on Tuesday or Wednesday, westward on Friday or Sunday; the south is avoided on Thursday. Wednesday is good for sowing, Tuesday for reaping. The Emperor Jahángír tells us in his "Memoirs" that it was the custom, when an emperor, a prince, or noble undertook an expedition to the east, that he rode an elephant with long tusks; when to the west, a horse of one colour; when to the north, he was carried in a litter; when to the south, in a carriage drawn by oxen. The strongest-minded men in India have been unable to shake off beliefs like these. Zálim Singh of Kotah, one of the ablest men in Rájputána, abandoned his palace and went to live in tents because he was scared by the ill-omened hooting of an owl.

OPIUM.—Of the early history of this drug in India we know little. There is no reference to it in Sanskrit literature, nor in the earlier Muhammadan historians. If known, it seems to have been confined to the coast within the sphere of Arab influence. Its cultivation probably spread from Europe, where one variety of poppy was grown by the Swiss lake-dwellers. The discovery of the value of its juice is usually attributed to the Greeks, who cultivated it as a garden plant, and it has been supposed that it was the Arabs who carried the knowledge of its properties to the East. Sir G. Watt believes it to be highly probable

"that the merits of the poppy seeds and poppy capsules were known to the Arabs and to the people of large tracts of Central Asia, and even of upper India, anterior to the supposed Greek discovery of opium. But the silence of the early Sanskrit authors leaves no room for doubt that right down to the commencement of Muhammadan influence in India the various wild poppies of the country attracted very little attention."

The first European writer who describes Indian opium is Barbosa (1511-16):

"If they leave off eating it they die immediately, that is, if they begin as children to eat it in such a small quantity that it can do them no harm, for some length, of time, and then increasing the quantity by degrees until they remain accustomed to it. This *anfion* is cold in the fourth degree, and on account of being so cold it kills. We call it *opio*, and the women of India, when they wish to kill themselves in any case of dishonour or despair, eat it with oil of sesame, and so die sleeping without feeling death."

Garcia de Orta (1574) says that the Cambay opium came from Málwa, and in the time of Tavernier, about the middle of the seventeenth century, the Dutch used to export the drug from Burhánpur, where they bought it in exchange for pepper. As tobacco-smoking came into use in the sixteenth century, it seems probable that opium-smoking began in imitation of it at a time long subsequent to the establishment of the habit in China. The first reference to Bengal opium is by Alexander Hamilton in 1727, and by the beginning of the next century Behár, where Warren Hastings created a monopoly in 1773, had become the chief source of supply.

In Moghul times Bernier describes the Poust as a common mode of assassination.

"This Poust is nothing but poppy-heads crushed, and allowed to soak for a night in water. This is the potion generally given to princes confined in the fortress of Goualier, whose heads the monarch is deterred by prudential reasons from taking off. A large cup of this beverage is brought to them early in the morning, and they are not given anything to drink till it be swallowed. . . . This drink emaciates the wretched victims, who lose their strength and intellect by slow degrees, become torpid and senseless, and at length die."

The Kusumbha-drinking in Rájput Durbárs is fully described by Colonel Tod and Sir J. Malcolm. The minister used to wash his hands in a vessel placed before the Rája, after which some liquid opium was poured into the palm of his right hand. The first in rank present approached and drank the liquid. The minister again washed his hands, and served a dose to the second in rank, and so on. To appease a feud they used to drink opium from each others' hands, an almost sacred pledge of friendship. Tod adds that, to judge by the wry faces on these occasions, no one could like it, and to get rid of the nauseous taste comfit-balls were served round. Even at the present day the Rájput of Cutch and Rájputána drinks a cup of opium water after he has smoked and bathed on rising, and this he shares with any friends present.

The opium traffic from India to China, and within the Empire itself, has been the subject of protracted controversy. Opium is eaten, drunk, and smoked in India; but after a careful review of the evidence, Sir G. Watt comes to the conclusion that, "far from having expanded since the advent of British rule, the total consumption of opium by all methods collectively has vastly declined." It is largely used as a drug, and is doubtless of much value in the various forms of malarious disease to which the people are so much exposed. It is chiefly used to flavour the prepared tobacco smoked in the *hookah*,* and many people all through life are moderate consumers, without showing any tendency to excess. The habitual opium-eater occasionally to be seen in the cities resorts to what is called Madak or Chandu, which are usually made by boiling down the rags in which the grower collects the essential juice of the product, and inspissating the infusion. The use of the drug in this form is undoubtedly demoralising, and the consumers of it come from the most degraded class. But, on the whole, the consumption of opium presents few of the terrible results which follow the excessive use of alcohol in Europe. The prohibition of it would certainly increase the use of spirits and the destructive drugs derived from hemp, and the loss of the trade would be ruinous to the large agricultural class which grows the drug. The quantity of land occupied in the culture is quite inconsiderable as compared with the area occupied by food crops, and the cultivation of the plant, which must be conducted with anxious care in the manner of the best market-garden holdings, not only gives much employment to women and children, but decidedly improves the standard of farming in the district where it is carried on. The Indian opium sent to China is valued like the choice vintages of Europe; and if the foreign trade ceased, China is quite able to provide herself with an ample supply, but of an inferior kind.

["Report of the Opium Commission," 1895; Watt, "Economic Dictionary," vi. Pt. I. 17ff.; "Calcutta Review," cii. 258, xcvii. 119.]

ORDEALS.—Trial by ordeal was fully recognised in early Hindu law. In the first volume of the "Asiatic Researches" (1798), Warren Hastings contributed an account of ordeals, based on information received from Ali Ibráhím Khán, Chief Magistrate of Benares, which may still be read with interest.

The early law recognised ten kinds of ordeal, some of which were assigned to special castes. Of these two offered a fair chance of escape—that of the balance, and that of drinking water in which an idol had been washed These were accordingly reserved for Bráhmans and their friends. In the case of the balance, the accused was weighed once, and then a second time after a short interval. If the second test proved him to be lighter, he escaped; if he was heavier, he was convicted. In the second form the accused was required to drink the water in which an idol had been washed, and if no bad effects occurred within a fortnight he was acquitted.

The ordeal for the Kshatriya, or warrior caste, was that of the hot iron. The man was required to stand within nine concentric circles. His hand was covered with a leaf bearing the name of a god, and after incantations a red-hot ball was given to him, which he had to carry over seven circles and place on the ninth. If his hand was found to be scorched he was condemned.

The ordeal of the Vaisya, or merchant class, was that of water. Three arrows were shot in succession; at the third a runner famous for his swiftness followed it, and the accused at the same time dived into a river or tank. If he rose to the surface before the shaft was brought back he was condemned.

For people of lower degree there were other tests. In the ordeal by poison the accused was given a dose, a bystander clapped his hands five hundred times, and if by that time no evil result appeared he was discharged. In the rice ordeal the accused was convicted if he showed distress after eating it, if his spittle was marked with blood, or if the rice remained dry. This last test is still sometimes used in cases of theft. In the oil ordeal, which was similar to that by fire, the accused plunged his hand into a vessel of boiling oil. The Dharma-Adharma test was really a mode of decision by lot. The image of Dharma, "Right," was made of silver; that of Adharma, "Wrong," of iron. Both were placed in a box, from which the accused had to draw one. For the Chandála, or outcast, was reserved the test of taking a venomous snake from an earthern pot. Even if the wretch passed this test, he was thought to have succeeded by some charm or incantation, and was liable to be tried again in another way.

Nicolo Conti, in the fifteenth century, accurately describes three forms of ordeal—licking a hot iron with the tongue, carrying a red-hot iron plate some paces from the idol, and, most common of all, plunging the hand in boiling *ghee*. Barbosa, in the sixteenth century, also speaks of the oil ordeal, and adds that if the accused were a Musalmán, he licked a red-hot axe.

Some of these ordeals were in use down to quite modern times. The ordeal of boiling *ghee* * was used in Madura as late as 1813. The ordeal of weighment is still resorted to in Malabar as a mode of deciding cases connected with caste. The accused is weighed, goes to a neighbouring tank and bathes, and if, on returning to the scale, he is lighter than when he entered the water, his innocence is established.

In remote places among the jungles of Chota Nágpur ordeals are still used. When a woman is accused of incontinence, two balls of calves' dung are made by a Bráhman; in one is placed a small silver coin, in the other a piece of charcoal. They are laid under the sacred tree of the village, and if the woman selects the former she is free. The boiling oil ordeal is used in similar cases, but only when the proof of misconduct is very strong, and it is intended to be in itself a punishment. Among the Khásis and in Burma the ordeal may be done by deputy, and hence, in the case of the water ordeal, the value of a long-winded advocate is obvious. In Cochin it is sometimes unpleasantly varied by making the accused swim across a tank infested by alligators. The Kandhs of Bengal have a modified form of the ordeal by hot iron for the detection of witches. A bar of iron is placed in the smelting furnace, the tribal priest works the bellows and repeats incantations. The names of all the suspected women are called out, and she whose name is mentioned just as the iron melts is convicted.

At Dabhoi, in Baroda, there is a holed stone which is supposed to act like the opening of the crypt of Ripon Cathedral, through which only the virtuous can pass. At Riwakantha, in the Bombay Presidency, a sacred tree is used in the same way. Its intertwined branches form a loop, through which suspected persons are made to pass;

every one believes that it grips the guilty, and allows the innocent to pass unscathed.

Disputed boundaries are often settled by a kind of ordeal. In Mysore the village watchman used to put on his head a ball of earth, with some water in the centre, and march along the line. If he wilfully turned from the true boundary it was believed that the ball fell to pieces, that he would die in a fortnight, and his house become a ruin. In other places a goat is made to walk along the line, and the favour of the god is assured if the animal shivers at the proper place—a result which is made certain by a douche of water poured on its ear. In Burma two candles are lighted, and the party is worsted whose candle goes out first. The Gurkhas, during their rule in Kumaun, used to decide cases by laying a piece of earth from the disputed land before an idol. One of the parties took it up, and if no death occurred in his family within six months, he won the case.

Such tests are also used in elections. In the Panjáb a Musalmán selects his Pír, or spiritual guide, by writing the names of the candidates on scraps of paper, which are thrown into water. The first that sinks is selected. The Kurambas of Madras choose their priests at their annual feast by placing the candidates in front of the idol, and breaking on each man's head cocoa-nuts offered to the god. If the head of a candidate bleeds, he must undergo purification; if the same result follows on a second trial, he is rejected as impure. The man who passes through the test unscathed is appointed for the coming year.

Like the European ordeals of the Middle Ages, these tests are in the hands of priests, and whenever a criminal escapes, the result is settled by previous arrangement.

PARIAH.—The Paraiyan of Madras, whose name means "drummers," are the great agricultural caste of the Tamil country, and number at the present time 2,500,000.

"The term," writes Mr Francis, "is now almost a

generic one, and the caste is split up into many sub-divisions, which differ in manners and ways. For example, the Koliyans, who are weavers, and the Valluvans, who are medicine-men and priests, and wear the sacred thread, will not intermarry or eat with the others, and are practically distinct castes."

The old Tamil poems and writings of the first centuries of the Christian era do not mention the name Paraiyan, but contain many descriptions of a tribe called the Eyinas, who were quite distinct from the rest of the people, and did not live in villages, but in forts of their own. Mr Francis regards these as probably ancestors of the Pariahs of our day.

All the traditions represent the Pariahs as a caste which has come down in the world, and the names of many of their sub-divisions are those of respectable castes —a fact which has been held to confirm the popular belief. This is corroborated by certain privileges which they still enjoy. Thus, at the Feast of Ammál, the mother-goddess, a Pariah youth is fed and clothed in the temple, and solemnly married once a year to the goddess—a rite which is probably intended to secure the fertility of the crops. A Pariah is married in the same way to Egattál, the tutelary goddess of the Black Town of Madras. Privileges of this kind are claimed by outcast tribes all over the country. In Mysore a Holiya, one of the lowest castes, is said to have discovered the idol of the Tirunáráyana Temple, just as it was a Savara who found the image of *Juggurnaut* * on the sea-shore. To this day a Holiya is allowed to enter the temple three times in the year. At the bull-games at Dindagal a Kallar, one of the thieving castes, acts as priest. Facts like these point to the conclusion that many of the idols and rites of modern Hinduism are really those of the non-Aryan tribes which were adopted into Bráhmanism. The aboriginal priest, in fact, accompanied the god to his new home.

Mr Nelson regards the Pariahs of Madura as descendants of the aboriginal tribes, swollen by the accession of outcast people and illegitimate children of other castes. They are employed on degrading work: their very touch defiles, and their mere presence taints the air. They live apart from the natives of high caste, and must never approach their superiors. Buchanan-Hamilton describes the Whalias of Mysore as so impure that "a Bráhman, if he be touched by a Whalia, must wash his head and get a new thread, and a Súdra must wash his head. A Bráhman throws a thing on the ground for such people to take." Europeans, he adds, from eating beef, are regarded as a sort of Pariah, "and nothing but the fear of correction prevents them from being treated with the same insolence."

But it would be an error to suppose that at the present time Pariahs are down-trodden, or in a state of slavery. All over the country no castes are more tenacious of their rights and privileges than those of the lowest rank. The spread of sanitation, for instance, has led to an increased demand for the services of the scavenger-castes, and the result has been that in recent years they have become much more independent and exacting. The influence of our law, the support of the missionary bodies, who draw a great number of their converts from the degraded tribes, and the fact that in Madras most of the servants of Europeans are recruited from this class, are gradually working an improvement in their social position. The old idea that their innate stupidity debars them from any occupation where intelligence is required is rapidly passing away, and they are gradually pushing their way towards a higher status. An indication of progress appears in their aptitude for colonisation. When they cross the sea to Burma or Ceylon they start a new life, removed from the degrading associations of their native land, and rise rapidly in wealth and social life.

In religious matters they are naturally little under the yoke of the Bráhmans. Many of them profess to be worshippers of Siva, but their creed is really a coarse form of Animism, in which the worship of their tribal gods is performed by priests drawn from their own body, with the usual accompaniment of a crude demonaltry and obscene rites such as devil-dancing and exorcism.

["Census Report," Madras, 1901, i. 172; Nelson, "Manual of Madura," ii. 75.]

PÁRSEE, PÁRSI.—This enterprising race, whose name records their origin from Persia, forms a small community, numbering 95,000, whose headquarters are the trading cities of the Bombay Presidency, whence small bodies of emigrants have established themselves in the chief trading cities of India and the East.

Before the dispersal of the Indo-Aryan races, the united people practised a common religion. Mazdaism, the faith of the Pársis, is thus closely allied to that of India, as we find it in the Vedic poems; but its conceptions are more archaic, and it more closely approximates to a pure elemental worship than that of the Indo-Aryans. The gods of the two allied races were, in name at least, identical; but the community broke up into two branches before the religion was fully developed, and, as often occurs in such cases, the gods of one branch became the devils of the other. The two races again came into contact for a short period when Darius, about 500 B.C., occupied part of north-western India. But by this time the religion of Irán, or Persia, under the teaching of Zarathustra, or Zoroaster, had entirely cut itself adrift from Indian Bráhmanism. It suffered temporary obscurity when Persia came under Greek influence, and again revived for a time under the Sassanian dynasty, only to be finally overwhelmed by the advancing tide of Islám, in the seventh century of our era.

The history of the Indian Pársis starts from the refugees, who were forced to choose between massacre and apostasy. A part of them landed on the Indian coast to the north of Bombay in A.D. 717. There they conciliated the Hindu tribes, who permitted them to build places of worship, and to preserve their ancestral faith in the land of their adoption. They soon displayed the trading ability which has always characterised them.

They entered into friendly relations with the Moghul Court, and Akbar dallied with Pársi priests as he did with Portuguese Jesuits. Their influence with the Emperor Jahángír is shown in the Persian names of his sons, Khusrau, Khurram, Jahándár, Shahryár, and Hoshang—a habit which continued in the royal family of Delhi until its downfall in the catastrophe of the Mutiny.

Garcia de Orta speaks of them as resident at Bombay in 1554; and when we took over the island from the Portuguese, Dosabhai Nanabhai, a Pársi, served in turn both its old and its new masters. By 1674 their first Dakhma, or "Tower of Silence," was erected. In the next year Fryer has a good deal to say about them But this traveller, who usually shows so much sympathy with natives of the country, did not appreciate "the Parseys, who were made free Denizens by the Indians before the Moors were masters." Speaking of their manner of living, he says:

"These are somewhat whiter, and, I think, nastier than the Gentues; and Live, as they do, all of a Family together; as if the Father be living, then all the Sons that are Married, and Men grown, with their Wives and Children house it with the Father, and have a Portion of his Stock; if he die, or be absent, the Eldest Brother has the respect of his Father shown, and so successively, they all Rising up at his Appearance, and sit not till he be seated. These are rather Husbandmen than Merchants, not caring to stir abroad; they supply the Marine with Carts drawn by Oxen, the Ships with Wood and Water."

It was in the eighteenth century that they selected Bombay as their headquarters. While they had lived dispersed among an Animistic population, their religion became gradually assimilated to that of their Hindu neighbours. But as they advanced under British rule, they renewed intercourse with the oppressed remnant of the race in Persia. Copies of the sacred books were obtained and translated into Gujaráti, the Indian tongue which they have adopted. The original Zend remains only the liturgical language. Scholars are now devoting themselves to the study of the Scriptures in the ancient speech, and many of the more important have been translated into English.

A community like this, perhaps the most prosperous in India, might be expected to increase rapidly. But they marry late in life, and, as they object to improvident unions, their progress in numbers is slow. There are two divisions among them, which are separated on the question of the calendar; but this difference is unimportant. The priesthood is a distinct Levite body, to which a layman cannot attain.

The popular conceptions of their belief—that they recognise a dualism of a good spirit contending with the evil one for control of the universe, and that they are worshippers of fire—are strongly resented by the modern Társis. According to Dr Haug, Zoroaster

> "having arrived at the grand idea of the unity and indivisibility of the Supreme Being, undertook to solve the great problem which has engaged the attention of so many wise men of antiquity and even of modern times—viz., how are the imperfections discoverable in the world, the various kinds of evils, wickedness, and baseness, compatible with the goodness, holiness, and justness of God? This great thinker of remote antiquity solved this difficult problem philosophically by the supposition of two primeval causes, which, though different, were united, and produced the world of material things as well as that of the spirit."

"Fire," writes the last historian of the race, "is the emblem of refulgence, glory, and light, the truest symbol of God, and the best and noblest representation of His Divinity. . . . The sacred fire is not the fire burning on our hearths. It has undergone several ceremonies, and it is these ceremonies, full of meaning, that render the fire more sacred in the eye of the Pársis."

The method of disposal of the dead is discussed under the head of TOWER OF SILENCE.

The Pársi community in Western India is particularly

distinguished by the liberal donations which they have made to the scientific and charitable foundations of the cities in which they reside. Their widespread commercial influence has been exercised with a view to secure for their depressed brethren in Persia the privileges which a Muslim Government is always unwilling to grant. In seasons of famine and other calamities their aid to this despised remnant has been liberal and timely.

[Dosabhai Framji Karaka, "History of the Pársis;" "Census Report," Baroda, 1901, i. 493; "Bombay Gazetteer," ix. Pt. II. 183ff.]

PEARLS.—Pearls have always been valued in India. In ancient times those of a rose tint were most highly esteemed; it was necessary to use pearls of this colour to ornament Buddhist reliquaries, and to distribute them at the building of a Dagoba, or relic-shrine. In Europe the ancients obtained their supplies almost entirely from India and the Persian Gulf, in which latter locality the fishery has been carried on from Macedonian times. The Indian Herakles, Megasthenes says, appreciating the beauty of the pearl as an ornament, caused it to be brought from all the seas into India, that he might adorn with it the person of his daughter. And he tells the curious story, also found in Pliny, that the

"oysters, like bees, have a king or a queen, and if any one is lucky enough to catch the king, he readily encloses in his net all the rest of the shoal; but if the king makes his escape, there is no chance that the others can be caught."

Linschoten, in 1596, visited and described the fisheries in the Persian Gulf, and speaks of Ormus and Goa as the chief marts. Nearly a century later Tavernier explored the fishery. He says that most of the pearls found went to India, some to Bassora, and some to Russia. The best pearl of his day was that owned by the Arab prince who took Muscat from the Portuguese.

"It is perfectly round, and so white and lively that it looks as if it were transparent, but it weighs only 14 carats. There is not a single monarch in Asia who has not asked the Prince of Arabia to sell him his pearl."

Friar Jordanus, who visited the Indian fishery in the Bay of Manár in 1330 says that 8,000 boats were employed. Cæsar Fredericke gives a good account of it at the end of the sixteenth century. The only mistake he makes is in exaggerating the depth at which the divers worked, which he says was as much as eighteen fathoms; as a matter of fact, they seldom go beyond ten fathoms. Linschoten, about the same time, tells of the way in which the Portuguese managed the fishery. The captain in charge supervising "yearlie three or four thousand duckers, yt live onlie by fishing pearles, and so maintain themselves." Tavernier, in the next century, reports that it was only by good fortune good pearls were found, the majority being only *Aljofar*,* or seed pearls, sold by the ounce, and ground into powder.

"Finally," he writes, "all the Orientals are very much of our taste in matters of whiteness, and I have always remarked that they prefer the whitest pearls, the whitest diamonds, and the whitest women."

In 1794-6 the fisheries in the Gulf of Manár fell into British hands, and for some time past have produced pearls worth about £6,000 per annum.

Pearls have long been valued as medicine. The calcined powder is used in bilious diseases. Dr Ainslie, quoted by Sir G. Watt, states that

"Arabian physicians suppose the powder of the pearl to have virtues in weak eyes. They have, besides, this strange notion, that when applied externally, while in its embryo state in the shell, it cures leprosy."

The finest pearls in the country are said to be those of the Great Necklace, which is an heirloom in the family of Scindiah.

["Calcutta Review," lxii. 289; Watt, "Economic Dictionary," vi. Pt. I. 118.]

PILGRIMAGES.—To the stranger in India, nothing is more impressive than the constant movement of vast crowds of pilgrims to visit the many sacred places scattered throughout the country. Some of them are, no doubt, under the influence of strong religious enthusiasm; but to the women and children the pilgrimage is the one annual outing which breaks the dreary monotony of village life—a chance of amusement and shopping, as a race-meeting or a cattle show is to the English rustic.

Probably the earliest object of pilgrimage was the sacred rivers. Many sites on their banks have been occupied by the worshippers of special gods; but the great rivers are, as a rule, unsectarian, and the right of bathing is shared by all classes of Hindus. Many of the holy places of Hinduism along the rivers have been occupied by one religion in succession to another. Thus, in Upper India, Mathura, now a centre of Krishna worship; Benares, of the Siva cult; Hardwár, shared by votaries of Siva and Vishnu, were all holy places of Buddhism. The fact is, that the pilgrim visits the sacred site, not the temples of the gods who reside there. Each of these sites has a sacred area, a Kshetra, or "field," as it is called, sometimes marked, as at Benares, by a Via Sacra, the Panchkosi, ten miles long, round which the pilgrim must march. When he goes to such a place, he worships, of course, the temples and images of the gods who are established there. But it is the inherent sanctity of the place which has made it the fitting abode for the gods. It is the place itself, which, within certain well-defined limits, exhales an odour of sanctity. As he bathes in the holy water or tank, he symbolises the purification of his soul from sin by the cleansing of his body.

Few of these sacred places are appropriated exclusively to one deity, and some are even common to more than one religion. At Sakhi Sarwar, in the Panjáb, Musalmáns visit the tombs of one of their saints; Sikhs, a monument of their Guru Nának; Hindus come to bathe in the holy water.

To turn to actual records of pilgrimage. In 1792

Jonathan Duncan, in the "Asiatic Researches," recorded the travels of a Bráhman Sannyási ascetic. He was by race a Panjábi, and was born while his mother was on a pilgrimage to Juggurnaut. When he started on his travels, he went into the Himálaya through Nepál and Tibet; thence to the sacred lake of Mánasarovar, and so on to the fire-temples of Baku on the Caspian. Returning through Afghánistán to Peshάwar, he went to Sind and Hingláj, the furthest western point to which Indian polytheism extends. Thence he went down the Ganges to Juggurnaut, and so south to Rameshwaram, situated on the island which lies between the extreme south point of the Peninsula and Ceylon. Next he came round to Súrat on the west coast, thence by sea to Muscat in the Persian Gulf, and so back again to Benares, where the tale of his wanderings was recorded. This enormous journey, save one sea voyage, was performed on foot. Many a palmer of our days has visited all the chief holy places, and, like our Sannyási, has crossed the Himálaya and Hindu-kush, bathed in the waters of Mánasarovar, at Puri on the Orissa coast, and at Cape Comorin.

Hindus give various classifications of their holy places Some say that there are four of the first rank—Badarinárάyan on the upper waters of the Ganges, Rameshwaram at the extreme south, Dwárka on the coast of Káthiáwár, and Juggurnaut. Others name five—the sacred junction of the Ganges and Jumna at Prayág, or Alláhábád; Gaya, in Behár; Pushkar, in Ajmír-Mhairwára, with one of the few Brahma temples; Bithúr on the Ganges, associated with the infamous Nána Sáhib; and Násik, where the Godávari passes out of the hills.

Some places, again, are closely associated with the sectarian beliefs of Hinduism. Siva has famous shrines at Kedárnáth, in the Himálaya; Madura, in Madras; Omkár Mandháta, on the Narbada; Somnáth, in Káthiáwár; Tarakeswar, in Bengal; and, perhaps greatest of all, Benares. Vishnu is specially worshipped at Badarinárάyan, in the Himálaya; Pándharpur, in the Deccan; and in

South India, at Seringapatam, Srirangam, and Tirupati. To his incarnation as Krishna are dedicated the scenes of his early life in the holy land of Mathura, and Somnáth, the place of his death. The cult of Ráma and his faithful wife, Síta, leads their votaries to Ajudhya in Oudh, Chitrakot in Bundelkhand, and Rameshwaram in the south.

The shrines of the blood-stained goddess known as Devi, Káli, or Durga often hide themselves away in the dense forest or hill country, whence her cultus was probably imported into Bráhmanism. Such are the fires of Juálamukhi, in Kangra; Hingláj, on the western frontier; Devipátan, under the lower Himálaya; Bindháchal, the Thug temple, where the Vindhyan range meets the Ganges valley.

The retiring character of the worship of the Jains also fixed its shrines far from the haunts of men—at places like Mount Abu, in Rájputána; Párasnáth, far to the east in Bengal; Palitána and Girnár, to the west in Káthiáwár. Of Buddhism, once the dominant creed, there remain only in the Plains the Tree of Wisdom at Buddha Gaya; and for Himálayan worshippers, the Mahúta Stúpa in Nepál; the great Gompas of Sikhim; and other shrines in the hills.

Rivers, and more particularly the confluences of holy streams, attract the largest crowds of pilgrims. Greatest of all is the Ganges. A legend predicted that Mother Ganges was to lose her sanctity a few years ago, and be replaced by the Narbada. But she is still as sacred as ever, and is in little danger of decay. The Narbada priests say that, to derive spiritual benefit, you must bathe in the Ganges water; while even a distant view of the Narbada purifies the sinner.

The most efficacious way to worship a holy river is to measure your length from where it joins the ocean to its source, and down the other bank. But you must keep the river to your right by beginning the journey on the right bank, and so move in the course of the sun. Many a man, oppressed by the burden of a sin like that of killing a cow, has thus painfully followed the course of the Ganges, or spent a year or two in tracing the Narbada from its outlet in the western ocean to its source at Amarkantak. Mrs Postans tells a story of five Bráhmans, converted to Christianity at Delhi, who purchased restoration to caste by undergoing the penance of measuring with their bodies the road between Delhi and Dwárka, a distance of 700 miles as the crow flies. She reasonably concludes that, when no one was looking, they were not careful about the way in which they performed their march. General Mundy saw a man who had journeyed from the Upper Provinces to Juggurnaut in this way, and spent a fortnight in doing the last 55 miles. He did not seem much the worse of a pilgrimage of nearly 1,000 miles thus completed. Akbar, when he visited the saint at Ajmír, always went on foot. His family also walked, but for them the road was spread with carpets, and canvas screens were erected on each side to conceal the beauty of his ladies from the eyes of the vulgar.

The sanctity of rivers, again, sometimes depends on their direction. The Ganges, when its course is east or north; the Jumna flowing to the west; the Godávari to the south, are all most sacred. One river alone is accursed —the Karamnása of Behár, and the Hindu who touches its foul water loses his hopes of salvation. It may have marked for a long period the eastern limit of Aryan colonisation, when to cross it meant entering the land of the barbarian, or the horror attached to it rests on some tragedy long forgotten.

Each of these holy places has its special priests, who send out their emissaries to conduct bands of pilgrims. These men keep the names of visitors carefully recorded in their books, and thus assert hereditary right to act as guides to the mysteries. One has only to watch the squabbles and intrigues of these harpies, who beset the roads by which the pilgrims enter the holy ground, to see how much that is sordid enters into the Hinduism of our day. Most rapacious and insolent of all are the river-priests, like those of Mathura or Benares, or, worst of all, the temple officiants at Gaya, where a pious Hindu should go to perform the rites to save the souls of his ancestors. As he starts on his journey to Gaya, he walks five times round his village, and calls on the spirits of all his forefathers to accompany him on his pious errand. To prove that a pilgrimage has been duly performed, the visitor is either branded by the mark of the god, as is done at Dwárka; or at other places he is marked with vermilion on the forehead, and with the sign of the red hand on his shoulder. Whatever be the form of the mark, he preserves it carefully till he returns to his village, to prove to his neighbours that he has performed this great religious act.

Musalmáns, too, have their own places of pilgrimage. The rich devotee goes to Mecca, or, if he be of the Shiah sect, to the Kerbela at Meshed, in the Euphrates valley. But the ordinary Indian Musalmán is obliged to content himself with a visit to the tomb of one of the great Saints, like him of Ajmír, Fatehpur-Sikri, or Pákpattan. As a special mark of honour, the custodian, for a consideration, allows him to touch or smell the turban or shoes of the Saint, and thus absorb some of the holiness which such relics exhale.

It is certain that under our rule pilgrimages have much increased. Crowds larger than ever attend the great bathing-fairs at Hardwár and Alláhábád. This is the result, not so much of a sudden awakening of religious fervour, but because the railway has opened the way to pilgrims, who in the old days did not dare to attempt such laborious journeys. Pilgrim-hospitals have been established at Jeddah on the Red Sea, and at all the local shrines. Roads and bridges have opened the routes to the sources of the Ganges and Jumna. The lumbering ox-waggon, crowded with laughing girls, forces its way through clouds of dust in ever-increasing numbers. Though the rustic may growl at the unaccustomed sanitary rules to which he has to submit in such places, and may even run the risk of having the fair prohibited while plague or cholera is about, still there is nothing which has tended more to popularise our Government than the peace and tolerance which enable them to visit in comfort and safety the sacred places of their faith.

PINJRAPOLE.*—This is the term used in Western India to denote the animal-hospitals, which are supported mainly by the Jains, in imitation of the humanitarian edicts of Asoka, in some of the cities in Bombay.

A good account of an institution of this kind is given by Pietro della Valle, writing in 1623:

"We caus'd ourselves to be conducted to see a famous Hospital of Birds of all sorts, which for being sick, lame, depriv'd of their mates, or otherwise needing food and care, are kept and tended there with diligence. . . . The House of this Hospital is small, a little room sufficing for many Birds; yet I saw it full of Birds of all sorts which need tendance, as Cocks, Hens, Pigeons, Peacocks, Ducks, and small Birds, which during their being lame, or sick, or mateless, are kept here, but being recover'd and in good plight, if they be wild they are let go at liberty; if domestick they are given to some pious person, who keeps them in his House. The most curious thing I saw in this place were certain little Mice, who being found Orphans without Sire or Dam to tend them, were put into the Hospital, and a venerable Old Man with a white Beard, keeping them in a box amongst Cotton, very diligently tended them with his spectacles on his Nose, giving them milk to eat with a bird's feather, because they were so little that as yet they could eat nothing else; and as he told us, he intended when they were grown up to let them go free whither they pleas'd."

Tavernier saw a similar hospital for monkeys at Mathura, where the Banians fed them. All sorts of animal life found shelter in such places. It is to Ovington we owe the story of the hospital at Súrat where insects were supported, and a poor man was now and then hired to rest all night upon a cot or bed, "and let the animals nourish themselves on his carcass." Of this the only trace remaining is a loft, where weevils and other vermin are collected and fed on grain.

Hospitals of this kind are now open at Súrat, Cambay,

Poona, and Ahmadábád. Forbes saw an aged tortoise at Súrat, which for seventy-five years had enjoyed this refuge for the destitute. A writer in 1848 thus describes this institution:

"Some lively poultry," he says, "cackle in pensioned happiness, and an able-bodied camel lolls his head in all the hopelessness of ennui. Really wretched animals are found only in the cattle-wards; and Bishop Heber would not accuse the Bráhmans here, as he did at Broach, of keeping up the institution for the sake of the good milch cows and buffaloes with which it provided them. A more miserable, famished set of animals can hardly be conceived."

The account by Professor Wallace in 1887 is not less unfavourable:

"I have heard of as many as 5,000 four-footed beasts of one kind and another being congregated in one of these places. Although the intention held by their native supporters regarding them is good, it is easily seen that it must be quite impossible to carry out a proper system of feeding and management on a very extensive scale in times of scarcity, when there is no one personally interested. It is not to be denied that these institutions do not always convey to one the idea of either comfort or plenty to the inmates."

The movement in its most senseless form is shown in Sir M. Gerard's account of the proceedings at Broach. Here, whenever a police edict was issued for the destruction of ownerless dogs, the pious merchants used to ship them across the river to save them from destruction. But they were absolutely indifferent to their suffering death by slow starvation, and never thought of providing funds for their sustenance.

The notorious cruelty of the Hindu to his cattle cannot be repressed by any system of this kind, and it may be hoped that the classes which support the Pinjrapole will soon transfer their contributions to the Societies for the Protection of Animals, which are now doing excellent work in the larger cities.

PLAGUE.—The early accounts of plague in India are too vague to enable us to judge of its symptoms or incidence. But there is ample evidence of outbreaks which caused enormous loss of life. The great Black Death of the fourteenth century is said to have depopulated the country, but the Musalmán historians give little information on the subject. The traveller, Ibn Batuta, states that the army of Muhammad Tughlak (1325-51) was nearly destroyed in South India by a pestilence, probably plague, and at the end of the century the districts through which Timúr's armies passed were visited by the disease. In 1443, when he was in Málwa, plague caused such loss to the army of Sultán Ahmad I., that he left the dead unburied and returned to Gujarát. The disease appeared again, side by side with famine in 1595, and reached the Deccan in 1618. Terry, who accompanied the Mission of Sir T. Roe, describes this outbreak. Writing of the epidemic of 1619, the historian, Mu'tamad Khán, gives an account which clearly identifies it:

"When it was about to break out, a mouse would rush out of its hole, and, striking itself against the door and the walls of the house, would expire. If, immediately after this signal, the occupants left the house and went away to the jungle, their lives were saved; if otherwise, the inhabitants of the whole village would be swept away by the hand of death. If any person touched the dead, or even the clothes of a dead man, he also could not survive the fatal contact."

In modern times it ravaged Cutch in 1812-21. But the first outbreak, which seriously attracted the attention of the British authorities was that at Páli, in Rájputána, in 1836. It was dealt with by Sir Charles Metcalfe, whose measures, as laid down in his Minute printed by Kaye, much resembled those enforced in our time.

Meanwhile, in 1823, a disease had been recognised and investigated under the name of Mahámari, "the great death," on the lower Himálayan slopes. Though some believed at the time that it was a form of malignant typhus, it is now certain that it was true plague, which has been endemic in that part of the country for a long period, and that its persistence is largely due to the filthy habits of the people. Why it has not constantly spread from this centre to the Plains is a mystery. Dr Hankin believes that the habit of the people of abandoning their houses at the first appearance of infection, for instance, on the finding of a dead rat, prevents the dispersion of the disease. He also suggests that Garhwál was one of the sources of the present epidemic, usually traced to China, and that it was brought by Fakírs from the Himálaya to the great fair at Násik, in the Deccan. If this be so, it is difficult to explain why it did not appear long before at the gatherings at Hardwár, which numbers of hill-men regularly attend.

As has been said, the present outbreak is usually traced to Hong-kong, and the disease is said to have reached that port from China, where its appearance has been connected with the loss of life in the suppression of the Panthay rebellion, or to inundations of the great rivers. At any rate, the Hong-kong outbreak of 1893 was followed by its appearance in Bombay in 1896. Thence it spread over that Presidency, especially the Deccan and South Mahratta country. There, and particularly in the great cities of the west coast, up to the date of the Census of 1901 330,000 deaths were recorded. But Mr Risley estimates that the actual mortality may have been double that amount. Thence it spread into other parts of the country, and up to the present time the loss of life has been continuous and enormous.

It is now generally admitted that plague has become well established in the country. The rate of mortality decreases with the advancing heat, but increases again with the setting-in of the cold season. The subsoil of the older cities, soaked with sewage, provides a particularly favourable nidus for the plague bacillus, and there seems little hope that the disease can be stayed by any sanitary measures. Previous experience seems to show that the pest gradually loses its virulence. It is probable that it will gradually become less deadly, and eventually disappear. But no one dares to estimate how long it may continue.

In the discussion which followed Dr Rankin's paper read at the meeting of the British Association in 1904, Dr Copeman remarked that

"plague could be caught by monkeys and rats, and possibly the fleas on rats assisted in disseminating the infection. Fleas deserted a dead organism, and one of the fleas peculiar to the rat could also exist on man. The reason that natives were so much more liable to infection than whites might be that so much more of their bodies was exposed."

Since then it has been suggested that rats suffer from two forms of plague—one acute, the other chronic, each produced by a different bacillus. The real plague bacillus dies rapidly, and would entirely disappear were it not kept alive in the bodies of rats and human beings. The true remedy, then, is to destroy rats, not when plague is raging, but during the interval between two outbreaks, when the bacillus is sheltered in these animals.

The system of quarantine and examination of travellers, which was enforced at the beginning of the outbreak, gave rise to so much irritation that the rules were gradually relaxed, and at present little beyond enforcement of sanitary regulations is attempted. Of the three forms in which the disease occurs—the pneumonic, septicemic, and bubonic—the first, acting through the lungs, is the most deadly and easily communicable. According to Dr Hankin,

"pneumonic plague, after passing through a few individuals, lost its virulence, as it did after passing from one rat to another. Except in cases of pneumonic plague, isolation of the patient was useless."

As the first shock of terror has passed away, and the people, in their usual fatalistic spirit, have become accustomed to the continuance of the disease, they are gradually learning the benefits of isolation and disinfection which the influence of any Government, unsupported by public opinion, is unable to enforce.

[Dr W. J. Simpson, "A Treatise on Plague."]

POISONING.—Poisoning is a very ancient crime in India. Manu prescribes a fine for machinations with poisonous roots, and for charms and witcheries intended to kill. A high-caste man was not to deal in poison, on pain of falling in seven days to the rank of a Vaisya, or merchant. The legends of Siva tell of his intoxication with deadly drugs, and how his neck became blue from drinking the deadly poison produced at the churning of the ocean, by which he saved the world from destruction. One of the tales of Krishna describes an attempt to poison him. Strabo tells us that Suttee was introduced to prevent the poisoning of husbands, and Alexander Hamilton reports that in his time the same story was current at Canara. An Indian king is said to have sent to Alexander a fair woman fed on aconite.

Many cases of deliberate poisoning are recorded by the historians. Mahmúd Begada, King of Ahmadábád (1459-1513), was the original of the "Macamut Sultan" of Cambay described by Purchas. "Like to the Pontic monarch of old days, he fed on poison." His daily food was "asp and basilisk and toad."

"His father," Barbosa tells us, "desired that he should be brought up from a child and nourished with poison, in order that it should not be possible to kill him with poison; for the Moorish kings of those parts often have one another killed with poison . . . for which cause he became so poisonous that if a fly settled on his hand, it swelled and immediately fell dead."

If he only breathed on one of his many wives she died forthwith. Mahmúd of Ghazni got rid of a gang of robbers by poisoning a camel's load of apples. The Búndi legend, with strange ignorance of the real character of India's greatest monarch, tells how Akbar tried to poison Rája Mán, and the pills getting mixed, he swallowed those intended for his guest, and so met his death. Sháh

Jahán poisoned one of his courtiers in open Durbár with a packet of betel. Fryer, Tavernier, and Bernier give curious accounts of the poisoning of princes by means of Poust or opium. General Maitland, while a prisoner, was poisoned by Tippoo in 1793.

Poisoning is certainly not infrequent at the present day. To quote Dr Chevers:

> "The abundance in which a variety of deadly plants spring up in the hot and moist atmosphere of Bengal, and the unrestricted freedom with which nearly all the most potent kinds of mineral and vegetable poisons can be purchased in every Indian bazaar, added to the familiarity with the action of narcotics, which has arisen from the daily habits of opium-eating and hemp-smoking, sufficiently account for the prevalence of the crime of secret poisoning among a timid people, who, except when wrought up to a state of frantic excitement, always prefer treachery to violence in the execution of their crimes."

The Zenanah system renders crime of this kind easy, and advantage has been taken of cholera epidemics to poison by means of arsenic.

During the early years of our rule the poisoning of horses and cattle was common along the Ganges, then the main route to the Upper Provinces. From the accounts of Lieutenant Bacon and others, it appears that the halting-places were infested by wretches who made a trade of poisoning officers' horses. The Chamárs, or curriers of our day, often poison cattle for the sake of the hides, which are their perquisite. The poisons generally used are arsenic, administered in a ball of sugar, which is placed in the animal's feeding-trough; or the seeds of the Rati [*Ruttee* *] or *Abrus precatorius*, rubbed down into a paste, and applied to a sore or gall in the skin. These seeds may be eaten boiled, but when used raw in this way furnish an active poison. The only practical remedy is to slash the skins of all dead animals, so as to render them valueless to the tanner.

When by the operations of General Sleeman and other officials, Thuggee was repressed, its place was taken by

Road Poisoning. The system under which the poisoner works very closely resembles that of the Thugs, of which some account will be found under the head of THUGGEE. The poison generally used is Dhatúra, or stramonium, which produces insensibility and delirium. A native pharmacopœia prescribes bruised Dhatúra, mixed with a person's blood, and smeared between the eyes, as a potent love-charm, which causes any one who sees a woman thus decorated to become her slave. The use of the plant, which is common all over the country, has thus become familiar to the people. Dr Chevers believed that no drug known at the present day represents in its effects so close an approach to the system of slow poisoning, supposed to have prevailed in the Middle Ages, as does Dhatúra. Burton, in his "Anatomy of Melancholy," says: "If it be eaten for twenty-four hours following, it takes away all sense, grief, makes them incline to laughter and mirth." It was perhaps from this drug that Linschoten derived his belief in "a certaine poyson or venome, which shall kill the person that drinketh it, at what time or houre it pleaseth them; which poyson being prepared, they make it in such sort, that it will lye sixe years in a man's body, and never dow him hurt, and then kill him, without missing halfe an houres time." So Grose tells of a seed produced on the banks of the Ganges, "that if once swallowed, will adhere closely to the coats of the stomach, where it vegetates, and spreads its ramifications so as to destroy a man, without its being in the power of medicines to extirpate or obstruct its growth."

Colonel Tod tells several stories of princes being poisoned in Rájputána by means of a venomed robe, like that smeared with the blood of Nessus which slew Herakles.

> "Of course," he adds, "it must be by porous absorption; and in a hot climate, where only a thin tunic is worn next the skin, much mischief might be done, though it is difficult to understand how death could be accomplished."

As an irritant poison, pounded glass has been often used. But diamond dust enjoyed a still higher reputation.

Colonel Wilks says that it is believed among Musalmáns of rank in South India to be at once the least painful, the most active, and infallible of all poisons. It was kept as a last resort in times of danger. Colonel Tod tells how, when Ajmír was invested by the French adventurer, De Boigne, the governor swallowed diamond dust.

"Tell the Rája," said he, "thus only could I testify my obedience; and over my dead body alone could a Southron enter Ajmír."

In our own time, when Mulhar Ráo of Baroda attempted to poison Colonel Phayre, diamond dust, mixed with arsenic, was used. The prevalence of poisoning led to the use of many antidotes, such as that of Madura, which Fra Paolino took when he believed he had been poisoned; while natives, and even the early English settlers, relied on special vessels to warn them against poison. Jade is supposed to possess this property; rhinoceros horn, believed to be that of the unicorn, was still more efficacious. "The hornes in India," says Linschoten, "are much esteemed and used against all venime, poyson, and many other diseases." Venetian glass was said to possess this property, and the Anglo-Indians of the seventeenth century used a particular kind of chinaware, which was supposed to crack when poison entered the cup. Fryer, writing of the Anglo-Indians of his day, says:

"At Meals their Domesticks wait on them with Obeisance suitable to great Potentates, enclosing their tables, which are strewed liberally with Dainties served up in Plate of China: *nam nulla aconita bibuntur fictilibus*, says Juvenal, which crack when poysoned, which, whether true or false (since it is so much practised in this country by way of revenge), it is but a necessary caution by all means to avoid."

There is a parasitical plant in the Himálaya which causes knots in the maple and oak. Some of these knots are made into cups, which are believed to detect poison. Sir J. Hooker had to pay a guinea for a specimen.

[Chevers, "Indian Medical Jurisprudence," 103ff.; a long list of poisons in Watt, "Economic Dictionary," vi. Pt. I. 309ff.]

POLO.—Polo has its origin in the East. It was a favourite game of the Kings of Persia, as is shown by the illustrations in old copies of their Epic, the Sháhnameh. In one of the early stories of the "Arabian Nights" the tale is told of the cure of the king's leprosy by the use of a polo-stick, in the handle of which potent drugs, enclosed by the sage Dubán, passed into the royal hand. The early Musalmáns brought this game of Chugán to India, and one of their kings, Kutb-ud-dín, was killed in 1210 by a fall during a game. Abul Fazl, the courtly historiographer of Akbar's Court, writes in his usual style:

"Superficial observers look on the game as a mere amusement, and consider it mere play; but men of more exalted views see in it a means of learning promptitude and decision. Strong men learn, in playing this game, the art of riding; and the animals learn to perform feats of agility, and to obey the reins. It tests the value of a man, and strengthens bonds of friendship. Hence His Majesty is very fond of this game. Externally the game adds to the splendour of the Court; but viewed from a higher point, reveals concealed talents." Akbar used to select the players by the cast of a die, "as he never orders any one to be a player." Ten played in a set, two being relieved every twenty minutes. Two varieties of the game are described. In one, the player got hold of the ball with the crooked end of the stick, and moved it slowly from the middle of the field to the goal. In the other "the players may either strike the ball with the stick in his right hand, and send it to the right forwards or backwards; or he may do so with his left hand; or he may send the ball in front of the horse to the right or to the left. The ball may be thrown in the same direction from behind the feet of the horse, or from below its body; or the rider may spit it when the ball is in front of the horse; or he may lift himself upon the back leather of the horse and propel the ball from between the feet of the animal."

This account, as translated by Professor Blochmann, is not very clear, and indeed the clerkly author knew little about the game. As he says himself, "it is impossible to describe the excellence of the game. Ignorant as I am, I can say but little about it." As curiosities of the game, he describes Akbar's skill in hitting the ball in the air, and tells how, on dark nights, he used to play by the light of fire-balls.

"For the sake of adding splendour to the games, which is necessary in worldly matters, His Majesty has knobs of gold and silver fixed to the tops of the Chugán sticks. If one of these breaks, any player that gets hold of the pieces may keep them."

This Moghul polo has quite disappeared, and when, about 1864, Europeans learned the game, it was found to be played only in two widely-separated tracts—at Manipur, on the borders of Assam and Burma; and at Balti and Chitrál, on the upper course of the Indus. Whether in these places the game was independently invented, or reached India by some agency other than that of the Moghuls, is uncertain. The fact that Japan has its own form of the game, which is described by Mr Chamberlain, may not imply that it was discovered there; possibly it may have come to them from the Mongol Court.

The present Manipur game is very like Polo in its modern form. The ground is 300 yards long and 250 wide; the ball and sticks resemble those used by Englishmen; but the biggest pony used is only 11½ hands high. They play seven a side, with no goal posts, the whole end-line of the ground being the goal. When a goal is hit, all the players get into the middle, and a new ball is thrown in. The match is the best of eleven games. The niceties of "offside" are unknown; but "riding off" is understood and practised. Such used to be the enthusiasm for the game, that many a wife was sold into slavery to provide a pony for a needy husband.

Lady Dufferin saw the game played at Manipur in 1888. She was struck with the smallness of the ponies, and the amount of harness on them. The men had lacquered shields curled in at each side, which protected the riders' legs. "As the Viceroy approached to inspect them, all the men went down on their knees."

Mr Drew gives a full account of the Baltistán game. The difficulty is to got a level ground sufficiently wide and the game is usually played in a field 200 yards long by 30 or 40 wide, enclosed by loose stone walls to prevent the ball from going beyond bounds. When the game is arranged, all the players collect at one end, and one starts the game by taking the ball in his hand and galloping to the centre, where he throws it in the air, and strikes it as best he can towards the enemy's goal. Sometimes he makes a goal at once in this way. The winners start afresh from the goal which they have won. "There is no law against getting in front of the ball or waiting at your enemy's goal; this last is commonly done by some wily players, while staying at one's own goal to defend it is never even thought of." The losers have to walk up the ground, and bow to their adversaries at every 20 yards or so. At the last point the victors rise and politely return the salutation.

["Ain-i-Akbari," tr. Blochmann, i. 247; Lady Dufferin, "Viceregal Life," 402; Drew, "Jummoo and Kashmír," 380ff.; "Early History of Polo," in "Baily's Magazine," 1900; "Badminton Library," "Polo"; Chamberlain, "Things Japanese," 3rd ed. 333.]

POLYANDRY.—This system of marriage, in which a woman has more than one husband, exists in two forms—the matriarchal in the south, the fraternal in the north. This identity of custom in tribes so widely separated has led some to recognise an ethnological affinity. Mr Fergusson, for instance, was struck by the curious identity of architectural style in Nepál and Canara; others, on quite insufficient grounds, have suggested that the Newárs, or the inhabitants of Nepál before the Gurkha conquest, were identical with the Nairs of Malabar. But the resemblances are merely superficial. The Tibetan tribes, in their absence of compact organisation, and their system of prohibited degrees, are widely different from the South Indian Nairs. Among the Tibetans two brothers often marry a single wife; but such a connection would be regarded as incestuous among the Nairs, and a Nair who married the widow of his deceased brother, or two sisters, would be promptly expelled from caste.

Polyandry is undoubtedly an old institution, but there is no evidence to show that it was one of the necessary stages in the evolution of marriage. Where we find it mentioned in the older literature, it is confined to frontier tribes, and not general among the Aryan community. Thus, in the Mahábhárata, where we meet the well-known case of Draupadi and the Pándavas, there is reason to believe that the latter were an alien tribe from the north, which occupied the land of the Aryans. The same Epic seems to refer to the southern form of the practice when it speaks of Agni, the fire-god, ordaining that the women of that region should lead a dissolute life in public, independent of their husbands.

The earlier accounts of South Indian polyandry come from the eleventh century travellers. Abd-er-razzák speaks of a class of men

"with whom it is the practice for one woman to have a great number of husbands, each of whom undertakes a special duty and fulfils it. The hours of the day and of the night are divided between them; each of them for a certain period takes up his abode in the house, and while he remains there no one is allowed to enter."

In the present day the matriarchal system is confined to the Todas of the Nilgiris and the Nairs of the Malabar coast. Among the Nairs in former times the girl was formally married in her own caste as a child, and when she grew up chose a group of men either of her own, or more commonly of the Nambutiri branch of Brahmáns, with whom she lived.

"Polyandry," says Mr Logan, "is nowadays scouted by all respectable people, and the fashion now is for the girl to go with the husband of her choice (not her merely nominal husband), whom she selects when she comes of age. But he occupies no legal relation involving rights and responsibilities to his wife or children."

This, in fact, is not polyandry in the strict sense of the word. The woman transfers herself from her *de jure* to her *de facto* husband. Mr Logan adds:

> "Nowhere is the marriage-tie, albeit informal, more rigidly observed or respected, nowhere is it more jealously guarded or its neglect more savagely avenged. The very looseness of the law makes the individual observance closer; for people have more watchful care over the things they are most likely to lose. The absence of ceremonial has encouraged the popular impression; but ceremonial, like other conventionalities, is an accident, and Nayar women are as chaste and faithful as their neighbours, just as they are as modest as their neighbours, although their national costume does not include some details required by conventional notions of modesty."

The result of this marriage system is that succession follows the female, not the male line. A man's heirs are his sisters and their children. A man without a sister is a man without heirs. This matriarchal polyandry is falling into disuse. It is being replaced by the fraternal form, which is now the common rule among the Todas.

Fraternal polyandry prevails more or less along the Himálaya, from Kashmír to eastern Assam, and chiefly among tribes with Tibetan affinities. Along the upper course of the Ganges, when much difference exists in the age of the brothers—for example, when they are six in number—the three elder marry a wife, and when the younger brothers come of age they marry another, but the two wives are regarded as the common property of the whole group. This curious family system has given rise to much speculation. It is not caused by a dearth of women, the surplus girls becoming nuns in the Buddhist monasteries, or adopting a less reputable course of life. The real object of the arrangement seems to be the prevention of family disputes arising from the division of property, and the poverty of the land contributes to maintain the system. The country is unable to support a number of separate households the members of which refuse to migrate, and congestion would soon result were it not for the custom of polyandry.

Strange as it may appear, the custom among these Himálayan tribes does not prevent romance. Colonel Dalton describes a pretty Dafla girl falling at his feet and claiming protection. She had fled, she said, to escape a detested marriage, and had eloped with her beloved. Assured of protection, she dressed herself in her best clothes, and looked very pretty and happy. But "the beloved," who had kept in the background, was summoned ; the romance was dispelled. She had eloped with two young men.

We have seen that the usages of Hinduism have checked polyandry in Malabar. In Baltistán, a tributary district of Kashmír, Islám has exerted the same influence, and there polyandry is now being replaced by polygamy, In Lahaul the custom is a great obstacle to Mission work, If a wife with four or five husbands is converted to Christianity, the husbands refuse to support her. She will not live with the first husband alone, as she says she is equally married to the others. It is on account of this difficulty about means of living that the people are unwilling to listen to missionary teaching.

If polyandry at the present day exists in a decaying condition among only a few isolated communities, there is evidence, from the study of survivals, that it must at one time have prevailed much more widely. Whether group-marriage does or does not exist in Malabar has been disputed. If it does exist, it springs from polyandry. When we find that the Khásis and Gáros of Assam still adhere to the rule of succession through the female, and that among some of the lower Hindu castes of North India the sister's son acts as priest, and that the marriage arrangements are made by the maternal uncles of the parties, we may reasonably conclude that the system of polyandry formerly prevailed among people who at the present day retain no traditions of the practice.

["Census Report," India, 1901, i. 447ff. ; Panjáb, i. 223 ; United Provinces, i. 121f. ; Cochin, i. 150ff. ; Fawcett, in "Bulletin of Madras Museum," iii. 234 ; Logan, "Manual of Malabar," i. 135.]

POLYGAMY.—Monogamy, says R. von Ihering, was the rule with the early Aryans, and was due to the limitation of the number of women who followed their migrations. But when they settled down in India, we find in the Rig-veda clear instances of plurality of wives, especially in the case of kings and great men. Even in later times Hindu law placed no limit on the number of wives; but gradually the habit of being content with a single legitimate spouse grew, and the custom of joint-sacrifices performed by husband and wife had an influence in the same direction.

So far from being a polygamous people, the natives of India, with some few exceptions, practise monogamy. The question is thus summed up in the last Census Report:

"In practice, except among wealthy Muhammadans, a second wife is very rarely taken unless the first one is barren, or suffers from some incurable disease; even then, in the case of Hindus, a man has frequently to obtain the consent of his caste Pancháyat (or tribal council), and occasionally that of his first spouse also. In the Empire, as a whole, amongst all religions taken together, to every 1,000 husbands there are only 1,011 wives, so that, even if no husbands have more than two wives, only 11 per 1,000 indulge in a second helpmate. The excess of wives is greatest among Animists, and next greatest among Musalmáns; in the case of Hindus and Buddhists it is only 8 and 7 per mille respectively, whilst among Christians, who are, of course, strict monogamists, and of whom many are foreigners, the excess is on the side of the husbands. As regards locality, polygamy appears to be more common in Madras than in any other large province; but it must be remembered that there is extensive emigration from the Presidency to Ceylon, Burma, and elsewhere, and that among these absentees males, and therefore husbands, are in very marked excess."

The tradition of the prevalence of polygamy in the East is no doubt based on accounts of the enormous harems kept up by some native princes. Nicolo Conti, in the seventeenth century, says that the King of

Vizianagram had 12,000 wives, of whom 4,000 went on foot and served in the kitchen, 4,000 on horseback, and 4,000 in litters. Of the last, 2,000 were selected as special wives on condition that they would burn at the king's death. Later on, the Emperor Jahángír says that Fíroz, the Bahmani King of the Deccan, had Arabian, Circassian, Turk, Georgian, Chinese, and Russian ladies in his harem, besides women of the country. With each of these foreign ladies he could converse in her own language.

Polygamy, in the case of Hindus, involves this difficulty, that with them marriage is a sacrament, equally binding on both parties. A man of good family finds it difficult to procure a second wife, even if the first be dead ; and people object to give a girl to a man already married, lest she may fall into the detested position of a co-wife. In parts of the Panjáb the boy's hand is examined at his first marriage, and if the lines show that he is fated to have a second wife, he is first married by full rites to an earthen pot, and then to his betrothed. In rural life, generally speaking, if polygamy occurs, it is due to the custom of taking over the wife of a deceased brother, who is regarded as part of the family chattels. The case is different in royal families, as in the house of Mewár, in Rájputána, where it used to be the habit for the Mahárája to have a queen for every day of the week.

The worst form of polygamy is that of the Kulin Bráhmans of Bengal. This is like the "sealing" of wives in the Mormon Church.

"Amongst the Turks," it has been said, "seraglios are confined to men of wealth ; but here a Hindu Bráhman, possessing only a shred of cloth and a piece of string, keeps more than a hundred mistresses."

Ward heard of a Kulin who had 120 so-called "wives," many had 40 or 50. It is said that this marriage system has become very uncommon. But cases occur even now, and Mr Gait records an instance of a Kulin with 9 wives. The cause is, of course, hypergamy. Owing to the extortionate demands of the higher groups, the bridegroom-price is so high that a Kulin has to choose between giving his daughter to a man of inferior rank and leaving her unmarried.

In some places the first wife strongly objects to her husband taking another mate. For instance, in Kulu, on the lower Himálaya, for a husband to take to himself another wife is frequently a cause of his losing the one he has already. Among ordinary Hindus it often leads to dissensions in the family, arising from the selection of an heir. In Northern India, however, among the agricultural classes, where the women have to undergo a life of ceaseless drudgery, the first wife, as she advances in years, sometimes welcomes a helper in household work. But, generally speaking, the country proverbs which dwell on the misery of the younger wife and the jealousy of the elder, accurately reflect popular opinion on the matter.

["Census Report," India, 1891, i. 254; 1901, i. 447; Drew, "Jummoo and Kashmír," 251f.; "Census Report," Panjáb, 1901, i. 208; "Census Report," Bengal, 1901, i. 251f.]

POTTERY.—The earliest form of Indian pottery is hand-made, without the use of the wheel. This still survives among the Andamanese, who have circular unglazed cooking-pots built up by hand, and either sun-dried or partially baked in the kiln. Sometimes they are encased in wicker-work for the sake of protection. This reminds us of some Stone Age pottery which still bears on its surface the marks of the wicker with which it was surrounded. It is only the more remote jungle tribes who are ignorant of the potter's art. The Lusháis of Assam generally use leaves and gourds, but occasionally acquire earthen or metal vessels from the people of the Plains in exchange for the produce of their forests.

The large collection of prehistoric pottery in the Madras Museum, much of which was procured by Mr Breeks and others from primitive graves in the Nilgiri hills, and which has been catalogued by Mr Bruce Foote, seems to belong to the Iron Age. Some of the vases and figurines show considerable mechanical skill. Many of the vases are fashioned to rest on pottery ring-stands, like the amphoræ of classical times. On the lids stand or sit figures of the most varied kind, men or animals, rarely inanimate objects, all modelled in a grotesque style. The interest of them chiefly lies in the light which they throw on the dress, arms, and implements of the people who made them. When we come to historical times, the vessels depicted on the Buddhist monuments, like those of Sánchi, Bharhut, and Bhuvanesvara, display a style of moulding and decoration which has hardly been reached in modern times.

The degradation of the common Indian earthenware is mainly due to the custom which prescribes that an earthen vessel should not, through fear of contamination, be used more than once. Yajnavalkya, one of the early lawgivers, lays down that a pot touched by food can be purified in the fire, but not if it be touched by any filth, or by a Chandála or out-caste, in which case it must be thrown away. In Benares alone, says one of the older teachers, an earthen pot can be used for three days without contamination. Hence a sure indication of a long-inhabited site is the pile of pot-sherds which cover it. In contrast to this Hindu contempt for earthen vessels Musalmáns in their laws are enjoined to use them in preference to metal vessels: "Those who keep earthen vessels in their houses are visited with respect by the angels."

The degradation of the craft is reflected in the contempt bestowed upon the craftsman. He, the washerman, and the gipsy alone use the ass, that despised creature, as a beast of burden. But he himself regards the making of his vessels as a semi-religious art; the wheel he worships as a type of the Creator of all things; and when he fires his kiln, he makes an offering and a prayer. He also makes the funeral jar, in which the soul of the dead man for a time takes refuge. Hence he is a sort of funeral priest, and in some parts of the country receives regular fees.

The primitive pottery is all unglazed. The surface

is never covered with a vitrified enamel, but it has been smoothed by friction, the clay being first prepared with a vegetable juice, probably that of the *Abutilon indicum* —a kind of mallow, which resists water and acids, but leaves the surface soft enough to be scratched with a steel point. There is plenty of kaolin in the country, but caste prejudice prevents the Hindu from using glazed ware. The art of glazing came with the Musalmáns from Persia, but it was probably borrowed in the first instance from Tartar or Chinese sources. Mr L. Kipling remarks that an examination of the rubbish-mounds at Lahore shows that glazed and coloured pottery must at one time have been more common than it is at present. He thinks that this pottery may have been introduced when the Panjáb was ruled from Kábul, where glazed earthen vessels are habitually used for domestic purposes. When the art of glazing was introduced into India, it was used almost entirely for architectural decoration. The use of tiles came down to the Saracens from the times of the Chaldean monarchy, and their use by Musalmáns dates from the conquest of Chingiz Khán, early in the thirteenth century. To quote Mr L. Kipling:

> "The glazed faience of Multán is a relic of the times, when mosques and tombs were covered with this beautiful material. Until a comparatively recent period the work was exclusively architectural, and consisted in tiles painted in dark and light blue, with large geometrical patterns for wall surfaces, the Muhammadan profession of faith painted in bold Asiatic characters for tombs, and panels of various sizes for door-jambs, and the like."

The Sind pottery had the same origin, but differs from that of Multán in some technical details. The colours used are a dark blue obtained from cobalt, and a very fine turquoise from copper. The Pesháwar glazed pottery for native Musalmán table use is very ancient, and nowhere else in India is glazed table-ware made, though European pottery is making way among Musalmáns. Here, as elsewhere, the trade is being injured by attempts to imitate European patterns. The only true porcelain made in India is that of Delhi, with a rich blue or rough duck egg-like coating, which is much admired. The paste is, however, bad, as kaolin is not used, although there are large deposits of the mineral near Delhi and in the adjoining Himálaya.

There was a considerable early trade in pottery from China. Pyrard de Laval tells of large importations by the Portuguese at Goa, both for themselves and for sale to natives. Nowadays, in the Panjáb, a certain quantity of celadon-tinted Chinese cups without handles is sold for use by Musalmáns.

Under present conditions of caste among Hindus the prospects of Indian art-ware are not promising. Art-schools have done something to improve the form and decoration; but there has been too much servile copying of foreign design, and too much production of cheap rubbish. Another cause of failure is the jealousy of the native craftsman. If he discovers a new method of manufacture, or a novel glaze, he keeps the secret to himself, or tries to hand it down to his own relations. The result is that many valuable discoveries are lost to the world by the death of the inventor.

[Bruce Foote, "Catalogue of Prehistoric Antiquities in the Madras Museum," Intro. viii.ff; Rajendralála Mitra, "Indo-Aryans," i. 270ff.; L. Kipling, "Mooltan Gazetteer," 106; Birdwood, "Industrial Arts of India," 301; Mukharji, "Art Manufactures of India," 283.]

PRAYER-WHEEL.—This is the European name for the curious device employed by the Buddhists of the Himálaya. It generally consists of a cylinder revolved by hand or by machinery, and containing a long roll of paper with the formula, "Om ma-ni pad-me Hung," "Hail! the Jewel in the lotus-flower!" This is really a form of address to the Bodhisat Padmapani, who, like Buddha, is represented as seated or standing within a lotus-flower, and is regarded as the patron-god of Tibet and controller of metempsychosis. To himself the Grand Lama now appropriates the invocation. The origin of the formula is obscure. According to Colonel Waddell, the oldest date yet found for it is the thirteenth century of our era. On some of the larger prayer-wheels it is printed 100,000,000 times.

These prayer-wheels are of various sizes, varying from the hand-machine, in which the cylinder is made to revolve round the axis by the momentum of a weight attached to a short brass chain, up to those which work by the agency of wind or water. Sir J. Hooker describes the small variety in Sikhim as "a leather cylinder placed upright in a frame; a projecting piece of iron strikes a bell at each revolution, the revolution being caused by an elbowed axle and string." A larger variety was placed in a house over a stream, and made to revolve on its axis by a spindle which passed through the floor of the building, and was terminated by a wheel.

From Kunáwar, in the western Himálaya, Captain Gerard describes the same machine:

> "Cylinders, called Mane, are very common; they are nothing more than hollow wooden barrels, inside which are sacred sentences printed on paper or cloth; they are closed up, and are generally a foot long; they are placed on a perpendicular axis in a niche in the wall, and are always turned from the north towards the east. There is a smaller sort, with a projecting piece of wood below, turned about in the hand."

He saw another in a house, adorned with curtains and hangings of China silk and satin. This was turned by ropes fixed on a winch below, requiring two people to work it properly.

Though China and Tibet use this simple means of performing their religious duties, it has not been adopted in Burma.

> "There," says Sir J. G. Scott, "you must pay your devotions in person, and unless you supplement these by almsgiving, your prospects towards a next existence are not such as your friends can regard otherwise than with concern."

[Hooker, "Himálayan Journals," ed. 1891, 119, 220; Gerard, "Koonawar," 127; Waddell, "Buddhism of Tibet," 149; Simpson, "The Buddhist Praying-Wheel."]

PRECIOUS STONES.—Precious stones were, from the earliest times, valued in India, partly as a form of ornament, partly for the mystical virtues which they were believed to possess as scarers of evil spirits. These beliefs survive in the folk-lore of our day. Thus the Nauratna, or jewel of nine stones, is a much-valued amulet. The torquoise protects the wearer from boils and from snakes; the onyx, called Sulaimáni, or stone of Solomon, repels demons.

Barbosa, writing early in the sixteenth century, gives a learned account of the ruby:

> They "are for the most part gathered in a river which is called Pegu," the Burma mines of our day. "In order to know their fineness, the Indians put the point of their tongue upon them, and that which is coldest and hardest is best; and in order to see its purity, they take it up with wax by the finest point, and so look at it by the light, by which they see any blemish which it may have got."

That learned jeweller, Tavernier, informs us that

> "there are only two places in the East where coloured stones are obtained—namely, in the kingdom of Pegu, and in the island of Ceylon. The first is a mountain twelve days or thereabouts from Sirin [*Syriam* *] in a north-east direction, and is called *Capelan*.* It is the mine from which is obtained the greatest quantity of rubies, spinelles, or mothers of rubies, yellow topazes, blue and white sapphires, hyacinths, amethysts, and other stones of different colours."

It was from here that the great Burmese ruby came, which the finder broke into three pieces. One of these was stolen, one was sent to Calcutta, and the third was said to be so brilliant that the woman who found it was able to spin cotton by its radiance at night. At last it fell into the King's hands, and when he heard the story he was so enraged that he had all the people of the village in which it was found burned upon a stage.

Aurangzeb used to wear in his head-dress, says Bernier, only a single jewel, "a beautiful Oriental topaz of matchless size and splendour, shining like a little sun." He had two chains, one of pearls and rubies of different shapes pierced like the pearls; the other of pearls and emeralds round and bored."

"In the middle of the chain of rubies," adds Bernier, "there is a large emerald of the old rock, cut into a rectangle, and of high colour, but with many flaws. . . . In the middle of the chain of emeralds is an Oriental amethyst, a long table, . . . and in perfection of beauty. Also a balass ruby cut in cabuchon, of fine colour, and clear."

Besides the Burma ruby-mines, the main source of the gem is Badakhshán, where the mines producing the spinel ruby were, in the time of Marco Polo, in the hands of the King of Balkh, who kept up the value of the stones by checking exportation.

The only Indian sapphire-mines are in the valleys of the Cauvery and Godávari and in Kashmír. The best garnets come from the Banás river in Jaypur, where they are cut and worked into various kinds of ornaments. Jade of an inferior kind comes from Mirzapur, the best specimens from Turkestán and Burma. It was highly valued by the Emperors Jahángír and Sháh Jahán, who prided themselves on the lovely cups which ornamented their palaces. It is now little worked except in South India, but a jade-like serpentine comes into the Panjáb from Kábul, and is cut into handles for daggers.

Coral necklaces are a favourite ornament with Hindus, and coming from the great ocean it is supposed to possess talismanic properties. Some white coral is found on the coast of Káthiáwár; but the Mediterranean is the chief source whence the inferior grade of coral used in India is obtained.

In the chalcedony-quartzoze group of minerals we have rock-crystal of which some splendid cups, now at Dresden, were looted at the capture of the Delhi palace in the Mutiny. When of a violet colour, it is the Indian amethyst; when yellow, the cairngorm. Next comes the jasper or agate group, to which reference is made in the article on *Cambay Stones;* and lastly, the opal. The taste for these stones spread largely in Moghul times, when they were used for the lovely inlaid work, now sadly damaged, which adorns the Diwán-i-ám or reception halls of the palaces at Agra and Delhi, and the beautiful screen of of the Táj Mahal. Agra, Broach, Cambay, and Jabalpur still maintain the industry of inlaying marble plates and cups with this work in stone.

[Watt, "Economic Dictionary," articles on various stones; Ball's edition of Tavernier's "Travels"; "Upper Burma Gazetteer," Pt. II. vol. iii. 8f.]

PROCESSIONS.—The custom of carrying about an idol in procession, which has its roots in the Animistic beliefs of the lower races, and is still practised in a rude way by the forest tribes, was revived and popularised by Buddhist and Jains. It is among the Hindus of South India and the Jains that the custom of parading images of the gods is most common, and the practice dates from the era of Buddhism. The procession of the image of Juggurnaut (*q.v.*) merely represents the Buddhist rite to which his worship succeeded. The object of the ceremonial is to bring the god personally in contact with his worshippers, and by carrying him round the area over which he has control to scare demons and other evil influences.

An early account of such a procession is given by Strabo, who probably received his information from Megasthenes:

"In processions at their festivals many elephants are in the train, adorned with gold and silver; numerous carriages drawn by four horses and by several pairs of oxen; then follows a body of attendants in full dress, bearing vessels of gold, large basins and goblets a fathom in breadth, tables, chairs of state, drinking-cups, and lavers of Indian copper, most of which were set with precious stones, as emeralds, beryls, and Indian carbuncles; garments embroidered and interwoven with gold; wild beasts, as buffaloes, panthers, tame lions; and a multitude of birds of variegated plumage and of fine song."

Barbosa tells how the Bráhmans of Malabar used to take out their idol morning and evening:

> "He who takes it out first washes thoroughly, and carries it on his head with the face looking backwards, and they walk with it three times in procession round the church, and certain wives of the Bráhmans carry lighted lamps in front, and each time that they reach the principal door, they set the idol on that stone, and then worship it, and perform certain ceremonies; and having ended the three turns with music and rejoicing, they again place it in the chapel."

Tavernier describes how, on his way to Golconda, he met a large party with more than twenty palankeens, each of which contained an idol. There was a man to fan each image, and prevent flies from settling on it, and another carried an umbrella to protect it from the sun. From time to time a man with a shield shook it so as to ring the bells attached to it, in order that the god might be amused.

In other cases the god is taken periodically to be bathed, perhaps as a rain-charm. The idols at Rameshwaram, in the extreme south of the Peninsula, are carried in state on an elephant and bathed in the sea. At Udaypur the great annual Rájput festival is the Ganggor, when the image of the goddess Gauri is taken to be bathed in the lake.

Sometimes the idol takes his walks abroad with the practical object of collecting money. Buchanan-Hamilton, in South India, once met an image of Hanumanta, the monkey-god, who was on a mission to collect money that some persons had vowed in time of trouble to his master, the god at Tripati. When the evil passed away they were slow in paying, and had to be reminded of their obligations by a junior god in person. A particularly troublesome god, named Mahásu, used some years ago to make incursions into Dehra Dún, accompanied by a host of followers, who from their rapacity were a serious burden to the district. At last, Major Young, the British officer in charge of the district, was bold enough to issue an official order banishing the god from his jurisdiction. He even still sometimes tries to repeat his visit, and continues to give trouble.

In parts of Northern India processions of Jain images have led to serious disturbances between the votaries of that creed and orthodox Hindus. Similarly when, owing to the luni-solar calendar, the date of the *Mohurrum*,* the Musulmán mystery-play, coincides with one or other of the leading Hindu festivals, breaches of the peace have occurred. The Mohurrum is almost entirely confined to the Shiah sect, but in some places Sunnis and even Hindus take part in it. The procession consists of *Tazeeas*,* or representations of the tombs of the martyrs Hasan and Husain, the shouting of whose names in the course of the ceremony has given rise to the familiar phrase, "Hobson-Jobson." The wild shouts of the excited fanatics, combined with the frantic beating of the breast, which is often lacerated in their wild enthusiasm, form a savage but impressive scene only to be compared with the performances of the Dancing Dervishes of western Islám. Part of the show consists in parading a copper representation of the open hand, a well-known charm against evil spirits, but here specialised in the service of Islám as the hand of the martyr, while the fingers symbolise the five great Saints. These processions are no part of the religion preached by the Prophet, but are derived from the practices of the Animistic tribes adopted by Islám on Indian soil.

[For the Mohurrum, see Pelly, "Miracle Play of Hasan and Husain."]

RÁJA.—This is one of the many titles of dignity which in later days have suffered degradation. As the independent States were gradually absorbed into the Empire, the Rája within British territory came to be little more than a noble with no functions higher than those of an ordinary land-owner. The title has still further lost dignity since the Indian Government adopted the practice of conferring the rank of Rája on some of its native officials, and many of those not even belonging to the Rájput tribes, who were originally in sole possession of the title.

The Rája, as we find him in the Vedas, is very different

from the autocrat of later times. He was the over-lord of a confederation of clans, each of which had its own chief. The office was, as a rule, hereditary, but there are signs that it was in some cases elective. The Rája was dependent on the advice of the clan council; he had no assigned revenue, but received a share of the booty gained in a successful foray. In later times, with the gradual weakening of the clan organisation, the power of the monarch increased. He occupied a central domain, provided with a fort, in which he lived with his family and dependants, and stored his goods and cattle. The outlying districts were ruled by chiefs, with one special Lord of the Marches to guard the most dangerous frontier. By the time of Manu, the Rája has a share in the harvest, and collects these through special officials. The Bráhmans are now his advisers, in place of the tribal council, except where, as in Rájputána, the monarchy was established on the tribal basis.

It is not easy to ascertain the grades of dignity attached to regal titles, as they seem to vary in different parts. In Western India the order of rank was usually Rája, Rána, Ráwal, the last often applied to the head of a temple, and thus, perhaps, suggesting the old idea that priest and king were one. Jahángír, in his "Memoirs," states that the old Mewár title was Rája; then Rúp, "the handsome one"; then Ráwal; and finally Rána. This last change, which has lasted to our time, took place in the beginning of the thirteenth century. At present, in Rájputána, we have a diversity of titles, of which the relative precedence is difficult to determine. The chief of Sirohi is Ráo; of Kotah and Bundi, Mahárái; the Banswára chief is Ráwal; he of Dungarpur and Jaysalmír, Maháráwal; Mahárái Rána represents the dignity of Jhaláwar and Dholpur. Udaypur, the greatest of all, who claims descent from the god Ráma, and has a pedigree dating back to 144 A.D., calls himself Mahárána.

Coronations begin with the Rájasúya, as we find it in the Mahábhárata. Seventeen, or as some say, eighteen kinds of holy water from sacred places were collected;

the king was bathed; a bow and arrows handed to him; sacred verses were recited by the priest, and the king was made symbolically to conquer the four quarters of the earth and sky. He was seated on a stool over a tiger skin, holy water, usually mixed with honey, butter, and spirits, was poured on his head, which was adorned with stalks of holy grass and ears of corn. He was then driven in a chariot amidst a herd of cows, one of which he touched as a sign of a successful raid. He was saluted by the priests, and handed a sacrificial knife. Finally, he quaffed the juice of the Soma and rice-spirit. The whole ceremonial is an excellent example of sympathetic or mimetic magic. With this rite was often combined the Horse Sacrifice, a sign of universal dominion.

The modern ceremonial is in many ways similar to this. The King of Madura was anointed with Ganges water. In the case of a Rájput Rája, the anointing is done with sandal paste and rosewater mixed together, and the priest marks his forehead with the middle finger of his right hand. But it is not till the family priests are re-elected in the service of the new Rája that they perform the unction. The giving of the Tíka, or forehead mark, is one of the chief parts of the rite. Sometimes it is given by one of the forest tribes, who thus assert their ancient right to rule, and accept the Rája as their viceroy. Abul Fazl tells us that the sign of institution of the Rána of Mewár was done in human blood—a survival of the blood-covenant. When a Rája of the jungle-dwellings Bhuiyas is crowned, one of the chiefs winds a flexible creeper round his head-dress to signify that he is lord of the forest. As has been elsewhere mentioned, the rite includes a remarkable survival of human sacrifice.

The Moghul Emperors used regularly, as over-lords, to send the Tíka, or sign of sovereignty, to the princes of Rájputána, and their officers used to smear the chief's forehead with sandal paste. The custom prevailed even in the days of the decline of the Empire, and in 1807 Rája Mán Singh anxiously entreated the British Government to get that *roi fainéant* Akbar II. to invest him. The request was refused. Our Government, in its turn, claims the same power of investiture, which is usually performed by the British Resident and sometimes confirmed by the Viceroy in person. The Kings of the late Burmese dynasty were solemnly towed in a barge round the city moat to signify that they thus occupied the capital.

The Moghul Emperors seem to have had no special rite of coronation. Akbar, we are told, on his father's death, was raised to the throne by Bairám Khán, the commander-in-chief, with the concurrence of the ministers and nobles. In the same way his successors were solemnly seated on the *Musnud** by the State officials. Some sign of dignity seems to have marked his accession, because Tavernier states that Aurangzeb asked from his father only a jewelled cap, and it was much debated whether his wearing it amounted to the rite of investiture or not.

The Vedas record that the Rája was seated on his royal throne, and then went through the rite of initiation. The form of the ancient throne is perpetuated in the hour-glass shaped *Mora*,* or reed stool, which is a common piece of furniture in every house. The grandest existing throne is, perhaps, that of Mysore, which some say descends from the Pándavas of old, while, according to another and more probable story, it was conferred on the dynasty by Aurangzeb. It is of fig-wood, inlaid with ivory and covered with plates of gold. Tippoo seized it, but on his downfall it came back to the ancient house. When the last Mahárája took his seat, he was pelted with roses till they lay in piles around him. Then he was sprinkled with holy water, and made to do reverence to the State elephant, ox, and horse, all of which must bear auspicious marks. If one of these animals dies, the Mahárája can eat only once a day till a successor with the lucky signs is found.

The late Burmese kings had no less than nine thrones, each used when the monarch performed a special duty or ceremonial, and each was adorned with a special emblem. The chief throne of state was made in the archaic hour-glass pattern.

The elective character of the Hindu monarchy is shown by the rule that the heir has, or ought to have, on his feet the lucky signs of the god Vishnu. When the throne of Idar was vacant, the silver forehead mark on an image of Krishna fell into the lap of one of the claimants, who was forthwith elected. In the folk-tales it is very often the elephant which bows to the rightful heir, or a cobra shades him from the sun with his hood.

In olden times it was the rule in Mewár that the prince, after installation, made a foray into the dominions of some enemy, sacked a town, and returned with the trophies. In these days of peace there is still a mock performance of this rite. A survival of the custom is shown in the rule at Gwalior, which was carried out as late as 1886, by which the shops of some corn-chandlers in the town are plundered at each coronation. When the owners made the usual Hindu appeal to the Mahárája the looting ceased, and they were compensated by the State. Here it marks the period of licence during the interregnum; when the new prince is acknowledged they look to him for redress, or it is a survival of the valour test imposed on the new Mahárája.

The old Hindu rule was that a Rája, twice defeated by his enemies, made over the kingdom to his successor, and burned himself in his royal robes. Jaypál, Rája of Lahore, did this when he fled before that arch-raider, Mahmúd of Ghazni. A symbolical rite marks a Rája's relinquishment of sovereignity. When the Rája of Búndi was deposed in 1771, an image of him was made and cremated with the usual solemn rites. His successor shaved as mourners do, and offered his locks to the Manes of his predecessor. After the usual period of mourning he was duly installed.

The regalia of a king, says Mr J. G. Frazer, are but the conjuring apparatus of his predecessor, the magician. We may learn what the old Hindu regalia were by the rule of the Burmese Court, which slavishly followed Indian practice. They were divided into eleven classes, each in charge of a special spirit-maiden. Chief among these were the umbrellas and the *Chowries*,* or fly-flappers, the sign of rule in the East; a betel-box, which was said to have come down from the great Buddhist Emperor, Asoka; the great bells and drums which proclaimed the accession of the monarch. Besides these were the royal boats, each assigned to a special function, and provided with various animal figures and decorations.

RICE.—We first hear of rice in China. Here, in the very earliest times, the importance of the crop was recognised in the rule that the reigning Emperor had to start the sowing himself, while the princes of his house sowed the other four kinds of grain. It is indigenous in India, where its cultivation dates from the earliest time. The knowledge of it came to Europe after the conquests of Alexander. In the oldest literature only rice and barley are recognised as sacred, the latter being frequently alluded to in the Vedas as the food of the Aryans, while by the time of Manu rice has become synonymous with food. No sanctity attaches to wheat in the Hindu domestic rites, and the natural inference is that it was imported later, and was unable to deprive rice, the older grain, of its recognised sanctity.

The varieties of rice are infinite; they vary from district to district, even from village to village. The peculiarities which distinguish them can be comprehended only by the native grower. Burma, a great rice-land, recognises red, black, white, green, and yellow kinds, which again are subdivided into those with a rough or smooth grain and husk, long or short, round or flat, and each sub-variety has its peculiar name.

Wild varieties have been found in many parts of the country, but their relation to the cultivated kinds is still obscure. Sir G. Watt accepts the view that all the forms of cultivated rice could not have come from a common ancestor, but he thinks:

"There is no necessity to believe the independent wild stocks as botanically anything more than varieties of a common species. But, if this position be admissible, they are varieties that have preserved their individual characters, even when carried to the most diverse conditions of climate and soil. If species, we are confronted with a problem which demonstrates the defective nature of botanical characters and terminology, since, according to all accepted notions of species, they are practically inseparable."

There are in Bengal three great rice harvests—the broadcast, sown with the first fall of rain; the transplanted, a later and superior crop; and thirdly, the tank rice. A man with a farm of mixed soil might in Bengal have a succession of crops ripening nearly all the year round. In this part of India the importance of the cereal may be gauged by the fact that the population, as shown in the census returns, is in exact proportion to the productive powers of the soil, measured in rice. But, as we know by experience, the crop is most precarious, and a failure of rain at any of the three critical periods leads to failure. The broadcast sowings must have steady rain with short intervals of sunshine during the whole three months of its growth. For the transplanted variety there must be light rain for sowing in May-June; heavy for transplanting in July-August; moderate in September-October to swell the ear. It is to the failure of this last supply that disaster is generally due. Excessive rain is seldom hurtful, save by over-swamping the fields or beating down the ripening grain.

It is well for the peasant that rice can be grown year after year on the same land, because the crop is deficient in mineral matter and nitrogen, which the other cereals remove from the soil. Besides this, it is grown in low levels with a plentiful water supply, which replaces, by the substances it brings from higher ground, the slight exhaustion of the soil caused by the crop itself.

It may be suggested that the transplanted crop was an Aryan invention, superseding the broadcast Dravidian sowing. The Hindu legend tells that the latter was the work of Visvakarma, the divine architect, while the former was invented by Brahma himself. Hence the transplanted is more pure than the broadcast variety, and it alone is used in the service of the gods.

Much of the rice sold in shops and exported to Europe

is steam-boiled to facilitate husking, and it is dried in the sun before being pounded in the pestle and mortar. High caste Hindus accordingly cannot use it, as it may have been boiled in water touched by impure hands. But it does not matter who may have fried it in *ghee*,* the sacred product of the cow removing the risk of pollution. Even the jungle tribes have their prejudices regarding rice. It must be cooked at a man's own fire and by himself; a Santál will not eat rice cooked by a Hindu—even by a Bráhman.

Our use of rice to throw over the bride and bridegroom seems to have come from India, where it is a long-established custom. The rice scares demons, and in particular those which check the fertility of the union. Barbosa describes how they used to sprinkle rice on the head of a new Rája after he had taken the oaths. The old marriage ritual prescribes that bride and bridegroom pour rice from their hands on the marriage fire. Hence comes the usage of presenting rice tinged with turmeric by way of invitation to wedding-feasts. In a modern Hindu wedding the pair stand, each on a pile of rice, and as the service proceeds, the relations, at the close of the recitation of each text, keep silently throwing a few grains of rice over them. The Burmese, as usual imitating Hindu usage, shower saffron-coloured rice over the married pair as they go to the wedding-chamber.

[Watt, "Economic Dictionary, v. 465ff.; Wallace, "India in 1887," 203ff.; Shway Yoe, "The Burman," i. 290ff.]

ROADS.—The art of road-making, according to R. von Ihering, came from Babylonia. But when we speak of early Indian roads, we must not compare them with a magnificent bridged and metalled highway, like our Grand Trunk Road, running from Calcutta through the Panjáb. The early road was what we should now call in Upper India a *Cutcha** road—that is to say, a track imperfectly levelled, unmetalled, and with here and there some sort of causeway over the smaller ravines and streams, and perhaps a ferry where it crossed the larger rivers. We hear of roads for carts and waggons in the Vedas; in the Epics of wide, spacious urban roads; and the Rámáyana tells of the custom of watering the streets. Manu speaks of the king's highway, of tolls on waggons, and of foot bridges. Strabo, probably quoting Megasthenes, says that "they construct roads, and at every ten stadia [the *Coss* * of our day], they set up a pillar to show the by-roads and distances." This was under the rule of the Mauryas.

The Greeks found what was called the Royal Road, running from the Indus to Palibothra or Patna. Skirting the junction of the Beás and Sutlej, it crossed the Jumna, and so through the Doáb to Patna. The Buddhists also had an extensive road system, of which Professor Rhys Davids gives a full account. Their roads were chiefly designed to permit the journeys of pilgrims to the sacred sites associated with the life and death of Buddha. The early invaders selected one or other of two routes—one down the Indus, round the Gulf of Cutch, and so up to the great city of Ujjain; the other from Kashmír along the foot of the Himálaya to the Holy Land of Buddhism, and so on to the Bengal Delta.

When we come to notices of trade with the West, we find a different state of things. This trade, originally started from the Euphrates-Tigris valley, was then taken up by the Arabs, and when the nations of the West began to have a share in it, was established at ports like Cambay and Broach on the western coast. Now the two lines of mountains known as the Western and Eastern Gháts, which bound the Deccan plateau, differ greatly in character. In the latter there are mere groups of hills more or less isolated from each other; in the former, the range is continuous, and only pierced here and there by difficult passes. It was, therefore, these western passes which controlled the trade from the sea. The most important of these was the Bor or Bhor Pass, which now carries the railway from Bombay to Poona. Its early importance is shown by the number of Buddhist caves and shrines to which it gave access. The military road through it was begun by Wellesley, carried on by Elphinstone, and finished by Malcolm in 1830. This, and the Nána Pass leading to the north, opened out the Deccan to western trade. By the Thall Pass was secured the route to Agra, which is still used by road and rail. The more western route by Indore to the Narbada valley was masked by the great fortress of Asírgarh, which was and is one of the most important strategical points in Central India.

In Malabar, in the same way, the course of trade was determined by that remarkable break in the chain which is called Palghát, the great highway of old times, which now carries the railway from Calicut to Madras.

When we come to Moghul times, the first great road-builder was Sher Sháh. To him India owed at least four great roads, which opened up the Ganges Delta to the Panjáb and Rájputána. He built, we are told, no less than 1,700 *Caravanserais*,* or hostelries, on these roads, and planted the sides with shady trees. This policy was continued by Akbar, who made the highway from Upper India to the Deccan through a gap in the Sátpura range. These great works excited the admiration of the early travellers. Terry, Sir T. Roe's chaplain, says:

> "Agra and Lahore are the two principal and choice Cities of the Empire, betwixt whom is that long walk of 400 miles in length, shaded by great trees on both sides. One of the rarest and most beneficial works in the whole world."

Bernier speaks of

> "the double row of trees planted by order of Jehan-guyre, and continued for one hundred and fifty leagues, with small pyramids or turrets, erected from Kosse to Kosse, for the purpose of pointing out the different roads."

Aurangzeb, who was constantly on the march, gave much attention to the roads by which his army was supplied during his protracted campaign against the Mahrattas. But in the days of confusion which lasted from the decay of the Empire to our days, like everything else, they were neglected.

In these days of railways we can hardly realise the delay and discomfort experienced by the early generations of Anglo-Indians. The Ganges and Jumna were the usual route to Upper India. We have many accounts of the horrors of this journey, especially to women and children, in the boats supplied for the use of troops. In 1834 Mrs Fanny Parkes spent fifty-one days travelling from Alláhábád to Agra, now a night's journey by rail. In 1824 Bishop Heber found it impossible to drive his gig from Alláhábád to Meerut, and as late as 1852 Lord Roberts spent three months going from Dumdum, near Calcutta, to Pesháwar. Times have certainly changed when India has 26,000 miles of railway—2,000 miles more than the mileage in France.

ROSARY.—The use of the rosary is universal among Hindus, Buddhists, and Musalmáns. Its introduction in the Church of Rome is comparatively modern, and it seems probable that it was originally invented by the Hindus, passing from them to the Buddhists, later on to the Musalmáns, and probably introduced from them to Christianity during the period of the Crusades.

There is hardly any class of substance which has not been used in India for beads—minerals, as glass, stone; products of the animal kingdom, coral, shells, bones; vegetable, seeds and fruits, prepared pieces of wood or other natural botanical structures. Beads of all kinds have been imported from time immemorial. The Aggry beads found from eastern Asia to western Africa have been attributed by some to the Phœnicians, by others to Egypt. China and Venice have both supplied India with glass beads, and some are locally made. Most of the curious rough stone necklaces worn by Fakírs come either from local sources such as supply the CAMBAY STONES (*q.v.*), or from Ceylon, Burma, or from beyond the Himálaya.

Each material used for the rosary has a specific purpose; but these vary infinitely among the sects which use beads. One rule lays down that the beads used in the worship of one of the goddesses should be of coral; pearls for that of Brahma; turmeric root to subdue the passions. The favourite bead of Siva worshippers is that called Rudráksha, or "eye of the god Rudra." This is usually supposed to come from the *Eleocarpus ganitrus*, and to be chiefly imported from Singapore; but Sir M. Grant-Duff throws doubt on this last belief, and says that the Mahárája of Vizianagram sent him two plants procured from Nepál, where the plant seems to be indigenous, as well as in Assam and the Concan. In the Panjáb, however, the name Rudráksha seems to be applied to the seeds of the Jujube tree, and there special attention is paid to the number of facets on the seed. The celibate Jogis wear beads with eleven facets; those who are married beads with only two; while those with five facets are sacred to Hanumán, the monkey-god. The worshippers of Vishnu, on the other hand, prefer the wood of the *Toolsy*,* or sacred basil, for their beads. The Sáktas, or goddess worshippers, break out into greater extravagance, having rosaries of dead men's teeth, and other relics of the same kind. Fakírs often carry rosaries made of snake-bones, as a sign that they know a charm to cure the bite, or they tie one of the beads round the wrist of a person afflicted with quartan ague. Snake-charmers, as a protective, sometimes hang such rosaries on the pipes which they play before snakes.

The sects differ also in the number of beads which their rosaries contain. A Siva worshipper wears 32, or that number doubled; a Vishnu worshipper, 108. Some believe that this number was intended merely to assist the worshipper in repeating the name of his god 800 times, each of the 8 extra beads marking a 100. But it is more probable that some symbolism of sacred numbers —3-3-12— may be at the root of the matter. The Tibetan Buddhists have adopted the same number, 108, for the beads of their rosary, and they, too, in default of any better explanation, say that the object is merely to repeat the spell by hundreds, and that the extra 8 beads are added to make up for any omission, owing to absent-mindedness or loss of beads through breakage.

The Sáktas have a way of counting the number of recitations of a charm in a more primitive manner than by the rosary. They count up to a 100 on the three joints of each finger of the right hand, marking off each 10 on a joint of one of the left hand fingers. When they have reached a 100 they lay before them that number of millet grains, and so go on to make up the number required. The Atíths of Bengal combine various numbers of beads for their prayers, wearing a string from the elbow with 27, a wristlet with 5, and strings of 3 beads hanging from each ear.

The Lamas in Sikhim use rosaries of onyx, turquoise, quartz, lapis lazuli, glass, amber, and wood, especially that of the yellow berberry and sandalwood. The chief Buddhist priest of Nepál, called the Vajra Achárya, "Thunderbolt Teacher," has 108 beads round his neck. Threaded on one side of his necklace is a Vajra or miniature thunderbolt, and on the other a small bell which he rings as each circuit of prayers is finished.

Among some Indian sects the beads are carefully concealed while being used in prayer, in order to avoid the risk of magic or the Evil Eye injuring the worshipper. For this purpose pretty little bags, beautifully embroidered, are sold at Benares, known as Gaumukhi, or "Cow's Mouth," which is also the name of the ice-cavern from which the Ganges flows out of her parent glacier. In the monastic fraternities the novice is directed to be most careful not to lose his beads. If he does lose them, he cannot eat or drink till they are found, or until he is invested with a new rosary by the Superior.

The Musalmán rosary is chiefly used by old men and women, or by those who are particularly careful in religious duties. If the wearer be a Shiah by sect, he wears a rosary made from the earth of the Kerbela at Meshed; if he be a Sunni, one of dark stone. Wooden beads are used by people of all sects, while Fakírs prefer glass of various colours, yellowish stone, amber, or agate.

[On Rosaries generally, articles in "North Indian Notes and Queries," vol. iii.; Buddhists, Waddell, "Buddhism of Tibet," 202; Watt, "Economic Dictionary," iv. 42.]

SACRIFICE.—Among the early Aryans the house-father was the priest, and made his simple offerings to the gods of nature or the ancestral spirits whom he worshipped. But when the race became settled on Indian soil, the idea of sacrifice which appears in the Vedic hymns rapidly developed, and with that later stage of religion to which the title of Bráhmanism has been given it became of supreme importance. The greater intricacy of the ceremonial, when "every word was pregnant with consequences, every movement momentous," gave occasion for the growth of a special Levite class, the Bráhmans.

The theory of sacrifice was based on the anthropomorphic conception of the gods. Man is gratified by presents, therefore he offers them to the gods; he needs food himself, therefore he pretends to feed them. At the outset the sacrifice was an act of communion between the worshipper and the totem, or natural object supposed to possess supernatural power; then it became a simple thank-offering; next a means of nourishing the gods, and strengthening them for their work of maintaining the universe; lastly, it was intended to make man a divinity himself, and able to coerce the gods to do his will. Strange to say, the theory of sacrifice as an atonement for sin seems never to have taken hold of the Hindu mind.

As we find it in its earliest stages, the whole system is pervaded by practices that breathe the spirit of the most primitive magic. What was originally a meal intended for the deity gradually dwindles down into a feast for the worshippers, to which the gods are ceremoniously invited. Such a blood-sacrifice is mainly the result of a compact that, if such an event does or does not take place, the deity shall receive his reward; if he fails on his part, he gets nothing.

The great Vedic sacrifices, like that of the horse, are now obsolete. We can hardly realise the elaborate nature of the ceremonial. Some lasted for three generations —over a hundred years. The poets of the Mahábhárata speak of one that extended to a thousand years. Myriads of priests and victims appeared at rites like these, which were organised and supported by the ruling power.

In modern times sacrifice is an individual act, not periodical, but performed, as a rule, when the worshipper is beset by any special trouble, or seeks to win a special boon from the god. What the sacrifice may be depends on the sect and personal wish of the worshipper. He who follows Vishnu or Siva does no blood-sacrifice. The Vishnu ceremonial is more elaborate, and hence is preferred by the wealthy trader; that of Siva is more simple, and involves little or no expense. The fire-offering is made to both gods; Vishnu, as Krishna, is honoured with cooked food; Siva asks nothing but a water-offering or a few flowers.

It is among the forest tribes and the Sáktas, or Mother-worshippers, that blood-sacrifice hold its ground. When the jungle man slays a goat in honour of his village or tribal god, the head, which was probably the god's share, falls to the priest. The deity must be content with a few drops of blood sprinkled on the rude stone which forms his altar, and the rest of the meat is eaten then and there by the worshipper and his attendant friends. Dr Oppert thus describes the ritual in South India:

"When an animal, a black goat, or any other goat, or a buffalo is to be sacrificed, the Pujári or priest walks from the right side round the fire-pit, binds the beast on the flagstaff to the east of the temple, and the sacrificer, possessed of the demon, waits until it indicates the consent of the deity by shaking its body, and then kills it with a sword by one stroke, otherwise it is regarded as unpropitious. This done, he cuts off its foot, and places it in its mouth. On its head is arranged an oil-lamp, which is lighted with a new cloth wick."

The rite ends with dance and song, and the congregation

take the flowers, leaves, and other things offered to the god, and place them on their heads.

The subject of the Sákta sacrifices is repulsive, and few Englishmen care to explore those shrines of Káli or Devi, which reek with the blood of victims. The Sákta ritual is much the same as that of the jungle man. The animal, usually a goat, is brought before the temple, and caused to tremble all over by squirting water into its ear. It is then slain with a single blow, severing the trunk from the head, which, with the blood, is laid before the altar. The accounts of rites like these show a horrid cruelty and disregard of the sanctity of life most abhorrent to our ideas. Those who are curious in such matters will refer to Ward's account of the Bengal sacrifices. The Rája of Nadiya, according to this authority, at a feast to Durga, began with one victim and doubled the number daily till at the close 65,000 animals had been immolated. The degraded so-called Buddhists of Nepál, in utter disregard of the injunctions of the Master, have a blood-sacrifice, accompanied with orgies, of which Dr Oldfield gives a distressing account.

[Hopkins, "Religions of India," chap. ix.; Oppert, "Original Inhabitants," 461; Oldfield, "Sketches from Nepál," ii. 297.]

SALT.—Hunting and pastoral tribes do not need salt, their diet supplying them with an abundance of alkalis; but this is not the case with agricultural people, who live mainly on a vegetable diet. Hence the use of salt marks the transition to settled life. The Aryans, during their wanderings, are believed to have been ignorant of salt, as were the writers of the Rig-veda; but when they settled in India they must soon have discovered the enormous supplies of rock-salt in the Panjáb, and have come in contact with Dravidians who learned the use of it when they reached the sea. This is corroborated by the fact that Lavana, or sea-salt, first appears in the Atharva-veda, written when the Aryans had advanced down the valley of the Ganges. The only people at the present day who do not use salt are the Koos of the eastern frontier, whose chief food is

Indian corn, and who live in an isolated hill-country far from the sea-coast, and are little influenced by the races of the Plains. The wild Veddahs of Ceylon are also ignorant of its use.

The rock-salt of the Sind frontier was named from its place of origin, Saindhava. The old Hindus also used Romaka salt, from the Sámbhar Lake in Rájputána, and Pansuja salt, derived from the alkaline earths found all over North India, which to this day, if the manufacture were not prohibited, would yield a considerable supply. But they valued chiefly, as being in their opinion the purest kind, the sea-salt produced by evaporation at various places along the coast. Even to this day

"the orthodox province of Orissa," writes Sir W. Hunter, "will have nothing to say to an article made by the impure hands of the infidel. The solar salt has taken a firm hold on the religious feelings of the people. Their whole life is one round of observances in meats and drinks and washing clean of platters, and the use of solar salt is an important aid to the salvation of their souls."

Possibly on account of its preservative qualities, mystical properties are ascribed to salt. It is waved over the heads of the married pair and of babies, to scare demons. Many ascetics bury their dead in salt, and among the Indian Jews, the minister, following the precedent of the salt of covenant, dips bread in salt, and it is handed round. In North India, in swearing friendship, each one throws a lump of salt into a water-pot and says, "If I am false, may I melt away like this salt!" Some of the ideas regarding it which prevail in Madras are not easily explained. Mr Fawcett describes men executing a devil-dance before a temple, carrying baskets of salt on their heads. Here the idea is possibly to scare evil spirits. In another case a Nair's house was plundered, his family idol knocked down, and salt put in the place where it had stood. This was regarded as an act of extreme profanity.

From at least the time of the expedition of Alexander, it was the policy of the rulers of India to derive a portion of their revenue from the taxation of a commodity which is produced in more or less abundance in most parts of the country, and which, in the simple conditions of native life, is one of the few urgent necessities of life, an impost on which compels the lowest class to contribute their quota to the support of the Empire. At one time what was known as the Salt Hedge stretched for hundreds of miles, from Attock on the Indus to the river Mahánadi on the north limit of the Madras Presidency. An army of 14,000 officials patrolled this barrier, which was intended to shut out the salt of the west from Northern India. This was removed in 1879, and since then the taxation on salt has been steadily reduced. In 1904 the gross revenue from this source was about £5,000,000. Western India is now largely supplied with salt from the mines of Cheshire and Germany. Probably less salt is used in the north than in the south, because the diet in Upper India largely consists of pulse and other nitrogenous food, which needs a condiment less than the rice of Bengal and Madras. The ordinary Hindu of the Plains mixes the salt with his food as it is being cooked. The people of the northern hills use it with their cooked food as we do.

[Watt, "Economic Dictionary," vi. Pt. II. 393ff.; Fawcett, "Bulletin of Madras Museum," iii. 259; for People who do not use Salt, Frazer, "Pausanias," ii. 108f.]

SERVANTS.—Writing of Surat in 1623, Pietro della Valle says:

"Servants cost very little, in regard to the multitude of people and the small charge with which the common sort are maintained; for a simple servant, who is not an officer, commonly in the best houses, between wages, victuals, and clothing, stands not in more than three Rupia a moneth, amounting to about the value of a Venetian Zecchine, or ten shillings sterling."

In 1751 we have a list of servants kept by Adam Dawson, "President Governour" of Bengal. His servants cost him exactly 500 Old Sicca Rupees per mensem, and the wages were much below the present rate—9 "cooleys," costing Rs.16; 2 washermen, Rs.6; and so on. In 1759 a head cook received Rs.5; a coachman the same; a head bearer, Rs.3; a grass-cutter, Rs.1½. Hadley, in 1780, says that a Captain in Garrison at Calcutta required 20 servants, costing Rs.140 per month. At the end of the eighteenth century, in Upper Bengal, wages were much lower than they are at present. A great Sahib's cook was paid Rs.20; table attendant, Rs.8; but they could buy much more for their wages. Mr Douglas shows that, at the beginning of the nineteenth century, in Bombay the table servant was paid Rs.12; a butler and tailor the same, "from which scale there has been little departure down to 1883." But since that time wages have steadily increased. This is largely due to recent famines, which have increased the price of food. It was Lord Clare who first improved cooking in Bombay by importing a French cook. He gave lessons to a number of Goanese, and the style of cuisine has since that time much improved.

In our day there has been some reduction in the number of servants employed in an Anglo-Indian household, as compared with the early period of our rule. The number might be still further reduced were it not that caste prejudices prevent a servant from doing more than one kind of labour. In 1824 Mrs Fanny Parkes tells of a dinner-party with 23 servants to 8 guests. At one time, she, a Civilian's wife, had 54 servants; at another she tells us that her 57 servants cost Rs.290 per month, "or about £290 per annum." The young officer of those days kept up a liberal establishment. General Mundy, when a subaltern in 1827, travelled with 3 tents, 2 elephants, 6 camels, 5 horses, a buggy, and 24 domestic servants, besides camel and elephant-men and tent-pitchers. The magnificent Lord Valentia in 1803 took with him on his march 287 servants, including 120 Sepoys and their followers. Sir G. Lawrence says that an officer in the 16th Lancers, during the Cabul war of 1838, had 40 servants in his train. The officer on field-service at the present day is allowed only a small "Cabul" tent and a very limited scale of baggage, and is thus able to make a corresponding reduction in his servants and transport.

SHAWLS.—Changes in taste and fashion have much reduced the demand for the so-called "Cashmere" shawl in Europe; but shawl-weaving is still an important industry. The craft owed much to Akbar, who delighted in shawls, designed the patterns of some himself, and introduced more richness and variety of colour. The chief seats of the industry were then Kashmír and Lahore; and to Kashmír it was in a great measure confined, until a famine in 1820 drove numbers of the weavers into the Panjáb, where they settled at Amritsar, Ludhiána, and other places, now centres of a thriving trade. It was Akbar, too, who introduced the custom of wearing shawls double, which explains the references in our older books where the "pair of shawls" is the standard gift of distinction.

Another variety of the shawl, the *Rampore Chudder*,* was originally made of the fine Pashm, or goat's wool, from the Basahir valley on the upper Sutlej, of which Rámpur is the capital. It should be made of thin, plain, single thread or twist Pashm; but now the demand for cheapness has caused this to be replaced by soft Cabul wool, which is used to adulterate the real shawl material.

Sir W. Lawrence gives a depressing account of the industry in Kashmír. The craft is said there to date back to the time of the Emperor Bábar, who died in 1530. The Moghul Emperors used to wear on their turbans an ornament called the Jigha, in shape like an almond, and over this a feather aigrette. A weaver imitated this design on a shawl for Bábar, and hence it became the established shawl pattern. It was M. Leqoux de Flaix who first introduced the Kashmír shawl into Europe, and in the early years of the last century it was a necessary part of a lady's dress. But fashions changed, and the trade was finally ruined by the Franco-German war of 1870. An eye-witness told Sir W. Lawrence "of the intense excitement and interest with which the Kashmíri shawl-weavers watched the fate of France in that great struggle, bursting into tears and loud lamentations when the news of Germany's victories reached them."

All hopes of a revival of the industry were dashed when the famine of 1877-79 visited the valley, and none suffered in this calamity more than the poor sickly shawl-weavers. "Some of the survivors migrated to the villages, where they still work for starvation wages in heated, unhealthy rooms, hermetically sealed in the winter."

Mr Johnstone gives a good account of the present craft in the Panjáb. The designer draws the pattern in ink on paper, the colours and other technical details being indicated by special marks. Then a second workman selects the proper coloured reels; and a third, at his direction, prepares the paper from which he reads out the instructions to the weaver. Formerly the double shawl was in fashion, and this was made by the Rafúgar [*Ruffugur* *], or darner, who displays extraordinary skill in sewing two breadths of the stuff together, or in replacing an imperfect piece in a finished shawl. But his occupation has all but ceased since the fashion of wearing single shawls has been adopted both by natives and Europeans. Mr Johnstone traces the causes of the downfall of the industry within our territories to the manufacture in England of shawls of the Rampore Chudder class, to the adulteration by the native manufacturer of the material, to want of ingenuity in the production of artistic patterns, but chiefly to the use of aniline dyes, and to the effect of hard water on the raw material.

[Lawrence, "Valley of Kashmír," 375; Johnstone, "Monograph on the Woollen Manufactures of the Panjáb"; Mukharji, "Art Manufactures of India," 341.]

SHEEP; GOATS.—India and Peru are the only countries where the sheep is used as a beast of burden. Sir J. Hooker describes the sheep in Sikhim, each carrying 40 lbs. of salt done up in leather bags, slung on each side, and secured by a band going over the chest, and another round the loins, so that they cannot slip off when going up or down hill. They are very patient, tame creatures, travelling twelve miles a day with ease, and indifferent to steep or rocky ground. In Nepál salt is imported on sheep from Tibet in bags of about 150 lbs. In the Western Himálaya, big, tall, shaggy he-goats, led by an old female, are used as beasts of burden. Nowadays we never witness an incident which Pietro della Valle records at Goa:

"I saw a Carnero, a wether without horns, which they told me was of the race of Balagat, not great but of strong limbs, harness'd with a velvet saddle, crupper, head-stall, bridle, stirrups, and all the accoutrements of a Horse, and it was ridden upon by a Portugal youth of about twelve years, as he went and came from his own House to the School of Giesu."

Among the splendid wild sheep of the northern frontier, so prized as trophies by Anglo-Indian sportsmen, the two Argalis, *Ovis ammon*, the Mongolian, and *O. hodgsoni*, the Tibetan species, cannot be regarded as Indian. And the same may be said of *Ovis poli* of the Pámírs, which takes its name from the traveller, Marco Polo, and its variety, *O. karelini* of the Thian Shan. The only unequivocally Indian species is *O. vignei*, which recalls the name of Vigne, another great traveller, represented by two varieties, *O. vignei blanfordi* in the trans-Indus hills, and *O. vignei cycloseros*, the Urial [*Ooorial**] or Sha of the Panjáb Salt Range. The *O. nahura*, the Bharal, or *Burrel*,* is hardly a typical sheep. According to Mr Blanford,

"in habit, as in structure, it is intermediate between sheep and goats. Like the former it is found on undulating ground, and frequently lies down during the day on its feeding ground, though generally amongst stones; but, like the latter, it is a splendid climber, perfectly at home on precipitous cliffs, and wont, when alarmed, to take refuge in ground inaccessible to man."

The domesticated sheep of Ladakh, according to

General Cunningham, are of two kinds, the black-faced Huniya, chiefly employed for carrying burdens, and a diminutive variety used only for food. The Huniya is much larger than any of the Indian breeds, while the Purik, or mutton sheep, is not larger than a Southdown lamb of six months. The mutton, says Moorcraft, is the finest in the world.

Professor Wallace, who has investigated the Indian breeds, regards the Madras hairy, red sheep as the variety most distinctly Indian. He observes that the Indian sheep in hard seasons is a foul feeder, while the goat is the only cloven-footed domestic animal in India which has the habit of cleanliness. This accounts for the orthodox Hindu preferring its meat to mutton. Towards Bombay we meet a black sheep, and this is the predominating colour of the Northern breed. He saw near Dárjíling a flock of English sheep, bred from Southdown rams and Leicester ewes. The climate does not suit them; they are liable to "scour" from internal parasities, leeches do them much injury; the wool has become coarse, like that of the indigenous variety, and they must be housed at night to escape leopards and jackals, which adds to the cost of keeping. "It would be vain," he decides, "to improve Indian sheep by crossing with those of Europe." The fighting ram, once essential to the Nawáb and the Musalmán young man of fashion, is now rapidly disappearing.

The sheep is regarded as sacred only by the Central forest tribes. The Parheyas use its dung to plaster their floors, as the Hindus do with that of the cow, and the Kharrias will not eat mutton nor sit upon a woollen rug.

The Indian goat is an admirable domestic animal, which is not valued as much as it deserves. The only economic objection to it is the damage it does to plantations. Its flesh is the staple food of the Musalmán all over the East, and many Hindu castes eat the flesh, particularly that of animals which have been sacrificed. It is a beautiful animal in its way, with what Professor Wallace calls "its strut of independence and portly bearing." There are many varieties, the finest in the Plains being found in North India, where they are much larger than in the South. Of the hill breeds, those of Nepál are distinguished by long, flapping ears and Roman noses. Many others from the Himálaya, whose peculiarities were fully investigated by Hodgson, have striking affinities to the wild species.

Of these we have many varieties. The genus Capra includes the Persian wild goat, *C. ægagrus*, of Sind and Balúchistán; *C. sibirica*, the Himálayan ibex; *C. falconeri*, the Markhor [*Markhore**] of the Pír Panjál range south of Kashmír, and thence through the hills of Afghánistán as far south as Quetta. In the genus Hemitragus are *H. jemlaicus*, the *Tehr*,* found along the Himálaya from Kashmír to Sikhim; *H. hylocrius* of the Nilgiris. In genus Nemorhædus we have *N. bubalinus*, the Himálayan Serow, and *N. sumatrensis*, the curious Goat-antelope of Burma. From an economic point of view goats may be classed as those yielding the *pashm* used in shawl-weaving found in the Himálaya and Tibet; those producing *pat*, the mohair-like fleece made into the fabric known as Pattu; those yielding goat's hair from Sind, Rájputána, and Balúchistán; lastly, the Indian village goat.

[L. Kipling, "Beast and Man in India," chap. v.; Wallace, "India in 1839," chap. xii.; Blanford, "Mammalia," 493ff.; Watt, "Economic Dictionary," vi. 549ff.]

SHIKAR.—India is still the paradise of the sportsman of moderate means, where, as yet, no game laws and preserving interfere with his amusement. But the gradual clearance of jungle, and the introduction of weapons of precision, have much diminished the amount of game. In North India, for instance, the destruction of the belts of jungle stretching into the Plains from the sub-Himálayan Tarái has considerably reduced the number of tigers. The first start in preserving game has been taken by the Forest Department, and native land-owners are beginning to follow their example. If measures of this kind are not soon adopted, sport will practically disappear in North India. We have only to read the accounts of the time of the

Moghul Emperors and in the early period of British rule to see that the range and supply of the larger game have become much reduced. We read of the great drives for game in the neighbourhood of Delhi by Ala-ud-dín; in one drive organised by Akbar, near Lahore, 15,000 animals were driven together; Jahángír, who kept his game-book carefully, records that he killed in all 28,532 animals, including 86 tigers, 889 *neelgye*,* 1,372 deer, 36 wild buffaloes 90 wild boars, and 23 hares, and 13,964 birds, of which 10,348 were pigeons, 156 water-fowl, and the balance sparrows, doves, crows, and owls.

One of the earliest accounts of Indian sport by Englishmen, given by Hedges in 1683, presents a curious picture:

"In ye afternoon they found a great Tiger, one of ye black men shot a barbed arrow into his Buttock. Mr Trenchfield and Captain Rogers alighted off their horses and advanced towards the thicket in which ye Tiger lay. The people making a great noise, ye Tiger flew out upon Mr Trenchfield, and he shot him with a brace of bullets in ye breast; at which he made a great noise and returned to his den. The Black Men seeing of him wounded fell upon him, but ye Tiger had so much strength as to kill two men, and wound a third before he died."

It is remarkable that at an early period of our rule Englishmen visited India for sport. A picture by Vandyke represents the first Lord Denbigh, dressed in a red Indian jacket and pyjamas, and attended by an Indian boy. This seems to commemorate his journey to India in 1630-33. Later on the gossiping Alexander Hamilton writes:

"This country about Carwar on the west coast is so famous for hunting that two gentlemen of distinction, viz. Mr Lembourg, of the House of Lembourg in Germany, and Mr Goring, a son of my Lord Goring's in England, went *incognito* in one of the East India Company's Ships for India. . . . They spent three years at Carwar, viz. from Anno 1678 to 1681, then being tired this Sort of Pleasure they took Passage on board a Company's ship for England;

but Mr Goring died four Days after the Ship's departure from Carwar . . . and Mr Lembourg returned Safe to England."

It is impossible at present to compile a complete list of record bags in India; but it may be worth while to collect some facts on the subject. Lieutenant Bacon tells of a native *Shikaree** who had been present at the death of more than a thousand tigers shot by Englishmen, and had killed 200 with his own hand. In our own time Sir M. Gerard knew a Sikh native officer who had probably been present at the death of 500 tigers. Mr Baker mentions Paul, a Dutchman, who, about 1782, near Plassey, killed in a week 23 tigers and several leopards. Miss Eden records that in 1838 Captain Osborne and a friend killed 36 tigers in a shoot along the lowlands of the Ganges—the largest number, she says, ever killed in that part of the country by two guns. About 1780 one of the Lindsays in Silhet used to kill 60 or 70 tigers yearly. Within the last ten years there were two Civilians in the United Provinces, Messrs Lumsden and Markham, each of whom had slain more than a hundred tigers. Such bags are not likely to be repeated. General Outram made a vow never to shoot a bird, and never to fire except with ball, and he kept it. In ten years (1825-34), in Khandesh and Mewár, he was present at the deaths of 191 tigers, 15 leopards, 25 bears, and 12 buffalos. There is a tradition in Bombay that he had a tent made of tiger skins. Another officer, "Tiger" Duff, gained his title from having met a tiger, or as some say a leopard, in his compound. The beast sprang upon him. The major thrust his arm into its mouth, seized its tongue, and while the beast struggled, Duff with his left hand drew a knife and cut its throat.

Passing to smaller game—Mr Baker's best bag of snipe in Bengal was 97½ couples to three guns. Three birds to four cartridges is, he says, a good average; but he knew a man who shot 17 birds in succession. Captain Hervey, who was in Madras from 1833 to 1844, says that at that time any tolerable shot could bag 20 couple, and he knew of 30, 40, and even 50 couple killed in a morning. Sir M. Gerard killed 53 couple of snipe and some teal in one day between 11 A.M. and sunset, and 73 couple snipe and 26 duck and teal in one day. Even bigger bags than this have been recorded in places near Calcutta. Captain Skinner about 1826, in the days of muzzle-loaders, describes an officer laying a wager that he would shoot 70 brace of quail in the Dún, and ride 100 miles between daybreak and 6 o'clock dinner. He won easily.

For large game-shooting the districts are fairly well defined. For tiger-shooting the best area is that between the Himálaya and Ganges, including the Tarái and Sundarbunds, and thence through Assam. Here the amount of swamp and jungle is so great that there is little chance of the extinction of the animal. Elephants are still found wild along the base of the Himálaya as far west as Dehra Dún; also in parts of the forest country between the Ganges and the Kistna, as far west as Bilàspur and Mandla along the Western Gháts, and in Mysore. Their destruction, except under special licence from Government, has now wisely been prohibited. Of the three species of Rhinoceros, the large one-horned variety is almost confined to Assam and the hills to the west of that province, where the Tista river enters the Plains; the smaller to the Sundarbunds and East Bengal; the two-horned to the East frontier, and thence into the Malay Peninsula.

The wild sheep and goats are discussed in the article on SHEEP.

Of the great Bovidæ, the *Gour,** or so-called *Bison,** is found all over the hilly forest country of the Peninsula, Assam, and Burma, and, according to Mr Sanderson, gives the best sport next to elephant-shooting. It is practically identical with the *Gyaul,** or Mithan, of Assam. The wild Yak is found on the Tibet plateau at a higher elevation than any other mammal. The wild buffalo is found all over the Peninsula in places which suits its habits, except in the south and west. Various kinds of antelope and deer, the Black Buck, *Sambre,** Chítal, *Chikára,** and many others are found all over the country, and can be shot by ordinary sportsmen who have not the means or opportunity of finding bigger game.

Pig-sticking, one of the finest of Indian sports, has been described in detail by writers like Baker, Newall, and Shakespeare, and need only be mentioned here.

Antelope-hunting with the Cheeta has been a favourite amusement of native princes since the days of Akbar; but it is very properly disliked by Englishmen. The remarkable point in it, as Sir M. Gerard says,

> "is, that from the moment the buck seems to realise his danger, and bounds off with perhaps 50 yards' start, until he has been rolled over in a cloud of dust, it is so almost instantaneous, that you scarce realise that the leopard has caught him up."

It has lately been the subject of keen debate whether some restrictions on the killing of game should be introduced. There is certainly much unsportsmanlike destruction of females and immature animals, and the native professional Shikaree is a wretched pot-hunter, who kills animals in the hot season at drinking-places, and spares neither age nor sex. On the other hand, there are obvious difficulties in fixing a close season, and defining the class of animals which furnish legitimate sport. Anything that would check the sporting tastes of the British soldier, the Gurkha Sepoy, and the Englishman with small pay, who finds in shooting the chief healthful amusement which the country affords, would be nothing short of a misfortune. Nor would it be possible to control the proceedings of the Shikaree, or the sale of game in the larger cities and cantonments, without an increase of the authority of the police or the addition of another body of poorly-paid officials, who would only find additional opportunities of rapacity and extortion. In many places, again, the farmer suffers heavily from damage to his fields caused by deer and wild pig; and it would be quite impossible for the State to deprive him of the use of fire-arms, or to prevent him from shooting animals which trespass on his crops.

[The following may be named among the large library of books on Indian sport:—Aflalo, "Book of Indian Sport"; Baker, E. B. "Sport in Bengal"; Baker, Sir S. W., "Wild Beasts and their Ways"; Blanford, "Mammalia of India"; Darrah, "Sport in the Highlands of Kashmír"; Forsyth, "Highlands of Central India"; Jerdon, "Mammals of India"; Maori [J. Inglis], "Sport and Work on the Nepál Frontier"; Newall, "Hog-hunting in the East"; Rice, "Indian Game from Quail to Tiger"; Sanderson, "Thirteen Years among the Wild Beasts of India"; Shakespear, "Wild Sports of India."]

SHIPS and BOATS.—Though the modern Hindu detests the sea, and thinks himself polluted if he is obliged to cross the "black water," this was not so in ancient times. The Rig-veda mentions "merchants who crowd the great water with their ships"; the Rámáyana speaks of merchants from beyond the sea bringing gifts to the king; Manu legislates for safe carriage and freights by river and sea. In some of the earliest Buddhist documents we read of voyages out of sight of land, some lasting six months, while later texts of the third century B.C. speak of voyages from the Ganges to Burma and round Cape Comorin.

But by the time the great Buddhist monuments were built in or after the time of Asoka (circa 250 B.C.), sea-voyages seem to have been for the most part discontinued. On the Stúpa of Sánchi we have only two boats, one made of rough planks fastened together with string, the other a royal barge. Even at Bhuvanesvara, near the sea, no marine scene is depicted.

In few things the people of India have been more conservative than in their shipping and boats. Mr Lindsay, who navigated a small boat down the Persian Gulf, noticed that everything nautical was as in the days of Nearchus; the silver models of boats at the Bulák Museum are counterparts of a Red Sea buggalow; the ships in the Gulf described by Marco Polo as having no iron fastenings, but stitched together with cocoa fibre, may be seen to-day in the harbour of Bombay.

Among the primitive Indian boats, the *Catamaran* * comes first. As used on the Madras coast, it consists of three logs and three spreaders and cross-lashings, the centre log being the largest, and pointed at one end. With wonderful confidence the boatmen steer these rude rafts through a terrible surf. A little higher development is the *Mussoola* * boat, which has no iron fastenings, and the elastic coir twine allows the timbers to yield to the force of the waves. The characteristic boat used for inland waters is the *Dingy*,* a name now added to the British naval vocabulary, which, in Upper India, is merely a dug-out, hollowed from a single tree trunk, but lower down the Ganges the name is applied to boats half-decked, half-waggon-roofed, built of planks. A curious boat is that used by the Bediya gipsies of Bengal, which is half covered over, the tilt cocoon or bottle-shaped, tapering gradually to the stem, where there is a small opening through which a man can with difficulty crawl. The country where many kinds of rude craft may be seen is the network of river-channels and swamps in the Sundarbunds and lower waters of the Bráhmaputra.

Next we have the coracle used on the Cauvery, Kistna, and other South Indian rivers. Tavernier, on his way to Golconda, writes:

> "The boats employed in crossing the river are like large baskets, covered outside with ox-hides, at the bottom of which some faggots are placed, upon which carpets are spread to put the baggage and goods upon, for fear they should get wet."

Coaches and carts were tied by the pole and wheels between two of these boats; but the horses had to swim across, a man driving the animal from behind with a whip, and another in the coracle holding it by the halter. Boats of exactly the same description are in use to this day.

Tavernier again describes the use of "the skin of a goat, which they fill with air and tie on between the chest and the abdomen." This is the *Mussuck*,* which is used in various forms in many places. On the upper Ganges, at Hardwár, it is called Sarnái, and consists here of a *charpoy* * or native bedstead tied across two inflated buffalo skins.

In the rapids two steerers, lying flat on similar skins, guide the crazy craft. Mr Drew describes the Sarna of Kashmír as

"a goat-skin carefully taken off and carefully closed wherever an aperture occurred; the end of one fore-leg only is left open for inflating; the skin is blown out tight, and the end fastened up with a bit of string; to the hind-legs are attached loops, through which the man puts his bare legs, and the stiff inflated goat-skin comes up in front of the chest; then, jumping into the river, the man balances himself on the Sarna, lying almost flat along it; by aid of his hands and a peculiar motion of the feet he can swim along at a fine rate, and fears not to trust himself to the waves and rapids of the swollen river."

On the Indus the same device, of which Mr Gore gives a graphic account, is called a Dren. Little changes in the East, and this device is depicted on the Sánchi sculptures; while the Emperor Jahángír, in his "Memoirs," tells how he used to travel in Kashmír on rafts of bamboo and grass supported on inflated skins. It is exactly the Kellek used on the Tigris and Euphrates, which is as old as the bas-reliefs at Khorsábád.

Tavernier tells a curious tale of a man putting his child in an earthen pot, and as he was swimming with it across a river, a snake jumped into the pot; the father in his terror lost hold of it, and it floated down to be finally recovered by a man and his wife; they got the child out safely, but the snake bit and killed their own baby which was close by. In Bengal a number of pots, the mouth of each closed by leaves, when covered with a bamboo framework, forms a primitive raft.

Some of the coast tribes are skilled sailors, like those of the west coast from whom we draw our *Lascars.** The canoes of the Nicobarese are skilfully rigged, made of one piece of wood hollowed out by burning. They are flat-bottomed, wide in beam, with long projecting bows, and the sails are made of the leaves of the cocoa-nut, or *Nipa** palm. With these they make considerable voyages round the islands.

The boats on the Ganges are generally broad in beam to avoid awkward squalls, and draw little water so as to escape the numerous shoals. The larger have a roof-like deck to protect the cargo from water. There is a single mast carrying a rude sail, a marvel of rents and patches, of a dull brown colour, dear to the eye of the artist. The captain, like the Chinaman, is careful to have two copper or gilded eyes on bow and stern, so that the boat may be able to see its way amidst the treacherous shoals. Going down stream, it is propelled by a long bamboo pole, and guided by a huge rudder of the most clumsy construction. On the back journey when the river is low, the boat is tracked up stream by ropes fastened to the top of the mast, and each tracker has a separate rope, so that the watchful eye of the skipper may detect if any man is shirking his work. The Ganges boatmen form a fraternity of their own, and are not in good repute. The goods of a native merchant often disappear in a mysterious way, and a convenient whirlpool or nasty shoal accounts for many an audacious robbery. In former days the dangers of the journey from accident and dacoity were great. A writer of 1844 says: "We scarcely know an individual who has made two trips on the Ganges without having been wrecked."

Another class of boats familiar to Englishmen are those of Kashmír, all built of *deodar** cedar, and peculiar in having no sails. Their variety is infinite, but those most used by Europeans are the *Dunga** which Kashmíris employ as a cargo and living boat, and English people as a commodious travelling conveyance, because it supports a convenient cabin. With separate boats for the cook and servants, a "six-manned" wherry and a swift punt for wild fowl-shooting, the wants of the traveller on the Kashmír rivers and lakes are fully supplied.

The Dundhis of the Indus, writes Mr Ross, "are well adapted to the peculiarities of that river. They are used for cargo, and some of them are eighty feet long, of sixty tons burden. The bow of the vessel rises at an angle of about twenty degrees with the surface of the water, and the stem is at double that angle; the sail is large, of lateen shape, and hoisted behind, not before the mast; the bottom is flat, and the whole construction of the vessel suited to lessen the violence of the shock when it runs against the bank, a very common accident."

SIKHS.—Sikhism is the result of a religious reform, which ended in becoming a political organisation. Its founder was Bába Nának, who died in A.D. 1469; he was succeeded by nine Gurus or high-priests, the last of whom died in 1708.

"In its origin," writes Sir D. Ibbetson, "Sikhism had much in common with Buddhism. Nának and Buddha alike revolted against a religion overladen with ceremonial and social restrictions, both rebelled against the sore burdens which the priests would have them bear, the tendency of both was to quietism. But the form which the doctrines of each assumed was largely influenced by the surroundings. Buddha lived in the centre of Hindu India, and among the many gods of the Bráhmans; these he rejected; he knew of nought else; and he preached that there was no God. Nának was brought up in the Province which then formed the border-land between Hinduism and Islám; he was brought up under the shadow of the monotheism of Mahomet, and he taught that there was one God. But that God was neither Allah nor Parmeshar, but simply God—neither the God of the Musalmán nor of the Hindu, but the God of the universe, of all mankind, and of all religions."

Had Sikhism been allowed to follow its natural line of development undisturbed, it would have ended in becoming one of the many theistic sects which find shelter in Hinduism. But it became connected with politics; the fifth Guru, Arjun, in the beginning of the seventeenth century, supported the rebel prince Khusrau, and incurred the hostility of Jahángír. He was imprisoned, and the treatment he received hastened, if it did not cause his death. He was thus the first Sikh martyr, and he, a priest and merchant, was succeeded by Har Govind, a warrior. The Moghul then began a course of brutal repression of these sectaries; but the Empire was in a state of decadence; the stout yeoman levies of the Panjáb more than held their own against the Musalmán armies; finally, the genius of Ranjít Singh, who died in 1839, built up a powerful kingdom. The crimes and follies of his successors provoked a conflict with the British, which ended in the annexation of their territories in 1849.

After their defeat, the Sikhs were governed by some of the best Indian officers the country has known—John and Henry Lawrence, Sir H. Edwardes, and others. Under their wise and conciliatory administration the population became thoroughly loyal to British rule, as was shown by their conduct in the Mutiny of 1857, and their services in our army from that time to the present.

The rules laid down by the Guru Govind Singh, who was the real founder of the Sikh polity (1675-1708), provided that five external marks—the five K's as they are called, from the initial letters of the native names—should mark the true Sikh: his uncut hair and unshaven beard, his short drawers ending at the knee, his iron bangle, his steel knife, and his comb. He was to dress in blue clothes, and especially to eschew red and saffron; to practise complete ablution; to eat the flesh only of those animals which were killed by decapitation; to abstain from tobacco; never to blow out a flame or quench it with drinking water; to eat with the head covered; to pray morning and evening, and recite passages from the *Grunth** or Scriptures of the sect; to abstain from worship of idols; and to venerate one God, without intervention of either Bráhman or Musalmán priest. Caste distinctions he condemned, and directed that at the meetings of the brethren the sacramental food was to be distributed to all present, to whatever caste they might belong.

No one can be admitted into the community save by the Pahul, or baptism, which is administered when the candidate has reached years of discretion, generally at the age of seven. The usual form is that, in the presence of the brethren, sugar and water are stirred up with a two-edged dagger, the novice repeats after the officiant the articles of his faith, some of the water is sprinkled five times over his head from the point of the dagger, and he drinks of it five times from the palm of his hand. He then repeats the watchword, "Hail! Guru!" and swears to obey the rules of his religion.

In recent times the tendency of the Sikhs has been to pay less heed to their special tenets, and to assimilate their practices more and more to those of orthodox Hinduism. But an attempt is being made to enforce the special ordinances of the faith, and at the holy city of Sikhism, Amritsar, increased attention is being paid to the initiation of novices, and to other rules established by the Gurus. There are thus three grades of Sikhism—first, that of the Akáli zealots, who follow all the ordinances of Guru Govind Singh; secondly, the true Sikhs, who observe his main directions against the use of tobacco and the cutting of the hair; thirdly, those Sikhs who retain many, or perhaps most, of the Hindu beliefs and usages, and yet profess devotion to the tenets of the Gurus.

Their numbers increase slowly with that of the general population. At present they number nearly 2,250,000. The great majority of them come from the sturdy Játs, the finest yeomen in the country. This tribe is closely allied to the Rájputs. In fact, in many parts of the Panjáb it is difficult to distinguish one from the other.

His disregard of caste rules, particularly of the futile restrictions which surround the eating and drinking of the ordinary Hindu, make the Sikh peculiarly valuable to our Empire. He does not, like the Hindu, object to leaving his village and crossing the "Black Water." Thus, we find him gladly volunteering for foreign service in China, the Malay Peninsula, and East Africa. Officers who know the three best types of the Indian Sepoy—the Sikh, the Panjábi Musalmán, and the Gurkha—tell us that, for rough mountain work on the frontier, the Pathán and the Gurkha are superior to the Sikh; but for steady, deliberate courage in the face of extreme danger, he is surpassed by no native troops in our Indian army.

Up to the time of the overthrow of their kingdom, the Sikhs had made little progress in architecture, but they had gone some way towards developing a style which, had it not been checked, might have presented some features of interest. Their buildings are small, and what beauty they possess depends on external plating with gilt copper and lavish internal decoration. The style is a development of that of the Musalmáns. Their great temple at Amritsar has the upper story sheathed in splendid gilt copper work, while the lower is encased in panelling of marble, inlaid with precious stones in the style of the Táj Mahal at Agra. The distinction between this and the Musalmán work lies in the introduction of animal forms—fishes, birds, and beasts.

"The designs," says Mr L. Kipling, "though over suave and flowing in line like all modern Indian work, are less Italian in character than those of Agra, and are marked by that local character of all Sikh ornament which is much easier to recognise than to describe."

They also developed an important school of wood-carving used for architectural decoration and the carved doors and windows found in old Sikh towns like Batála are admirable examples of the handicraft.

[Ibbetson, "Panjáb Ethnography," 134ff.; "Census Report," Panjáb, 1891, i. 148ff.; 1901, i. 122ff.; Cunningham, "History of the Sikhs."]

SILK.—It has been debated whether silk manufacture is indigenous in India or introduced from China. Sir G. Birdwood concludes that the manufacture of coloured silks was introduced from China, but at what period it is impossible to say. This suggestion is corroborated by the fact, pointed out by Sir G. Watt, that the mulberry, of which various varieties are found in India, appears to be an introduced and highly variable species. On the other hand, there are references to silk in the Vedas, and it was used in the most ancient of all rites—that of marriage. The mode of bleaching silk is mentioned by Manu, and in the Mahábhárata silk is said to have been brought as tribute by the Chínas. If these people were really Chinese, the fact of early importation is established; but even if this be admitted, it does not necessarily exclude the possibility of an indigenous kind, like the *Tusser** of our day, being cultivated.

The manufacture for which India had always been celebrated is the gold silk brocade known as *Kincob.** Sir G. Birdwood compares the variety of this fabric known as Shikárgáh, or "hunting ground"—that is to say, a cloth decorated with representations of sporting scenes—with Homer's account of the robe of Ulysses; and he concludes that,

> "when this passage is read with others in Homer, proof is added to proof of the traditional descent of the Kincobs of Benares, through the looms of Babylon and Tyre and Alexandria, from designs and technical methods, which probably, in prehistoric times, originated in India itself, and were known to the Hindus already in the Code of Manu, and before the date of the Rámáyana and Mahábhárata."

Such conclusions, however, must be received with some caution.

With the rise of Buddhism a reaction against the use of silk clothing seems to have arisen. Even at the present day the Puritans among the Burmese Buddhists denounce the habit, which is becoming very frequent, of the monks wearing silk robes. This objection to silk was also felt by the Musalmáns. "He that wears a silk garment in this world shall not wear it in the next," said the Prophet: this, however, in another passage he confined to men, while women were allowed to wear silk and ornaments of gold. In India both their sects, Shiahs and Sunnis, are prohibited from saying their prayers in clothing made of pure silk. To avoid this, it is usual to wear what is called Mashru [*Mushroo**], a mixture of silk and cotton.

The Parsi ladies probably wear silk more commonly than those of any other native race. Much of this comes from China or Japan, or even from France, but some of the printed silks worn in Western India are made at Súrat.

The centre of the indigenous or *Tusser** silk manufacture is in Bengal, at Cachár, Dárjíling, and Bhágalpur. The gold or silver woven into splendid fabrics is in its various forms specialised at different places. The gold-broidered loom embroideries come from Satára in the Deccan, and those with gold and silver stripes from Tanjore; the gold-figured Mushrus from Tanjore, Trichinopoly, and Hyderábád in the Deccan; the gold and silver tissues from Ahmadábád, Benares, Murshídábád, and Trichinopoly. The designs of these fabrics were, as Sir G. Birdwood points out, largely influenced by the Musalmáns:

"Kincobs are now made in Ahmedábád and Benares identical with old Sicilian brocades; and the Saracenic Sicilian silks abound in designs, which prove their origin in Assyrian, or Sassanian, and Indian art."

Kashmír had in former times an important silk industry. It was re-established in 1869, but failed. Sir W. Lawrence writes: "The whole business was too official, and the general public looked on it with hatred and disgust." Recently, under the management of Sir T. Wardle, its condition has improved, new stocks of eggs have been introduced from Europe; but it remains to be seen whether they will resist disease, and render annual importation unnecessary.

[Allen, "Silk Clothes of Assam"; Yusuf Ali, "Silk Fabrics of the N.W. Provinces"; Cookson, "Silk Industry of the Panjáb"; Watt, "Economic Dictionary," vi. Pt. II. 96ff.; Birdwood, "Industrial Arts of India," 261ff.; Mukharji, "Art Manufactures of India," 331; Lawrence, "Valley of Kashmír," 367ff.; Sir T. Wardle, "Kashmír and its New Silk Industry."]

SLAVERY.—Slavery has existed in India from the earliest times, and it was certainly one of the errors of Megasthenes to assert that there was no slavery in his days. In Buddhist times, however, slaves were certainly not numerous, being mostly household servants, and they were not harshly treated. In the time of the Periplus, about 90 A.D., there was a considerable importation of slave-girls from the West under the name of Yavanas, or Ionians, who probably came from the Græco-Bactrian region. In one of the dramas of Kalidása, we find them wreathed with garlands of wild flowers, and saluting the king with the welcome of their native land, "Chaire!" "Hail!"

Under the early Musalmáns the trade was actively pursued, and in the raids of Mahmúd of Ghazni and Timúr thousands of wretches, captured in India, were sold in the bazaar of Samarcand and other Central Asian cities. But under the rule of Islám the slave was generally regarded, not as a persecuted and miserable chattel, but as a well-treated household dependant, whose life was full of possibilities. He might end his career as *Vizier*,* or Prime Minister, or like Kutb-ud-din Aibak, who founded a dynasty in the beginning of the thirteenth century. Akbar, with his usual humanity, checked the trade.

"It had been the custom," writes the courtly author of his "Memoirs," "of the royal troops, in their victorious campaigns in India, to forcibly sell and keep in slavery the wives, children, and dependants of the natives. But His Majesty, actuated by his religious, prudent, and kindly feelings, now issued an order that no soldier of the Royal Army should act in this manner."

The slave-dealing of the Portuguese became such a scandal, that in 1599 the king issued an order calling attention to the cruelty with which slaves were treated. A clever observer, Pyrard de Laval, assigned slavery as one or the chief causes of the downfall of their power. He speaks of American slaves

"exported to Portugal, and to all places under the Portuguese dominion. The Portuguese carry off the children, seducing them by fair speeches, and leading them away and hiding them, both little and big, and as many as they can, yea, even though they be children of friendly races, and though there be a treaty of peace whereby they are prohibited from taking them for slaves; for all that, they cease not to kidnap them secretly, and to sell them."

He quotes instances of slaves committing suicide on

account of maltreatment. Tavernier says that the black slaves of Goa

"will blindly obey their master's orders to go and kill any one. . . . If it should happen that they spend too long a time in finding the man whom they wish to murder, and are unable to meet him in the fields or in the town, then, without the slightest regard for sacred things, they slay him at the altar."

One great hunting-ground was the Sunderbunds and the islands off the coast of Bengal, where the country was almost depopulated by the ravages of the slave-hunters. It is to the honour of the great Dalboquerque that he did his utmost to check the trade in slaves. It was almost a fitting retaliation for such acts when the Emperor Sháh Jahán, in 1629, had the whole Portuguese population of Hoogly sent as slaves to Agra.

The Dutch, too, largely dealt in slaves. They were mainly Abyssinians, known in India as *Hubshees*,* or *Seedees*.* They have left their trace in the curious mixed race in Canara on the West Coast, and these, later on, formed a dangerous body of pirates, which attacked our commerce. Under a Mahratta leader, Angria, they occupied the stronghold of Vijaydrug, or Gheria, which was finally destroyed by Admiral Watson and Colonel Clive in 1756. The little Seedee State of *Jungeera* * is all that remains to record the deeds of these Abyssinian freebooters.

When we first became connected with the country the slave-trade was active. The Musalmáns, says Grose in 1757, prefer the women of Kashmír for their seraglios,

"having the advantage in a delicacy of shape and make, which is chiefly in request among them. This taste they even push to such an extravagance as to scruple no price hardly for a female slave, which to her other beauties should have added that of a plumpness covering the smallest bones that can be imagined, for in the bone they think the weight chiefly consists, and therefore those who weigh the least are by them reckoned the rarest and delicatest pieces. Those who amongst us pass for comely majestic dames would not meet with admirers among those people."

They also valued Hubshees for their courage, fidelity, and shrewdness, and in the latter days of the Moghul Empire some of these men often rose to be governors of cities. As late as 1761 the Select Committee of the Court of Directors "particularly recommended" the Madras Government "to procure as many slaves from the French islands as possible"; and the kindly James Forbes, when at Anjengo, on the Malabar coast, in 1772, bought for Rs.20 a boy and girl as a present for an English lady in Bombay, the price, as he says, being less than for a couple of pigs in England. The English newspapers of the day have many advertisements of slaves, and they were openly sold in Calcutta about 1785.

Regulation of the trade began in 1811 with a law prohibiting the importation into British territory of slaves from foreign countries; in 1832 the buying or selling of a slave, brought from one district to another, was declared punishable; in 1843 claims to slaves were removed from the jurisdiction of the Civil Courts. The Penal Code of 1860 finally prohibited the trade.

Slavery in British India at the present day, though prohibited by law, exists in some parts of the country in the modified agrestic or predial form.

"A mitigated serfdom," writes Sir W. Hunter, "is indigenous in every country where the people increase, and the means of subsistence stand still. It represents the last resource of labour when placed by over-population completely at the mercy of capital."

To this day, he says, each of the chief Orissa families has nominally certain servile families attached to it. Under our rule the conditions of people like the Cherumárs of Mysore has somewhat improved, as compared with the account given of them by Buchanan-Hamilton in 1800; but they and some of the menial castes in thickly-populated tracts like Oudh are in a state little above that of serfage.

The petty kinglets of the Himálaya have a troop of

"ladies-in-waiting," who accompany the Ráni on her marriage. Such girls are technically slaves, but they are rather slaves to custom, following a way of life which has been traditional with them for countless generations, accepting their position without a murmur, as the girl of humble life in Europe accepts the work of a servant or factory-hand as a matter of course. What are known as Pagoda slaves in Burma are a well-recognised body, who are looked on as unclean, and with whom the rest of the community will have no intercourse. Even since our occupation, when they were released from compulsory service, they are looked on with aversion, and have to travel into districts where they are unknown before they can find employment even of the most menial kind.

For actual slavery we have to go to the wild tribes on the frontier, who are still practically outside our law. Thus the Aos of Assam now deal less in slaves than before our occupation. They still have some slaves who are usually well-treated, but if troublesome they are sold to more distant tribes among whom human sacrifice is not yet extinct. They are sometimes made over to hostile villages in compensation for heads taken. Not long since such people were invariably slaughtered as an offering to the spirits of the slain. The Lepchas of Sikhim have slaves often taken as security for a debt and treated kindly.

Dr Wright describes slavery as an institution in Nepál:

"Every person of any means has several slaves in his household, and the wealthy have generally a great number of both sexes. It is said that there are from twenty to thirty thousand slaves in the country. Most of them have been born slaves; but free men and women, with all their families, may be sold into slavery as a punishment for certain crimes, such as incest and some offences against caste. In a few of the wealthier households the female slaves are not allowed to leave the house; but in general, they enjoy a good deal of freedom in this respect. . . . The price of slaves ranges from 150 to 200 rupees for females, and for males 100 to 150 rupees. They are usually well-treated, and, on the whole, seem to be contented and happy. Should a slave have a child by her master, she can claim her freedom."

In Chitrál, on the north-western frontier, slavery was rife until quite recently. Part of the revenue was taken in Káfir women, who were brought to Pesháwar, and sold according to height, Rs.50 or Rs.60 per foot being the average price. This practice seems to have ceased. But among the Káfirs themselves many slaves are kept, partly the descendants of an ancient people subdued by the Káfirs, and partly of prisoners taken in war. Sir G. Robertson describes them as on the whole fairly treated. Sometimes their masters enter into blood brotherhood with them, and it is a curious fact that some are annually elected to the council of magistrates which regulates the affairs of the tribe.

Since British power was established in Balúchistán slavery has ceased. In former days the slaves were either Negroes from the Somáli coast, or Hazáras sold into servitude after rebellion by the Amír of Kábul. Most of the slaves have now been released and have become cultivators or paid servants.

[Buchanan, "Mysore," ii. 371ff.; "Calcutta Review," v. 269; Logan, "Malabar Manual," i. 148; Shway Yoe, "The Burman," ii. chap. xvi.; Wright, "History of Nepál," 45; Robertson, "Kafirs of the Hindu-kush," 100; "Census Report," India, 1901, "Ethnological Appendix," 213; Adam, "Law and Custom of Slavery in British India"; Peggs, "An Account of Slave Population in the Western Peninsula of India."]

SNAKES.—There is no animal in India more closely connected with the popular religion and folk-lore than the snake, and none regarding which more general ignorance prevails.

"The reptilian fauna of India," writes Sir G. Watt, "is remarkable for the great variety of generic types and number of species. The latter amounts to no fewer than 450, which is nearly one-third of the total number of species known in the world. They are referred to 100 genera, of which the majority do not range beyond the limits of India. Of the 21 families of Indian Ophidia only 4 are venomous, Elapidæ, Hydrophidæ (sea-snakes), constituting the Colubrine sub-order; and the Viperidæ and Crotalidæ (pit-vipers), forming the Viperine sub-order. Of the Colubrine snakes, the Cobra (*Naia tripudians*), the Ophiophagus or Hamadryad, the Karait (*Bungarus Cœruleus*), and of the Viperine snakes the Daboia Russelli are those most frequently met with, and the most destructive to life."

The widespread fear of the animal has prevented the native from investigating the varieties, and distinguishing those that are dangerous from the harmless. This fear is well founded, because snake-bite is a much greater cause of death than the attacks of wild animals, and the annual recorded deaths amount to about 20,000. But this certainly does not represent the total mortality. Women, from their habits of groping about in dark corners of the house, and walking abroad barefoot before dawn, are peculiarly liable to attack. Such deaths, to avoid an inquest, are often not reported, and, on the other hand, crime is often concealed under the pretence of snake-bite.

This ignorance of the people about snakes is illustrated by the quaint beliefs that prevail regarding them. Fra Paolino tells of the Malabar basilisk which kills by a look. In Coorg the whip-snake enjoys the sanctity of a Bráhman, and its skin gets blistered if the shadow of a man falls upon it. In Bengal this snake is believed to flick people on the back with its tail, thus causing a fatal wound. One variety in the Panjáb drinks the breath of sleepers; another ties up the hind-legs of buffalos with its coils, and then drinks their milk, in spite of the fact that suction is impossible without lips and a broad tongue, which no snake possesses. In Delhi they say that the house-lamp flickers when a cobra enters, as if it were fascinated. Snakes, as a matter of fact, have no powers of fascination. Most people believe that the *Mungoose* * is immune to snake-bite, and it is said to use the mungoose plant (*Ophiorrhiza Mungos*) as an antidote. But Sir J. Fayrer has clearly shown that the animal is not proof against cobra poison; if left to itself it is almost invariably victorious, and escapes being bitten by its wonderful activity, but if pushed on the snake will probably be fatally bitten. There is, however, some evidence to show that the animal is less susceptible to poison than other animals, and when bitten by a venomous snake that the effects are produced after a longer period than with other mammals of the same size. This is, according to some authorities, the result of hereditary transmission; according to others, it is due to slight inoculation with the venom during conflicts with snakes.

For snake-bite all sorts of marvellous remedies are in use. The snake-charmer depends on his skill in handling the snake and extracting the venom teeth. He has, it is true, a mantra or spell of his own, but he does not care to make rash experiments, lest, as he says, he might forget the text at the critical time. His piping is quite useless, as "the deaf adder closes her ears"; in fact, its auditory apparatus is imperfect, and it probably has little perception of sound. The many popular remedies are, needless to say, worthless. Many varieties of *Snake Stone* * are in use. Some are said to come from the head of the snake, but most of them consist of charred animal bone, which is supposed to suck out the venom. One is recorded as found in the detritus of the Sutlej valley; another, on investigation, proved to be a calculus taken from some animal's stomach. One of the simplest remedies is thus described by Albiruni:

> "It is a Hindu custom that, when a man has been bitten by a venomous serpent, and they have no charmer at hand, they bind the bitten man on a bundle of reeds, and let him float down a river, first placing on him a leaf on which is written a blessing for that man who will accidentally light upon him, and save him by a charm from destruction."

The usual treatment nowadays is by charms and exorcism, or to take him to some one regarded as immune from snake-bite, like one of the Rájput tribes of Oudh, who drops water on the head of the patient from a vessel suspended over him; or they send him to the shrine of one of the snake-gods, like Gúga or Mánasa Devi, and have charms said over him. At one of the Panjáb shrines the date trees have branches like twisted cobras, and on the principle that like cures like, one of these keeps snakes out of the house.

The worship of the snake is universal in India, but the two chief seats of the cultus are in Kashmír to the north, and in Malabar to the south. In the old creation myth the gods tie the great snake, Vásuki, round the Mount Mandara, and with it churn the ocean—a story localised at the Mandaragiri hill in Bhágalpur of Bengal, where the image of the serpent stands carved on the rocks. By another legend Krishna is seized by the Nága, or great dragon of the Jumna. This has been interpreted as a symbol of the contest between the new faith and that of the aboriginal Nágas, or serpent-men. They are supposed to have been a northern race akin to the trans-Himalayan people who had the snake for their totem, and were adopted into Hinduism in the guise of mermen and mermaids and as demons of drought. Animism associates them with streams and fountains, the living force which makes the waters flow. This Nága worship is widespread in north-western India and there are numerous Nága shrines in Nepál. In Kashmír the temples, according to General Cunningham, are placed in the middle of tanks, the abode of the Nága or dragon; but the fact has been disputed.

In Malabar respectable Hindus keep the south-west corner of their gardens undisturbed and overgrown with vegetation, as the Nága-kotta, or snake-shrine.

"Usually," says Mr Logan, "there is a granite stone carved after the manner of a cobra's hood set up and consecrated in this waste spot. Leprosy, itch, barrenness of women, death of children, the frequent appearance of snakes in the garden, and other diseases and calamities supposed to be brought about by poison, are all set down to the anger of the serpents. If there is a snake-stone in the garden, sacrifices and ceremonies are resorted to. If there is none, then the place is diligently dug up, and search made for a snake-stone, and if it is found it is concluded that the calamities have occurred because of there previously having been a snake-shrine on the spot, and because the shrine had been neglected. A shrine is then at once formed, and costly sacrifices and ceremonies serve to allay the serpent's anger."

One class of Bráhmans in Cochin, who tend and feed snakes in their houses, is supposed to be safe from poison. They are the snake-priests, and they alone can cut or make use of the trees of the snake's grove. No other Hindu will touch a twig of the holy trees.

In South India the snake-goddess is Durgamma, the "Mother." Her shrine is built over a snake-stone, and beside it is the snake-tree, the *Neem*,* or Margosa. A cobra's head in silver represents her in the domestic worship. In Bengal her place is taken by Mánasa Devi, who sits on the lily, surrounded by serpents. At her feast Mals, or snake-charmers, stand on bamboo platforms, and let all kinds of snakes bite them, while women offer milk to the goddess and implore her to spare their children.

Many cases have occurred of persons claiming supernatural powers over snakes. From them many snake-gods have sprung. In 1830, at Satára, in the Deccan, a man died of snake-bite. From a child he was said to be able to control snakes; he was an incarnation of Vishnu, and was to free the land from British rule. Even after his death he was expected to rise again, and a shrine was erected, where he is still worshipped.

The snake is the sacred animal of many tribes who claim descent from the dragon. Thus the Cheros, a wild tribe of Chota Nágpur, call themselves "Children of the Snake," and the coat of arms of the Maharájá is a cobra, with a human face under its distended hood.

In folk-lore the snake is a guardian of house and treasure. In a village of Káthiáwár, where seven brothers were slain by marauders, they have become guardian snakes of the village. They are seen at night lying in the village entrance, and no snake may be killed or even annoyed in the village. In the same way one of the gates of the Agra fort was said to be guarded by a snake, and when it was being demolished some years ago by European engineers, a great snake rushed out, and thus supplied infallible evidence of the truth of the legend. In particular, the snake guards treasure, and, when a rich man dies without an heir, he comes back as a snake to guard his wealth. If you know the proper charm, you may appease him, and then he goes back to the other world, and leaves his wealth to the finder. Jogis and quacks of that kind deal largely in such nostrums. The wood-cutters in the Sunderbunds make their Jogi give a practical test of his ability. When they enter the place, they send their Jogi in advance, and if he escapes, they know that the place is safe.

Though many jungle tribes revere the snakes, others eat them. In Bhotan, when they find a python's hole, they light a fire at the mouth and smoke it out, and then promptly eat it.

[Fergusson, "Tree and Serpent Worship"; "Calcutta Review," civ. 350, cxiii. 19; Fayrer, "Thanatophidia of India"; Oldham, "The Sun and the Serpent"; "Census Report," Bengal, 1901, i. 105; Panjáb, i. 104; Cochin, i. 24. For the Mungoose, Blanford, "Mammalia," 125.]

SUN-WORSHIP. — Sun-worship has appeared in India at various times and among various races. We find it among the Dravidian tribes of the Central hills, where the Sun is worshipped as Boram, or Dharm Devata, "the god of piety," in an open space with an ant-hill for his altar, where a white cock is sacrificed to him. When the Aryans entered India, they brought with them the cult of Súrya, Savitri, or Prajápati, "Lord of Creatures," which was part of their higher Animism, the cult of Nature. Again, in the time of the Greek successors of Alexander, and of the Indo-Scythians who followed them, votaries of the old Iranian Sun-worship entered the land as missionaries, and were adopted into Hinduism as the Sakadwípi Bráhmans. With his usual eclecticism, Akbar introduced the worship. He ordered the Sun to be worshipped morning and evening, at noon and at midnight; he had 1,001 Sanskrit titles of the deity collected, which he used to repeat daily, turning reverently to the Sun. As he did so, he used to hold both his ears, and then, turning quickly round, used to strike the lower parts of his head with his fists. His son, Jahángír, was also a Sun-worshipper, and the Mithraic symbolism on his tomb at Lahore corroborates, if further evidence were needed, the accounts of contemporary historians and Portuguese missionaries, who all notice the assiduous worship devoted to the Sun by the early Moghul Emperors.

In spite of all this, it is curious that so few temples are dedicated to him. Though he is revered in the domestic ritual, his image at the present time appears in shrines only in association with those of the newer and greater gods. His worship has been largely taken over by Vishnu, and wherever the cult of Siva is predominant, that of the Sun becomes neglected. One of his special temples is that of Kanárak, in Orissa, or, as Sir Monier-Williams interprets the name, Konárak, "the Corner Sun." This shrine, of which Sir W. Hunter says that the "luscious ornamentation forms at once the glory and disgrace of Orissa art," was built about the beginning of the thirteenth century of our era. Another famous shrine dedicated to him is that of Mártanda, in Kashmír, a building specially interesting, because "it reproduces, in plan at least, the Jewish temple more nearly than any known building." It has in all eighty-four columns, a singularly appropriate number in a Sun-temple, if, as has been supposed, the number is sacred to the Hindus, because it is the multiple of the number of days in the week with that of the signs of the zodiac.

"General Cunningham," observes a writer quoted by Sir W. Lawrence, "thinks that the erection of this Sun-temple was suggested by the magnificent sunny prospect which its position commands. It overlooks the finest view in Kashmír, and perhaps in the known world. Beneath it lies the paradise of the East, with its sacred streams and glens, its orchards and green fields, surrounded on all sides by vast snowy mountains, whose lofty peaks seem to smile upon the beautiful valley below. The vast extent of the scene makes it sublime; for this magnificent view of Kashmír is no petty peer in a half-mile glen, but the full display of a valley 60 miles in breadth and upwards of 100 miles in length, the whole of which lies under the ken of the wonderful Mártand."

The famous golden image of the Sun at Multán has been mentioned in connection with IDOLATRY. In North India few temples are dedicated to the Sun. There is one at Benares, another in Káthiáwár, and two or three in Bengal. The deity is represented in some by an equestrian image, in others mounted in a chariot drawn by seven horses, or merely by a circle painted red.

The pious householder bows to the sun as he leaves his door at dawn. Many of the higher castes worship him in the morning with a water oblation before the other gods or goddesses are adored. Sunday is sacred to him, and on that day many abstain from fish, flesh, or salt. In parts of Bengal girls worship him in the hope of getting a good husband, or what is even more important, a good mother-in-law. He is often credited with powers of healing in diseases like leprosy and consumption, while any contempt of his majesty is likely to be visited by illness. All over the country people do the "deazil," as the Highlanders call it, walking round a temple or sacred object in the course of the Sun—that is to say, with the right shoulder next the sacred place.

["Census Report," Bengal, 1901 i. 188; Crooke, "Popular Religion and Folk-lore," i. chap. i.]

SUTTEE.—Suttee is an ancient institution of the Indo-Aryan, based upon the primitive idea that in the shadowy life of the next world, which in a way resembles that of the present, the dead chief or king needs the service and companionship of his wife or wives. As early as the Atharva-veda, it is described as "an old custom." The text in the Rig-veda, which in later days was quoted as a religious sanction of the practice, was, it is true, to use the words of Professor Max Müller, "mangled, mistranslanted, and misapplied." At the same time, the rule that at the cremation of her husband the wife was to be placed on the pyre with his corpse represented, as Professor Tylor shows, "a reform and reaction against a yet more ancient savage rite of widow-sacrifice, which they prohibited in fact, but yet kept up in symbol." A further modification of the early practice appears in a passage in the Rig-veda, which shows that the widow sometimes, as is now the rule with the inferior castes, married her husband's younger brother, and thus as a family chattel remained, with whatever goods she possessed, in the family of her adoption. The historians of Alexander found the custom prevailing at Taxila; but the earlier law books do not prescribe it, and Manu enjoins the widow to lead a life of ascetic austerity. It may have lingered in remote corners of India. At any rate, about the sixth century of our era, it was revived and recognised in Hindu customary law.

It is interesting to speculate why this old savage custom was now revived after many centuries of disuse. Mr Risley suggests that

"closer contact with more barbarous races, the growth of the sacerdotal spirit, the desire, as Sir H. Maine has suggested, to get rid of the inconvenient lien which the widow held over her husband's property, may have all contributed to this result. But when widow-sacrifice had been thus re-introduced, it is *primâ facie* unlikely that it should have been enforced with that rigid consistency which characterises the true savage; and, in fact, the texts prescribed for the widow the milder alternative of a life of ascetic self-denial and patient waiting to join the husband who had gone before. According to some authorities, they recognise, though as a less excellent path than the two former, the alternative of re-marriage."

But two causes contributed to check the growth of widow-marriage. In the first place, it was felt inexpedient that a stranger should assert rights over the widow's property, which by her marriage had passed to the family of her late husband; secondly, the sacramental theory of marriage grew stronger with the spread of

Bráhmanic ritual. The widow was taught to recognise the spiritual benefit which would arise from the annual performance of the death-rites. Being now a member of a new kin, there was no one to give her away a second time in marriage, and the property having passed from her control, no means of paying to get her married again.

Suttee under these conditions held its own through the Middle Ages, when European observers began to supply numerous pictures of the horrors attending on the rite. But it never prevailed with the same intensity all over the Empire. For instance, it was never very popular in the Panjáb. Cases occurred, of course, in later times, as when 300 women were cremated with the corpse of Suchet Singh of Kashmír, and four wives and seven concubines perished with Mahárája Ranjít Singh. As might have been expected, the rite was more common in the neighbouring hills. For instance, at the town of Nagar, in Kulu, there are many Suttee monuments, one containing as many as seventy names. But the real feeling of the people was shown in the touching verse of the Adi Granth, the Sikh Scriptures:

> "They are not Satis who perish in the flames, O Nanak!
> Satis are those who live with a broken heart."

It never extended, as a well established, popular institution, fully south of the river Kistna. Pyrard de Laval, who records the burning of five or six Bráhman widows at Calicut, could not have referred to the Nambútiri or Malabar Bráhmans, among whom the custom was unknown. He probably meant to describe them as women from the Concan. The case of the widow described by Pietro della Valle was probably that of a lady from the country north of the river Kistna. Dr Burnell shows that wherever the custom prevailed in South India it was not derived from indigenous tribes, but was directly introduced by the Bráhmans. This was probably the case at Vijayanagar, where numerous cases occurred, and some archæologists identify the "Cinder mounds" at Bellary with these sacrifices. The practice, again, was limited in many ways. In Madura it was only the wives and concubines of princes who were expected to immolate themselves. These women maintained the tradition that it was right for daughters of the old Indian royal race to do so, and some Bráhman widows followed their example. But some princesses, like Mangammál, the famous regent, lived on, and she, in spite of her amours, left an honoured name. Much the same feeling extended over the Deccan and the West Coast. It was in the country where Bráhmanism was most powerful, in Bengal and along the Ganges valley, past Benares and into Oudh and Rájputána, that the rite was common.

When it was at its height in Western Bengal, Buchanan-Hamilton states that the Bráhmans, in their eagerness for sacrifice, used to overlook many irregularities as, for instance, allowing to Bráhman women the privilege of dying, to which, by near relationship to the dead, they were not entitled, and permitting Suttee when the husband had died at a distance. This last case sometimes involved awkward results. General Sleeman tells of a woman, who, when her husband was supposed to have died in a foreign land, was burnt with his turban. But he returned home soon after the tragedy. The habit extended even to the menial castes, and Buchanan-Hamilton speaks of a Musalmán weaver's widow burying herself alive in the grave of her husband.

The methods of immolation varied in different parts of the country. In South India, whenever it did occur, the woman jumped, or was forced into a fire-pit, in which her husband's corpse had been previously placed. In Western India she was laid in a grass hut, supporting her husband's head with her right hand, while she lighted the hut with a torch held in her left hand. Along the Ganges valley, she lay, or was forced upon, the already-lighted pyre. In Nepál, where the rite still survives, she is laid beside the corpse. A pile of inflammable materials is placed behind their heads, and when these are lighted both bodies are kept down by long poles of green wood, which are held and pressed by relatives on either side.

It was the custom in Rájputána, when the Suttee

started on her death-journey, to mark the gateway with her hand steeped in saffron. These marks were after her death carved in stone, and they still remain to show the number of the women who devoted themselves to death. Colonel Hervey, from investigation of the Bikanír records, traced 152 cases in the family of the chief; Colonel Tod records that 84 women died with the Rája of Búndi, and 64 with Mahárája Ajít Singh of Márwár. The records show 237 Suttees with nine Maháráos of Búndi, the largest number in any case being 95. It is remarkable that in the island of Bali, where Hinduism has taken root beyond Indian limits, the rite did and does prevail to an extent unknown in the parent country.

The first movement for the repression of Suttee was made by Akbar, who directed that, if a Hindu woman wished to be burnt with her husband, his officers should not prevent her, but that she should not be compelled to immolate herself. Under our rule the question was first raised at the end of the eighteenth century by Sir C. Malet and Mr Jonathan Duncan. In 1817 the Government merely gave effect to the decision of the Pundits that the widow of a Bráhman should not burn except with the corpse of her husband, and the relations were threatened with punishment if these orders were violated. The reason of this order is illustrated by a case recorded by General Sleeman of a woman burning herself with the corpse of a man to whom she alleged that she had been married in a previous birth. Further agitation and enquiry led to the total abolition of the practice in 1829. That popular feeling was generally moving towards abolition is shown by the case of the famous Ahalya Bái, the Mahratta princess, who, shortly before her death in 1795, endeavoured to prevent her daughter from sacrificing her life, but in vain.

In later times, Jang Bahádur discouraged the rite in Nepál, and directed that widows with young children should not be burnt, and that intending Suttees might alter their decision even at the pyre. In spite of this, at his death in 1877 three of his widows immolated themselves. Even when Europeans used their influence against it, such scenes have often occurred. Tavernier records a case of a woman at Patna who asked permission from the Dutch Governor to burn herself, and allowed her arm to be severely burned in proof of her courage. General Sleeman states that in 1829 he was reluctantly forced to allow a woman to become a Suttee, because she would otherwise have starved herself to death. Alexander Hamilton tells the strange tale of Job Charnock, the founder of Calcutta, rescuing a Suttee from the fire. The lady lived with Charnock for many years as his wife, and made him, as Hamilton alleges, "a Proselyte to Paganism," so much so, that, in imitation of the Pachpiriya sect of Behár, he used to sacrifice a cock on her tomb at each anniversary of her death.

From time to time, in modern days, cases of Suttee have occurred in isolated parts of the country. Early in 1905 the relatives who assisted in the cremation of a widow in Behár were sentenced to long terms of imprisonment. If our rule disappeared from India, it is certain that the rite would be revived.

A curious explanation of Suttee is given by Strabo, that it was intended to check the poisoning of husbands by their wives. It is remarkable that the same theory was revived by Alexander Hamilton, apparently from local tradition at Canara, which he visited between 1688 and 1723. Barbosa, again, reports that it was the custom of the Lingáyats of South India to bury the widow on the death of her husband. In the voyages of Sindibad, as recorded in the "Arabian Nights," we have the curious story of the inhumation of the husband on the death of his wife. It has been suggested that this was a perverted account of the Lingáyat custom brought to the west by Arab merchants. But no instance of male Suttee has yet been discovered in India. In the kingdom of Ashanti, in West Africa, the husband of the king's sister is expected to commit suicide when his wife or an only male child dies. On the other hand, we have many instances in India of male immolation, but not of the Suttee type. Thus,

Barbosa records that, besides his widows, many men, confidants of the King of Malabar, used to burn themselves with the royal corpse, and Masúdi mentions similar cases in the Konkan. Suttee pillars in Rájputána testify the deaths of male servants with a beloved master, as well as of female slaves dying with their mistresses. This also is the only part of India where we have continuous evidence of mothers burning themselves with their dead sons. Buchanan-Hamilton tells of an isolated case at Gorakhpur, in the United Provinces, where a woman did not burn with her dead husband, but some time after she lost her son, and was cremated with his remains.

[Chevers, "Indian Medical Jurisprudence," 665; "Calcutta Review," xlvi. 221; Nelson, "Manual of Madura," Pt. II. 83, 246.]

SYMBOLISM.—A symbol has been defined as "a representation which does not aim at being a reproduction."

"Most religions," writes Colonel Waddell, "teem with symbolism, which is woven so closely into the texture of the creeds that it is customary to excuse its presence by alleging that it is impossible to convey to the people spiritual truths except in material form. Yet we have only to look at Muhammadanism, one of the great religions of the world, to see that it appeals successfully to the most uneducated and fanatical people, although it is practically devoid of symbolism, and its sanctuary is a severely empty building, wholly unadorned with images and pictures."

The other Indian religions abound in symbolism of many kinds. First, we may consider the Swástika. This symbol, which by some curious blunder in etymology has received in England the name of Fylfot, is the Cross cramponnee, the Gammadion of Byzantine ecclesiastical architecture. It is not found in Assyria, or Chaldæa, but the assertion of Max Müller, adopted by D'Alviella, that it is absent in Egypt, has been proved incorrect by the excavations of Flinders Petrie. Many explanations of it have been given: that it represents the union of the male and female elements; that it is a Páli monogram; that it denotes water, storm, lightning, fire, or the Arani or fire-drill, the sun, or a solar god. It appears constantly in India on the oldest Hindu coins, on the footprints of Buddha, on various textile fabrics; in Western India on the wooden ladles used in the worship of the fire-god, and on every Hindu invoice and book of accounts, where it is associated with Ganesa, the god who prospers undertakings. It is probably connected with the motion of the sun, and the production of fire by means of the Arani or fire-drill.

Most nations represented the Sun as a circle or cruciform sign.

"This symbolism," writes Count D'Alviella, "doubtlessly renders the idea of the solar radiation in the four directions of space. But the Sun does not restrict itself to darting its rays in all directions; it seems, further, animated by a circular motion from East to West. The latter action may have been symbolised, sometimes by changing the disk into a wheel, sometimes by adding to the four extremities of the solar cross feet or broken lines usually turned in the same direction."

He concludes that the Swástika came to India from Greece, the Caucasus, or Asia Minor, by ways which we do not yet know, and, being adopted by the Buddhists, thence reached Mongolia. It is also found in the reverse form among the Bonpas of Tibet, who circumambulate an image, not from left to right like Buddhists, but from right to left. This was believed by Max Müller to symbolise the retrograde motion of the autumnal Sun, in opposition to its progressive movement in the spring.

The Buddhist wheel seems to be a modification of the Swástika. But it is not, as some have supposed, peculiar to Buddhism, being held sacred also by the Jains. It was an old Hindu symbol of the Chakravartin, "he whose wheels roll all over the world," the Universal Emperor, and was then, by a natural metaphor, connected with the preaching of the Law of the Buddha.

The trident appears as the emblem of Siva, and also

in Buddhism. It seems to have been derived from the primitive Animism, and implying the flashing lightning or three-tongued flame, is thus emblematical of fire or Sun-worship. Connected with this is the thunderbolt, the Dorjé of Buddhism, which, according to Count D'Alviella, came to India through the Greek invaders. But Indra, the Vedic god of the firmament, has his thunderbolt, and to this day stone celts, supposed to be thunderbolts, are worshipped in village shrines. It is constantly found in Buddhist art of the Gandhára type. In fact, the modern school of symbolists has perhaps gone too far in deriving these Indian emblems from Western sources. They meet us in the oldest Sanskrit literature, but as Indian stone monuments are all comparatively late, early physical representations of them are wanting.

The tree of life, again, was a favourite Buddhist symbol, and probably reached India from Babylonia. It has survived as a common form of decoration on modern textile fabrics. The lotus-flower, too, which some believe to signify "the mysterious sanctuary into which the Sun returns every evening, there to acquire fresh life," was adopted in Buddhism, Buddha and Vishnu, who took over much of his cultus, being represented as seated upon it. It is graven on the hands of images of the Hindu gods, and by the rules of native cheiromancy implies universal sovereignty.

The open hand seems to be a Semite symbol, representing the divine might; but we find it on Buddhist sculptures decorating the pedestal of the sacred tree. It frequently occurs in Islám, where it is the standard of the Martyr at the *Mohurrum* * Festival, the five fingers denoting the five great Musalmán Saints. It is a common form of signature, and peasant women dip their hands in lime and decorate the walls of their huts in the belief that it scares demons.

Another form of symbolism appears in the things which represent the gods. Thus a small oval agate represents Siva; a globular carnelian, Ganesa, god of luck; a crystal taw, the sun; a metallic ball, Devi; the Sálagráma Vishnu. This last is a fossil ammonite with perforations, which are popularly supposed to be the work of the god in one of his manifestations. This and the Bána-linga, the symbol of Siva, enjoy the unique distinction of being essentially sacred, and entitled to divine honours without any rite of consecration. In fact, of their own nature they are occupied by the special presence of deity. So far symbolism is carried, that some pious Hindus annually marry the Sálagráma, as representing Ráma, one of Vishnu's incarnations, to the *Toolsy*,* or holy basil, the pretty little shrub which symbolises Síta, the faithful wife of the god. Much depends on the colour of the fossil. If it borders on violet it means that the god is angry, and no one will dare to keep it in his house. The Sálagráma is kept carefully wrapped in a clean cloth, frequently perfumed and bathed, and the water in which it was washed is drunk for its sin-dispelling qualities.

Next come the symbols of the various sects. Thus the mark of a Siva worshipper is three horizontal lines in the shape of a half-moon, one above the other, representing the trident of the god. It is made of Ganges clay, sandal-wood, or cow-dung ashes, the last symbolising the disintegrating power of the god. The votary of Vishnu is marked with three lines, one perpendicular down the forehead and two oblique meeting at the base, made in Ganges clay or sandal powder, the symbol representing the footstep of the god. The Sáktas, or goddess-worshippers, often do not bear any mark, as the cult is unpopular; when they are marked, they wear a small semicircular line between the eyebrows, with a dot in the middle made of charcoal or lampblack. Other sectaries have marks of their own; but, as Sir G. Birdwood writes,

"considerable latitude is allowed to individual taste and caprice in painting these dots, lines, and circlets; and generally the whole character of a Hindu is betrayed at a glance by the manner in which he is marked on his forehead—whether he is orthodox from conviction, or merely from fashion or caprice; or whether latitudinarian and unbelieving; and in conduct loose or strict; and in temper sober, hard, or gay."

The object of these sectarial marks is based on a form of magic. They are intended to be the outward and visible sign that the wearer is under divine protection, and demons and evil spirits would be well advised not to interfere with him.

Lastly, a form of symbolism which has not as yet been fully investigated is concerned with the marks used in lieu of signatures. In Bengal, according to Mr Gait, a Baishnab, or Vishnu worshipper, has for his sign the bead-necklace of his sect; a carpenter, a hammer; a hill-man, an arrow; and so on. Hindu women use the sign of a ring; Musalmán men, a dagger, and their women a bracelet. Probably this form of symbolism, which utilises the tools or appliances characteristic of the bearer's trade, is more or less common all over the country.

[D'Alviella, "The Migration of Symbols"; Mrs Murray-Aynsley, "Symbolism of the East and West"; Kern, "Manual of Indian Buddhism": J. Wilson, "The Swástika." For Caste Marks, Birdwood "Industrial Arts of India," 97; "Census Report," Central Provinces, 1901, i. 83; Baroda, 1901, i. 122.]

TANK.—The word Tank is used in India to describe two very different kinds of reservoirs; first, the malodorous excavations near villages from which the clay to form the mud walls has been removed. These, when filled with water, are used indiscriminately for the purposes of drinking and ablution. Sanitary officers justly attribute to them much of the cholera and other epidemic disease which ravage the country. Secondly, we have the magnificent artificial reservoirs at sacred places, or those specially constructed for irrigation.

This latter class of reservoirs includes some of the finest native works in the country. They are generally made by embanking a river valley, and the dams are often adorned with *ghauts*,* or flights of steps, *kiosks*,* or temples, which sometimes form as perfect a piece of architectural combination as any presented by the art of the Hindus.

The great artificial reservoirs of India fall into three main groups—those of Madras, the central parts of the Peninsula, and of Rájputána. Of the Madras tanks the finest are generally admitted to be that of Cumbum, in Kurnool, with an area of 15 square miles; that at Gangaikundapur, in Tinnevelli, with an embankment 16 miles long, now partially ruined; that at Rájasingamandalam in Madura, nearly 20 miles round; that of Chembrambakam near Madras, covering some 11 square miles. Mysore has the Sulekere or "Dancing Girl" lake, which is variously described, probably from observations at different seasons, as 20 or 40 miles in circumference. In this province there are no less than 39,000 tanks, or, on an average, more than one to each square mile of the area. They are generally mutually dependent works situated in the same catchment basin, the surplus water from the high-level reservoirs feeding the lower. If the embankments are neglected, sudden floods often cause breaches destructive to life and property. Near Hyderabad, the capital of the Nizam's dominions, is the Pakhal lake, which, Sir R. Temple says, "is probably the largest sheet of water in the Peninsula"; but it does not seem to surpass those already described.

Passing on to the central part of the Peninsula, we find a vast series of irrigation works, remarkable as having been constructed at a time when the resources of the country were limited. They were the work of the early Gond Rájas, the only aboriginal tribe which has ever founded a stable dynasty, and their successors, who called themselves Kshatriyas, or members of the warrior caste. Probably they were built by a liberal use of corvée. Such tanks fall into two classes: first, those in the higher hill-country, where a basin is formed by a dam following the contour of the ground; secondly, those found in the flatter country, where a long low dam surrounds a portion of a gently-sloping plain, in the centre of which is a natural or artificial depression forming a permanent reservoir. Such irrigation tanks are sufficient to provide a two months' water supply for the rice. When the rainy season is over, the bed is often sown with wheat or linseed.

Sir R. Temple thus writes of the Lake Region of Central India:

"An irrigation tank is not a piece of water with regular banks, crowned with rows or avenues of trees, with an artificial dyke and sluices, and with fields around it; but it is an irregular expanse of water; its banks are formed by rugged hills, covered with low forests that fringe the water, where the wild beasts repair to drink; its dykes, mainly shaped out of the spurs from the hills, are thrown athwart the hollows, a part only being formed by masonry; its sluices often consists of chasms or fissures in the rock; its broad surface is often, as the monsoon approaches, lashed into surging and crested waters."

This is much the character of the tanks further north in Bundelkhand, constructed by the Chandella dynasty between A.D. 800 and 1200, or by the earlier Parihár kings. Most of them were not built for irrigation, but as adjuncts to palaces and temples. One of the finest of these is the Barwa Ságar tank in the Jhánsi district, with an embankment three-quarters of a mile in length, and containing two lovely wooded islands.

In Rájputána, along the wild hills of Mhairwára, numerous tanks, built or improved, are due to the genius of Colonel Dixon, one of the early British officials. Others, like the splendid lakes at Debar and Kankrauli in the Udaypur State, are the work of native rulers. One, the Jaysamand lake in this State, is described by Tod as the largest lake in India, with a circumference of 30 miles. Finest of all was the great Bhojpur lake, near Bhopál, which covered an area of 250 square miles. The dam was cut in the fifteenth century by the Muhammadans, and the bed of the old lake is now a fertile plain, traversed by the Indian

Midland Railway. Marble embankments, pavilions, and shrines decorate these splendid reservoirs.

The distinction between the work of the earlier and later native builders is clearly marked in the shape of the reservoir. The oldest have their greatest length from east to west, the later from north to south. The Musalmáns, who did little tank-building, chose the earlier form.

In beauty few surpass the Kankariya tank at Ahmadábád, which, says Pietro della Valle,

"hath about the middle an Island, with a little Garden, to which they go by a handsome Bridge of many Arches, very well built; upon which, I believe, two Indian Coaches may go abreast. Indeed these Indian Lakes are goodly things, and may be reckon'd amongst the most remarkable Structures of the World."

Many of them are naturally sacred, like that at Amritsar, "The pool of immortality," the headquarters of the Sikh faith. At Tháneswar, in Umballa, during eclipses the waters of all the holy pools of India collect, and the happy pilgrim secures the concentrated merit of a visit to many a shrine. Others have all sorts of wondrous qualities. Some, discovered by a Rája affected with leprosy, cure that disease; others are so deep that they reach down to Patála, or the nether world; others have underground connection with the Ganges, or some sacred river; some of them hold enormous treasures in their depths, guarded by a dragon. As the well is wedded before its waters are held fit to fructify the crops, so the tank is solemnly married to a plantain tree. On no ornament of his town or village does the Hindu look with greater pride than on reservoirs like this, and no sight is pleasanter at dawn than to watch the files of graceful girls passing and repassing with water-pots on their heads; the Bráhman muttering his prayers at the shrine close by; the Fakír telling his beads; the great, soft-eyed cattle drinking at the *Ghaut** reserved for them; the men bathing, smoking, gossiping on the banks. Like the village well, it is the centre of rural social life, and the name of its builder is handed down with grateful honours from one generation to another.

TATTOOING.—"Not one great country," says Mr Darwin, "can be named, from the Polar regions in the North to New Zealand in the South, in which the aborigines do not tattoo themselves."

There appears, however, to be no evidence of tattooing among the Indo-Aryans, but it prevailed, as well as a modification of the practice in the form of wood-staining, among the Indo-Germanic peoples. The habit of face-staining persists among the women of Tibet. In India, when we come to the early age of Buddhism in the days of Asoka, we find it frequently depicted in the bas-reliefs. From a comparison of the forms then used with those of the present day, General Cunningham concluded that the builders were of Dravidian race. Marco Polo states that in his day people used to come from Upper India to Zayton, now Chinchew in Fokien, to be tattooed; and Nicolo Conti, writing of the Irawadi valley in the fifteenth century, says:

"All the inhabitants, as well men as women, puncture their flesh with pins of iron, and rub into these punctures pigments which cannot be obliterated, and so they remain painted for ever."

Some Burmese women, it is true, do not now tattoo, but among their Khyen neighbours, who have more carefully preserved the primitive tradition, it is almost altogether confined to females.

It is little in favour with the Nairs of Malabar, and in Travancore it is said to have come in under Moghul influence as late as the seventeenth century. But in most parts of the country the habit prevails to the present day. Some ethnologists have treated it as a survival of the rites of blood-letting common to many savage tribes at the worship of the gods, at marriage, and other ceremonies. Mr J. G. Frazer has suggested that the tattooing of women is a relic of the custom of beating girls as a test of endurance, and to drive away the demons which surround them. The symbol used is very often that of a protective deity, and in some parts it is regarded as a sort of initiation performed when a girl comes of age. In Bengal a respectable Hindu will not take water from the hands of a girl who does not bear the mark on her forehead. Generally, however, at the present day, it seems to be purely ornamental. Among the Chins of Burma the beauty of a woman is guaged by the number of her tattoo marks, and it is believed by them that the object of so marking the faces of women was to conceal their attractions, and render them less liable to abduction by hostile tribes. In some cases there are traces of distinct tribal marks which may have been intended to distinguish members of one group from those of another. Such is the case among the Aos of Assam, who define tribal distinctions by special marks on the arms and calves of the leg. Among the Red Karens of Burma there is a suggestion of totemism. Each of them bears the rising sun, "the crest of his nobility," tattooed on his back.

In Northern India the art of tattooing is specialised by the Gipsy tribes. Tavernier says of the Banjára women that,

"from the waist upwards, they tattoo their skin with flowers, like as when one applies cupping glasses, and they paint these flowers divers colours with the juice of roots, in such a manner as it seems as though their skin was a flowered fabric."

The Gipsy women nowadays who practise the art carry about with them a set of patterns which they submit to their patrons, and those which seem most becoming are selected. The operation is performed with two or three English needles, the points of which project only a short distance from a sheathing of thread. The pigment used is indigo or vermilion, dissolved in human milk, or the leaf of a common weed (*Eclipta alba*) is rubbed on the punctures, producing a deep bluish black. An officer riding through a village will often hear the dismal howls of some wretched damsel on whom the operation is being performed. There is a widespread idea that, while her clothes do not go with a women to the next world, her tattoo marks survive death. Low caste women believe that if they die without these marks their parents will not recognise them in heaven; others say that Parameshwar, the Great God, when they arrive in heaven, asks them to show these signs as a proof that they have lived on earth; if they are wanting, he causes the woman to be reborn as an evil spirit, or has her dragged through thorns to supply the marks which she neglected to assume in this world.

Among the jungle tribes, some, like the Bhíls of Rájputána, are not addicted to the practice; and among the Kisáns of Bengal a woman who decorates herself in this way is expelled from the tribe. But every Gond woman tattooes her legs as far as she allows them to be seen with indigo or gunpowder blue, and the figures they execute are the only form of ornamental art attempted by these people. Further east the Juáng and Kharria women make three parallel lines on the forehead, the outer lines terminating in a crook with two lines on each temple.

While in continental India the tattooing of males is practically unknown, in Burma every male in his boyhood is tattooed from waist to knees; in other words, he has a pair of breeches tattooed on him.

"The pattern," says Sir H. Yule, "is a fanciful medley of animals and arabesques, but is scarcely distinguishable, save as a general tint, except on a fair skin."

Women tattoo themselves between the eyes and on the lips and tongue as a love-charm. The mark is often made in some place not easily seen, to avoid the imputation that the wearer is an old maid on the look-out for a husband. In Rangoon, Sir J. G. Scott says, when a woman is seen tattooed, it means that she wants an Englishman for her husband.

But the talismanic idea is the most potent. Burmese boys have a special tattoo which prevents them from feeling pain when caned; all men are tattooed with cabalistic words or numbers to protect them from some special ailment, or, more frequently, to save the wearer from bullet wound or sword-cut. These charms to secure invulnerability must be tattooed in red above the waist, with a mixture of vermilion and human fat, and, to give extra potency, the candidate must hold a bit of human flesh between his teeth while the operation is being performed. A Musalmán is forbidden to use indigo to form the mark.

Among tribes like the Nágas of Assam tattooing is a mark of dignity, and without the mark no youth is allowed to marry. The intention seems to be to give additional fierceness to the warrior's appearance. The disfigurement is carried to such an extent that it gives them an unnatural darkness of complexion, and that fearful look which results when a white man blackens his face.

It has also been used as a form of punishment. In the days of native rule an offender was often led about mounted on an ass, with the name of his crime tattooed in blue upon his forehead. Under the authority of the Burmese kings incorrigible offenders were tattooed with a circle on the cheek, or the title of their offence was inscribed on their breast.

Tooth-staining, a kindred practice, used to prevail among the Kadus of Burma. It is said to have come to them from the Chins, who state that, like tattooing, it was introduced to disguise the beauty of their women.

[Shway Yoe, "The Burman," i. 46; "Census Report," Mysore, 1901, i. 556, with photographs of markings; Baroda, i. 526, with drawings; Burma, i. 146; and a series of articles in "Indian Antiquary," 1892, 1897, 1902, 1904.]

TEA.—Tea is said to be mentioned in Chinese literature as early as 2700 B.C., but there is no reference to the infusion till the fourth century of our era. Thence it spread to Japan in the ninth, and to Europe in the sixteenth century. The earliest authentic account of it in

Europe is found in 1545 in Ramusio's Introduction to Marco Polo's "Travels," who says he heard of it from a Persian merchant, Háji Mahomed. It probably reached Europe in the first instance through the Portuguese, who had dealings with the Chinese from the beginning of the fourteenth century.

Much controversy has arisen on the question who first discovered tea in Assam. Sir G. Watt, after a full discussion of the evidence, is inclined to assign the honour of founding the Indian tea industry to Sir Joseph Banks; next to Colonel Kyd, who in 1780 procured and cultivated the first China tea ever grown in India; then to David Scott, who acted on the suggestion of Banks, and aroused interest in the matter. But without the active aid of the Governor-General, Lord W. Bentinck, who left nothing undone to acclimatise the best Chinese plants, no success would have been attained.

> "But," Sir G. Watt writes, "if credit of an exceptional character be necessary for any one of the pioneers who have first seen the indigenous Assam plant, there would seem little doubt that credit must be given to Major R. Bruce."

His brother, Mr C. Bruce, first started the cultivation in 1838. Among those to whom the development of the industry in later years is specially due, the names of Mr R. Fortune, who studied the plant in China, and Dr Jameson, who experimented in Dehra Dún, are prominent.

Sir G. Watt regards Manipur and the Indo-Burman and Chinese adjacent regions as the true home of the plant and concludes that it was introduced from that district into Assam and Cachár. He suggests that the crude method of burying the leaves in the ground so as to produce the required fermentation, as practised at the present time by the Sháns of Upper Burma and on the borders of Manipur, may be the primitive mode of preparation, and that the danger of decomposition when tea was carried long distances may have suggested the habit of baking it into bricks. This brick tea, to be used, requires to be softened by boiling, and hence may have arisen the Tibetan method of eating the tea leaves mixed with flour and butter after they have been boiled. The Chinese, he supposes, may have improved on this process by preparing an infusion from the leaves, instead of eating them. This theory is to some extent corroborated by the earlier writers, who express astonishment that the Chinese only pour boiling water over the tea, instead of either eating the leaves or drinking the infusion. In the hills about Kashmír cardamoms are used instead of sugar to flavour tea, and in this region shepherds smoke tea, instead of either eating it or drinking the infusion.

It would thus seem that the use of tea spread from the Burman region both to China and India. As there is no mention in early Chinese literature of eating the leaves or drinking the infusion, it is possible that the tea-plant, or some allied Camellia, may have been used for some purposes different from that for which it is now grown, and this suggestion is to some extent corroborated by the fact that we have no evidence that the properties of the plant were known to the enlightened people of India.

It is certainly remarkable that even at the present day tea is so little used in India. Musalmáns occasionally drink it, but more as a medicine or stimulant in malarial fever than as a part of the daily meal. If it were generally used by the village population, it would obviate some of the dangers resulting from a foul water supply, and would tend to check malarial fever, the chief source of mortality. There seems some reason to believe that the prejudice against it is being gradually overcome. If the use of tea became general throughout the vast native population, the conditions of the industry would be revolutionised.

Even when natives use tea, they seldom succeed in preparing it. They do not use boiling water, stew it too long, use inferior tea, smoked milk, or add sugar in excess. The result is a mixture which the European who has ever been invited to tea by a native gentleman recalls with horror. The Uzbegs of Central Asia, Burnes tells us, mix it with salt and fat. This method, if it was ever familiar to the Moghuls in their original home, was abandoned by them in India. But some of the modes of preparation still employed by the border tribes seem to us equally barbarous. In Spiti, a district of the Western Himálaya, the tea is placed in a pipkin with a little cold water and some soda, and then boiled; some hot water is next added, and the hot tea, with a little butter and milk, is poured into the tea-churn. It is then well churned and served up with the froth on. The tea of this region comes from Lhása, and is used only by the richer classes, who dislike Indian teas. In Kashmír, tea from India or brick tea from Ladakh is largely used. The Samovar, or Russian tea-urn, the model of which was brought many years ago by a travelling merchant, is now common in most Kashmíri houses. The Lepchas of Sikhim, who cannot afford tea, drink a decoction of the leaves of the maple, wild vine, and other trees and herbs.

Another curious preparation is the Le'h-pet, or pickled tea of Burma. According to Sir J. G. Scott, the leaves which form the base of this preparation are not those of the tea-plant, but of a shrub called *Elæodendron orientale*, or *E. persicum*. There are, however, reasons for believing that this is incorrect, and that tea-leaves are often used. There are two ways of serving it. In the first the leaves are prepared with a little oil, salt, garlic, or assafœtida, and eaten in small quantities after dinner as we eat cheese. It is believed to promote digestion, but Europeans find in it little more than an overpowering flavour of assafœtida. It is also used on ceremonial occasions, as at the conclusion of a lawsuit, where the bill of costs is always rounded off with a charge for "pickled tea." By the second method the coarse leaves of the first crop are dried and steamed over a cauldron, a process which removes a certain amount of tannin and glucose. The compressed leaves are then thrown into pits or small masonry wells, and weighted down. The result is "salad" or "pickled tea."

[Watt, "Economic Dictionary," ii. 70; vi. Pt. III. 417; Shway Yoe, "The Burman," i. 357; "Upper Burma Gazetteer," Pt. I. vol. ii. 357.]

TEMPLE.—The gods of the Aryans dwelled not in temples made with hands; in fact, the Aryans were not builders in stone. Most of their structures were of wood, to which was perhaps sometimes added a masonry plinth, and hence the early history of architecture in India, if we except the rude stone monuments, is a blank. It was only when the relic-worship was adopted into Buddhism that the Stúpa came into existence. This accounts for the absence of great ancient temples in Northern India; they have not been destroyed; more probably they never existed. When Bráhmanism overcame Buddhism, the interval was too short up to the time of the Musalmán invasion to allow the creation of a distinct style, or the erection of stately buildings. Thus the Indo-Aryan style was adopted by the Hindus directly from that of the Buddhists and Jains, and the buildings, except in special cases like those of Khajuráhu and Bhuvanesvara, were seldom magnificent in size. It has been suggested that the small size of the modern North Indian temple is the result of the iconoclasm of Aurangzeb. More probably the builders followed the earlier tradition.

In South India the case was different. Here Bráhmanic Hinduism had a longer existence, and the resources of the powerful local dynasties were devoted to temple-building. But even here these splendid buildings show the course of their development in the smallness of the central shrine. Many of them, like Seringham, for instance, grew up round a petty village shrine by a process of incrustation, one grand court, or boundary wall, or gateway being added by the piety of successive generations. In the same way the magnificent Egyptian temple of Karnak grew by successive additions to the original nucleus. The parent shrine, in fact, was considered too holy to be moved, and the god, like the men who worship him, desires privacy. Further, there is in Hinduism no congregational worship like that which fills the cathedrals of Europe. It is only when the god deigns to go abroad in procession that his votaries, as a body, have a chance of observing and venerating him. The devotion paid at the ordinary temple is a personal not a congregational act. The Bráhman acts as proxy for the worshippers, and needs no space for his ministrations. The permanence of the original petty shrine round which the temple grew is secured by the feeling that to demolish the existing house of the god would destroy the merit of the original builder, and bring no gain to the restorer. The god, who in bygone days took shelter in the rude menhir or pillar-stone of a half-forgotten race, still abhors the sound of hammer and chisel, and prefers to abide, as he was wont to do, in the uncarved stone or shabby cell. This incrustation of buildings round a petty shrine is also a characteristic of modern Buddhism. The great pagoda at Pegu is said to have been originally only one cubit high.

The most primitive temple is found in the rude erections of the forest tribes. In the highlands of Central India the Bhíl or Gond sometimes raises a rough straw shed over the fetish stone or rude image stained with red ocre which represents the tribal god. More usually he is content to pile these stones or fetishes under the shade of a sacred tree, and here the simple worship is performed.

But it was not from shrines like these that the modern temple was developed. Some have held that the temple had its origin in the tomb or relic-shrine of the Buddhists, and the case at Jhánsi noticed by General Sleeman has been quoted as an example.

> "The family of the chief," he says, "do not build tombs, and that now raised over the place where the late prince was burned is dedicated as a temple to Siva, and was made merely with a view to secure the place from all danger of profanation."

This may account for the origin of some temples, but the explanation of growth of the modern temple lies in another direction.

The Chaitya, or cave-temple, of the Buddhists has been regarded by some authorities as the parent of the modern temple. These remarkable structures are distributed in a curious way, nine-tenths of those known being in the

Bombay Presidency. As for the remainder, there are two unimportant groups in Bengal, those of Behár and Cuttack; one in Madras, and some insignificant examples in the Panjáb and Afghánistán. They have no connection with similar constructions in Egypt, and their distribution is determined simply by the suitability of the rock formation for excavations of this kind.

The Chaitya in character presupposes a still older style of wooden building, the details of which, in construction and carving, it closely follows. This is specially the case with the Bráhmanical cave-temples, which generally copied buildings, while the Buddhist caves were always caves and nothing more. In form the Chaitya much resembles the Basilica of Europe. There is a long, lofty nave, with ogival roof, terminating in a semi-circular apse, which forms a choir occupied by an altar or relic-shrine. Two lateral aisles meet behind the choir. What would be the west end of a Christian cathedral has a great horse-shoe window, and beyond it an imposing façade, with wooden galleries and balconies for musicians. So careful were the Buddhist builders to follow the tradition of a wooden structure, that they even inserted an inner carved roof. The finest of these Chaityas is that of Kárli, the date of which is fixed by Mr Fergusson at 78 B.C.; but the series really starts from the time of Asoka, about 250. That at Badámi was built in the seventh century of our era. In some examples the animal capitals show a strong foreign, probably Persian element.

"The Hindu temple," says General Cunningham, with perhaps some exaggeration, "is generally a sort of architectural pastry, a huge collection of ornamental fritters huddled together, either with or without keeping, while the Jain temple is usually a vast forest of pillars, made to look as unlike one another as possible by some paltry differences in their petty details. On the other hand, the Kashmírian fanes are distinguished by the graceful elegance of their outlines, by the massive boldness of their parts, and by the happy propriety of their decorations."

He believes that several of the Kashmír forms and

many of the details were borrowed from the Greeks of Kábul, while the arrangement of the interior and the relative proportion of the parts were of Hindu origin.

To describe the three styles of temple defined by Mr Fergusson as the Dravidian, Chalukyan, and Indo-Aryan is beyond our limits. The Dravidian, or southern style, is characterised by massiveness, by the absence of the arch, which is replaced by a brick vault, and by the great Gopuras, or storied gates, which give entrance to the enclosure. The Chalukyan, originating in a kingdom occupying what is now the Dominions of the Nizam, has more ornamentation and higher spires. The Indo-Aryan of the north is less massive and more highly ornamented, the modern Jain style adopting the bulbous dome of the Musalmáns. The most marked distinction is that the northern spire has curved, the southern straight lines.

A great modern temple, like that of Juggurnaut, to quote Sir W. Hunter,

"consists of four chambers, opening one into the other. The first is the Hall of Offerings, where the bulkier oblations are made, only a small quantity of choice food being admitted into the inner shrine. The second is the Pillared Hall, for the musicians and dancing-girls. The third is the Hall of Audience, in which the pilgrims assemble to gaze upon the god. The fourth is the Sanctuary itself, surmounted by a lofty conical tower."

Temples differ so widely in style and feeling that it is impossible to class them in order of merit. The Black Pagoda of Orissa has been considered to be the finest extant Hindu temple, and Mr Fergusson is of opinion that here is no roof in India where the same play of light and shade is found with an equal amount of richness and constructive propriety, nor one that sits so gracefully on the base that supports it. That of Govind Deva at Brindaban is perhaps the most impressive religious building that Hindu art has ever produced, at least in Northern India. As groups of splendid buildings, more graceful in design and less ponderous than their South Indian rivals, nothing surpasses the Jain temples at Palitána. For grandeur of scale and lavishness of ornament, the great fanes of Madras, like Rameshvaram, Chillambaram, Madura, and Tanjore, are unrivalled. The only temple in this style in North India is that recently erected by the Seth bankers of Mathura at Brindaban.

[For the Buddhist Buildings, Cunningham, "Mahábodhi," "Bharhut," "Sánchi"; for Hindu Temples generally, Fergusson, "Architecture," chaps. iv., v., vi.; Cave Temples, Fergusson-Burgess, "Cave Temples of India"; Orissa, Hunter, "Orissa"; Mathura, Growse, "Mathura," chaps. vi., ix., x.]

THREAD, SACRED.—The use of a thread, with various mystic knots, is common to the folk-lore of many races. Everywhere we meet the idea that a knotted cord tied round a joint cures a sprain; fastened round a child's neck is a remedy for cough and similar ailments. The Rájput father binds round the arm of his new-born son a string made of the sacred *Doob* * grass, to ward off evil influences. The sacred cord of the twice-born castes of India seems to be based on the same principle. Like the magic circle, it forms a barrier across which demons cannot pass and interfere with the rites of the priest. Hence it came to be the outer mark of the higher Hindu castes.

The first cords used were probably strips from the skin of the sacrificed victim. The material out of which the early cord of the Bráhman was made appears to have been the Kusa, or sacred grass; while for the Rájput the Bow-string hemp (*Sansevieria zeylanica*), and for the Vaisya, or merchant, wool were prescribed. Later, Manu directed that the Bráhman's cord should be made of Karpasa, which was probably the fibre of the *Gossypium arboreum*, still planted near temples and hermitages, and used for this purpose.

The thread is made in various ways in different parts of the country. Among the Madras Bráhmans, who are most careful in such matters, it is of fine country-grown cotton, not foreign, and spun by hand. Three very fine threads are twisted by a Bráhman into a single cord, 16 feet long. He then squats on the ground, winds it thrice round his knees, and fastens the ends in a special knot known as that of Brahma. This is the sacred triple thread, worn over the left shoulder and hanging loose under the left arm. It is blessed by having the holy text, the Gáyatri, recited over it: "Let us meditate on the excellent glory of the divine, vivifying Sun; may He enlighten our understanding!"

In North India the four fingers of the hand are closed, and a thread is wound back and front over them 96 times. This thread forms one strand of the cord, three of them making it complete. During worship of the gods it remains over the left shoulder; when the wearer is unclean, or when he performs the rites for the dead, he shifts it from its usual position to the right shoulder.

The thread is girded on a boy between his eighth and twelfth year, and marks his initiation into full religious rights and obligations, and his assumption of all the authority and duty of a Bráhman. As the thread is assumed, the boy makes a pretence of leaving the house to commence the ascetic stage of a Bráhman's life, but he is persuaded to return and live as a layman. The whole rite, with its endless purifications, sacrifices, and symbolism, is a piece of primitive mimetic magic.

Nowadays the wearing of the cord has lost much of its significance, because many castes which have no real claim to be regarded as twice-born assume it. In the Panjáb, even the barbers of castes entitled to wear it follow the example of their employers. They will not deign to use the single cord to which their inferior status alone entitles them, but strut about with the cord on the model of that worn by their masters. Here, too, the Jogi Fakírs wear a cord, but it is made of three strands of black wool, each of eight threads, and it is worn not over the shoulder, but round the neck. Round the waist they carry a similar cord, and to it is attached a sort of whistle made of deer-horn, whose weird note, heard as they pray or meditate in the night season, scares the evil spirits which would mar their devotions.

The Pársi Kushti is a thin woollen cord of seventy-two

threads, each representing one of the chapters of their Scripture. It is passed round the waist three times, and tied with four knots, two in front, and two behind, while a hymn is chanted. At the tying of the first knot the wearer says:

"There is only one God, and no other is to be compared to him." At the second: "The religion given by Zoroaster is true." At the third: "Zoroaster is the true Prophet, who derived his mission from God." At the fourth and last: "Perform good actions, and abstain from those that are evil."

When he gets out of bed, the orthodox Pársi unfolds the cord round his waist, turns his face to the Sun, and, giving the cord three vigorous flaps, cries out: "Defeat to Shaitán, the Evil One!" When he dies, the cord is tied round his waist by a relative, and the corpse is then made over to the professional watchers of the dead.

A curious development of the Indian sacred cord is the Sa-lwé of Burma, which was the only approach made by the late dynasty in the direction of European orders of knighthood. It is described by Sir J. G. Scott as a sort of shoulder-belt formed of chains of gold, fastened in four places, in shields or bosses, and worn over the shoulder like an officer's sash. The number of strings or threads marked the rank in the order, and when King Thibaw sent one to Mr Gladstone, then Prime Minister, it had twelve strings.

[For Madras, Fawcett, in "Bulletin of Madras Museum," iii. No. I. 41, 82; "Census Report," Panjáb 1901, i. 130, 338; Dosabhai Framji Karaka, "History of the Parsis," i. 168; "Upper Burma Gazetteer." ii. Pt. I. 134.]

THUGGEE.—It has been remarked that an interesting book might be written on the crimes in India which have been "repressed," only to appear again in some novel form. This is the case with Thuggee, which, when put down by General Sleeman and the officers who worked with him, has appeared again in the form perhaps quite as dangerous of Road Poisoning. [*See* POISONING.] Both these forms of crime, however, seem to have gone on side by side from a very early period.

The early Hindus were familiar with the use of the Nága-pása, or "dragon noose." We find in the Epics that the demons who fight with the gods are thus armed. Strangling of travellers prevailed from a very early time. In the Ellora cave-temple, which was constructed about 760 A.D., we have a Thug represented strangling a Bráhman who is worshipping the emblem of Siva, whereupon the god comes to his rescue and kicks down the Thug. Fíroz Sháh, near the end of the fourteenth century, captured some thousand Thugs near Delhi, and in his usual merciful way contented himself with deporting them to Bengal.

Early in the last century, to quote Sleeman,

> "the annually returning tide of murder swept unsparingly over the whole face of India, from the Sutlej to the sea. One narrow district alone was free, the Concan beyond the Ghauts, whither they never penetrated."

One gang lived close to his court-house, and he often encamped in the grove near Narsinghpur, one of the greatest places of slaughter in India.

The river Thugs committed fearful slaughter among the boating population.

> "Two hundred and fifty boats full of river Thugs," writes Sir J. Hooker, "in crews of fifteen, infested the Ganges between Benares and Calcutta during five months of the year, on pretence of conveying pilgrims. Travellers along the bank were tracked, and offered a passage, which, if refused in the first boat, was probably accepted in some other. At a given signal the crew rushed in, doubled up the decoyed victim, broke his back, and threw him into the river, where floating corpses are too numerous to elicit even an exclamation."

All along the main routes Sepoys returning home on leave, merchants conveying treasure, dancing-girls on their way to marriage-feasts were ruthlessly murdered. Sleeman's Thuggee map of Oudh shows no less than

274 murder stations; one man confessed that he had been engaged in 931 cases.

These gangs of assassins regularly took the field after the Dasehra Festival at the close of the rainy season. They acted, as they believed, under the sanction and with the aid of the goddess Káli, who has her most noted shrine at Bindáchal, near Mirzapur, where the Vindhyan hills overshadow the Ganges valley. Here the *Roomál*,* or handkerchief used in strangling, and the mattock with which the grave of the victim was dug, were solemnly blessed by the temple priests, who received a liberal share of the plunder. The Musalmán Thugs in the same way owed allegiance to the Saint Nizám-ud-dín Auliya, whose beautiful tomb is one of the chief architectural gems of old Delhi. One class of these Thugs, known as the Tasmabáz, or those who played the game of "Stick and garter" familiar at country fairs, where the player has to push a stick into the exact central fold of a twisted strap, are said to have owed their skill to the teaching of an English soldier named Creagh.

At length, when the matter was taken up by our Government, informers were induced to reveal the organisation of the gangs. They were hunted down by the police like wild beasts. Many were executed, and the less guilty were interned for life. By these operations this form of crime disappeared for a time. How far these miscreants were connected with the road-poisoners of our day has been much debated. James Forbes, a good authority in such matters, was of opinion that the more experienced Thugs used the cord, the less intelligent poison; and Dr Chevers believed that when the raid began, the Thugs abandoned strangling and had recourse to drugs. But while these two classes of crime are in some respects similar, there is a clear difference in the methods. The road-poisoners formed small isolated gangs, and never possessed the elaborate organisation characteristic of the Thugs. It is only Thevenot who describes the Thugs of his day taking women with them to entice travellers. This Sleeman denies to have been the habit of the Thugs, and it is probable that Thevenot's Thugs were really poisoners. Thugs, again, were specially directed to spare women, while the chief victims of the poisoners were dancing-girls. Lastly, there is no word for poison in the Thug argot. A connection between these two classes of crime has been traced in the custom of sacrificing to a god or making offerings to a saint before undertaking an enterprise. But this is a habit with other classes of criminals, and has no resemblance to the organised religious meetings of the Thugs.

The methods of the modern poisoner much resemble those of the Thug. Sometimes he is accompanied by a family, real or pretended; sometimes he masquerades as a wandering Fakír, or to facilitate his operations as a Bráhman cook, from whose hands any traveller may eat. Sometimes he pretends to be a pilgrim tout, or a marriage agent in search for a bride, or he hangs on to a band of dancing-girls, or a party of Kábul merchants bringing Turkestán horses for sale. His chief hunting-ground is the *Serái*, or native inn, where he offers to assist travellers in procuring or cooking food, and is thus enabled to drug their cakes or rice. He almost always uses Dhatúra or Stramonium, occasionally Nux vomica. General Sleeman believed that the road-poisoners always intended to take life; but Colonel Hervey denies this, and asserts that their real object was to promote insensibility sufficient to cover their escape. This is probably the intention of the criminals of our time; but often, through a mistake in the amount of the dose, fatal results follow the administration of the drug. The extent of their operations may be judged by the case of Sharaf-ud-dín, the most noted poisoner in recent times. He had been a policeman, and learnt the trade in jail. He confessed to sixty-nine cases of poisoning, and said that he had committed hundreds, the details of which he could not remember.

The extension of railway travelling has, by providing facilities for escape, greatly assisted this class of crime. It is checked only by the constant efforts of a well-organised detective service, and when repressed in one direction soon reappears elsewhere. If the vigilance of our police were relaxed, it would soon become as serious an evil as the old associations of the Thugs.

[Thornton, "Illustrations of the History and Practices of the Thugs"; Sleeman, "Report on Depredations committed by the Thug Gangs"; Hervey, "Some Records of Crime"; Arthur [A. T. Crawford], "Reminiscences of an Indian Police Official"; "Calcutta Review," xxxv. 371; Wilson, "History of British India," iii. 277; Chevers, "Indian Medical Jurisprudence," 576.]

TIGER.—The earliest home of the tiger was probably the marshes and heavy jungle of Bengal. The Rig-veda, which seems to have been compiled in the Panjáb, does not mention the animal, and it is not till the time of the Atharva-veda, written when the Aryans had reached the Ganges valley, that his name occurs. It was in comparatively late geological times that he reached South India, his absence from Ceylon proving that he migrated southwards after the island was severed from the mainland. Nor is he mentioned in the Avesta, one of the ancient Iránic Scriptures, and it was probably at a relatively late period that he spread to West and North Asia and into the Malay Peninsula.

There is no well-known animal about whom more diverse impressions prevail. For instance, Captain Forsyth, whose book is a classic on the subject, asserts that the tiger, in killing his victims, seizes by the nape of the neck, and uses his paws to hold the animal and give a purchase for the wrench that dislocates its vertebræ. Mr Sanderson, on the contrary, depending on the evidence of herdsmen, believes that he sometimes seizes his victim by the nape, but that this is not his usual way. He does not spring upon his prey, but,

"clutching the bullock's forequarters with his paws, one being generally over the shoulder, he seizes the throat in his jaws from underneath and turns it upwards and over, sometimes springing to the far side in doing so, to throw the bullock over and give the wrench which dislocates the neck."

This view is accepted by Mr Blanford; but Sir S. Baker, on native evidence, seems to believe that the tiger springs on the animal, and,

"when well fastened upon the crest, by fixing his teeth in the back of the neck at the first onset, continues its spring so as to pass over the animal attacked. This wrenches the neck suddenly round, and as the animal struggles the dislocation is easily effected."

From the experience of the present writer, Sanderson's account seems the more probable. The idea, again, that he sucks the blood of his victim is now quite abandoned.

About the maximum size of tigers also there is much difference of opinion, resulting partly from the modes of measurement, and partly from the varying dimensions of the animal throughout the country. Sir J. Fayrer fixes the size of the full-grown male at from 9 to 12 feet or 12 feet 2 inches; of the tigress, from 8 to 10 feet, or very rarely 11 feet. The old joke of "twelve-foot tigers" is shown to be not an over-statement of facts by the instances recorded by Sir J. Fayrer and Mr Sterndale of animals exceeding that measurement. But other good observers record an average of much smaller animals. Captain Forsyth says that a tiger 10 feet 1 inch is unusually long, and that the skin of such a beast will stretch to 13 to 14 feet; Sir S. Baker fixes the average at 9 feet 6 inches, which agrees with the experience of the present writer in the United Provinces. The largest specimens killed by Mr Sanderson were 9 feet 6 inches for a male, and 8 feet 4 inches for a female. On the whole, in North India, except perhaps in parts of Bengal where the beast attains a larger size, a tiger measuring 10 feet by a cord stretching from tip of nose to end of tail, and following the lines of the carcass, is a fine specimen.

A "kill" by a tiger can generally be distinguished from one by a leopard. The latter makes for the forequarter, drinks the blood from the throat-vessels, and tears out the heart, liver, and lungs. The tiger eats the hindquarters first, does not drink the blood nor tear open the pleura when he makes his first meal on the "kill." If undisturbed on a second or third visit, he devours the entire carcass. A tigress with well-grown cubs will eat the animal in a single meal. According to Captain Forsyth, a tiger will kill an ox about once every five days; if very hungry and undisturbed, he will eat both hindquarters the first night, and will return and finish the beast by the third day.

The area over which a tiger ranges varies according to the character of the jungle and the abundance of game or cattle. In Bengal, where he easily finds the cool damp reed-beds which are his favourite shelter in the hot weather, and where deer, wild pigs, and domestic cattle are abundant, he wanders little. But on the arid Vindhyan hills or the hot plateau of the Deccan, where game, water, and shade are scanty, he will sometimes habitually cover in his nightly wanderings an area of 40 square miles or more. In such districts the difficulty of bringing him to bag is largely increased.

Authorities differ widely as to the power which the tiger possesses of dragging animals over a fence or palisade. Colonel Walter Campbell records a case of a tiger jumping clean over a 6-foot hedge of prickly pear with a bullock in his jaws; not a twig of the hedge was broken. Sir S. Baker believes such tales incredible:

"I have heard it positively stated by persons who should have known better that a tiger can carry off a native cow simply through the strength of his jaws and neck. This is ridiculous, as the height of the cow exceeds that of the tiger, therefore a portion of the body must drag on the ground."

On the other hand, Sanderson writes:

"The enormous muscular power of the tiger is shown by the way he can transport large carcasses of oxen or buffaloes over rough ground, up and down steep banks and through thick bushes. He sometimes completely lifts the body off the ground."

He mentions a case in which a bullock weighing about 400 lbs. was thus carried for 300 yards. This is, however, very different from jumping, with the victim in his jaws, over a 6-foot fence. But Mr Webber, a careful observer, speaks of a tiger jumping with a cow over a deep ravine 8 or 10 feet wide.

Many causes contribute to turn a tiger into a man-eater. Sometimes he is an animal too fat, heavy, disabled by old age or crippled by wounds, and thus loses the activity necessary to catch wild pigs or deer, his normal food; so he takes to man-killing, because it is an easier form of sport. A few years ago, in the Mirzapur district, a tiger took to man-killing, because, in the course of a beat, a random bullet broke his larger teeth and rendered him powerless to capture game. If the animal be a tigress, she sometimes kills men because she has to bring up a family of cubs in a district where game is scarce. As Captain Forsyth pointed out, the districts in which man-eating is most prevalent are those where cattle are sent to graze for only a part of the year; they keep down the game supply, and when they depart the tigers have to kill men or starve. Where cattle are to be found all the year round, tigers rarely take to man-killing. But once a tiger acquires the habit, the ease with which he can procure food, and perhaps its superiority to his ordinary diet, confirms him in the practice. When a tiger becomes a man-killer, no animal is so crafty and none so often baffles the sportsman. General Douglas Hamilton tells of such a tiger in South India which evaded him for years, and was finally killed by a European, who followed up the trail immediately after the beast had slain a woman drawing water at a stream. It was known to have killed two hundred human beings. Even more destructive was the Himálayan tiger, said to be the son of a man-eating mother, slain by Mr Webber after it had killed some two or three hundred men, women, and children. Sir M. Grant-Duff tells how, on a railway in North Arcot, the pointsman had at one time to be immured in a cage to protect him from tigers, thus reversing the usual order of things.

The days of great tiger bags have passed away with

the retirement of the animal to the more inaccessible swamps and jungles. But, for the present at least, there is no reason to fear that the breed will become extinct. In the dense marshes and reed-beds of Bengal and the Tarái, and in the rough country of Central India, with large areas of almost impenetrable scrub jungle, the beast will doubtless long survive. For these two areas two different methods of sport are necessary. In Bengal and the Tarái the sportsman depends on a line of howdah elephants, reinforced by a number of pack-animals, which on the announcement of a "kill," endeavour to beat a large area of grass or swamp, and finally surround the beast. This method is impossible in the Central Indian tract. Here, as a preliminary measure, the position of the tiger must be fixed by "tying up" a number of young buffaloes in likely places, such as the bed of a ravine close to which there is a supply of water. In warm weather especially, a gorged tiger, unless he be a very experienced beast who has been driven on some previous occasion, seldom wanders far. All likely exits from his lair must be guarded by *Mucháns* *, or platforms, and the tiger is then beaten towards the rifles by a large gang of coolies provided with drums, *cholera horns* * and other "musical" instruments. The danger is that the tiger, if he understands the game, may break back through the coolies and injure some in his retreat, or may slink up some smaller ravine and escape without passing a Muchán. This last manœuvre is counteracted by posting men as "stops" on trees along the higher ground, who are instructed merely to tap the branches as the animal approaches. Many sportsmen in Central India have habitually killed tigers on foot, or with no more protection than the shelter of a bush or rock at the entrance of the ravine. It is only in sport of this kind, and, in particular, by yielding to the temptation of following up a wounded tiger on foot, that fatal accidents occur. As sport, the Bengal method of beating up a tiger with elephants is infinitely superior to shooting him from a Muchán. The interest of the latter form of sport consists in the fact that no two tigers break in the same way. One may charge past the rifles with a roar, another will slink through grass or bamboo, the shades and colours of which admirably match his stripes, and make it often difficult to detect his movements. Even when he is seen it is not easy to kill him. The bullet must strike him fairly in one of the chief organs —brain, heart, or lungs; and such is the vitality of the beast, that a wound in the belly or hindquarters never stops him, and if he escapes to die, his skin is seldom fit to be preserved as a trophy.

From time immemorial tigers have been captured and partially tamed for purposes of display, and for use in the animal-fights which were a common amusement of Indian princes. The first tiger seen in Europe was a present to the Athenians from Seleucus Nikator, about 300 B.C. Later on, Augustus showed the example of exhibiting them at Rome. The Emperor Jahángír is said to have possessed the power of taming animals, and when the King of Persia sent to ascertain if this were true, he found the Emperor stroking two great tigers, which were as tame as cats, and Terry saw tame lions at his Court. When Captain Basil Hall visited Linga Rája of Coorg in 1813, two large tigers were led in, held by men with long ropes on each side. Suddenly the Rája ordered them to be loosed.

"There we sat in the middle of the open court, with a couple of full-sized tigers in our company, and nothing on earth to prevent their munching us all up. The well-fed and well-bred beasts, however, merely lounged about, rubbed their noses together, and then, tumbling on the ground, rolled about like a couple of kittens at play. I could, however, detect the Rája spying at me out of the corner of his eye, and half-smiling at the success of his trick. After a time the men were recalled, and the tigers dragged off."

The Karáoli Rája. Lord Roberts tells us, appeared at Lord Canning's Durbar in 1859 with four tigers, each chained on a separate car.

Naturally, a beast like the tiger is worshipped by people exposed to his attacks. When a hill-man is killed by a tiger, no one will visit the spot until the Baiga priest attends and goes through a series of antics supposed to represent the animal in his fatal spring, and ending by taking up with his teeth a mouthful of the blood-stained earth. One of the forest tribes in Baroda has a sort of pantomimic worship of the tiger-god. A man is covered with a black blanket, made to bow before the god's image and walk round it seven times. Then he is slapped on the back and chased into the forest by children, who fling balls of clay at him, and finally bring him back. The idea clearly is to expel the dangerous beast by a sort of mimetic magic. As Baghwat Deo, or Bágh Bhairon, the tiger is often worshipped. The most remarkable rite is that in Coorg, where, at a tiger-hunt, the carcass is raised on a wooden frame, and the lucky sportsman is solemnly wedded to the departed soul of the tiger. The show finishes with a dance round the dead tiger, and with singing and feasting. Henceforth the tiger-slayer is entitled to wear a long moustache, in the fashion of the Rája.

[Sir J. Fayrer, "The Royal Tiger of Bengal"; Sir S. Baker, "Wild Beasts and their Ways"; E. B. Baker, "Sport in Bengal"; Sanderson, "Thirteen Years among the Wild Beasts of India"; Forsyth, "Highlands of Central India"; Sterndale, "Seonee"; Rice, "Indian Game, from Quail to Tiger"; Blanford, "Mammalia of India."]

TOBACCO.—It is as difficult to imagine how the Indian peasant before the seventeenth century existed without tobacco as to conceive that the boy in medieval Europe had little sweets except honey.

The original home of the plant Sir G. Watt supposes to have been Ecaudor, where its present name was derived from that of the pipe, not of the herb. Francisco Hernandez first brought it to Europe in 1560, and Captain Ralph Lane introduced it to England in 1586. About 1605 the Portuguese carried it to the Deccan, and thence it reached Upper India. Tavernier says that in his time (1659) the herb was grown so abundantly about Burhánpur that the people used to leave half the crop to rot in the fields. It was Asad Beg, the historian, who first brought it to the Court of Akbar. The Emperor was disposed to use it, but his physicians succeeded in inducing him to abstain from this strange drug. The nobles, however, quickly approved of it, and its use rapidly spread. Jahángír, like our James I., issued a ukase against it, and so did the great Sháh Abbás of Persia; but neither monarch succeeded in checking the consumption.

There are still some Indian castes which object to it. Buchanan-Hamilton says that in Bengal, at the beginning of last century, only one division of Bráhmans, the Gayawáls, or low temple priests of Gaya, smoked. Chewing seems in a great measure to have disappeared, except in parts of North India where the tobacco used is called Súratí, or "that of Súrat." But smoking is universal, and in recent years even the use of cigarettes has spread through the rural tracts. Sikhs are forbidden to use it, and one of them told Burnes that tobacco and flies were the greatest evils of this degenerate age. Though Musálmans regard it as an "act indifferent," because it came into use after the time of the Prophet, the Wahhábi Puritans, who have made some way in India, strictly prohibit it. The Burmese monks are forbidden to use it, and some Tibetan monasteries have, in large letters over the gateway, a notice that smoking is not allowed. Some of the higher castes in the Deccan will not grow the plant, supposing that its narcotic properties are due to an indwelling spirit, which, when volitalised in the smoke, brings disease on their children.

Buchanan-Hamilton found that snuff-taking was much more prevalent in the Carnatic than in Bengal; in fact, the pipe there was unknown to all except Musalmáns. The lower classes, he says, used to smoke cheroots, and the word, with the habit, has come from Madras. The first cheroots seen by Columbus were made from the spathes of maize, and among the Central Indian tribes the leaves of the *Bauhinia racemosa* and those of the *Saul* tree are used for the same purpose. Out of these was evolved the modern cigar. Developed in another direction, we have the leaf-pipe, which people like the Gonds and some of the Himálayan tribes still use. The former make it of the leaf of the Palása (*Butea frondosa*), a special twist making the bowl and its narrow stem in the most perfect way. No European has ever been able to learn the knack. But though made of frail materials, they are very effective. Some sent home to the Pitt-Rivers Museum at Oxford smoked excellently after their voyage.

Another very primitive mode of smoking is common in the Himálaya. Two holes are made in the snow or in the earth of a sloping bank, connected together by an underground channel. In one hole is placed the lighted tobacco, and the smoker, crouching over the second hole, sucks out the smoke. A reed is sometimes inserted in the "mouthpiece" end to save the smoker from the necessity of stooping. Convicts in Indian jails, where tobacco is taboo, use the same device.

There is reason to believe that in India, at least, the tobacco-pipe was made in imitation of that employed for hemp and opium, the use of which dates from very early times. In fact, the habit of tobacco-smoking spread rapidly in the conservative East, because the people were already habituated to drug-smoking. The coarseness of the Indian tobacco made it necessary to filter the smoke through water, and hence comes the Persian *Caleeoon*,* with its artistic stand and long, elastic "snake" through which the smoke, perfumed and cooled, reaches the smoker. This was the article without which Jos Sedley refused to move. Grose, writing about 1757, says:

"The Moors are also much addicted to smoaking, and the great ones among them all affect the Persian luxury of that article of callioons, which are made like decanters of transparent glass, with enamel flowers in their proper colours adherent to the bottom of them. These are full of water, and plugged up with a machine that at once holds the tobacco artistly caked and lighted, and the insertion of a leather pipe wired round, of two or three yards length, pliant and coilable like a snake, by which name it is known among the English. Through this pipe they suck in the smoke, so managed as to receive a coolness and a mildness, by passing first through the water, which causes it to gurgle, so as to form a not unpleasing noise."

The early Anglo-Indians followed the native practice in using the *hookah* * in its more elaborate form; and a very splendid article it was, with a special servant to tend it. Lord Roberts says that in 1852 Mr Lowther, Commissioner of Allahabad, was one of the very few Englishmen who smoked the hookah, and by the time of the Mutiny in 1857 the practice of smoking the hookah in public seems practically to have ceased. But many an old "country-born" lady still finds that the hookah is infinitely more soothing than either cigar or cigarette.

The pipe of the poor man is the rude hookah or hubble-bubble, in which a coco-nut, or in the Eastern Himálaya a hollow joint of bamboo, serves as a water bowl, and a pipe connects this with an earthenware cup or *Chillum.**

The tobacco used by the poor differs widely from that of the rich. The peasant in Upper India cuts the tobacco leaf into shreds, and kneads it up with treacle and water till it becomes a black, sticky mass, which has to be kept alight by a lump of red-hot charcoal placed upon it. A day's smoking costs him half-a-farthing. In some places the smoking material is half tobacco and half molasses and impure carbonate of soda. To make the superior article, all sorts of ingredients are mixed with the tobacco—preserved apple, rose leaves, betel leaves, sandalwood, cardamoms. It is from the Musalmán cities, like Delhi or Lucknow, that the connoisseur draws his supplies.

While the native of the Plains filters his tobacco in water, the hill-man on the East frontier thinks nicotine-water one of his greatest luxuries. It is the women who smoke the pipe and make the supply of essence for the men. The Chin women of Burma are always smoking, partly because they like it, and partly to supply the men with nicotine. It is, in fact, a lazy form of chewing, and a mouthful of the nasty beverage is retained in the mouth as long as possible. The Nágas and Shindus of Assam think that it preserves their teeth, and they carry about gourds full of it. It is an act of common courtesy to offer a sip of it, like a pinch of snuff, to a friend. In the same spirit, well-to-do men in Rájputána carry about their tobacco in an oval wooden box, and if a gentleman has a long wooden handle fixed to his box, it shows that he will give a pipe-full to any one who asks for it.

In the village rest-houses you will see three or four "parish" pipes, which any one may use. Each has a special coloured rag attached to it, which shows that one is allotted to Bráhmaṇs, one to low caste people, and one to Musalmáns. Woe betide any one who violates these conventions. The really hospitable smoker uses a movable mouthpiece for his pipe, which he is able to change, and supply a man of a different caste with smoke from the reservoir, and thus avoid the risk of pollution. Smoking is hedged in by other rules of etiquette. The younger should never smoke in the presence of the elder brother.

" Facetious people," says Sir J. G. Scott, " have declared that Burmese babies blow a cloud while they are still at the breast. This is a scandal. They never indulge till they are able to walk without needing the assistance of their hands."

Ward tells us that the Bengali boys begin to smoke when they are four or five years old. But though the Burmese are always smoking, it amounted to *lèse majesté* to smoke in the presence of the King.

[Watt, "Economic Dictionary," v. 353. For nicotine drinking, Lewin, "Wild Tribes," 284; Dalton, "Ethnology of Bengal," 44, 52; "British Burma Gazetteer," i. Pt. I. 470.]

TOMBS.—The earliest Indian tombs are the Dolmens (*q.v.*) of South India. The Hindu, who usually cremates his dead, is, of course, not ordinarily a tomb-builder; but in many places he erects as a home for the ghost the Chatri, or cenotaph, in memory of the departed, and in these he has gradually adopted the model designed by the Musalmáns. The idea of the cenotaph comes down from the Buddhist Stúpa. The ostensible object is to keep sacred the spot on which the body had been burnt. Some of these Chatris are among the most beautiful examples of Hindu architecture, like that of Sangrám Singh at Udaypur, or of the Ját leader, Súraj Mal, at Brindaban. These are open kiosks, raised on a platform decorated with some sacred emblems, the discus, skull, sword, or rosary, which mark that the site is in divine keeping, and avert the jealousy of the spirit from his descendants.

Hindu tombs of another kind are those known as Samádh, erected over the remains of members of the ascetic orders, who cling to the primitive rule of earth-burial. On the same model are the tombs of Jain priests at Mudbidri, in Canara, which Mr Fergusson considers unique in India, not so much, as he supposes, because tombs of priests are unknown elsewhere, the ascetic being usually buried, but because their design follows a model from the further north, introduced perhaps by Chinese merchants in the South Indian trade.

The Musalmáns brought with them their taste for natural scenery and the Tartar solicitude for the preservation of the remains of the dead. Hence came the lovely gardens, each containing the owner's tomb, which form one of the chief ornaments of our cities. Each man erected his own tomb in his lifetime, not so much from distrust of the piety of his heirs, as because his wealth was liable to confiscation on his death, and in any case was sure, under the Musalmán law of succession, to be minutely subdivided. If he made a fortune, it was the result of peculation or of the transient favour of the Emperor, and hence no hereditary estates were formed. While he lived he entertained his friends in his garden and in the tomb which he had erected, and here he and his successors were interred. The dead, in his opinion, were not to be hidden away in gloomy cemeteries far from the haunts of men. His tombs stand along the high road like those on the Appian Way, and the ghosts of the dead share the social life of their descendants.

The series of Musalmán tombs begins with that of Iltitmish, or Altamsh, who died in 1236. He is buried in Old Delhi, in a tomb which admirably illustrates the application of Hindu art to serve the needs of the conqueror. It now lies open to the sky; but the intention to cover it with a vault was perhaps never carried into execution. Close by is the still more beautiful tomb of Ala-ud-dín Khilji, erected seventy-four years later; and from that time to Sher Sháh (1539), who drove Humáyun from his throne, the tombs follow the stern, simple style of the Afgháns, or so-called Patháns. With the tomb of Humáyun (1554), we first meet the characteristic Moghul style. The external form is a square with the corners cut off, the dome of white marble and the rest of the building of red sandstone, with inlaid marble ornamentation. The chief innovation of the later style was the tower attached to each corner of the main building, originally stout and massive, but to develop later on into the graceful minarets at each corner of the platform of the Táj Mahal. The intervening links are the one-storied tower of the tomb of Itimád-ud-daula at Agra, a marvel of delicate ornamentation, the gateway towers of Akbar's tomb at Sikandra and the three-storied minarets of the mausoleum of Jahángír at Lahore. The tomb of Akbar at Sikandra differs in plan from that of other Moghul monuments. Contrary to usual Musalmán custom, the head faces the rising sun, not the Prophet's tomb at Mecca. The design bears the stamp of incompleteness. Akbar himself began the work, but his son Jahángír ordered part to be rebuilt. Mr Fergusson believed that it followed a Hindu, or rather Buddhist model, and supposed that the original intention was to cover the cenotaph, which now lies open to the sky at the summit of the tomb, with a domed canopy which would have given to the upper story the finish which now is wanting.

The Táj Mahal at Agra marks the culmination of the sepulchral art of the Moghuls. Some critics have seen a "weakness of femininity" in the building; to others it represents the supreme triumph of Moghul art. Lady Sleeman best expressed this feeling when she said, "I know not how to criticise such a building, but I would die to-morrow to have such a building over me"; or in

Bishop Heber's epigram, "They built like giants, and finished their work like jewellers."

"The Táj," writes Mr Havell, "was meant to be feminine. The whole conception, and every line and detail of it, express the intention of the designers. It is Mumtáz Mahal herself, radiant in her youthful beauty, who still lingers on the banks of the shining Jumna, at early morn, in the glowing mid-day sun, or in the silver moonlight. Or rather, we should say, it conveys a more abstract thought: it is India's noble tribute to the grace of Indian womanhood—the Venus de Milo of the East."

It is almost certain that the building is of native design, but that some of the ornamentation was done by foreigners. Manrique asserts that he learned on good authority that the design was the work of a Venetian architect, Geronimo Verroneo, and it is pretty certain that the *pietro dura* work was executed under the superintendence of a Frenchman, Augustin de Bordeaux. But the inlaid marble decoration has no analogue in the earlier Indian art. It follows the Persian style, and there is no echo of the renaissance in the building. We may admit with some critics that there is no relation in its dimensions; that the outline of the dome does not suggest the form of the vault below; that the disengaged towers have no purpose; that the fenestration and exterior outlines give little play of light and shadow; that the building within is dark; and lastly, that its effect has been much improved by English landscape gardeners. Even granting much of this, it seems, to use the words of Lady Dufferin, "as if the building had a soul, as if it had been created and not made, so mysterious is its fascination."

Among other famous tombs may be mentioned that of the Saint Salím Chishti at Fatehpur-Sikri, in the best Moghul style, with its wonderful marble tracery, to which women hang rags to mark a prayer for a son. That of Mahmúd Sháh at Bijapur has a wonderful dome, which almost rivals that of the Pantheon, the Duomo at Florence, St Peter's, or St Paul's. The monuments of the kings of

Golconda form an admirable group. Aurangzeb himself rests under the plainest monument ever raised to a Muhammadan Emperor. After his time the style passed rapidly into decay until it was represented by the debased buildings at Lucknow.

Later rulers of the country have left few tombs of any merit. Quaintest of all are the Dutch tombs at Súrat, of which Ovington writes:

"In Súrat cemetery there was the tomb of a great Dutch drinker, a relation of the aforesaid Prince of Orange. At the top was a great cup of stone, and another at each corner. Opposite each cup was the figure of a sugar-loaf. Dutch drinking-parties used to frequent this tomb, brewing their punch in the large stone basins; remembering their departed companions, they sometimes forgot themselves."

[Fergusson, "History of Indian and Eastern Architecture"; Havell, "Handbook to Agra and the Táj"; Fanshawe, "Delhi, Past and Present."]

TOPE.—The Stúpa, or, as we call it, the Tope, is one of the most interesting forms of Buddhist architecture. These monuments were erected in the early stage of Buddhism to preserve the relics of the Master or other saintly personages, or to mark the scene of some event famous in the growth of the faith. When this form of relic-worship, which was unknown in Egypt, Babylon, Assyria, Greece, or Rome, first arose in India, we have no exact means of deciding. The Jains at an early date practised relic-worship, and with the Buddhists it seems to have commenced soon after the distribution of his relics, which followed the death of the Buddha at Kusinagara, an event which is now supposed to have occurred about 487 B.C. The remarkable Stúpa recently discovered at Piprávwa, in the Nepálese Tarái, seems to date about 400-450 B.C.

The Stúpas, according to Mr Fergusson's rather arbitrary classification, fall into two series, according to the purpose for which they were designed. There were, first, he supposes, the true Stúpas or towers erected to commemorate some event, or mark some sacred site; secondly, Dagobas, which were monuments containing relics of the

Master or of some famous Saints. But there is nothing to indicate a distinction between these two classes of monuments, and, from an architectural point of view, they must be regarded as identical.

It seems clear that the Stúpa is the lineal descendant of the sepulchral tumulus or burial mound. This appears to have formed the model of the most ancient Stúpas; but in later times the curvilinear shape of the structure seems to have imitated the ordinary hut, the outline of which was determined by the natural curves of two or more bamboos planted apart in the ground, and drawn together at the top. We may imagine that the first stage of development was to face the earthen mound with a casing of brick or stone, this being done partly to protect the mound from damage by weather, and partly, perhaps, as a mode of defining the holy site, or to serve as a "ghost-hedge," to restrain the ghost of the dead man from trespassing beyond his allotted domain. The material of the mound varied with the locality. Where stone was abundant, as at Sánchi or Bharhut, this was used; in other places the masonry was of brick. In the Piprâwa Stúpa the relation of height to diameter is as 21 to 116 feet, and, roughly speaking, the increasing height of the structure is an indication of a later age. The best example of this more modern type is the famous monument at Sarnáth, near Benares, erected in the Deer Park, a sacred site in the life of the Buddha. This monument General Cunningham assigns to the sixth century of our era; but from a comparison of the beautiful geometrical carvings, which much resembles Hindu work on the earliest mosques at Ajmír and Delhi, Mr Fergusson is inclined to date it early in the eleventh century.

From the evidence of Buddhist bas-reliefs, all these old Stúpas would seem to have been crowned with gilt, copper, or stone umbrellas, the sign of royalty—a design perpetuated in the Stúpas of Burma, where we have a succession of umbrellas one over the other, gradually diminishing in size. At the same time, figures of Buddha were placed in niches on each side of the square base, and the tiers of mouldings were separated by rows of sculptured figures, the forerunners of the modern anthropomorphic statues of Hindu and Jain worship.

Another interesting part of the design was the railing round the Stúpa, which seems to have been gradually evolved from the rows of stones placed for the purpose of protection at the base of the original earthen tumulus. Of these much the finest example is that of Amarávati; that of Bodh Gaya probably dates from the time of Asoka; at Sánchi the railing is plain, but the gateways are splendid examples of Buddhist art. The Jain Stúpas were also provided with railings. Many of these rails reproduce the designs in wood-carving from which they were immediately derived.

Besides the more modern Burmese Stúpas, best represented by the great *Shwé Dagon* * Pagoda at Rangoon, the type survives in the Ch'orten of Tibetan and Himálayan Buddhism. These were probably, as Colonel Waddell suggests, originally intended as relic-holders, but they are now merely cenotaphs in honour of the Buddha or some canonised Saints. Like their Indian predecessors, they were originally massive hemispherical domes, crowned by a square capital surmounted by umbrellas. Later on they became more complex in form, with numerous plinths, and much elongated. The Ch'ortens of the Lamas have depicted on them a pair of eyes, supposed to be connected with Sun-worship, one of the many foreign elements which the northern Buddhism has absorbed.

[Cunningham, Monographs on Mahábodhi, Bhilsa, Bharhut; Fergusson, "History of Indian and Eastern Architecture," 57ff.; Waddell, "Buddhism of Tibet," 263ff.; V. A. Smith, "Jain Stúpas at Mathura"; Rhys Davids, "Buddhist India," 80ff.]

TOWER OF SILENCE.—This is the English name for the Dokhma, or place in which the Pársi dead are deposited. Mr Dosabhai Framji, who gives a full account of them, rather unkindly compares them in appearance to "the large circular gasometers attached to gas-works."

He explains the internal arrangements which no European is allowed an opportunity of examining. Round the inside of the structure are arranged the niches in which the corpses are deposited, and in the centre a pit, into which, when clean, the bones are removed. To the Pársi the exposure of the corpse to the purifying agency of the Sun, and its destruction by birds of prey, seem quite natural. It is undoubtedly a practice descending from remote antiquity. "It is said," Herodotus tells us, "that the body of a male Persian is never buried until it has been torn either by a dog or a bird of prey." Mr Jevons suggests that the dog being a totem animal, the ghost would be pleased that he, as a member of the clan, should consume the body. Others believe that the idea was to relieve the bones as quickly as possible from the infection of corruption. Recently, however, Dr Waddell, accepting the suggestion of Bogle, shows that the real reason of the practice in Tibet and other parts of Central Asia is the extreme scarcity of fuel for cremation, and the impossibility of digging graves in the ice-bound soil during the protracted winter of these regions. There are some indications that the custom is now beginning to offend the feelings of some of the more advanced Pársis. [*See* PARSEE.]

The seclusion of these homes of the dead is most carefully preserved. Grose was told that if he looked into one he was sure to die, and when he determined to make the experiment, a Pársi warned him to desist, assuring him that if he dared to intrude he would not long survive his idle curiosity. In 1792 the Governor of Bombay issued a proclamation reciting that as

"a European inhabitant of this island, unobservant of that decency which enlightened people show to the religious ceremonies of the natives of India, had lately entered one of the repositories for their dead, to the great distress, inconvenience, and expense of the said caste," he issues orders "that whoever shall obtrude themselves on the Temples, Tombs, or religious ceremonies of the natives residing under the protection of this Government, will be suspended the Honourable Company's service, if in their employ, or if free merchants, mariners, or others, adjudged to have forfeited their licenses, and will be sent to Europe."

[Dosabhai Framji Karaka, "History of the Parsis," i. 199; Douglas, "Bombay and Western India," i. 147.]

TRADE. — It is certainly significant that the early accounts of the honesty of Indian traders differ widely from those of later travellers. Part of this was no doubt matter of tradition, but the respectability of merchants in old times is so constantly asserted that there must be strong foundation for the belief. The testimony of the Greek authors is favourable to the honesty of the trading class.

Marco Polo (1290) says that the Abraiaman or Bráhmans of Western India "are the best merchants in the world, and the most truthful, for they would not tell a lie for anything on earth." This view is supported by Friar Jordanus (1323), and, following them, Frederic describes the perfect trust which foreign merchants reposed in the Hindu brokers of Cambay. Pyrard de Laval (1610) says, though fine and subtle, they are neither cheats nor easily cheated.

After this a change occurs in the relations between the foreigner and the native merchant. Peyton (1615) calls the Súrat broker "subtle, and, unless well looked after, ready to deceive the buyer and seller"; and De Couto, about the same time, says that the Gujarát merchants must be descended from the Lost Tribes, because they were so religiously careful to swindle the Christian. Tavernier writes that the Banians could give lessons to the cunning Jews; and Fryer writes that fleas and Banians are the vermin of India, a mass of sordidness, blood-suckers, horse-leeches, liars, and dissemblers. Vincenzo, writing in 1675, speaks of the prevalence of fraud among traders. It was commonly said at Súrat that it took three Jews to make a Chinaman, and three Chinamen to make a Banian. Grose in 1757 takes a more reasonable view, that the chief merchants are as honest as Europeans, but that the underlings are rogues.

Tavernier describes the system of secret bargaining which still goes on in every horse and cattle fair in the country. The parties put their hands under a sheet, and "when the seller takes the whole hand of the buyer, that means 1000, and as many times as he presses it so many thousands of pagodas or rupees." Five fingers mean 500, one 100. By taking the finger only up to the middle joint, 50 is meant, and from the end of the finger up to the first joint 10. Fryer refers to the same practice in his very uncomplimentary account of the merchants of Súrat:

> "Though you hear, see, and understand them, yet you will be choased, they looking you in the face; for as a piece of Superstition they must place their hands under a Ramerin [mantle], when by their fingers they instruct one another, and by that slight often contradict their Tongues; Such a subtle Generation is this, and so fitly squared a place is Súrat to exercise their genius in."

["Bombay Gazetteer," vi. 190; Yule, "Marco Polo," 1st ed., ii. 303.]

TREE WORSHIP.—The worship of the sacred tree is an important branch of Indian Animism. It

> "may perhaps be regarded," says Mr J. G. Frazer, "as occupying an intermediate place in the history of religion between the religion of the hunter and shepherd on one side, whose gods are mostly animals, and the religion of the husbandman on the other hand, in whose worship the cultivated plants play an important part."

The tree cult in India is very ancient. In many passages of the Vedas the trees, or rather the spirits supposed to haunt them, are invoked as deities. The widespread belief in the World-tree passed to Buddhism in the cult of the Bodhi.

At the present day it assumes many forms. We have the tree embodying the spirit which influences the fertility of crops and human beings. Such a tree to which offerings are made at seed-time and harvest naturally turns into the sacred village tree, beneath which the local gods take shelter in a heap of rude stones. Here the people meet for worship, and the tribal council settles their affairs beneath its shade. It is thus closely connected with the religious and social life of the community.

Other trees, or collections of trees, again, are valued as representing the last relics of the primeval forest, the final resting-place to which the wood sprites ejected by the wood-cutter fly for refuge. Such groves, as we find them among the Kols and similar tribes, are kept highly sacred; no one dares to cut or destroy the trees, or even to collect dry wood within the precincts.

Some trees are valued for their mystic or useful qualities. The mysterious waving of the leaves or branches of one shows that it holds a spirit; another is evergreen, and a type of eternal life; others are connected with the spirits of the dead, because some of the forest tribes bury their dead in trees; from the wood of others, fire, a divine being, is created; from the leaves or bark of some things intoxicating, and therefore a sign of indwelling demons, are produced.

Hence the unwillingness to cut trees. The idea is as old as the ancient Bráhmanic books. The tree for the sacrificial post was cut with the incantation, "O axe, harm it not!" In one of the clearings done by the English in Bengal, no wood-cutter would ply his axe till the European overseer struck the first blow, and thus took the wrath of the spirit upon himself.

Of all the sacred trees the most important are those of the fig species. We have seen why the Banyan is sacred. The *Peepul** waves its leaves in an uncanny way. It is said that once some Hindu merchants objected to have one of these planted in their bazaar, because they could no longer lie and cheat under its shade. The *Saul** is one of the many trees held sacred by the forest tribes. The *Bael** is the tree of those who worship Siva, the *Toolsy** of the votaries of Vishnu. The Asoka is sacred to Káma, the god of love, and a pretty piece of folk-lore tells that the buds will instantly open in full splendour if the foot of a beautiful woman touches its roots. Grimmest of sacred trees is the gigantic *Adansonia*, an importation from Africa, which is regarded with awe at Bijapur as the site of executions under native rule. In gigantic girth of trunk it must surpass any existing trees, except those of California. In height Dr Brandis never saw anything to rival an *Antiaris*, allied to the *Upas** tree of Java, and a *Deodár** cedar at Kulu, each of which was about 250 feet high.

Many customs illustrate the cult of trees. The jungle tribes of the Central tract dance round the Karam tree at their agricultural feasts, as the emblem of the tree spirit which promotes fertility. Close to many shrines may be seen a pair of trees of different species, such as fig and a Margosa, which, when they reach the age of twenty, are solemnly wedded to each other with the regular rites. The curious custom of marrying human beings to trees has been discussed in connection with MARRIAGE. Equally curious are the rag trees which are found in India and in various parts of Europe. The worshipper, by tying a fragment of his clothing to the tree, brings himself into sacramental communion with the spirit occupying it, and thus secures relief from disease. With the same object shepherds in Kulu select the pencil cedar, and if any one is in pain he transfers his malady to the tree by driving a nail into its trunk.

The tree is thus the natural abode of the spirit of the place. When a village is being founded in North India, two men, who represent the gods of the earth and of the trees, and who are known respectively as the "Earthman" and the "Treeman," become possessed of the local deity, who has been summoned to the spot by tuck of drum. Suddenly the wizard clutches at the spirit hovering in the air around him, and pours grains of sesame through his hands into a hole in a piece of fig wood. He promptly closes the hole, and the wood is buried at the spot which is intended to be the shrine of the local village gods. He is thus closely immured in his sanctuary, and is incapable of doing mischief, provided offerings be duly made in his honour.

[Frazer, "Golden Bough," iii. 26; Fergusson, "Tree and Serpent Worship"; Mrs J. H. Philpot, "The Sacred Tree."]

TWICE-BORN.—The ideal division of Hindus is into the "twice-born" who wear the sacred thread, and all other castes who are regarded as "once-born."

"As the egg," says Ward, "at one time impregnated with life, is afterwards hatched by the mother, so the receiving of the cord and Gáyatri [SUN WORSHIP] is accounted the second birth of Bráhmans, who are from that time denominated Dwija, or twice-born."

Manu goes further when he says:

"According to the injunction of the sacred texts, the first birth of an Aryan is from his natural mother; the second happens on his tying on the girdle of Munja grass; and the third on the initiation to the performance of the Srauta [the elaborate Vedic rites] sacrifice."

A Bráhman, in fact, is not born, but raised to that dignity by his Karma, which means not only the merit acquired in previous births or by rites performed during life, but a disciplinary process leading to spiritual development, by which he becomes "twice-born," and of which the initiation is the outward and visible sign.

The rite of girding on the sacred cord is, as has been shown in connection with the SACRED THREAD, a form of magical initiation. In the rite, as described in the Bráhmanical books, the symbolism of actual re-birth was carefully followed. The old kings of Madura used to undergo re-birth by passing through a cow of bronze, and the rite is still retained as being most efficacious in removing sin and impurity. Fra Paolino, who was in India at the end of the eighteenth century, tells how the King of Travancore was required to creep through a golden cow because he had burned some Hindu temples. In the modern form of the rite, which was solemnised in

1854 and again in 1894, the Mahárája entered a large golden vessel filled with water, which had been mixed with all the products of the sacred cow. A cover was put on the vessel, and he bathed four times in the liquid, while Bráhmans chanted hymns. On emerging, he bowed before the tutelary gods of his kingdom, and the crown was placed on his head. The object of the rite is to elevate the Mahárája from the lower caste to which he rightfully belongs to the dignity of a Bráhman, or as near this as it is possible for him to reach. After the "Regeneration ceremony," the Prince can no longer partake of food with the members of his own family, to whom he is now superior in caste as well as rank. But he is admitted to the privilege of being present when the Bráhmans are fed, and he may eat in their presence. Formerly the Mahárája passed through a golden image of the cow. More recently a representation of the holy lotus of Vishnu was selected. After the rite the image is broken up, and the fragments shared between the Bráhmans and the temple treasury.

The same rite is performed in North India when the horoscope of a child shows that he committed some crime in a former birth, or that some serious calamity is impending over him. The child is clothed in scarlet, and tied on a new corn sieve, which is passed backwards and forwards beneath the legs of a cow. The usual worship with aspersion follows, and the father smells his son as the cow smells her new-born calf. Quite recently the ambassadors of a native prince, who had become polluted by crossing the "Black Water," were purified by passing through the golden image of a cow.

We may perhaps connect rites like these with the custom common in Europe and elsewhere of passing people through the holes in a dolmen, or through a cloven ash-tree as a cure for rupture or rheumatism, or as a chastity test, as at "St Wilfrid's Needle" in Ripon Cathedral. Such is the crevice in the rocks at Malabar Hill, near Bombay, of which Grose says:

"This place is used by the Gentoos as a purification of

their sins, which they say is effected by their going in at the opening and emerging out of the crevice, which to me seemed too narrow for any person of any corpulence to squeeze through, though I have been credibly assured that several very fat persons have achieved it."

Many shrines, like that of the Panjáb Saint Faríd-ud-dín, have openings so narrow that at the lucky hour many pilgrims have been crushed to death in an attempt to reach the grave.

[For the Travancore rite, Nelson, "Madura," iii. 188; Mateer, "Land of Charity," 169; "Calcutta Review," cxi. 334; Frazer, "Golden Bough," i. 22, 307.]

VILLAGE.—Much attention has been devoted to the constitution of the Indian village community, partly because it has been recognised as an important factor in the social stability of the country; partly because, since the researches of Sir H. Maine, it has been identified with similar forms of land tenure in Europe.

As regards its stability, the famous words of Sir C. Metcalfe are nearly as true as ever:

"Village communities seem to last when nothing else lasts. Dynasty after dynasty changes; revolution succeeds revolution. Hindu, Pathán, Moghul, Mahratta, English were all masters in turn, but the village community remains the same."

But since the writer's day the community has been much weakened under the rule of English law, which has tended to substitute personal for corporate right in property.

The constitution of the village community is a subject too wide for our space. Briefly speaking, we have two types, the Aryan or joint village characteristic of North India, and the Dravidian or *Ryotwarry** village of the South. The former is the result of the Aryan clan system, a body of settlers occupying a tract, part of which they allot to the householders as separate farms, while part is held in common by the entire community. Such a form of land-holding was specially adapted to the dry Plains of Northern

India, where co-operation was needed for the provision of a water supply, and there were little facilities for communal agriculture. But in date of development the Dravidian village is clearly earlier. While in the Aryan village the *patria potestas* has passed into clan organisation, with the Dravidians it continued to exist; and we find here an influential hereditary head-man, who allots the free lands among the cultivators, and provides for the remuneration of that hereditary staff of servants by whose ministrations the village becomes a community independent of aid from outside. Unlike the North Indian village, there is no common holding of the occupied land: it has all been allotted to tenants, and enjoyed independently from the first.

The form of the village, again, indicates whether the modern history of the tract in which it is situated has been peaceful or disturbed. Where anarchy and rapine have prevailed, the villages are large associations of people banded together for the purpose of self-defence, and the village site is itself fortified. Thus Buchanan-Hamilton writes of a Mysore village:

"The defence of such a village consists of a round stone wall, perhaps 40 feet in diameter and 6 feet high. On the top of this is a parapet of mud, with a door in it, to which the only access is by a ladder. In case of a plundering party coming near a village, the people ascend into the tower with their families and most valuable effects, and, having drawn up the ladder, defend themselves with stones, which even their women throw with great force and dexterity."

Under the reign of peace such fortified villages have now disappeared from Mysore; but in the Afrídi villages on the Afghán frontier a fortified tower is essential to every settlement, and in our expeditions across the frontier the destruction of these towers by our engineers is one of the severest forms of punishment which we can inflict on these wild caterans who periodically make raids on our territories.

In other cases the village is found to be protected

by a dense hedge of thorns or bamboo. In Upper Burma the Wá villages are surrounded by a rampart covered with cactus and other thorny plants, and outside is a deep fosse, carefully masked, intended to stop the rush of the enemy. Up to quite recent times the capital of the Native State of Rámpur in the United Provinces was protected by a dense bamboo hedge, which could not be destroyed by artillery. In Assam we find side by side the two types of village, the open and the fortified; the former in the settled Plain country, the latter on the border-land, with stockaded fort to protect the people from raids for women and heads.

In some of the older towns we find survivals of a similar state of things. Each craft occupies a separate quarter, and these are divided off by gates, which are kept locked at night. The closely-huddled houses and narrow lanes of the villages in the north mark the same condition. Buchanan-Hamilton, writing in the beginning of the nineteenth century, says that in Behár these narrow lanes were deliberately adopted from reasons of jealousy, to prevent people of rank from molesting the women; in other places the object was to check the rush of armed bandits at night, and to enable the villagers to rally in defence of their herds and other property. The appearance of a village, again, often shows the character and occupation of the race which colonised it. In the Panjáb, villages of the three great agricultural tribes, Kambohs, Játs, and Arains, are easily distinguishable. The first are compact, with houses solidly built of mud and the roofs flat, with a small yard surrounded by a wall large enough to hold the farming implements and plough teams; the second straggling, the houses thatched and often with walls of wattle, but each provided with a great yard to hold the herd at night; the third presenting the characteristic of the first and second, modified to some extent to meet local requirements.

Some of the sites of villages in the Plains must have been inhabited from a remote antiquity. They stand on a high mound formed of broken pottery and the *débris* of the mud walls which are repaired after each rainy season. These mounds cover the relics of the ancient civilisation of the country, and the investigation of them will be the task of the archæologists of the future.

It is in the old settled tracts, like Bengal and the West Coast that the open village has been the result of a long period of tranquillity. In Bengal the communal system has long fallen into decay, and the houses are so dispersed that it is hard to say where one village begins and another ends, or to distinguish the hamlet from the parent village. On the West Coast the stringent rules of personal purity compel the people to live in scattered homesteads, each surrounded by its own fence, rather than in a compact group of houses.

This tendency to separateness is most apparent in the villages of the jungle tribes in the central hills, where shifting cultivation prevents the growth of a compact village. Thus, writing of the Kandhs, Captain Sherwill says:

> "In choosing the site of his habitation, the Kandh displays great taste. His village lies embedded in a leafy grove, or at the foot of finely-wooded hills, or crowns some little green knoll in the valleys, well raised above flood-level. The hamlet consists of two rows of houses, forming a broad curved street, and closed at the ends by a strong wooden barrier. The patriarch has his house in the very centre of the hamlet, close to the cotton tree which the priest plants and dedicates to the village god as the first necessary act in building a hamlet. The low caste properly live at the extremity of the street, but in some cases erect their miserable clusters of houses just outside it."

Each enclosure is made of green branches or wattled pailings, and contains a man and his wife with their married children and their families, a pig-stye, and buffalo shed. This is the type of jungle village we find all through the central part of the Peninsula. The people are so peaceable, and there is so little crime that their houses stand scattered about in convenient spots where water and grazing are available, like the farm-steadings on an English country-side.

One of the prettiest sights in India is a Ját village in Northern India on a morning in the cold weather. The fields round the site are masses of green, darker and more luxuriant near the houses, where a plentiful supply of manure is forthcoming. The oxen work the creaking wheels at the numerous wells; the air is full of the song of men and boys as the bag is hauled full of water to the surface. The stream trickles along innumerable channels, and is directed into each little plot by the ready hands of the girls. The spare yokes of cattle chew the cud lazily at the mangers close by. The old people sit under the trees, the women spinning, the men smoking and gossiping. All displays a scene of rural peace and prosperity, which it would be hard to equal in any country in the world.

In sharp contrast to this is the Rájput or Gújar village. The one is a rearer of cattle, the other a cattle-thief; the one is too dignified to work his fields, and employs labourers to cultivate for him; the other spends most of his time, when he is not on the prowl after the oxen of his neighbours, in grazing his herds of buffaloes on the rank pasturage by the river-bank. There he erects a rude shanty of reeds, in which he shelters until the periodical rains drive him back to his squalid village founded on the high ground beyond the reach of the floods.

More resembling the Ját village is that of the market-gardener class near the larger cities. Here every inch of ground is under cultivation, sown with opium or pepper, yams or onions, and pot-herbs of many kinds. The owner's well is constantly at work to supply water to his varied crops, and every member of the family, down to quite little children, is occupied in digging or sowing, watering or weeding, or piercing the poppy capsules, and the other many forms of work which this form of *petite* culture involves.

[Maine, "Village Communities in the East and West": Baden Powell, "The Indian Village Community."]

WATERFALLS.—It is remarkable that more attention has not been paid to the magnificent waterfalls of India. In the Himálaya slopes, as a rule, the character of the rocks produces many rapids, but few great waterfalls although one on the Bhagírathi, and another near Simla deserve a visit. Finer than these are the falls on the Chináb in Kistwár, a dependency of Kashmír, where the water falls in a series of leaps over 2,500 feet high. The first two falls are each of 500 feet.

"In the greater leaps," writes Mr Drew, "the water, although in volume not little—for the river is distinctly heard at a distance of two miles—becomes scattered into spray; again it collects and comes over the ledge in a thick stream; in part it divides into various lines, which at a distance seem vertical, immoveable white threads. In the morning sun the spray made in the greater leaps shows prismatic colours, visible even at the distance of our chosen point, a phenomenon attributed by the people of the place to fairies who bathe in and display the strange hues of their bodies through the showers."

Jahángír, Bernier tells us, had a pavilion made where his Court could enjoy the view of the Núr-i-chasm, or "Stream of Light," the Kashmír waterfall, which pours down from rock to rock with a final mighty leap of nearly 70 feet. It was on the Gori river, on the west frontier of Nepál, that Mr Webber, by counting the seconds, and watching a particular spot in the white water descend to the bottom, found the height of the fall to be 1900 feet.

But it is where the rivers pour down into the Plains from the central plateau that the waterfalls are most remarkable. Here, in the area of the trap and other igneous rocks, the strata are firmer and the precipices more sheer. To begin from the north—some of the rivers of the table-land pour into the Ganges valley with falls of more than 400 feet over the mural precipices which form the northern scarp of the Vindhyan Hills. Of these one of the most beautiful is the Chánpatthar on the ill-omened Karamnása. That of the Suvarnarekha, in Lohárdagga, has a measured height of 320 feet, but this does not represent a sheer drop except in the rains. Further south the Narbada, at Amarkantak, tumbles over a black basaltic cliff, a sheer descent of 70 feet, showing a glistening sheet of water against the intensely dark rock.

Passing on to Southern India, we have the splendid fall of the Incharna, in the Nizám's territory, with one perpendicular fall of 398 feet. It is best known to English readers by the account of it in Colonel Meadows Taylor's novel of "Seeta." There is another on the Kistna 408 feet in height, the roar of which can be heard at the distance of thirty miles. A Bedar, one of the jungle folk, told Meadows Taylor that it was "like all the white horses in the world fighting together and tossing their manes," thus reproducing the old Animistic myth which attributes these wonders of nature to a spirit.

Still further south, two waterfalls are the most magnificent in the country—those on the Cauvery and the Gersoppa, or, as Englishman have distorted the name, the "Grasshopper" Falls on the Sherávati. At Sivasamudram, where the Cauvery leaves Mysore territory, is the famous Fall of Gangana Chuki. Here, to quote Mr Bowring,

"one sees the stream rushing precipitately over the face of a tremendous abyss, and dashing over vast boulders of rock in a cloud of foam, till it hurls itself into a steep pool below, 300 feet from the summit. The noise made by the roar of waters is deafening, and as one's ears are stunned by their loud thunder, so one's sight is blinded by the steam of mist which hides from view the sacred stream as it rushes furiously forward over great rocks to meet the sister fall below."

The Sivasamudram Falls have recently been utilised to convey electrical energy to the Kolár gold-fields of Mysore.

Still greater is the famed Gersoppa Fall, one of the wonders of the world. Though the volume of water is less than that of the Cauvery, the immense height of the chief fall is almost without a parallel. The chasm through which the "Rája" Fall precipitates itself in one unbroken column is 830 feet deep. Half-way down it is encountered by the "Roarer," which hurls itself into a tremendous basin, and then rushes on to meet its comrade.

"A third, called the 'Rocket,' shoots downward in a series of jets; while the fourth 'Dame Blanche,' is an Undine-like cascade gliding gently over the mountain-side in a sheet of foam."

Some years ago a party of naval officers from Bombay got a rope across, and hauling themselves out in a cradle, ascertained the depth by letting down a plumb-line. For sheer beauty nothing perhaps exceeds the Courtallum Fall, but here the height is only 100 feet.

WEAVING.—This, one of the earliest and up to modern times the most widely spread rural industry, is now in a state of decline. Machine-made fabrics have displaced the native cloths, and though much less durable, their low price has secured control of the market. The causes of the ruin of this once flourishing industry were the exclusion in the eighteenth century of Indian fabrics from England; the change in fashion in the West Indies after the abolition of slavery, which led to the loss of the valuable trade in *Bandanna* * handkerchiefs; improvements of machinery in Lancashire; and, lastly, the rise in the price of cotton during the American War. But even now the industry is of some importance. It has been estimated that of the cotton cloth used in the country, two-fifths are imported and three-fifths woven at home from native thread or imported yarn.

Of all the Indian cloths, the most famous were the muslins of Dacca and Arni. The rise of this trade dates from the establishment of the luxurious Moghul Court at Delhi and Agra, which held the monopoly of all the finest fabrics produced. Sironj, in Rájputána, was also a place where these delicate cloths were manufactured. Tavernier tells us that this was

"a description of muslin which is so fine, that when it is on the person, you see all the skin as though it were uncovered. The merchants are not allowed to export it, and the Governor sends all of it for the Great Moghul's seraglio, and for the principal courtiers. This it is of which the Sultánas and the wives of the great nobles make themselves shifts and garments for the hot weather, and the King and the nobles enjoy seeing them wearing these fine shifts, and cause them to dance in them."

Many tales are recorded of the delicacy of the material. Tavernier tells of the ambassador of the King of Persia, who, on his return from India, presented his master with a coco-nut of the size of an ostrich egg, which contained a turban sixty cubits long, so fine that you would scarcely know that it was in your hand. This, considering the size of an ostrich egg, is not so very wonderful after all. Bolts says that the Emperor Aurangzeb was "angry with his daughter for showing her skin through her clothes, whereupon the young princess remonstrated in her justification that she had seven suits on." Another story is that a weaver was chastised and turned out of Dacca by the Nawáb for his neglect in not preventing a cow from eating a piece of muslin spread to dry on the grass, she mistaking it for a spider's web.

Spinning, it has been said, is the only industry in India that is performed by persons of all castes, and concerning which there seems to be no caste prejudice. James Taylor, in his valuable account of the Dacca industries, says that the finest thread was spun by women under thirty, and was made early in the morning when the air was comparatively damp; in particularly dry weather the necessary moisture was obtained by working over a shallow pan of water. One skein weighed by Taylor was found to contain thread 250 miles long to a pound of cotton. The finest modern work of this kind recorded was made at Chánda in the Central Provinces, one pound of cotton producing 117 miles length of thread.

In the Plains the work of spinning is confined to women, that of weaving to men; but Colonel Harcourt remarks that in Kulu, on the lower Himálaya, the men alone do the weaving, whereas in Lahoul and Spiti it is undertaken by both sexes. The thread is arranged for the loom on a series of reeds erected in rows under the shade of trees near the house of the workman.

"When the warp has been laid," writes Mr Hoey, "it is dressed with a paste of flour and dried. It is then taken to the loom, and each alternate thread is drawn through a hole in one leaf of heddles, and the other threads drawn through the interstices of another. Then all the threads are drawn through the interstices of the batten, and the ends are finally fastened to the beam. The other end of the warp is attached to a hook or peg or other contrivance, swung from, or fastened to, the ceiling. There is but one beam in the loom; the place of the second is taken by three reeds, which are disposed so as to prevent the threads becoming confused behind the heddles. To the heddles are attached treddles, and by their movement the 'shed' is produced through which the shuttle flies."

It is impossible here to discuss the numberless products of the Indian loom. The taste for Oriental art fabrics, like *Phoolkarees* * and chintzes, has given a certain stimulus to the trade. The prints of Farrukhábád, Kanauj, and Lucknow are specially beautiful, and vie with the *Palempores,** or bed-covers, of Sadras and Masulipatam. Old-fashioned natives still rightly prefer, on account of its durability and artistic qualities, the country to the imported cloth. Fashion, it must be remembered, has little power in India. There are changes in the appreciation of colour or in the use of special fabrics, but the form of dress is much the same as it was in the time of the earliest sculptures, two centuries before our era.

[J. Taylor, "A Descriptive and Historical Account of the Cotton Manufacture of Dacca, in Bengal"; Hoey, "Monograph on Trade and Manufactures of N. India," 123; Francis, "Monograph on Panjáb Cotton"; Johnstone, "Monograph on Wool"; Cookson, "Monograph on Silk"; Silberrad, "Cotton Fabrics of the N.-W. Provinces"; Pim, "Monograph on Wool"; Yusuf Ali, "Monograph on Silk"; J. F. Watson, "The Textile Manufactures and Costumes of the People of India."]

WELLS.—In the rural economy nothing is more important than the well, and the builder of a well is honoured as a benefactor by succeeding generations.

Asoka proudly records in one of his edicts that he planted trees and dug wells along the highways. To make a well is not, as in Europe, to clear out the entrance of a perennial spring and construct a reservoir. Even in the Tarái, where in the rainy season the water bubbles out of the wells, some sort of fencing is required to prevent the friable soil from choking the source. This is the *Cutcha*,* the first form of well, which, where the soil is fairly firm, need only be excavated till the percolation level is reached; if the soil be loose, it must be supported by cables of wattle, or fenced round with wooden planks. Such wells can only be built in alluvial soils, where the water is close to the surface. The later and more elaborate form of well, the *Pucka*,* or that formed by sinking a masonry cylinder, could only be made by the co-operation of the members of a settled community, and can hardly be much earlier than the beginnings of stone and brick-building, a couple of centuries before our era. The masonry cylinder is first built a few feet high, on a frame-work of wood of a kind proof against injury by water action. The soil within is gradually excavated, and the cylinder built up as it sinks to the spring level. This is a work of some difficulty and danger, and various devices are employed to secure the perpendicular sinking of the well through the friable soil. Similar in construction, but of much greater size, are the cylinders sunk in the treacherous bed of an Indian river to support a bridge like that which spans the Ganges at Benares. When the spring is comparatively near the surface, the sides are sometimes protected by shaped cylinders of earthenware.

A later development of the Pucka well is the *Bowly*,* some of which supply examples of the best form of Indian buildings. The finest wells of this class are found in Gujarát and other parts of the country west of the Jumna. The Bowly consists of a series of flights of steps, balconies, and rooms built round an underground spring or reservoir. One in Kaira, said to have been built by the famous Mahmúd Begada as a summer retreat, is now partially ruined. Above are two stone arches, from which his swing bed was hung, and underground are four winding stairs and eight chambers, the roofs supported by elegant columns, and the walls decorated with bas-reliefs. Sometimes the stairs do not lead to a simple well, but to an underground tank fed by many springs.

It is in the desert of Rájputána that the deepest wells are found. They are generally built in a depression between two lines of sand-hills, a site which offers the best chance of water. Colonel Tod speaks of some as much as 700 feet deep. A well in the Jaysalmír State is 490 feet deep, and several of a greater depth than 300 feet have been recorded. These great wells are farmed out to speculators, who work them with their own cattle and gear, and exact a small payment from all except the poorest travellers for every bucket of water they supply. The historian of the wanderings of the Emperor Humáyun tells an extraordinary tale of the depth of a well. The rope by which the water-bag was hauled up from the bottom was, he says, so long, that a drum was beaten to give the driver notice when the bag reached the surface. As he moved on with his team, he was then so far off that a call would not reach him.

Some wells are excavated in the solid rock, like those in the hill-forts of Dátegad and Károad in Satára, the latter of which has a splendid flight of eighty steps leading down to the water-level. Another fine well is that cut through the rock on which the Cathedral Mosque of Delhi stands. It was built by Sháhjahán, and the water comes from the Canal by a long underground passage. Some of these old Musalmán wells are provided with balconies, from which men dive into the water from a considerable height. The two best known wells of this kind are those at the tomb of Nizám-ud-dín Auliya in Old Delhi, and that near Akbar's palace at Fatehpur-Sikri.

Along the western frontier another device for supplying water is in use, the Karez or Kanát, an underground channel by which water is brought from long distances One of them is described by Marco Polo in the Kermán desert. Mountstuart Elphinstone heard of one in Kábul 36 miles in length.

Among famous wells may be mentioned that at Goa, which Pietro della Valle says is

"one of the greatest wells that I ever beheld, round, and about twenty of my Paces in Diameter, and very deep; it hath Parapets or Walls breast-high round about, with Gates, at one of which is a double pair of Stairs leading two ways to the bottom, to fetch water when it is very low."

This seems to be the well now known as that of St Francis Xavier, in which the Saint is said to have washed, and in the water of which miraculous reflections are seen. A second splendid well is that in the old garden at Agra, 220 feet in circumference, and so deep that it makes one dizzy to look over the parapet into the water. A very ancient well in the fort of Rai Bareli, in Oudh, is 108 yards in circumference. Mrs King describes another well at Patiála:

"The wonder of the garden is a well, which might rank with an old Roman work; it is built of very small bricks, such as the Romans used, and has a diameter of fifty feet clear, besides three storeys of arched galleries running round it, contained in the thickness of the well."

Robertson Smith suggested that in Semitic countries property in water was older than property in land, and this seems to have been the case in India. In Cutch it was the old rule that a man might build a well wherever he pleased, and was entitled to all the land which he could water from it. Round the sites of ancient ruined cities a lucky man often comes across a deserted well and makes his fortune from it. In the Panjáb are men known as "smellers," the Oriental representatives of the "dowser" of England, who are able to select a good site for a well. They are said to mark down deserted wells by driving a herd of goats, which are supposed to lie down at the place where search should be made. In parts of Rájputána there is a prejudice against building new wells, and the people search for old wells on the sites of ruined cities. These wells, they say, were all built by a Rája of old days, who had an army of demons whom he kept employed in "smelling" out water. Since his time the art has been lost, and new wells never succeed. Needless to say, no one dreams of digging a well without taking omens and feeding Bráhmans.

Many wells are sacred. Some are supposed to have underground connection with a sacred river; one as far south as Tinnevelli is said to draw its supply from the Ganges. Others were used by the god Ráma and his wife Síta in their wanderings. Benares has two very holy wells, one the Manikarnika, which was produced by an ear-ring of Siva falling into it; the other, the Jnána-vápi, which to drink brings wisdom. Some are holy because the water at times bubbles up in an uncanny way, or changes its colour from time to time like the changing hues of shot-silk. This is due to the minerals at the source, but the Bráhmans, of course, say that a spirit is at the root of the matter. Other wells by their flow foretell the prospect of the season; others are famous for the cure of disease.

When there is only one well to serve all the castes in a village, from Bráhmans down to sweepers, trouble often arises. In Bengal a great deal depends on the kind of vessel used, and the nature of the well itself. With a reasonable subordination of caste prejudices to practical considerations, it has been decided that a masonry well is not so easily defiled as one lined with clay cylinders; and if it be more than five feet in diameter, so that a cow may turn in it, the lowest castes may use it without defilement. The use of a metal vessel, again, does not pollute it so readily as one of earthenware. At Amritsar, in order to meet the religious difficulty, the well is divided into sections at the top by means of wooden partitions which run some distance down the well. The vessels may touch at the bottom, but so long as each caste sees its vessels come up in its own section, they are quite satisfied. In Gujarát the rules are very stringent. If an animal falls into a well, the water must be purified with a mixture of all the products of the cow. If a woman drawing water meets a funeral she will cover her head, or, if extra careful, will throw away the water she is carrying. Everywhere, of course, a well is defiled by a corpse. These open, unprotected wells are a constant source of accident, and offer facilities for murder. Many a jealous woman has contrived that her hated rival should stumble and fall in, and many a luckless infant is thrown down a deserted well for the sake of the paltry jewellery which it wears. Suicides in wells are common. Some years ago an epidemic of suicide among girls broke out at Delhi, and was checked only by the issue of an order that in every case a *post-mortem* examination should be made. In the troublous times in Nepál, Jang Bahádur practised the art of jumping down a well, and on one occasion saved his life by his dexterity.

WINE.—The use of wine in India at an early time is attested by many references in post-Vedic literature.

"The possession of an extensive vocabulary of names," writes Sir G. Watt, "both in the classic and modern languages of India, for the plant, its fruit, its wine, and its spirit (brandy), when viewed in the light of the historic evidence which can be produced, and when taken in conjunction with the existence of several wild species which yield edible fruits, and are even partially cultivated along side of the true vine, are facts that leave little reason for doubt that India manifests a strong claim to an ancient cultivation of the vine."

The legend of the Eastern origin of Bacchus may thus have some historical foundation.

Prior to the Muhammadan conquest, we have little precise knowledge of the cultivation of the grape. While in other countries the spread of Islám tended to repress vine-growing, this result did not occur in India till the close of the sixteenth century, and after the death of Akbar. He actively fostered its cultivation, and greatly improved the stocks throughout Northern India. The earlier Moghuls were fond of the pleasures of the table, and paid little heed to the religious ordinances which prohibited drinking. The revival of fanaticism in the time of Aurangzeb put a stop to all progress, and even the vineries of Kashmír were destroyed. The justification for this action rests on the many accounts which we possess of the debauched habits of the grandees of Akbar's Court, and of many of his successors. Later on, in the Panjáb brandy was largely distilled, and Ranjít Singh drank it to excess.

It is in Kashmír alone, in modern times, that viticulture has been revived with some measure of success. A stock of vines was procured from the Bordeaux district in the time of Ranbír Singh, who in 1857 succeeded his father, to whom we surrendered the country after the Sikh campaign of 1846. Sir W. Lawrence thinks that the vines of Burgundy would have been more suitable.

"In spite of lavish expenditure," he writes, "the vineyards did not seem to flourish, and in 1890 it was evident that the vines were suffering from Phylloxera. American vines were at once imported, and are now gradually replacing the unhealthy Bordeaux plants." Wines of the Medoc and Barsac type are produced, but "the vineyards are under the direct management of the State, and, in spite of supervision, the vines do not receive the sedulous cultivation which alone can give success. The cultivators of the country have not taken up viticulture, and . . . I do not think that the wine industry of Kashmír will ever attain real importance until the villagers engage in wine-growing. The only market at present for the wines is Srínagar, as the long road carriage and the duties levied at the frontier make it difficult to land Kashmír wine in India at a moderate price; and, briefly, the business in present circumstances does not pay."

[Watt, "Economic Dictionary," iv., Pt. IV. 258; Lawrence, "Valley of Kashmír," 351.]

WITCHCRAFT.—This, one of the most primitive superstitions of India, prevails even at the present day among the lower and less advanced races. The witch, as Sir A. Lyall has pointed out, differs from the person who works through the agency of a fetish in that he does everything without the help of the gods.

"The witch is one who professes to work marvels, not through the aid or counsel of the supernatural beings in whom he believes as much as the rest, but by certain occult faculties which he conceives himself to possess."

The continuous existence of witchcraft is probably due to "the power of suggestion gained through the credulity of its victims"; and it specially prevails among the jungle races, exposed to sudden attacks of malaria or wild beasts, oppressed by the mystery of the forest, its dark recesses and deep hill-caves, which the boldest hunter will not enter. In the belief of such people, disease and death are supernatural, and nothing seems to them more probable than that such sudden calamities are due to the malignity of the Evil Eye, or to the machinations of a witch. As is the case in Europe, such powers are specially attributed to the mysterious Gipsy races.

This power is generally exerted either in wishing something out of, or wishing something into, the victim. Thus the Jigarkhor, or "liver-eater," described by Abul Fazl, is able "to steal away the liver of another by looks or incantations." In the Deccan she can produce star-shaped or cross-like marks on her victim's body.

As to the prevalence of the belief, Mr Beighton writes:

"There is scarcely a village of rural Bengal which does not possess its witch. The anxious mother snatches up her child as soon as the witch is seen to approach, and she murmurs some simple incantation to naught the charm of the Evil Eye. The witches are popularly supposed to possess the power of sucking the blood of healthy children and animals. The belief is, no doubt, a variant of the Vampire incubus of Eastern Europe. . . . There are other arts employed to counteract their malignity besides the bestowal of alms. They are detected sometimes by salt being put upon their heads, which causes them to turn round and mutter incoherent words, and to deprive them of their skill, they are persuaded to eat sweetmeats in which dung has been surreptitiously inserted. . . . If a child suffer from illness caused by the curse of a witch, one orthodox mode of cure is to mark the forehead of the patient with burnt turmeric. Water, on which spells have been muttered, is also sprinkled over the child, and the forehead is rubbed with burnt wicks of earthen lamps fed with mustard oil."

Various leaves of holy trees are also waved over the patient.

But in wilder times and among wilder races more drastic measures were and are taken against a suspected witch. The ordeal of plunging the witch into water, or making her walk on hot iron, was often employed; or a bag of cayenne pepper was tied over her head, or her eyes were rubbed with a well-dried capsicum. Among the jungle tribes of Central India the witch-finder flourishes. One of his methods is to light a little earthen lamp, and then repeat the names of each woman in the village. He fixes on the witch by the flicker of the light when her name is mentioned. In Bastar, one of the most remote districts of the Central Provinces,

"a fisherman's net is wound round the head of the suspected witch, to prevent her escaping or bewitching her guards. Two leaves of the Pípal or sacred fig-tree, one representing her and the other her accuser, are thrown upon her outstretched hands. If the leaf in her name fall uppermost, she is supposed to be a suspicious character; if the leaf fall with the lower part upwards, it is possible that she may be innocent, and popular opinion is in her favour."

The final test is the water ordeal.

The Gáros of Assam, when a woman is charged with witchcraft, put her into a long narrow basket with a cat, and the basket is so secured that she can put only one hand out of it. She is then thrown into a river, and if she can secure a handful of sand without being scratched by the cat, she is held to be innocent. If she fails, and escapes drowning, she is banished as an outcast. A more lenient method is to pass a bamboo pin through her shadow, which in popular belief is part of the woman herself. If she moves away easily, she is acquitted. These Gáro witches are said to become burning hot at night, and one way of detecting them is that they are unable to sit on a log cut from the sacred tree of the tribe.

When a witch is condemned by the witch-finder, the punishment awarded to her displays a diabolical ingenuity. It is significant that when British authority was relaxed during the Mutiny, there was an epidemic of witch-hunting and cruel outrages in the wilder parts of the country. One method of dealing with a witch is as common in India as it was at one time in Europe. She is pricked in the tongue with a needle, and the blood is dropped on some rice which she is forced to eat. The witch often takes the form of a man-eating tiger, and the remedy in such cases is to knock out some of her teeth to prevent her from doing any more mischief.

A witch is supposed to be able to work evil to a person if she can procure a lock of his hair, or the parings of his nails. Hence no careful native leaves such things about; rather he burns them or otherwise secretes them. Or she may take the measure of her victim's footsteps in the dust, and by this means bring disease upon him.

The belief in witchcraft has held the most heroic minds of India in bondage. Grose tells how a witch, "about forty, very corpulent, and not of an ill presence," frightened Sivaji, the Mahratta leader, who proposed to put her to death.

"She ordered two fowls to be produced, the one a cock, the other a hen. The cock was set down on the ground, full of life and spirits; then taking the hen, she desired the Rájah to mark the consequence. At these words she wrung the neck of the hen off, when at the same time the cock, though untouched by any one, imitating all the convulsions and agonies of its death, accompanied the hen in it. 'This, Sir,' said she to the Rájah determinately, 'remember to be a type of your fate and mine.' The Rájah struck by this, not only desisted from his intentions, but entreated her to be near his person, settled a considerable pension on her, ordered her a palankin and tendance, and, in short, treated her henceforwards like a person with whose life his own was wound up."

["Calcutta Review," lxxxiv. 188; Chevers, "Indian Medical Jurisprudence," 817; Crooke, "Popular Religion and Folklore," ii. 259; Shway Yoe, "The Burman," ii. 125.]

WOLF-CHILDREN.—The destruction wrought on village children by wolves is very great, particularly in some parts of the United Provinces. The number of these baby-eating brutes is small; according to the last official report a vast number of deaths in the districts of Cawnpore, Budaun, and Fatehpur, in the United Provinces, were traced to one or two animals. The wolf generally lurks in a thicket close to the village, and charges in the dusk down the street, carrying off one of the children playing outside the house. Sometimes they work in pairs, and while one distracts the attention of the people, the other carries off its prey. Captain Forsyth gives a good account of his successful attack on a pair of brutes of this kind which had taken up their quarters near a village. The people, as usual, with the apathy of fatalism, did not care to take the trouble of helping to beat them out. Indeed, General Sleeman believed that the prejudice which he found to exist among some classes in Oudh against killing wolves was due to the income which they derived from finding the silver ornaments of slaughtered children near the animals' dens.

More extraordinary are the tales of children who have been brought up by wolves, which are universally believed by the people of Oudh and the United Provinces. The following description of a child of this kind was given by Mr Lewis, Superintendent of the Secundra Orphanage, near Agra, in 1885:

"We have had in this Institution from time to time

three wolf-boys, two of which have died, and one still remains. . . . He was received by us in 1867, having been found by a Mr Lowe, the then Collector of Bulandshahr, in his district. At first, I am told by an old workman and resident that the boy would persist in walking on hands and feet, and had a strange fondness for raw meat. At present he is free from such peculiarities. He cannot talk, and though undoubtedly *págal* [imbecile or idiotic], still shows signs of reason, and sometimes actual shrewdness. I may also say he is fond of gnashing his teeth in true animal fashion, and clawing with his hands; otherwise he is harmless and decent, and never gives trouble. His one great liking is for cigars, which he smokes, when presented with one by visitors, with great gusto."

Many similar cases are recorded by General Sleeman, Dr Ball, and others who have investigated the question. The general conclusion is that the children alleged to have been nurtured by wolves present the symptoms of cretinism or congenital idiocy. The boys are said all to have become brutalised by association with wolves, to be dirty in habit, and to have acquired the taste for raw meat. Similar tales are told in Europe of children nurtured by bears, which are of the familiar Romulus-Remus type. Such children are said to have been suckled by the female animal, and to have escaped the demoralising influence of their brute foster-parents. One of these so-called bear-children was said to have been found at Jalpaigúri, in Bengal, so late as 1893. She was two or three years old, and walked on all fours, bit and scratched any one who approached her, and was unable to articulate. This seems to be the only recorded case of a girl being found under such circumstances, and the fact that the recorded cases of wolf-children belong to one sex throws suspicion on the narratives.

The legend probably depends on the habit of wolves carrying off and devouring children. Idiot children may have been found in places which wolves frequent, but the evidence of actual fosterage by wolves seems to break down in all or most of the cases which have been examined, and the accounts probably rest entirely on the credulity and mythopœic tendencies of the native population.

[Blanford, "Mammalia," 139; Ball, "Jungle Life," 455; Sleeman, "Journey through Oudh," i. 208; Forsyth, "Highlands of Central India," 74; Thornhill, "Haunts and Hobbies of an Indian Official," 279.]

WOMAN.—Much sentimentalism has been needlessly expended on the Indian woman. Like most women in other lands, she is not slow to give expression to the pathos of her life; but she, not less than her husband, would resent the belief that she is down-trodden and degraded. In a land where the affairs of life are regulated by custom, she is quite content to repeat the experiences of the heroines of old times, whose docility and reverence for the man with whom they were linked is an ideal which she is proud to follow. She has no conception of any grievance with which the greybeards of her caste, assembled in council, are not competent to deal. Of course, her range of matrimonial choice is limited, but this, she well knows, is the result of inexorable conventions, the ordinances of her religion, the rules of caste, the tone and conditions of social life.

In early Aryan times she was not secluded. Even Manu, who represents the Bráhmanical reaction, does not recommend it: "By close confinement and observant guardians women are not secure; but those women are truly secure who are guided by their own inclinations." We have many accounts of the custom known as the Svayamvara, in which girls of rank publicly selected their husbands. Arrian, probably quoting Megasthenes, says that

"the women, as soon as they are marriageable, are brought forward by their fathers and exposed in public, to be selected by the victor in wrestling or boxing, or running, or by some one who excels in any other manly exercise."

The custom of maintaining female guards in the royal harems dates from very early times. "The care of the King's person," says Strabo, writing of the Mauryan dynasty, about 300 B.C., "is entrusted to women," and such was the rule in the Court of the King of Malabar, of which Barbosa gives a quaint account. "All the attendance on the King is done by women, who wait upon him within doors, and amongst them are all the employments of the King's household." This custom survived to recent times. Ranjít Singh had a regiment of seventy Amazons, who were paraded before Lord W. Bentinck dressed in yellow silk, and marshalled by a female commandant armed with a long cane. Mountstuart Elphinstone saw the female guards of the Nizám of Hyderabad in 1801, dressed like Madras Sepoys. To this day the palace is guarded by well-dressed, good-looking young women, who now usually act as State musicians, though they occasionally appear as sentries at ceremonial functions.

Some modern women of rank have enjoyed considerable liberty. Sir John Malcolm describes Mahratta women, like the notorious Tulsa Bai, who were excellent riders. If they had estates of their own, they did much as they pleased, seldom wearing the veil, entertaining their friends, and spending their money on clothes and jewellery. Bhíma Bai, daughter of Jaswant Rao Holkar, told him that, as she had neither husband nor son, it was her duty to lead her troops in battle—an example followed by the Ráni of Jhansi in the Mutiny. The Mahrattas, in fact, never submitted to the Musalmán custom of keeping their women under restraint. Even modern Musalmán princesses, like the Begum of Bhopál, have appeared unveiled in public, and attended to the duties of administration. Among the wilder Muhammadan tribes, women enjoy much liberty. Sir H. Edwardes tells how the Pathán girls at Bannu used to stand laughing round the wells, careless of concealing their faces or ankles from the gaze of a Feringhee. The Pársi woman of our day drives with her husband, or takes the air on the Bombay Esplanade. "The Burmese lady," says Sir J. G. Scott, "enjoys many rights which her European sister is even now clamouring for." In South India the *Purdah* * restriction is comparatively modern. In 1623 Pietro della Valle was admitted to audience by the King and Queen of Calicut, the latter being unclothed above the waist. Alexander Hamilton had a similar experience about a century later. But Bráhman influence has changed all this. The Nambútiri woman of our day must not look in the face of any man but her husband. When compelled to go abroad, she is accompanied by a Nair woman, who, with a long-drawn shout, warns all male travellers to leave the road, and the charms of the lady are protected by the great palm-leaf umbrella which she carries.

Nowadays the most obvious evidence of a man's rise in social estimation is that he secludes his wife. None are so careful in this respect as the upstart traders who batten under our rule. Nothing, says Mr Rose, writing of the Panjáb, impresses the Indian visitor to Europe more than the extent to which women are employed, and there is no greater obstacle to progress in India than the senseless prejudice against the employment of women in occupations for which they are naturally adapted. All over India the real working peasant woman walks abroad uncontrolled, and though she may through prudery try to veil her face before a European, it is little more than a formal concession to popular prejudice. Bernier slyly tells how he used to catch a glimpse of the Court beauties of his day by walking behind an elephant, the tinkling of whose silver bells used to make the shy damsels put their heads out of the windows of their litters. Her want of delicate reticence, her propensity to discuss her private affairs in public with a liberal use of bad language, are the worst points in the working-woman of our time.

It is, of course, a breach of courtesy to refer in conversation to the ladies of a native gentleman's family, and he oddly fails to understand that this objection to reciprocate courtesy is the main barrier to his reception into intimacy with Anglo-Indians. This feeling was stronger a century ago than it is now. In parts of Behár, Buchanan-Hamilton

"found it considered by certain classes, even of Hindus, an intolerable outrage, not only to speak of a person's own female connections, but even to mention the sex in the most general manner, and any discussion of the female customs gave many persons the utmost disgust."

In the more remote places the rustic still turns away his head when an English lady passes, following the Persian etiquette when the ladies of the royal household go abroad.

The lower we go in the social scale, the more freedom the woman claims. The wife of the Bunjára carrier stalks with a fine dignity ahead of the caravan; and among the jungle tribes, particularly when, as is not uncommon, the wife is older than her mate, she regards him as no whit superior to herself, and no business is done without her sanction. Among the Lusháis of Assam the widow becomes mistress of the family, but has to do all the hard work. Many of the vagrant gangs of North India are under female leadership, but this is accounted for by the fact that so many of the adult males are in jail. Colonel Dalton gives quite an idyllic picture of the Ho women in Chota Nágpur. There is no quarrelling, and a woman, unless she be a reputed witch, is well treated. It used to be a fine trait of the Bhíl women to pose as advocates of order, to show humanity to prisoners, and oppose crime and debauchery.

Even the woman of higher rank who does not appear in public takes good care to keep herself acquainted with all that goes on, and exercises an influence which is not the less potent because she does not show it openly.

"In Kashmír," says Sir W. Lawrence, "the husband sometimes chastises the wife, and the men talk somewhat boastfully about the necessity of maintaining discipline in their houses. But, as a matter of fact, the wife, both in Musalmán and Hindu houses, is all-powerful, and I believe that, as a rule, the Kashmíri lives in awe of his consort. The Kashmíri wife is a real helpmate, and joint work and joint interests give rise to a camaraderie between man and wife which is very healthy."

When the English first settled in Súrat, some of them

were married. But the Anglo-Indian lady of the time was not looked on with much favour by the authorities, on account of her waywardness and extravagance. Sir T. Roe in 1616 bluntly told one of his subordinates that "his wife would cause many inconveniences, and that he must live frugally and like a merchant, and send his wife home." Della Valle in 1623 could not bring his wife to the factory because there was no lady there; and a few years later, when Mandelslo was entertained there, only men joined the party to drink the health of their wives at home. It was the wise President Aungier, at the end of the seventeenth century, who suggested to the Company that their servants should be encouraged to marry, and succeeding travellers, like Ovington and Fryer, speak of English ladies at Súrat. At the time of the Black Hole there were several ladies at Calcutta, and one, an East Indian, was among the sufferers. In the same year Ives tells of a supercargo who met his death from a cold caught by dancing with ladies just arrived from England.

The native ideal of female beauty is that of Sarada, daughter of the god Brahma:

> "She was of a yellow colour, had a nose like the flower of the sesamum; her legs were taper like the plantain tree; her eyes large like the principal leaf of the lotus; her eyebrows extended to her ears; her lips were like the young leaves of the mango tree; her voice like that of the cuckoo; her arms reached to her knees; her throat was like that of the pigeon; her waist narrow like that of the lion; her teeth like the seeds of the pomegranate; and her gait like that of an excited elephant or of a goose."

Few women nowadays reach this height of perfection. The Bengali still finds his ideal of beauty in Lataf-un-nissa, the mistress of the infamous Síráj-ud-daula. Her skin was golden-hued, and so transparent that when she ate *pawn*,* the red colour could be seen passing down her throat. She weighed only 64, or, as some say, 44 lbs. In beauty, tradition always places the Kashmíri above her sisters. Mr Drew describes them as decidedly good-looking, with well-shaped faces, good brows, and straight noses, black hair coming rather low on the forehead, their figures tall and well-developed, but this is obscured by the looseness of their dress. They have, however, little of the delicacy of form that many other native women possess, and the well-turned arm and small hand are not common. The best Kashmíri women object to be photographed, and the pictures we have are usually of Bátal dancing-girls, who are not the finest specimens of the race. Sir W. Lawrence is not so complimentary. Out of thousands of women he has seen, he

"cannot remember, save one or two exceptions, ever seeing a really beautiful face"; and he thinks that the "old and prevailing idea among the natives of Hindustan as to the beauty of the Kashmíri women is probably due to the healthy, rosy cheeks that many of them have, so different from the wheaten hue of India."

Their dress certainly does not enhance their charms. The prevailing colour is drab, which means that their clothes would be white if they washed them.

Men from Madras declare that there are no women more beautiful than those of the Nairs, or Nambútiri Bráhmans. Others swear by the Bant women of Canara, with their lovely dark eyes, pencilled eyebrows, low, narrow foreheads, and soft glossy hair, often falling to the knee. The shapely Grecian foot, with slightly-arched instep, is said to be common among them. In Northern India the best specimens of beauty are to be found among the higher Rájput tribes and some of the better classes of merchants—probably one of the purest races in the country. The figure, uncontrolled by the corset, is often admirable, and the bright eyes and soft wheat complexion are finely set off by jewellery and gorgeous dress. But early marriage and lack of medical care soon destroy their beauty, and a woman of thirty is usually a hag.

[Miss Billington, "Woman in India"; for Burma, Shway Yoe, "The Burman," i. 98; South India, Logan, "Malabar," i. 127; Fawcett, "Bulletin of Madras Museum," iii. Pt. I. 3; Mahrattas, Malcolm, "Central India" i. 316; Fanny Parkes, "Wanderings of a Pilgrim," ii. 32; Kashmír, Lawrence, "Valley of Kashmír," 277; Drew, "Jummoo and Kashmír," 182.]

WOOD-CARVING.—Wood-carving is a very ancient Indian art. The earliest forms of stone architecture reproduce the style and construction of the original wooden buildings. As early as the sixteenth century, Barbosa describes the workmen of Cambay as "great artists with the turning-lathe, who make large bedsteads," a splendid example of which, wrought with gold and mother-of-pearl, was given by the King of Melinda, in East Africa, in 1502, to Vasco de Gama.

Modern wood-carving takes various forms. We have, first, the splendid examples of carving applied to architecture still to be seen in some of the larger cities, like Gaya, or Násik, the old Sikh towns of the Panjáb, the temples and private houses of Nepál and Burma. Next comes the Black-wood furniture of Bombay in a style obviously derived from the Dutch.

> "Although," as Sir G. Birdwood remarks, "it is highly probable that the excessive and ridiculous carving on old Dutch furniture was itself derived from the sculptured idols and temples which so excited their astonishment when they first reached India."

Thirdly, the sandalwood carving of Western India, which assumes various forms. To quote the same writer:

> "The Súrat and Bombay work is in low relief, and the designs consist almost entirely of foliated ornament; the Canara and Mysore work is in high relief, the subjects being chiefly mythological; and the Ahmadábád work, while in flat relief, is deeply cut, and the subjects are mixed, floral, and mythological."

The Burmese work forms a school of itself, derived immediately from the decoration of Buddhist monasteries and pagodas. The design largely consists of figures of birds and animals, and of the Náts, or spiritual beings, which Buddhism has adopted from the indigenous Animism. In animal forms the elephant is depicted with the highest realism, and the grotesque head of a Belu, or wild man, is often introduced. The effect is more bold and realistic than any Indian work. It was introduced into Upper India by the dacoits, who were sent to Indian jails during the outbreak which followed annexation.

The spread of the taste among Europeans for specimens of art-work has largely encouraged the production of all kinds of articles of use and beauty. Such are the tables, brackets, and picture-frames of Sahåranpur; the ebony-work of Nagína; the Benares toys, decorated with lacquer; the cabinets of Ahmadábád; the lovely panelled ceilings of Kashmír, made of thin strips of pine-wood, the various shades of which blend in perfect harmony. These carved articles are frequently decorated with inlays of ivory, horn, brass, or silver, among which one of the most interesting developments is the work in inlaid wire of Mainpuri. While the establishment of Schools of Art has encouraged various kinds of wood-carving, they have, on the whole, tended to debase the native styles by the introduction of incongruous designs.

Even in the conservative East fashions change, and this is reflected in some handicrafts. Thus bow-making, up to recent times, was an important industry, but it has entirely disappeared since the introduction of fire-arms. The workmen of this craft have now turned their attention to furniture, and have applied their old methods of decoration to this new industry. Their foliated patterns in tin, coloured yellow to simulate gilding, or left white like silver, are now used in a new direction with considerable success.

The reckless destruction of forest before conservation was commenced by the State has caused a scarcity of the more valuable kinds of timber, and the roughness and inequality of the carver's work are often due to the difficulty of procuring wood of the necessary quality and dimensions. Even admitting this, the carelessness of the workman in detail often spoils the artistic effect of his work. Once the carving is done, he often scamps the fitting of the pieces, or the joinery, and neglects to provide suitable metal-work in the form of locks, hinges, and the like.

Thus the product often wears a look of want of finish which seriously detracts from its beauty.

[Birdwood, "Industrial Arts of India," 199; Mukharji, "Art Manufactures of India," 230; O'Dwyer, "Monograph on Wood-carving in the Panjáb."]

WRESTLING.—Wrestling is one of the most popular forms of Indian athletics. A match between two famous champions is as attractive as a football contest in Europe, and in the villages of North India there is generally an arena in which the youths contend amidst the applause of the assembled grey-beards.

The sport has always been patronised by Indian Princes. Akbar had wrestlers and boxers from Persia and Turán attached to his Court, besides champions from Hindustán and Gujarát. Every day two well-matched pairs used to contend before him for large rewards, and Abul Fazl is careful to give a list of the most famous athletes of the day. In later times the most celebrated band of wrestlers was that maintained by Zálim Singh of Kotah, in Rájputána, and those in the pay of chiefs like the Guicowár of Baroda, the Ráo of Cutch, and the Nawáb of Oudh. Many famous wrestling schools, like those of the burly Chaubés of Mathura, those of Behár and Cuttack, enjoy more than a local reputation. The system of training differs from that of Europe, the object being not to bring the athlete into a state of "fine" condition, but to produce weight of brawn rather than of sinew. The Indian combatant relies on a diet of milk and *ghee*,* which would not commend itself to a European trainer.

The North Indian wrestler, before entering the arena, smears his body with clay, and struts about with inflated chest and solemn gait. The crouching position, head to head, is adopted, and each combatant uses every art to secure a favourable grip, in the intervals slapping his arms and thighs with his open hand. A fair fall consists in being thrown flat on the back, both shoulders touching the ground. This, owing to the suppleness and agility of the combatants, is seldom reached. There is no disgrace in a side fall; in fact, the man who is getting the worst of the contest often throws himself on his face to recover breath, and thus defies all the efforts of his antagonist to turn him, like a turtle, on his back. General Mundy, a good authority, was of opinion that the Cuttack wrestlers seemed to understand the mechanical applications of their strength better than those of Britain. Owing to the difference of style, whenever a British soldier contends in the native way, he is usually beaten. To the European the whole performance seems monotonous and uninteresting. As Fryer says: "They weary one another only by pure Strength and Luctation, not by Skill and Circumvention."

The Mysore contests, as described by Colonel Wilks, were much more brutal than those of Northern India, where injury seldom occurs. The Mysore style was more like that of the Roman arena, the combatants being armed with a weapon made of buffalo horn, fitted to the hand, and pointed with four knobs resembling very sharp knuckles, with a fifth of greater length over the little finger.

"This instrument, properly placed, would enable a man of ordinary strength to cleave open the head of his adversary with a single blow. But by their arrangement he could do so only at the risk of dislocating the joints of his fingers."

Hence the combat was a sort of mixture of wrestling and boxing, the blows being aimed at the head of the adversary, and a wistful glance in the direction of the royal balcony was the usual symptom of acknowledged defeat.

[Mundy, "Pen and Pencil Sketches," 321; Wilks, "Historical Sketches," i. 33; Blochmann, "Ain-i-Akbari," i. 253; Mrs Postans, "Cutch," 41; Prinsep, "Imperial India," 180; Rousselet, "India and its Native Princes," 104.]

WRITING.—The earliest literary evidence of writing in India is found in Buddhist books about 450 B.C. From these references it is clear that the art was already well developed. It is also certain that some of the oldest Indian letters are identical with those on Assyrian weights, and the so-called Mesa inscription of the seventh and sixth centuries B.C. Much controversy has arisen as to the route by which these letters reached India—that is to say, whether from the North Semites, or from those of the South in Lower Arabia. Professor Rhys Davids, rejecting both these routes, suggests that they were derived from the pre-Semitic form of writing used in the Euphrates valley. It seems clear that an extensive trade intercourse from this region to India grew up in the seventh century B.C. The merchants who brought this script to India were probably Dravidians, and it is to them, and not to the Aryans, that India is indebted for its alphabet. Mr V. A. Smith believes that the knowledge of the art of writing may have reached the south-west coast as early as the eighth century B.C., whence it gradually reached North India during the seventh century. The oldest MS. from Khotan, in Central Asia, is in the Kharostri script, so-called from the country of Kharostra, or Kashgar, and introduced overland into north-west India about 500 B.C. When this script came to India it was not immediately adopted. Bráhmanism was then the ruling faith. Its priests had been accustomed to commit their sacred texts to memory, and were not inclined to allow this knowledge to spread among the people. Further, no form of writing material had then been invented in India. This began with the use of birch bark, such as was used in the MS. recently discovered in Khotan.

Meanwhile, in the time of Asoka, we find his edicts recorded in stone about 250 B.C., and from this script the modern letters used in India are to a large extent derived. The character of these modern scripts was determined by the material on which they were written. In Southern and Eastern India where the material was the leaf of the palm, the use of the stylus perpendicularly, or following the grain of the leaf, would have torn its texture. To avoid this, the circular form of writing, as we find it in Tamil or Burmese, was evolved. Both the Tamil and the Telegu script of Madras sprang directly from the old Bráhmi alphabet used by Asoka. Speaking of another kindred script, the Oriya of Orissa, Dr Grierson writes:

"Oriya is handicapped by possessing an extremely awkward and cumbrous written character. This character is in its basis the same as Deva-nágari [*Nagaree**], the Hindi script of North India, but is written by the local scribes on a *talipot** palm-leaf. The scratches are themselves legible, but to make them more plain, ink is rubbed over the surface of the leaf, and fills up the furrows which form the letter. The palm leaf is exceptionally fragile, and any scratch in the direction of the grain tends to make it slit. As a line of writing on a long narrow leaf is necessarily in the direction of the grain, this peculiarity prohibits the use of the straight top line, which is a distinguishing peculiarity of the Deva-nágari character. For this the Oriya scribe is compelled to substitute a series of curves, which almost surround each letter. It requires remarkably good eyes to read an Oriya-printed book, for the exigencies of the printing-press compel the type to be small, and the greater part of each letter is this curve, which is the same in nearly all; while the real soul of the character, by which one is distinguished from another, is hidden in the centre, and is so minute that it is often difficult to see. At first glance an Oriya book seems to be all curves, and it takes a second look to see that there is something inside each."

The Musalmán raids on the west frontier, beginning early in the eighth century A.D., introduced the Arab-Persian alphabet, which is used not only for the pure tongues of that region, but for the *Oordoo*,* or mixed language, which is rapidly becoming the *lingua franca* of the Peninsula. During recent years Hindu popular feeling, which loses no chance of asserting itself, has rebelled against the use of a Musalmán script in legal proceedings and village records. In deference to this claim, in parts of Bengal and the United Provinces the *Kythee*,* or writer's script, has been allowed where the population is largely Hindu, and uses the so-called *Hindee** tongue as its vernacular. Sindhi uses both the Arabic and Deva-nágari script, but the latter is so corrupt and incomplete, that, when written, it can seldom be read by any one except the original scribe. This fault of illegibility extends to the modern banker's script, of which many amusing tales are told. In the Panjáb Mr Rose remarks that Hindu writing changes every twelve miles, and the script of one tract becomes illegible even a few miles away.

The use of writing materials came into vogue, as we have seen, in comparatively modern times. Writing in ink is as old as the relic-caskets recovered from the Sánchi Stúpa, built some time after the reign of Asoka, in the third century B.C. Paper of the native kind made in Nepál, of a species of Daphne, and in Kumaun of a plant like butcher's broom, is still preferred by bankers for bills of exchange and account books; but everywhere rags, hemp, and other fibres are coming into use.

In South India and Burma we have the *Parabyke*,* which is mentioned by Abd-er-razzák in the fifteenth century. It is either white or black, made from fibrous bamboo or bark, and when intended to be black is coloured with starch and teak-wood charcoal made into a paste with some vegetable juice; sometimes it is merely a cloth stiffened with gum. The writing is done with a pot-stone or steatite pencil, the marks of which can be washed out, but not removed by friction.

The order in which the materials are used in the village schools of Bengal is more primitive. First, the characters are made in the dust of the floor, and the pupil is promoted successively to a wooden board and chalk, palm-leaves, plantain leaves, and finally to paper.

All over India grants of land were often recorded on copper plates, held together by a copper ring, or on stone slabs. Such were the plates on which treaties between the Greek States were recorded. The brass plates are comparatively modern, many of those in the Museums coming from the Panjáb, and recording grants by Ranjít Singh. The grants recorded on these plates are all Hindu or Buddhist, as the Musalmáns never used them. In support of claims to property they have been freely forged from time to time. The art of engraving characters on metal is very old. The copper-silver seal of Kumára Gupta, found at Bhitari, in the Gházipur district, may be dated about 530 A.D.

Passing to regions where Buddhism now prevails, we find that in the Himálaya the script is of Indian origin. There are two Tibetan scripts, the religious and the commercial. Buddhist women learn the sacred character, as Sikh women do the Gurmukhi, in which the Granth, their Scripture, is recorded. In Tibetan there are such a number of silent consonants that the spelling of every word has to be committed to memory, and it is quite impossible from the sound to know how a word should be spelt. The words are so full of consonants that they can be articulated with almost semi-closed mouth, the intensity of the cold making it necessary to keep the lips closed against the piercing wind. In the Burmese monasteries copies of the sacred books are written either with a style on palm-leaves, or, if more highly valued, on strips of well-sized white chintz, which looks like ivory. The folds of the cloth are joined together with black-wood oil; the outside is coated with gum, and, when wet, overlaid with vermilion. On this the letters are formed with gum, and margin ornaments and scroll-work of liquid gold are added.

The pious Hindu seldom seals his letters, but he writes on the folds of the back what is equivalent to an imprecation against any one who tampers with the contents—symbols to indicate the seven seas, the four Vedas, the Sun and Moon. No one would dare to open such a letter. The historian Rashíd-ud-din, writing of the Mongols, says:

> "It is usual in Cathay, when any contract is entered into, for the outline of the fingers of the parties to be traced upon the document. For experience shows that no two individuals have fingers precisely alike."

Similarly the Musalmán custom of stamping the mark of the hand and five fingers as a particularly solemn mode of attesting an important document is said to have been adopted by the Prophet. We have here a remarkable anticipation of the modern method of identifying offenders by their fingers-marks.

[Dr Grierson's admirable chapter on the languages of India in "Census Report," India, 1901, vol. i.; Bühler, "Indische Palæographie," of which an English version is now appearing in the "Indian Antiquary"; Hoernle, "An Epigraphical Note on Palm-leaf, Paper, and Birch-bark," "Journal Asiatic Society of Bengal," 1900.]

INDEX